MOTIVATION & EMOTION

ADVANCED PSYCHOLOGY TEXTS

Lyle E. Bourne, Jr.
Series Editor

Advanced Psychology Texts (APT) is a series of intermediate but highly readable textbooks and monographs in the core areas of psychology. The primary objective of the series is to give undergraduate student majors and beginning graduate students in psychology a basis for evaluating the state of the science and a springboard into further guided or independent scholarship in a particular area. Each volume will center on the current issues and the basic concepts of a core content area of psychology. Students who use these books are expected to have some general background in the field. The textbooks take advantage of that background, building it into a sophisticated contemporary understanding of the facts and of the important yet-to-be answered questions. Each text focuses on recent developments and the implication of those developments for future research. Although the emphasis is on psychology as an evolving systematic scientific discipline, applications of basic research findings are also included. Authors have been asked to present clearly and thoughtfully what it is that each sub-area of psychology has to contribute to human knowledge and welfare.

Volume 1 *Skill Acquisition and Human Performance*
Robert W. Proctor and Addie Dutta

Volume 2 *Cognitive Psychology*
Ronald T. Kellogg

Volume 3 *Motivation and Emotion*
David C. Edwards

MOTIVATION & EMOTION

Evolutionary,

Physiological,

Cognitive,

and

Social

Influences

David C. Edwards

ADVANCED PSYCHOLOGY TEXTS

SAGE Publications
International Educational and Professional Publisher
Thousand Oaks London New Delhi

For information:

 SAGE Publications, Inc.
2455 Teller Road
Thousand Oaks, California 91320
E-mail: order@sagepub.com

SAGE Publications Ltd.
6 Bonhill Street
London EC2A 4PU
United Kingdom

SAGE Publications India Pvt. Ltd.
M-32 Market
Greater Kailash I
New Delhi 110 048 India

Printed in the United States of America

Library of Congress Cataloging-in-Publication Data

    Edwards, David C.
      Motivation and emotion: Evolutionary, physiological,
    cognitive, and social influences / by David C. Edwards.
       p. cm. — (Advanced psychology texts; volume 3)
      Includes bibliographical references and index.
      ISBN 0-7619-0832-3 (hardcover: alk. paper)
      1. Motivation (Psychology) 2. Emotions. I. Title. II. Series:
    Advanced psychology texts; v. 3
      BF503 .E38 1998
      153.8—ddc21   98-19717

99 00 01 02 03 04 10 9 8 7 6 5 4 3 2 1

Acquiring Editor:	C. Deborah Laughton
Editorial Assistant:	Eileen Carr
Production Editor:	Diana E. Axelsen
Editorial Assistant:	Denise Santoyo
Typesetter/Designer:	Danielle Dillahunt
Cover Designer:	Candice Harman

Brief Contents

1. INTRODUCTION AND HISTORY   1

2. PHYSIOLOGY, RHYTHMS, AND SLEEP   27

3. EATING   61

4. EMOTION   97

5. ANGER AND AGGRESSION   129

6. PAIN, FEAR, AND STRESS   159

7. SEXUAL MOTIVATION: POLITICS AND BIOLOGY   201

8. EROS, LOVE, AND COMMITMENT   237

9. SOCIAL INTERACTIONS   269

10. MOTIVATED COGNITION   295

11. ADDICTION   329

12. WORK   361

13. PLAY AND LEISURE   395

 EPILOGUE: MOTIVATION IDEALS   427

Detailed Contents

PREFACE　　　xvii

1. INTRODUCTION AND HISTORY　　　1

Psychology's Past　　　2

Founding of Psychology　　　2
Theoretical Schools of Psychology　　　4
SECTION SUMMARY: PSYCHOLOGY'S PAST　　　7

Ideas in Motivation Theory　　　7

Motivation as Substance　　　8
Motivation as Energy　　　9
Evolutionary Models　　　11
Describing Motivated Behavior　　　14
Awareness of Motivation　　　16
A Motivation Definition　　　19
SECTION SUMMARY: IDEAS IN MOTIVATION THEORY　　　20

Modern Motivation Science　　　21

Cognitive Science　　　21
Motivation Topic Development　　　22
SECTION SUMMARY: MODERN MOTIVATION SCIENCE　　　23

Chapter Conclusions　　　24
Study and Review Questions　　　24

2. PHYSIOLOGY, RHYTHMS, AND SLEEP　　　27

Nervous System Components　　　29

The Nervous Systems   29

Spinal Cord   30

Hindbrain   31

Midbrain   32

Forebrain   32

SECTION SUMMARY: NERVOUS SYSTEM COMPONENTS   34

Chemical Communications   **34**

Endocrine Functions   34

Neurochemistry   34

Biological Rhythms   **35**

Natural Rhythms   36

Selling Biorhythms   43

SECTION SUMMARY: BIOLOGICAL RHYTHMS   44

Sleep   **45**

Why Sleep?   45

Sleep Patterns   46

Sleep Length   50

REM Sleep   54

Dreaming   54

SECTION SUMMARY: SLEEP   57

Chapter Conclusions   **58**

Study and Review Questions   **59**

3. EATING   **61**

Nutrition   **62**

Food Materials   62

Natural and Modern Diet   67

Starting and Stopping Eating   70

Long-Term Weight Regulation   71

SECTION SUMMARY: NUTRITION   72

Appetite   **72**

Physiological Programming   73

Personal Experience With Food   75

Social Regulation of Eating   78

Culture and Eating Habits   81

SECTION SUMMARY: APPETITE   86

Motivation Foods   **87**

Popular Beliefs About Foods   87

Foods and Brain Chemistry   88

Aftereffects of Meals   88

SECTION SUMMARY: MOTIVATION FOODS   88

Overeating and Obesity   **89**

Components of Overeating   89

Obesity   90

Weight Loss Principles   91

Dieting Programs   93

SECTION SUMMARY: OVEREATING AND OBESITY   94

Chapter Conclusions   **94**

Study and Review Questions   **95**

4. EMOTION   97

Phenomena and Experiences   **98**

Emotion Experience   98

Primary Emotions   102

SECTION SUMMARY: PHENOMENA AND EXPERIENCES   103

Biological Foundations of Emotion   **104**

Inherited Function Theories   104

Conditioned Response Theories   107

Brain and Nervous System Theories   108

SECTION SUMMARY:
BIOLOGICAL FOUNDATIONS OF EMOTION   112

Developmental Elaboration   **113**

Emotion Identification in Children   113

Emotion Functioning in Child Development   114

Emotion Expression   115

SECTION SUMMARY: DEVELOPMENTAL ELABORATION   119

Cultural Order   **119**

Cognitive and Social Theories   120

Social Construction   122

Gender Expectations   124

SECTION SUMMARY: CULTURAL ORDER   125

Chapter Conclusions   **126**

Study and Review Questions   **126**

5. ANGER AND AGGRESSION   129

Aggression Ideas   **130**

Defining Aggression   130

Forms of Aggressive Acts   132

SECTION SUMMARY: AGGRESSION IDEAS   133

Physical Foundations for Aggression   **133**

Biological Structures   133

Genetic Animal Nature   136
Genetic Human Nature   139
SECTION SUMMARY: PHYSICAL
FOUNDATIONS FOR AGGRESSION   141

Emotional Aggressive Acts   **142**

Drive Sources of Aggression   142
Impulsive Aggression and Feeling Bad   143
SECTION SUMMARY: EMOTIONAL AGGRESSIVE ACTS   145

Anger   **145**

Brain Activity of Anger and Aggression   145
Social Rules of Anger   146
SECTION SUMMARY: ANGER   148

Instrumental Aggressive Acts   **148**

Defending One's Self   148
Social Sources of Aggression   149
Aggression as a Stable Trait   151
Men's and Women's Aggression   151
SECTION SUMMARY: INSTRUMENTAL AGGRESSIVE ACTS   153

Learning Anger and Aggression   **153**

Modeling and Imitation   153
Rewards and Punishments   154
Acquiring Social Rules   154
Historical Emotionology of Anger   155
SECTION SUMMARY: LEARNING ANGER AND AGGRESSION   156

Chapter Conclusions   **157**
Study and Review Questions   157

6. PAIN, FEAR, AND STRESS   **159**

Experiencing Pain   **160**

Describing Pain   161
Interpreting Pain   162
SECTION SUMMARY: EXPERIENCING PAIN   165

Pain Physiology   **165**

Nociception   165
Neural Complexities   166
Spinal Cord Pain Gating   167
Brain Dimensions of Pain   168
Mechanisms of Chronic Pain   169
SECTION SUMMARY: PAIN PHYSIOLOGY   170

Managing Pain   **170**

Medical Treatment   170
Psychological Control   173

Pain Clinics   174
SECTION SUMMARY: MANAGING PAIN   175

Fear   **175**

Fear Phenomena   175
Elicitors of Fear   176
Response to Fear   177
SECTION SUMMARY: FEAR   178

Anxiety   **178**

Anxiety Phenomena   178
Anxiety Theories   178
SECTION SUMMARY: ANXIETY   180

Stress   **181**

Stress Concept Origins   181
Outlines of Stress   182
Factors of Stress   182
SECTION SUMMARY: STRESS   183

Physical Bases of Stress   **183**

Emergency Physiology   184
Stress Physiology   185
SECTION SUMMARY: PHYSICAL BASES OF STRESS   187

Life Applications of Stress   **187**

Life Change Stress   187
Crowding   188
Coronary-Prone Acts   188
Clinical Anxiety Disorders   189
Depression   191
SECTION SUMMARY: LIFE APPLICATIONS OF STRESS   192

Control and Coping With Stress   **193**

Coping Resources   194
Coping Acts   194
Symptom Therapies   195
SECTION SUMMARY: CONTROL AND COPING WITH STRESS   196

Chapter Conclusions   **197**
Study and Review Questions   197

7. SEXUAL MOTIVATION: POLITICS AND BIOLOGY   **201**

Western Social History of Sex and Love   **202**

Greek, Roman, and Christian Ideals   202
Sexuality and Feelings   203
Gendering Love   204
Individualism and Romanticism   205

SECTION SUMMARY: WESTERN SOCIAL HISTORY
OF SEX AND LOVE   206

Scientific Studies of Love and Sex   **207**

Affirming Social Beliefs   207
Sexuality and Gender Differences   208
SECTION SUMMARY: SCIENTIFIC STUDIES OF LOVE AND SEX   210

Politics of Sex   **211**

Sexology Studies   211
Ideology of Sex   213
Modern Western Sexual Culture   214
SECTION SUMMARY: POLITICS OF SEX   216

Dissecting the Sexual Acts   **217**

Stages of Sexual Acts   217
Neural Mechanisms   218
Hormone Foundations   219
SECTION SUMMARY: DISSECTING THE SEXUAL ACTS   223

Sensual Arousal   **224**

Libido   224
Sexual Stimulation   224
SECTION SUMMARY: SENSUAL AROUSAL   226

Gender Differences   **226**

Evolution Theories of Sexuality   226
Sexual Attraction   227
Sexual Interest and Orgasm   230
SECTION SUMMARY: GENDER DIFFERENCES   233

Chapter Conclusions   **233**
Study and Review Questions   **234**

8. EROS, LOVE, AND COMMITMENT   237

Erotic Sexual Arousal   **237**

Ultimate Arousal Origins   237
Scripts of Love and Sex   238
Modes of Erotic Arousal   240
Personal Sexual Motivation   244
Social Roles of Love and Sex   245
SECTION SUMMARY: EROTIC SEXUAL AROUSAL   246

Images of Love   **247**

Romantic and Pragmatic Love   247
Romantic Passion's Role   248
John Lee's Styles of Love   250
Robert Sternberg's Three-Component Love   251
SECTION SUMMARY: IMAGES OF LOVE   252

Attraction to Others   **253**

Familiarity   253
Physical Features   253
Positive Regard   254
SECTION SUMMARY: ATTRACTION TO OTHERS   255

Relationship Development   **255**

Personality Patterns   255
Forming the Relationship   256
SECTION SUMMARY: RELATIONSHIP DEVELOPMENT   260

Functioning of Love Relationships   **260**

Experiences in Love Relationships   260
Patterns of Intimacy   261
Challenges to Love Relationships   263
SECTION SUMMARY: FUNCTIONING OF LOVE RELATIONSHIPS   265

Chapter Conclusions   **266**
Study and Review Questions   **266**

9. SOCIAL INTERACTIONS   269

Social Order   **270**

Manners and Propriety   270
Fads and Fashions   272
SECTION SUMMARY: SOCIAL ORDER   274

Accounts of Conduct   **274**

Facework   275
Motive Talk   276
Attributions of Responsibility   278
SECTION SUMMARY: ACCOUNTS OF CONDUCT   279

Social Order Disruption   **280**

Altruism and Helping   280
Crowd Acts and Mobs   282
SECTION SUMMARY: SOCIAL ORDER DISRUPTION   283

Bound to the Majority   **284**

Influence Experiments and Analyses   284
Mechanisms of Influence   285
Seductions of Dissent   286
SECTION SUMMARY: BOUND TO THE MAJORITY   287

Practical Social Influences   **288**

Authority   288
Attraction   289
Conformity   290
Commitment   291
Reciprocation   291

SECTION SUMMARY:
PRACTICAL SOCIAL INFLUENCES   292

Chapter Conclusions   **292**
Study and Review Questions   **292**

10. MOTIVATED COGNITION   295

Experiencing Consciousness   **296**

Stream of Consciousness   296
Agency   299
SECTION SUMMARY: EXPERIENCING CONSCIOUSNESS   301

Theorizing Mind   **302**

Consciousness: A Persistent Problem   302
Eliminative Materialism   303
Cognitive Closure   304
Representing Reality   305
Dennett's Parallel Brain Machine   306
SECTION SUMMARY: THEORIZING MIND   309

Controlling Awareness   **310**

Meditating   310
Experiencing Hypnosis   311
SECTION SUMMARY: CONTROLLING AWARENESS   313

Thinking   **314**

Reasoning   315
Deciding   316
Producing Consistent Thought   321
Staying Happy   325
SECTION SUMMARY: THINKING   326

Chapter Conclusions   **326**
Study and Review Questions   327

11. ADDICTION   329

Components of Addictive Acts   **330**

Physiological Effect   330
Psychological Dependence   331
Habitual Action   332
Cultural Origins   333
Social Response   334
Economical Affect Maintenance   334
Self-Representation   335
SECTION SUMMARY: COMPONENTS OF ADDICTIVE ACTS   335

Addiction Theory and Change   **336**

Models of Addiction   336

Abstinence Versus Moderation   337

SECTION SUMMARY: ADDICTION THEORY AND CHANGE   339

Taking Drugs   339

Narcotic Drugs   340
Social History of Drug Use   341
Politics of Illegality   344

SECTION SUMMARY: TAKING DRUGS   347

Drinking   348

Early American Alcohol Drinking   348
Politics and Consumerism   349

SECTION SUMMARY: DRINKING   353

Smoking   354

Social History of Smoking   354
Health and Politics   355

SECTION SUMMARY: SMOKING   356

Dieting   356

SECTION SUMMARY: DIETING   357

Chapter Conclusions   357
Study and Review Questions   358

12. WORK   361

Images of Work   362

Reluctant Producing   362
Work Motivation Theory   363

SECTION SUMMARY: IMAGES OF WORK   364

Worker Character   364

Fulfilling Needs   364
Personality Styles   366

SECTION SUMMARY: WORKER CHARACTER   368

Conditions of Work   368

Hygiene and Motivator Factors   368
Job Enhancement   370
Intrinsic Motivation and Rewards   372
Equity Theory   374
Fatigue   375

SECTION SUMMARY: CONDITIONS OF WORK   382

Work Organization Systems   383

Management Participation   383
Outcome Expectancies   385
Accepting Goals   386
Motivation-Performance-Satisfaction Cycle   387
Reward Systems   388

SECTION SUMMARY: WORK ORGANIZATION SYSTEMS 390

Chapter Conclusions 391
Study and Review Questions 391

13. PLAY AND LEISURE 395

Foundations of Play 396

Natural Bases 396
Social and Cognitive Concepts 397
SECTION SUMMARY: FOUNDATIONS OF PLAY 398

Looking for Experience 399

Curiosity 399
Boredom, Optimum, and Overload 401
Absorption 404
Consequences 406
SECTION SUMMARY: LOOKING FOR EXPERIENCE 406

Theories of Ritual, Play, And Leisure 407

Ideas of Ritual 407
Views of Playing 408
Conceptions of Leisure 411
SECTION SUMMARY: THEORIES OF RITUAL, PLAY, AND LEISURE 413

Forms of Playing 413

Social Interactions 414
Play in Language 414
Games 415
Sport 416
SECTION SUMMARY: FORMS OF PLAYING 417

Forms of Leisure 418

Time in Leisure 418
Leisure Variety 420
Touring 420
SECTION SUMMARY: FORMS OF LEISURE 423

Chapter Conclusions 423
Study and Review Questions 424

EPILOGUE: MOTIVATION IDEALS 427

REFERENCES 433

INDEX 461

ABOUT THE AUTHOR 467

Preface

The tradition of a preface demands I tell you why I wrote the book, what its contents are, and who helped in the project. A few moments here will help you understand the variations in content and format I have chosen.

I prepared this textbook primarily to introduce students to the fascinating ideas of motivation and emotion. After I had presented psychology's motivation materials to students for a few decades, I found that the topics of most interest and general application were not well covered, if at all, in the standard textbooks. The content most valuable to students has been slowly developing and is no longer served by focusing on psychological theories formed in the 1960s and earlier. I came to believe that many of those older ideas deserved to have a respectful burial rather than continued recycling in detail in textbooks. The proliferation of unneeded content, along with escalating textbook prices, led me to build this book of ideas about motivation.

This textbook has been a long time in development because new ideas are always appearing that make a revision in order. I do not pretend that this is a handbook or review of all we know and have done. Instead, I have chosen what I believe to be the best topics relating to motivation and emotion, researched them for facts and ideas, pared them down where necessary, and put them in a good order.

The structure, content, and presentation of this text all aim at students learning concepts of motivation and emotion. I assume that my readers are college and university students with a few years of experience and some familiarity with logical methods of science, concepts of social science, and basic ideas of general psychology. No specific knowledge is a prerequisite, but I expect most students will benefit occasionally from a review of additional sources. The names of the topics are specific and instructive. There is a prospectus at the end of the first chapter; I don't see a further need for an overview of the contents here. My biases, personal preferences, and choices are clearly explicated as each topic first appears.

Each chapter begins with a concise overview and ends with a personal summary. Material illustrating some ideas is shown in sans serif type like this. Important terms and concept names appear in boldface type. Major sections conclude with a summary. At the end of each chapter is a set of questions to facilitate study. By outlining the basic structure of a multiple-choice examination, these ideas answer the perennial student question, What do we have to know for the exam?

What you won't find in this book are unneeded figures, multicolor illustrations, and numerous boxes and the like that have overwhelmed textbook publishing over the years. My goal is simplicity. No illustration should distract the reader from the chosen material or give undue emphasis to weaker or rejected ideas. I believe illustrations should make a special point, being reserved for material that is visual in form or not easily described in words.

The primary help I must acknowledge is that of the countless researchers and thinkers whose work I have humbly tried to put together in a coherent way. In addition to arrangement and order, I have inserted a few new ideas, giving objective meaning to my title of professor, meaning "one who professes."

Specific thanks are due my daughter and former Iowa State University student, A. J.

Edwards, who carefully applied her writer's eye to my early efforts and motivated me to keep the student reader in mind. Of course, she can't be blamed for any remaining problems. Thanks are also owed to developmental editor Ann West, Sage Senior Editor C. Deborah Laughton, and series editor Lyle E. Bourne, Jr.

The several creative illustrations are the work of Melissa Cheeseman, a recent graduate of Iowa State University's biological illustration program; her signature appears on her artwork.

Finally, I thank those colleagues who have supported my writing over the years in various ways. Particular thanks are due Camilla Benbow for encouraging me to complete this book; I may well have gone on forever in revising and changing as I discovered more ideas. Even now I am thinking about doing a couple of things differently in Chapter. . . .

CHAPTER 1

Introduction and History

Motivation is a language concept we use to help account for our lives. We will study motivation from the viewpoint of natural science accounting for choices, intensities, and feelings of human activities.

Psychology has developed as a blend of scientific philosophy and physiology. German laboratory experiments and American practical study of mental experience led the way for a set of theoretical schools—structuralism, functionalism, psychoanalysis, and behaviorism—each adding a component to modern psychology's thought about motivation. Traditional theory has pictured motivation in a variety of ways including as a biological substance or process, a condition of the nervous system, and a set of inherited functions. Modern study describes motivation using biological, social, and cognitive information.

Psychology's Past

Ideas in Motivation Theory

Modern Motivation Science

*M*otivation is a word we use to describe and account for how we do things. But the study of motivation does not come with a clear definition to mark its domain and boundaries. Even so, we want an established definition because we think that is the way it *should* be done. Our intellectual habits and myths take over. Aren't definitions supposed to start us on common ground, eliminating confusion at the beginning of our study? But the concept of motivation is a little bit peculiar: Experts don't agree on just what it is or isn't. We could look at many samples of attempts to define *motivation*, but that would not be helpful without an explanation of each writer's personal history and point of view in the wonderful world of psychology theory. In spite of this, we will outline some concepts later in this chapter that amount to a rough definition, a working definition.

Where then shall we start? Perhaps the best beginning is to establish common ground about what psychology was and is. This leads us to some history that may seem remote from the ways we conduct our daily lives. But we have a clear purpose. Many topics involving motivation make better sense when their origins are understood. Most educated Western readers know something about Darwin, Freud, and Pavlov, and those who have studied some psychology recognize words like *behaviorism, psychoanalysis,* and *cognitive science.* Each of these terms and many others had a direct influence on how psychologists imagined and developed the ideas of motivation.

After looking at that history, where do we go? The next part of the chapter leads us into the general conceptions we have about motivation. Is it a thing, a force, a biological condition, a behavior choice, an energetic performance, a thought pattern, a feeling of energy, a pleasure, a pain, or what? We will examine these ideas and, along the way, describe the ground rules for the rest of the study. Finally, we conclude this chapter with a brief sketch of some recent developments in the study of motivation.

In the remainder of the book, we will explore topics common to the investigation of motivation. The topics were chosen partly by what is traditional, and, just as important, by this guiding question: What can we learn about motivation that will make a difference in our lives? We will try to answer that.

PSYCHOLOGY'S PAST

The work in motivation represents a curious collection of information. There are bundles of facts and principles about particular topics, whereas others have scarcely been touched. In general, theories from diverse parts of psy-

chology have dictated the notions of what motivation must be. Furthermore, certain philosophical viewpoints have proposed what should and what should not be studied. To understand this curious collection, it is helpful, if not necessary, to have in mind some background of psychology. A selective history of a few relevant ideas will guide our thinking about motivation and its theories. More details can be found in the many good history of psychology texts (e.g., Heidbreder, 1933; Leahey, 1992; Schultz & Schultz, 1996).

Founding of Psychology

By the latter half of the 1800s, several studies of mind by philosophers and a few topics of physiologists were focused in their parent fields. Individuals with these emerging ideas called themselves psychologists. Their goal was to establish psychology as a new science, a purposeful attempt to repeat the previous successes of physiology and physics. The forms of science—its methods, its language, and its philosophy—were thought to be useful to answer psychology's questions as well. The choice of how to do and think about psychological problems, however, came from a combination of different traditions in German rationalist and British empiricist philosophy. Within that general context, the separate academic area of psychology developed in and around two cultural movements: Wilhelm Wundt's laboratory science and William James's science of experience.

Wundt's Laboratory Psychology

In the middle 1800s, research laboratories were just beginning to be the proper places to examine questions of science. Nowhere did laboratory science grow so fast and become so powerful as in Germany. Following this tradition, in the 1870s, Wilhelm Wundt (see Figure 1.1) at Leipzig University established physiological (experimental) psy-

Figure 1.1. Wilhelm Wundt (1832-1920).

SOURCE: From the Archives of the History of American Psychology. Reprinted by permission.

Figure 1.2. William James (1842-1910).

SOURCE: From the Archives of the History of American Psychology. Reprinted by permission.

chology to be, in part, the laboratory science of mental experience.

His laboratory became famous for experimental studies of various visual and auditory perceptions, response times for different thoughts, chains of associated memories, the dimensions of feelings, and a host of other topics. Wundt's purpose was to construct a comprehensive theory of human functioning, but Wundt's personal objective was forgotten by those excited by the idea of a laboratory science of psychology. In the years before 1900, American students discovered the new laboratories of psychology run by Wundt and others in Germany, earned their degrees, and returned to develop psychology in American colleges.

James's Science of Mental Life

The second cultural movement affecting psychology was American in origin. Even before Wundt's influence rose to its peak, William James (see Figure 1.2) and others in America were teaching and writing about the new experimental philosophy called psychology. James's influence was especially strong, both personally and because of his masterful handbook of psychological topics, *Principles of Psychology,* published in 1890. His perspective was that psychology is the science of mental life and that psychologists need to base their knowledge upon a scientific examination of that mental experience.

American psychologists did not entirely follow either Wundt or James. They incorporated more topics than did Wundt and had philosophical differences with the perspective of James's mental experiences. The method of the Americans was primarily science as they saw it, but selection of topics and problems soon followed practical interests. In a word, they broadened psychology. Among the new topics they looked at were education, child psychology, old age, abnormality, and social behavior. American psychologists also paid attention to mental illness and problems of everyday life, and so an applied psychology developed.

Through all of this early development, there was a strongly self-conscious concern for making psychology into a legitimate and respectable science. Its methods were carefully argued and analyzed. From these arguments, divisions began to form based on interpretations of what scientific psychology should be and what it should not be. This set the stage for a procession of "schools" of psychology.

Theoretical Schools of Psychology

Psychologists did not seriously question how to address the understanding of human functioning. They assumed that scientific methods, as interpreted by empiricism and positivism, would be adequate by themselves. That is, only directly observed and simple experience could provide facts for scientific psychology. (In the opinion of some philosophers of psychology, their assumption was just a philosophical hypothesis, and I believe that remains a fair judgment of today's psychology as well.) Thus, the history of formal psychology is one of minor variations in scientific methods and big differences in what material to apply those methods to. The scientific method was supreme; the subject floated.

Structuralism

The first systems of psychology, which most loudly proclaimed themselves to be scientific, were little more than extensions of the associationist position found in British philosophy. In that view, mental content and operations were believed to come from a succession of associated experiences. Structuralists, most influential from about 1895 to 1920, proposed that psychology examine such contents of mind by using the methods of the laboratory. The idea was to build a firm

Figure 1.3. Edward Bradford Titchener (1867-1962).

SOURCE: From the Archives of the History of American Psychology. Reprinted by permission.

understanding of the elements and processes that occur in the mind.

The structuralists' leader, Edward B. Titchener (see Figure 1.3), saw their role as similar to that of scientists who study the body. Anatomists describe parts of the body, and so psychologists must discuss the elements of mind with a descriptive vocabulary. Like physiologists finding body mechanisms of action, psychologists can and should be examining the workings of the mind by careful experiment. They are to describe the structure and flow of normal mental content. Although there was no distinctly motivational component in this approach, the structuralists did begin to describe the mental states underlying positive and negative feelings.

There are many logical and political reasons why structuralism did not produce a foundation for psychology, but it had one strong and lasting legacy. Its proponents established the attitude that the only valid psy-

Figure 1.4. Robert Sessions Woodworth (1869-1962).

SOURCE: From the Archives of the History of American Psychology. Reprinted by permission.

chology was an experimental one. As a result, a measure of mystique and prestige became attached to the methods and topics of experimental psychology.

Functionalism

Functionalism is a broader and longer lasting school of thought, which also has an informative name. The majority of American psychology was functionalist in its early years. Functionalism essentially began with the first generation of American psychologists in the 1890s and never really disappeared. The intent was to study the functions of the mind. What does the mind do? How does it work?

There was a strong evolutionary flavor to early functionalism. Functionalists assumed that the purposeful mind must have evolved to assume its present role of guiding adaptive behaviors. Functions such as learn-

ing, thinking, perceiving, adjusting, and so on were studied with methods that had been successful in other sciences. Functionalists produced the first formal ideas of motivation.

Rapid growth of American universities around the turn of the century provided an employment opportunity for new psychology professors. Large and strong programs developed at the University of Chicago and at Columbia University in New York City. These departments educated the bulk of the doctoral students, who then spread the functionalist perspective across America.

Functionalism was especially compatible with the innovative applications to which psychology was being directed. For example, a motivational emphasis in functionalism was given at Columbia University by Robert Woodworth (1918) in his *Dynamic Psychology* (see Figure 1.4). In what he called a "motivology," he saw drives as energy sources that motivate changes in behaviors and feelings. He pictured dynamic behavior as made up of mechanisms and drives. Mechanisms, whether learned or innate, form how a behavior is done; drives determine why. A "look for food" mechanism is activated by a hunger drive.

Psychoanalysis

An especially popular school of thought was based on the psychoanalytic psychology of Sigmund Freud (see Figure 1.5). Freud began systematic writings just before 1900, but he reached the peak of his personal influence in the 1920s. By that time, he had visited and lectured in America (in 1909) and the national animosities of World War I were over. In psychoanalytic thought, the primary causes of acts are unconscious. Freud believed that the structure of one's personality forms in childhood experiences within sexual contexts. Psychoanalysts discovered these unconscious formational forces through careful construction of cues from behavior, dreams, and the method of free association of ideas. Even though these methods of psychoanaly-

Figure 1.5. Sigmund Freud (1856-1939).

SOURCE: From the Archives of the History of American Psychology. Reprinted by permission.

ety, resulting from childhood isolation and helplessness in a potentially hostile world.

A new generation of psychologists became excited by psychoanalytic ideas. Henry Murray (1938) led a project attempting to comprehensively account for individual personalities. Among his theory elements was a set of 20 needs that provide motivation to behavior. He saw needs as brain forces that organize mental forces to satisfy them. Among the 20 needs, achievement, power, and affiliation have been used by researchers in theories of work motivation (see also Chapter 12).

Behaviorism

Beginning about 1900, protests appeared against parts of the structuralists' program that based psychology exclusively on a study of the contents of mind. John Watson (see Figure 1.6) and others argued that psychology should include the study of behavior. As this thesis strengthened in the 1920s, Watson went further. He rejected the study of mental experience altogether and proposed

sis developed in the clinic rather than the laboratory, Freud proposed them as a scientific thesis.

Many of Freud's ideas were attractive, especially those relating to motivation. Although ideas of unconscious processes were commonplace in the 1800s, his development of them as sources of motivation added to their wide acceptance. Hidden forces and urges provided excuses for what we do, in his thinking. The many defense mechanisms that he described appeared in psychology as part of the popular subject called adjustment.

Other psychoanalysts developed similar themes. Carl Jung (1936) proposed what came to be labeled *analytic psychology* and included varieties of collective and personal unconscious motivations. Alfred Adler (1930) stressed the motivational potential of striving for superiority and compensating for feelings of inferiority. Karen Horney (1937) believed motivation springs from basic anxi-

Figure 1.6. John Broadus Watson (1878-1958).

SOURCE: From the Archives of the History of American Psychology. Reprinted by permission.

that psychology be strictly the investigation of public behavior.

Behaviorism significantly changed the goal of psychology, even though this shift was subtle. Psychology was no longer attempting to understand human functioning. Instead, it proposed merely to predict and control subjects' behavior. This difference in worldview not only influenced the subject of what one does, but also affected the kinds of thoughts psychologists were permitted in their newly limited science.

By the 1930s and lasting through the 1950s, behaviorism was the most outspoken if not the dominant thought in psychology. A 1930s' generation of behaviorists, called the neobehaviorists, provided theories and programs of research for psychology. The major laboratory topic of the neobehaviorists was learning, adopting conditioned reflexes as elements of primary theory. Behaviorists readily employed animals as subjects, motivated in these studies by biological conditions of hunger and pain-forming drives. Most neobehaviorists held a simple mechanical picture of behavior that followed from the dynamic psychology of functionalism; learned habits (the machinery) were motivated by drives coming from biological needs (the energy).

SECTION SUMMARY: PSYCHOLOGY'S PAST

The study of motivation in psychology is built on the strategies and plans of groups of psychologists holding definite points of view. It began as a blending of philosophical questions and laboratory methods, but this blend was manifested differently in Wilhelm Wundt's Germany and William James's America. We remember Wundt for his methods and James for his ideas.

Americans first developed the new psychology along two lines. Structuralists asked the question, What are the contents and processes of mind? Functionalists asked, What are the evolved functions and uses of the mind? These two schools of thought were challenged by two narrower points of view. Sigmund Freud's psychoanalysis focused psychology on mental abnormalities and their presumed sources in unconscious motivational dynamics. John Watson's behaviorism challenged the validity of scientific studies of the subjective mind, proposing instead only objective observations of behavior. Each of these views shaped the terms of the study of motivation.

We turn next to some general background ideas about motivation that came in part from our psychology heritage. Is motivation a substance? Is it energy? Is it inherited? Is it a way of acting? Is it a personal mental awareness?

IDEAS IN MOTIVATION THEORY

Among theorists and researchers in psychology, agreement has not been reached concerning the nature of motivation. In rough summary, a hundred years ago, it was be- lieved that motivation arose from "springs of conduct," an accepted part of human nature (Romanes, 1886). Fifty years ago, motivation was tightly linked with theories of "needs" and "drives" (e.g., Hull, 1943; Murray, 1938). In recent years, psychologists have been less interested in using motivation in any central role in their theories, and the result has been a disintegration and breakup into narrower topics and theses. There is still no real consensus among psychologists, but in an everyday sense, they agree that motivation has to do with what makes people act the way they do (e.g., Beck, 1990; Franken, 1993). Theories of motivation are said to consider two kinds of questions about human acts: Why? and With what energy?

Motivation as Substance

As we noted at the beginning, *motivation* is an idea word, and it is part of the human story. We use motivation ideas to describe and account for the things we do and how we do them. Going deeper, motivation in all of its appearances is part of an idea of things being caused to happen. At this point, we bring in habits of thought.

If motivation is an idea about causes, it must be some *thing*. In our physical world, we believe that only things that are real can have influence on other things, because "nothing" can't cause things to happen. We talk of motivation causing us to do things, so motivation must be a thing. And if it is a thing, it must be possible to define it or at least make it appear in some way for our inspection and study.

This is a common, although hidden, chain of thought about motivation, but it also gives us false expectations. The roots of motivational acts *are* physical, but it may not be helpful to approach understanding the motivation idea that way. The thing-status of motivation is nonsense to the degree that we force our thinking along the lines of physical machinery.

Mechanical Models

We have a long tradition of using physical models to explain how things work. The idea is seductive. We seem to know so much about the ways physical forces cause things to happen. Powers of attraction and repulsion, expansion and contraction, heat and cold, electrical events and chemical changes—all

of these are commonly accepted, with only the fine details to be studied by each of us. Our vague picture of the physical world is certainly causal, even if the specifics of what we each know are coarse and fuzzy. The conclusion people habitually come to is that real science is nothing more than physical things and their properties. That conclusion is soundly defensible and generally accepted philosophy.

The next step creates problems for motivation philosophy and perhaps much of psychology. That step assumes that any *ideas about things* can be reduced to *existence of physical things* and their properties. We get our word labels mixed up with our physical things. Because we speak of motivation as causing things to happen, we want to see motivation as a real, physical thing that has substance and properties in a physical world. This is what some philosophers call making a *category mistake*.

Sometimes, for example, we poke around in the brain for that special organization of matter called motivation. If motivation is real stuff causing things to happen, it must be in there somewhere. The problem is that this is not where motivation can ultimately be found. Body machinery is all that will be seen to exist. The difficulty comes from our simplifying a great deal of complex and diverse functioning into a word, thinking that the word represents a thing and then looking for its physical image. It isn't anywhere because motivation does not exist in that way.

The logical path goes further. After we have agreed on the word and assumed it must be physical, then we turn to studying it with the traditional and practical tools of physical science, especially those of analysis. That describes things and what they do in terms of properties of their pieces. How do the pieces fit together and affect each other? In physics, we see that powers of things come from the relations among the pieces. This has worked very well in early studies of the physical world. If that type of analysis works for physical things, it must surely be a proper method for studying anything. In a sense, that may be so, but analysis is not the only useful way to study ideas about how things function.

Biological Models

Mechanical models of motivation often look to biology for their pieces. The functions of the body can be divided into mechanistic elements and energizing elements. This logical approach supposes that there will be systems, or areas, or fluids in the body's communication systems that are the source of that energy. One example is brain and brainstem neural structures that appear to regulate general arousal. We will look at examples of these arousal ideas next. But the thalamus and hypothalamus are also major centers in several theoretical ideas about motivation that will be mentioned in topics in later chapters. Endocrine gland secretions and specific neurotransmitters likewise are found in descriptions of motivated activities. Each of these carries the danger of being seen as *the* motivation center, the one physical image that determines motivation.

If we do not rely solely on physical or biological substance, then what *do* we use? Does this mean we are going to turn away from science? Some motivation theorists have suggested that we must resort to new ways, taking a different philosophical path to understanding. We will not follow that trail, because it has not yet proved productive. Our choice is to remain in the domain of natural science but establish a broader explanatory strategy. To do that, we look at other ways the idea of motivation is used.

Motivation as Energy

Energy is a good, functional word. We find it very useful. Energy is part of Einstein's formula of $e = mc^2$, and we describe energy resources in oil reserves and solar radiation. There are countless ways we speak of the effects of energy and its sources. But energy is not a thing. It makes no concrete sense to talk of pure energy except as an idea. It exists in our description of events, but it is not real in any other sense. Energy is a concept, an abstraction we find useful. The forms that energy ideas take are many, and no one should believe that one kind is the real energy in which we can see all the others. That is, we can't find a specific energy instance that is its true essence.

Energy as a concept reaches into just about every domain of our thinking. In a sense, with space, time, and perhaps a very few other dimensions, energy is a part of every topic with which we deal. Wherever there is change, we find it compelling to speak of the sources and effects of energy. In this basic sense, we find it easy to view life as an energy-based function. Mere existence as a living thing implies a flow of energy changes. The more complicated the living thing, the more kinds of energy effects we can describe. In a sense, this is a logical circle, but as that is so, it is also an important lesson about our common understanding of things.

It is soon apparent, as we think in these ways, that the forms of energy and what they do in human bodies are basic to existing as living things. Energy forms are the means by which we can describe the important ways our bodies function. It is easy to abstract and combine these notions of body energy. We can feel the intensity of our body's functioning. That mental experience is obvious in everyone's intuition and makes up part of what we feel is our motivation of the moment. As this is a common and frequent experience, it would seem to be an obvious way to approach the concept of motivation. But the concepts with which we make up the idea of motivation do not reduce to any simple form of body energy. Furthermore, there has been no success in finding a simple measure of body energy as we commonly conceive of it. We need to explore some of the general features of body energy and energy changes to see why that is so.

Physiological Arousal

Physiological components have existed side by side with psychological ideas since the first writings in psychology. This stems in part from the origins of psychology as philosophical ideas of certain physiologists. Wilhelm Wundt and William James were trained as physiologists, and Sigmund Freud was a physician. Physiology continues to hold a fascination for psychologists with its implicit promise of holding secrets of the causes of human acts. The concept of physiology that most directly resembles the idea of pure motivation is overall body energy. As facts and theories of physiological energy accumulated, psychological theory borrowed them. In this vein, psychology's energy ideas developed.

Muscle tone and tension seem to account for strengths of actions. The body as a whole appears to vary in energy tone. Ideas of tonic processes were named **energetics,** activation, and arousal. Of these, activation is a term more commonly used in the description of biological and chemical processes. **Arousal** has become the most-used energy term in general psychology.

Arousal as a Theory Idea

A thorough summary of the history and variety of concepts of arousal may never be written. It is difficult to chronicle an idea used so widely in psychology. The popularity of arousal rests on its peculiar dimensions. First, we like arousal because it suggests what seems to be patently true: People vary in their body energy level. That simple abstract idea strongly suggests a single process. Belief in arousal has become implicit, nearly unchallenged.

Second, a variety of possible measures of arousal were illustrated in the works of physiologists. Apparent measures of arousal abound. Physiological changes and self-reports can be measured and compared with changes in physical and psychological performance. In 1929, Walter Cannon proposed the idea of energy mobilization in various body states such as pain, hunger, fear, and rage. Psychologists in the 1930s followed with similar energy models. Elizabeth Duffy (1951) described energy mobilization as "the

energy used in tensing the muscles in preparation for overt response as well as that used in the overt response itself. Figuratively speaking, it is the rate at which the bodily engine is running" (p. 32).

The metaphor was commonplace and seemed obvious. "Bodily engine-running" energizes motor acts. Arousal energy was measured directly as muscle tension and indirectly as the electrical activity in muscle tissue and electrical conductance of the skin. Neither muscle tension nor skin conductance was meant to be identical with energy mobilization, but "the general direction which such measurement should take is clearly apparent, and only the details remain to be worked out" (Duffy, 1951, p. 33).

Psychologists were quick to use measures that were simple and quantitative, such as heart rate or electrical skin responses, often paying little heed to their validity. Where there are patterns of data that conform to what one wants to see, there is little incentive to be critical. However, none of these often used measures of arousal is without major problems and concerns about other aspects of functioning they may be reflecting.

Third, there tends to be intellectual confusion about the kind of concept arousal is. In one view, arousal is a general state of body energy, a tonic condition that reflects all aspects of performance. This is perhaps the kind of idea most psychologists accept in using arousal measures and ideas in their work. Another view shows arousal to be a brief period of changed condition and performance, a phasic state that reflects the immediate situation. Most typical of phasic arousal are some of the energetics studies of the increased muscle intensity we recruit to do difficult tasks (see the "Energetic Acting" section later in the chapter).

Although arousal appears as a single dimension of body energy available for psychological performance, the many pieces proposed to make up arousal do not correlate well. Several theorists have noted this fact. John Lacey (1967) expressed early doubt that arousal is a unitary dimension. He noted that correlations among autonomic nervous system measures of arousal are low. Brain-stem activation

(Reticular Activating System or RAS) and brain-wave (Electroencephalograph or EEG) (see Chapter 2 or the Index) measures of arousal are not always related to those of the autonomic nervous system or to performance measures. He also elaborated a *directional fractionation* of measures under certain conditions. For example, in response to an arousing stimulus, the heart reduces its rate of pumping blood for a time.

Other theorists have proposed physiological systems of arousal that serve different specific functions. We will briefly list some of them for emphasis, without explanation. One early scheme separated response-organization functions of the brain stem's Reticular Activating System (RAS) from rewarding consequences of the limbic system of the brain (Routtenberg, 1968). More recently, two theorists proposed three controlling subcortical brain systems. One determines the basic readiness to respond, a second sets the level of the response, and the third coordinates the other two through the effect of effort (Pribram & McGuinness, 1975). In another recent theory, the action of different neurotransmitter systems establishes readiness and level of response (Tucker & Williamson, 1984). Still another approach to arousal is through self-reports of mood; this has resulted in a theory of energetic and tense arousal. Energetic arousal is body mobilization, such as that coming from productive work or exercises combined with conscious awareness of attentive vigor and expectation of competence. Tense arousal is defensive body mobilization combined with conscious awareness of possible danger and readiness for distraction (Thayer, 1989). Together these theories and others like them illustrate the complexity wrapped into the arousal idea. More theory and problems with arousal are presented below in the section "Energetic Acting."

Evolutionary Models

Biology has another model to consider, as well, one that does not reduce motivation directly to substance or simple process. In-

Figure 1.7. Charles Darwin (1809-1882).

SOURCE: From the Archives of the History of American Psychology. Reprinted by permission.

stead of focusing on what motivation *is,* we may focus on how the conditions it describes evolved. Now, the better model may be evolutionary biology instead of simple physics. The new themes are biological ones of process and of change that have a past as well as a present. This evolutionary perspective makes us think about the structures that stand behind the life patterns we call motivation.

Charles Darwin's book, *On the Origin of Species by Means of Natural Selection* (1859; see Figure 1.7), began a wave of excitement that infected all of academic thought by the turn of the century. Many psychologists were enthusiastic proponents of ideas of instinct, adaptation, and evolutionary selection. They quickly saw in evolution a set of answers to questions about motivation. Commonplace body and mental functions alike were assumed to be based on inheritance. Some of these ideas now seem fantastic at best. For example, it is in the nature of dogs to love their masters. People naturally respond with sadness to loss of a child. Women are biologically ordained to bear and raise children rather than acquire education. Primitive peoples are less fully evolved than those of Western society and hence feel less pain. A stronger instinct for pugnacity leads some men to fight.

The "instinct" label was applied recklessly to nearly everything people do, and reaction developed. Some behaviorists led a successful fight to make the word and idea of instinct forbidden in proper scientific psychology. Consequently, there was poor development in psychology of principles of Darwinian evolution, and that allowed new misapplications.

Human Nature Misconceived

It's natural to look to our biological roots to understand why we do things. We know we are animals, although very special ones. If we are animals, there might be some causes for what we do in our biological nature. Few people would seriously object to that. Yet, there are problems of philosophy and attitude in finding and interpreting that biological human nature. The modern study of evolutionary psychology provides the best approach.

Evolutionary psychology can tell us the way we are, and that can be seductive. Sometimes, we buy the implications of being animals to the degree that we see ourselves as *only* animals. At the root of these extreme beliefs is a mechanical theme of fatalism. We can fall into believing that some acts are part of our physical nature; that they are caused by something inside us; and that until we learn enough to change our bodies, we must provide some relief for their insistent urges. The seduction comes from how some of these ideas make things we do seem acceptable because we cannot control ourselves. Fatalism allows us to assign responsibility to a hidden biological nature for some things we do.

If these things are a part of human nature, then we are in a sense free from responsibility for their having happened. "I couldn't help doing it, I'm only human" or "Human nature made me do it!" The biological theme is compelling when it provides these justifications for us, excusing our periodic excursions into acts that the social rules of civilized society may disapprove. These prejudices suggest that we look more closely at what we commonly call our human nature.

Myths of Nature Versus Culture

Our human nature is typically contrasted with our culture. The presumption is that human nature is fixed and can be no different than what it is, whereas human culture is arbitrary and can be readily changed and resisted as situations are presented. The natural themes, those of nature, are unalterable, competitive ones, whereas those of culture have cooperative flexibility. Once this general myth is assumed, and one side or the other is taken regarding some topic, the search for confirming examples is easy.

The ease of this nature-culture contrast is disarming. When we inspect it more closely it gets more problematic and can easily lead us astray. What have we evolved to do? What are some specific adaptations? In this perspective, we eat, sleep, walk, smile, and do all manner of other things that are biologically structured, not formed by early life experience. We use spoken, abstract language. We prefer what is sweet in part because a sensitivity to certain substances probably helped us to select substances rich in sugar energy. Others are just tendencies that were selected by their success in aiding reproductive fitness and that now provide a basis for specific acts or functions.

Evolutionary Psychology

The key in evolutionary psychology is building defensible knowledge of adaptations as they would have formed in ancestral environments and describing how those adaptations would respond to current conditions. Our sweet tooth for lemon drops was formed by events unrelated to the package of candy we find in the store. In general, our present culture plays a necessary role in eliciting our natural response, but our reaction may serve a different role from that on which our nature was formed.

A proper analysis following evolutionary psychology will present (a) a design of adaptations that (b) would have led to a reproductive fitness advantage (more reproducing offspring) (c) over a long period in the ancestral world of adaptation. To escape the circularity of just making up any adaptation to match a current pattern of acts, the design must be tested by demonstrating how other implications of those adaptations should also appear as they operate in the conditions of the modern world (Tooby & Cosmides, 1992).

The resulting adaptation design reflects historical facts of reproductive success; these facts hold no implication for continuing to serve in the same way. For example, we can consider the following example design of adaptations: Men who selected and invested in women showing high mate value had a reproductive advantage. Women who selected men with evidence of willingness to invest in their children had a reproductive advantage. They each evolved adaptations for such selection and investment.

These adaptations should and do predict the patterns of choices that men and women now make in their choices of mating partners (Buss & Schmitt, 1993). The adaptations were established historically. There is no reason, however, to suppose that they continue to affect fitness, and there is no reason at all to assume that anyone seeks a mate now because of the urge to increase reproductive success. Neither do the adaptations hinge on whether they still have reproductive success as they are presently used. In fact, many adaptations are no longer heritable. That is, like the form of the eye or DNA chemistry, too little difference exists within the species for selection to work. These are ideas we will revisit in content chapters as we entertain possibilities of evolutionary adaptations.

To compound easy and direct observation of evolutionary adaptations, we each have a long period of experience forming our individual natures. So the genetic expression depends in part on the kind of development and learning we have had and the ways we have made use of what we think of as the "hard-wired" components. Any particular act that is partly human nature was formed in a cultural-social setting. It depended on individual development and learning for its formation and unfolding.

Understanding evolutionary adaptations is confusing when we blend in the myth that human nature is fixed and only culture can readily change. Expressions of genetic adaptations of the kind that affect our psychology are usually very flexible. Essentially, any adaptation of this kind is and has been modified both by individuals and by cultures. Adult human acts take place in culture by individuals with years of social training. Each and every feature can be and is altered from one group, individual, event, time, or place to another. The aspects we want to call human nature are no less changeable in their actual expression than those we call human culture. To believe that human nature is inflexible is simply factually wrong. It persists as philosophical preference founded on prejudice.

By the same token, neither can differences coming from culture be taken as evidence that there is no genetic adaptation. A common theme of criticism has been to scour the cultures of the world for evidence of just one that doesn't appear like the others in the feature being examined, and thereby conclude that there can therefore be no inherited adaptation. A better method looks for common features in widely different cultures. Any exceptions can be accommodated after a sound understanding is formed of the prevalent evolutionary adaptations.

Studying Animals

Another place of difficulty with human nature ideas is our relationship to other species. Some nineteenth-century biologists assumed that there is a single, grand order of the species from one-celled entities at the simple end to human beings at the most complex. That single order is an idea many of us still hold, and it is the hidden source of many a curiosity. For example, if we are higher than dogs, why can they follow a scent trail we can't detect? For that matter, why can't we fly, or swim under water for 10 minutes at a time? The questions quickly reveal that there are many dimensions of difference. The single chain is absurd because it presumes some single quality being ordered. Species differ in an amazingly complex set of ways.

Still, species can be lumped together when we look for similarities. Some of the similarities reflect possibilities from shared ancestry. At some point in evolution, the mammals were likely a single or very few species and all modern forms trace back to these few. There may then be a collection of adaptations from this early period that persists in all mammals. And so we trace shared ancestors to the present time.

In the family-tree picture, we are tempted to pick out our nearest relatives in terms of likely shared ancestry. In using this concept, we take a mental shortcut. Instead of thinking—as we should—that we descended from a common ancestor, we think we descended from primates like those with whom we now share the world. We forget, especially when we look at them for clues to our biology, that these other species also diverged from the common ancestor, and perhaps changed in some ways and amounts greater than we. Evolutionary selection works on all species to make them fit the world in which they lived.

The puzzles of our biology and adaptations are too complex to read a direct answer in the makeup of other current species. Still, that does not write off learning from the biology of animals. It just demands that we be cautious. The picture we can grasp must look at some broad strokes of (a) how other animals do things, (b) what causes lie in their biology, and (c) how those are similar to or different from what we do and what we can determine of our biology. Even after we find close comparisons of acts and causal physiology, we must be wary. The human species has taken a different path of adaptations and shows elaboration of brain structure and function shared with no other species. Even as we share, for example, limbic system structures, it is not certain that these systems do the same things in the same ways in the brains of rats, monkeys, and humans.

Describing Motivated Behavior

A valid understanding of whatever we agree to call motivation will be formed of descriptions made up of meaningful words. Word meaning comes from its successful history of use, so the approach we will now take examines some of that successful use of words about motivated behavior.

Language Descriptions

First, we will focus on the broadest ideas of motivation words, beginning with some general observations. Psychologists seek to know the reasons for the acts of others, to predict them with accuracy, and to understand the causes for them. But this is what we all do, just to get along in daily affairs. Everyone is a practicing psychologist. We must deal with other people, and that requires at least a moderate success in knowing what they will do and think. The psychologist's purpose is not different, although perhaps the product of scientific understanding will be in a different form than our usual experiences.

The basis for being successful with others lies in knowing oneself. Life is a continuous flow of acting in consort with others, but the key to being successful is predicting and understanding your own acts and perhaps describing them with inner language. Social existence is filled with language. We use language to describe the things we are doing or plan to do, and in social arenas, we use a similar description of others' acts and intentions and verify them in conversation. We can see most of our common understanding of daily affairs as made of that personal language.

Motivation is a common word for part of that understanding. It labels some features of the view everyone holds of their own thoughts and actions. We commonly detect variations in our personal motivation, and we know when someone else is motivated. At the same time, the features of that motivation, like those of many complex features of life, are not easy to clarify. Some of the meaning of motivation is a sense of spirit or energy. We can look in a thesaurus or two. The entries for *motivate* show these synonyms: animate, arouse, embolden, excite, goad, impel, incite, inflame, innervate, inspire, provoke, quicken, rouse, spur, and stimulate. The energy part of the motivation idea becomes clearer. Other parts of motivation involve personal will and the choices that we make. Thesaurus listings for *motive* include these: cause, consideration, ground, reason, and spring. Putting the two together, it becomes clearer that motivation labels ideas of energy and of choices. These agreements we have about word use mark one basis from which to begin a study of motivation.

Making Choices

We may pursue these motivation ideas as questions. We begin by looking at why, in the sense of reasons for choices of acts. Much of psychology seems to be trying to answer the question, What is typically done or what can one do? The perspective of motivation adds its unique question, Why does one do it at all? What are the forces provoking people to certain acts? The essence of the matter is choice. For example, Why are eating and drinking included in most social gatherings? Why do people seek sexual interactions? Why do politicians fund water diversions onto marginal lands to aid just a few ranchers? Why don't people spend all of their time in useful and productive work? Each of these questions of motivation seeks a description of why specific behaviors were chosen.

Energetic Acting

Arguably the more basic of the common motivation questions is With what energy are these things done? Motivated people usually do things with energy, forcefulness, and vigor. Those without motivation are often sluggish, weak, and listless. In the midst of action in a game, we are energetically motivated. We have more vigor in working at three in the afternoon than at three in the morning.

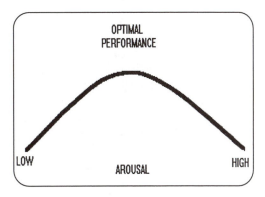

Figure 1.8. The inverted-*U* theory of arousal.

We use greater force to correct people who make us angry. Persistence in achieving a career goal shows motivation. These kinds of variations in energy indicate another part of what motivation commonly means.

In the 1950s and before, theorists developed energetics, mentioned above, as a motivation model (Duffy, 1951; Freeman, 1948). The most famous application of simple energetics is the idea that performance increases with arousal only up to a point and then worsens with greater arousal. Performance is pictured against some measure of body arousal as an inverted *U*-shaped curve (Hebb, 1949; see Figure 1.8).

The model implies that there is an optimal energy mobilization for maximum performance. Based at first upon a study of mice motivated by shock to learn to discriminate perceptually (Yerkes & Dodson, 1908), the inverted-*U* model grew to the status of a major principle. The principle was easily accepted because it made intuitive sense and fit in with the pattern of theory that was common. Everyone knows of times when increases in arousal gave them better performance, like the quick cup of coffee that made reading easier and clearer. We also can remember times when we got so overwrought that we could not perform. Put these together and there is a logical middle ground of optimal arousal.

Several thoughtful studies have exposed the oversimplification of the relationship (Neiss, 1988). One issue is whether there is an actual downturn in performance with increasing levels of arousal, or whether the observed performance worsens by some other consequence of trying to produce greater arousal. The studies reporting inverted-*U* curves have all failed to escape the latter condition. The operation required to produce the arousal directly impaired the measured performance. Some condition other than pure, increased arousal was responsible for the downturn in the curve (Naatanen, 1973).

A second, and more serious, issue is at the heart of the arousal concept as a single dimension of body energy. Neither the notion of arousal nor the idea of difficulty of task performance is a simple increasing function. In every specific instance, these are simplifications and abstractions of the actual variables and conditions.

An allied but largely unexamined assumption has been that the domain of arousal and the domain of task performance are entirely separate, so that it is simply a matter of checking the change in one against that of the other. Detailed study, however, has shown they are not independent. The causes of arousal are found to affect not just the intensity of the performance, but they also alter the *way* that the task is done, a qualitative change in the psychological function (Sanders, 1986). Despite the criticism, the inverted-*U* arousal theory persists.

Awareness of Motivation

We are going to be imprecise in our philosophy so that we can approach what we know about motivation from common experience. (For instance, "inside the mind" and "acts of mind" are commonplace phrases, but they are not a correct foundation on which to build a scientific explanation. We will try to clarify that in Chapter 10.) Several kinds of experience make up the view from within, but it is what we loosely call *feelings* and *expectations* that are closest to ideas of motivation.

Feeling is, first of all, a common label for our mental experience. News reporters constantly ask people they interview, "How did you feel?" when they want a report of the events from that person's perspective. We often speak of how we feel about an issue when we hope we are really talking in a logical way. A fuzzy complex of mental experiences is mixed up in that word *feel*.

Second, some of this mixture of ideas follows from language use that blends feelings with perceptual sensations (Coulter, 1989). Sensations of the outer world are the model for our language of experience. We directly sense *blue, large, rough, cool,* and *moving* as stimulation features and learn their names without difficulty in a common social group. Sensations of the outer world are caused by physical events, and there is little doubt of their origins. Physical stimulation from a green tree makes sensations that in themselves are clear and distinct, for example. There is little question as to the "what" that is occurring, but such occurrences have a different nature from sensations arising from "inside."

In more technical language, feelings name private body events for which there are no specific public references. We describe body sensations with the word *feel*: I feel cold, I feel tired, I feel sore, or I feel hungry. No one can know another's feelings, nor are there simple sources for stimulating feelings in the sense that there are instances of blue, large, rough, cool, moving, or green trees that can be identified for everyone in concrete ways. Yet, it is obvious that we do communicate our private feelings to others.

That gives us an important problem. On what is feeling language based? How can we come to agree on a word for some experience that is private for each of us? A reasonable answer is that the words for body feelings are based on natural actions that come from the conditions yielding those feelings (Harré, 1988; Wittgenstein, 1953). Feeling tired, I notice my slowed reactions and limp limbs. Having a pain in the head, I hold my head and moan. Being cold, I wrap my arms tightly about my body and shiver. Words come to replace those natural consequences and are acquired by use in communication with others.

Feelings of Energy

Motivation feelings can be divided into those that involve sensing some degree of energy, potential, and activity and those of the pleasure-pain value of the moment. Feelings of doing something with energy are basic to what we call motivation. Language words of intensity, as we described earlier, are reflections of those internal assessments. The more private aspect of this same complex is the feeling we have of being able or not being able to do something. Here the feeling is of potential, of being full of excitement and energy to do something, or of being unable to carry out what needs to be done. These feelings can exist and still not be communicated in what we do or say. We may know that we are not feeling energetic, for example, but we may carry on as if we were, to save face or position. Or we may hide our enthusiasm if we believe others may disapprove.

Seeking Pleasure, Avoiding Pain

Some feelings are of pleasure and others are of pain, and many others are somewhere between those ends. Pleasures and pains describe the natural dimension we call **affect.** (A related philosophical label is hedonism: holding that what is pleasant or has pleasant consequences is the highest good.) No one has had to learn what a pleasure is, or what it means to be pained. Immediate and inescapable pleasures and pains have been called "hidden beasts" of human life. They are beasts because they seem to have origins in our bodies, but also because they appear to rule our lives without respect for the reasoning that we would like to have in charge. (They are beasts, too, in the sense of having been difficult for psychologists and philosophers to tame.)

Based on foundations of natural experience, other aspects of life can take on affective meaning. Social events or mental problems or listening to music become attached to a quality of feeling. These attached pleasures and pains may become the valued aspects of human life. The irony is that the beast often underlies the valued meaning of living.

In our ordered and intellectual society, we claim that the beast of feelings sullies the purity of thinking. It has become a dogma of mental discipline that feelings must be suppressed. Real life of the workday world is to be controlled, free from passions and emotions. Being mature and in control means that feelings are to be disciplined in favor of intellect. But that is not possible, because feelings are always attached to what we are thinking and doing. They are an inherent part of all thought and action. Every choice we make among thoughts and actions pays tribute to those relative feelings (Solomon, 1976, 1989).

Explaining Experience

To understand the awareness phenomenon of motivation, we need to continue with a closer look at some of our assumptions. We will be talking about the kind of philosophy we agree to hold. There is nothing particularly difficult in philosophy. Doing philosophy is just persistence in trying to think clearly. Some psychologists, particularly those who cloak themselves under their science hood, see any look at philosophy as akin to poking a sleeping dog with a stick. They believe that the need for any philosophy has long since passed, and some even proclaim that the narrow form of philosophy called science sets the standards by which any other philosophy shall also be judged. We must be wary of the dizzy circle that this idea proposes and of the minds that are thereby closed in the name of science.

Wipe away the special shorthand jargon of the professionals and what is left are pictures of what we believe about what exists, how things work, and how we know about it all. Knowing how and what we are thinking is especially crucial in psychology because our beliefs shape the kind of questions we ask. As we find some answers, the questions are refined. There is no magic in scientific methods that stops the feedback process. Science is a current fashion of disciplined thinking having considerable success; it is not the end of philosophy.

We will explore one illustration, but a very important one.

I ask, "Who are you?"

"I am myself; I am me," you reply, perhaps adding your name.

But I persist. "What makes up your self as you know it? What are the pieces and what really exists of your self?"

Now you begin to defend what you know. You may talk of the sensations you now have and have always had, the narratives of the past you can bring out of your memory, and the pattern of things that you say and do.

But what is the meaning of this, really? There is nothing in your picture of yourself for others to know as you know it. Others can see you and see what you are doing. They can talk with you and get some measure of the communications you will share and volunteer. But cannot a machine be built to display these things as well? Does the machine then have a self just like yours? Is there nothing of your self but a pattern of machine-like activities coming from an essentially unchanged object?

How can we think more clearly about this particular problem and construct some ideas that are useful? That is one value of philosophy, and we look in Chapter 10 at some philosophy applied to just that problem. In many ways, this problem lies at the heart of motivation, if not all of psychology.

First, some ground rules for this book. We assume that psychology is a natural science, focusing on the functioning of human beings. Using natural science means that we will examine any objective evidence about the structure and nature of the focused subject. If we agree on that, there are several ways we can proceed. Human functioning can be examined from different directions. Some focus may be on cell organization and biological functioning. Other evidence comes from observing stimuli and consequent responses. A content peculiar to psychology is objective evidence of personal experience. Mental experience and social relations intertwine in how we use language. Any of these kinds of evidence are acceptable as they contribute to our coherent understanding of human functioning. Using natural science means we will develop the accumulated natural facts in a way that is consistent with those of other subjects of the natural world. No special standpoint or philosophical exceptions are needed.

Nonetheless, the peculiarities of studying ourselves do invite some caution. Our personal experience is part of what we must understand and explain. It will be especially challenging to observe from a natural science position. Some may despair that an experiencing scientist cannot objectively examine that ongoing experience. There appears to be a circle of sorts. But by rigorously maintaining a natural science vantage point, we will not be easily tripped up by subjective experiences. Mental experience is in the same causal dimension as other human functioning. We must be wary of assumptions that try to make it something different and mysterious. There is enough legitimate mystery without making some up as we go.

None of our sources of evidence has a privileged position. They must all conform to rules of evidence and add to our coherent understanding. Mental experience can be handled by removing its implication of incorrigible truth. We are used to assuming that experience is the most fundamental and direct apprehension of what is real and true. Instead, as natural scientists, we must insist that experience gives nothing more than evidence of what reality seems to be to a person (including ourselves). From there, we must build a picture of those facts of experience. Those facts are part of the evidence of human functioning.

No details of our personal mental experience must be allowed to have trump powers. We cannot allow ourselves to evaluate our collected scientific evidence by thinking, "But that is not the way that it seems to me." Our personal view cannot countermand the verified evidence and the coherent statement we are building. The criterion of psychological science cannot be, "How true does that seem to be in my personal experience?" That road leads to endless argument founded on the worst possibilities of subjectivism. Unfortunately, it is also the method of some of psychology's history (e.g., structuralism as noted above) and a major part of psychology's reputation with the public. By allowing ourselves that method of critical evaluation, we grant the same right to anyone, knowledgeable observer or not.

Our natural science stance is that of observers and organizers of facts. We must see our experience not from the inside but from the perspective of someone else. The title of an early psychology text (Meyer, 1921) captured that idea as *The Psychology of the Other One.* Daniel Dennett (1991) explains it with the metaphor of a piece of literary or media fiction. We can know the world and experiences of the people in that fiction. The depth of that knowing is limited only by the skill and extent of the author's work. Like the construction of the fictional world, a view of human functioning can be built. Mental experience is part of that functioning, and as we "know" the mental experience of our fictional characters without living their lives, we can build a natural science of human functioning without turning to introspection.

A Motivation Definition

We noted at the start that it is difficult to devise a definition of motivation. A definition is a good idea, but if we do not accept its meaning, it may just get in the way. In texts and other writings, we can find dozens of definitions for motivation, but none presents agreement beyond our conversational language. Perhaps, there is no simple definition because that is the reason for the whole area of study. Or perhaps the area of motivation is too complex and too inconsistent to bear a single precise definition. Why then make the attempt?

A definition can be a way of setting some boundaries and rules. It forms a sort of outline map of ideas, even though the map doesn't have much substantive detail or color. A definition can set limits. What we will consider is not an elaborate theoretical definition. What we propose does little more than put together what we know to be the common meanings we have for using the word *motivation,* but that is a very good place to begin.

The definition proposed is this:

Motivation is the collection of accounts of choices, intensities, and feelings of acts.

The five ideas in this definition are neither profound nor explicit. But there is more to them than first appears. We have already explored three of the components of our definition: the language-based elements of choices, intensities, and feelings. Now we can consider the remaining words: *accounts* and *acts.*

Accounts

Motivation ideas describe what we know about choices and intensities of different acts and the feelings that we experience with them. These ideas take form in our language. In this sense, motivation is an account—a description in words. This takes us back to an argument we began earlier. Motivation is a language concept in use, not an entity. Motivation is not a thing or process made of special events or materials. It is not substance or existing stuff. There is no reservoir of motivation in the body or the mind that is waiting to be tapped or to be filled. Motivation is the label we use for certain aspects of what we do. There is no more to it than being a means of communicating thoughts about actions.

Each description of motivation is an account of what we know, but the form of an account reflects choices of specific terms and principles. Here is where the account builders show what they believe. Each writer selects certain information and places it in a particular order. The theory held by an account writer focuses on some aspects of actions and excludes others. Therefore, because motivation psychologists have different perspectives, they cannot agree on rules for what form an adequate account must take. The form of their motivation accounts and the kind of information in them will vary. As a reader, it is important to be aware of the perspective from which writers construct accounts of motivational acts. That inherently gives importance to the historical dimension of all scientific descriptions of motivation. Our personal and collective history, no matter how widely shared, is always a biased product of our history of experiences. This fact bears on the choice of the last of the definition terms.

Acts

Motivation concerns acts. Deliberately and with caution, we will use the word *act* as the broadest category of events interesting to motivation psychology. *Behavior* and *responses* are more common terms, but behavior is of relatively recent origin, implying a behaviorist philosophical perspective and denoting a more narrow selection of activity. Response, too, implies a narrower action and has the additional meaning of being blindly determined. Both behavior and response also have slightly negative connotations, implying a *re*activity rather than a *pro*activity. Some of our acts are clearly responses and others are behaviors, but we must be careful not to limit our thought to what those forms mean and lock out their other implications.

Such a simple matter as choice of words can have a powerful influence on what materials will be a part of the motivation story. Behavior and response suggest that topics of normal communication about motivation such as meaning, purpose, and human intentions may be ruled out. These common forms of language about motivation may not be needed in the eventual natural science description of how we function, but they are surely a part of the beginning material that must be accounted.

We must note also that not everything we do is important for motivation. Our less precise, common language helps us make this final distinction. The word *act* covers a wide range of human performances, but we will restrict it to those that are organized and significant. One way to express this is "Acts are those human events that have meaning and value." Meaning and value are difficult to define, but most often we see them coming from social relations in which the acts are embedded. We will discuss those social dimensions wherever they appear.

Putting the definition pieces together, we focus our study of motivation variation on acts that concern choices, intensities, and feelings.

> **Motivation is basically *accounts* of ideas about differences in *acts* from one occasion to another. The main classes of variation are those we describe in common language: *choices* of acts, their relative performance *intensities*, and the affective *feelings* accompanying them.**

What things are done, with what energy, and how do they feel?

SECTION SUMMARY:
IDEAS IN MOTIVATION THEORY

Common ways of thinking might lead us to believe that our useful word *motivation* is something real, and being real it must exist in some physical form. Similar mechanical models have been useful throughout science. Perhaps, we may conclude, there could be some physiological event that is motivation's source.

The idea of motivation is too diverse to identify in some simple, singular way. A prime component is energy, and energy is not a thing. From there, it is a small step to look for differences in body energy. The concept of arousal emerged for a time as nearly synonymous with motivation. Arousal is too diverse to identify in some simple, singular way.

Sometimes popular and sometimes decidedly unpopular, inherited sources of human functioning trace their first great enthusiasm in science to the works of Charles Darwin and his followers. The notion of human nature versus human culture as competing influences is persistent. The modern view of evolutionary psychology is that these are complementary concepts. There are distinct and subtle inherited bases of our functioning that are often shaped by their development in specific cultural environments. We are formed both from the way we are and from what we experience. Specific evolutionary adaptations will be part of our motivation descriptions in the content chapters to come. Occasionally, animal biology and function will be useful in our study.

Our successful use of the word *motivation* in common communication can be divided into two ideas. One is to indicate how we choose what we do, illustrated by the question "Why did we do that?" The second is to describe acting energetically. The arousal concept enters in the inverted-*U* theory, proposing optimal performance at intermediate arousal levels.

Personal experiences of motivation are made partly of our feelings of energy level and their changes. Another part is the collection of pleasures we seek and pains we avoid. These experiences, although very real to each of us, must be examined carefully from the ground of natural science.

We concluded this section with the working definition: **Motivation is the collection of accounts of choices, intensities, and feelings of acts.**

We finish the chapter with some recent history of motivation in psychology and a few common examples of theory.

MODERN MOTIVATION SCIENCE

From the 1950s to the present, psychology has had marked growth, both in its academic subjects and applications. The number of psychologists has doubled nearly every decade until recently. Great numbers of approaches allow for some diversity, but the basic psychology strategy has remained true to its established methods and topics. The traditions during the rapid growth years of psychology were essentially study of (a) observable behaviors with (b) experimental methods. Learning theory has been the favored topic and explanation for most complex functioning.

Those two particular methods of science, as formulated over the years, became an unimpeachable authority in all matters of psychology. Behaviorist and experimentalist biases have been most evident. But attitudes change as new topics and different perspectives appear. Some changes are substantive and some only present a different way of talking about the same material.

Cognitive Science

Over the last three decades, the label for the theory and methods of much of psychology has been *cognitive science*. The new ideas have been those of information processing, using computer and calculation examples. These were offered as both the tools for doing scientific psychology and as a way of thinking about psychology's questions. The metaphor of machine calculation opened the behaviorist lock on topics of mental function and thinking. The language in use has definitely changed with cognitive concepts emerging as respectable psychology.

Has psychology's fundamental philosophy of method changed or is it only that the language and the model images have been broadened? We have used models of simple machines for many years, and now we have massive calculation devices based on information nets. Is the change real or just a matter of language? Some historians suggest that there is not much change in ideas, certainly not enough to justify pronouncing it a "cognitive revolution" in psychology (Leahey, 1992). Everyone agrees, however, that the new cognitive psychology allows a broader range of topics than its more austere neobehaviorism ancestor. We will see limitations and problems of both the older and newer views throughout the book.

Motivation Topic Development

Establishing the Area

Motivation was merely an aspect of specific theories in psychology until several publishing events occurred a few decades ago. Beginning in 1953, faculty at the University of Nebraska held an annual symposium on "motivation" topics and published the papers of the selected participants. These Nebraska faculty views of motivation topics were fairly broad, and until the middle 1970s, the symposium volumes were valued sources of motivation concepts. (After that period, the title "motivation" on the symposium series has not been very descriptive.) The first volumes helped to establish motivation as an area of psychology. Another noteworthy publishing event was the intentionally comprehensive textbook of motivation information by Charles Cofer and Mortimer Appley in 1964. Since that time a regular flow of textbooks has provided evidence of evolving concepts of motivation.

Motivation texts have largely moved beyond championing special theories. The most common strategy now is to divide the broad forces of motivation into those ideas from biology, from social psychology, and from cognitive studies. This trend simply follows the strengths and emphases of current work in psychology. Motivation always remains an aspect of the language of psychology and follows the broad path cleared by psychological ideas. Specific textbooks often tend to emphasize one perspective much more strongly than others, leading to calling one a "social" text and another a "physiological" text. The choice of topics and the kinds of information emphasized suggest these labels.

In this text, we will try to avoid a bias concerning the evidence used to validate the topics discussed. The direction of emphasis will follow the strength of the evidence and information that the author has found. When there appears to be a good quantity of physiology information supporting a motivated function, we will use that; if the best evidence is from social interaction study or from cognitive analyses, we will use that. The primary guide is the selection of the major topics themselves. In that choice, this text is different from others. The topics were selected not because of their traditional coverage in motivation texts nor because they complement a theory position. They were chosen because they are major aspects and venues of motivated functioning. Sleep, food, emotion, aggression, pain, fear, love, sex, other people, thought, addiction, work, and play make up the list. What do we know about how we are motivated by these things?

Theory Patterns

To further set the stage, we will close the chapter by mentioning some motivation theory ideas. Each theory idea is used with specific topics but has a broadly useful logical form. Sometimes these logical forms take on a life of their own and are thought of as a hidden reality. Like hot and cold, light and dark, and up and down, commonly used dimensions or patterns come to be thought of as real mechanisms beyond their reality as merely description. With that caution, we can still note and use them as descriptions.

Homeostasis is a pattern of changes to keep an equilibrium. Because our bodies regulate cell functions to keep a core body temperature, and because we take in food to hold an adequate level of nourishment to our cells, we may describe these and other systems as motivational mechanisms. Walter Cannon (1915) called it the "wisdom of the body" in his early textbook. We will meet this again in the next chapter.

Also from physiological thinking is the motivation idea based on needs and their satisfaction. Biologists described such needs for food, drink, air, and reproduction as drives and that idea was enthusiastically adopted by psychologists in the early to mid-twentieth century. Needs were freed from physiology in theories of Henry Murray (1938) and Abraham Maslow (1970) and became psychological necessities as well. Motivated acts were driven by needs. The more purely physiological concept of *drive* was elevated to be the central motivation component in mechanical analysis of behavior by certain functionalists and the neobehaviorists (e.g., Hull, 1943; Woodworth, 1918).

A range of theories were related by their use of patterns of *consistency*. From Fritz Heider's (1944) description of balance in social relations through Leon Festinger's (1957) use of the motivating powers of cognitive dissonance, the consistency idea was the key to describing and understanding human motivation. We will elaborate this in Chapter 10. In each of its forms, some kind of mental consistency is the desired state, and we are motivated to achieve it in the face of life events.

Finally, some events can be described in terms of actions and reactions. Richard Solomon and J. Corbit (1974) proposed an *opponent process theory,* in which conditions that increase positive affect have an associated but hidden increase in negative affect. The interplay of these two establishes one way of viewing motivated behavior. Michael Apter (1982) describes *reversals* in states such as arousal and hedonic tone (pleasant-unpleasant). These patterns of description use the ends of dimensions and opposites to anchor motivated acts.

Many other general and specific theoretical ideas from psychology will be developed and used in the chapters that follow. And, of course, motivation is a theoretical idea itself. Theory is the way we build mental pictures about things. We have a lot of constructing to do in motivation and psychology.

SECTION SUMMARY:
MODERN MOTIVATION SCIENCE

In the past 30 to 40 years, we have seen major changes in the kind of topics favored in motivation studies. Most obvious throughout psychology is the move to examine mental functioning directly instead of pretending it is hidden and revealed only by studying various behaviors. The new language includes cognitive psychology as a science.

More subtly, the range of topics has evolved over those years from heavy reliance on specific theories to more eclectic collections of topics, guided perhaps by biases of certain researchers toward either social or physiological choices and accounts.

CHAPTER CONCLUSIONS

Motivation has been an integral part of psychology and its history, focusing essentially on what we choose to do and how energetically we do it. The many forms of thought about motivation have followed the changing fortunes of the parent psychology. Special problems impede clear thinking about motivation because its essence is itself many-faceted and sometimes vague. Like many topics we will meet in the next chapters, motivation began as a commonplace concept in verbal communication. Using our experiences, we try to analyze motivation into its essence, perhaps imprudently trying to make it into something simple.

The real essence of motivation emerges from careful examination of a collection of accounts of what we do and why. As an emergent concept, it naturally defies pinning down to any conclusive particulars. Rather than attempting to do that, our task will be to consider all of the facts and ideas we can put together bearing on what we do and why. A first problem is what the target human functions shall be. We will partly follow traditional topics and build from there into interesting related areas.

There is a rough idea behind the topic order of the following 12 chapters. We begin with attractive features of our functioning that seem rooted strongly in biological functions: sleep and eating. From there, we move to the general condition of emotion. With that base, we elaborate the emotional and other bases of anger and aggression; of pain, fear, and stress; and of sex and love. At this stage, we are heavily into social elements, opening us to direct view of selected social motivations. That bridges to a careful view of our thinking and its foibles in motivated cognition.

The final three chapters take up specific motivation applications to complex parts of our lives. By studying addiction, work, and play, we reinforce elements of motivation outlined in earlier chapters, and we also see some new principles and ideas emerge.

That is where we are going. In the next chapter, we first take a brief excursion into physiological elements and terminology. Then, we work out some of the understated facts of biological rhythms, followed by influences from that third of our lives we spend asleep and dreaming.

Study and Review Questions

1. When and by what events was psychology founded?

2. What was Wilhelm Wundt's role in psychology's founding?

3. What was William James's role in psychology's founding?

4. How does a structuralist view psychology?

5. How does a functionalist view psychology?

6. What motivational concepts were developed in functionalist psychology?

7. How does a psychoanalyst view psychology?

8. What motivational concepts were developed in psychoanalytic psychology?

9. How does a behaviorist view psychology?

10. What motivational concepts were developed in behaviorist psychology?

11. How and why do we develop descriptive words into mechanical things?

12. What have been the typical views about how arousal is defined?

13. Is there one best way to identify arousal of body energy?

14. How does a fatalist view of human nature provide an excuse for some acts?

15. What is proper evidence of an evolutionary mechanism?

16. What is not appropriate evidence against an evolutionary mechanism?

17. Why should psychology include some limited study of animals?

18. What ideas about motivation emerge from looking at common use of that word?

19. Why is the inverted-U theory of aroused performance an inadequate theory?

20. What different kinds of feelings contribute to ideas about motivation?

21. Does describing our own experience give good psychological explanation?

22. From what evidence standpoint should psychology describe human mental functioning?

23. What is the proposed working definition of motivation?

24. Why is motivation an "account"?

25. What does homeostasis describe?

26. Which schools of psychology identified motivation in terms of drives?

CHAPTER 2

Physiology, Rhythms, and Sleep

As living beings, humans have survival adaptations that are biologically rooted. Some are fundamental, others are conditionally evoked, and many depend on information and experience. We will outline the nervous systems and chemical communicators that organize these adaptations, noting the motivationally relevant functions of the selected parts.

Delicate biological rhythms affect our sensitivities and performances in direct and subtle ways. They can be desynchronized by life events, revealing both their complexity and their practical importance.

Sleep is an overpowering biological rhythm in our lives, but one with many unknowns. "Why sleep?" is the implicit question of sleep research. Study has shown that sleep is an active period of cyclic patterns of brain activity and other body actions. Rapid-eye-movement sleep seems most associated with narrative dreams though some mental activity exists in every part of the sleep period. Each of sleep's components motivates certain aspects of life.

Nervous System Components

Chemical Communications

Biological Rhythms

Sleep

We begin with basic functioning, starting with a question: Why should we think about simple life functions and physiology when we want to know about adult human motivation? Our answer: We must use a reasonably complete understanding of how and why we are constructed in our unique human way. To ignore our structural roots is to beg the question of what our biological human nature truly is. We must try to see what lies behind our present form and functions.

Functions	Strategies	Acts
Constructing	Assimilation	Breathing Drinking Eating
	Reproduction	Seeking sex Nurturing young
	Maintenance	Sleeping Preventing damage
		Seeking benevolent environment Grooming Being nurtured
Sensing	Perception	Using senses
	Orientation	Finding location
	Exploration	Identifying Manipulating Thinking
Defending	Aversion	Fleeing Hiding Not moving Emitting
	Removal	Destroying Threatening Forcing away

Figure 2.1. A logical division of acts, strategies, and functions necessary for mammals to survive.

Any living form has some basic survival functions. To exist and to continue to exist demands that certain things be done. Three inescapable functions are constructing, sensing, and defending. In **constructing,** life entities must form, maintain, and reproduce their structure. In **sensing,** they must perceive and interact with features of their environment. And in **defending,** most life forms must avoid or remove threats to their existence. A species that fails at any of these things over time will not survive.

After sorting through the species to focus on mammals, we can discuss strategies of each of the basic functions. There are strategies of construction, of sensation, and of defense. Still staying at the most general set of ideas, we can consider acts that help accomplish each strategy. Some suggestions are shown in Figure 2.1, including eight strategies and some 22 acts.

If we agree this is reasonable so far, the next step is to consider how each of these acts is biologically constructed. Some functions are relatively primitive. Those will be the most strongly predetermined and the least moldable. We can select breathing, sleeping, using senses, and fleeing as good illustrations of the primitives. Other acts will have a tough core that emerges under provoking conditions. In this group are seeking sex, preventing damage, and destroying. For some acts, particularly by human beings, a nearly seamless veneer of culture makes the biological roots somewhat difficult to assess. Nurturing young, being nurtured, identifying, and threatening are some in that group.

But too much can be made of this. We must start with a clear idea of basic functions. Then, we will tie them to their biological roots and build from these basics. The building materials are the functioning parts of our bodies.

	Somatic voluntary and conscious	Autonomic visceral and life-support	
Central brain and spinal cord	perception and thought body control		
Peripheral body function	sensation muscle action	Sympathetic aiding action	
		Parasympathetic restoring energy	

Figure 2.2. Divisions and general functions in branches of the nervous system.

NERVOUS SYSTEM COMPONENTS

A sketch of our nervous system, its form and functions, may be a necessary beginning. Nervous systems are the organizing structures for communication within bodies. Nothing is more basic than nervous system functioning. That being so, we will draw some pictures, name the parts we will use later, and then outline some functions (a) of the autonomic (or self-governing) nervous systems, (b) of the brain stem, (c) of forebrain central areas, and (d) of the cerebral cortex. We will see how those structures control or limit many motivation basics. We will also be selective, focusing primarily on those parts whose functions play some part in our discussion of motivation.

The Nervous Systems

We begin the picture by labeling several systems of nerve fibers. The nervous systems can be divided by location and by function (see Figure 2.2). The central nervous system, made up of the brain and spinal cord, will be treated in more detail after we outline the peripheral nerve fibers and functions.

The peripheral nervous system includes the nerves extending from the spinal column to body areas. One part of this system includes somatic fibers providing communication path-ways from senses and to muscles. They underwrite voluntary or conscious activity. The other major part of the peripheral nerve fibers is the autonomic nervous system, which operates primarily visceral (body organs) and life-support functions that have little or no conscious control or report.

Autonomic Functions

Autonomic means self-governing. The **autonomic nervous system** uses smooth muscles, glands, and cardiac muscle to maintain the organs of the body, responding to changing environments and the body's maintenance needs. Smooth muscles (as compared with the voluntary, body-moving, striated muscles) control action in blood vessels, operate digestive and elimination organs, open the pupil, and focus the eyes, along with performing functions in the skin and hair. All gland secretions, whether exocrine (flowing outside, such as tears and sweat) or endocrine (transported inside, such as cortisol and testosterone), come from autonomic regulation.

Sympathetic-Parasympathetic Balance

For most of this century, the autonomic nervous system was pictured to operate in two coordinated but largely opposing divisions. Energy mobilization was described as the function of the **sympathetic division.** In

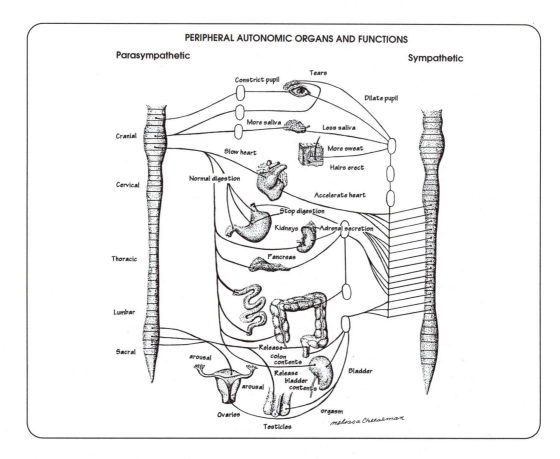

Figure 2.3. Peripheral autonomic nervous system functions at different levels of the spinal column.

general terms, the sympathetic division prepares the body for action and expends energy. The **parasympathetic division** restores energy supplies and maintains functioning in a normal resting state. These two divisions operate in coordination.

The sympathetic process is catabolic (using energy), the parasympathetic process is anabolic (storing energy), and together, they make up body metabolism (the sum of use and storage).

When the sympathetic division is dominant, many observable and measurable changes may occur:

- Increased heartbeat strength and pulse rate
- Changes in the pressure, volume, and composition of blood
- Changes in respiration or breathing cycles
- Changes in temperature
- Sweating
- Tearing
- Increasing size of the pupil of the eye
- Dry and pasty saliva
- Muscle tension and tremor

Many of these changes are complex, however, and there is large variation among responses of different people.

Spinal Cord

The **spinal cord** is the body's information superhighway to and from the controlling brain. The cord is enclosed in a line of 24 bony vertebrae that vary in size and shape.

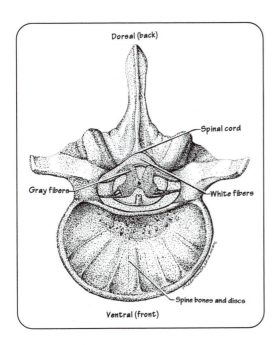

Figure 2.4. A typical cross-section of a spinal column.

Topmost vertebrae are called cervical, next are thoracic, then lumbar and sacral at the lower end. The same labels are also used for fibers in and connecting these areas, which are pictured in Figure 2.3.

A typical cross-section of the spine (see Figure 2.4) shows the spinal cord in a protected dorsal (back) passage attached to the ventral (front) weight-bearing and articulated spine bones and discs. The spinal cord nerves appear oval in cross-section, with an *H*-shaped pattern of grayer fibers in the center of white ones. In simplified description, the **white fibers** are tracts along the spinal cord and the **gray fibers** are cell bodies and short, local-connecting neurons. Sensory information enters through dorsal roots, and controlling signals exit by ventral roots. Protective membranes shield the spinal nerves and the brain from outside body processes. The central nervous system is inside these membranes.

Hindbrain

The spinal cord enters the brain as the brain stem, extending through the hindbrain,

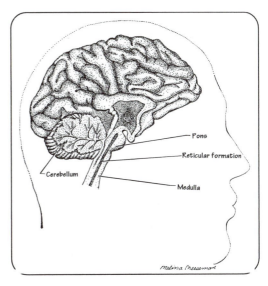

Figure 2.5. Major brain stem areas (hindbrain and midbrain).

midbrain, and forebrain. White fiber tracts reverse sides in the medulla oblongata of the **hindbrain,** and the gray matter there (now called tegmentum) regulates life-supporting respiration and cardiovascular functions. The tegmentum in the next area, the *pons,* seems to be involved in arousal and sleep.

At the center of the spinal cord is the reticular formation, a complex of neural tissue extending through the midbrain. It has been called the **ascending reticular activating system (ARAS** or sometimes just **RAS)** for its work in receiving signals from the sense organs and transmitting signals that arouse the higher brain centers of the cerebral cortex. At the hindbrain level are also some fiber routes to the cerebellum that coordinate motor function and balance. (See Figure 2.5.)

In the late 1940s, researchers found that electrical stimulation in a brain stem area produced activation in the cerebral cortex brain. Destructive cuts in this area seemed to prevent further activation in the brain and made animals appear slow and inactive. The name *ascending reticular activating system* was indeed appropriate. ARAS function seemed to be communication of some information of the general level of sensory excitation, perhaps

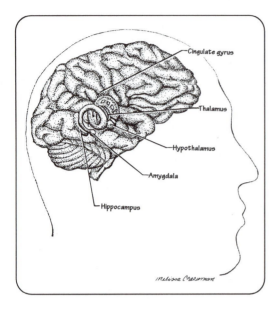

Figure 2.6. Major interior areas of the forebrain.

serving a toning function (Moruzzi & Magoun, 1949). The more sights, sounds, and touches we are getting, the more excited and ready is our brain for receiving them.

Midbrain

The brain stem continues into the **midbrain.** Besides the reticular formation, the tegmentum of the midbrain includes the **periaqueductal gray matter,** which has roles in pain and in fundamental species-specific aversive reflexes of defense or flight. On the top of the midbrain are the superior **colliculi** (coordinating vision reflexes) and inferior colliculi (involved in hearing).

Forebrain

The **forebrain** is what we typically mean by "the brain." The outside layer of the brain is the cerebral cortex or **cerebrum.** Inside are structures of the **diencephalon** including the thalamus, hypothalamus, limbic system, and basal ganglia. (See Figure 2.6.)

Central Forebrain Functions

The interior forebrain structures are the thalamus, hypothalamus, and limbic system.

Fibers from the two-lobed **thalamus** control, with cerebral cortex feedback, the information reaching cortex areas. Almost all of the neural information to the cortex, sensory and motor feedback, is relayed through the thalamus. Sensory and other information is transformed as it passes through. Sensory signals may be moderated by inhibiting them, essentially adjusting the flow in accordance with body arousal and possibly other nonspecific conditions.

The **hypothalamus,** below the thalamus, is a structure of many parts regulating nerve and hormonal information. The small hypothalamus makes up for its size by performing large, vital functions. The autonomic nervous system and body glands are under its direction. That is a large domain, which controls the bases of many survival tasks, including eating and drinking, mating, defending and fearing, and sleeping.

The **limbic system** is an interconnected set of structures including the mammilary bodies, hippocampus, cingulate gyrus, amygdala, and septum. The basal ganglia are the caudate nucleus, globus pallidus, and putamen. All of these are closely connected to the adjacent cerebral cortex. Experts have disagreed about which of this diverse group of forebrain structures are part of the limbic system. Its functions are important in emotion, attention, arousal, and memory. The **amygdala** associates sensory information with affective elements. In a similar way, the hippocampus controls memory of space and time features of sensory information.

Cerebral Cortex

The **cerebral cortex** is a sheet of neural tissue lying over the lower brain. It is 2 mm to 6.5 mm thick and appears convoluted and folded. Six layers of cells make up the cerebral cortex, and these function in vertical columns. (See Figure 2.7.)

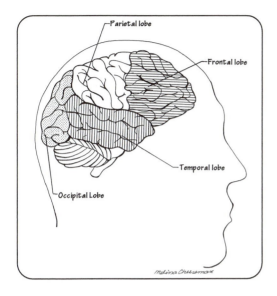

Figure 2.7. Lobes of the forebrain's cerebral cortex.

For convenience, the major fissures of the cerebral cortex help in dividing it into lobes. At the front is the frontal lobe, and at the rear is the occipital lobe. Between them is the parietal lobe, and wrapping over them from below are the temporal lobes. Several systems have been used to distinguish, number, and name different areas of the cerebral cortex.

Because of its immense numbers of neurons and connections, we haven't, until recently, had many good ways to see what the cerebral cortex is doing. The function of general areas was discovered by correlating changes in behavior with tissue destruction from accidents and disease. Some stimulation during brain surgery added to the picture. Recent study has examined patterns of blood flow during specific brain activities.

Early tools also assessed the brain's general level of activity over large areas. When instruments were developed to amplify its very small electrical voltages, brain study was boosted by the electroencephalograph. The **electroencephalograph** or **EEG** is a graphic recording of changes in voltage measured by electrodes near brain tissue. The EEG is the sum of those electrical properties that reach the electrode from the brain neurons. The activities of many neural cells add together—the pattern we see is primarily the influence of the strongest cells nearest the electrode. EEG records are described by their appearance on the record. In the original instruments, the total voltage reaching the electrode was amplified electrically to force movement of a pen, as paper was moving beneath it. Different EEG patterns made pen movements of different magnitude, frequency, and regularity. Some common EEG patterns related to arousal were arbitrarily named beta, alpha, theta, and delta.

As you read, alert and awake, your brain shows primarily beta waves. **Beta waves** are small magnitude, more than 13 Hz (hertz or cycles per second) but typically 18 to 30 Hz, irregular in form, and strongest on the frontal lobe of the brain. As you rest with your eyes closed, essentially mentally idle, your brain shows **alpha waves** of fairly large magnitude, 8 to 13 Hz, and clear regularity of motion. Alpha waves appear strongest on the back, occipital lobe of the brain. Reopening your eyes or becoming mentally engaged, your alpha waves disappear and beta waves again appear. If you sit longer with your eyes closed, you may become drowsy. In the early stages of sleep, there appear **theta waves,** fairly regular, 3 to 8 Hz, and strongest on the sides of the brain. A sleeping brain shows periods of **delta waves,** very large amplitude, less than 4 Hz but typically 1 to 2 Hz, and with a very clear regularity. These EEG wave forms are illustrated later in the chapter as we use them to describe stages of sleep.

In 1929, the discoverer of the EEG, Hans Berger, found that alpha activity changes to beta following an unexpected stimulus. Names for this change are *activation pattern, alpha blocking, beta rhythm, desynchronization,* and *arousal reaction.* **Activation patterns** occur with meaningful stimuli, significant changes in stimuli, and cognitive acts like solving an arithmetic problem. Activation also occurs occasionally in sleep, and then when awakened, sleepers report dreams. From the EEG, researchers have found evidence that the beta wave may show an aroused brain.

These brain system properties made a strong case for one way of measuring energy level of the body. Brain waves correlate well with obviously different states: sleep, rest, and alert functioning. The brain waves follow the degree of sensory stimulation flowing. Although these ideas promised to bloom with potential, they wilted in practicality. In the past, typical EEG measurements have been cumbersome and intrusive, wave forms were not easily quantified, and they were not sen- sitive to rapid and continuous changes in body state. Furthermore, there was no subtlety at all among different changes in brain function. There can be drastically different levels of specific functions that will not be detected in the slow 30 sec or 1 min sampling process of the EEG.

Additional specific techniques have been developed to measure brain response to simple stimuli. Spikes of change can be averaged to show how they are received. These **average evoked potentials** trace the brain's response to a flash of light or similar trigger.

SECTION SUMMARY: NERVOUS SYSTEM COMPONENTS

Our nervous system has several anatomical and functional divisions. *Central* and *peripheral* are obvious labels. *Somatic* names the voluntary and conscious control and *autonomic* includes the automatic visceral and supporting functions. The sympathetic division of the peripheral autonomic system controls an assortment of body functions when the body is physically or mentally active.

The spinal cord collects and transmits information from body parts into various fiber tracts. Near the brain, the spinal fibers elaborate into the hindbrain (arousal systems) and the midbrain (defense reflexes and pain).

The forebrain is made up of several central structures covered by the cerebral cortex. The forebrain regulates most body functions through combinations of neural and chemical stimuli. Important structures include the thalamus, the hypothalamus, and the pieces of the limbic system. The convoluted, thin cerebral cortex is divided into regions and has been studied largely by measuring patterns of electrical activity. Patterns of decreasing alertness are named *beta, alpha, theta,* and *delta waves.*

CHEMICAL COMMUNICATIONS

Endocrine Functions

Hormones are secreted by endocrine glands and have some kind of control function in the body. Hormones are carried in body fluids to communicate conditions and changes. They vary from being widely effective to having a specific target location and function. Table 2.1 gives some examples but is not a complete record. Many hormones affecting cell function and very specific targets are not included.

Neurochemistry

The most powerful regulators of the nervous system are the chemicals used in neurotransmission. A very small gap separates neurons; **neurotransmitters,** specific emitted chemicals, bridge the gap (see Figure 2.8

TABLE 2.1   Selected Endocrine Hormone Sources and Functions

Source Gland	Hormone	Function or Target
hypothalamus	releasing hormones	controls pituitary hormones
hypothalamus/ pituitary	vasopressin	kidney water retention
anterior pituitary	ACTH	adrenal cortex
	growth hormone	growth in most cells of the body
	thyroid-stimulating hormone	thyroid
	FSH = follicle-stimulating hormone	ovary follicles; testes sperm
	LH = luteinizing hormone	ovulation; ovary hormones; testes hormones
	prolactin	breasts; breast milk
pituitary	oxytocin	attraction, affiliation, satisfaction, bonding, milk release
thyroid	thyroxine (T_4) triiodothyronine (T_3)	bodywide cell energy
adrenal medulla	epinephrine	metabolism; stress response
	norepinephrine	metabolism; stress response
adrenal cortex	cortisol	foods metabolism; stress response
	aldosterone	kidney sodium and potassium excretion
	androgens	growth; women's libido
kidneys	renin	adrenal cortex; blood pressure
pancreas	insulin	carbohydrate metabolism; blood glucose release
	glucagon	liver glucose release
ovaries	estrogen (β-estradiol, estrone, estriol)	reproduction; breasts; female growth and development
	progesterone	uterine milk; breast development
testes	testosterone	reproduction; male growth/development; men's libido

for a partial list). The energy pulse flowing along a neuron forces the release of a chemical. When there is enough of it on the membrane of another neuron, that cell's energy pulse begins. Different kinds and quantities of neurotransmitters, as well as chemicals that aid or block their action, regulate the body.

Some neurotransmitter chemicals have been divided into family groups. Acetylcholine operates the skeletal muscles. A group of monamines includes epinephrine, norepinephrine, dopamine, and serotonin; these have functions in sleep, mood, and feelings of pleasure. A collection of amino acids includes aspartic acid, GABA, glutamic acid, glycine, and substance P. Peptides include beta-endorphins and enkephalins, these having a role in producing and moderating pain.

BIOLOGICAL RHYTHMS

We begin a look at biological rhythms with what is obvious. Nature has rhythm! Our environment has repeating cycles, and to live with those rhythms, we adopt cycles of our own. The most obvious is our daily sleep, the major topic later in this chapter. But we

Group	Family	Specifics
Fast-acting, small molecule types	Acetylcholine	acetylcholine
	Amines	norepinephrine dopamine serotonin histamine
	Amino acids	GABA glycine glutamate
Slow-acting neuropeptides	Hypothalamic-releasing hormones	thyrotropin-releasing hormone luteinizing hormone-releasing hormone somatostatin
	Pituitary peptides	ACTH β-endorphin prolactin luteinizing hormone thyrotropin growth hormone
	Gut and brain peptides	leucine enkephalin methionine enkephalin substance P gastrin vasoactive intestinal polypeptide neurotensin insulin glucagon
	Other tissues	angiotensin bradykinin sleep peptides

Figure 2.8. Selected neurotransmitters presented in groups and families.

will start with other, less noticed cycles of sensitivity.

Natural Rhythms

Solar energy has daily and annual changes. Cycles of light, heat, and other energy produce a host of more subtle changes in the environment. Life forms adapt to these changes, often with function changes of their own. This is what biological rhythms are all about. **Biological rhythms** are regular patterns in body change, and the time when something happens during a biological rhythm cycle can make a significant difference.

The regularities of body rhythms have been known in a general way for a long time, but since about 1960, a variety of functions and actions has been more closely examined. More than 100 aspects of human functioning follow a daily rhythm. Research has shown that nearly every aspect of human function has a daily rhythm: sleep, body temperature, adrenal gland function, sex hormone production, pain sensitivity, time judgments, and so the list goes on. It may now be noteworthy if a careful study indicates that an important feature of life does not have a daily rhythm. In a short time, the belief has changed from holding that things are normally constant to accepting that many processes vary in a regular way. The implications for theory and practice of these many biological rhythms are being sorted out.

Biological rhythms are important to us for several reasons. First, the facts of cyclic variations in sensitivities and performances are motivation-relevant because they affect the possibilities of actions. These are the sorts of changes that partly determine how we are able to perform.

Second, biological rhythms are important because specific rhythms must be considered when sensitive actions are measured for other purposes. We may inadvertently make tests at different times of the day and contaminate the comparisons with additional variability. A more serious error is testing experimental groups at different times and not recognizing that the effects are caused by biological rhythms. The practical values of understanding biological rhythms are significant.

Rhythm Basics

In this context, the words *rhythm, cycle,* and *oscillation* are interchangeable and describe one complete appearance of a repeating change. The duration in time is its period; the extent of change is its amplitude. Biological rhythms may be smoothly changing variations in a single dimension such as temperature; they may be the presence and absence of complex phenomena of functioning such as sleep or the seeking of food; or they may be bursts of activity such as some hormone secretions.

The most spectacular biological rhythms seem to be those that follow approximately the period of a day. First used by Franz Halberg in 1959, the term **circadian** (*circa* =

about, *dies* = day] applies to daily changes. Sleep is the most obvious of the circadian rhythms, but many other changes occur in physiological functions, sensitivities, and performances over a day's time. Most changes in performance can only be determined during waking hours, and in recognition of that, **time-of-day** or **diurnal variation** (day-active) has been the traditional label for changes having a daytime variation.

Biological rhythms of periods other than circadian are also studied. These include annual changes, a period of roughly 90 min (sometimes called a physiological hour), cycles in women's fertility, and cycles of long-term emotional tone.

Physiological Rhythms

The greatest research effort has focused on changes in biological processes and substances. This is, after all, a biological discovery. After locating daily rhythms, researchers try to find the causes of the changes and relationships among them. We won't pursue studies of underlying mechanisms. Instead, we will sketch the basic circadian rhythms and their known relations to features of human action. The most easily acknowledged circadian rhythms are those of activity and sleep and of body temperature. It is reasonable to suppose that these two rhythms reflect two different oscillators or clocks that provide the bases for many of the observed circadian changes (Minors & Waterhouse, 1981). The activity-sleep cycle is the most obvious circadian rhythm, and that will be the major topic later in this chapter. But first we will look at daily temperature and the many rhythms we describe in reference to it.

In 1845, J. Davy described a regular variation in body temperature. Recently, body temperature has been used as a reference change in biological rhythm studies. Its pattern and variations have been thoroughly studied and described.

The average daily temperature rhythm (see Figure 2.9) is at a low of about 97.4° F just before awakening, rising rather rapidly in

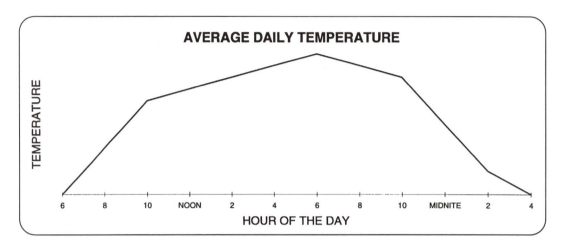

Figure 2.9. Typical average temperature variation in a day from an average low of 97.4° to a high of 98.6°.

the morning and more slowly in the afternoon to a peak of about 98.6° at 6 p.m., and then declining slowly at first and then more rapidly during sleep to the early morning low (Colquhoun, 1971). The average change is about 1.2° F. These averages are just that; we each have our own normal high and low temperatures, but our individual patterns of change are fairly smooth and with a single maximum and minimum. The temperature rhythm comes close to being a smooth function with a single peak and a single valley. The temperature rhythm appears not to be entirely immune to influences from the outside environment, but its pattern is largely **endogenous,** generated from inside the body.

Of the many body physiology rhythms, heart rate and brain waves give good illustrations of being in synchrony with body temperature. Heart rate has long been known to vary with body temperature. Physicians often confirm the presence of a fever by a check of the blood pulse rate; high temperatures go with a fast pulse. Heart rate circadian rhythms mirror those of temperature, normal and abnormal. But there is also evidence that hearts have internal clocks of their own. **Brain waves** also appear to follow the circadian temperature rhythm. Records of brain waves show that speed and perhaps amplitude of alpha waves are greater with higher temperature (Frank et al., 1966).

Gland functions are more complicated in their rhythms. Circadian rhythms are a feature of the endocrine gland secretion systems (Minors & Waterhouse, 1981). These secretions set and adjust the levels of functioning of aspects of the body as diverse as cell growth, emotional response, digestion and elimination, and sexual activity. The circadian rhythm of certain key endocrine secretions is different from that of temperature, however.

Adrenal cortex production of **cortisol** reaches a rapid peak just before awakening and then falls away during the waking day to a low after midnight. Actual secretions occur in 7 to 13 bursts of different durations and magnitudes. Cortisol is part of a chain affecting nervous function. Cortisol increases the availability of amino acids and fat from their storage areas. Amino acids improve protein metabolism, and, with the available fats, the liver can produce glucose for general body nutrition. This available glucose provides energy for the nervous system. In this way, cortisol affects relative calmness or irritability.

Growth hormone secretions also appear in a circadian rhythm in young people in a normal activity-sleep environment. Large releases of growth hormone occur just after the onset of sleep. Study has shown, however, that control of growth hormone may be primarily produced by external or **exogenous**

events. The fundamental stimulus appears to be the onset of sleep.

Testosterone is an androgen responsible for male body characteristics and has an important influence on sexual motivation. Testosterone secretion increases to a peak near the end of sleep and then falls somewhat, remaining essentially constant or decreasing slightly during the day.

These few physiological processes are but a sample found in the rich, growing, and somewhat complicated research literature. Circadian rhythms, for example, are present in the cardiovascular and respiratory systems, in the kidneys, in the gastrointestinal system, and in other parts of the endocrine system. For an early, but still useful review, see Minors and Waterhouse (1981).

Many human functions follow the circadian rhythm, often in rough synchrony with body temperature change, although others follow a different diurnal pattern. Here are some processes and sensitivities that follow the daily temperature change. With higher temperature, there is increase in the following:

- Resistance to damage by X-ray, bacterial and viral infection, noise-induced stress, and hazards of serious illness or surgery

- Response to allergy-producing substances

- Speed of disappearance of active drugs including nicotine, barbiturates, amphetamines, salicylates, strychnine, and alcohol

- Sensitivity to sensory pain

- Grip strength

Physiological process, sensory sensitivities, and basic physical actions are included in the above list, which mentions just a few of those that have been reported. There are also rhythms in sensitivity that do not mirror the daily temperature change. At about 3 a.m. and again at 5 to 7 p.m. our sensations of hearing, taste, and smell are sharpest.

Because so many physiological processes appear to follow the temperature rhythm, an early hypothesis was that temperature change was the basis for an increased arousal, which in turn formed the diurnal patterns. The suggestion was that higher temperature made faster chemical reactions or faster metabolic rates of brain cells, the body energy notion again. This led to a general myth that all performance rhythms follow body temperature (Kleitman, 1963).

Performance Rhythms

Many simple performances, those that use direct sensory-motor acts, do closely follow temperature. Among those are the following:

- Simple reaction time

- Muscle coordination

- Speed of card dealing, card sorting

- Speed of canceling digits or letters

- Maze tracing

- Visual search speed

Temperature-paralleling performances are commonly those that use immediate processing. That is, they are direct and mentally uncomplicated acts responding to simple changes in stimulation. The extent of their diurnal variation is typically 7% below the daily average at 8 a.m. to 5% above average at 8 p.m. (Folkard, 1983).

Recent research moved beyond description and lists and has been more critical and analytical. Even the arousal concept itself has come under question. In some studies, volunteers rated their arousal at different periods during the day. These self-ratings follow a pattern similar to that of temperature but reach a peak much earlier. Because rated arousal and temperature did not vary together, it is hard to explain the rhythms in terms of arousal. Furthermore, direct physiological measures of arousal, troublesome as we saw them to be in Chapter 1, have also not mirrored the temperature pattern (Folkard, 1983).

Study of memory, especially the practical memory of life events, illustrates the complexity of diurnal performance rhythms.

Short-term memory performance steadily decreases from morning to afternoon. Short-term memory is the ability to hold material briefly in mind, and it is tested in a practical way by memory of contents shortly after reading a short article. The magnitude of this variation is much greater than that for immediate processing performances, being 15% above the average daily at 8 a.m. and 15% below at 8 p.m. Furthermore, delayed tests for that memory, essentially a practical long-term memory, showed better memory of material presented in the evening than in the morning. In summary, immediate memory is better in the morning than the evening, and long-term memory is better for materials learned in the evening than those learned in the morning (Folkard & Monk, 1980).

A finding that either helps sort out these diurnal memory patterns or confuses them even more is another diurnal variation: attention to different aspects of stimulation. In the morning, more attention focuses on the physical features of materials, but as the day passes, there is increasing notice of meaning. Immediate memory most readily uses the physical bits of sounds and sights of the memory stimuli, but these cues disappear in a short time. Long-term memory relies on embedding the material in nets of meaningful experience. Afternoon learning, having less focus on sensory events and greater focus on meaning, results in greater retention. This concept also is consistent with the greater size of diurnal variation for more meaningful practical memories and other performances (Folkard, 1982). For now, these are primarily descriptive studies; there are no deeper theoretical pictures explaining our sharper attention in the morning or our better use of meaning in the late afternoon.

Rhythm Disruptions

Biological rhythms are fragile. The normal synchrony of biological rhythms is easily disturbed. One common example is jet lag, rapid transportation to a different time zone, which produces a discrepancy between our existing rhythms and the daylight and activity cues of the new place. Patterns of systematic change of work schedules are another source of repeated changes in the correspondence between our activity-rest schedule and stable environment cues. But, also, some onetime life events such as illness produce lasting changes in rhythm harmony, and intentional rhythm disruption has been studied in people who experience prolonged isolation.

Some of the best evidence about biological rhythms has come from isolation studies. People have cut themselves off from daily light-dark and social activity cues. The purposes have been many. Some studies were primarily tests of endurance in unconventional environments (Mills, 1964; Siffre, 1975). In others, the main concern was finding the cause for certain biological rhythms (Wever, 1979). Is the temperature rhythm stimulated by some feature of daily activities outside the person (exogenous), or is it a persisting feature having internal (endogenous) cues? Some of these tests have attempted to experimentally impose a cycle different from the 24-hour one, such as either longer or shorter days, for a time. Others have left the individuals to keep their own schedules. From these tests, some interesting patterns have become apparent.

As we see in the idealized Figure 2.10, after 5 days of normal day-night cues, volunteers are left to form their own activity and rest patterns. On the average, individuals left to decide their own activities in an isolated environment adopt a 25+ hour day in the activity and sleep cycle. For most people tested, their temperature followed the new pattern; but, significantly, for some, it did not. These others maintained a few days of synchrony of temperature and activity and then began a pattern of increased length of daily activity. Their temperature rhythms remained at the 25+ hour cycle, and thus their temperature and activity rhythms desynchronized. A few individuals began this desynchronization immediately. This and other studies suggest that activity and temperatures have independent

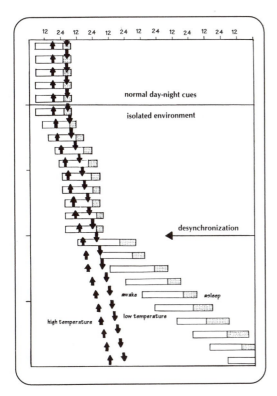

normal day-night cues

isolated environment

desynchronization

awake ☐ asleep

high temperature ↑ low temperature

Figure 2.10. Daily activity and sleep patterns during (top panel) and without normal day and night cues and desynchronizing from temperature. Idealized pattern based on experiments by Wever (1979).

clocks (different endogenous rhythm sources), but that they are normally coordinated by certain environmental time cues.

Isolation studies, particularly with animals, have been used to look for the natural cues for cycles. The time cues, or **zeitgebers** (time-givers in German) *entrain* (cue, drag, or carry along) the rhythm functions. Change in daily activity routine can also disrupt body rhythms. Traveling to a different time zone and changing the time of one's work to a new shift are alterations in zeitgebers that may desynchronize circadian biological rhythms. The practical questions are how and how soon will one become entrained to a specific new time environment.

Travel to a different time zone affects body functions and performances, but a complete picture is not yet ready. The first rush of findings produced a long list of potential dis-

abilities from a single large change in time zone. Heading the list of jet-lag symptoms were sleep disturbance, fatigue, and slow mental performance. Frequent time-zone travelers reported headaches, burning eyes, digestion upset, unprovoked sweating, menstrual irregularities, and possibly premature aging (Luce, 1971). These studies of aviation professionals also introduced the problem of separating time-zone changes from symptoms of work stress, including irregular rest periods.

Among the most predictable effects and perhaps the dominant factor of time-zone change is sleep disturbance. Change in timing breaks the laws of sleep. A traveler is either awake at the time of normal sleep or expected to sleep after too short a period of being awake. The effects are those of being sleepy at inappropriate times and difficulty getting sufficient sleep when the social schedule in the new time zone dictates. Together these effects lead to feelings of sleepiness and fatigue, perhaps partly the cause of subnormal mental performance.

The practical questions are how to deal with time-zone, activity-rest disruptions, and how long does it take to adapt to the changed time. Some partial answers are available. There are differences in adaptation to time-zone change depending upon the direction of the change. Change to a longer day works more rapidly than change to a shorter day. In travel, this means that westward travel is more tolerable than an equal change to the east. One explanation uses the fact, found in isolation studies, that people tend to have a 25+ hour natural activity day. Going from Chicago to Denver is the same as adding an hour to the day; from Chicago to New York subtracts an hour. A day longer by 1 hour would be unnoticed on arrival in the new time zone. A shorter day is a little harder to accommodate, but roughly 1 hr or less of change is usually assimilated with little effect, at least for activity-sleep functioning.

The time required to become completely adjusted to a new time zone is not known. Again the picture is somewhat complicated.

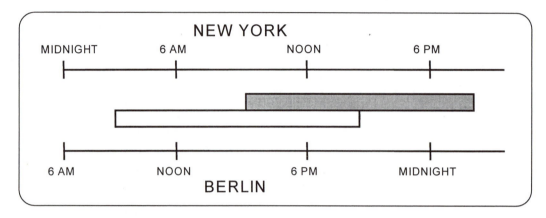

Figure 2.11. A typical jet-lag event with bars showing best times in each time zone before adaptation to the new time.

The rate of adaptation is not the same for all circadian rhythm functions. There are different schedules of resynchronization. For example, mental performance adapts more quickly than body temperature. We believe that these differences depend upon the extent of endogenous as opposed to exogenous influence on each function. Functions with more exogenous control change more rapidly to the new zeitgebers.

By following two principles, a traveler can compensate for jet lag and adapt most rapidly. If the visitor is in the new time zone for more than a few days, the first principle to reduce jet lag is to maximize the strength of the new zeitgebers. Activities of the new time zone must be carried out with normal vigor. Eating should be at the new meal times, sleeping according to the new time, and so on with all daily activities in a normal fashion. The tendency to remain apart to rest must be avoided. Some plans suggest trying to begin the new schedule before leaving the old one, but the success of this has not been definitively evaluated. This is partly a personal choice between interrupting activities either before or after the trip.

The second principle to avoid weak performance under jet lag is to compensate by using good times of day in both the new and the old places to schedule important activities (see Figure 2.11).

Assuming time was advanced 6 hours by flying from New York to Berlin, sleepiness and low efficiency will appear during the night hours of the old time. Important things should be avoided at these times. Performances should be scheduled at times of waking in both time zones, say 3 p.m. to 9 p.m. at the Berlin times. And if the first principle has been followed, we can assume that the two will come closer together at the rate of 1 to 2 hours each day.

Irregular work shifts have effects similar to those of time-zone change. Shift work is necessary for a variety of safety, production, and efficiency reasons, but there are an amazing variety and complexity of shift schedules. The three primary formats are: (a) permanent shift assignment, (b) rapid shift-change schedules (most common in continental Europe), and (c) slow rotation schedules (typical in Britain and the United States). Biological rhythms are disrupted as each new shift is begun.

Under slow rotation schedules, change starts a slow entrainment of temperature rhythms to the new activity-rest pattern. A stable condition will take about 2 to 3 weeks. Like that of time-zone changes, clockwise changes toward later activity periods give quicker adjustment than changes to earlier periods that initially shorten the awake time.

On a rapid shift-change schedule of two or more different time shifts in a pattern over 4 or 5 days, biological rhythms do not have a chance to follow any of the schedules. Instead, they follow the most dominant schedule, usually the regular day-night zeitgebers but with another twist. With rapid shift changes, the day-night circadian performance patterns have reduced magnitude.

Performance on night shifts depends on the circadian rhythm change and on the type of task. On night shifts, easy immediate-processing work follows body temperature and, hence, if the temperature is low, performance is poorer. Performance is worse during the period of adjustment to a new rotated-shift schedule. Working on rapid-change shifts, quality worsens with lower circadian rhythm temperature, although in this work pattern, because the rhythm magnitude is muted, the performance decrement is less. Complex task skills, such as those requiring a heavy memory load or cognitive complexity such as computer programming, seem not to vary with temperature. Such performances often are better, with fewer errors made during the night shift, but perhaps this is also because there are fewer distractions then.

We have been focusing on the biological rhythm changes from work schedules. The reality of shift work is that it also disrupts many aspects of life, especially social activity, sleep length, and sleep quality. Social demands are competing zeitgebers, interfering with rhythm adjustment to night work schedules. Sleep interference is common during daylight hours when working the evening or night shifts. Rapid-rotation work schedules typically yield less total sleep and a poorer quality of sleep (Monk & Folkard, 1983).

Biological rhythms also desynchronize from therapeutic drug use, illness, and life stress. Antibiotics and barbiturates are drugs that have been so implicated. Well past the period of taking the drug, there remain subtle traces of desynchronization. Feelings of weakness are common, perhaps from continued sleep alteration. Illness and stress also make a lasting disruption of biological rhythms. These are new areas that are typically neglected by medical researchers.

It would seem that an optimally synchronized state of affairs is a rare event. Perhaps it is, and perhaps it underlies those peak periods when we feel great and do exceptionally well. But we must be wary of patently simple explanations such as those from sellers of "biorhythm" myths.

Selling Biorhythms

In recent years the implications of biological rhythms have been successfully marketed. This commercial venture, called **biorhythms,** comes from a quite different background. Biorhythm supporters make suggestive reference to research in biological rhythms and make general quotes about the value of rhythms. However, they ignore the research and facts. Biorhythm is not an application of biological rhythms research. What is it, and from what did it develop?

The commercial biorhythm theory assumes that everyone has three rhythms that began at the moment of birth. A cycle with a 23-day period is said to influence our physical ability, along with a 28-day cycle of emotional state and a 33-day cycle of intellectual capacity. Each cycle follows a smooth and simple path, and hence the highs and lows of each can be splendidly and precisely calculated. We will not examine the theory predictions further.

At the beginning of this century, William Fleiss, a friend and confidant of Sigmund Freud, and Herman Swoboda studied the rhythms of repetition of various illnesses and proposed the 23- and 28-day cycles. Alfred Teltscher in Switzerland proposed the 33-day cycle from a small sample of students' examination performances. Several others over the years have simplified the basic idea, primarily by improving and promoting the calculation devices.

A few dozen studies in the late 1970s examined large populations for relations between biorhythm critical days and accidents or other evidence of poor performance. The bulk of the studies shows no relationship (e.g., Kurucz & Khalil, 1977; Persinger, Cooke, & Janes, 1978; Wolcott, McMeekin, Burgin, & Yanowitch, 1977). Proponents (Thommen, 1973) tend to select individual cases that fit their predictions and hold them up as ad hoc proof. There has been no search for the mechanisms that might produce these proposed rhythms, and there is no serious discussion of how the rhythms affect performance. Biorhythms appear to be another of those attractive nuisances of science that proclaim to give easy answers to very complicated prediction problems.

The assumptions of the biorhythm idea are very difficult to accept by anyone versed in the nature of biological rhythms and general knowledge of the human body. First, all cycles are assumed to start at the moment of birth, but there is little that is biologically beginning at that moment. When do the cycles begin for those who experience premature, medically induced, surgical, and trauma-induced births? Second, the cycles are said to be invariant with life events, yet, all known biological processes respond to environmental events and traumas—except, supposedly, biorhythms. Third, the cycles are identical in all people and are precisely of the stated periods, but variability is the nature of life and its functions. We can easily see that biorhythm notions are so deviant from accepted knowledge that we must insist that a systematic program of evidence be provided. No one has done that.

The commercial biorhythm proponents have taken their ideas to business managers and to the entertainment marketplace. It can be entertaining, although not necessarily harmless. As entertainment, it is similar to long-standing enterprises. Note the continuing profitability of horoscopes and similar self-deluding features. Although biorhythms are now fading as a popular newspaper filler item, many work managers continue to be enthralled by the idea. The "success" that they attribute to biorhythm critical days is a variant of the well-known principle of self-fulfilling prophecy. People examine the predictions and act so that they appear to be true. They look for, and magnify the importance of, events that conform to the predictions.

SECTION SUMMARY: BIOLOGICAL RHYTHMS

Body systems are never unvarying. Many functions change predictably over the waking day (diurnal) or the 24-hour period (circadian). Deep body temperature is circadian, as is heart rate, cortisol and testosterone flow, and the normal sleep-awake pattern. Various sensitivities and performances have diurnal variations of 5% to 15%, including short-term and long-term memory. Without day-night cues, some rhythms adopt different cycle lengths: Sleep-awake patterns tend toward 25+ hour "days." Disruption (desynchronization) of rhythms also results from rapid change to new earth time zones (jet lag), resulting in poor sleep, worsened mental performance, and fatigue. Desynchronization also comes from irregular work schedules that alter the normal sleep-awake timing, from illnesses, and from some therapeutic drugs.

Biorhythm charts and predictions of optimal physical, mental, and emotional performances are pseudoscience, having no validity in natural science. Apparent successes can be accounted for by principles of self-fulfilling prophecies or post hoc data selection.

◈

SLEEP

Repeating periods of activity and sleep are the most obvious of the circadian rhythms. Everyone follows approximately the same daily cycle of awake activity and sleep. The exceptions from a routine day of activity and a night of sleep, despite their frequency, serve to emphasize the normal pattern. Although sleep is a break in our consciousness, it is not a time-out from living. By taking 30% or more of our time, the inevitable demands of sleep force the way we conduct our lives. Therefore, sleep is an important factor of motivation.

Far from being just a period of rest, sleep is a complicated phenomenon—an active pattern of muscle action, physiological process, and mental operation. To understand the role of sleep in shaping what we do, we must explore both the phenomena of sleep and the consequences of alterations in sleep.

Why Sleep?

Why sleep? Research and thought about sleep are approaches to answering this brief question. Webb (1979) outlined several distinct types of theory, which are less competing viewpoints than they are different collections of observations and thoughts about sleep. Restoration theory and evolution theory are well studied.

Restorative Hypotheses

Restorative theory answers the common, practical question, Why sleep? with an equally common answer: that sleep replaces something lost. Restoration theories are simple metaphors of life and the world (Hartman, 1973; Oswald, 1974). We talk of recharging batteries and refilling fuel tanks. The normal fatigue in muscles recovers overnight. We know some things have changed during sleep, but what exactly has happened? We hold our waking life to be sacred for the opportunity it gives us to do things. Sleep wastes our valuable time. If the sleep change mechanisms can be found, perhaps we can eliminate sleeping, make it more efficient, or at least control when it takes place.

The research problem for restorative theorists is to find evidence of changes before and after sleep, focusing on the immediate conditions leading to sleep. Is there a substance or the lack of a substance that accumulates as need for sleep increases? The restorative theories lean toward neurochemistry and physiology. In animal studies, different substances have been found that affect sleep onset, sleepiness, sleep duration, and specific stages of sleep. It appears that each substance is part of a chain of biochemical responses, but finding the beginning and end of such chains and tying them to the periodicity of sleep is difficult. Much more detailed research is necessary to build confidence in biochemical descriptions of sleep.

Closely related to restorative theory is the proposal called **protective theory.** The point of protective theory is that sleep prevents damage caused by constant activity (Pavlov, 1927). Periods of sleep allow specific cells and other elements to recover.

James Horne (1988) recently proposed two concurrent functions of sleep. **Core sleep** allows periods of inactivity of the cerebral cortex for neural maintenance and repair. Such maintenance takes the controlling brain partially off-line for a time. That repair takes place in cycles early in the sleep period. Core sleep is thought to be necessary, and little loss of it is tolerated. **Optional sleep** is proposed as an urge to sleep, serving nonspecific needs to be inactive during the unproductive night hours or perhaps to conserve energy. Its loss need not be made up, and it can be shortened or lengthened with relative ease.

Evolution Hypotheses

Evolution theorists assume that sleep is one of the evolved patterns of life, an adaptation that aided survival, in the past at least. Related notions are the energy conservation hypothesis and the instinctive theory (Webb, 1979).

Evolution theory assumes that sleep is still useful for species survival (Meddis, 1977; Webb, 1975). Sleep perhaps had a historical role for each species, developing as an effective response to ecological pressures. Ethologists, those who study and compare activities of different species, look for sleep causes in current survival factors. For example, some animals are less exposed to danger when asleep than when foraging. For others, sleep may provide useful periods of not responding. Essentially continuous activity with little sleep may be best for others. Sleep may still have a role in individual survival in some fashion or other.

The **energy conservation hypothesis** concentrates on the survival value of reduced sleep metabolism. A correlation across species between sleep time and metabolic rate supports the hypothesis (Zepelin & Rechtschaffen, 1974). Sleep, in general, may be conserving body resources.

Proponents of the **instinctive theory** classify sleep as one of the several life patterns of a species (McGinty, Harper, & Fairbanks, 1974). Sleep is a complex of organized action similar to eating, mating, or locomoting. Each species' nervous system is formed to operate that way. The origins of evolved sleep may be obscure so that looking for its purpose may be useless; there may be no remaining function or purpose to it in a practical, individual sense. It is an adaptation that has persisted simply because there was no reproductive fitness advantage to not sleeping.

Sleep Patterns

Modern sleep study became productive by using the EEG to define brain activity, along with records of muscle activity. Muscles are at times inhibited from action and at others directed to move. One special form of muscle action is **rapid eye movement** or **REM.** Beneath closed lids, our eyeballs twist and turn as if we are looking around vigorously. EEG patterns, muscle activity, and REM are the features we use to define qualitative differences in sleep.

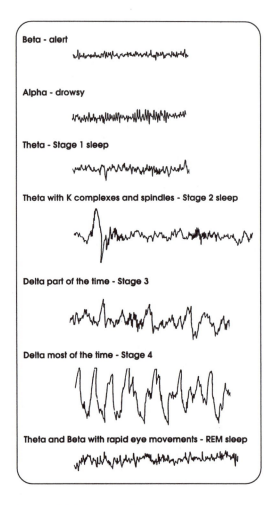

Figure 2.12. Typical EEG records of brain stages from awake to deep sleep.

Stages or Depth of Sleep

EEG recordings describe five stages of sleep. We examine brain functioning in 30 sec or 60 sec periods for the presence or absence of specific wave types, but the records are seldom perfectly clear. Changes in stages of sleep are not abrupt. Stages of sleep are just labels we put onto what are typical periods of brain waves during sleep. What they are and what they mean depend on our definitions in scoring EEG records. One set of standards is published by the National Institutes of Health (Rechtschaffen & Kales, 1968). Using these standards, we see the defined stages following a regular cyclic pattern in a night of sleep,

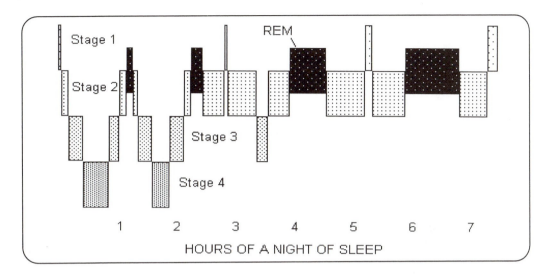

Figure 2.13. Pattern of stages in a typical night of sleep.

within certain limits. (Figure 2.12 shows EEG patterns in each sleep stage.)

Stage 0 is a quiet wakefulness showing low-voltage, fast beta waves but with appearances of alpha rhythm half of the time or more. Alpha waves are of 8 to 13 hz (Hz = cps) regular form and medium magnitude (at least 40 microvolt amplitude).

Stage 1 is a period of sleep-entry drowsiness showing an irregular pattern of theta waves and usually lasts only a few minutes. Theta waves range from 3 to 8 Hz.

In **Stage 2,** we are asleep, and the EEG shows the appearance of occasional **sleep spindles** and **K-complexes.** Spindles are 12 to 14 hz bursts of larger voltage lasting from $1/2$ sec to 2 sec; the name *spindle* comes from its appearance on the record. K-complexes are high voltage spikes of brain activity. The K-complex in the brain is similar to a sharp stimulus in an alert person.

Stage 3 adds the occasional appearance (20% to 50% of the record) of large, slow delta waves to the continued patterns of Stage 2 spindles and K-complexes. Delta waves are of 1/2 to 3 Hz and at least 75 microvolt amplitude. In **Stage 4** sleep, delta waves appear more than half of the time. Stage 4 is the deepest sleep, from which we usually awaken only with the greatest diffi-

culty. Taken together, Stages 3 and 4 are **slow-wave sleep** or **SWS.**

REM usually begins after a half hour or more of sleep, as sleep changes from SWS to Stage 1 or 2 and the eyes begin a series of rapid movements. These eye movements are recorded on the same polygraph and are scored for presence or absence. Along with the bursts of eye movements, we see an EEG pattern of theta and beta waves.

This fast, low voltage, and irregular activity of the EEG has been called **paradoxical sleep** because it suggests that the sleeper has awakened but actually the sleeper has not. During REM periods, there may be irregular breathing and blood flow, appearance of perspiration, sex organ arousal, and inhibited movement of large muscles of the body. Awakened during periods of REM, sleepers usually report narrative dreaming.

Nightly Cycles of Sleep Stages

When young adults sleep, the cycle of stages (1, 2, 3, 4, 3, 2, 1 REM) repeats through the night (see Figure 2.13). Each cycle takes about 70 min to 110 min to complete, and four or five sleep cycles occur each night. Occasionally, the sleeper awakens for a brief time, often in response to external stimulation. The pat-

TABLE 2.2	Characteristics of a Typical Sleep Night
Number of cycles through stages	4-5
Slow-Wave Sleep, SWS	mostly early
REM and Stage 2	mostly late

tern of stages of a typical or ideal night's sleep is shown in Table 2.2. Note that slow-wave sleep (SWS) is most extensive in the first few cycles of the night. REM increases to become most lengthy in the later cycles of the night.

The purpose of the cycles of relative arousal during the sleep period has been a matter of considerable interest, but it is not well understood. One hypothesis is that a **basic rest and activation cycle (BRAC)** occurs, not only during sleep but during waking hours as well. Building on the BRAC, Lavie proposes a summarizing theory: that during waking hours, there are periodic increases in sleepiness. During sleep, the cycles of stages reflect periods of increased arousal. Lavie believes that these gating periods facilitate a change in state, allowing more control over the length of sleep, particularly concerning natural zeitgebers. Breaking the waking periods and the rest periods into shorter units pro-

vides more opportunities, or gates, to move easily into the other state, as circumstances of the body or the environment may dictate (Lavie, 1985; Schulz & Lavie, 1985).

Another speculation about the purpose of sleep cycles is James Horne's (1988), following his core-optional sleep theory. Horne defines core sleep to include the first few cycles of stages, including both the SWS, the REM, and the lighter sleep periods in those cycles. The cerebral cortex is functionally off-line during SWS for necessary neural repair and maintenance. Horne suggests that the cycles allow periodic testing of the adequacy of cerebral cortex repair during core sleep. REM is testing and toning the brain. Thus, a test follows a period of repair, followed by more repair and then a test. This cycling continues until the repairs are adequate, as shown in the reduced length of SWS repair time as the night goes on and increased REM toning.

The time we spend in each stage is a useful measure of the quality of sleep. We can most easily compare the time spent in each stage in a picture like Figure 2.14.

In this format, we can easily see that the greatest time is spent in Stage 2 sleep. SWS (Stages 3 and 4) totals about 110 min or one quarter of the 450 min and is about equal in total length to REM sleep time.

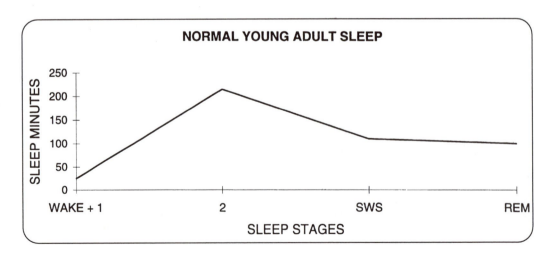

Figure 2.14. Time spent in each stage in a normal young adult's sleep.

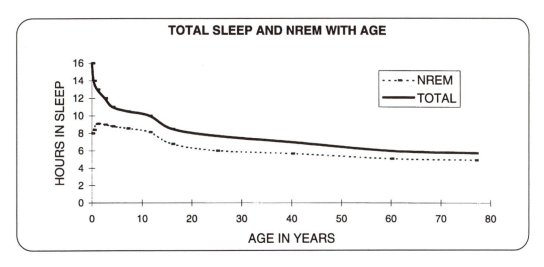

Figure 2.15. Changing patterns of No Rapid Eye Movement (NREM) sleep and total sleep over a lifetime; REM sleep is the difference between the two lines.

Sleep Changes With Age

A basic pattern of sleep is tied to age. How do sleep patterns change with aging? (See Figure 2.15.) Newborn infants sleep about 16 hours a day. Their cycle is more rapid, at about 60 minutes, and has a less predictable sequence. About half of their sleep time is REM. They spend much less time in Stage 4 sleep than adults.

Sleep patterns change gradually over the growing years to those typical of the young adult (Roffwarg, Muzio, & Dement, 1966). Much of the information about sleep comes from studies of young adults, and thus most facts and statistics about sleep reflect sleepers of that age.

Through the adult years, slow change of sleep patterns may take place, but it is less remarkable. By age 60, certain features of sleep during the night seem to have changed in subtle ways. There is evidence that average sleep length shortens by something approaching 1 hour. Other study has indicated (a) a more even pattern of REM periods over the night, (b) slower sleep onset, (c) more Stage 1 and awakenings especially near the end of the sleep period, and (d) less deep sleep. These patterns suggest that there is a change

in the quality of sleep with age (Kahn & Fisher, 1969).

Each of these findings about aging has been questioned, and the study goes on. For example, using the same criteria for identifying wave forms as those for young adults, there is less slow-wave time in sleepers over 60 years old. It may not be, however, that older people have less time in deep sleep. The magnitudes of EEG slow waves decrease with age. Because the criteria for delta waves include a requirement that they be of a specific magnitude, fewer slow waves are counted in the sleep of older adults. With the magnitude criterion relaxed, there appears to be no reduction in slow-wave sleep (Webb, 1982).

Among the other factors to consider in examining sleep changes with age is the structure of life during the active day. Sleep time shortens or lengthens in response to lifestyle demands. Such forces are common in life. Our work and recreation schedules may lead us to reduce sleep to a minimum. In later years, as we change our lifestyle toward fewer demands, particularly in retirement, sleep may increase to fill time. With more time available for sleep, and with other qualitative lifestyle changes such as increased time in daytime naps, the pattern of nightly sleep

TABLE 2.3 Three Methods of Determining Average Sleep Length Along With Their Noted Problems

Method of Determining Length	Duration of Sleep	Problems With Method
Sleep Log	7 hour 29 min	When did sleep begin? Naps?
Questionnaire	7 hour 4 min	What is expected of me? Naps?
Sleep Laboratory	6 hour 51 min	Reluctance to remain? Naps?

will likely change. These forces also mask any purely physical aging causes of changed sleep.

Sleep Length

Length of Normal Sleep

How long is normal sleep? That is an easy question without an easy answer. We start with being vague. People differ in how long they sleep. For each of us, average daily sleeping time is reasonably constant, but there can be a large variation across nights. There is no standard, best length of sleep for everyone. Some of us sleep long, and some sleep a short time. The usual summary is that the average young adult sleeps 7.5 hours, with a standard deviation of 1 hour. That means that about two thirds of young adults average between 6.5 and 8.5 hours, and all but 5% fall between 5.5 and 9.5 hours.

Finding how long we sleep is not easy. Several studies have presented population statistics of sleep length. These studies illustrate several ways to find sleep-length averages, but none is without contamination. Each method has its unique problems of interpretation. Fortunately, the statistics are not markedly different among these methods, and the variations are understandable.

We can keep sleep logs for a time. A **sleep log** study of 509 recording volunteers yielded an average night's sleep of 7 hours and 29 minutes (Tune, 1969). Sleep logs require the respondent to know how long each sleep episode actually lasted; for example, what time did sleep actually begin?

We can simply ask people how long they typically sleep. A questionnaire study of 659 respondents showed average reported sleep length to be 7 hours and 4 minutes (Zepelin, 1973). The questionnaire responses depend upon memories influenced by what each person believes to be the "correct" length of sleep. Napping time is typically underestimated or ignored.

Volunteers can be monitored in **sleep laboratories** in which EEG and other measures are recorded. Measurement of 127 people in a sleep laboratory found the average sleep to be 6 hours and 51 minutes (Williams, MacLean, & Cairns, 1983). Sleep laboratory measures probably underestimate normal sleep because of the unaccustomed sleeping conditions, the reluctance of volunteers to snooze longer in the laboratory bed, and the absence of data on napping during the day. (Table 2.3 compares the findings of sleep logs, questionnaires, and sleep laboratories.)

From these studies, sleep researchers also find that some people normally sleep very long, and some sleep a short time during the night. In his University of Florida sleep laboratory, Bernie Webb compared these two kinds of sleepers against a control group of normal 7.5-hour sleepers (Webb & Agnew, 1970; see Figure 2.16).

There was little difference in SWS among them. The differences were in Stage 2 time and in REM sleep. Long sleepers had added REM and Stage 2 time, with somewhat longer Stage 1 time. Short sleepers, 6.5 hours, had no difference from normals in REM time; all the difference was in Stage 2. Very short sleepers, under 5.5 hours, had Stage 2 reductions and less REM. Researchers could find no personality differences associated with the length of sleep.

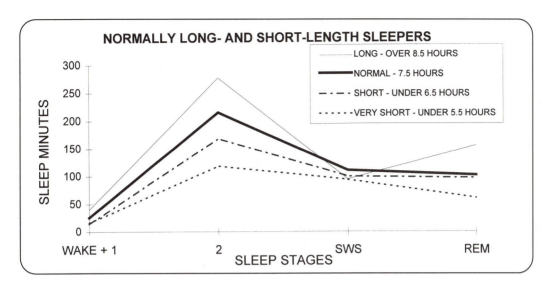

Figure 2.16. Time spent in each stage by normally long- and short-length sleepers.

Several studies have shown that physical work and exercise have little effect on the need for sleep or one's sleepiness. Extent of physical activity, controlled for mental work, is not a factor in the amount of sleep one needs or the quality of that sleep, but it does create feelings of tiredness (e.g., Angus, Heslegrave, & Myles, 1985).

Mental activity, however, is very important to the need for core sleep. James Horne entertained sleep-deprived volunteers with trips to visually and mentally interesting places such as zoos and gardens. Horne's thesis was that these mental engagements work the cerebral cortex harder and thus lead to a greater need for the maintenance and repair of the core sleep. The mentally stimulated but sleep-deprived volunteers were sleepier following these busy days than following confinement in the monotonous laboratory environment. Recovery sleep had 40% more SWS time following busy versus boring days. The greater the normal mental life during the sleep deprivation, the greater were the feelings of sleepiness and SWS in recovery sleep (Horne, 1976). This suggests that, contrary to common wisdom, a day filled with challenging mental work will make us more sleepy than a day of repetitive physical labor. Need for sleep is different from fatigue of muscles.

We will look more at this in Chapter 12, "Work."

Altering Sleep Length

We can choose when to go to sleep and when to awaken, but are there limits? How short can average sleep be? Sleep shortening has been studied in different ways that give us important ideas. In one study, normal sleepers shortened their sleep to roughly 4 hours to 6 hours per night and maintained that sleep length for long periods. Webb and Agnew (1974) abruptly reduced sleep length in their volunteers and found that after a period of some difficulty in adjustment, REM time reduced, but there was no change in the Stage 4 total.

Sleep researchers in San Diego (Friedman et al., 1977; Mullaney, Johnson, Naitoh, Friedmann, & Globus, 1977) more gradually shortened the sleep of three couples who normally slept 8 hours per night. Reductions were by ½ hour every 2 weeks and then after every 3 or 4 weeks. There were no important performance changes during the period of the studies, but the volunteers did report an increase in feelings of sleepiness and fatigue and a corresponding feeling of decreased vigor as the nightly sleep shortened to below

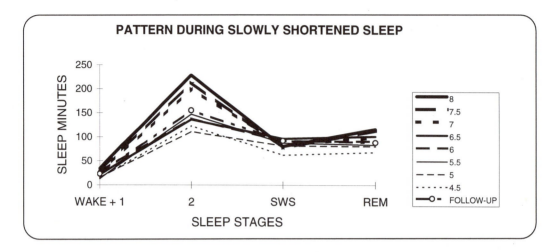

Figure 2.17. Time spent in each sleep stage by sleepers who gradually reduced their sleep length.

6 hours. At 5 hours and below, there was evidence of irritability, daytime sleepiness, and poorer efficiency at work.

Shown in Figure 2.17 are the times in sleep stages as the three couples' sleep was reduced by ½-hour steps. Similar to the pattern seen in normally short sleepers, reduction in sleep time came primarily from the Stage 2 and then the REM time. An interesting side note is that volunteers who experienced a gradual reduction of sleep from 8 hours to about 5 hours were still, a year after the study was over, sleeping only 6.5 to 7 hours per night. This suggests that such an experience can lead us to establish a comfortable minimum sleep length.

According to core-optional sleep theory, sleep reduction appears to be entirely in the optional sleep. Reducing optional sleep produces optional-sleep sleepiness, but fundamental capabilities remain unchecked. Reductions to sleep lengths below that required for core sleep are not tolerated. If cerebral cortex maintenance and repair are necessary, need for core sleep sets the lower limit of long-term nightly sleep length.

Forcing a longer sleep period by sleeping or at least staying in bed longer than normal also does not change the Stage 4 total but will increase Stage 2 and REM time (Feinberg, Fein, & Floyd, 1980).

Sleep Deprivation

The most direct effect of not sleeping at the accustomed time appears at once. We feel sleepy. Sleepiness is one good index of sleep loss, but this measure is not without problems. The sleepiness we feel depends on not having slept and also on the time of the day. We feel most sleepy at those times of typical sleep; the biological rhythm of activity and sleep moderates the sleepiness. From the late-evening time of normal sleep, we feel a gradual increase in willingness to sleep. In addition, there is good evidence we will feel moderate sleepiness in the mid afternoon and marked lack of sleepiness in the early evening (Lavie, 1985).

A second direct effect of not sleeping is that sleep occurs more rapidly. That is, the latency of sleep shortens the longer we are awake. With a long period of sleep deprivation, sleep latency reaches near zero; we fall asleep immediately. The biological rhythm of normal sleep-activity patterns also moderates sleep latency. Falling asleep when deprived of sleep is quickest at times of day we usually feel sleepy or fall asleep.

Beyond making us feel sleepy and speeding up sleep onset, there will be some small changes in other physiological functions. For example, we feel periodic difficulty in focusing our eyes and our eyelids droop, but these may be fatigue effects of specific muscle systems not accustomed to continuous activity. Those who have looked for consistent evidence of body impairment coming solely from sleep loss have not been able to find anything (Horne, 1988; Kleitman, 1963).

Changes in performance potential with sleep deprivation are subtle but real. Most life tasks and simple performances can be accomplished at acceptable standards. It appears at first that sleep deprivation has no real effects, but differences occur in lapses or absences of responses. With greater sleep loss, we have more frequent periods of not responding. Thus, errors, omissions, and measures of poorest performance are the most sensitive indicators of sleep deprivation.

A simple sensory-motor test shows this, comparing the 10 best reaction times with the 10 worst when rested against those measures during sleep loss. The best reaction times are unchanged over the days of the tests, but the averages of the worst reaction times directly increase with sleep loss. Another way to see sleep loss deficits is during periods of sustained performance. A brief task may not be affected, but a longer task will show periods of lapses caused by sleep deprivation (Williams, Lubin, & Goodnow, 1959).

The nature of the sleep-loss assessment task is also important. It matters whether a task is self-paced or work-paced. We are able to direct our own progress in doing self-paced tasks. In these tasks, sleep deprivation will lead to slower speed of performance but with no effect on quality. We monitor the lapses and slow or redo the work properly. We take more time but still can keep a high standard. Work-paced tasks allow no such flexibility, and hence, in situations demanding speed or having a high mental load, we make errors of omission.

There are many factors that bear on measuring performance after sleep loss. Sleep deprivation studies are especially complicated by problems of fatigue, task variables, subject motivation, and others. Fatigue, for example, is a particularly difficult factor to specify and control. Of course, fatigue is a part of sleep loss in most situations. It is all but impossible to deprive people of sleep for a reasonable period while ensuring that they are physically and mentally rested. Continuous exertion is the only practical way to prevent sleep.

Despite some speculation (seemingly supported by a few media events), there are no serious changes in personality resulting from sleep loss. Occasionally, a period of bizarre activity will occur in a long-deprived volunteer, but the pathology seems to be part of that individual's unique reaction to the mental stress of the situation rather than to the sleep deprivation specifically.

One additional interesting example of sleep deprivation was a teenager's attempt at breaking the world record of nonsleep, then thought to be 260 hour. No subtle testing was planned for the spontaneous event, but sleep psychologists monitored him in the last days of the attempt. When he did go to sleep, he slept for 14 hours and 40 minutes. His following nights of sleep were of normal length (Gulevich, Dement, & Johnson, 1966). The studies of total sleep deprivation of other volunteers show a similar pattern. There is only a slight temporary increase in subsequent sleep time. Total sleep loss is not made up with anywhere near a one-for-one recovery time. However, the quality of sleep in the makeup period emphasizes significant amounts of SWS. In line with the concepts of necessary core sleep and optional sleep, it appears that sleep recovery is essentially the needed core sleep. Most of the lost core sleep (cerebral cortex repair time) is regained in subsequent sleep recovery.

SWS Sleep Deprivation

An interesting test of core sleep theory, deprivation of SWS, is difficult to accomplish. We need a procedure that will raise the sleeper to higher sleep stages but not all the way to awakening. Webb and his colleagues found a technique that worked—giving light shocks to the sleeper's foot at the appearance of SWS. Sleepers did not awaken nor did they appear to notice the shocks. An average of more than 200 shocks per night were required to stave off deep sleep. Over the 7 days and nights of the experiment, the SWS-deprived volunteers reported being sleepy during the day, and they also were described as "physically uncomfortable, withdrawn, less aggressive, and manifested concern over vague physical complaints and changes in bodily feelings" (Agnew, Webb, & Williams, 1967, p. 856). This is intriguing, but more evidence is needed about SWS deprivation.

REM Sleep

Sigmund Freud developed in Western culture the potent but misleading idea that most dreams have a disguised meaning and are a way to understand unique and personal mental functioning. The damage is now done; a psychoanalytic view of meaningful dreams is firmly lodged in common folk psychology. Following the Freudian logic, if dreams are an important piece of mental functioning, then they are in a sense necessary.

With the discovery of REM, researchers found that people reported that they had been dreaming when awakened during REM. An exciting hypothesis about deprivation of REM sleep time followed the assumption that REM indicates dreaming time. If Freud was right and REM time is psychologically vital, then its loss may produce bizarre consequences. Researchers tested the notion by awakening volunteers whenever the REM appeared, through several nights of sleep. The loss of dreaming did not appear to be important (Ellman, Spielman, Luck, Steiner, & Halperin, 1991); not so with REM itself.

REM deprivation has its major influence on sleep quality. One effect was REM pressure. **REM pressure** is the quicker appearance of REM sleep in the night of sleep. There seems to be a greater urgency for REM. Another consequence is **REM rebound:** an increased total time of REM during sleep nights after the deprivation operation stopped. A certain amount of lost REM time apparently will be made up as long as sleep time is available (Dement, 1960). There is no agreement that

REM deprivation has other reliable effects. REM sleep, like sleep itself, seems strongly determined, but its effect outside sleep is yet to be established.

Recall that newborn infants sleep about 16 hours a day. Their cycle is more rapid and has a less predictable sequence, and about half of their sleep time is REM. Horne, in his coreoptional sleep theory, has proposed that REM stimulates the growing infant cerebral cortex. REM provides the constant activity needed for growth of brain function. Thus, adult REM may be just more of this kind of function, either continuing a necessary brain activity or simply being a vestige of a once-useful function.

A related idea we noted earlier is that REM provides a toning and testing service to the cerebral cortex brain areas. Horne proposes that a continuous toning activity maintains the brain in a ready condition during times when understimulated. The REM periods are a kind of self-test, a checking routine to show that all the processing functions are operating in an acceptable manner. Some evidence for this self-test notion comes from studies of the nature and contents of dreams.

Dreaming

Dreaming permits each and every one of us to be quietly and safely insane every night of our lives.

W. Dement, quoted in *Newsweek,*
Nov. 30, 1959

In Sigmund Freud's psychoanalysis, dreams have meaning, sometimes disguised so that interpretation is necessary for a complete understanding. The focus of Freud's dream study is on what is in the dream, its content (Freud, 1950). Many volumes of dream study have been published in his tradition. Dream anecdotes from earlier home sleep are recalled and analyzed with a psychoanalyst in a clinical setting.

By contrast, a cognitive scientist approaches the dream as a kind of mental process, and the question is changed to what it tells about brain function and thinking. Dreams are sometimes obtained immediately by awakening dreamers during laboratory sleep. In this manner, David Foulkes (1985) has developed a process-oriented analysis of dreaming and its function, arguing that dreaming is involuntary thinking. In a different but related way and from his systematic study of dreams, Harry Hunt (1989) believes that dream study depends upon first having a valid analysis of the forms that dreams take. He has proposed that dreaming is an immediate synthesis of results from different forms of brain information, without the logical and judgmental aspects of thinking about them.

Perhaps Shakespeare said it pretty well:

I talk of dreams;
Which are the children of an idle brain,
Begot of nothing but vain fantasy.

Romeo and Juliet, 1.4.96

Describing Dreaming

Dreaming during the first sleep period, the sleep-onset transition through Stage 1 sleep, is somewhat different because of its transition from waking ideation and because of its limited duration. Foulkes (1985) describes a set of stages of mental content when entering sleep, beginning with losing control of waking mental imagery. The loss of voluntary control is intensified, leading to a loss of orientation as well, a period of hallucinating. Mental content then becomes disordered in context, a state the psychoanalysts have called regressive. In a regressive dream, one loses the "I" so that the mind no longer exists. After this, the lower sleep stages are entered and the dream content becomes that of **no rapid eye movement (NREM)** sleep.

The first students of REM sleep and dreaming tried to link the observable changes of the sleeper to the content of the sleeper's dreaming. They soon found that dreaming could not be read from such physical clues. Eye movements did not always reflect visual inspection, and male erection did not indicate a sexual dream content. What was clear, however, was that when in REM, 90% of awakened sleepers reported that they had been dreaming. Foulkes (1985) also found that dreams were reported equally often during awakening from Stage 1 sleep just at sleep onset (90%) and somewhat less often on awakening from NREM sleep (60%).

Foulkes's studies of NREM dreaming showed some interesting phenomena. About one fifth of these reports were just that the dreamer had been thinking about something, but there was no narrative. The recalled NREM images were not organized; they were disconnected. NREM dreams tended to be fragments or of smaller scale than those during REM. For example, Foulkes and Schmidt (1983) showed mental content in 93% of REM awakenings but only 67% in NREM. In REM, about 80% of the mental content had dreamlike themes, compared with 40% in NREM. The average REM report had 5.5 units; the NREM had 1.3. Foulkes suggests that the NREM dreams are more discrete and diffuse memories, and there is no need to invoke what he calls the *dream production system* to make sense of them.

Hunt (1989) has a different view of NREM dreaming. He believes that what pass for dreams among people awakened in NREM periods actually reflect a kind of defensive reaction of people who are not sleeping well. The dream is a response to the pressures of the sleep laboratory setting and the demands of being awakened. The defense amounts to a continuous low level of mentation that keeps the sleeper on guard for the anticipated events. Similar NREM activity happens to people facing life pressures or who fear falling asleep. Hunt believes that the NREM mental activity was overlooked in the earlier studies because the awakened sleepers were asked for their dreams rather than for what was "in their minds" at the time. The NREM material is not what most sleepers typically call a dream.

Repetitive Dreaming

William Domhoff (1993) has analyzed many studies of dreams for elements of repetition. He suggests that in repetitive dreams and repeating dream themes we may be dealing with our problems. That is a familiar psychoanalytic (e.g., Sigmund Freud or Carl Jung) theme, but we may consider it without that theoretical baggage. Domhoff suggests a dimension of repetitive dreaming, anchored at one end by repeated dream elements that are ordinary and mundane people, things, and activities. Next are repeated dream themes that appear in long sequence dreams. Further toward the other end are recurring dreams that produce fear and situations not related to current life events. At the extreme end of the dimension are overwhelming and traumatic dreams that reproduce disturbing experiences again and again.

Domhoff concludes that repeated dreams reflect problems in life, usually unpleasant emotional ones. Being so, they may be cautiously explored for evidence of problems and unfinished or unsolved emotional business. There is no evidence that repeated dreams actually solve those problems, nor that such solutions are the function of dreams. That repeated dreams exist, and that they often highlight aspects of our lives, seem to be factual statements.

But we cannot conclude that all dreams have meaning nor that any particular dream, no matter how emotionally shocking or painful, has any necessary connection to our cognitive nature. Some dreams are inventions made up of experienced cultural fiction and perhaps combined with or made exclusively of life images put together in ways not actually lived. Such dreams harbor nothing but evidence that such images are a part of our possible mentality.

Dreaming as Thinking

We generally acknowledge that dreams are not under our control. The contents and the changes just happen without an awareness that we play a personal role. We accept the mental happenings but not as events we personally intend.

In a related way, Foulkes believes that the dreaming is not a matter of just perceiving; it is a thinking process. Dreaming is an abstraction of past events, bringing together different memories and other items, but the dreams are not merely memories, however disorganized or random. Memory of pre-sleep events is rarely reproduced accurately. Neither are dreams a simple response to current happenings. In laboratory studies, stimulation during sleep may be used in dreams in different ways, but most common stimulation is blocked (sleepers do not see), and REM sleep is not begun by external stimuli. As Foulkes (1985) states,

> Dreaming is memory-based, but it generally is not, in the conventional sense, mere "remembering." It is a form of conscious recollection in which bits and pieces from various memory "files" seem to have been caught up together, although they pose, in the dream, as fitting together naturally in some unified impression. (p. 28)

When we think about dreams, we bring to mind ideas of sensory imagery, hallucinations, and bizarre content. In contrast to this usual view of dreams, Foulkes's major finding from laboratory study of REM dreams is that they are typically ordinary and mundane. They follow an organized narrative. At each moment, the dream experiences follow from the prior ones in a coherent fashion. We experience narratives as though they were actually happening rather than as though we are merely thinking about them. It is in this sense that he says that they are "believable analogs of the world."

But in dreaming, we are not conscious of our typical self actively monitoring the happenings, as we are in waking life. Foulkes believes that this loss of the sense of the self may be the most important difference between waking and dreaming acts of ideation. It is interesting that the source of the dream is entirely from within, but there is little of the unique self and its purposeful acts revealed in the dream. Yet, we have an unshakable conviction that each dream is our own and is personal. In dreaming, we do not control the conscious contents, we are not aware of where we are or what we are doing, and we have no self-reflection that assesses the reality of it all.

Dreaming as
Partial Consciousness

Hunt (1989) accepts the suggestions of many observers of dreams that there is not a single form for dreaming, dreams are not likely to have a unique set of causes, and dreams have no single purpose. To understand dreaming, one must accept and account for the wide variety of reported dream experiences, attaching no special validity to those that are found in sleep laboratory settings. In this wider context of study, we find dreams of intense emotion and great personal significance as well as repetitions of commonplace daily events. Some dreams reflect complex syntheses of old and new memories, sometimes disguised in metaphors. There are lucid dreams in which the dreamer is aware of dreaming during the process, and they may include intense, titanic experiences of aggression, sexuality, monsters, or movements like flying and falling.

Hunt (1989) describes dreams as the regular working of the mind when "all that is sequential and sustained, the judgmental, the logical-intellectual, is slowed and derailed" (p. 206). The material presented to the mind, coming simultaneously from many different channels of information, is synthesized and parts are presented in the dream in primarily visual-spatial patterns. The dreamer passively receives that great complexity of mind activity as a chain of immediate sensations.

The purposes of dreaming are as varied as the purposes of the working of the mind. There is not likely to be any simple answer as to what any particular kind of dream means. Dreaming offers us a lot to learn and perhaps to think through in new ways. The motivational relevance of dreaming is similarly not clear. The state of dreaming lacks the normal element of intentionality, and there is little agency exercised by the dreamer. However, examining the general nature of dreaming and its many varieties makes it less mysterious. Indirectly, that knowledge is a part of other expectations that are aspects of motivation.

SECTION SUMMARY:
SLEEP

Sleep theories have elements of two factors. Restoration theories focus on physical changes that sleep repairs. Biochemical indicator substances are the focus of physiological work. Brain-repairing core sleep provides a useful model to organize sleep facts. Various evolution theories make up the second set, ranging over studies of sleep's use in protection, ensuring optimal nutrition, conserving energy, and vague adaptation origins.

Stages of sleep are defined by EEG and eye movement records. We pass through an irregular pattern each night, but that pattern has some identified consistencies. We cycle through the stages four to five times each night; most deep sleep occurs in the first cycles, and most REM comes later in the sleep night.

Average young adult sleep length is 7½ hours, with normal variation between people of an hour or more. Longer sleepers spend more time in REM and Stage 2 sleep. Short-length sleepers lose Stage 2 and REM sleep. The amount and pattern of slow-wave, deep sleep does not vary. Sleep can be shortened by making very slow changes, and the pattern becomes like that of very-short-night sleepers—less Stage 2 and REM. Sleep deprivation yields brief periods of not responding, which show up as increased errors, missed signals, and measures of poorest performance in a series. Deprivation of SWS has effects similar to those of total sleep deprivation. Loss of REM sleep has little known effect except increased tendency to go into REM sleep and having more REM in subsequent sleep nights. A day of mental work increases sleep pressure more than does physical work.

Mental activity of some sort is reportable during almost any sleep time. Awakened during REM, sleepers nearly always report dreams and relate multiple themes and elements in them. From NREM, mental activity is harder to identify and report in a way that "makes sense" to the dreamer. Typical nights of dreams bring together multiple memories without control. They are "followed" as if there were a theme, but the elements and theme often change. Dreams that are repeated seem to involve unpleasant, unfinished life events.

CHAPTER CONCLUSIONS

We must always build on the fact that we are biological organisms of wonderful complexity. We construct, sense, and defend in multiple ways, all having roots in existing body mechanisms. We often focus on our unusually developed cerebral cortex, tending to underrate the reality that it administers and is served by complex mechanisms lower down in the brain and the body. It all works together, and we must constantly look to what physiological information is there as we try to understand motivation topics.

Although most people know about daily rhythms, we rarely take account of these patterns in our sensitivities and performance, unless they become a problem via jet lag or work schedules. Optimal scheduling of learning, of fine motor performances, or of problem solving could improve our life efficiency, were we to make the necessary changes.

The causes and fundamental reasons for sleep remain largely unknown, but we do know how our typical night of sleep occurs. Instead of falling into deep sleep and coming back out, we experience several cycles down and up, nearly awakening a few time during the night. We can do without much of what happens later in the sleep night, but those deep sleep time periods are protected and, if absent, are responsible for negative feelings and poor performances of the following waking day. The hypothesis that significant parts of the brain go off-line for repair during deep sleep fits these facts. It also accounts for mental work making us sleepier than physical work and the powerful consequence of slow-wave sleep deprivation.

We commonly hear media stories about how we would be better off with more sleep, but the evidence seems to show that we do nicely with less sleep, as long as we protect those periods of slow-wave sleep. How do we know if we are sleeping long enough, and how can we ensure the most efficient, restful sleep? The answers are related. Awaken at the same time every day, without exception, no matter when sleep was attempted. Over time, body functions adjust to that schedule and the hour to begin sleep will be obvious. In this way, we use the regularity of circadian rhythms to support good sleep. Try to treat unusual events that disrupt normal sleep with little accommodation. "Sleeping in" merely weakens good sleep habits and does little else, although it obviously feels good at the time. Sleep loss is not life threatening. Brief naps and subsequent sleep nights will put things back to normal.

Industrial strength myths abound concerning dreams. Dreaming tells us more about general mental processes than about deeply buried controlling forces of our minds. Without outside stimulation and need for body action, the mental content in dreams is left to run without controls. Most dream stuff involves recent, somewhat random memories, but imagined possibilities are also constructed and worked into dreams. Freud was right that dreams tell us a little about ourselves, but perhaps they are more a collection of disorganized history and imagination potential than a foretelling of the future.

Study and Review Questions

1. What are the three proposed major groups of survival functions?

2. What is the general role of the sympathetic nervous system?

3. Where is the ascending reticular activating system, and what does it do?

4. What structures make up the forebrain?

5. What is the general role of the thalamus?

6. What is the general role of the hypothalamus?

7. In what functions does the limbic system participate?

8. What type of EEG waves show an alert, active brain?

9. How do hormones differ from neurotransmitters?

10. What do neurotransmitters do?

11. What is a biological rhythm?

12. When is body temperature high and low?

13. What functions change in synchrony with temperature?

14. What functions change in a circadian rhythm that is different from temperature?

15. At what time of day should we learn material for long-term memory?

16. What length day do people follow when day-night cues are removed?

17. What are zeitgebers?

18. What is jet lag, and how can it be minimized?

19. What are biorhythms?

20. What is the restorative theory of sleep?

21. In the core-optional sleep theory, why is core sleep needed?

22. What are some reasons for sleep according to evolutionary theories?

23. Describe the several stages of sleep during a normal night.

24. How do beta EEG waves differ from alpha EEG waves?

25. When do theta EEG waves appear?

26. What are sleep spindles, and when are they seen?

27. What are K-complexes, and when are they seen?

28. What is slow-wave sleep (SWS)?

29. How is Stage 3 of sleep defined compared with Stage 4?

30. How do we describe the patterns of phenomena in a night of sleep?

31. When and how much REM is in our typical night of sleep?

32. When and how much SWS is in our typical night of sleep?

33. What sleep stage takes up most of the sleep night?

34. Who has more REM sleep in a night: infants, young adults, or those of advanced years?

35. How long should a person sleep?

36. What, in total length of stage time, is lost in shortened sleep?

37. What, in total length of stage time, is added in lengthened sleep?

38. By what procedure can people find their shortest optimal sleep length?

39. How could you test someone for sleep loss?

40. What happens with REM sleep loss?

41. What happens with SWS sleep loss?

42. What do we report when awakened from REM sleep?

43. What mental experiences do we have during NREM sleep?

44. What is the likely source of repetitive dreams?

45. In what ways is dreaming like thinking?

46. In what ways is dreaming just partial consciousness?

CHAPTER 3

Eating

Foods and eating are woven by our thoughts and acts into the fabric of human society. Although not as colorful as violence, sex, power, and the other features attracting attention as news and history, eating is an undeniable and relentless part of daily life. It makes up in frequency and necessity what it lacks in excitement. Being so common, eating's influence is easily overlooked.

Eating is a powerfully motivated activity, and it provides motivation for other human acts. Strong feelings are connected to eating. It presents fascinating questions. What biological necessities control eating? What are our eating habits, and why do we have appetites for specific foods? How do culture and other people affect our eating? Do specific episodes of eating have motivational consequences? For what reasons do we gain unwanted weight, and how might we lose it? Answers to these questions outline our study of the motivation of eating.

Nutrition

Appetite

Motivation Foods

Overeating and Obesity

Our need to eat is unrelenting and thereby is fundamental to our biological and social natures. Some basic dimensions of eating are what we eat, when we eat, and how much we eat. We begin with a brief look at food materials, our inherited needs and acquired diet, storage of nutrients, and the biology of starting and stopping a meal. What food materials do we need and with what urgency? How do we use food? How is food energy stored in our bodies?

What we eat is part of our food appetites. Appetites for specific foods depend on both genetic mechanisms and personal learning. Both biology and eating experiences form our tastes for foods. But the roots are deeper. Eating, being a major event in human societies, has social rules. Each culture sets what, when, and how eating is done. We will explore several dimensions of cultural effects on our eating habits.

We have ideas about the motivational potency of eating specific foods, but little direct evidence has been found. The problem is difficult to study. We do know that the time since we have eaten influences the energy of our performances.

Episodes of eating are obviously sources of overeating and building of unwanted body weight. Attention to these abuses of eating will show us that much of the problem is in lifestyle choices of what we eat compared with what body energy we use.

NUTRITION

Eating is a major part of our physical and social lives, but we tend to dismiss the details of what we eat until they affect how we feel or what we can do. Those details are matters of nutrition, the study of food requirements. In this section, we examine the various food materials and how the body uses them, what we know of our inherited diet needs, and our modern diet. Then we briefly examine mechanisms of nutrient storage, physiological factors in starting and stopping eating, and body mechanisms of long-term weight regulation.

We turn first to the fuel sources for our body machinery. We will outline the different components of foods and their digestion and then make an interesting comparison of our modern diet with that of our ancestors—the things we eat now are not those we ate as we evolved into our present form.

Food Materials

Nutrition scientists have developed a solid foundation of knowledge about human food needs, but not without some controversy over details of quantities. Similarly, we understand many of the details of food processing in the body. Still, some of the most interesting questions under study concern ways that food energy accumulates in the body and how that energy moves from storage to nourish body cells. Storage and retrieval mechanisms are important in understanding appetite and weight control, among other motivation topics.

Food substances are arranged in five groups: carbohydrates, fats, proteins, minerals, and vitamins (see Table 3.1). Our look will be simplified to get an overview of some essential ideas, using a few foods as representative examples. Readers interested in more detail should consult a recent nutrition textbook.

Carbohydrates

Carbohydrates are the major sources of energy for people. They are the least difficult to obtain, and the most abundant. Their major function is giving energy for action and providing heat. Carbohydrates divide into monosaccharides (or simple sugars), disaccharides (or double sugars), and polysaccharides. **Monosaccharides** such as glucose, fructose, and galactose require no digestion and absorb directly. **Disaccharides** such as sucrose, lactose, and maltose change into simple sugars for absorption. Together, the mono- and disaccharides make up the collection of sugars we consume in honey, various forms of packaged sugar, and many prepared foods from soup and bread to cakes and ice cream.

Polysaccharides are complex compounds of monosaccharides found in starch and cellulose forms. Grains and vegetables contain starch, which appears in prepared foods such as breads, cereals, potatoes, and corn products as well as in beans, peas, and fruits. Considerable digestion energy is used in breaking these complex carbohydrates into useable components. Complex carbohydrates digested into simple sugars are absorbed into the bloodstream and converted in the liver to

TABLE 3.1   Types of Food Nutrients, Their Forms, Their Uses, and Their Results

Carbohydrates

Forms	monosaccharides (or simple sugars)	
	disaccharides (or double sugars)	
	polysaccharides—complex compounds	
Use	energy source for body cells	
Results	excess stored as glycogen in muscles and the liver or converted to fat by insulin	

Fats

Forms	saturated	
	monounsaturated	
	polyunsaturated	
	hydrogenated	
Use	provide and store energy essential in cell structure and some hormones	
Results	stored as adipose or fat tissue	

Proteins

Forms	chains of amino acids	
	essential amino acids	
Use	building materials for body cells	
Results	excess converted to fat	

Minerals and Vitamins	provide no energy but play vital role in a body process

glucose. Glucose is the main energy source for body cells, along with fatty acids. Excess is stored as **glycogen** in muscles and the liver, or is converted to fat. **Cellulose** comes from the cell walls of plants and is an indigestible form of carbohydrate that provides fiber bulk or roughage to slow and normalize the digestive transport process.

Fats

Fats, akin to carbohydrates, provide and store energy and are essential to cell structure and some hormones. Fat is a loose label for the materials more precisely known as forms of lipids. The nature and uses of fats are complex, but we can outline the essentials.

Most food fats, called triglycerides, are made of three chains of fatty acids attached to a glycerol molecule. Lumped with fats under the name *lipids* is cholesterol. **Cholesterol** comes from animal sources and is more wax-like, being technically an alcohol. Dietary fats and cholesterol are absorbed through the lymph system, entering the bloodstream in sac-like particles. Fats, not being water soluble, flow in the bloodstream in combination with lipoproteins to the cells for metabolism. Lipoproteins are low density (LDL) or high density (HDL). HDL, carrying less fat and cholesterol, is determined by genetic makeup and can be increased by body exercise. We judge it good because it carries cholesterol away from tissues. LDL increases when we eat saturated fat, and LDL carries cholesterol to body tissues. Excesses are deposited, making a special health problem when accumulated in blood vessels.

Structures of the fatty acid chains distinguish types of food fats. Pure fats are either saturated, monounsaturated, or polyunsaturated, defined by the presence of the chemical element hydrogen. Fatty foods have different proportions of the three forms of fat, and there are many kinds of fatty acids of each form. **Saturated fats** carry all the hydrogen possible at the bonds in the chains; they are usually hard at room temperature. Saturated fats are in greater proportion in lard, farm animal meats, dairy products, palm and coconut oils, and chocolate. **Monounsaturated fats** have one bond where hydrogen could be attached. Olive oil and cashew nuts have primarily monounsaturated fats. **Polyunsaturated fats** have two or more such places for more hydrogen and are liquid at room temperatures. Polyunsaturated fats are in greater proportions in most vegetable oils, fish, and peanuts. An additional type is **hydrogenated fats** where bonds are filled by forcing hydrogen in processing. The purpose of hydrogenation is to solidify liquid oils (as in margarine) and to reduce their speed of deterioration.

Two kinds of fatty acids must be supplied from food to form prostaglandin hormones that are vital for many body processes. These essential fatty acids are the linoleic and linolenic groups, the latter including Omega-3 family members found in significant quantities in certain fish oils.

Fats not immediately needed will lodge as adipose or fat tissue in many body places. Storage just beneath the skin provides heat insulation, but much of the fat deposits from our affluent living have become a health liability.

Proteins

Proteins are the fundamental materials making up cells. Protein supply is always needed. Body cells suffer damage in action, and sources of different proteins are necessary for that repair. Body cells also regenerate continuously; the protein in cells is always being replaced in a somewhat inefficient process. Proteins themselves are chains of **amino acids** in different arrangements of a three-dimensional structure.

Nine of these amino acids must come from foods and thus are essential amino acids. Proteins are not stored (excess is converted to fat), and new protein must be eaten daily to meet our needs. Proteins from animal products and some vegetables like soybeans contain all nine essential amino acids and are called complete proteins. Plant food proteins, such as nuts, grains, corn, and legumes, lack one or more of the essential amino acids and must be combined with others to get complete nutrition.

Minerals and Vitamins

Minerals are inorganic chemical elements that provide no energy but play some role in a body process. Required in larger amounts are calcium, sodium, and chlorine, among others. Smaller or trace amounts of 14 elements, including iron, copper, iodine, and silicon, are required.

Vitamins, like minerals, provide no energy directly but are necessary for essential processes. Vitamin groups B and C are water soluble, easily break down by air or heat, and require continuous replenishment. Vitamins A, D, E, and K are fat soluble, absorbed by fat in foods, and stored in fat. Most minimum vitamin needs have been defined negatively, stating how little we can consume without deficiency disease. In this sense, they can be supplied by a varied diet of nutritious foods, assuming those vitamins are not destroyed by processing. Optimum amounts of vitamins are contentious questions of science, politics, and individual experiences. Some hold the view that vitamin amounts must be considered in terms of individual needs based on body uniqueness and health condition, within some limits. The typical Western diet, although above deficiency levels, may give far less than what a person needs of specific vitamins—and that diet gives far more than the necessary calories.

Digestion

Foods convert to body nourishment by digestion, absorption, and metabolism. Mechanisms at each stage play some part in regulating eating. **Digestion** is both a mechanical and a chemical process. Digestion begins in the mouth with chewing food to smaller pieces, mixing it with water, and adding the first of several digestive enzymes. An **enzyme** is an organic substance capable by its presence of producing changes in other organic substances. The muscled walls of the system move the material along in a process called **peristalsis.** Digestion continues in the stomach, then in the small intestine, and finally to a small degree in the large intestine. Ten more enzymes enter the stomach and small intestine, helping to break the food particles into usable nutrients: glucose from carbohydrates, amino acids from protein, and fatty acids and glycerol from fat, as well as minerals, vitamins, and fiber. These simple statements fail to convey the complex orchestration of triggers and processes involved with specific foods, digestive organs, and movements.

Aiding digestion is dietary fiber from plants in two forms: water soluble and insoluble. Resisting digestion, insoluble fiber of plant walls takes on water in the intestines, dilutes and increases material bulk, and thereby slows the movement. Digestion efficiency and stable bowel function result. Water-soluble fiber from pulp in fruit, beans, vegetables, and other sources supports intestinal bacteria growth that adds bulk and also affects cholesterol metabolism.

Absorption

Absorption moves the nutrients to body tissues in the forms of glucose molecules from carbohydrates, amino acids from protein, and free fatty acids and glycerol from fat. It occurs primarily through small projections called villi in the 22-foot-long small intestine. Blood capillaries and lymphatic vessels in the villi transfer the nutrients to the bloodstream and thus to body cells.

Insulin is a major factor in absorption. Our pancreas produces insulin in response to the presence of blood glucose (and in response to a nervous system conditioned to eating cues). Insulin must be present for all cells (except in the nervous system) to take in glucose. It also functions in converting excess glucose into fats, moving amino acids to sites of protein synthesis, and moving fats into fat storage locations.

Complementary to insulin is another pancreatic secretion, **glucagon.** With low

levels of glucose, insulin production is shut down, and secreted glucagon breaks stored fats into fatty acids and glycerol, giving glycogens to the brain, nervous systems, and the muscles. In this way. needed energy then comes from stored fat (triglycerides).

Metabolism

Metabolism is an idea we often use in describing the components and rough functioning of our bodies. In this sense, metabolism is the sum of the processes of constructing, using, and consuming our bodies. More exactly, **metabolism** is the process of changing nutrients into energy in the cells. Some nutrients combine with oxygen, producing energy and heat and leaving primarily carbon dioxide, nitrogen, and water. Using metabolic energy to build or repair tissue is **anabolism**; breaking tissue down and using it is **catabolism.** Normal body maintenance, including respiration, circulation, temperature regulation, and cell activity, use energy at the **basal metabolic rate.** Resting metabolic rate seems to be set by the body's amount of lean mass—body weight minus body fat.

Some of the energy available in food is lost through excretion of waste products. Net energy is that available for the primary body missions of body maintenance, including replacement of tissues, growth, reproduction, and work. The energy unit used in nutrition is the kilocalorie (kcal), shortened in common use to simply **calorie.** The energy in proteins or carbohydrates is 4 kcal per g; fat sources give 9 kcal per g.

Energy Storage

Nutrient energy from glucose, amino acids, and free fatty acids not used immediately in cells accumulates in two forms: glycogen and adipose (fat) tissue. Glucose is the primary source of energy for all tissues, including replenishing needed glycogen in muscles (and the liver). Excess glucose, via carbohydrate-evoked insulin, is converted into fatty acids and hence into **adipose tissue.** Amino acids used in muscles and other lean tissue

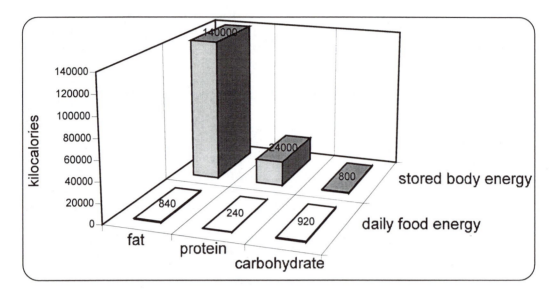

Figure 3.1. Comparison of amounts of stored body energy in different forms and the amount of similar energy consumed in average daily foods. Note that needed carbohydrates are not retained in that form and require daily intake or conversion from other forms.

reconstruct body protein; excess amino acids convert to fatty acids in the liver. Nutrient glycerol and fatty acids store together in adipose tissue as **triglyceride molecules.**

Muscle activity sets the limit to the glycogen stored in active muscles for use as an energy reserve. Active training can increase the glycogen storage in a muscle to about eight times more than that in inactive muscle. Fat is not so limited and can accumulate to an impressive degree. The size and number of fat cells increase to store energy-rich material.

Ignoring gender and cultural differences (which are, nonetheless, important moderators of diet patterns and body processes), a typical adult human being has, in simple numbers, about 164,800 kcal of stored energy. Just 0.5% (800 kcal) is carbohydrate forms, 14.5% (24,000 kcal) is protein, and 85% (140,000 kcal) is fat (Bray, 1994). Using Eaton, Shostak, and Konner (1988) estimates of modern diet components and assuming a diet of 2,000 kcal, we take in 920 kcal of carbohydrate, 240 kcal of protein, and 840 kcal of fat each day. Compared with what is stored, our daily eating of carbohydrates is somewhat more than what is stored, protein in our meals

is about 1% of that in our body, and the fat in our food is less than two thirds of 1% of existing body fat. (See Figure 3.1.)

From this we can suspect that gains or losses in body carbohydrates should have an immediate effect on what we eat, whereas short-term changes in either body protein or fat are not likely to be large enough to immediately influence meal choices.

When at rest, parts of the body have very different energy needs for maintenance. The simplifying rule is that most maintenance energy goes to the active organs. The liver uses about 27%, the muscles, 20%, the brain, 19%, the kidneys, 10%, the heart, 7%. The remaining 17% is in the lungs, skin, and digestive tract. Fat cells take very little maintenance energy. (See Figure 3.2.) These energy factors play a role in overeating and dieting discussed later in the chapter.

Complementary body systems are those of intake control. Nutrient intake is not continuous, and thus physiological mechanisms of starting and stopping eating must be at the root of regulating periodic meals. What makes us start and stop each time we eat? Important to these mechanisms is knowing

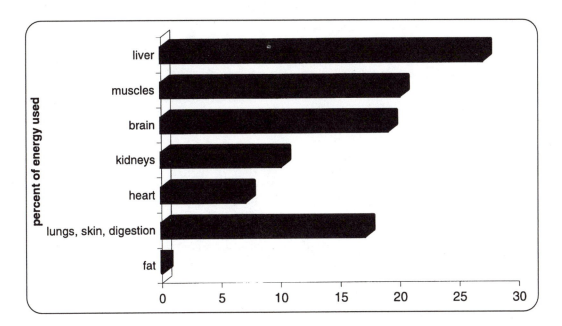

Figure 3.2. Energy needs to maintain normal functioning of different body tissues. Note that little energy is needed to keep fat reserves.

how much we have eaten, both during a particular meal and over a long time.

Natural and Modern Diet

Our human bodies evolved to use food available in our ancestral environment, but it is likely that the food we commonly eat is different from that of our ancestors. If we are now ignoring our bodies' real adapted needs, the consequences are obviously important. That introduces important questions: What *was* our ancestral environment? What food was at hand in our common ancestors' environment 10,000 to 2 million years ago? At the least, we can make educated guesses of what food resources might have existed in our history. We begin with an idea useful to this discussion, which has the virtue of being founded on recent expertise in nutrition science.

Seaside Origins

The usual theory holds that our species evolved its large brain from a smaller one after reaching roughly our present size. Michael Crawford and David Marsh (1989) propose that it was the other way around. As our ancestors became larger, their brains grew in proportion; other species had proportionately less brain size as they grew. Relative brain size is not everything, but it does count for a lot. A certain minimum of brain size is dedicated to basic life functions, but if that is all there is, nothing is left over for more complex activities. Our excess brain structure is mostly cerebral cortex, the material least dedicated to simple life support activity.

Why did our ancestors grow brains along with their bodies whereas their competitors and our cousin apes did not? Crawford and Marsh (1989) suggest it had to do with our diet—using the available foods in the niche our ancestors filled. They suggest our ancestors did not come down from the trees to occupy the grassy savannahs, but instead they settled at the edges of water and took food from both land and water. These survivors were our ancestors, and we should look to them for clues to our inheritance. The key to growing larger brains may be ingesting food from the water.

Brains and their supporting vascular system require nourishment from fatty acids, especially so during the prenatal and early childhood years. Essential fatty acids found in the brain include arachidonic acid, an Omega-6 fatty acid, and docosahexaenoic (DHA), an Omega-3 fatty acid. Optimum brain development comes from a 1:1 balance of Omega-3 and Omega-6 families of fatty acids. Omega-6 comes from "the sticks," from seed-bearing plants and the bodies of animals that eat them. Omega-3 comes from "the sea," from sea vegetables and from marine animals. Bodies of land animals have from 3 to 6 times more Omega-6; fish have about 40 times more Omega-3. As a consequence, whether they are grazers or carnivores, savannah species will not have the optimum fatty acid balance to grow large brains. (Large-brained sea mammals such as dolphins have the opposite problem of getting enough Omega-6, and they apparently do so by seeking squid, a unique source of it.) The story adds another level in noting that the foods in the sea begin as long-chain (20 and 22 carbons) Omega-3 acids like those the brain needs; plant materials on land are short-chained (18 carbons).

> Had man been a savannah species he would, like all other savannah species, have found it difficult to obtain long chain fatty acids in his food, especially docosahexaenoic acid. He would have had difficulty in satisfying the nutrient requirements for his brain and nervous system: which may well have happened to certain hominid offshoots.
>
> Had he occupied the vacant niche between land and water, things would have been different. He would have had available Omega-6 fatty acids from land seeds, protective antioxidants, and high concentrations of arachidonic acid preformed, from small land mammals, from freshwater foods and coastal seafoods as well as from marine mammals. He would also have had an abundance of the docosahexaenoic acid which is missing in the food chain of large land mammals. The land-water interface was an incredibly rich ecological niche which would otherwise have been unexploited. To achieve a ratio of 1:1 would have presented no problem.

> Furthermore, nutrition is not just about fatty acids. The same location would have undoubtedly been a superior source of foods rich in vitamins and especially rich in trace elements. The interface quite simply provided the best of both worlds." (Crawford & Marsh, 1989, pp. 183-184)

With success comes prosperity, which produced both greater size and increased population. As the best niches at the edge of water in the best climates were filled, people moved away from the warm climates and away from the water. The result was less food abundance and a growing need for reliable food sources. Domestication of animals and plants followed.

> The "Neolithic Revolution" that produced agriculture was the basis of civilisations that followed, and it seemed to have occurred at about the same time, around 10,000 years ago, in widely separated places in Western Asia, in America and elsewhere. In isolated areas across the world, separated from one another by mountains, forests and deserts, the beginnings of settled cultivation started to appear. (Crawford & Marsh, 1989, p. 192)

These last 10,000 years or so of civilization are the times we look at for our patterns of culture, including eating. We must keep in mind also that our ancestors relied on wild foods for the first 98.5% of their history. There is little if any adaptation in our biochemistry in these last few millennia, at least not in the basic contributions of amino acid building blocks and body mechanisms for absorbing and storing nutrients. It is likely, too, that in the last 10 generations, human evolutionary change has in all respects been arrested by medical advancement, laws, and ethics making up our culture. The question we must examine is whether our cultural eating practices supply our natural nutrient needs. An interesting analysis of the differences is that of *The Paleolithic Prescription,* by S. Boyd Eaton, Marjorie Shostak, and Melvin Konner (1988). We will summarize several of their descriptions.

TABLE 3.2	A Comparison of Our Average Modern Diet With That of Our Paleolithic Ancestors, as Presumed by Eaton et al. (1988)	
	Paleolithic	*Modern*
Diet energy		
Fat	21%	42%
Carbohydrate	46%	46%
Protein	33%	12%
Ratio of polyunsaturated to saturated fats	1.41	0.44
Fiber	100 gm	20 gm
Sodium	690 mg	2500 mg
Calcium	1500 mg	740 mg
Vitamin C	440 mg	90 mg

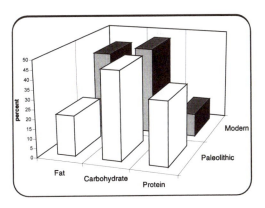

Figure 3.3. Percentage of the three food types making up modern and Paleolithic diets.

Paleolithic Diet

Plants and animals from the native environment differ from cultivated plants and animals in nutrient density, micronutrients, and proportions of fats and carbohydrates. In Table 3.2 are estimates based on Eaton, Shostak, and Konner (1988), comparing likely late paleolithic and modern diets.

Foods of our preagricultural ancestors had less fat, fewer carbohydrates, and more protein, vitamins, minerals, and fiber than what we now eat, but with greater bulk for the same number of calories. Carbohydrates came from high-fiber fruits and vegetables that were only minimally cooked; usually, they were eaten raw. The only refined carbohydrate was from the occasional honey cache. Fats were less saturated (usually nonhydrogenated) and formed a lower percentage of the diet. With seasonal variation, this early diet was 20% to 25% fat, 40% to 50% carbohydrate, and 25% to 35% protein.

Modern Diet

Our average diet today in simple numbers is close to 40% fat (mostly saturated), 50% carbohydrate (refined to simple sugars and free from micro nutrients), and 10% pro-

tein. In specific micronutrient differences, our preagricultural ancestors' food had more iron, double our calcium, and a drastically lower sodium-potassium ratio. (See Figure 3.3 for a comparison of paleolithic and modern diets.)

The source of our modern diet is domesticated plants and animals; domestication is a practice forced on our ancestors by increasing population in a limited environment. Penned-up animals lose muscle and develop fat. In small grazing areas, grasses never produce the stems and seeds characteristic of mature plants. Young growing grasses have more energy, leading to faster animal growth, but that also makes heavy saturated fat deposits. Wild beef animals have about 4% fat; domesticated beef animals have 25%. The difference is made up by increased lean meat and protein in wild beef. Because fat gives 9 cal of energy per g whereas protein and carbohydrates give only 4, the obese domestic beef also supply more energy. In terms of energy source, a useful measure is the ratio of energy coming from fat versus lean sources. In wild animals, that ratio is about 0.5:1; in domestic animals it is 5.6:1. Similar results appear in comparing wild and domestic pigs and fowl. The energy ratio of fat to protein in a wild partridge is 0.56:1; a broiler chicken gives 5:1.

Parallel changes in the nutrients of food resulted from domestication of grain sources of carbohydrates. Sugar comes from grasses, but all of the nutrients except simple carbohydrates disappear in the refining. Wheat and rice varieties were bred and refined for the size of the white endosperm with its rich carbohydrate, ignoring the germ and coatings holding the majority of other essential nutrients.

An important but unfortunate consequence of our modern diet is a long list of disorders with ties to eating. On the list are diabetes, atherosclerosis (fat in the arteries), heart attacks and strokes, obesity, hypertension (high blood pressure), bowel cancer and perhaps other cancers, osteoporosis (weakening bones), and tooth decay. According to current statistics, about 1 in 4 men (and increasingly women) will have a stroke or heart attack before they retire from work, many dying within a year. Not all of those medical events are attributable to diet, but cultural comparisons suggest that the bulk of them are so tied. Next in frequency on the diet-caused disorders list are nervous system and brain disorders (Crawford & Marsh, 1989).

One recent proposal for change in eating is based partly on the idea that our bodies have continued unchanged from evolutionary design in the paleolithic times. Barry Sears (1995) has proposed that the major key to optimal nutrition is maintaining the paleolithic energy balance of 30% protein, 40% carbohydrate, and 30% fat in every meal. His specific plan includes many elements, but he bases every meal on that collection of foods being composed by weight of 7 units of protein, 9 units of carbohydrate, and 3 units of fat (fats have more energy than the others). Daily food is spread over three meals and two significant snacks, to keep the balance of insulin and glucagon smooth. Eating in this way he describes as being in the zone.

With our typical heavily carbohydrate meal, high insulin is produced, leading it to store the excess glucose as fat. Continued high insulin inhibits glucagon with its ability to release fatty acid energy stored in the liver and as fat. In this way, high carbohydrate meals are said to "lock in" the fat and inhibit use of fatty acid energy. With an optimal balance of carbohydrate and protein, the insulin

and glucagon production by the pancreas also is balanced. The possibility of too much insulin is moderated both by the digestion requirements of the protein foods and by choosing slowly digested carbohydrates, avoiding quick release forms such as sugar, pasta, potatoes, and other refined starchy foods. Food fat, primarily of the polyunsaturated and monounsaturated forms, is also required. In addition to meeting nutrition requirements, food fat products are slow to be absorbed, giving a longer full feeling.

There is irony in this picture. The fats we have been told to avoid do not make fat, but are actually necessary to keep us from becoming so. And the recent "food pyramid" encourages eating from the base level, a variety of carbohydrates that are our undoing. We can examine for a moment what it is farmers provide to cattle to give them rapid weight gain. They feed them large amounts of low fat cereals and grains. Grains were rare components of our ancestral paleolithic diet. Processed grains, and all of their derivatives, now are major sources of our food. For us, too, they give rapid weight gain and are at the root of many health problems.

We should be seeing that our cultural eating practices are not serving our bodies, but we have many habits and social practices that keep us from accepting this fact. Those habits and practices make up our acquired motivations concerned with eating, which we will examine later.

Starting and Stopping Eating

Several theories of short-term food regulation appeared in a wave of research in the 1950s. Low level of blood sucrose is an important, direct stimulus to eating. Several hours after last eating, glucose from the meal is used or stored, causing a slight lowering of the glucose concentration flowing in the blood. Sensors, some in the brain and others in the liver, respond to that lowered glucose concentration and signal brain mechanisms that control eating. This is the essence of the

glucostat hypothesis of hunger (Mayer, 1955).

How to stop eating is more complicated. Cues to stop eating, called satiety cues, include glucose, insulin, and amino acids that appear with food digestion. Nutrient metabolism produces elevated body temperature as another stimulus, the thermostatic theory (Strominger & Brobeck, 1953). Hormones in the gut may provide more signals. Glucagon stimulates the liver to produce more glucose; the increased glucose leads the brain to produce satiety. Stretch receptors in the stomach also provide direct brain messages to cease eating. Most important are our experiences of eating. We associate the taste, smell, sight, and texture with the nutrient value of foods we have eaten. Over time, we learn to regulate how much to eat to get the required effect (Booth, Lee, & McAleavey, 1976).

But, of course, there is much more to the physiology of eating and digestion than just starting and stopping. For example, the food we present to our senses sets off body changes that prepare us for eating. Visual, tactile, olfactory, and gustatory senses produce what are called **cephalic phase responses,** meaning that brain processing initiates something in the digestion. These responses are thought to prepare us for the best processing and storage of the nutrients (Booth & Westrate, 1994; Nicolaidis, 1977). One important process is salivation because it adds chemical substances that lead to enzymatic action, helps in forming food for swallowing, and slows the emptying of the stomach. Production of saliva is easy to see and record. Gustatory (sweet, sour, salt, bitter) stimulation gives the greatest amount of saliva, olfactory (smell) stimulation gives less, and sight of the food gives the least (Pangborn, Witherly, & Jones, 1979). Cephalic phase responses of saliva may also be affected by our hunger and how much we like a food.

Other cephalic phase responses release digestive enzymes and hormones throughout the digestive tract. These processes are begun before food reaches the places where changes and breakdown into usable nutrients are be-

gun. A review of these is given by Richard Mattes (1987).

Long-Term Weight Regulation

Long-term eating control is part of the regulation of body weight. Some theories of how we maintain body weight use accounts of fat storage, generally labeled the **lipostat** notions (Mayer, 1955). The most intriguing of these notions uses the set-point theory described by Richard Nisbett in 1972.

According to the **set-point theory,** we each have a specific weight that our body attempts to maintain: the set-point weight. Our body defends that weight by doing things to store energy when weight is below the set point and doing things to reduce the storage of energy when weight is above the set point. Those things the body does to hold set-point weight are (a) encouragement or discouragement of eating, (b) encouragement or discouragement of exercise, and (c) change of the efficiency of metabolism, or all three. The set-point idea suggests how people tend to remain at the same body weight without really being aware of it.

Other theorists propose that fat storage mechanisms underlie the set-point notion. These ideas follow from the question of what causes people to have different set points. The theory's answer goes like this. We know that some people have more fat storage cells than others, and each person's set point weight is that at which the body fat cells are full. The earliest of these theories stated that the fat storage cells form in infancy, depending upon the amount of energy to be stored and perhaps on genetics. Thus, fat babies have more fat cells and thereby establish their weight for life.

More recent work in Sweden cued the idea that the number of fat cells increases at any time that all the existing cells are full and there is more energy to be stored. In this way, periods of weight gain lead to more fat cells and raise the set-point weight. Periods of weight loss do not as readily reduce the number of cells but just lower the amount of fat carried in some cells. This idea is distressing for people trying to lose weight through dieting alone (Sjostrom, 1980). We will use these ideas and paint a more complete picture of the problems and solutions of weight regulation later in the chapter.

SECTION SUMMARY: NUTRITION

Few people are unaware that foods are made up of protein, carbohydrate, and fat. The varieties of each of these are somewhat more esoteric, and the need for adequate levels of vitamins and minerals tends to be underplayed. The foods we take in are processed in the body successively by digestion, absorption, and metabolism. A critical point for aspects of motivation is control of absorption by pancreas secretions of high carbohydrate-stimulated insulin and low carbohydrate-stimulated glucagon.

Our bodies' food needs were established in our ancestral, natural environment and have not changed despite a few thousand years of civilization and a modern diet that incorporates domesticated animals and grains. One reasonable speculation about optimal food resources suggests a blend of plants and marine animals, resting on the optimal brain development we might get from their micronutrients. By most accounts, we now eat too little protein, too much fat, and the wrong forms of carbohydrates, compared with our ancestral diet. The consequence is stored body fat from quick-digesting carbohydrates that stimulate insulin.

The premier glucose-level theory of why we start eating remains largely valid. Why we stop eating is more complicated, involving a number of chemical, physical, and learned factors. Sensing foods by sight, smell, and perhaps thinking about them can begin some digestion processes before the food material actually arrives. Long-term patterns of how much we eat may be set by mechanisms that sense fat storage.

APPETITE

Appetite is desire; in this case, it is desire for food or drink. With appetite, we move beyond the bare need for food. What sensations lead us to choose to eat, what tastes do we seek, and what leads us to eat certain things and in certain ways?

Appetite has been analyzed from a variety of perspectives. One writer distinguished food liking, food preferences, and food choices. Often there may be differences between foods we like, foods we prefer, and foods we actually choose. **Likes and dislikes** are the physiologically based feelings arising from eating a food. For most of us,

pleasant feelings come from sweet foods, and bitter things are unpleasant. **Preferences** reflect what we would like to have, considering the facts we believe about ourselves and the food. We may like the sweet cheesecake, but we have already eaten one piece, and it comes at a high cost to our diet. **Food choices** introduce the elements of food availability and what we must do to get a particular food. Fresh asparagus tips in December may not be a possible choice, so we settle for frozen green beans. Likes reflect our genetic programming, preferences form from life experience in a culture, and choices reflect practicalities in the environment (Logue, 1991).

We will separate the appetite concept into four major parts. First, evolved physiological mechanisms stimulate basic desires for food and drink, and those desires change depending on immediate experiences and needs of the body. This part of appetite has been physiologically programmed. Second, most of human appetite develops in a context of personal eating experiences. Food selection is a matter of extensive experience with foods and their effects following a unique personal history of eating. Third, eating is a common social activity with extensive social rules and influence. Fourth, cultural setting controls a lot of what and why we eat. We begin with our inheritance.

Physiological Programming

Natural Liking

Food tastes come from evolved structure of the body. Certain fundamental gustatory (true taste) sensations produce pleasant sensations, and others produce unpleasant sensations. We speculate that sweet and salty tastes evolved to have pleasant sensations because they influenced survival in the distant past. Sweet tastes make attractive foods. The first reasonable guesses were that sweet things attract because they represent carbohydrates, foods rich in energy. A similar evolution mechanism is suggested for our liking for salt. Sodium ions in salt are necessary for cell function. Especially in the presence of food need, these two tastes should be fundamentally attractive. As one writer summarized it, "Human beings will eat anything if you just put enough salt or sugar or both on it" (Watson, 1985, p. 35).

These plausible ideas are too simple, however. Other facts must be considered to build a better picture. We share our sweet tooth with other omnivores, with rats, and with some invertebrates, but carnivorous mammals do not prefer sweet foods. We like a weak saltiness but not foods strongly salty, and we also like glutamate, a primary ingredient of flavor enhancers. Sour and bitter tastes are unpleasant and usually repellent.

Sour tastes are present in many spoiled and rotting foods, such as fruit. Bitter tastes often come from poisonous nitrogenous plant materials. What is missing in this list of four gustatory sensations is sensitivities to fats and to protein.

Some alternative ideas have been offered for even the simplest of positive sensations. For example, the nature of our human preference for sweet may lie in the need for something to make mother's milk more palatable. We are repelled by certain nitrogenous compounds commonly found in poisonous alkaloid plants. Some amino compounds in milk are bitter because they stimulate those same receptors, but present also in the milk are other amino acids that are sweet or bittersweet. The hypothesis is that we have evolved sweet sensitivity, not to seek out carbohydrate foods but primarily to counteract the natural bitterness of certain protein components in mother's milk (Booth 1990, 1991; Booth, Conner, & Marie, 1987). Carnivores have no evolved aversion to plant materials, no amino acids are bitter for them, and so they evolved no sweet preference adaptation to counteract any taste in their mother's milk (Booth, 1990).

Another kind of structural food preference is that for milk. Milk digestion requires the enzyme lactase. Without lactase, milk decomposes in the large intestine, producing gas and discomfort. Infants have lactase, but adults may or may not have sufficient lactase, depending upon their genetic heritage. The simple rule is that milk-cow people of northern Europe, parts of Africa, and northwestern India are more likely to produce lactase than others. People having lactase have a biological basis for milk preference. Adults of the Far East and most of central Africa are lactase-deficient and often believe milk is a repulsive food that makes them sick (Simoons, 1982).

Biological roots of preference can change over time. Fast change may come with body development, as in the case of the lactase enzyme. Others are more gradual and general. Taste sensitivities decrease with age (Murphy, 1986). Sweet, salt, sour, and bitter sensations weaken, and that may lead people in their late maturity to prefer a greater variety of more strongly flavored foods.

Food Selection

Food preference rests on experience, but certain aspects of experience depend on another aspect of the biological heritage. Humans are omnivores. That is, our species has evolved to eat a variety of plant and animal food. However, some foods are of value and some are not; some are harmful, and some give desperately needed nutrients. Even as they follow their natural liking, foraging omnivores must have a way of establishing the consequences of eating specific foods. How is that done? Speculation is that omnivores evolved ways to sample new foods and permanently establish a feeling in regard to each one depending on its nutritional effects. Few such studies have tested adult humans, but the principle has been shown with animals. Animals learn to choose the one of two foods that has a needed nutrient. Animals also use cafeteria-like arrangements to satisfy nutritional needs from offered foods. Their choices are formed on the effects those foods have on their well-being (Rozin & Kalat, 1971).

As omnivores, people probably have a similar mechanism. There is anecdotal evidence that we come to prefer or avoid specific food sources depending on what we have felt after eating them (Pelchat & Rozin, 1982). If we become ill, for whatever reason, immediately after eating a novel food, the taste of that food may become unpleasant and we avoid trying it thereafter. Or a new food may remain especially attractive after we eat it during an unusual, pleasant circumstance.

Eating experiences may also change biologically based preferences in the short term. Eating some foods may change the physiological basis for preference for others. Eating a meal of one kind of food material may increase our preference for another that is now needed. For example, if we eat nothing but carbohydrates for lunch, will we feel a stronger liking for protein in the next meal (Murphy,

1986; Vazques, Pearson, & Beauchamp, 1982; Wurtman & Wurtman, 1984)?

We start with a more basic question. Do we "keep track" of the foods we eat through the day and alter our food selection according to body energy needs? The simple answer is "Sometimes, but it depends." We first look at what a high-energy snack does to noon lunch food selection. Nutritionists at the University of Toronto (reported in Black & Anderson, 1994) found that children given a 180 or a 360 kcal sugared gelatin drink 90 min before lunch did not alter what or how much they ate. But at 30 min before lunch, that energy preload caused them to eat less food and choose more bread and meat rather than cookies. And the more sugar drink they consumed, the more radical the consequence.

These and other studies suggest that modest amounts of readily digested energy eaten well before meals will not affect meal choices but will increase the normal daily energy intake. Yet, changing the energy content of regular meals will alter food choices in subsequent meals that day. For example, a bigger breakfast will suppress food choices at midday lunch, and a large lunch will weaken our appetite at the evening meal (Booth, 1994). We appear to be sensitive to what goes into our regular meals, but we overlook modest between-meal snacks when calculating energy totals. This suggests a strong learning component that is mealtime sensitive. It also implies what many of us already know: Quick-digesting snacks often go to "waist"!

Considerable study has been made of how sensitive we are to additions or reductions of specific nutrients in our foods. Several studies asked whether we detect fats and adjust our eating to control our energy intake. This research manipulated the fat content in otherwise equal and normal foods over weeks at a time (studies reported in Levitsky & Strupp, 1994; Rolls & Shide, 1994). They showed these patterns:

> Sufficient food was selected by the participants to maintain carbohydrates according to daily needs. (Recall that body carbohydrate stores are about the same as the level

present in a day of normal diet; little loss is tolerated.)

With a diet of reduced fat (about 15% to 20% fat), little notice was taken and a stable volume of food was consumed. Weight loss accumulated, but over a long period, there was a slow increase in total daily energy intake.

With a diet of increased fat (about 40% to 50% fat), again little notice was taken and a stable volume of food was consumed. Weight gain accumulated, but over a long period, there was a slow decrease in total daily energy intake.

Therefore, it is likely that in eating normal meals, we select food primarily according to a need to replenish carbohydrate stores we have consumed. Insensitivity to total daily energy intake (carbohydrate, fat, and protein) suggests poor unconscious control over our overall eating patterns from meal to meal. This leaves us open to following mealtime habits instead. More on this below.

One last concept with a physiological root is the matter of desires for specific nutrients, made popular by the "carbohydrate craving" idea with its proposed serotonin-deficiency explanation. This notion was proposed as being one root of obesity and a variety of other disorders (e.g., Wurtman, 1984, 1988). Adam Drewnowski (1994) suggests that certain foods rather than specific nutrients are what people choose to eat. Studies and example anecdotes of cravings use ice cream and chocolate rather than carbohydrate-richer potatoes and carrots. Food cravings usually aim at doughnuts, cookies, cakes, ice cream, breads, and rolls. All these are tasty combinations of fat with the carbohydrate sugar. Foods with high carbohydrates and low fat are less commonly chosen. Fat in foods adds preferred flavor and palatable texture, suggesting that such craving is based on pleasant eating rather than brain serotonin chemistry.

Personal Experience With Food

We know that some hunger and satiety come from our body mechanisms, and we se-

lect or reject certain foods because of genetic heritage and physiological consequences. Although these forces have undoubted power, strong psychological factors also operate in the wide gap between physiological hunger and physiological satiety.

Acquired Taste

The general process of acquiring tastes for foods can be described with the logic and current wisdom of psychological theory. Our expectations build with experiences and become mental guides for our action choices. Perceptions of foods form on experiences of eating. Eating involves all sensory systems, and over time a collection of information attaches to each food and the conditions of eating it. Among the most salient of those associations is the complex of sensations called taste, actually composed of tastes, odors, textures, pains, and temperatures. How a food is expected to taste and the way it feels most directly determine our choosing it.

David Booth (1991, 1994) asserts that almost all of our normal eating control is learned. We have acquired liking for foods by tying together their sensory elements, their effects on our bodies, and the social circumstances of eating them. For the most part, we eat for reasons only loosely or occasionally connected to physiological needs. Our motivations to eat involve feelings other than hunger. Examples of bitter drinks and of irritating chili peppers are instructive.

We may object to the claim in the "Natural Liking" section above that we don't like sour and bitter sensations. Many foods we like to eat are basically sour or bitter. The difference between physiological aversion and our personal preference comes from food experiences that have moderated the basic tastes. We all reject sour and bitter sensations in their strong and pure forms, but their presence in common foods is another matter. We modify and cultivate these natural reactions. We initially reject foods that are bitter or that irritate our mouth and throat tissues, yet we come to readily consume them. Bitter or irritating foods and materials include coffee, tea,

TABLE 3.3 Examples Along a Continuum Using Different Dimensions From Which We Judge the Relative Attractiveness of Foods

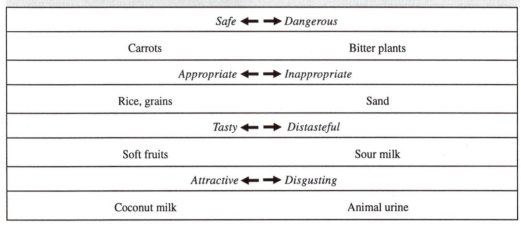

Safe ⬅ ➡ Dangerous	
Carrots	Bitter plants
Appropriate ⬅ ➡ Inappropriate	
Rice, grains	Sand
Tasty ⬅ ➡ Distasteful	
Soft fruits	Sour milk
Attractive ⬅ ➡ Disgusting	
Coconut milk	Animal urine

alcohol, beer, tobacco, chili peppers, and other spices. Why do eat these things and other foods like them?

No other omnivore species eats against its initial sensations, as far as we can tell. Some answers to our peculiar tastes rely on food aftereffects. We know that drinks and tobacco change the way we feel for a time. But that doesn't work for all initially rejected tastes. Among the most widespread are strong spices, such as chili peppers. They have no disguised consequences: what we taste is what we get. Some explanation puts liking chili peppers in the class of "noxious but safe" experiences (Rozin & Schiller, 1980). The taste sounds an alarm that we can learn is not serious. Similar experiences are sky-diving, taking amusement park thrill rides, watching horror movies, and the like. The safe thrill is perhaps the key. Still another answer is even simpler. We eat the foods of fashion in our cultures, and the original reasons for choosing them may be lost in history. They now are simply habits.

Our most preferred foods are those that we are used to, that have been socially approved, and that have shown us good nutritive results. These preferences are not fixed; they undergo continuous modification with life experiences. Booth (1990) notes that we would not notice a one-fifth reduction in sugar or salt or both in many of our foods.

After an experience with the new food, we would adapt to it, and another reduction could be made. Over time, our food tastes would be modified.

Finally, we should keep in mind that our attraction to and revulsion from foods has several psychological dimensions as illustrated in Table 3.3. Moving down the table, we begin with essentially genetically controlled and end with essentially socially moderated factors.

Food Sensation

Food sensation is a conglomerate of experience elements. Chemical taste, odor, texture, temperature, and appearance are all important pieces of the combination (Lyman, 1989).

We examined the chemical sense of taste earlier. Usually, the general term *taste* includes a large odor component. Food-related odors can be judged and ranked from the most liked (strawberry, honeysuckle, raspberry, orange, and lemon) to the least liked (sour milk, vinegar, fish oil, burnt, and sulfurous). Yet preference depends on the food and surrounding experiences of meal. A cheese that smells of strawberry is not correct, even though the odor is much preferred to the sulfurous smell of a good limburger cheese. It is a matter of appropriateness that builds with our experi-

TABLE 3.4 Some Dimensions of Texture Making Up the Sensations in Eating Foods (adapted from Lyman, 1989)

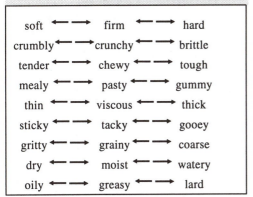

soft	←→	firm	←→	hard
crumbly	←→	crunchy	←→	brittle
tender	←→	chewy	←→	tough
mealy	←→	pasty	←→	gummy
thin	←→	viscous	←→	thick
sticky	←→	tacky	←→	gooey
gritty	←→	grainy	←→	coarse
dry	←→	moist	←→	watery
oily	←→	greasy	←→	lard

ences. A Brussels sprout ice cream or doughnut will probably not sell, but chocolate always will. Coconut in scrambled eggs also doesn't sound appealing, but perhaps chives or garlic does. Each kind of food, appetizer, main dish, salad, vegetable, and dessert, has its own collection of odors that is appropriate or not. New foods in each category must conform to those broad guidelines of experience we share.

Textures of foods are associated with the feelings of foods in the mouth as they are chewed and swallowed. Some dimensions of texture we experience upon first receiving a food include those in Table 3.4, inspired by Lyman (1989).

A similar list of dimensions can be used to describe the feeling of liquids in the mouth, including the effects of later stages of mastication.

The texture of a specific food is often included in its definition. Crunchy breakfast cereal, thick milk shake, juicy fresh oranges, chewy caramel candy, meltable chocolate, firm but chewable carrots, mixed vegetable of a salad, and tender, meaty beef steak are expected. We would not be pleased to find these qualities confused and discover a meltable salad or a steak-like chewing resistance in a fresh carrot. For some foods, the precise mouth feel defines its quality, and substitutes fail to make the grade.

Temperatures contribute a great deal more than we often recognize to how we like a food. Many odors are released at specific temperatures; too cold and the flavor doesn't appear, and too hot drives it away quickly. Some drinks, such as tea, are preferred by most tasters only when the liquids are quite hot or very cold. Other beverages, such as coffee, seem to be preferred hot. Soft drinks must be cold. Cool spaghetti seems unattractive, and a hot lettuce salad is absurd.

The appearance of a food is a matter of size, shape, color, and the circumstances of place and any other foods with which it is presented. A square block of purple mashed potatoes or small, round pieces of blue meat may be artistic statements but will not likely be seen as pleasant invitations to eat them. We usually are most attracted to foods in a standard portion, in a traditional form, of their natural color, or at least the way they have been consistently manufactured and presented. We prefer margarine colored to appear like butter, and breads and rolls should have a brown crust. Salads and vegetables are usually greens, yellows, oranges, and reds. Meats are best liked in browns, whereas fish looks freshest when white. The matter of artistic arrangement of foods and their positioning and timing in presentation can also have considerable influence, especially for those seeking "fine" dining.

A wide collection of personal and socially shared associations form the perceptions each of us brings to food choices. New foods are judged by what we know of them and how their sensations rate in that collective experience. Mango and okra illustrate such acquired food perceptions.

Mangoes are rather large, somewhat ugly, green, red, and yellow fruits with very sweet, distinctively flavored and juicy orange flesh surrounding a slippery, fuzzy, and large pit. Once having eaten them, most of us like their taste. If that experience with mangoes is very positive, we may choose them over other foods, even when we don't feel hungry.

A different initial experience is common with okra. The cooked pod of the okra plant is unusually mucilaginous (slimy) and is used in stews and gumbo soups. Although its flavor is typical of green vegetables, the most salient

TABLE 3.5	Foods We Are Likely to Choose When We Feel Certain Emotional Events (selected and revised from Lyman, 1989)

Food	Most Often Chosen When
Salad	Loving
Meat	Happy
Fast food	Friendly
Fruit	Happy
Vegetables	Happy
Dessert	Joyful
Healthy snack	Bored
Junk snack	Amused
Soft drink	Loving
Nothing	Fearful

perception is that slimy texture many people find unpleasant. Perhaps other ideas of slippery materials form the negative feeling attached to the okra.

Food and Feelings

Some of our eating follows from how we feel just then. Very strong states of rage, terror, lust, or whatever get in the way of eating. Neither our digestive system nor our mental state will allow it.

Lesser emotional states of mind and body may set us up for mindless eating. At the low extreme, eating is something to do when we are bored. Another candy or bowl of popcorn gives us something to do. Even when there is something happening, we may eat because we are just observing and not doing anything. Snacks at movies disappear quickly. A few drinks and bowls of finger food are consumed in an evening of television watching, sometimes without real awareness. These are dangerous mental states and habits for people with weight-control problems.

Middle-level emotional intensities, such as loneliness, guilt, and anxiety states, also can underwrite a period of eating. Eating takes the place of facing the hardship. The food is a comfort, sometimes formed on past experiences. Parents may have comforted a lonely child with a piece of cake or pie and a glass of chocolate milk. Adult loneliness now can be assuaged by more of the same. An offering of food is made to remove the guilt of something done or not done to another person. The food treat now comes to mean the easing of guilt for oneself. These kinds of food attachments are as widespread and complex as the varieties of lives.

In compiling Table 3.5, people were asked what kind of food they would like as they imagined themselves to be feeling each emotion. Turning the data around, we can look at which emotion most often determined each kind of food (selected from report in Lyman, 1989).

Social Regulation of Eating

Appetite is based on biological programming using specific experiences of eating, but it is with others that we form most of our specific tastes and eating preferences. Food is nearly always produced, prepared, and served with others. Social regulation of eating is a process that concerns the ways other people, their presence and their acts, determine when, where, and what we eat. The process of social regulation is partly passive and partly directed. Passive regulation accumulates through mere exposure to others and the foods they eat. Being a part of a midwestern American farm family is sufficient to establish both the particular kinds of foods eaten and the social habits of eating. Growing up in a Central American farming culture establishes different choices in eating. But directions from others also train our eating. As children we learn the acceptable foods and eating manners. Errors are corrected by specific instruction. However, there is no clear line between passive and active social education in eating. Active social training depends upon living in a society structured by fundamental, passive influences.

The ways of social regulation of eating are the topics of this section. Most important is the often-overlooked centrality of eating in social life. The power of interpersonal influence and ones' cultural eating habits are complex, and they are powerful because they are important dimensions of what it means to be human.

Eating: A Prime Social Act

Eating is a direct or indirect part of nearly all social activities. We can try making a list of significant social groupings and events that have no eating associated with them. If we list only activities that do not directly use eating or have supplemental eating opportunities, we will not find many. Eating is always there. We serve snacks at a dance. Food stands are at every public gathering including sporting events, fairs, and street parties. Clubs, churches, and workplaces have kitchens, canteens, or snack bars. An invitation to someone's home contains an implicit assumption of some sort of refreshment. Of course, food is a periodic physiological need, and any social activity taking an appreciable time will necessarily be integrated with eating. The interesting social fact, however, is the extent of eating in all social interactions, especially those without hunger. Can it be true that there are no social gatherings without food? If so, and even if there are just a very few, why is this so?

Perhaps the most direct explanation is that there are just a few original and fundamental activities of life. Eating and mating are primary for continuance of a species. With more complexity of a species, we also see needs for shelter, the raising of young to their breeding maturity, and defense from predators. Even these are built on the social foundations of the original functions, and eating is the clear leader in consuming our time. The result is that all aspects of social life have elements of the foundational and routine activity of eating.

Another view is that we expect to have good feelings from eating in the company of others. The pleasure of company and the pleasure of eating are strongly associated. The association is reciprocally reinforcing. That is, the pleasure of company reinforces the attraction

to eating, and the pleasure of eating reinforces the attraction to others. That is a typical behaviorist explanation, but it may not be the most important factor. There is more to our social eating.

A third explanation is a more subtle one, building on the first. We have a great deal of time to fill, outside of essential life activities. Eating is something to do, especially in the company of others. The list of possible social activities is quite limited. Interactions must have some pattern that the participants anticipate. We find it abhorrent to do nothing or to do the same thing for long periods. Talking face-to-face with others, for example, is a social interaction with a finite length. And just talking also does not satisfy our need to make meaningful actions with the rest of our bodies. More vigorous games, sports, and other physical activities also operate in a limited time period, and when they end, the immediate social question is what to do next. Eating is an act satisfying that need to do something and pass time meaningfully with others.

If eating is a prime social activity, then a major part of each culture will center on foods and eating. Major roots of appetite will be in food preferences set by social experiences. The centrality of foods and eating in determining major structures of human motivation becomes apparent.

Social scientists describe the many and varied uses of food and eating within societies, beyond the value of merely nourishing the body. This short list is instructive (adapted from Fieldhouse, 1986, Preface).

Starting and maintaining relationships

Focusing communal activities

Expressing love and care

Expressing individual uniqueness

Marking the separateness of a social group

Coping with stress

Rewarding or punishing acts of others

Exercising power

Preventing or treating illness

Symbolizing emotional experiences

Displaying piety

Expressing moral sentiments

Showing social status, security, and wealth

Any of the items on this list may be the primary source of our eating motivation. Eating's entanglement in social affairs is extensive and thereby significantly connected to study of motivation.

Interpersonal Influence

In specific social groups, people obviously influence one another, and it is no surprise that people can affect others' eating. Influence begins in infancy with communications from caregivers. Personal relationships throughout life continue the process. What to eat, when to eat, how much to eat, the feelings from food and specific foods, the meanings of food, and the purposes of eating are taught. Each of these topics of social learning contributes a part of the stimulus conditions to motivate our eating. Like any complex social activity, we know just the beginnings of origins and causal effects. The following research examples represent attempts in that direction.

We describe children's avoidance of new things as neophobia, a phenomenon that appears at about 2 years of age and lasts for about 3 years. Children of these ages increase their preferences for novel foods from mere exposure to them. Such change is limited to specific food and flavor patterns and does not generalize to foods that are similar to newly acquired preferences. In fact, eating of similar foods but with different added flavors actually declines. We speculate that increase in preference follows a decrease in fear because of newness, but also because the child is learning what is an appropriate food (Birch & Marlin, 1982; Sullivan & Birch, 1990).

Children adopt the food preferences of those around them. Infants in a nursery formed preferences for the juice consumed by the person regularly feeding them. In a carefully staged sequence of shared mealtimes, preschool children began to eat a non-preferred vegetable that the others at the table had chosen. There is also evidence to support the general parental lore that a child will more likely try a food if an adult first demonstrates eating it (Birch, 1981; Escalona, 1945).

Young children have some natural ability to know when and how much to eat, but they must also learn connections between the cues of eating and the consequences of eating. Eating does not begin automatically when food is needed nor does it shut off when a period of eating fills physiological needs. Each child learns to use internal cues to start a meal (Birch, McPhee, Sullivan, & Johnson, 1989) and to connect the consumption of foods with their aftereffects (Birch & Deysher, 1985; Birch, McPhee, Shoba, Steinberg, & Krehbiel, 1987). Examined negatively, external control by others that disregards eating consequences can disrupt that learning. Emphasis from caregivers can be on "cleaning" one's plate rather than on stopping eating when one feels full. The results may be that we do not know when to stop eating. Such modeling can form a foundation experience for poor eating control later (Birch, 1987; Costanzo & Woody, 1985).

In most families, the principles of what to eat at particular meals appear as early as 3 years of age. Children correctly identify preferred breakfast and dinner food, and they make those choices more strongly at the appropriate times of day (Birch, Billman, & Richards, 1984).

One of the most interesting influences on how we learn about foods involves rewards. The rule is counterintuitive at first. When food is a reward, preference for that food increases (Birch, Zimmerman, & Hind, 1980). When eating a food is rewarded, preference for that food decreases (Birch, Marlin, & Rotter, 1984). The rule makes sense if you think of what the fact of being rewarded means. If you have to be rewarded to eat a food, that means the food is less valuable than the reward. In the other case, if the food is used as the reward, that means the food is of more value than the other act.

Adult relationships continue the process that influences eating, but it is difficult to find systematic evidence. Some descriptive observations come from therapeutic situations. For example, in studying mealtime conversations of women desiring to lose weight, (a) husbands initiated food-relevant topics of conversation 7 times more often than their wives, (b) husbands offered food to their wives almost 4 times more often than wives did to husbands, (c) wives rejected those food offers about 2 times as often, and (d) husbands offered criticism of their wives' eating 12 times more often than they praised it. All of these acts show a social influence of encouraging overeating by the women (Stuart & Davis, 1972).

The intertwining of social regulation and personal experiences provides the structure and habits of how and what we eat. We can consider the shifts among kinds of foods in a multicourse meal. We begin with some kind of appetizer, soup, or salad or a combination of these, change to an entrée with side dishes, and then move on to a dessert. Why not begin with the most palatable, the dessert? These eating patterns are based in experience with some attention to consequences. The sequence has the effect of giving us a range of nutrients in roughly their appropriate proportions. If we began with high fat and refined carbohydrate desserts, we would be soon sated, leaving little interest for the important roughage and specific nutrients in greens and other vegetables, complex carbohydrates, proteins, and essential fatty acids. The tendency to add sugar, salt, and tasty fats to nondessert foods defeats the purpose of this useful pattern. Making all foods dessert-like may be destroying an important way to achieve essential nutrition. Our historical habits of eating have rarely been well designed, as we will describe later.

In another example, we regularly eat particular snack foods in specific social settings. Beer and pretzels after bowling each week, buttered popcorn at the movies, doughnuts and coffee at morning break. These patterns strengthen and yet may be time- and event-limited. The pretzels, popcorn, or doughnuts just seem much more attractive at those times and places and may actually be disliked out of those contexts. The palatability of foods is a personal thing for each of us, and much of that attraction is founded in the social origins of our experiences.

Culture and Eating Habits

Nutritionally adequate meals come from limitless combinations of foods, but choices follow our experiences with those foods in social settings in accordance with cultural habits. Food choices are an integrated part of every culture. Eating serves roles in religion, social ritual, and economics. Food is also a part of the aesthetic values of people and is an important subject of communication. These cultural traditions make up enduring laws of each society, and these laws guide the "textbooks" that instruct each member in what to eat and the circumstances of the eating. Cultural traditions contribute to the motivational complex surrounding eating.

Whatever their source, and whether nutritionally valid or seductive nonsense, major parts of human personal appetite are formed on cultural communications. Each of us lives in a defined culture and abides by the food habits of that social group. Even when we know them to be wrong by another context of thought, our group's ways of eating are powerful sources of motivation nonetheless. Not to follow them can be a social source of unhappiness.

Foods Choices and Group Markers

What foods do U.S. college students say they like and don't like? The top 10 in each category, according to a very large survey done in the middle 1960s are those in Table 3.6 (Einstein & Hornstein, 1970).

Similar choices are found among U.S. armed forces personnel and in the guidebooks for institutional cooking and restaurants. Allowing for shifting tastes and fashions, young people today probably have similar preferences, at least in what they say they like and dislike.

TABLE 3.6   An Old, but Perhaps Still Informative Survey of College Student Food Preferences (From Einstein & Hornstein, 1970)

Most Liked	Least Liked
Ice cream (best)	Chicken liver (worst)
Soft rolls	Turnips
Beef steak	Liver
Hot biscuits	Fried eggplant
Milk	Cabbage
Orange juice	Pickled beets
Roast turkey	Baked squash
Roast beef	Stewed tomatoes
Apple pie	Carrot-raisin salad
Fried chicken	Stewed rhubarb

We use cultural food preferences to separate ourselves from others. Many derogatory labels use the terminology of a group's preferred food. Germans are called krauts, British are limeys, Italians are spaghetti-eaters, Mexicans are tamales, and French are frogs. The ridicule keeps the border strong. French people's contempt for any other kind of cooking, especially British, is legendary. Eating habits are important markers for such stereotypes.

In our own food culture, we like only our foods. Anything new and markedly different, regardless of taste or nutrition, is usually abhorrent. From our North American perspective, eating ants and other insects is repulsive. Americans also firmly reject puppy-ham meals eaten by some Eastern people or decayed birds eaten by Polar Eskimos.

We especially are repelled by things we don't believe to be primarily foods. When led to eat something by disguise or guile, we can become ill when we find out its true nature. Tasty pieces of chicken are just fine—until we learn they are rattlesnake. We won't accept stir-fried insects, but we happily eat a nutritionally similar batch of nut pieces and grains. Cultural habit partly determines what we hold to be edible.

Anthropologists seek the roots of cultural eating practices and find them often based on a substantial reason. We select certain foods and ignore others because of their relative reliability as sources or the energy costs in obtaining them. Availability of food is basic to food traditions. Central Americans may find their food entirely in readily available vegetables such as beans, corn, and melons. A nutritionally equivalent meal in the U.S. Midwest may include pork, potatoes, and apples. !Kung Bushmen may eat native animals, roots, and insects. The differences originate in the foods available to each group, but the local fare becomes an enduring preference for the individuals of that society. No people use all the food materials available to them. What we eat is a matter of tradition. The !Kung Bushmen, for example, eat only 17 of the 223 species of animals in their area and 23 of the 85 edible plants. Countless food sources are simply ignored (Lee, 1979).

Foods that are not efficient to gather will be ignored. We can build optimal foraging models that take into account the ease of getting the food. Plentiful materials that stand up to continual harvest will come to be most preferred. Native Americans of the plains could build their life around the plentiful bison (before the European settlers destroyed them for reasons of political domination). Rare and elusive foods, even though they are rich sources of nutrients, are not worth the effort over time.

The origins of other cultural food preferences are in politics, economics, and religion. People believe that their own choices of food are reasonable but that foreign peoples' choices are dictated by taboos and magic. An example is eating horseflesh. Most Western people do not eat horsemeat in spite of its availability and high-quality protein. It was commonly eaten until the eighth century. Then the pope ordered Christians in Germany to stop eating it to separate their society from the Pagans, who used horseflesh in religious rites. Eating horsemeat became the basis for marking a political and religious separation between peoples. The tradition remains and is reinforced by our modern romantic human partnership with horses (Simoons, 1961).

In market economies, the political interest of the wealthy in maximizing profits affects food availability and eventually establishes a society's eating traditions. English landowners had control over most Irish lands in the eighteenth century and used those lands to produce cattle for England's markets. The peasants grew potatoes to get an efficient return on the small parcels of land available to them. By the mid-nineteenth century, the Irish peasants depended almost entirely on the potato while those owning the land continued to export beef and grains.

Choices of development of foods look to profit, not protein (Harris & Ross, 1987). Our eating habits are formed partly as a result of the centralization of the U.S. food industry and its close ties with government-funded policy.

Eating Fads, Science, and Advertising

Before the mid-1800s, there were no clear ideas of nutrition. The prevailing Western society supposed that it was how much you ate that mattered and that different foods were about the same. Americans ate what was available and tasted good to them, even though they heard from those who preached about how much to eat, what to eat, and how to eat it. They did not usually follow such advice, instead eating what was traditional in Britain. The American diet was heavy on meat and some grain porridges; vegetables were used in small amounts to accompany the meat; and little fruit other than apples was eaten. Cooking was typically also heavy, with the boiling of meats and vegetables for long periods or else frying in thick layers of lard or butter, suggesting to one historian that the national curse was constipation (Levenstein, 1988). Eating tended to be a serious business with little conversation and a style of getting large amounts of food in the stomach rapidly.

Because of more variety in living arrangements, class, and ethnicity of immigrants during the latter half of the 1800s, it is risky to make generalizations about food at that time. Among the new urban working middle class, food variety actually declined. Grains were baked into heavy breads and pastries to be eaten along with heavily cooked meats. There was considerable distrust of vegetables and fruits, probably justified by spoilage due to the slow trip between farm and consumer. *Constipation* was replaced by a catchall term *dyspepsia* to refer to the apparent digestive disorders of the times. These various upsets were partly caused by what people ate, partly caused by how much they ate, and partly used as an excuse for whatever ailed them; and there were many cures and medicines offered (including various forms of opium, setting the stage for a small wave of regular use by middle-class people).

In each of these eras, there were those who promoted different ideas of eating. Vegetarianism appeared in the 1830s, based partly on animal rights, partly on health ideas, and partly on the fact that meat and spices were thought by some to unduly arouse sexual urges. Sylvester Graham was popular on the alcohol temperance lecture circuit before he turned to the reform of eating practices. Grahamism became a popular fad especially at boardinghouses where members were offered his special Graham bread, meatless meals to be chewed thoroughly, and frequent hot baths. His ideas helped spread vegetarianism to others, including the founder of the Mormons, Joseph Smith; *Walden* author Henry Thoreau, and the leaders of the New York Oneida Community experiment in communal living. By the 1850s, his personal influence had subsided and left in its wake Graham flour, bread, and crackers along with increased attention to what and how people were eating.

Vegetarian influence took on a definite moral position as it was organized during the 1850s. "Flesh-eaters" were viewed as sinners who were unable to think clearly because their minds were obscured. Attitudes of moral superiority and arrogance were common among food reformers, appearing regularly in their lectures and written statements.

In the mid-1870s, there were more vegetarian groups, including the Seventh-Day Adventists. John Kellogg took control of their sanitarium in Battle Creek and used individual diet treatments, some rather bizarre, but this became the refuge of the rich and famous who were ill. By aggressive self-promotion, Kellogg became known as a leading scientist by the end of the century. He devised some unusual foods, including a breakfast grain of wheat flakes. His brother, Will, crafted and patented Toasted Corn Flakes and developed the famous breakfast food business. The idea spread, with Charles W. Post formulating a grain drink called Postum and then the cereal food Grape-Nuts.

Alongside Kellogg, and only slightly less famous, was Horace Fletcher, who proposed an odd idea of tediously chewing each mouthful of food 100 times, holding liquids in the mouth for 30 sec before swallowing, and eating only when hungry. Chewing food thoroughly was not a new idea, but this was extreme and would have been ignored had Fletcher not gotten the attention and support of the medical community through research physiologist Russell Chittendon. Chittendon verified that Fletcher had reduced his protein to a remarkable 45 grams per day (about one third of the recommended 125 grams) while remaining in good health. Again, a variety of famous and reputable people supported the new food ideas. Fletcherism became fashionable and was adopted as one of the techniques of Kellogg's sanitarium, which he named San.

Another of the influences on foods and eating at this time was by the man who computed the nutrient values of specific foods and promoted their use in scientific cooking and eating. Wilbur Atwater was working on these measures in the mid-1880s at his academic position and later as director of the federal Office of Experiment Stations, using techniques developed by German chemists 40 years earlier. While analyzing the nutrient components of foods, examining the common diet, and studying metabolism in a specially designed live-in chamber, he concluded that American eating was wasteful and unhealthy. He became a part of the informal movement to make food and eating an informed and regulated practice, adopting the stern tones and moral righteousness not untypical of food reformers. His work was useful, however, and his Department of Agriculture food charts and many of his ideas became a part of the new domestic science of nutrition, applying chemical science to family cooking (Levenstein, 1988).

Working side by side with, if not coordinated with, scientific cooking was legitimate concern with the quality of food sources. Adulteration and spoilage were common problems dating from the increased needs to transport food to centralized consumers beginning about 1850. Traditionally, foods that families could not grow for themselves were supplied in bulk to local grocers from regional producers. Better transportation in the late 1800s changed that, allowing factories to make foods available almost anywhere. That depended on new ways to preserve foods, primarily canning, jarring, and sealed packaging.

H. J. Heinz used canned horseradish to begin his trademark line of 57 Varieties that he could ship nationwide. But others could and did compete, and thus food advertising by brand developed. Advertising asserted that the quality and purity of brand foods was backed by the reputation of the company.

As an example, National Biscuit Company introduced In-Er-Seal packaging of its Uneeda brand biscuits in 1899. Soon thereafter, the grocery store's traditional cracker barrel was outdated and faded away. Food producers played on consumers' fears of contamination and spoilage by using the somewhat twisted logic that the machine-processed foods were more fresh, pure, and natural.

The trend was then set. Most food advice now comes from food advertisers. Marketing influences our food preferences and choices. It has become established and probably necessary to maintain our food system. In a 1980 work of the Peoples Food Commission, the founder of General Foods, Charles W. Post, was quoted as saying, "You can't just manufacture cereal. You've got to get halfway down the customer's throat, through advertising. Then they've got to swallow it" (quoted in Fieldhouse, 1986, p. 12).

Advertising works two ways as one of the cultural bases of our food habits. First, it is itself a cultural phenomenon. In the large scale of Western society, primary communication comes from the different forms of mass media. Electronic and printed messages are efficient ways to advertise. Media communications, replacing the cultural communities of the past, are the keys to establishing and maintaining culture-based food habits. Media become powerful sources of food information simply because we buy most of our food. Through advertisement, sellers of food and food preparation materials are our primary educators about eating. We see thousands of food advertisements, and most are effective influence mechanisms.

Advertisements focus on images of the food itself, its economics, and what it may accomplish. Advertising is designed to influence people to purchase and use a specific food. It presents sensory and rational appeals of the food itself. Consuming the food promises enjoyment. Foods are shown to be flavorful with pleasant aftereffects. Soup tastes good and warms and refreshes a tired body. Coffee gives both a pleasant aroma and increased alertness. Rational appeals (and many that may not be rational) present evidence of nutritional benefit or of economy and convenience.

Second, advertising uses other pieces of culture to affect food choices. Food advertisements show social meaning. Effective messages claim a food will make a person thinner (low-calorie mayonnaise), stronger ("milk does a body good" [sic]), more attractive (soft drinks liked by the opposite gender), or prestigious (mustard handed from one luxury car to another). People appear eating the advertised product in a setting that encourages positive feelings in the viewer. Groups of people eating, popular people endorsing the food, and reminders of parental advice are other effective social influences. Effective appeals tie foods to established cultural habits. Cultural symbols and myths appear with the advertised food. Sunday-dinner chicken, Thanksgiving turkey, and wholesome steak and apple pie have been used as a pervasive cultural background to display a food choice.

Some but not all of that advertising gives misleading and inappropriate information about when, where, and why people should eat. Nutrition themes may be used cynically and fraudulently to promote processed foods that have marginal value. In the culture of Western society, food is primarily a business commodity, and we must remember the age-old mercantile imperative, "Let the buyer beware!"

Food in Lifestyle and Magic Foods

Patterns of change in Western eating habits illustrate another dimension of culture. We know these patterns as modern lifestyles. A simple list will illustrate topics having patterns of choice, and because we share this culture, we need not elaborate on them:

> Eating away from the home
>
> Fast-production, limited-menu restaurants
>
> Prepared food delivered to the home
>
> Take-out food
>
> Pre-prepared food
>
> Microwave cooking
>
> Food preparation machines
>
> Cooking outside
>
> Ethnic foods
>
> Snack foods
>
> Diet foods
>
> Health foods
>
> Organic foods

The concepts of this short list overlap, and there are perhaps ways of organizing them, but the emphasis of the collection is the style and changes in the modern Western culture of eating. Each of these changes has roots in multiple dimensions of society's ideas and forces.

More specific and directed eating makes up our long-standing cultural style of looking for perfect foods or foods that will cure our afflictions. There have always been foods or food types that were promoted with enthusiasm as solutions to life problems. In our modern scientific institutions, promotion of each idea and finding is rapid and offered with breathless excitement as of major importance. Small differences in cancer rates correlated with a specific food lead to an almost ludicrous eagerness to incorporate it in our diet. That kind of food enthusiasm is not a new pattern of society.

In the late 1880s, the grape was thought to have digestive and curative powers. The prescriptions ran from encouraging dyspeptic eaters to include grapes in their daily diet (along with suitable food) to taking a Grape Cure of 5 pounds or so of grapes a day. Kellogg used the Grape Cure as part of his San regimen. It is quite likely that such quantities of fruit would have a cleansing action of sorts, but few would want to continue it for long.

Jump ahead to the 1980s and 1990s, and we have sugar substitutes, oat bran, broccoli, high beta-carotene carrots, Omega-3 fatty acids, and low-fat and no-cholesterol everything. All are foods claimed to heal or prevent the disorders we have from eating "bad" foods. The magic foods should solve the problems. And by all the evidence, people in general continue in diet habits leading to increasing difficulty. At the same time that we have more knowledge of proper nutrition, many of us continue to eat the wrong proportions of nutrients, and we still follow the pattern noted in the 1800s of eating large amounts of food, good and bad. Meats, al-

ready too fatty, are most often prepared in restaurants by frying in saturated fat. Premium (high-fat) ice creams, salty snacks, high-fat dips, pizza, and sugar-laden pastries are all growing in sales. Some restaurants promote how big their meals are or provide vast quantities of food for customer selection in long troughs.

At the same time, shoppers claim to be health conscious and want food low in fat and sugar. Sugar-free soft drinks sell well—to wash down the 600-calorie piece of high-fat cheesecake. One answer to this paradox is obvious. We intuitively believe that we can compensate for our eating sins by a piece of magic food that will even it out. We assume that the 1-calorie drink gives us some virtue to balance against the 600-calorie cheesecake; that broccoli compensates for the high-fat hamburger to prevent a tumor; and that oat bran in a cookie will reduce cholesterol in the blood vessels. Michelle Stacey (1994) reports an advertiser's finding that 74% of Pepsi drinkers would switch to Coca-Cola if it had oat bran in it. In a kindred controlled study, women were given yogurt shortly before a meal. Those given cartons with low-fat labels chose more calories for lunch than those whose cartons had high-fat labels. The difference came from what they believed, not their bodies, because all of the yogurt was the same (Rolls, Shide, Hoeymans, Jas, & Nichols, 1992). The motivation seems to be compensation with magic foods.

SECTION SUMMARY: APPETITE

The four elements of appetite are based on physiology, experiences, social relations, and culture. Physiological bases of appetite are based on natural liking for some tastes (sweet and salt) and natural aversion to others (sour and bitter). Some variation exists concerning the ability to metabolize milk, apparently based on a rather

recent genetic addition. Furthermore, physiological mechanisms prepare us to select beneficial foods and avoid dangerous ones, based on small samples and weighing the consequences. In the short term, we are affected in our food choices by what we have recently eaten. Eating carbohydrates depresses interest in more carbohydrates for only a short time; after a 2-hr delay, there is no effect. Changes in dietary fat have no immediate effect on food choices, but over the long term, we will select foods to moderate those changes.

We acquire tastes for foods not just because we naturally like them. We develop a preference for sour and bitter foods and sometimes seek materials that are scalding hot or painful to mouth membranes. Eating such foods becomes a habit for many personal reasons unrelated to nutrition. Our resulting tastes are mixtures of natural and acquired food sensations. We seek and enjoy foods having a certain appearance, texture, and personal meaning.

Eating is part of nearly every social organization and event, and hence the motivation for much of our eating becomes established in social ways. This is so perhaps because it is a fundamental life activity, because eating is mutually reinforcing with so-cial relations, and because it is a meaningful way to pass time with others. Much of the detailed structure of our eating habits comes from experiences in social groups by direct influence or by showing us examples.

Our home culture sets the broad limits of what, when, and with whom we eat. We feel most secure when we follow those traditions. Furthermore, we identify ourselves with that culture in part by aspects of foods and eating. Recent fads in American eating illustrate cultural influences. Government interest in foods was a recent addition, founded on new nutrition information and concern with food safety. It was food producers and their need for advertising, however, that made food a primary focus of our affluent and consequently overweight society. Food now is a major vehicle for self-definition and establishing a lifestyle. We look to magic foods to solve social problems, including those brought on ourselves by other foods.

MOTIVATION FOODS

This section asks a different kind of question: Does eating some foods affect our motivation? We know that at the extreme, the absence of specific needed substances such as vitamin C produces diseases, for example, scurvy. Certain temporary effects also result from eating excessive amounts of foods such as canned beans and stewed prunes. These affect what we feel and do but are not the kinds of motivation factors intended in the question.

Anecdotes and convictions abound, but there are no controlled studies that give simple, consistent results about the motivation effects of foods. This could mean that there are few such effects, that effects are very weak, that a wide range of individual sensitivities are masked in group experiments, or a combination of these reasons. One review divided the evidence into three sorts of studies: (a) popular beliefs about food effects, (b) food effects on brain neurotransmitters, and (c) aftereffects of eating meals (Spring, 1986).

Popular Beliefs About Foods

Researching popular beliefs about foods is difficult. When people make casual observations and tests, they often allow more than a single food to vary, making interpretation difficult. Studies administering foods generally yield much less effect than those testing single nutrients, and even the single-nutrient studies show small changes.

One example is, Does sugar cause hyperactivity in some children? A variety of clinical sources and parent observations suggest that eating sugar-rich foods leads to a bout of hyperactivity. This question is very difficult to test, even with proper design. Double-blind procedures, where neither the eater nor the person assessing the effects knows which condition is being administered, are appropriate but rare. With a double-blind test employed, no reliable increase in activity appeared with the sugar, but instead there was a suggestion that the sugar quiets some hyperactive children. This is still an unsolved question with complicating interfering conditions such as content and recency of prior meals and the place and circumstances evoking the actions (Behar, Rapoport, Adams, Berg, & Cornblath, 1984; Spring, 1986).

Foods and Brain Chemistry

If a food does alter performance, it most likely alters the balance of the neurotransmitters in the brain. Foods affect brain neurotransmitter levels through **precursors,** complex molecules converted by enzyme action to specific neurotransmitters. Thus, the chain of food to precursor to neurotransmitter must be shown. Just a few such food-neurotransmitter connections have been demonstrated. One that has direct motivational effect is that of tryptophan-serotonin, but the mechanism is not direct.

The precursor tryptophan comes from protein but its amount is small, compared with competing large amino acids from that food. Hence, tryptophan has poor access to the molecules that carry it from the blood to brain tissues. Protein food will actually lower the amount of brain serotonin. A carbohydrate meal without protein, on the other hand, causes the competing large amino acids from earlier eating to move into muscle, leaving an increased opportunity for the tryptophan to reach the brain and convert to serotonin. What does serotonin do? Studies show a pattern of reduced sensory sensitivity, increased sleepiness and calmness, and some reduced task performance. Thus, the level of tryptophan under certain conditions of eating can reduce alertness.

Aftereffects of Meals

Does a meal improve or impair work performance? Interest in the effect of eating meals comes from industrial managers. They focus on breakfast and the midday meal. The midday meal, especially if it is heavy, seems to many people to lead to a drop in their performance and increased sleepiness afterward. This is the traditional nap time or formal work break in some cultures. The decrease in alertness after a midday meal is a stable finding. A dip occurs in physiological functions of pulse rate and body temperature as well as in performance measures and self-reports of sleepiness and motivation. Breakfast has had less study, but the general finding is that it has a much smaller aftereffect (Spring, 1986). Even fewer studies have examined aftereffects of a larger evening meal.

SECTION SUMMARY: MOTIVATION FOODS

Does eating some foods affect our motivation? Direct evidence is elusive. Adequate double-blind testing of food elements like sugar is nearly impossible. Some effects come from temporary alterations of brain chemistry (low serotonin) by certain patterns of foods (low protein). The most robust answer responds to a slightly different question. Eating a meal heavy in certain nutrients (in other words, "heavy" meals) depresses work performance for a part of that digestive period.

OVEREATING AND OBESITY

We have examined some of the facts and principles of motivated eating. We saw that motivations to eat have many roots. Consequently, control of overeating will have many challenges, along with motivation conditions and components of its own.

Components of Overeating

To review, first, some motivations to eat and overeat lie in complicated matters of nutrition and energy storage mechanisms. Second, genetic programming and acquired perceptions give attractive taste experiences we anticipate in eating. These two roots amount to strong physiological bases for unhealthy choices in today's food markets. For example, specific preferred foods are often high in simple sugars, fats, and refined wheat flour and consequently supply little of the body's nutrition needs. Overeating follows wanting those tastes, eating substantial amounts of such foods, and still receiving body signals of hunger because of lack of adequate nutrition.

The third major root of overeating is in the intertwining of eating with culture and current social relationships. These are powerful mechanisms based on social motivations of normal eating. The major points were these. Social habits determine when, where, and what people eat. Eating is a prime social activity that is directly or indirectly a part of nearly all social activities. Eating is rewarded by the pleasure of being with others and provides an important set of actions for each to perform in the company of others. Eating is used to accomplish a wide range of social goals, such as wooing or displaying wealth. The details of eating are learned by imitation and through direct instruction. Food choices are set by many political, economic, and religious proscriptions. Eating is a major form of society style, and food advertising has an important effect on propagation of such style. Any of these social factors of normal eating can assume a major role in a person's overeating.

A fourth root of overeating brings us to new ground. This amounts to the defenses that bodies marshal to maintain current weight and prevent weight loss, processes that are related to withstanding famine and starvation. Briefly, reduced food intake alone, without increased exercise, can be countered by more efficient body use of energy. Because fat requires the least energy to store, other tissues are first sacrificed during a diet. Metabolic rate is slowed to require less energy, and physical effort is discouraged by feelings of reduced vigor and energy.

The message of one recent book is that dieting makes you fat (Cannon & Einzig, 1985). The argument is that a simple account of obesity and its control won't work. Most dieters assume that their body works at a set speed. They believe that they have eaten too much and that the excess has been stored as fat. Although that is essentially true, their logic continues that eating less than necessary for normal body needs will lead to loss of fat. It is not that simple because the body has evolved ways to compensate for brief periods of reduced food intake and it also matters *what* is eaten and when.

It is useful to think that the body reacts to a crash diet as it does to starvation and to a prolonged diet as it does to famine. In both cases, the principle is that the body will shed the nonvital tissues, those that consume a lot of energy, and will protect the efficient storage of energy in fat tissues. (See the "Percentage of Energy" values in Figure 3-2.) When a resource is threatened, the efficient response is to reduce the consumption of it and to conserve the stores. Thus, the human body responds to reduced food energy by slowing the processes of metabolism. The constant change of tissues in the body requires considerable energy and specific nutrients. Muscle cells need great amounts, but fat storage requires very little. A more energy-efficient body will result if energy-using muscles are reduced, and food energy is stored instead as fat. Only the muscles and tissues that are in use or are vital to body function are spared. The body of a dieting, sedentary person loses muscle with time because it is not needed. With a prolonged diet, there will be losses of lean tissue from muscles and other organs as well as fat. The more severe the diet, the greater the proportion of lean tissue lost. That loss of lean tissue leads to a slowed metabolic rate, which slows the weight loss as the diet continues.

On-and-off diets condition the body to endure diets by shedding lean tissue and replacing it with the fat needed during periods of starvation and famine. Fat is a more efficient user of energy, needing less fuel than other organs. The metabolic rate drops from one diet to another, and the body needs less and less food. Loss of lean tissue diminishes the need for oxygen as well as food, and the body establishes a lower energy balance. To this may be added the concept of number of fat cells. With each failure of the diet and return to overeating, more fat cells may be added to the body. Those additional fat cells increase the set-point standard of weight. The result is that dieting slows the body down and sets the stage for getting fatter, and doing it on less and less food. Cultural and social habits of what we eat and how we exercise intensify the problem.

Obesity

The four components of overeating are strong root forces that, collectively, affect motivation to eat, and each is an important component of addictive overeating leading to obesity. In one sense, the problem of obesity has its origins in overeating. It is almost trite to note that overeating causes people to be overweight. To imply that that is all there is to it, however, is also very misleading. Saying that removing fat and holding a lower weight is nothing but a matter of eating less is somewhat like saying that preventing vehicle deaths is just a matter of eliminating body impacts, ignoring everything that caused the crash.

Still, it remains true that having too much body fat is caused by taking in and storing more energy than the body needs over a long period of time. Few obese people gained their weight rapidly or did so intentionally. It usually began with habits of living in our modern society of abundance and labor-saving technology. In both cases, we are led by perhaps liking too much some foods that were rare in our ancestral environment.

By all accounts, the business of living during our evolutionary history took considerable strength and stamina. Whether capturing and bringing in meat or seeking and harvesting fruits and vegetables, the necessary work was hard and demanded well-conditioned muscles that used considerable energy (Eaton, Shostak, & Konner, 1988). Ways that lessened that burden and foods that supplied good energy were attractive; they gave pleasure. We were evolved to use our brains to conserve energy and eat good energy sources. These inclinations remain in our modern abundance.

Increased use of tasty purified fats, concentrated sugars, and simplified grains, combined with cooking practices that intensify the preferred tastes, make foods of high palatability easy to get. They are also high in energy sources—too much food energy for the quantities that we wish to eat. At the same time, our work roles are low in physical requirements, actually sedentary in the majority of cases. These are exactly the conditions that we learned were correct for fattening up domestic animals: Keep them confined and feed them high-energy food. Should we be surprised the principles work on us as well?

Our bodies' needs are not met until sufficient food of needed quality is ingested. We may eat a little or a lot and still not meet those needs. It depends on the nutrients. As a rule, foods lose aspects of nourishment when they are developed and processed for nonnutritional reasons such as efficient production and shipping, cooking characteristics, or special flavor and taste. For example, refined elements such as sugar, white flour, and purified fats become very narrow-spectrum sources of nutrients. When consumed alone or in combinations, although they may be tasty, they supply little or none of the body's needs except for simple energy. That is what is meant by **junk food.** Without the proper proportions of quality protein, essential fats, fiber, vitamins, and minerals our bodies need, we will experience hunger and, if that lasts a long time, deficiency diseases with symptoms of depression, exhaustion, mood swings, anxiety, periodic pains, sleeplessness, and sometimes irrational activity.

The body defends itself against these deficiencies. The body of a sedentary person eating high-carbohydrate, processed foods and sugar will dump insulin into the bloodstream. That heavy load of insulin signals cells to take in glucose and then converts the remaining glucose to fat. Glucose levels then fall rapidly, again signaling hunger. Without some moderation of the insulin secretion by the presence of protein, we pass through rapid cycles of hunger and eating. The result, of course, is that too much food is eaten. Sedentary people overeat and gain fat because they truly feel hungry. The body will always signal hunger when glucose level is low, even though adequate energy is stored in the body.

Still, a noteworthy truth is that some people do exert control over their weight. Many people maintain a fairly constant weight over time, and others change to a desired weight (Schachter, 1982). Studies of weight histories have revealed that people commonly change from obesity. About half of the people found to be obese at one point in their adult life were not obese 10 years or 20 years later. Children and infants found to be obese are even less likely to be obese as adults. Furthermore, the relationship between obesity in both children and their parents increased with the children's age until the children left home in their early adult years (Garn, 1985). These social facts make it difficult to consider set-point and hereditary theories as the sole causes of obesity.

Within groups of similar people, there are standards of weight that indicate some cultural control. According to research studies, women of low socioeconomic means were found to be six times more likely to be obese than those of higher means, and those of Italian heritage were obese three times as often as those of English backgrounds; obesity tends to lessen the longer immigrant populations live in the United States (Goldblatt, Moore, & Stunkard, 1965).

Social factors appear to have some influence on the weight people maintain. The principle is the same as that underlying personal control or lack of control over choosing addictive acts, as we will see in Chapter 11, "Addiction." People try to maintain their weight according to who they see themselves to be and what sort of weight controls they are expected to maintain.

Weight Loss Principles

There are two keys to lifetime weight control, and both tend to run counter to the habits that have currently developed as general practices in Western society. First, select a variety of whole foods that are nourishing and eat them in moderation. There are many accounts of the science and practice of nutrition, but we must always be careful about who influenced them and what their motives might be. Cookbooks from food producers rarely have optimum nutrition as a goal. Even our own government panels and their publications make compromises, bowing to entrenched commercial interests at the cost of sound nutrition. We must be mindful that politics funds science, and scientists move slowly to change ideas that have been entrenched by years of political support.

Some practical nutritional rules to start with are very simple but may take discipline to follow. It may be wise to remember that our bodies were designed for paleolithic habitats and habits, not plentiful, high-profit, prepared foods. We can put together few principles of body energy control based on that concept.

First, avoid easily digested carbohydrates, including most grains and grain products. Carbohydrates are not poison. Actually, in modest amounts mixed in with protein and fat, they are necessary. But moderation is fast destroyed by their overrepresentation in nearly every prepared food we buy and meals that are designed for us in cookbooks and by restaurants. The carbohydrate form we should select is that of a variety of fresh vegetables and fruits. These have more of what we really need and will satisfy our nutrient hungers. But beware of how even these good forms may be processed or prepared. When mixed with heavy doses of salt, sugar, and hard fats, we add trouble.

The second principle is to acquire an adequate level, but not an excess, of protein and fat in every meal. Not only the absolute level, but also the balance and sequence is most important for our body needs to be met. The difficult trick here is to get adequate protein without getting too much saturated fat. A casual glance at food composition tables on grocery store packages will illustrate the problem in meal planning. Sequence also matters, because easily digested carbohydrates, such as bread and potatoes, give a quick shot of insulin, beginning the potential for storage of excess as fat. Every meal and every snack should be balanced in protein, carbohydrate, and fat, as we noted earlier in the chapter.

The third principle is cultural and will help us to follow the first two: Don't get nutrition advice from product advertisements. Advertisers are some of the cleverest applied psychologists around. When we think about it, why should they tell us what we need rather than what makes their greatest profit? Carbohydrates are more plentiful and less expensive than protein. Adding lots of sugar, salt, and hard fats to anything makes it tasty and last a long time on the shelf, but it also can become dangerous to our nutritional health. Which of these is important to selling products: taste or nutritional need? In the metaphor of advertising, real nutrition has no sizzle. But times change and better ideas of nutrition emerge. These too become ideas that motivate us. We often come to realize that we have been making poor food choices. As we assume guilt about what we eat, we are drawn to advertised products that *claim* to have greater nutrition or provide magic cures. Again, we must beware.

The second key to weight control is body activity. Dieting tends to slow the body down. Exercise of the right type will speed up metabolism and also demand preservation of muscles and tissues other than fat. In comparing diet alone, exercise alone, and a combination of the two over a period of 16 weeks, researchers found that body weight losses were about the same for all groups of volunteers. But the two exercise groups lost more body fat and actually gained lean body mass. Diet alone removed less fat and also some lean body mass (Zuti & Golding, 1976). This is a robust finding demonstrated over and over.

The next question is about the amount of exercise. The effect of exercise must be considered over a long term. This can work in at least two ways. First, slight increases in activity will accumulate to significant gains. Small changes can be made in ways of doing things so that more energy is used in routine daily activity.

Second, the effects of exercise do not stop when the activity stops. Long-term benefits do not usually come from fits of intense exercise. Short periods of very great energy use tend to consume almost all stored carbohydrates (glycogen) before fatigue stops the activity. It takes long-term, less intense exercise to use both carbohydrates and fat. There are many misleading views about exercise and what is needed to lose a unit of weight. A simple deduction can begin with the units of exercise and food energy. Caloric values of exercise are usually computed on the basis of measures of increased body activity above that required for quiet rest. Dividing that increase into the caloric value of a pound of weight loss, roughly 3,500 kcal, gives formulae suggesting, for example, 7 hours of wood chopping to lose a pound. Tables of such examples are interesting but misleading because body effects don't stop. The effects of exercise are greatly underestimated. After the exercise activity, there is a continuation of the increase in energy use. Immediate effects come from the energy needed to return the body to resting levels of energy resources. Additional, long-term energy consumption comes from the metabolic requirements to maintain the increased muscle tissue formed during the exercise.

The question of what is the right amount of exercise is answered by the current wisdom of exercise physiologists. Exercise of moderate intensity should be done for at least 30 min, at least three times per week. Moderate exercise is defined as that leading to a sustained heart rate of 60% to 70% greater than normal. That level can be attained by activities that burn about 10 kcal per min, such as jogging, bicycling fast, basketball, hockey, squash, handball, and swimming. Such exercise will develop the muscle that uses fat as fuel and will also strengthen other systems of the body and reduce the malnutrition malaise. The result is a loss of fat and a gain of lean tissue.

Dieting Programs

Selling weight loss, diets, and related ideas and materials is a solid part of the marketplace. Estimates are that it is a $10 billion annual business. Surveys show that about 20% of the Western population is on a diet at any one time. Most diets will not have a lasting effect. How can so many fad diet schemes survive? Why do we try them? Some of the reasons we try new diets are similar to those that led us to needing them. We prefer what is pleasurable, quick, easy, and not painful. Commercial diets promise fast, painless, effortless, and satisfying weight loss. Long-term effective weight control requires something different—sound management of body energy.

A scheme offered by psychologists develops the life management necessary for weight control. It offers a way to help us retrain ourselves. There is no magic or hidden mechanism in it. The plan amounts to sound analysis and control of our actions. The steps we will review can be used for essentially any activity with suitable modifications—for example, weight gain, if that is the problem.

1. Establish your baselines. You must have accurate, quantitative records of what you are doing now. To begin, record everything you eat and drink for a period of a week or so. The baseline records should note where you ate, the events that occurred just before and after

the eating, and, most important, who was present and their response to the eating. Who is interested in your being fat or thin?

2. Identify your rewards. A list of rewards will be useful to motivate you. A rewards list includes the many personal pleasures to be realized by achieving weight control.

3. Set a diet. A nutritionally adequate diet of balanced protein, carbohydrates, and fat in frequently spaced meals and snacks attends to all of the body's needs. Record everything you eat and the food elements in it. Make it quantitative and in a form you can examine easily. Make a diet list to stay aware of what and how much you are eating. A quick way to overeat is to become distracted from absolute control over thinking about your eating. Snacking while distracted is devastating to a diet (Herman & Polivy, 1993).

4. Increase your exercise. Establish a gradual program of increased physical effort. Note that attrition rates from exercise programs average 50%, perhaps higher in obese persons and with abrupt exercise changes. Slow changes with quantitative, visible records are more effective.

5. Include others. Involve others in your program by telling them your goals and intentions. Encourage them to monitor your diet and exercise progress and reward you.

6. Rein in your dreams. A major source of failed motivation in weight loss comes from inappropriate expectations. First, we expect fast results, something we have learned from diet plan advertisements. True weight loss does not appear quickly. The weight gain took a long time and so will its loss. A rapid weight loss is about 2 pounds per week. Second, weight loss itself is an inappropriate long-term expectation. The process is actually one of managing your life activities, and weight control is one consequence. Permanent weight control comes only from permanent change in life activity.

SECTION SUMMARY: OVEREATING AND OBESITY

Overeating, like other types of eating, rests on matters of food nutrients consumed and absorbed, genetic and acquired tastes for foods, and social and cultural influences. When overeating occurs, an additional element is the body's natural response to reduced food nutrients. An efficient and optimal mechanism will conserve stored energy most efficiently (burn unused muscles but protect fat), and reduce the need for energy (lower the metabolic rate creating lethargy). On-and-off (yo-yo) diets condition the body for periodic starvation with these responses and store even more fat during the "off" times. Food in proper nutritional proportions cancels hunger feelings and other negative feelings.

Weight control is based on adequate nutrition and body activity. Neither one will work alone. Nutrition is based on three principles. Choose moderate amounts of complex carbohydrates, avoiding the quickly digested forms. Eat an adequate level of protein and fat in every meal and every snack. Don't rely on advertisers to give sound nutrition advice. Body activity must be adequate to maintain all muscles and lean tissue. Literally, we use them or lose them. Weight management does not require intense exercise, although other health benefits come from periodic aerobic activity. Weight can be managed, but there are no magic tricks. All it takes is the will to carry it out as a life change.

CHAPTER CONCLUSIONS

Modern foods—made of protein, carbohydrates, fats, vitamins, and minerals—are in a dramatically different form than what was found in our ancestral environment. Although modern foods are energy efficient and capable of sustaining great populations, they may also be at the root of many of our life problems. With civilization, foods were shaped to serve many functions beyond life preservation. Taste, social relations, and lifestyle came to be more important than what those foods do to our bodies. Ironically, we look for magic in special foods to solve problems our food choices have given to us.

Heading the list of greatest concern (although perhaps not the most dangerous) is obesity. With copious supplies of refined, high-energy/density food materials, we are led to consume too much and, more important, dangerous kinds and proportions of nutrients. The cure is easily stated, but personally challenging to carry out as long as we must make choices about what we eat and what we do. Because the marketplace encourages modern eating problems, it should be obvious that it will not supply the cure. The fundamental interest of advertisers is in reducing the weight of our wallets. The real magic is our personal change of attitude about eating and activity.

Study and Review Questions

1. What are the food material types?

2. What are common forms of monosaccharides and polysaccharides?

3. Distinguish saturated, monounsaturated, polyunsaturated, and hydrogenated fats.

4. For what normal body process is protein essential?

5. In what stages is food processed in the body?

6. What does insulin do?

7. What is the consequence of eating unneeded carbohydrates in the absence of protein?

8. What proportions of the three basic food material types were we adapted to eat?

9. Compare the presumed paleolithic and modern diets.

10. In what proportions are body energy types stored?

11. What are rules of the glucostat theory?

12. What are cephalic phase responses?

13. In what ways is body set-point weight defended?

14. Why are sweet and salt tastes pleasant?

15. Why are sour and bitter tastes unpleasant?

16. How do we naturally form food aversions?

17. When should a dieter eat a "rich" carbohydrate snack?

18. What is the result of reducing and increasing the amount of fat in our diet?

19. Why might we choose to eat hot and spicy foods?

20. For what three reasons is eating a prime social activity?

21. How can you get a child to like a new food?

22. Will giving a reward for eating it increase liking for a food?

23. What factors make up cultural food choices?

24. What did the 1890s diet reformers see as the primary eating problem?

25. What was wrong with foods that led to the turn-of-century food labeling laws?

26. With what influence mechanisms does food advertising structure our food choices?

27. Why are we attracted to "magic" foods?

28. Are there specific foods that are motivators?

29. How does our body protect energy resources when we reduce the amount of food we eat?

30. What happens when we cycle between fasting and binge eating?

31. What are the two key elements of maintaining a desired weight?

32. What are the steps for an effective program to control weight?

CHAPTER 4

Emotion

Emotion words and concepts reflect experiences and actions in our social lives. William James presented a provocative idea of emotion as a peculiar experience. Some modern philosophers continue that tradition.

The biological elements of emotion experience are obvious. Theories and research explore the possibilities of emotions as inherited, adaptive expressions, as fundamental body processes, and as systems of brain function.

A traditional exploration into emotion is through children, charting the appearance of emotion as life experiences are acquired. From there, it is an obvious step to consider the bigger picture of emotional expressions and their role in the progress of emotional experiences.

Emotional dimensions form most of our social interactions. Most emotion has a social context that defines each emotional experience. The social context is no better illustrated than in the different gender roles of emotion.

Phenomena and Experiences

Biological Foundations of Emotion

Developmental Elaboration

Cultural Order

In this chapter, we explore the feelings dimension to motivation ideas that we outlined in the beginning of the book. We start the study of feelings with general concepts and theories of emotions and then follow with four chapters focusing on aspects of life heavily involved with emotional experiences.

PHENOMENA AND EXPERIENCES

Rage, love, terror, revulsion, and the like are not ordinary daily affairs. Such intense emotional experiences are obvious and distinct episodes of life. As we experience a time of anger or deep affection or fear or thorough disgust, we know a piece of life that has something different to it. Having a strong emotion means doing some unusual things. We may attack, hug, flee, or vomit. Yet, it isn't just what we do that makes an emotion. To make the experience an emotion, we also have drastically altered feelings and noticeable body changes. In an emotional episode, our feelings are strong and distinct, or they are at least distinctly different from what we have been feeling. Along with and sometimes trailing what we feel and do, we notice tense muscles, tearing eyes, or other involuntary body events from a legion of possibilities. Acts, feelings, and body changes seem to be the essence of experiencing an emotion.

Some of those acts, feelings, and body changes that we perceive in ourselves can be seen by others present. Conversely, we can see evidence of other people's emotion episodes. We are social beings, and emotion is important content of our social lives. We all are interested in and want to talk about our emotion experiences. We describe strong emotional experiences to one another and to ourselves.

Furthermore, we have extended our emotion ideas to more subtle experiences. In those subtler, less intense, but apparently similar forms, emotion gives human substance to simple life events. We report, for example, feelings of enjoyment or annoyance or apprehension as we are thinking or acting or both. Much of this is abundantly clear to anyone who reflects on it.

Yet, studying emotion has always been difficult. Understanding emotional life has been a central problem in disciplined human thinking, and in psychology, it has been especially troubling and annoying. Some psychologists have tried to limit what we call emotional experience and show its simple essence. Whether as physiologists, behaviorists, cognitivists, social constructionists, or psychoanalysts, psychologists have treated emotion to serve other ends and decided it is "nothing but" one feature or another of a system of psychology. That literature is filled with simplifications, polemics, and dogma. Few people have examined emotion broadly and with strict natural science methods. It is not easy to do.

Several myths of fact and theory have become ingrained, and to question them is to invite peril. In particular, the role of our feelings in emotional experiences is at the core of philosophical and psychological beliefs. Perhaps the key question is broader: What events arouse an emotion and make each particular complex of acts, feelings, and body changes? And then we must address why. Examination of emotion goes to the heart of understanding human psychology, and thus motivation's basic question: Why do we want to do that? If we can understand emotion and feelings, we will add a great deal to our understanding of motivation principles.

Emotion Experience

Patterns of life are never without emotion roles. Narratives of emotion supply the bulk of what people think is interesting about living. No one wants to be without emotional feelings. Although emotions are elusive and fuzzy events to define, all of human society acknowledges that there are such experiences, and feelings are communicated with accuracy in human life. Everyone uses emotion and descriptions of emotion. What are the ways of that use? No easy answers or simple summaries will do. The richness of emotion literature, both technical and general, is overwhelming and was so more than 100 years ago when William James complained about it. Thus, for anyone to make a definitive summary of that scientific and literary description, or even a very complete abstract, is presumptuous. We can instead look to the scientific theories that hope to find emotion's essential nature.

The modern complexity of emotion is shown by the dozens of theories that address the elusive question of what exactly constitutes an emotion. In traditional naturalism, many theorists present emotion as a physical response, as a function that evolved naturally and is common to all people and many animals. Within this category of physical theories, some trace the origins of emotion to certain survival mechanisms. Others see emotion as built by conditioned responses from a base of a few natural responses. Still others believe emotion to be the function of certain structures of the brain. Theorists who see emotion in all social life believe it to be a fundamental narrative of human functioning. They stress its cultural roots and the cognitive events on which it depends.

Before any of these, however, there was the misunderstood and often-ridiculed body-reaction feelings thesis of William James.

William James's Body-Reaction Feelings

In the early development of psychology, there were differences of opinion as to whether its major task was to study mental phenomena as they appeared or to examine mind as it functions. William James included both, but he was most concerned that the full richness of many topics be a part of psychology. On occasion, he presented an original theory but within the system of ideas that he had championed. His theory of emotion was one of the most famous of those and one that continues to be mentioned, although negatively. William James's unique theory is worthy of a close look because its most important elements have been misunderstood and attacked with evidence and rhetoric that missed the mark.

William James (1890) based his view of emotion on his well-developed notion that all acts are instinctive in their original roots.

The actions we call instinctive all conform to the general reflex type; they are called forth by determinate sensory stimuli in contact with the animal's body, or at a distance

in his environment. (Vol. 2, p. 384; italics in original)

Man has a far greater variety of *impulses* than any lower animal; and any one of these impulses, taken in itself, is as "blind" as the lowest instinct can be; but, owing to man's memory, power of reflection, and power of inference, they come each one to be felt by him, after he has once yielded to them and experienced their results, in connection with a *foresight* of those results. (p. 390; italics in original)

In speaking of the instincts it has been impossible to keep them separate from the emotional excitements which go with them. Objects of rage, love, fear, etc., not only prompt a man to outward deeds, but provoke characteristic alterations in his attitude and visage, and affect his breathing, circulation, and other organic functions in specific ways. When the outward deeds are inhibited, these latter emotional expressions still remain, and we read the anger in the face, though the blow may not be struck, and the fear betrays itself in voice and color, though one may suppress all other signs. *Instinctive reactions and emotional expressions thus shade imperceptibly into each other. Each object that excites an instinct excites an emotion as well.* (p. 442; italics in original)

The natural response is the fact on which emotion depends, in James's view. In describing that pattern, he used language that, although accurate, was perhaps unnecessarily provocative and in some ways misleading. He reversed the sense of common description of emotion narrative, and he tied his theory to an overly simple set of examples that opened his theory to easy but inaccurate criticism. The fateful passages are in a section informatively titled "Emotion follows upon the bodily expression in the coarser emotions at least."

The bodily changes follow directly the perception of the exciting fact, and . . . our feeling of the same changes as they occur IS the emotion. Common-sense says, we lose our fortune, are sorry and weep; we meet a bear, are frightened and run; we are insulted by a rival, are angry and strike. . . . The more rational statement is that we feel sorry because we cry, angry because we strike, afraid because we tremble, and not that we cry, strike, or tremble because we are sorry, angry, or fearful, as the case may be. Without the bodily states following on the perception, the latter would be purely cognitive in form, pale, colorless, destitute of emotional warmth. . . . *Objects do excite bodily changes* by a preorganized mechanism. . . . *The changes are so indefinitely numerous and subtle that the entire organism may be called a sounding-board,* which every change of consciousness, however slight, may make reverberate. . . . The immense number of parts modified in each emotion is what makes it difficult for us to reproduce in cold blood the total and integral expression of any one of them. (James, 1890, pp. 449-450; italics in original)

Emotion, in James's view, is formed on an instinctive response of the whole body to "normal instigating causes." People perceive and act, and the emotion is the feeling sense of all of the natural body activity. Take away the feelings of that body activity and what remains is not an emotion. An important component, often overlooked, is that these body acts and feelings are natural responses, or as James labels them **instincts.**

In his section titled "The subtler emotions," James (1890) takes up what he calls the moral, intellectual, and aesthetic feelings. Critics claimed that in hearing music or seeing a landscape, an emotional feeling forms directly and the bodily expression arrives later. James's reply:

That aesthetic emotion, *pure and simple,* the pleasure given us by certain lines and masses, and combinations of colors and sounds, is an absolutely sensational experience, an optical or aurical feeling that is primary and not due to the repercussions backwards of other sensations elsewhere consecutively aroused. (p. 468; italics in original)

Other parts of the flow of feelings over time are added as a result of experience. These are called the "secondary pleasures."

These secondary emotions themselves are assuredly for the most part constituted of other incoming sensations aroused by the diffusive wave of reflex actions which the beautiful object sets up. A glow, a pang in the breast, a shudder, a fullness of the breathing, a flutter of the heart, a shiver down the back, a moistening of the eyes, a stirring in the hypogastrium, and a thousand unnameable symptoms besides, may be felt the moment the beauty *excites* us. And these symptoms also result when we are excited by moral perceptions, as of pathos, magnanimity, or courage. The voice breaks and the sob rises in the struggling chest, or the nostril dilates and the fingers tighten, whilst the heart beats, etc., etc.

As far as *these ingredients* of the subtler emotions go, then, the latter form no exception to our account, but rather an additional illustration thereof. In all cases of intellectual or moral rapture we find that, unless there be coupled a bodily reverberation of some kind with the mere thought of the object and cognition of its quality; unless we actually laugh at the neatness of the demonstration or witticism; unless we thrill at the case of justice, or tingle at the act of magnanimity; our state of mind can hardly be called emotional at all. (James, 1890, pp. 470-471; italics in original)

The complete history of the attacks on James's deceptively simple theory is something for another text. This state of affairs was an instance of clashing eras and ideals in which certain studies became classical critiques, although they were really only excuses to shift to a preferred set of ideas. James's "sins" were several, including proposing an instinctive basis for human acts, denying human reason a role in forming what is emotional in experiences, and being unaware of what were to be the future fashions of psychology, especially psychology's enthusiasm for simple physiological models.

One major attack on the theory, however, had the effect of discrediting it, even though the evidence for doing so was plainly inadequate. The primary evidence used against James's theory was a centralized model of nervous system function built on incomplete study. Walter Cannon (1927) provided the major attack, which was readily accepted, although that attack did not really confront James's emotion theory. James also was no longer around to respond to criticism, having died in 1909. Cannon began each argument with a numbered statement. We will briefly consider the validity of each point.

1. Total separation of the viscera from the central nervous system does not alter emotional behavior. (p. 108)

James did not limit his theory to viscera as was commonly assumed. He viewed body reaction much more broadly, including acts such as fighting and fleeing.

2. The same visceral changes occur in very different emotional states and in nonemotional states. (p. 109)

Perhaps, but it is the pattern of differences that is the emotion.

3. The viscera are relatively insensitive structures. (p. 111)

This is not important because emotion comes from what *is* there.

4. Visceral changes are too slow to be a source of emotional feeling. (p. 112)

Again, Cannon focuses on the viscera, and speed doesn't matter because it is what eventually happens that is the emotion, and only then.

5. Artificial induction of the visceral changes typical of strong emotions does not produce them. (p. 113)

This is not a test James would allow, and the results actually *support* James's position. See Pananicolaou (1989) for more detail and references on Cannon's critique.

All in all, James's "body-reaction feelings" theory of emotion has stood up well to argument and test, as the evidence and actual theory are examined. In addition to its robust-

ness, both as an allegedly discredited curiosity and as a coherent statement, James's emotion theory is among the very few that have addressed the fundamental problem. He clearly theorized what an emotion *is*. James believed that the incorrigible natural fact that defines an emotional experience is the presence of feeling, and James theorized its origins and consequences. It fails in a modern natural science view, however, because, typical of James, his truth criterion is personal mental experience and in its most subjective form.

A philosopher of recent times gives us another example of basing emotion on examined experience. This philosopher sees emotion as a way of being, founded on judgments.

Robert Solomon's Emotions as Judgments

Robert Solomon (1976, 1989) writes with the professional expertise of a philosopher who has been studying emotion. He views emotion as a source of meaning in human life that depends on a broad view of **judgment** as unfolding in a conceptual analysis within a cultural context. Solomon (1989) writes of emotion as a "way of being in the world."

> Every emotion is a way of being, a partial self, a set of values and expectations. . . .
> Emotions as judgments are basic to the self itself, nothing less. (1989, p. 136)

A judgment is prereflective in that it need not be deliberated or even articulated; it is often "spontaneous," if we notice making it at all. . . . A judgment is constitutive insofar as it does not only interpret but *defines* our experience; seeing someone as hateful or offensive is not the superposition of a value judgment onto a neutral perception. It is the hatefulness or the offensiveness that structures the perception. . . . To be *very* angry must be understood not in terms of some overwhelmingly physiological accompaniment but rather in terms of the significance or harshness of the judgment. . . . Finally, to say the emotions are composed of evaluative judgments is to make the point . . . that, although the logical presuppositions of emotions might be any number of purely factual judgments . . . , the emotion itself is composed almost entirely of value judgments, though these can be enormously varied and complex. (pp. 140-141; italics in original)

Solomon (1989) emphasizes that emotions are part of a system of judgments, and then asks how emotion judgments are different from other kinds of thought and mental content. His answer begins with the common-sense notion that in emotions we are taking something personally.

An emotional system of judgments is defined . . . by a kind of self-involvement, by an essential link with desire and action. . . . The criterion (and quantitative test) of such self-involvement is *excitement,* the fact that one is inspired or exhilarated or otherwise "moved" in judging a certain state of affairs. (p. 143; italics in original)

The desire component of emotion is essential and inescapable, for to have a self-involved judgment that makes up an emotion is the same as having the appropriate desire to act. We cannot judge the event of an approaching bear without the desire to avoid it or judge the acts of another as insulting without the desire to correct them. The combination *is* the emotion, and neither the mental process alone nor the desire alone is sufficient.

One-line examples fail to describe the complexity and multidimensionality of real life. Each emotion is made of a complex of judgments at different levels of complexity and from different perspectives of oneself. In Solomon's view, emotions are completely describable with detail and precision that lay out the fabric of experience. There is nothing held back as inherently indescribable. Although emotions are describable, that description will be complex, each perhaps taking a book itself. Solomon begins by proposing an analysis using 10 key judgment categories, such as direction (other-directed,

inner-directed, or bipolar) and intentions (benevolence, malevolence, or others).

Solomon (1989) has sketched the outline of an encompassing theory of emotion in which he sees the other "nothing but" theories to be inadequate if not philosophically unsound.

Judgments, not feelings or physiology, give the characteristic structure, significance, and variety to our many emotions. And it is emotion, not reason or simple desire, that gives significance to lives. (p. 146)

We cannot deny the reality that emotion is the essential color in our lives. We can doubt, however, that analysis of phenomenal experience, no matter how disciplined, will give us the basic principles of emotion we seek. In his way, Solomon has narrowed emotion to another form of "nothing but" that complements rather than replaces our natural science methods. From work such as Solomon's, we can better know the complexities of mental experiences allied with emotion.

We briefly turn now to questioning the different kinds of emotions that theorists have proposed. The first question is, Are there primary emotions? If the answer to that is yes, then the obvious next question is, What are they? This is an ancient and ongoing debate without a clear resolution yet. We will be selective for both logic and efficiency reasons.

Primary Emotions

The logic of talking about primary emotions is controversial. Two psychologists (Ortony & Turner, 1990) made that clear recently when they challenged the idea of basic emotions and lit a firestorm of illuminating rebuttals that strengthened our understanding of biological bases of emotion (Ekman, 1992a; Izard, 1992; Panksepp, 1992). Many, if not most theories and commentaries build on ideas of a few fundamental emotions from which more complex emotional life is constructed. Finding absolute criteria for select-

TABLE 4.1 Most Commonly Listed Different Emotions in Several Popular and Historical Theories

James	Ekman	Izard	Plutchik	Watson	Panksepp
fear	fear	fear	fear	fear = X	fear
rage	anger	anger	anger	anger = Y	anger
grief	sadness	distress	sadness		panic
	joy	joy	joy		
love			acceptance	love = Z	
		interest	anticipation		expectation
	surprise	surprise	surprise		
	disgust	disgust	disgust		
		contempt			
		shame			
		guilt			

ing them has been difficult. The idea of wanting to use some set of primaries may rest on the fact that some emotional experiences have very clear referents and strong agreement in communications about them. The domains of happiness, fear, and disgust are less fuzzy and ambiguous than those of pride, distress, and guilt. Sharper word use leads to clearer concepts, and clearer concepts suggest simple and discrete real events causing them. Regardless of the dimensions that have been used by theorists to propose such a list, the existence of primary emotions is well established in language, and the literature of emotional experience tends to be concentrated on the most common labels.

Six theories mentioned in the chapter are shown in Table 4.1. From this format of emotion lists, we can see just which names appear most often. If this kind of sampling has any validity, it appears that most writers see a use for fear and anger, with variants of grief or sadness, joy or love, interest or surprise, and disgust also very common as basic emotion labels. But natural science is not an opinion poll. At this level, the most we can get is what has been common in our collective thought.

We next move on to the best evidence for a natural science of emotion, finding among it some old classics and some fresh and very recent looks at biological systems underlying what we experience as emotion.

SECTION SUMMARY:
PHENOMENA AND EXPERIENCES

Emotion, being part of the essence of life, has traditional elements of feelings, noticeable body changes, and acts that we try to simplify and discount with theories. William James tied these elements together by assuming we instinctively react after perceiving some events. Emotion *is* the resulting experience, the feeling, we have of this happening. His view ran up against the new anti-instinct attitudes, and psychologists seemed to fall over themselves in the rush to show James to be wrong. Yet, their evidence typically was not relevant, and James's perspective remains important in declaring emotion to be based in natural, body reactions. A modern philosopher, Robert Solomon, believes emotions to be based in meaningful judgments we make in our personal lives.

He proposes extensive, disciplined study of experiences of living to understand these emotional elements.

Traditionally, researchers have studied emotion by dividing it into certain clear and basic types. The listing of primary emotions partly follows our common language labels and partly uses the logic that, in their extreme form, emotion experiences seem to be clearly distinct. Beyond a few basics, however, we don't agree on what makes up the list of primaries. The theories in the following sections will illustrate those differences and why they are that way.

BIOLOGICAL FOUNDATIONS OF EMOTION

An appropriate introduction to the nature of biological systems of emotion is through the biology-based theories. A good place to start is with biological theory ideas of inherited functions that emotions serve.

Inherited Function Theories

As we noted, many theories of emotion include a core of basic or fundamental emotions. The key to the inherited-function theories is in how they select the core emotions; these theories value the role of emotions in survival. Ideas about survival function date at least from Charles Darwin's 1872 book, *The Expression of the Emotions in Man and Animals*. His theory was that emotions are adaptations or inherited functions that at least once had survival value for the species.

Paul Ekman's Pan-Human Expressions

Paul Ekman (1977) suggests a model of emotion in which

> emotion refers to the process whereby an elicitor is appraised automatically or in an extended fashion, an affect programme may or may not be set off, organized responses may occur, more or less managed by attempts to control emotional behavior. (p. 61)

Emotional responses occur quickly but in a complexly organized fashion. Ekman calls the units of this complexity **affect pro-grams**; they are genetically given. The various pieces of movement, face responses, sounds, and nervous system changes are each inherited affect programs, and some of them are presumed to work together naturally. This is similar to William James's natural response. It is our nature to act in particular ways when meeting certain kinds of situations. Next, Ekman considers how those affect programs are set off.

Affect programs are called into action through the automatic action of an **appraisal mechanism.** The roots of appraising are part of the natural response, the adaptations we share in the human species. With life experience, each individual adds depth and dimension to appraisals. The appraisal makes use of imagination and memory and foresees the possible outcomes of situations. Included are the display rules (noted below) and attempts at coping with the situation.

Elicitors are the stimuli specific to different emotions that are appraised. Ekman believes that there are no specific elicitors for affect programs but that there is evidence that the elicitors for each emotion share some characteristics. Elicitor situations for anger have in common some blocking or aggression. Fear elicitors present the real possibility of harm or pain. Disgust elicitors refer to something noxiously unpleasant. The appraisal mechanisms are sensitive to these kinds of general features. There is still room for culture to determine specific instances of what is anger-provoking, feared, or disgusting. Elicitors are appraised that suggest specific affect programs, but those affect programs are modified or inhibited according to other parts of social rules.

Display rules are what Ekman calls the social regularities that control the emotional response. The social environment dictates what we do in each emotion situation, but some personal latitude is also tolerated based on our experiences. Anger in the normal affect program is displayed with threatening postures, "angry face," and specific sounds and words. But some of society's display rules involve disguising the degree of emotion experienced. We may meet the angering situation with a clenched-teeth smile and questions of the intentions of the responsible person. Or we may exaggerate the display to communicate our power and authority in the situation.

From a base of extensive study and analyses of human expressions (e.g., Ekman, 1973, 1977, 1984, 1992a), Paul Ekman has focused specifically on the essence of an emotion state in its distinctive facial expression. Without such a universal facial signal, he proposes that the state should not be called an emotion. Ekman (1984, pp. 530-539) lists 10 characteristics to aid that distinction:

1. There is a distinctive pan-cultural signal for each emotion.

2. Distinctive universal facial expressions of emotion can be traced phylogenetically [by evolutionary history].

3. Emotional expressions involve multiple signals, involving the voice as well as the face.

4. There are limits on the duration of an emotion.

5. The timing of an emotional expression reflects the specifics of a particular emotional experience.

6. Expressions are graded in intensity, reflecting variations in the strength of felt experience.

7. Emotional expression can be totally inhibited.

8. Emotional expressions can be convincingly simulated.

9. There are pan-human commonalities in the elicitors for each emotion.

10. There is a pan-human, distinctive pattern of changes in the autonomic and central nervous system for each emotion.

These descriptors clearly imply that emotions are natural, inherited event patterns. Ekman further states that he has assumed that emotions have evolved to deal with fundamental life tasks. Specific patterns of acts are called out that are appropriate in content and in timing for each prototypic situation, and it is this coherence that allows common labels of anger, fear, joy, and the like.

In Ekman's view, emotions are always of rather short duration. Most last but a few seconds, and no emotion lasts more than a matter of minutes. His assertion is that the natural emotional response, seen in its facial and other expression, is always brief. After that period, both the expression and the other aspects of the experience change into other forms, following other demands of the situation and strategies of the person.

Ekman's view, after reviewing decades of evidence of facial expression, is that extensive agreement is found on five emotions (happiness, surprise, fear, sadness, and anger), with a lot of support for three or four more (Ekman, 1992a). There are specific muscles associated with some basic emotions, patterns of autonomic nervous system action are associated with some emotions, and patterns of central nervous system activity are beginning to be found as well.

Among his most intriguing recent demonstrations is that of feedback from the expression to build patterns of emotion physiology (Ekman, 1992b). Voluntary movements of face muscles appear to generate specific physiological patterns of emotion. This has been dubbed the *facial feedback hypothesis,* which we will consider later.

Carroll Izard's Fundamental Emotions

Without speculating as to their original causes or ancient purposes, Carroll Izard (1971, 1977, 1984) has deduced, in part from cross-cultural studies of expression, that 10 basic emotions have emerged in human evolution: interest, joy, surprise, sadness, anger, disgust, contempt, fear, shame or shyness, and guilt. These 10 are unique and separate. Each has its distinctive experience, physiology, and body activity (especially facial and gestural). Each emotion is inherited as a set of neurochemical processes as revealed in unique motor (facial) and mental (feeling language) expressions. Izard (1991) appears to reject using some concept like arousal to build an underlying unity in emotions. He discourages the general use of the term *emotion* in favor of the study of specific fundamental emotions.

In Izard's (1993) view, each emotion has potential to be activated by four systems: neural, sensorimotor, motivational, and cognitive. In the neural systems, unique patterns of neural transmitters and brain structures are involved for each emotion. Sensorimotor systems include feedback from muscles of posture and action. Izard's motivational systems include other emotions as well as drive states and direct sensations such as pain. Cognitive systems eliciting emotion include appraisals, evaluations, comparisons, judgments, attributions, memories, and anticipations. The point is that Izard sees specific emotions as components of a complex system. We will review more of Izard's views on emotion later.

Robert Plutchik's Survival-Based Core

Robert Plutchik (1980, 1984) has suggested that core emotions derive from survival functions. Plutchik's emotion theory uses evolutionary logic, assuming that emotions evolved as parts of natural experiences that helped adapt individuals to change in the environment.

Plutchik (1980, p. 129) stated his theory in 10 declarative postulates.

1. The concept of emotion is applicable to all evolutionary levels and applies to all animals as well as humans.

2. Emotions have an evolutionary history and have evoked various forms of expression in different species.

3. Emotions serve an adaptive role in helping organisms deal with key survival issues posed by the environment.

4. Despite different forms of expression of emotions in different species, there are certain common elements, or prototype patterns, that can be identified.

5. There is a small number of basic, primary, or prototype emotions.

6. All other emotions are mixed or derivative states; that is, they occur as combinations, mixtures, or compounds of the primary emotions.

7. Primary emotions are hypothetical constructs or idealized states whose properties and characteristics can only be inferred from various kinds of evidence.

8. Primary emotions can be conceptualized in terms of pairs of polar opposites.

9. All emotions vary in their degree of similarity to one another.

10. Each emotion can exist in varying degrees of intensity or levels of arousal.

The first three points state most clearly the evolutionary theory approach. Plutchik's next four postulates provide the starting place for a taxonomy of emotion. He believes that certain patterns of action are common among many species, and aiding these adaptive acts are a few primary emotions. The notion of primary emotion is an old one, but he places conditions on how they are to be identified. Plutchik insists that primary emotions be adaptive for all levels of animals and be defined by acts, not physiology or mental experience. The eight functions that Plutchik holds to be basic and the primary emotion associated with each are shown in Table 4.2.

Plutchik's remaining postulates provide for a formal model to describe the relations among the core emotions. Plutchik purposefully follows an analogy to color mixture theory and proposes a solid inverted cone figure to represent the interdependence. Emotions across the circular dimension are opposite,

TABLE 4.2　Robert Plutchik's Survival-Based Emotions, Their Original Function, and Their Original Form of Pathology

Function	Emotion	Pathology
incorporation	acceptance	histrionic
rejection	disgust	paranoid
destruction	anger	antisocial
protection	fear	passive
reproduction	joy	manic
reintegration	sadness	depressed
orientation	surprise	borderline
exploration	anticipation	obsessive

adjacent categories are similar, and vertical levels are differences in intensity, with lessening excitement toward unemotional at the apex.

In further development, Plutchik described the pathology that arises from abnormal emotional events that endure as traits of personality. The third column of Table 4.2 shows some symptoms that may appear. Clinical attention can then be directed to likely functional and emotional causes of the pathology.

Although they have differences in emphasis, the ideas of Ekman, Izard, and Plutchik basically agree. Emotion is a useful design feature that had survival value for a variety of species. It remains a part of human brain design that shapes some of our functioning.

The behaviorists also found it necessary to start with some kind of core on which emotional responses could be built. We turn next to the early ideas of John Watson, behaviorism's early outspoken proponent.

Conditioned Response Theories

Behaviorists generally avoided the topic of emotion in its full breadth, and instincts became a symbol of incorrect thinking for some of them. Their theories of emotion focus on acts and their stimuli. There is some mention of physiological change, but mental feeling is ignored entirely. John Watson's (1929) notion was of this sort.

John Watson's X, Y, and Z Emotions

Watson (1929) started with a few natural basics.

> An emotion is an hereditary "pattern-reaction" involving profound changes of the bodily mechanisms as a whole, but particularly of the visceral and glandular systems. By pattern-reaction we mean that the separate details of response appear with some constancy, with some regularity and in approximately the same sequential order each time the exciting stimulus is presented. (p. 225)

Watson proposed three fundamental emotional reactions:

> *fear, rage, and love* (using *love* in approximately the same sense Freud uses sex). We use these terms which are current in psychology with a good deal of hesitation. The student is asked to find nothing in them which is not fully statable in terms of situation and response. Indeed, we should be willing to call them emotional reaction states X, Y and Z. (p. 229, italics in original)

These fundamental reactions are attached to new situations through the learning principle called conditioning, thus enlarging "the range of stimuli capable of calling out emotional activity" (p. 229).

By conditioning, the complexity of adult emotional life is thought to be constructed through individual life experiences.

Conditioned Emotional Reactions

Following the traditional view that emotions are real and separate entities, such emotions are described by behaviorists as being attached to new stimuli by conditioning. That some sort of learning or experience factor is at work seems obvious from casual observation of life experiences. We fear what we did not fear, love what we did not love, or become angered by what was not angering. In behaviorists' theories, the wealth and variety of experiences of emotion are said to be formed automatically by the conditioned response learning process.

John Watson put this into an especially narrow model that fit with the theory fashions of the times. Watson claimed to have conditioned the emotion of fear in his laboratory. Watson's famous demonstration (Watson & Raynor, 1920) apparently made Albert, an 11-month-old hospital clinic patient, afraid of white furry objects. Tests showed Albert to be at first unafraid of a white rabbit, a white rat, a dog, a fur coat, cotton wool, or a Santa Claus mask. The rat was then placed in front of Albert. As he reached for it, Watson made a loud noise by striking a metal bar with a hammer. The noise made Albert fearful, and he fell over on his mattress and whimpered. After a second pairing with a similar result, Albert was not tested for a week. Then five more pairings were given. The sixth time the rat was placed in front of Albert that day he cried, fell, and scrambled away. Five days later the objects were again placed in front of Albert. The rat, rabbit, and fur coat produced fear. Albert made milder responses to the dog, cotton wool, and Santa Claus mask.

Watson appeared to show that fear could be learned and thereby gave an intellectual boost to an idea that he helped develop into wide currency—that the mechanism of conditioning forms the complexity of adult emotion from the simple, natural infant reactions. It was widely assumed thereafter that conditioning is the primary mechanism of emotion development.

Watson's fear conditioning was promoted as proof of the behaviorist ideas. The reality, however, is that it was little more than a preliminary demonstration using a single child. There was no real measurement of pre- versus post-conditioning acts, no isolation of conditions. Furthermore, others have not been able to repeat it despite many attempts to do so, but that critique was irrelevant to theorists who wanted desperately to display an example to support the theory that they were already convinced was correct. Many psychologists thought that Watson's conditioning was a valid explanation for all learning of emotional attachment. Why? Because conditioning was the favored idea of the times to explain the formation of all human and animal acts. The legacy of that ideology remains in psychology.

Brain and Nervous System Theories

One of the most obvious features of experience in a strong emotion is the way our body changes. James recognized that feeling those changes in body functioning was the most important part of emotion experiences. It is no surprise that emotion theorists have tried to identify emotions by measuring bodily changes or, at the least, have focused specific body changes in their schemes. Some physiological findings suggested that parts of the nervous system act as a whole during preparations for action and in carrying out specific acts. Other researchers have looked for direct links between named emotions and specific body changes.

Many physiologists assume that emotions are automatically formed by brain function. That may be correct, but we are just beginning to draw clearer pictures. We find a complexity that challenges description of the brain areas, specific brain circuits, and particular neurochemical changes. The explosion of research and accumulating information seemed for a time not to be converging on answers but instead diverging into more questions. Some of that is beginning to change.

To get at least something suggestive from the wealth of increasing information, we can examine a few of the older and some of the bolder summaries and speculations that have been offered.

Walter Cannon's Central Reactions

Walter Cannon (1915) proposed that the physiology of emotion is expressed in actions of the autonomic nervous system. He believed that the sympathetic and parasympathetic parts of this nervous system act in a balance in nonexcited states. Each exerts opposing forces on a number of motor and glandular functions of the body. He believed that when the balance has been upset, the sympathetic nervous system activates those parts of the body that prepare for specific actions and mobilize emergency and stress resources. The sympathetic system then stimulates what was called the fight, fright, and flight activities. These activities were said to expend body resources and usually operate in concert; many sympathetic responses acting together. This system is useful for an adaptive response to noxious events and stress. The parasympathetic system, conversely, was believed to be most active during resting states, acting in piecemeal fashion when needed, and serving to conserve the resources of the body.

One of the responses of the sympathetic system is increased secretion of epinephrine into the bloodstream. Cannon believed that epinephrine further excites the sympathetic system and maintains the sympathetic-parasympathetic imbalance for extended periods of time. Epinephrine was thought to be the agent responsible for many of the lasting effects observed after emotional stimulation has passed. Muscle tremor, pounding heart, and blood distribution at the skin are some of the lasting results from epinephrine-prolonged sympathetic arousal.

Cannon's theory provided one set of roots of the growing idea that emotion is a general state of the system rather than a word for a collection of different systems. From Cannon's sympathetic nervous system and epinephrine, it is an easy step to believe emotion is merely an aroused nervous system as Elizabeth Duffy (1941) held. Stanley Schachter and Jerome Singer (1962) added that the different experiences we have are merely cognitive interpretations exaggerated by sympathetic nervous system arousal.

Paul MacLean's Triune Brain Structures

A traditional goal of biological psychologists is linking functions and structures of the brain to emotional phenomena. The assumption is that there must be physiological roots to what we call emotional experience, and it is not unreasonable to look for brain and nervous system centers that control emotions. Among the first, James Papez (1937) tried to identify three different brain structures that handle action, consciousness, and feeling. The feelings were thought to be processed in the hippocampus, a part of the limbic system.

Paul MacLean (e.g., 1949, 1970, 1993) carried speculation farther along similar lines using increasing neuroclinical evidence. MacLean (1993) located the operations of emotion feelings in the limbic system and put this notion in a larger context of dividing the brain into three parts: reptilian (the oldest and most centrally located brain regions), paleomammalian (limbic system), and neomammalian (cerebral cortex): "In evolving to its great size, the human forebrain has retained the anatomical organization and chemistry of three formations that reflect a respective relationship to reptiles, early mammals, and late mammals" (p. 67).

His speculation is that these three brain parts, interacting yet independent, function in all of human action, but each has its own kind of intelligence, memory, sense of time and space, and motor and other functions. One consequence of the functioning triune brain is what is called emotion.

The reptilian brain is formed of the brain stem. It evokes stereotyped acts, "such instinctually determined functions as establishing territory, finding shelter, hunting, homing, mating, breeding, imprinting, forming social hierarchies, selecting leaders, and the like" (MacLean, 1970, p. 131).

The paleomammalian or limbic brain includes those structures bordering the brain stem. MacLean proposed in 1970 that it has much the same functions in all mammals: "elaborating emotions that guide behavior with respect to the two basic life principles of self-preservation and preservation of the species" (MacLean, 1970, p. 132). In a 1993 description, MacLean has elaborated on limbic functioning.

Factors related to the evolutionary development of the forebrain of early mammals (the paleomammalian brain or so-called "limbic system") were responsible for the honing of emotional feelings that guide behavior required for self-preservation and the procreation of the species. (p. 67)

Three subdivisions of the limbic system were identified as coherent by location, connections, and behaviors. The amygdalar division relates to finding and ingesting food and aspects of anger and defense in getting food. The septal division involves specific parts of procreation including aspects of courtship, sexual responses, and feelings of pleasure. The thalamocingulate division concerns maternal activities and some elements of play.

MacLean (1980) finds evidence for the functioning limbic system in clinical studies of neuronal discharges in the limbic cortex that give vivid feelings to epileptic patients.

The *basic* and *general* affects are usually of the kind associated with threats to self-preservation. . . . More rarely, there may be affects of an agreeable or ecstatic nature, possibly reflecting a spread of the seizure to other subdivisions of the limbic system.

The *basic* affects include those of hunger, thirst, nausea, and feelings associated with the emunctories [waste elimination]. . . . the *general* affects are usually "free-floating" insofar as they are not identified with any particular person or situation. . . . Ironically, it would seem that the ancient limbic system provides free-floating, strong affective feelings of conviction that we attach to revelations and beliefs, regardless of whether they are true or false! (pp. 20-21, italics in original)

Those general feelings appear as epileptic auras in the absence of any specific objects or contexts. They include feelings of fear, desire, anger, dejection, affection, and gratulance. These last, gratulant feelings, are of discovery, revelation, enhanced reality, importance, and absolute truth.

MacLean believes that the neomammalian brain has evolved toward specialization in perception of the external environment. The cerebral cortex is crucial for interpretation of events outside of the body. Most directly involved in emotion is the front half of the frontal lobe, the prefrontal cortex. Lobotomy studies showed its role in planning and anticipation.

Prefrontal cortex connections project most directly to the thalamocingulate parts of the limbic system, those specializing in care of young. As breeding success improved with effective anticipations of events affecting family life, this cortex area grew and added specialties. The feeling elements of suffering when separated from family members and joy when reconnected were elaborated into anticipation of loss and of recovery. Crying and laughing are expressive elements of these situations.

Other neocortex areas would activate the gratulant feelings as more elaborate aspects of anticipation and discovery became possible. Especially important are reflections of self-discovery and self-awareness. Anticipation of loss and the like can progress into concepts of future suffering, and with culture icons, concepts of suffering in all living things.

Joseph LeDoux's Amygdala Focus

Joseph LeDoux (1987) states the brain systems thesis clearly: "*Emotion* is . . . a general term referring to a group of interrelated brain functions" (p. 419; italics in original). In his later summary of emotion in the nervous system, LeDoux was more specific.

2. Neurons in the limbic forebrain, particularly the amygdala, code the biological value of sensory stimuli arising from the external environment and from the body.

3. The evaluation of the emotional significance of sensory stimuli by limbic neurons occurs unconsciously.

4. Stimulus evaluation in response to exteroceptive and interoceptive sensory stimu-

lation plays a causal role in the expression of changes in emotional behavior and accompanying visceral responses. (pp. 449-450)

LeDoux's (1993) recent focus has been on the amygdala:

The amygdala receives a wide range of inputs about immediately present, imagined, and remembered stimuli. Its anatomical connections suggest that it can be activated by simple features, whole objects, the context in which objects occur, semantic properties of objects, images and memories of objects, and the like. Any and all of these may therefore serve as the critical trigger information for emotional arousal.

. . . the amygdala is somewhat blind as to the nature of the stimulus that activates it, since primitive sensory features are potentially as capable of activating the emotional system as complex thoughts. (p. 112)

Jaak Panksepp's Command Circuits

Jaak Panksepp (1982) offered four categories of emotion system in a general psychobiological theory. He suggested that rapid action is required for each of these broad functions and that their actions are genetically "hard wired" in the visceral-limbic brain. Positive incentives evoke **expectancy** with its varieties of anticipation, hope, and desire. Body surface irritation, restraint, and frustration produce **rage,** including indignation, hate, and anger. Pain and threat of destruction elicit **fear,** with its accompanying anxiety, alarm, and foreboding. Social loss yields **panic** in forms of loneliness, grief, and separation distress. Each of these systems has an information flow that passes through the hypothalamus, and at this site, they are systematically studied. (See Chapter 2 for a rough reference of the physiological terms here and following.)

The expectancy system, for example, tunes an individual to investigate and deal with the world. Mood disorders of reduced interest, inability to plan, and the like appear when it malfunctions (Panksepp, 1985). Named areas involved in the circuit include the basal ganglia and basal forebrain, and the system appears to be sensitive to levels of acetylcholine (cholinergic circuits).

The rage system defends an individual with acts of anger, threats, and evidence of irritation. Uninhibited rage leads to aggressive violence. Temporal lobe brain areas and the nearby corticomedial amygdala are the higher end of the circuits through the hypothalamus. Testosterone influences some of this system (Panksepp, 1985).

Fear systems yield flight and escape acts. Fear circuits seem to be near and comingled with those of rage in the temporal lobes and stem from the basolateral and central amygdala and then through the hypothalamus (Panksepp, 1986).

Distress from separation from a caretaker or loved one stimulates the panic system. Higher areas of the system include the bed nucleus of the stria terminus and the anterior cyngulate gyrus. The system is inhibited by brain opioids like endorphins (Panksepp, 1985).

Neuroendocrine Patterns

James Henry (1986) summarized emotional functioning in five systems with special attention to the neurochemistry evidence. His work is perhaps best seen in a visual layout. Table 4.3 is an abstract of it.

These glances at brain functions of emotion show us the complexity involved and the challenges yet to be undertaken. But despite the seemingly hopeless complications, the more information we accumulate, the better we can understand how the patterns we call emotion are based in our natural function. It both gives us new insights and destroys simplistic guesses of the past. Next, we look at emotions in another realm of complexity, human development.

TABLE 4.3　James Henry's (1986) Picture of Various Body Changes Typical of Five Emotion States

Limbic System	Anger Amygdalar Central Nucleus	Fear Amygdalar Basal Nucleus	Depression Hippocampus Septum	Serenity Amygdala	Elation Hippocampus
Blood pressure	↑	↗		↓ ↘	
Pulse	↑	↗	↘	↓	
Norepinephrine	↑	↗		↓	
Epinephrine	↗	↑		↓	
Testosterone	↑		↓		↑
Cortisol		↗	↑		↓
ACTH			↑		↓
Endorphins			↑		↓

NOTE: ↑ = strong increase; ↗ = moderate increase; ↓ = strong decrease; ↘ = moderate decrease.

SECTION SUMMARY:
BIOLOGICAL FOUNDATIONS OF EMOTION

With an implicit nod to William James, and more formal credit to Charles Darwin, many modern emotion theories are rooted in the concept of inherited functions. Three popular examples were presented. Paul Ekman describes complex affect programs in which elicitor situations are appraised, leading to social displays. Carroll Izard proposes 10 inherited emotions in a complexity of neural, sensorimotor, motivational, and cognitive systems. Robert Plutchik postulates eight emotion types emerging from eight survival systems common to all mammals.

A different biological tactic was that of John Watson, speaking for the new behaviorism school of psychology. He assumed that principles of conditioning form all of our reactions, based on three hereditary pattern reactions given at birth. The simplicity of this view was attractive to those who tried to see us as nothing but simple learning machines.

Looking at physiological reaction has a lot of appeal, given the obvious body changes we experience during strong emotions. Walter Cannon highlighted the aroused, energy-using aspects of the sympathetic nervous system. Paul MacLean developed emotion in the context of evolutionary stages in brain development labeled reptilean, paleomammalian (limbic brain), and neomammalian (developed cerebral cortex). Emotion is essentially in the middle, limbic brain stage. Joseph LeDoux focused emotion in the amygdala portions of the limbic brain. Jaak Panksepp identified brain systems that underwrite four emotion functions: expectancy, rage, fear, and panic. James Henry put emotion into five systems based on differences in neurochemistry. Although they appear to be different, these physiological theories are quite similar, moving us slowly in the direction of coherent factual pictures of emotion.

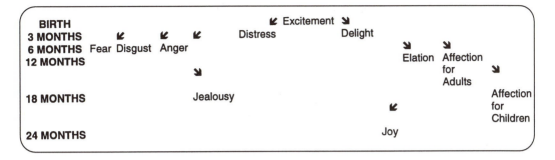

Figure 4.1. Appearance of different emotions in very young children (based on Katherine Bridges, 1932).

DEVELOPMENTAL ELABORATION

What emotions are expressed by children, and how are they used? That deceptively simple question starts us along a path from a too-simple idea of emotion entities appearing and being expressed in growing children to the important matter of social functioning of emotions.

Emotion Identification in Children

Nearly all theory positions about emotion acknowledge that emotions have roots in earliest life. Whether as inherited functions or as acquired styles of response or as features of learning the patterns of normal social interaction, infant and child emotional roles are believed to be important. Consequently, study and thought has been focused on them (e.g., Izard, 1984; Plutchik & Kellerman, 1983; Scherer & Ekman, 1984). Two kinds of content have been considered. First is the old and elusive question of the earliest appearance of emotion expressions. This question is answered by studying the expressions and the contexts of states presumed to be affective or emotional. Second is the complicated problem of placing affect and emotion in the developing social relations of children. What is the nature and function of emotional interaction?

Finding First Expressions

Evidence about what are primary or fundamental emotions may come from looking for their first appearances in young children. In what is perhaps the earliest systematic study, Katherine Bridges (1932) sampled the emotional actions of 62 infants in the Montreal Foundling and Baby Hospital. Infants of less than 1 month and up to 2 years of age were observed over several months. Her focus was on description of expressions, reporting in great detail the kinds of actions of children at each age. She then summarized the study with a chart that indicated her view of a differentiation of emotional actions toward adult types with aging. A picture of her differentiation is shown in Figure 4.1. At the earliest age, she wrote,

> The emotional reactions of the tiny infant are certainly not highly differentiated. The most common response to highly stimulating situations seems to be one of general agitation and excitement. . . . This vague emotional response to a large variety of circumstances must surely be one of the original emotions, if not the only one. (p. 326)

Though Bridges's descriptions are impressively detailed, it is difficult to label the resulting pattern as changes in emotional states rather than developing capacities for expression. It is also hard to accept that Bridges's observations weren't influenced by knowing that the children were maturing and *should* therefore show adult types of emotion;

it is easy to read into actions what one wants to find.

Charting Development Patterns

Emde, Gaensbauer, and Harmon (1976) summarized a yearlong longitudinal study of infants, using a description of three developmental steps they called levels. Their work revealed consistency in appearance of certain forms of expression of emotions in infants.

The first level is marked by **fussiness**, an unprovoked crying or restlessness. It is strongest at birth and declines in occurrence over the first 6 months. The observers suggested that fussiness serves the purpose of communicating biological need and facilitating attachment bonds to the caretaker. Paradoxically, the fussiness does not strengthen with receipt of attention; reinforcement with attention seems to reduce the frequency of appearance of crying (Ainsworth & Bell, 1977; Bell & Ainsworth, 1972).

In the second level, **smiling** begins after a month or two and develops to full strength by about 8 months. Human faces, particularly the caretaker's, produce the response. Comparable stimuli (caretaker's voice and touch) produce smiling in blind babies, suggesting a genetic or maturational rather than a modeling source. Smiling adds to the attachment bond by communicating mutual pleasure. After about 4 months, the smile is responsive to stimulus control including reinforcement procedures. The smiling indicates that the child is responding to the environment.

In the third level of development of expression, **stranger distress** in infants begins at about 6 months, reaches a peak at 8 months, and declines in strength thereafter. The stranger distress response begins with expression of interest toward an unfamiliar person followed by a sober perplexity. There are then signs of fear, frowning, and crying, terminating in avoidance by turning away. As the attachment bond strengthens, **separation distress** is produced in response to the caretaker's withdrawal and absence.

These observations outline specific emotional patterns of infants. Some exist from birth

with aging changes, and others appear at particular early life periods. Recent attention has been given to how these emotional patterns function to aid the child, especially in communication with caregivers.

Emotion Functioning in Child Development

Newborn human infants have no language except emotional expressions. Those expressions are their messages to caregivers about conditions. Such expressions are native to human infants and appear in natural rhythms and in response to changing events. In earliest infancy, crying and the like give the general message of distress with something that must be changed. Smiling conveys pleasure with what is happening that should continue. Specification of the length of this earliest period depends on the kind of question asked and the perspective of the observers.

Robert Emde and his colleagues (1976) believe that after 2 months, infants begin modifying their reactions in accordance with outside events. Colwyn Trevarthen (1984) cites studies with his colleagues showing interaction with caregivers of face and vocal expressions and gestures at 6 weeks of age. Both Emde and Trevarthen believe that infants perceive meanings in others' facial expressions during the middle of their second month. These expressions appear to be communications soliciting confirming faces and acts from the caregivers. Considerable experimental work has demonstrated this kind of function, called social referencing.

Social referencing uses expressions from caregivers, beyond their mere presence, to influence what very young children will do and what emotions they will express. For example, work by Mary Klinnert (Klinnert, Campos, Sorce, Emde, & Svejda, 1983) used the visual cliff table, a glass-topped table with a checkerboard pattern immediately under one side and at some distance below the other. The child is encouraged to cross from the former to the latter, moving out over what appears to be a drop-off. Most infants crossed over when their mothers showed a smiling face; none crossed when their mothers showed a face of fear. Social referencing is also shown in children's willingness to explore further and tolerate more novelty when they are being actively watched by a caregiver who is showing supporting emotional expressions.

Jerome Kagan (1984) describes four types of emotional reaction during a child's first 3 to 4 months. He labels them surprise to the unexpected, distress to physical privation, relaxation to gratification, and excitement to assimilation of the unexpected. He also notes smiling to familiar faces during the third month, which is part of a joy of understanding. From these and similar beginnings, as language is begun, and with maturational changes in cognitive capabilities, emotional expressions become more diverse, and they play increasingly important roles in social communications. As they approach 8 months of age, children react to unfamiliar happenings with expressions of fear or anxiety, as noted above by Emde and colleagues (1976). Strangers are compared with caregivers, and the child reacts with a sobering of expression and a cessation of activity followed by withdrawing from the stranger and crying. Kagan believes that these reactions depend on newly formed memory and evaluation functions, and they possibly are there to protect the child from harm. At about this age, children begin to respond with anger to being interrupted or to losing an interesting object, perhaps forming the basis for resisting rather than yielding to others. These reactions also depend on being able to relate desired objects and events to a memory of them.

Kagan goes on with speculations about emotional development through the later childhood years. During the second and third years, the sources for affective reactions are less from outside events. Internal emotional concepts seem designed to restrain the child. Depression and sadness typically follow the prolonged loss of something or someone to which there was strong attachment. Those emotions may function to keep a child close to familiar people and objects. Challenging tasks at which failure is likely will generate anxiety and withdrawal. Tasks and activities

are also at the heart of emotional responses to seeing that something is done wrong or that something was done well. These emotional task orientations support group goals of cleanliness and orderliness, against destruction and aggression. In the fourth year, children are able to realize their separate identities and recognize that they can make choices between acts. With this capacity, a child can experience shame for what was done and guilt over what might have been done. In later years, each child begins to make comparisons with others and forms reactions, such as inferiority, pride, and humility.

Emotion Expression

We are now set to develop what we are learning about a persisting idea: that much of the substance of emotion is wrapped up in communications of the participants. How is an emotion communicated? Specifically, what is the form and development of facial expression of emotional experience?

An obvious aspect of emotion is its expression. Emotional states are communicated to others. Expressions constitute the social aspects of the experiences and would be functionally unnecessary without social purpose. The nature and variations in expression must then be tied in direct ways to social existence and enculturation.

Facial expressions and movements make up the most direct means of communication. Two points of view have been defended since the time of Darwin in the 1870s. One position holds that there are universal facial expressions that are inherited responses to specific types of emotional experience. Faces of anger, joy, fear, and a few other emotions are adaptations we have inherited. Darwin presented this thesis in 1872. The other position is that the expressions are culturally based and have no direct inherited attachments to emotional experiences (e.g., Mead, 1975). This belief asserts that faces of joy and the others were learned by example and reinforcement, presumably in our early development.

Early studies presented stereotypical emotional faces to observers for their emotion identification. Within a culture, of course, the agreement among judges was very good. Comparing different cultures, there was also substantial agreement. The empirical problem is not that direct, however. There is more that must be known than just the apparent identification. The weight of current research and opinion has gone beyond the simple yes or no question of inherited expressions. We now find a rich literature of the patterns and development of expressions that blends the two. There is no doubt of the innate mechanisms of emotions and their social communication, and likewise there is clearer description of how those forms are modified with maturation and life experience in a culture.

A Developmental Perspective

We will summarize the work of Carroll Izard and Carol Malatesta for an overview. For citations and details, consult Izard and Malatesta (1987). They presented seven principles. First, they asserted and defended the idea that "the mechanisms of emotion expression are innate and preadapted" (p. 511).

> *Principle 1*. Innate emotion-specific neuromuscular patterns (facial expressions of basic emotions) show regularity in form and time of emergence and serve crucial adaptive functions in development.

> *Principle 2*. The pre-adaptedness of emotion-specific expressive behaviors enables the emotions systems to function independently of the cognitive system, but the interaction and interdependence of the two systems becomes more complex with development. (Izard & Malatesta, 1987, p. 501)

Infants have all of the specific muscles needed for facial expression of the basic emotions. Furthermore, the very young infant seems to be preprogrammed to display facial expression of distress, interest, disgust, and social smiling. In their next few months, expressions of anger, fear, surprise, and sadness

appear. Good evidence and argument has been presented that each of these plays an adaptive role in the infant's survival and that each appears directly from neural processes without thinking in between.

The end of their Principle 2 blends with Principle 3. Maturation and experiences shape emotion expressions.

> *Principle 3*. Biological and social forces gradually change full-face instinct-like expressions to more restricted and controlled emotion signals. (Izard & Malatesta, 1987, p. 501)

Change is possible both by additions to the conditions that set off the emotions and in how the emotions are expressed. Expressions will change in their frequency and in their range of magnitude. Younger children have more changes between discrete emotions, but as they mature, more blends of emotion expressions appear. Furthermore, expressions become compressed into fragments and minimal cues.

> *Principle 4*. An innate expression-feeling concordance ensures effective communication with the prelingual infant but learned expression regulation increases the flexibility of expression-feeling relations. (p. 501)

The fourth principle establishes a foundation of emotion: that perceiving emotional expressions as well as making them is innately connected to appropriate emotional feeling. From that foundation, we learn to manipulate our expressions so as to stimulate specific emotional feelings in others. But do we control our own emotional feelings as well, simply by controlling our expressions? Izard and Malatesta's (1987) Principle 5 addresses that.

> *Principle 5*. The socialization of emotion expressions contributes to the regulation of emotion feelings. (p. 501)

Ample evidence demonstrates that expressing an emotion influences the development of the same emotion in others. By being excited, we recruit excitement in those watching. Children watch the expressions of adults for clues to how to respond to a situation. Izard and Malatesta suggest that this power of emotions may be why most cultures have rules for moderating emotion expressions. With time, each culture teaches children its emotion-expression rules by examples and feedback. Specific patterns of development have been documented in several non-Western cultures.

> *Principle 6.* Emotion feelings are invariant over the life span but their causes and consequences change with development. (Izard & Malatesta, 1987, p. 501)

Feelings come from a specific neural pattern that provides vital sources of information about the world. Feeling patterns are part of the stability we use to know ourselves. As such, the feelings themselves do not change; it is their attachments to new cues and new action that change.

> *Principle 7.* Facial expressions and expression-feeling concordance facilitate the development of emotion-cognition relations and affective-cognitive structure. (Izard & Malatesta, 1987, p. 501)

Patterns of adult emotional life build from innate units that are elaborated in childhood experiences. At the innate root are neural patterns yielding feelings, and these are innately attached to expression, both cues from others and our own acts, primarily facial expression. These units are the mechanisms that build our emotional and motivational picture of the world and how to act in it.

Faces, Leakage, and Feedback

We return again to the old argument about facial expressions of emotion. From Izard and Malatesta's (1987) position, the question reduces to differences in how we have attached the natural emotion-feeling structures to new cues, and how we have moderated the expression of those feelings. There is no doubt that there will be cultural differences, and likewise there is no doubt that some fundamental feelings and expression-feeling concordances exist that are identical across all people. Evidence of difference is not hard to find.

Paul Ekman demonstrated both factors in a cross-cultural study. Volunteers watched two films without knowing they were being videotaped (Ekman, 1972). One film was a bland travelogue, and the other was stress-inducing. This plan was carried out with two different groups, Americans in California and Japanese in Tokyo. A very high correlation was found in facial movements of the two groups, with both making essentially the same movements at the same places in the films. In a second part, an experimenter in a white laboratory coat sat with each subject as he or she watched the stress film. The culture groups now differed; the Japanese displayed more smiling and polite facial response. When they knew they were being watched, the Japanese adopted their cultural rule of hiding from authorities their display of negative affect. Using close examination of the tapes, the researchers also found that the smile was often produced just after, and covering up, the beginnings of evidence of negative emotional expressors. Ekman calls this **leakage.** These studies show us both the normal cultural display rules and evidence of the innate expression-feeling concordance beneath them.

Returning to an idea we mentioned earlier, how does making an expression affect the emotion being felt? People can be directed to change specific face muscles, but will that form an emotion? The idea is called **facial feedback.** Interest in this question and numerous studies have appeared over the years. With the development of stronger biologically based theories such as those of Carroll Izard and Paul Ekman, the topic has had renewed interest. There now seems to be little doubt that directing people to move muscles in accord with the essence of a specific emotion, without mentioning that emotion or the emotion topic, produces strong evidence of their experiencing and feeling that emotion, and it produces appropriate differences in autonomic nervous system measures (Ekman, 1992a, 1992b; Levenson, Carstensen, Friesen, & Ekman, 1991; Levenson, Ekman, & Friesen, 1990). Paul Ekman views this as further evidence for natural patterns of expression based in physiological mechanisms resistant to being altered.

The power of this reversal of the normal flow is limited, but what is there gives some ideas of application in the normal course of emotional experience. First, making strong expressions of emotions will reinforce the ongoing experience, perhaps exaggerating and prolonging it. By adding to the cues for the event, the facial expression feedback gives support. Second, by purposefully limiting our expression, we may slow down or minimize the extent and duration of an emotional experience. By giving weak or false feedback cues from expression, some of the power of the physiological activation may be lost. Third, we may generate emotional experiences and general emotional mood by forming and holding appropriate facial expressions. The advice of "putting on a happy face" may have a biological mechanism aiding it. Similarly, presenting a scowl and angry countenance will recruit a testy and easily provoked mood. How we make ourselves look makes a difference in how we feel. Fourth, we tend to mimic the facial expressions others present. By mirroring that expression, we come to feel some of the other person's emotional experience. Sad people can make us sad because we adopt their sad look. Happy and energetic people make us smile and begin to feel happy ourselves. Some of our commonplace communication of emotion is likely rooted in facial expression feedback.

Managing Emotion Expression

Sometimes the demands of living presume a managed emotion expression. Being cheerful and uplifting is a commonplace requirement in many work settings. What are the costs and consequences of maintaining a particular emotion expression over the long

hours of a job day in and day out? How can contrary inclinations be managed? Will the expression-concordance remain or can a dissociation develop? These are topics of Arlie Hochschild's (1983) work, *The Managed Heart: Commercialization of Human Feeling.*

Hochschild focused her primary attention on the training and work of airline flight attendants, in which the business of emotion management is legendary. Corporate policy requires a pleasant flight experience for every passenger, and the attendants are the frontline employees. Their outward expressions must be positive, helpful, and friendly no matter what the situation or special provocation. Each flight attendant is encouraged to display a genuine smiling face or appropriate sympathy and concern. This skill is learned by practice until it becomes reflexive. This is surface acting where the expression is on the surface and does not necessarily reflect true feelings. But such expression will likely elicit some amount of appropriate feeling as it is put into practice. Both internal facial feedback and reflection of that expression from most passengers keeps the appropriate feeling going.

Another aspect of managed feelings and expression is a form of deep acting, a skill made famous by the art world's method acting. Attendants work themselves into the role psychologically each shift. Part of their deep acting is being ready for discordant events. They are trained and retrained in dealing with angering situations and passengers by rethinking what they mean to them. Annoying people are thought to be themselves suffering from personal tragedy and hence deserving of sympathy rather than anger. When provoked, the attendant deflects the normal response by seeing it with different causes. By changing the internal picture of the event, a different emotion feeling and expression are presented. Again, the expression is acting and amounts to corporate-policy emotion, which remains separate from the emotion and expression of the offstage self.

These managed emotions are easy when the attendant is feeling good and the passengers present no emotional problems. But that is not usually the case, and thus the job requires a heavy load of emotional labor. Both the requirements of maintaining the corporate emotion against the private emotion and the sheer length of acting time contribute to the labor. How does emotional labor change the worker? Some attendants report an increasing difficulty in separating the two emotional selves. They express doubt about which is real and report being emotionally numbed. Others report guilt over being phony or plastic in their reactions on the job. They see this as a failure of deep acting, and they resort to surface acting. They worry about becoming cynical.

Of course, not only flight attendants have emotional labor. Secretaries, salespeople, bill collectors, funeral directors, and a variety of others are essentially in the emotion-control business. Hochschild suggests that emotion management is more typical of traditionally women's work than that of men. We will explore the gender differences issue at the end of the chapter.

SECTION SUMMARY: DEVELOPMENTAL ELABORATION

Although it may not show us fundamental origins of emotion, watching children's expressions and reactions does tell us about their cognitive and emotional maturity. The growth and decline of aspects of distress, smiling, and fussiness in a child's first year give us some clues and practical advice about caring for children's emotional needs. Social referencing shows us how older children acquire emotion cues from others. The complexity of adult emotion builds from social models and self-models children slowly construct as they mature. The point is that emotion is a consequence of how children (and adults) are able to view the world.

One of the oldest conundrums of emotion is whether (facial) expressions of emotion are innate or learned. The problems in testing this question are nearly unsolvable, but the general evidence suggests that a few basic categories of expression seem to have universal emotional meaning. Carroll Izard and Carol Malatesta defend the idea that there is an innate, unchangeable, two-way connection between feeling and expression, at least in these simplest cases. Although we may alter our expression, we cannot destroy the original feeling-expression connections. Evidence comes from studies that show leakage of natural expression into controlled expressions. Furthermore, there is at least some, although weak evidence of facial feedback, wherein voluntarily making elements of an expression produces corresponding feelings and nervous system changes. This gives foundation to common advice: Act the way you want to feel and the way you want others to feel. The practice of managing one's feelings then becomes a social skill, an important part of some vocations.

CULTURAL ORDER

We turn now to a different kind of theory. In cultural contexts, some of the "nothing-but" aspects of the theories lurk more deeply. Because the focus of these approaches is closer to the stuff of daily experience and communication, there is pressure to think of them as more "real" or "true to life" than those theories relying on some neural process of emotion. In the cognitive and the social context, emotion is typically seen as part of a mature, well-functioning member of society. Theorists believe that experiences of emotion are events of normal social life.

Without a narrative in a social context, it is difficult to communicate emotion. Body changes, unique feelings, or facial expressions and movements have little or no role in the story except as they are a part of the communication language of that kind of experience. Human narratives and stories make up the core of the communication, and the listener responds with an understanding of the emotion. These kinds of observations lead to a focus on the cognitive and social settings that make up real emotional experience. The flow of the narrative naturally evokes appropriate emotional experience (although the conditions and mechanism of this are not discussed). Stories provoking our emotion can be in the happenings of the moment, or they can be supplemented by representations in language or other media. It is being in that provoking social context that constitutes the emotion.

Cognitive and Social Theories

Cognitive appraisal is one term for assessing situation elements that make a social happening an emotional experience. Such appraisals are natural and continuous in human functioning. A change in emotional experience can be introduced into a situation by natural events, by listening to a narrative, or by observing the examples of others. The emotion that results reflects the perceived happening along with how one is a part of it.

Richard Lazarus's Cognitive Appraisal

Richard Lazarus and his colleagues believe that emotion is a life process of perceiving and interpreting the flow of environmental events. In their early studies, they examined the role of mental states in the social narratives that make up emotions. One way they did that was by introducing interpretations of

film portrayals of life situations. In an initial study, volunteers watched two silent films. First, they saw a depiction of daily farming life (*Corn Farming in Iowa*), which was presumed to be only mildly arousing. Then, they saw a motion picture showing boys in an Australian primitive culture receiving cuts on their genitals with a sharpened stone (*Subincision*). Watchers appeared to be upset by the second film. Their disturbance was revealed by measures of skin conductance and heart rate, by interview results, and by mood checklists (Lazarus, Speisman, Mordkoff, & Davison, 1962).

In a second study (Speisman, Lazarus, & Mordkoff, 1964), different sound tracks were put with the disturbing film: trauma, denial, and intellectualization. The trauma commentary emphasized the horror and pain experienced by the boys. The denial commentary stated that the rite was not painful and was a happy experience for them. The intellectualization commentary gave technical description without emotional reference. Those watching with the trauma sound track showed greater indication of aroused emotions than those having no sound track at all, and those watching with the defensive sound tracks of denial and intellectualization had the least emotional response. Emotional experience appeared to be reduced by ideas that oppose what seems to be happening.

Another study (Lazarus & Alfert, 1964) showed even greater reduction of emotional activity if the denial message was given before the film. These experiments vividly illustrated the power of cognitive contributions to alter the intensity and quality of emotional experience. Specific emotional experience was established by structuring the viewers' thoughts.

Lazarus and Alfert (1964) labeled the process of linking cognitions to specific emotional experience as one of cognitive appraisal. In later developments of this view, Lazarus and his colleagues have added the processes of coping and reappraisal as aspects of an unfolding life experience (Lazarus & Folkman, 1984). Emotions are patterns of events that develop from the appraisal of situations and resources, attempts to cope with those situations, and continuous reappraisals and coping.

Lazarus and his colleagues have been particularly critical of past and present ideas of emotion as a thing with specific causes and powers (Lazarus, Coyne, & Folkman, 1984). To assert emotion to be an entity, they believe, is little more than holding that some aspects of acts define an emotion and that the presence of the so-defined emotion explains those acts. What is missing is an understanding of the actual origins of the labeled acts. It is easy, but circular, to hold that emotion is just a drive, a state of arousal, or a pattern of physiological measures without an explanation of their sources in social events. Emotions as concept entities or patterns of measures allow splendid empirical study of relations but make no progress on the basic question of the real nature of emotion in life events. They also believe that it is not necessary to dismiss the idea of emotion altogether (Brown & Farber, 1951) or to call it simply a strong motivation (Duffy, 1962) as some have done.

Cognition Plus Arousal

One of the most famous recent ideas of emotion led to an attempt to show that the intensity and labeling of an emotional experience is the result of a cognitive appraisal of that experience and that the same sympathetic nervous system action arises from all such emotional appraisals. This theory has been widely accepted by cognitive theorists and has been enshrined in textbook accounts of the experiments purported to prove it.

Stanley Schachter and Jerome Singer presented these ideas in a paper in 1962. In their words,

> Given a state of physiological arousal for which an individual has no immediate explanation, he will "label" this state and describe his feelings in terms of the cognitions available to him. To the extent that cognitive factors are potent determiners of emotional states, it could be anticipated that precisely the same state of physiological arousal could be labeled "joy" or "fury" or "jealousy" or any of a great diversity of emotional labels depending on the cognitive aspects of the situation. (pp. 381-382)

> Given the same cognitive circumstances, the individual will react emotionally or describe his feelings as emotions only to the extent that he experiences a state of physiological arousal. (p. 382)

Schachter and Singer aroused the sympathetic nervous system with injections of epinephrine but told the volunteers it was a vitamin to be tested for its effects on their vision. Others, in control conditions getting the same social treatment, received placebo injections of a neutral solution. With each person in a room, waiting for the effects of the "vitamin" to develop, was another (a confederate of the experimenter) who, for some volunteers, carried out an act of playing in a humorous fashion with the paper and materials in the room. In other experimental conditions, volunteers were asked to answer questions on a form during the waiting period, and the confederate began a display of anger about the insulting nature of the questions. (They *were* insulting.) The volunteers who received epinephrine reported more euphoria or anger than those who got the placebo. Variations on this plan were carried out in other experiments by Schachter and his colleagues as well as others. The general agreement has been that these experiments show that the labeling of the emotion and its perceived strength depend on the general arousal of the sympathetic nervous system.

If we take a critical stance, we can see logical problems with both Schachter and Singer's theory and with the interpretation of the experiments themselves. One way to illustrate these problems is in contrast with William James's (1884, 1890) body-reaction theory. James asserted that the emotion *is* the pattern of body reactions to an ongoing situation. Schachter and Singer hold that emotion is a cognitive appraisal to which a non-unique body reaction has occurred. The problem for Schachter and Singer is how to account for the source of the body reaction that does occur. On what basis is a body reaction aroused from one appraisal and not from another? Schachter and Singer, along with most cognitive theorists, have given up the "natural reaction" ground that James used. Instead, they have supposed that a cognition develops it all.

The problem is left unsolved, but according to the cognition-plus-arousal theory, a real-life emotional situation must evoke both a label and a body reaction. On what basis is the body reaction produced? In those situations that do give body reactions, Schachter and Singer believe that the pattern of arousal is always the same. If so, what role does it play? An answer might be that body arousal marks the intensity of the reaction. But why is body reaction needed at all? If all informative content of the emotional experience comes from the cognitive appraisal, what information is added by the body response? Particularly, the assumption of a common body arousal flies in the face of what we know of brain and body systems of arousal, emotion, and feelings. Schachter and Singer's cognition plus arousal oversimplifies the body events in emotion.

Logical tangles abound in purely cognitive views of emotional experience. Although some theorists have essentially denied that there are any body feelings at all in what people call emotion, they typically illustrate those ideas with emotion concepts such as envy or loneliness, which are deeply entrenched in complex social relations and for which the feeling components are said to be less clear or to have less "heat." That work has value in sorting out the social narrative bases of the richness of emotional experience, but it denies the primary problem of accounting for the experience and role of such feelings in the classical emotional situations. The soft spot in the cognitive views is their handling of the facts of the body feelings of emotional experience.

Social Construction

Social constructionism theorists have developed alternative approaches to aspects of psychology for several decades. Their label effectively summarizes their approach. They try to picture our functioning as a construction of existing social events. By doing that, they have reminded us of the complexity of social factors bearing on our lives. In their excesses, they have proposed we reject any structural stability or search for timeless laws of our functioning. In place of those laws, they propose a descriptive account of the social appearances of the moment. In extreme form, emotion would be just another social interaction process, formed entirely of shifting social forces.

The immediate data for social constructionists' study of emotions are the words and meanings by which we communicate the situations we face, our thoughts and feelings about them, and the actions we deem appropriate and sometimes produce. Emotion situations are thought about and compared, and the material of that thought is descriptive language. Social constructionists approach emotion by studying accounts using language.

Social life is a part of emotion that cannot be ignored. Without social narrative, emotions become trivial events. Theorists who have developed this fundamental assumption into the next step are social constructionists. Social constructionists view emotion as a collection of ways of interpreting and acting on social situations. In this view, emotions are not things. There is not an entity called anger, for example, but there are angry individuals in angering scenes. Social constructionists believe emotions are labels for happenings with affect, not for something one has.

Social constructionists assume that emotional experience is a matter of responding to and reflecting the rules and norms of one's society. Emotions are labels for what one is doing. Although not independent of biological elements, emotional experience depends primarily on evolution of one's culture and on the social structure that now exists. The word *anger* means just what people in a real social world use it to mean. These ideas are illustrated by social philosopher Rom Harré, who describes the components of adult emotional life.

Rom Harré's Conditions

Rom Harré (1986) describes three conditions that typically define the use of an emotion word. First, there is some form of physiological disturbance, or **bodily agitation,** as he calls it. This disturbance is not sufficient, however, to define the use of different emotion words. Second, there is some form of **intentionality.** Emotions are "about" something. People are fearful *of,* sad *about,* proud *of,* or joyful *because.* Emotions cannot exist without intentions and intentional objects. One is not angry or grieved except in a social context. Third, emotion words only make sense in some sort of **social or moral order.** The emotional experiences are based on systems of rights, duties, and obligations and other social systems of personal evaluation. The emotion words come from language that reflects human moral order. Harré sees emotional experience as a matter of having bodily agitation while intentionally acting in a moral order.

James Averill's Rules Approach

James Averill (1980, 1982, 1984) has written the most detailed social constructivist theory of emotion. In that theory, he has given a logical system of the type and scope of emotion rules that are followed. He uses an analogy to a complex task like playing chess to illustrate the system. Averill proposes three types of rules (constitutive, regulative, and heuristic) and four scopes of rules (appraisal, behavior, prognosis, and attribution) in his game metaphor of emotion. This division is meant only to separate some dimensions of emotional experience to aid in its study; it is not proposed to be an exact analysis to account for all of emotional reality.

Constitutive rules are those that make up the fixed plan. The rules of chess are established, and in playing, we do not alter them. Constitutive rules of emotion form the fundamental appropriateness of the experience in a situation. We "fear" objects that present danger, not harmless objects like flowers. We "enjoy" the close attentions of others; we do not "grieve" over those attentions. "Anger" is the proper emotional experience to another's purposeful blocking of a life goal; we do not experience "envy" during that event. We see these constitutive rules when they are violated by individuals whose emotional learning has been deficient or seriously disturbed; the bizarre appearance of emotional actions illustrates the normal social rules.

Additional rules, such as time limits for a chess move and constraints on permitted distractions, are **regulative.** These may be transient or relatively permanent fixtures of the activity, but they only change the way the game is played. They do not change the nature of the game as it is constituted. Expressions of emotional experience are regulative. The patterns of changing face expression, gestures, body posture, and verbalizations regulate the flow of the experience.

Heuristic rules are plans and schemes for playing the game and involve the process of improving our success with experience. With life experience we use heuristic rules to refine the ways we interpret situations emotionally, respond to them, define their time course and conclusion, and explain the occurrences to ourselves. We may learn to suppress anger experiences in traffic events. It is not really an attack when another driver steers a car close in front of ours; it is not appropriate to seek revenge. Psychotherapists make a good business in emotional "skills training" to help people to develop heuristic rules to interpret and respond to situations more adaptively.

Appraisal rules of scope interpret and evaluate the situation. In emotional experience, we use appraisal rules to assess the instigation, the target, and the response goal. **Behavior** rules include the organized responses one uses. Actions, including mental experience and physiological happenings, are set by behavior rules of expression. Rules of **prognosis** include the time course and consequences of the action. Rules of **attribution** are the connections we hold between the instigation, our actions, and our self. Attributions are the ways that the experience is accounted for in a social and a personal context.

The three types and the four scopes of rules can be crossed to determine a matrix of 12 combinations for analysis, for example, constitutive appraisal rules, heuristic prognosis rules, and so on. Only some of these logical categories of rules of emotion experience have been examined in detail. They may not all be important. Specific emotional experiences may use some forms of rules more heavily than others. For example, Averill notes that grief depends heavily on rules of prognosis, envy on regulation, and love on heuristics. It is not likely that all of the theoretical cells of the matrix will have meaning for each emotional situation. It does provide a way to separate different functioning components of what makes up an emotional experience, and it takes into account the changing nature of the individual's emotional life.

Social constructionists see emotions as more than static events. Change is typical in emotional experience. We acquire new emotions (like pragmatic love), refine the nature of many others (like what makes us angry or jealous), and mute others. There is a continuous development of some but not all features of emotion experience through life. The social constructivist view, by emphasizing the life context of emotional experience, connects emotion to the experiences we live.

Gender Expectations

Part of the culture of emotion is different gender roles. What do we commonly believe about men's and women's emotion? Men are expected to have different control over their emotional experiences than women, men's permitted emotions are viewed as more positive and less dangerous than those of women, and men's emotions are thought to be formed by events, whereas women's are said to result from biological determination. These are the cultural patterns that we accept, both men and women. Like many of our ideas, these are thought to have been proven by scientific studies. We don't yet have good evidence of the reality. As long-standing cultural patterns, they may have an element of evolutionary adaptation in them. It may be also be that such

beliefs are merely cultural and political positions that have been corroborated by scientists who wanted to find them. Or both may be partially true. For the moment, we explore the cultural stereotypes and then some of the social science evidence.

Emoting Women and Stoic Men

The social fact seems to be a double standard (Shields, 1987). Women are believed to be more emotional, and that is held against them in the work world. At the same time, they are expected to express those emotions more than men, except in the case of anger. Digging deeper, we find other deviance from the rule. Women's emotions are expected to be primarily passive, reactive, and dependent in form, but not expansive and outgoing. A woman is expected to show happiness, but not an active sense of humor. She may show feelings of fear but not of superiority.

The idea that emotion must be controlled is part of the shared Western culture of men and women. Emotionality has become one of the ways that power is evidenced, and there is no strength revealed in withdrawal displays of emotion. The power one has to control emotion is thought to be partly a matter of one's gender. Women withdraw into emotion and therefore are weaker, whereas men mark their strength by controlling their emotion, except when a particular kind of expression serves a power purpose. The tie to social power is not accidental. Emotional roles mark gender differences in power.

The language of this description illustrates the assumed reality. Women's typical emotion is a matter of withdrawing into themselves, falling apart, losing control, or resorting to tears. Men's socially approved emotion is, for example, an outward display of anger to dominate or control a situation. Men (Real Men) do not act the woman's emotional role, and women who act a man's emotional role are said to be cold and "bitchy." Part of the explanation for our cultural gender differences is rooted in some biological theories we have assumed.

Women's "Dangerous" Internal Biology

By first assuming that women are *naturally* emotional, scientists then look for the biological causes. If women's emotion is rooted in female body functions, then a certain fatalism results. The obvious female biology on which to focus is that of reproduction and motherhood. A premenstrual syndrome (PMS) can be defined as a disease caused by cycles of hormones. Although there is little doubt that many women experience varying levels of pains and cramping during this period, its extent and generality have been questioned. Critical studies of the mood disturbances and emotional responsiveness in the premenstrual period also have been shown to lack strong evidence (Archer & Lloyd, 1985; Fausto-Sterling, 1985). Some of the identification of the syndrome relies on women's reports of their condition. Those reports reflect their knowing the cultural wisdom in connecting their female hormones and their emotion. In short, some women report what they know they are expected to report, and their PMS can be used as an excuse for other personal and social acts.

In a more general vein, women are assumed to be more emotional by cultural tradition. Biological gender differences are sought to illustrate how emotion is tied to their generally smaller and weaker bodies, which are periodically disturbed by waves of hormones. This makes them weak and potentially dangerous if they cannot control themselves.

Catherine Lutz (1990) illustrates these ideas in structured conversations she had with individual men and women about their emotions. Women speak more often than men about the need to control their emotions and how their emotions may be a danger to themselves and their families. But more important, they have accepted the cultural theory that they are more emotional and that there is a need for constant striving to control their expressed feelings.

Western Gender Roles of Emotion

A fairly brief summary statement can be made of differences in emotion expression, experience, and recognition between men and women following a recent analysis (Brody & Hall, 1993). Women express more intensity in their emotional experience, report a greater variety of emotion, and are better at recognizing emotion in others—with these exceptions. Men are stronger in expressing and recognizing anger, pride, and contempt.

SECTION SUMMARY:
CULTURAL ORDER

Cognitive and social context theorists see emotion as a part of normal life narratives. Their focus is on identifying emotional kinds of life situations. Richard Lazarus showed that different emotional reactions emerge when instructions give social events altered interpretations. The key element here is the appraisal we make. Stanley Schachter and Jerome Singer showed that people will exaggerate their emotional responses and feelings when their sympathetic nervous system is excited by a drug. Their conclusion, widely accepted, was that emotion was nothing but a cognition that has been "aroused." This cognitive approach sidesteps the real question of what sort of events naturally evoke the elevated arousal and why.

Social construction theorists build emotion from life narratives following systems of rules. Rom Harré suggests emotional narratives can be identified from bodily agitation, intentionality (aboutness), and a system of social/moral order. James Averill elaborated that social/moral order in terms of the rules by which we operate. In an analogy with games, he suggests that we have rules that constitute, regulate, and develop emotions. Emotions exist in the flow of life according to meeting and breaking these rules.

Some of the more interesting social rules of emotion are those that traditionally separate men and women. Modern Western thought holds women to be more openly expressive of their emotions and the experts on things emotional.

CHAPTER CONCLUSIONS

Emotion is a difficult topic to study because it is so commonplace in our thought and language. We also have strong ambivalence about the value and necessity of emotion. We see emotionality as weakness, and Western thought regularly describes the best logic to be unemotional. The reality may be that there is no human activity without undertones or overtones of emotion. Our brains work the emotional systems constantly and every function, especially logic, works to respect the emotional value of the current contents. To be human is to be emotional.

Yet, we try to devalue emotion and make it be "nothing but" some piece or other of a psychological and physiological system of information. From being just a judgment, an inherited function, a brain structure, or a place, to being a social narrative, a cognition, or a set of social rules, our theories try to minimize emotion by simplifying it. From the theory collection, however, a pattern of information has been emerging that gives emotion a central place in our lives. And that is where we really knew it was all along.

Study and Review Questions

1. What three components make up an emotion, in the traditional view?

2. What did William James claim an emotion to be?

3. What makes an emotion for philosopher Robert Solomon?

4. What are the six most commonly listed primary emotions?

5. What do emotions do in inherited function theories?

6. What is an "affect programme" in Paul Ekman's view?

7. On what are emotions based in Robert Plutchik's theory?

8. With what kind of scheme did Robert Plutchik picture relations among emotions?

9. How did behaviorist John Watson theorize the formation of adult emotional life?

10. In what nervous system did Walter Cannon believe emotions are activated?

11. What are Paul MacLean's triune brain categories, and in which is emotion located?

12. Where in the brain are Jaak Panksepp's command circuits, and how are they formed?

13. What was the error in watching children to see when different emotions first appeared?

14. When do children show fear of strangers?

15. What is "social referencing" of emotion?

16. What is meant by Izard and Malatesta's "innate expression-feeling concordance?"

17. What does Carroll Izard believe emotional "leakage" tells us?

18. What happens in "facial feedback" of emotions?

19. What do cognitive and social context theorists believe an emotion to be?

20. What does a cognitive appraisal do in a potentially emotion-arousing situation?

21. What three conditions are necessary for an emotion, according to Rom Harré?

22. What kind of metaphor does James Averill use to describe the complexity of emotion?

23. In James Averill's view, what kind of rule defines the basic nature of each emotion?

24. In traditional Western culture, how is women's use of emotion different from men's?

25. How do men and women differ in emotion expression, experience, and recognition?

CHAPTER 5

Anger and Aggression

Fighting is exciting, but we claim not to like it. Aggression and violence are part of the way things are. Although our history, our cultures, and our ancestors' adaptations may support many anger and aggression tendencies, we want them controlled.

Psychologists have followed the obvious link of anger and aggression. Some kind of emotional arousal seems to be a part of aggression, and those feelings play a strong role in its excitement and its control.

Aggressive acts affect others. We build our selfhood and manage our affairs by a style of aggressive tendencies that defines us. Rules of anger and aggression are part of our enduring culture, but with gender differences.

Because aggressive acts are clearly physical and done by many species, we look for natural causes to excuse them. The "beast within" is sought in brain function, neurochemistry, and genetic heritage. Lessons from animal study have been especially influential but are often misleading.

Aggression Ideas

Physical Foundations for Aggression

Emotional Aggressive Acts

Anger

Instrumental Aggressive Acts

Learning Anger and Aggression

Few topics are as rousing and confusing at the same time as one person intentionally hurting another. We won't try to analyze what is exciting about such aggressive acts right away, but we must focus on the confusion. All books on aggression begin with a chapter or long preface trying to define what the word *aggression* means. Of course they don't agree, or they would each need only a short paragraph.

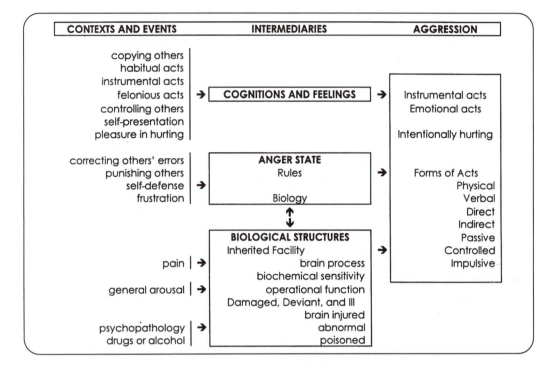

Figure 5.1. A graphic summary of the elements of human aggression.

Some of the confusion comes from the particular points of view about aggression the authors defend. Each tries to make the concept fit most closely the kind of aggression he has emphasized. That is understandable. Confusion about labels is not an unfamiliar topic for us. How might we sort it out this time?

AGGRESSION IDEAS

We will try to picture the many facets of aggression before we approach the mystery of what aggression really is. Some of the complexity can be seen in the spatial array in Figure 5.1. This picture gives an overview that may make the whole problem easier to grasp. The column of "contexts and events" contains the kinds of situations that provoke aggression. Each of these has been given serious attention. "Intermediaries" are the emotional states and biological conditions often

discussed as part of the cause of aggressive acts. The "aggression" column shows some ways of categorizing the aggressive acts themselves. Many of the items and links shown in the figure are topics examined in the chapter. As we look at separate topics, we won't shrink from the arguments; but alas, neither will we settle them. At the start, we should accept the truth that there is no one, true aggression.

Defining Aggression

Which of the following do you think are aggressive acts? Three-year-old Marilyn pushes Danny and takes the sand shovel. Barry pulls abruptly into the next lane of cars. Terry yanks a weed from the flower bed. Barbara shoots a squirrel. Carleen sets a land mine along the enemy's road. Nancy throws a frying pan at her husband. Winnifred puts exceptional energy into raising the factory's production level. George, a dismissed employee, plans acts of revenge. Ronald turns away from a seedy-looking customer. Maggie watches as children throw broken bottles into the road. Which of these are aggressive, and which are not? What are the rules for using the label a*ggression*?

The phrase *aggressive acts* has a variety of meanings to theorists. For some users, aggression implies an unconscious source of acts. Whether following an evolutionary heritage thesis or a psychoanalytic model, they believe that it is in the nature of people to produce aggressive acts, and they may also believe fatalistically that there is little that can be done to control those urges. To others, aggression means attacking and hostile actions, like the prototypical out-of-control angry person intending to inflict harm. The intention and the result is to harm another person and, in extremity, do violence. Still another view is that aggression labels a certain style of act. Such aggressive styles are nearly synonymous with high motivation. An executive is said to have an aggressive management style. We describe basketball players as aggressive in shooting. These and similar meanings imply that one person is acting to gain an advantage or achieve superiority over others.

At least some of the differences in defining aggression seem to come from whether aggression is seen as "a force producing harmful or violent acts" or as "a result of conditions and events" that have occurred. An extreme biological theorist may be more comfortable with aggression as a force or function that is primed and often engaged. An extreme social context position accepts some kinds of acts from social encounters as being usefully labeled aggressive. Still another position may propose an intermediary state of anger as the key to eliciting aggressive acts in a social encounter. These, of course, do not exhaust the possibilities.

Some aggressive acts are socially admired, whereas others are generally condemned. Evaluation of action fragments depends upon social aspects of the situation and of the evaluator. An act is seen as aggressive if the victims are "not willingly partici-pating or deserving of punishment." Thus, some theorists insert the idea of the aggression target being an unwilling participant. The winner in a boxing match is not condemned by sports enthusiasts as an aggressor, but exactly the same actions against a passer-by in the street would be thought a heinous mugging. People of more genteel thought might see both events as aggressive violence. The personal judgment we make depends on how we perceive the situation and how that relates to our accepted value systems.

Many psychologists define aggressive acts as those *intended* to hurt others. We will stay close to that tradition. A broader conception of aggression might add this language to the definition: "those acts intended to provoke conflict or to secure an increased competitive advantage." These additions are part of our social use of the aggression label, but many believe it wise to leave them out of our natural science approach to aggression, at least for now. There is a useful coherence to acts intended to hurt others, and it has been a good initial strategy to focus research efforts on them, leaving aside other possibilities.

An immediate and serious problem surrounds the word *intend*. How do we know when there is an intention? Is it enough that someone is hurt or that there is violence? What if 4-year-old Betty knocks down Cathy's sand castle and then says that she didn't mean to do it? The intention is denied, and that denial is plausible. We have all had experience with actions that unintentionally hurt others. We don't usefully call them aggressive because they fail to have what we know to be important, the element of intention.

On the other hand, aggression exists sometimes solely in thoughts of intending to hurt. The dismissed employee plans revenge. The only signs of aggression are the intentional thoughts. Thoughts of intending to hurt are the critical part of the motivational complex. But not all intentions to hurt get directly expressed, for one reason or another. Ineffective or neutralized aggressive intentions are made obvious in the Pink Panther movies or the Road Runner cartoons. Wiley E. Coyote intends to hurt the Road Runner but never succeeds. Inferring intentions is not easy.

In still other situations, we intentionally do violence but without an intention to hurt. Physicians cut and destroy tissue or stimulate pain in various therapies. Hunters kill animals. These examples reveal that the intention concept has two components. The specific act is not accidental—it was intended—but it was not intended to hurt.

In human psychology, aggression is primarily social. The implication of being socially founded is that fragments of hostile acts become meaningful when seen as part of an interaction among people. The concept of intention to hurt only makes sense in social relations. Harm or damage by itself, although interesting, is not evidence of aggression. People commonly speak of violent acts toward animals or property, for example, but these only become meaningful as aggressive acts if the recipients are identified as having human-like capacities or are the property of humans. With life experience, we may attach aggression to things and events other than people, but the roots are in intentions to hurt other people. Practical and efficient research strategy focuses on these basics.

Forms of Aggressive Acts

We routinely appraise specific situations. In each social arena, we try to calculate the consequences of our actions against those of others. There are many ways to be aggressive. Our intent to harm may be direct, indirect, or passive. The form of expression in each of these can be either physical or verbal action. The direct forms of aggressive acts require no special analysis because they are the obvious examples we think of as aggression. Any form of indirect or passive aggressive act requires some thought and analysis to understand the true aggressive nature of it.

We are good at skills of deception. That is, anyone can intend to harm while apparently doing acceptable things, causing actual harm without seeming to be responsible. Deception and related social skills are apparent in some common forms of aggressive acts. Practical jokes and gossip are not usually seen to be the aggressive acts that they are. The joker often claims to be just "having fun" or "telling good stories," harboring no ill will toward the victims. Such is the deception.

Passive aggression is one form of these subtle situations. In passive aggression, we act according to selected social rules, but the outcome is a damaging, aggressive act. Michele Cole (1980) made an interesting popular study of passive aggression, which she published under the title *Violent Sheep: The Tyranny of the Meek.* She begins with one of the indicators of passive aggression: the disguise by the aggressor that she calls the "whoops factor." People try to rationalize their passive aggressive acts with cover-ups such as "I didn't mean it," "Don't take it personally," "Anyone can make a mistake," and "It seemed like a good idea at the time."

Cole then works through a series of individual strategies of passive aggression she labels "violent sheep." A couple of examples will do. The type she calls "The Lummox" creates destruction by consistently being clumsy. "The Conspicuous Nonassumer" is one who lets violence happen and claims a cover-up philosophy about it. This person sees preschool kids fighting with a broken bottle and of course does nothing, saying parents should supervise their children. Seeing a burglar breaking into a neighbor's house, the conspicuous nonassumers claim to mind their own business. "The Babes" make people want to rescue them. They ask others to do things for them, feigning inability or ignorance. With time and a willing victim, they escalate the demands. If they are refused, they reject the person totally. Finally, "The Gentle Provocateur" provokes for the pleasure of immediate antagonism. This is the person who tells the accident victim to have a nice day or offers chocolate cake to dieters and makes them feel guilty if they refuse.

SECTION SUMMARY:
AGGRESSION IDEAS

There is no one "real" or "true" aggression. Aggression amounts to a fuzzy complex of life events that includes various contexts, intermediary states, and actions. Narrowing this complexity into scientifically manageable content, we assume that human aggression is intent to harm others. Aggressive acts vary from unfulfilled intentions to passively allowing things to happen to taking direct action against a perceived provoking source.

PHYSICAL FOUNDATIONS
FOR AGGRESSION

Anger and aggression are thoroughly a part of the way we are and of our social history. Their consistency and resistance to control suggest they are part of our design. In this section, we will explore some theoretical ideas about that design.

We have deep-seated beliefs about acting aggressively, founded in the aggregate of Western cultural history. Some are the male-oriented rules about using aggression. These beliefs and others are collected in "the myth of the beast within," which we believe to be part of human nature (Klama, 1988).

Jeffrey Goldstein (1989) lists these seven beliefs common in Western thought.

- We are instinctively aggressive.

- Expressing anger is healthy.

- Aggressive urges can be released in substitute activities.

- Children will be better behaved if they play aggressively to "get it out of their systems."

- Violent acts typically come from the mentally ill.

- Violence comes from an unusually strong aggressive drive.

- War is an unavoidable expression of our aggression instinct.

At the root of these beliefs is a mechanical theme. In holding them, we believe that aggression is part of our physical nature, that aggression is caused by something inside us, and that until we learn enough to change our bodies, we must provide some relief for its insistent urges. These prejudices share responsibility for making aggression acceptable and accountable. They allow us to assign responsibility to something else for our feared and disliked aggressive acts. If these things are a part of "human nature," then we are in a sense free of responsibility for their having happened. "I couldn't help doing it, I'm only human." We examined these ideas in Chapter 1.

Biological Structures

We have provided considerable evidence that aggression is not "nothing but biology." Nonetheless, biological mechanisms do underlie the fragments that make up aggressive actions. Kenneth Moyer (1985) proposes a working biological model. He assumes that we have neural systems that result in aggressive acts toward specific targets. The key to the action of these systems is in both the body conditions and situations faced. Normally, however, most unrestrained, reflex-like aggression is prevented or controlled.

Is there a biology of anger or aggression? How can we know if there is, and what it is? These questions are not easily answered. Furthermore, we must be wary of assuming that physiological fragments are aggression's true essence. We must also be wary of holding a simplistic philosophy that prejudices our view of links between aggressive acts and physiological events.

Brain Functions

In animal studies, the limbic system has been shown to be involved in fragments of aggressive acts. The limbic system (see the description and Figure 2.4 in Chapter 2 for a review) is a set of nervous structures appearing in cross-section like a letter *C,* making up the juncture of the brain stem and the cerebral cortex (*limbus* in Latin means border). It includes portions of the thalamus and hypothalamus, upper portions of the brain stem, and inner surfaces of the cerebral cortex. Named areas include the hippocampus, hippocampal gyrus, cingulum, and amygdala. Stimulation has produced attacking actions in many animals (e.g., Egger & Flynn, 1963). The target of the aggressive act is very specific, and that is quite important. The aggressive acts are narrow and unique parts of each species' repertoire. No generalized or unfocused attacking comes from limbic system stimulation.

Human studies are, of course, rarely experimental. Brain function is typically studied from accidents, disease, and exploratory surgery. What is known from these sources provokes continued study. A few patients with electrodes in the amygdala responded to stimulation with hostility, threats, and aggressive acts (King, 1961; Marks, Ervin, & Sweet, 1972). Yet, amygdala stimulation given to each of 80 temporal lobe epileptics did not yield any aggressive feelings or acts. Most sensations were related to body functions, general confusion, or nothing at all. A few reported fear (Jasper & Rasmussen, 1958).

Some hints about feelings underlying anger were given in studies that catalogued reports from people having epileptic brain seizures localized in the limbic system. Paul MacLean (1970) sorted the feelings into six categories: desire, fear, anger, sadness, affection, and gratulance (composed of gratification, triumph, success, and ecstasy). Other analyses examined the records of 100 people out of a total population of 2,100 having emotional content in their epileptic seizures. Of these 100, 61 showed fear, 21 showed depression, and the rest were spread over various other emotions (Ervin & Martin, 1986). There seems to be little evidence of spontaneous (epileptic) brain stimulation of the anger feeling.

Clinical studies of brain pathology are another source of clues. However, such studies give questionable evidence for obvious reasons: (a) lack of control over or knowledge of the person, (b) the fact that people with pathologies are likely to have correlated abnormalities of both their biological and psychological conditions, and (c) the lack of comparison data. Striking cases are held out as examples. The idea comes from (and is then strengthened by) striking, apparently clear instances linking specific pathology and violent aggression. In fact, there is no isolation of conditions that would justify a conclusion of cause. Another potentially misleading method (e.g., Moyer, 1985) is to describe many different cases and summary statistics without giving details of exact conditions or comparisons against base-rate frequencies of similarly disordered people who are not aggressive. Such information is one-sided and makes a poor base for understanding.

Consider the often-reported case of student Charles Whitman at the University of Texas in 1966 (Johnson, 1970). After some attempt to report his feelings to health professionals, he killed his mother and wife and then climbed to the top of the university tower and killed 14 people with his rifle, wounding 24 others before being killed himself by gunshot. He suspected a physical cause and asked in a letter written beforehand that he be examined. A malignant tumor was found in the temporal lobe area of the limbic system, but exact details were confounded by his gunshot brain wound. What might be concluded? Are there conditions in this individual case that mitigate the quick conclusion that temporal lobe tumors cause violent aggression?

Whitman's familiarity and experience with shooting and rifles was necessary for the violence to be carried out. How strong were those tendencies, and what might they indicate about his psychological tendency to use shooting acts when he felt badly? How might his developing physical discomfort have contributed to a general condition of irritability, which, in turn, magnified his tendency to act out his violent thoughts? What if Whitman had killed himself in private; would his case have even been noticed? These questions reflect lack of control or observation of the supporting conditions, and that lack of control severely limits the conclusions that we can make.

What records are there of people with similar tumors? There are certainly many of them. With what frequency are there exhibitions of aggression resulting from such tumors? Kenneth Moyer (1985, p. 87) reports a study by Sano of 297 people with tumors in the limbic system. Sano's reported conclusion was that there was increased irritability and rage attacks, but quantitative data were not given. A few other positive instances are given but without examination of negatives and base rates.

Another clinical study has been made of intentional destruction of parts of the limbic system. It involved 128 epileptic people with aggressiveness and hyperactivity. Their amygdalas were removed with the result that 9 had greatly reduced violence, some improvement was shown in 45, and the other 75 showed little change (Balasubramaniam, Ramanujam, Kanaka, & Ramamurth, 1972). This does show a weak link, but it is still not clear evidence for an aggression brain center in undiseased people. Especially noteworthy is anatomical study showing that the limbic areas are richly and complexly connected to the cerebral cortex, suggesting that there is extensive cognitive control in place over the limbic areas.

Our common idea of the brain is formed on what we know of modern machinery having computational "brains." We quietly borrow the implication that we, like these machines, have a fixed computational brain that receives inputs and produces behavior. Let us consider with Pierre Karli (1991) that the "function" of our brain is engaging in a dialogue with the environment, and this life-long dialogue has literally made our brain out of some early genetic potentialities of inheritance. Events, reactions, and feedback actually form the nature of the functions we have. The evidence for physical malleability throughout life has been well documented. The point is that there will be no nerve bundles or areas that have not been developed (or altered) by experiences. Some of these developed functions, or potentials for functions, have been selected by consequences to be part of our inheritance, but many have not. None escapes having been formed by necessities of use. In a physical sense, what we have done as individuals forms what we do and that in turn forms what we will do. In this view, aggressive acts may have a specific physical base, but that base comes from an individual's history, not a fixed design. We should not be surprised that there are no simple "centers of aggression" or critical areas for aggressive acts. The reality is complexity and diversity of physical vehicles of aggressive acts, and few of these will be pieces of inheritance.

Neurochemistry

Neurochemistry holds some distinct possibilities of physical influences on aggressive acts. Three categories of neurochemistry have been suggested to play a role: neurotransmitters, hormones, and chemical poisoning. We must be wary of undue simplicity here also.

The neurotransmitters thought to have some function in emotional and aggressive acts are serotonin, norepinephrine, and dopamine. These are present in high concentration in the limbic system and are known to change with activation of that system. No easy connection has been established, however, between neurotransmitters and specific aggressive acts. Any uncomplicated picture is unlikely. Structures and enabling chemistry enabling aggressive acts probably are tied to the emotional anger (or rage) limbic systems. The cerebral cortex control normally in place makes their use depend on the provoking situation and the individual's personal characteristics. In this mix, neurochemistry is at best a weak correlate rather than a switch.

Sex hormones have also been implicated in aggressive acts. A large and diverse literature has indicated that men are more likely to show aggressive and violent acts than are women. One major source suggested for this difference is the relative proportions of male and female sex hormones. As we will note in Chapter 7, "Sexual Motivation: Politics and Biology," men have a preponderance of male hormones but some amounts of female hormones, and women have a preponderance of female hormones but some male hormones. The tendency to aggression has been thought to be the result of the amount of male hormones, androgens (and particularly testosterone), present during brain development. Evidence is indirect: correlations of aggressive acts with levels of testosterone.

1. Some study has been made of children who have had unusual levels of androgens before birth. Both girls and boys who had high therapeutic levels of androgens before birth did not show more aggressive acts than other children who were suitable controls (Money & Schwartz, 1976).

2. Studies of castrated men show no consistent reduction in aggressive acts or pacification, and even if there were such effects, there is no suitable control group against which to compare. The psychological effects of such radical surgery on their self-image could easily be the source of major changes in their choice of acts.

3. John Archer's (1991) meta-analysis of studies showed at best a very weak correlation between measured levels of testosterone and aggressive acts or feelings. Some studies find a relationship, and others do not.

4. There is evidence that levels of testosterone and other hormones actually follow environmental events. Aggressive acts lead to higher levels of testosterone and being attacked lowers the levels (Archer, 1991; Kreuz & Rose, 1972; Mattsson, Schalling, Olweus, Low, & Svensson, 1980; Mazur, 1983; Meller, 1982).

Collectively, there is no reason to believe greater testosterone directly produces aggressive acts or feelings in men or women.

Brain Dysfunctions

Abnormal brain chemistry is sometimes connected to aggressive acts. For example, people having low blood sugar (or hypoglycemia) sometimes show aggressive emotion and acts, but many do not. Others may become depressed and withdrawn. There is no simple link. Some alcoholics become aggressive and violent, but many do not. Some normally aggressive people become passive when intoxicated. It is most likely that the brain disruption from alcohol is one of distortion of brain processing, such that one's normal moral and social controls are weakened. In an aggressive environment, intoxicated people act aggressively. It is not the alcohol that produces aggressive acts physiologically (Powers & Kutash, 1978; Taylor & Leonard, 1983). Gibbs (1986) concludes that "violence is the product of certain kinds of interpersonal interactions, and alcohol affects perception and cognition in ways that make the occurrence of these kinds of interaction more likely" (p. 137). Again, the link of aggression to presumed abnormal brain chemistry is not established.

Genetic Animal Nature

Genetics has long been known to be involved in aggression. The question is not whether there are such biological tendencies. What we need to learn is exactly what is different in strains and species that show differences in aggressive acts. From there, we can proceed cautiously toward understanding our biological aggressive roots.

Animal Evidence

The most direct genetic evidence for aggressive tendencies is our ancient practice of animal husbandry. Cats, dogs, chickens, and horses have been bred for aggressiveness or its lack. By simply mating only among the most aggressive offspring, a strain of more aggressive animals can be produced in a few generations. We don't really know what physiology was changed. The selectively bred offspring have a changed functioning, but the changed structure may be different in each species. It makes no sense to think that one strain has accumulated a greater quantity of aggression.

Ethology Theory

We must now recall the cautions of biological philosophy that we introduced at the end of Chapter 1. We find it easy to believe (although it is wrong) that a function that is regularly seen in many species and seems to have a purpose must be inherited. If we have been doing something for a long time, it must be a part of human nature. Furthermore, if a reason can be found for it to have aided our ancestors' survival, it must be genetically determined. These beasts within have become clichés of mass media, included in literature, arts, movies, and public commentary. It is a cheap and easy explanation for human acts, particularly those human acts that are not easily reconciled with a genteel image of humanity and its related social morality. Aggression fits this pattern perfectly. We excuse our aggressive acts by assuming that they are an inherited part of human nature. Careless ethologists give us those excuses.

The most provocative suggestions about aggressive human nature have come from those who study animal performances. In their popular writing, animal behavior theorists (often called *ethologists*) have proposed some logical models of aggression in the animal world and have declared that these are also the biological heritage of humans. They draw their conclusions from a few analogies. They add to the popularity of these ideas by illustrating them with parallel patterns of aggressive acts of selected species. Their writings are entertaining and give simple, satisfying answers to the very complex situation of human aggression. Examples are Konrad Lorenz's *On Aggression* and Robert Ardrey's *The Territorial Imperative*, both published in 1966.

Three specific theses have been proposed in the popular writing. Ethologists have not been uniform in their support of these ideas, but the notions have all been widely promoted as truth and regularly illustrated in numerous nature programs. It is hard to present an antidote to ideas that have such a broad appeal, particularly when they also give us views to justify what we are doing. The three popular ethology theses of aggression are those of territory, dominance, and an aggressive reservoir.

Some species define and protect a specific area from others of their species. The territory may be a specific place, or it may be a shifting one based on time cues. Borders are marked by species-specific means including visual landmarks, natural or constructed; sounds; and scents. The purposes of such territories are more often presumed than proven by research. The assumed goals are logical ones, such as protection of food supplies and the like.

The normal state of animals in territories is described by the ethologists to be nonaggressive. Aggressive acts only occur when there is a disturbance at the borders that must be adjusted. Borders are established through contests, and once they are settled, peace reigns.

The means of establishing the peace is a matter of making threat displays. After a period of species-specific posturing, which involves contact that is typically not harmful, one of the contestants withdraws and signals the other with species-specific submission displays. That settles the matter, and the individuals now respect the boundary and act in characteristic ways to one another.

Other species live in social groups organized by dominance ranking. The scheme of dominance rankings is very similar, except that it is a hierarchy among the individuals that is established rather than a territory. Threats and submission signals are the normal currency of social interactions that establish and reinforce the dominance relationships.

The ethology analysis of aggression in the human condition is based on the observation that the human species has produced too many members without a corresponding change in the genetic tendencies. Humans have been using socialization and culture mechanisms to suppress the strong signals for aggressive display that are nearly always present. Simply stated, people are overcrowded. Whether viewed as a territorial or a dominance-organized species, the same result appears. Ethologists speculate that people are too close together and their territories change too often to establish boundaries within which they can reside peacefully. The many and changing social relationships hopelessly confuse attempts at rankings (Lorenz, 1966; Tinbergen, 1968). The consequence is continued aggressive urges in each person.

Konrad Lorenz's view is that aggression is a fighting instinct. He believes that aggression serves important purposes. The aggressive mechanisms distribute animals over a territory and select the most powerful to breed and defend the young. He sees it as a constructive and life-preserving function. Lorenz views aggression as just one of the "big four" spontaneous and rhythmic drives (the others are hunger, sex, and flight). Lorenz proposed a sort of hydraulic model of aggressive potential. A reservoir of aggressive energy builds up until an appropriate signal appears and the energy is released as violent action (Lorenz, 1966). Some have pictured this less charitably as the "flush-toilet model" (Klama, 1988). Karli (1991) finds it difficult to imagine how an "'all purpose' aggressive drive" could have evolved, believing it to be "biological nonsense, liable to lead the animal kingdom rapidly to its disappearance" (p. 12).

There is no ethology evidence for a spontaneous aggressive drive. There is no evidence that ancestors of humans were embattled warriors. Anthropologist Richard Leakey believes that our view of ourselves as "killer apes" is unfounded and "one of the most dangerous pervasive myths of our time" (Leakey, 1981; Leakey & Lewin, 1977).

In particular, the various aggressive energy storage theories have no basis in biology. Logically, there is no way for the nervous system to store energy tied to a kind of action like aggression. At best, such notions are metaphors, and being poor ones, they explain nothing. There are, however, processes of sensitization that make aggressive acts more likely, if there is also a suitable provocation. But it is not useful to think that there is an accumulating necessity for aggressive action. Worse still, it leads us away from asking the specific questions we need to ask about causes and consequences of real activities.

Similarly, there is no physiological basis for the common idea of catharsis that has been popular in drive-reservoir theories of personal therapy. The catharsis idea is that aggressive urges can be worked out or eliminated by aggressive acts in safe situations. Is there an accumulation of aggressive necessity that acting aggressively is intended to eliminate? On the contrary, there is not only no biological basis for that, but the psychological evidence is that aggressive acts beget more and stronger aggressive acts. Cathartic therapy just practices and strengthens aggressive solutions to personal problems. Even large-scale social statistics show no catharsis-based reduction in aggressive acts. Homicide rates after a war are higher than before, even higher in countries that won or had high battle losses (Archer & Gartner, 1984). That is hard to reconcile with an aggression-release theory.

In contrast to the popular ethology writings, ethologists Richard Lore and Lori Schultz (1993) see aggression as a strategy of acts that can be used or not. The conditions of control appear to be as predictable in rats as people. Such balanced reviews of animal aggression have not been presented as well nor to as wide an audience (De Waal, 1992). The instinct extremists have found a willing audience; more cautious views are harder to promote. Cautious views also are ignored because they undercut the prime excuse from biological psychology, "My body made me do it."

Genetic Human Nature

Studies of human genetics of aggression follow different strategies. Some use twin studies. Identical twins are compared with genetically dissimilar fraternal twins. Identical twins are not more alike in their response to aggression models (Plomin, Foch, & Rowe, 1981). Identical twins are also not more alike than fraternal twins in their rate of violent crimes. No chromosomal abnormality (including the once popular studies of xyy-chromosome men) has been linked to aggressive feelings or violent acts. In short, there is no clear evidence for the genetic transmission of a tendency to aggressive acts in humans (Mednick, Pollock, Volavka, & Gabrielli, 1982).

Another set of ideas about genetic human aggression is based on evolutionary psychology theory.

Evolutionarily Stable Strategies

It is quite reasonable to believe that we come into being with some Evolutionarily Stable Strategies (ESSs) (Dawkins, 1989; Maynard Smith, 1982; and others) regarding confrontations with others. Richard Dawkins describes an ESS as one that is stable among others like it. An ESS cannot be bettered or removed by another strategy in the long haul of fitness. But an ESS is not "winner-take-all." Different kinds of balance are typical.

Suppose a simplified world of confrontations leading to a winner and a loser. There are several possible strategies. For illustration, consider the values in Tables 5.1 through 5.3 as measures of benefits and losses. The precise numbers do not matter as long as the underlying relationships are preserved. One strategy compares a warrior who attacks im-

TABLE 5.1 Confrontation: Warrior Meets Pacifist

winner	loser
warrior	+50
pacifist	0

TABLE 5.2 Confrontation: Warrior Meets Warrior

winner	loser
warrior	+50
warrior	−100

TABLE 5.3 Confrontation: Pacifist Meets Pacifist

winner	loser
pacifist	+40
pacifist	-10

mediately or a pacifist who merely threatens. When a warrior meets a pacifist, the confrontation quickly ends with the pacifist running away: warrior gains, pacifist loses nothing (see Table 5.1). When a warrior meets another warrior, there is a fight until one (or both) is injured or dead: winner gains, loser suffers great loss (see Table 5.2). When a pacifist meets a pacifist, there are equal threats with no action, wasting their time until one tires of it, but with no damage: winner gains with cost of time wasted, loser has cost of time wasted (see Table 5.3).

Gains and losses are shorthand for small effects on reproductive successes; they influence fitness advantages. Losing when there is no fight has no consequences. Time-wasting threat-fights are minor losses for both participants. Thus, in a warrior-pacifist contest, the warrior has a gain and the pacifist gains or loses nothing. In a warrior-warrior contest, the winning warrior has a gain and the losing warrior has a big loss. On the average, the warriors have a net loss. In a pacifist-pacifist confrontation, the winner has the gain minus the small loss from wasted time; the loser has only the minor time-waste loss. On the average, the pacifists have a net gain.

Clearly, the best world is the all-pacifist one. But suppose a mutation in the pacifist population produces a warrior. That strategy would win consistently and increase in the subsequent population of offspring. Eventually, the warriors would have a strong chance of meeting other warriors and the advantage would decline. When warrior numbers reach a certain proportion, the net loss coming from warrior-warrior confrontations would balance the net gain coming from confrontations with pacifists. At this point, the distribution should become stable. The exact proportions are determined by the absolute magnitude of the average gains and losses in reproductive advantage. In this example, we can see that two different types of inclinations to battle can exist in the population. and both are biologically underwritten as ESSs.

There is also no reason that there should be just two rather than several varieties that would reach equilibrium. Dawkins (1989) describes the work of Maynard Smith and others about retaliators who begin a meeting as pacifists but respond to attack as warriors and bullies who begin as warriors but change to pacifists when the attack is returned. Computer simulations show that mixtures of retaliators and warriors are evolutionarily stable.

Fitness Functions

If we want to know of the likely human adaptations related to anger and aggression, we must work out the ways in which certain patterns of action provided advantages in fitness; that is, how they gave advantages in more viable offspring. One beginning is in working out what needs to be done and how, who would do it and when, and the broader fitness function it aids. Some of the possibilities have been examined; others are waiting attention.

We begin by assuming a Pleistocene social environment of extended families in kinship groupings. Among the things anger and aggression might do are

Establish dominance and leadership

Maintain social order

Punish social violations

Eliminate rivals for resources

Remove barriers to resources

Repel attacks from outsiders

Each of these goals, and perhaps others, aid the genetic fitness of the genes of the breeding population.

Anger and aggression would be made of threats and attacks that are sufficient to achieve the goals. Actual damage to individuals will be weighed on the scales of fitness against its effect on genetic survival. Doing actual harm to outsiders who threaten the survival of the genes of the group would perhaps aid fitness. Damage by aggressive acts to individuals within the genetic group would not aid fitness. The likely outcome in a social group is a complex set of moderation of threats and aggression to meet the goals of the breeding population. Aggression will appear to be measured and deliberate, according to group rules.

Who would do these things and when they would do them is contingent on what is to be done and why. The majority of anger and aggression would be the work of males, particularly those in leadership roles and those in their youthful prime. Those males with established mates and those leading kinship groups have a fitness advantage in defensively protecting their property, resources, and access to them. Young males use threats and attacks relatively recklessly to get property and resources. The less they have, the more reckless in attack they can afford to be (Daly & Wilson, 1994).

Females too will defend their property, resources, and children. Humanity is just moderately dimorphic in gender; that is, men are not overwhelmingly larger and stronger than women. That state of affairs is different from what is the case in many species, including our closest relatives among the great apes. This means women have considerable physical bases for anger and aggression, although still somewhat less than those of men.

Some threats and attacks will be reflexes to kinds of situations. The roaming outgroup male will be challenged and kept away. Most threats and attacks will be memory-based interpretations of past experiences with a view to what the future conditions will be. That distant kin, for example, has taken food without sharing in the past; he will now be threatened whenever he approaches.

Much of anger and aggression involves protection of property. Property includes physical things and places such as food, clothing, artifacts, cooking facilities, and sleeping areas. These serve fitness by aiding physical survival of parents and by supporting children until they reach successful breeding maturity. Other aspects of property involve protection of genetic material in the form of defending the lives of children and breeding age kin. Furthermore, one must protect exclusivity of breeding with mates to ensure that efforts are supporting one's own rather than another person's children, and each parent must enforce the full efforts of the other toward support of children of the union.

A second major part of social functioning involves reputation. The roles and successes each has in social interactions depend on how others expect things to turn out. A person who defends a bargain with force is not likely to be cheated. A reputation for carrying out angry threats ensures compliance to requests. These, too, add to overall fitness.

SECTION SUMMARY: PHYSICAL FOUNDATIONS FOR AGGRESSION

More than most topics, we are inclined to assign aggressive acts to uncontrollable physical causes. To counter that, this section takes an unusually critical stance. Limbic brain areas, especially in the amygdala, are involved in emotionally aggressive acts, but no single place has special controlling or center functions. Clinical studies of localized epileptic seizures show a pattern of emotional feelings without an anger location. Similarly, some moderation of aggressive acts results with amygdala removal, but not enough to justify calling it an aggression control center. A variety of neurotransmitter chemicals are required for all meaningful acts, but testosterone is usually thought to be involved in aggression. The evidence is very weak, with some suggestion that testosterone increases are the consequence (rather than the cause) of aggressive encounters. Brain poisoning by alcohol also is culturally believed to produce violence; the violence of drunks is not forced by the alcohol but rather comes from the aggression-stimulating situations they frequent.

Human genetic variations have not been an important cause of differences in aggression. Studies of animals, however, have focused on their use of threats and aggression in their social lives. Second only to presenting their mating habits, nature programs most often show animals in aggression encounters. Ethologists have divided species into those that use aggression to mark territory and those that establish relative social ranking. Some have proposed a fighting instinct and generalized that to humans. The consequence has been the well-established public impression that we have an aggressive nature lying beneath a thin veneer of cultural control. That becomes our excuse for our occasional public displays of aggression.

Assuming anger and aggression are natural parts of our social interactions, we look for aggressive interaction strategies that would have benefited reproductive fitness. Evolutionarily stable strategies of aggression are those that survive against other strategies. Theoretical possibilities include warriors, pacifists, bullies, and retaliators. Simulation models show that a population mixture of retaliators and warriors will be stable.

Anger and aggression strategies keep social order, get and protect resources, and defend against outsiders. All of these strategies emerged because they aided reproductive fitness (produced more breeding offspring).

EMOTIONAL AGGRESSIVE ACTS

Emotional aggression labels the kinds of aggressive acts that come more from internal states than from conscious plans. They reflect "aggression as being impelled by intense physiological and motor reactions within the individual," as Leonard Berkowitz (1993) describes it. He pictures emotional aggression as an "internal agitation" that "'pushes out' the attempts to injure the target." These are acts of someone who is intensely aroused and carries out aggressive acts "with relatively few complicated thoughts and plans" (p. 26).

Emotional aggressive acts have been described from different collections of causes. These are some of the ideas we will explore. A variety of theories in the "drive" tradition have been proposed (see Chapter 1), the most elaborate examining the role of frustrating events. Arousal has been proposed as a general contributor. Leonard Berkowitz has developed well the idea of conditions of impulsive aggression. The intermediary of anger is another well-founded idea. Berkowitz uses the theme of "feeling bad" to tie many of these together, as we will discuss below.

Drive Sources of Aggression

Much early psychological study of aggressive acts was founded on the assumption that there is a drive called aggression. Notions of an aggression drive are loosely based on an instinct or a biological energy model. That aggressive acts are caused by aggression drive was part of Sigmund Freud's psychoanalytic concept of *thanatos* (death instinct), of some animal psychologists' notions of aggressive instincts, and of some behaviorists' models of biological energy (Freud, 1948). All these theorists shared the expectation that aggressive acts will come from the presence of a drive called aggression.

Frustration Conditions

Tests of psychoanalytic theory assumed that aggression is the result of frustration, according to Dollard, Doob, Miller, Mowrer, and Sears (1939): "The proposition is that the occurrence of aggressive behavior always presupposes the existence of frustration and, contrariwise, that the existence of frustration always leads to some kind of aggression" (p. 1).

Evidence was drawn from social statistics and from experiments. For example, researchers found a correlation between indexes of bad economic conditions and the numbers of lynchings and property crimes of violence (Hovland & Sears, 1940). In typical experiments, children were frustrated by being shown attractive toys that they were not allowed to play with. Later, they were allowed access to these toys and were found to play with them in a more aggressive manner than children who had not been so frustrated. The aggressive drive aroused by frustration was thought to be reduced by performing aggressive acts (Barker, Dembo, & Lewin, 1941).

The frustration-aggression thesis, as it came to be called, finds easy support in common experience. Everyone knows the feelings of being frustrated followed by urges to be violent. Further research and thought, however, shows that frustration and aggression are not always linked in this strong manner. Some kinds of frustration do not lead to aggression, and some aggression comes from situations that are not frustrating.

The most common way to measure aggression in laboratory experiments has been a technique developed by Arnold Buss (1961). He made a machine that appeared to deliver a range of electric shocks to a person in another room. The context for studying aggressive acts was a learning experiment in which wrong answers were to be punished by the "teacher," who was the real focus in the experiment. Aggression is measured by the strength of shocks the teacher selected to give to others.

Using this general setting, some laboratory researchers found frustration to be a weak condition for aggression and that aggression depends on several other conditions being present in the test situation (Baron, 1977). It is difficult to evoke aggression through frustration alone. Frustrating experiences do play a role in stimulating aggressive acts, but undoubtedly, they are not necessary or sufficient to do so.

Leonard Berkowitz (1989, 1993) argues that a few clarifying conditions will salvage the essentials of frustration. He notes that the essence of frustration is failing to get pleasures you have expected, so the strength of your aggression will be tied to the intensity of those expected pleasures. Furthermore, your aggression is linked to how unpleasant the frustration events appear to you. Unexpected blocking is unpleasant, especially if you believe it to be purposefully aimed at you and it is improper. Someone barring your passage to a restaurant for no apparent reason gives you unpleasant frustration, and that allows you to make an aggressive response. On the other hand, sports competitions generate many blocks to your potential pleasures, but because they are within the rules and an expected part of the game rather than personally aimed, aggressive acts are not evoked.

Arousal Influences

As drive theory declined in popularity, the word *drive* was avoided but substitute concepts appeared, including dispositions to be aroused. We saw in Chapter 1 that the ideas of arousal were formed from study of activating systems of the brain and came to be a general description for the arousal of our body. Some aggression researchers proposed that levels of arousal are produced by both the instigating psychological conditions and also by unrelated, arousing aspects of the environment. In the view of some theorists, arousal replaced drive as the source of aggression.

In the Buss experiment for measuring aggression that we just reviewed, higher shocks were given by people who were experiencing high levels of heat, of noise, of crowding, of physical exercise, and of sexual stimulation. Each of these conditions was assumed to produce high levels of arousal. None of these findings has been uncontroversial (Siann, 1985). Often the occurrence of the defined aggression depended upon an additional condition of provocation, such as insults or some gain to be realized through punishing the other person. Arousal by itself seems to be just one of several accounts of what is evoking stronger aggressive acts.

Impulsive Aggression and Feeling Bad

Leonard Berkowitz has maintained that certain conditions provoke attacks that occur "impulsively." Most homicides, for example, are not premeditated but are spontaneous and passionate, often arising from disagreements about relatively trivial matters. The threat of punishment has little deterrent effect in these cases because, in the rage of the moment, the consequences of killing simply are not anticipated. Laboratory tests showed similar effects. Using a form of the usual aggression protocol, impulsive aggressive acts may be produced by a variety of stimulus conditions. In addition to uncomfortable heat (Griffitt, 1970), unpredictable and uncontrollable noise (Donnerstein & Wilson, 1976; Geen, 1978), and pain (Berkowitz, Cochran, & Embree, 1981), greater aggression is shown when weapons are present. People who have weapons in view give higher shock levels (Berkowitz & LePage, 1967; Frodi, 1975; Turner & Simons, 1974; Turner, Simons, Berkowitz, & Frodi, 1977).

Berkowitz has also manipulated the perceived characteristics of the person to be shocked. After a prizefight film was shown, the target person in the Buss aggression protocol is identified as a college boxer. A stronger shock is given than if the target is identified as a speech major (Berkowitz & Geen, 1966). The degree of justification for the aggressive shocks was also manipulated by instructions. When the prize-fighter was described as deserving the beating, people shocked their target more than did others who were told that the beating was unfair (Berkowitz, 1965).

Leonard Berkowitz's (1993) most recent analysis has led him to suggest that unpleasant feelings are the key to whether aggressive acts will occur. To use the words of one of his chapter titles, "We're nasty when we feel bad." It isn't the factual conditions of pain, noise, heat, insult, or anger that evokes aggression. We act aggressively when these things also feel unpleasant to us.

In a more elaborate but tentative sketch, Berkowitz proposes that unpleasant events produce negative affect, which in turn is primitively associated with both aggression and escape tendencies. At the early stage of an episode, both attacking and fleeing tendencies are called up. The aggressive tendencies are partly a physical striking reflex and partly an idea of hurting someone. When we have strongly unpleasant feelings, we tighten our fighting muscles and are ready to hurt someone.

Collections of aggression tendencies are activated, including expressive and motor actions, physiological reactions, thoughts, and memories. These form rudimentary anger, and that is interpreted through social and cultural rules. The consequence is some level of irritation, annoyance, or anger. A similar development builds to differentiated feelings of fear. Anger and fear states develop in parallel with our tendencies to harm and flee, rather than cause the harming and fleeing. (In many ways, Berkowitz is reworking the basics of William James's analysis of emotions. Elsewhere is his book, Berkowitz acknowledges the inadequacy of the arguments trying to discredit James's theory.)

A number of different experiments demonstrate a priming effect. Present thoughts make other related thoughts available. Berkowitz believes that these thoughts also have associated feelings. When cues of hostility and aggressive acts are presented, they prime the emotional complex of anger, and in the presence of a succeeding instance of unpleasantness, aggressive acts are more strongly called out. Berkowitz and others have shown that physically uncomfortable people judge others more harshly and recall more negative and conflict events of their past (Berkowitz, 1990; Rule, Taylor, & Dobb, 1987). In another study, women first heard female job applicants make derogatory comments about university women, then listened to hostile comedy about women. They judged those female job applicants more severely than did others who heard neutral humor or neutral comments from the applicants (Berkowitz, 1970). When already feeling displeasure, we intensify our aggressive acts if we have had them primed.

In a similar way, once we are already feeling displeasure, getting contrary or mitigating information is not very effective. Being told that someone you are about to meet is feeling bad and is likely to be offensive will neutralize your displeasure, and your subsequent acts will not be aggressive. Getting that same information after you have gone through an interaction with the offensive person will not "cool you down," and you will act aggressively when given the chance (Zillman

& Cantor, 1976). This effect is likely to last as long as your present "heat." Over a longer time, you are likely to integrate the later information and hold no future grudge.

The expression of aggression is part of the information supporting aggressive feelings. For this reason, physically displaying threats and acting aggressively won't "get it out of your system" or be cathartic. Instead, it will strengthen your cues to be aggressive. Just making appropriate facial movements of anger will prime your anger or increase its intensity (Rutledge & Hupka, 1985).

SECTION SUMMARY: EMOTIONAL AGGRESSIVE ACTS

Early theorists suggested aggression was driven solely by frustrating situations. This frustration-aggression drive theory was overly simple, but Leonard Berkowitz has retained its theme in focusing on the unpleasantness of aggression-provoking situations. He suggests that aggression arises from bad feelings and will often appear impulsively in those conditions. Consequently, aggression control depends on cooling down the feelings or preventing "heating up" by the situation.

ANGER

Anger and aggression are linked, but not always and not necessarily. In Chapter 4, "Emotion," we saw anger as a label we use for emotional experience. Aggression describes a class of social acts. As we commonly see it, an angry person carries out aggressive acts, and aggressive acts are often seen to come from angry people. But the exceptions to the implied linkage give a deeper understanding to both concepts. There are social accomplishments of displays of anger that do not use aggressive acts. Some aggressive acts are carried out by people who are not angry. Neither term, *anger* or *aggression,* refers to a simple, single state or process. Their complexities give life to a variety of points of view and styles of analysis.

In this section, we will look at two contrasting styles of analysis. First, we consider the kind of brain processing that appears to underlie being angry and possibly carrying out aggressive acts.

Brain Activity of Anger and Aggression

Our brain's function is to make useful adjustments in our bodies and their actions. Current experiences are evaluated according to memories of past events and using plans that anticipate the future, all with the aim of ensuring survival. Not just survival of that body, but also, if not more fundamentally, survival of its genetic material. In this context, anger and aggression are in part organically based strategies. These strategies reflect an ancestral history of social interactions. Components of past, present, and future events are represented in the nervous systems. Brain activity is the heart of the matter.

The brain's design in anger and aggression, as in many of its functions, is a continuous cycle. Events are interpreted for affective feelings and space-time information by comparing them with memories and models of the environment. Objectives are formed and behaviors directed. Their consequences are evaluated and recorded, changing the environmental model as required. These elements go on seamlessly and continuously in accord with design strategies that have been moderated by individual plans and social experiences. Such plans and social records are, of course, part of the brain's processing.

Important parts of this brain activity of anger and aggression take place in limbic system structures. Sensory information of events comes from cortex processing and is compared with space-time memories in the hippocampus and compared with affective meaning in the amygdala. Interpreted information is then projected to the hypothalamus. The complete system is more than this, including ties to the prefrontal cortex of the cerebrum. Acts of choice seem to arise from the prefrontal cortex and other structures via the thalamus.

The key to emotional meaning in this system is the amygdala. Experimental stimulation of the amygdala yields emotional experience (Halgren, 1981), and lesions there diminish emotional reactivity (Karli, 1991). The amygdala has receptors sensitive to relevant hormones—testosterone, cortisol, and endorphins—allowing more general modulation of emotional experiences.

Human studies have had mixed results about whether testosterone is an indicator of aggression, but that hormone is more consistently tied to anticipations based on past events, producing anxiety states and liability to frustration and threat. Cortisol facilitates response to danger in unsettled conditions, especially in threatened individuals, disappearing when stability has become common. After defeat, the loser's cortisol falls, supporting memory of that encounter. Endorphins reduce the aversiveness of situations.

Anger and aggression function to reduce or stop the aversive feelings that are either anticipated or present in the current situation. Or they may produce or increase pleasant feelings that are anticipated or present. Those feelings are part of the record of the brain, based on evolutionary tendencies and on memories and models of experiences.

Social Rules of Anger

Now we turn to a different style of analysis of anger and its likely outcome in aggressive acts. The perspective here is the social context of modern Western society, with its traditions and formal rules about being angry and using aggression. James Averill (1982) made an extensive analysis of the nature, causes, and effects of anger, or what he calls the anger syndrome. In his view, anger is classed as a conflict emotion, having meaning only in a social reality. It is a human process in response to a social judgment. One judges that another person has violated appropriate social standards and committed deliberately harmful acts. The anger response is itself an open social communication of one's displeasure and right to make appropriate corrections. Anger is thus a form of discipline for acts judged to be wrong, because they violated human social rules. The socialized person feels anger at the rule violations and intends to correct the wrong with anger acts. (These judgments, acts, and feelings perhaps reflect an ESS for social order.)

Looked at in another way, there are also social rules for anger. Anger is discouraged except under certain conditions, and then it becomes permitted if not mandatory. A reasonable person should not be angry, but if certain social rules are violated by others, the passion of emotion is expected and will be displayed using socially determined acts. Social rules determine the class of angering violations of rules and the acceptable responses. Understanding anger depends on knowing the social rules and how they are related to the angered person. A partial list of Averill's rules, including types he called appraisal, behavior, prognostication, and attribution, are shown in Figure 5.2.

In appraising a situation, Averill's rules tell what are appropriate provocations, targets, and purposes. The rules of behavior suggest what can be done and what level of arousal and feelings is appropriate. Prognostication rules describe the sequence and

Rules	Objects	Principles of Anger
Appraisal	Instigation	right/duty at intentional wrongs, careless misdeeds; not if outside influence or otherwise correctable
	Target	at responsible persons; peers or subordinates; familiar persons; men rather than women
	Goal	to correct, restore equity, or prevent; not to injure or gain personal advantage
Behavior	Acts	direct and appropriate to the situation; not excessive or unfair
	Arousal	with appropriate heat of passion
	Mentality	spontaneous, deliberate; with commitment and resolve
Prognostication	Sequence	begin with verbal confrontation and proceed uninterrupted
	Duration	end with correction or restitution
Attribution	Events	connected to the instigation and target; not displaced
	Self	separated from the self-as-agent; not responsible when angry

Figure 5.2. The collected social rules of anger (abstracted from Averill, 1982).

duration of the anger, and rules of attribution form the causal connections among the angry person, the instigation, and the target. Following Averill's rule analysis, which we described in Chapter 4, "Emotion," some of these rules constitute the anger and some regulate it.

To be able to appraise a violation of social rules, the angered individual and the recipient of the anger must be functioning, sentient members of that society. One must know the rules, be aware that another person has violated them, and have sufficient self-awareness to interpret that violation as directed at oneself. Without self-awareness, there may be a retaliatory response, but there would be

little likelihood of anger at its root. Walking down a street you may see a wind-blown cardboard box land on the path and bounce against your leg. You feel no anger. If you saw that same box being thrown by another person, you would become angry and communicate your displeasure. Although in both events, the box inflicted the same objective pain, only that coming from another person having presumed harmful intent incites anger. The appropriate responses may include stopping, adopting a facial scowl, and perhaps asking, "What are you doing?" If you get signs the person accepted the correcting anger message, you will likely end the event. A rule was violated and your measured response righted

the wrong. Anger is a communication intending to rectify the wrong, and such a message implies comprehending senders and re-
ceivers.

SECTION SUMMARY: ANGER

Anger is the common emotional component during aggression. Emotional meaning
of ongoing events is signaled by the
amygdala's interpretation in the limbic system, and the amygdala's response can be
modified by current hormones such as testosterone, endorphins, and cortisol. Anger
and aggressive acts modulate those experienced and expected feelings.

In our culture, anger corrects violations
of rules. James Averill outlined the details of
how we appraise rule-breaking events, act
to correct them, and think about the situations. Anger and appropriate acts are expected to occur under these social rules.

INSTRUMENTAL AGGRESSIVE ACTS

James Averill's social rules of anger provide
a bridge to social aspects of aggressive acts.
In our elaborate personal, social, and cultural
constructions, aggressive acts have functions
that can be many times removed from their
biological roots in feelings and reflexes. We
form our individual selves partly on the ways
we use aggressive acts and respond to them.
We develop our aggressive repertoire as we
learn to eat, speak, love, and do countless
other things. We turn now to the ways aggressive acts become instrumental in our social
lives.

Defending One's Self

Many aggressive acts are attempts at defending one's self. This is much more complicated than the word *self-defense* in common
use. Self theory is a mature and elaborate set
of notions that attempts to find understanding
of many different kinds of interpersonal relationships. From William James in 1890 to
Mary Calkins in 1900 to George Mead in
1934 to Carl Rogers in 1963 and beyond, self

theory has been entertained and developed.
Many of its tenets are implicit, unstated
pieces of common sense. We each hold a personal self-picture. It is the collections of beliefs, likely actions, and feelings that make up
what we believe is true of ourselves. It is our
personal identity.

The self is formed of different life experiences. Some of the self is common in many
others, having been formed in facing the same
social realities. Part of the self is made up in
our unique social interactions. Each of us
learns of the self through others. We become
self-aware by what we see reflected by others.
Part of the self also comes from the many
comparisons we make with others. Competition with peers, for example, lets us learn of
personal differences and uniqueness.

Membership in groups also gives some
of the components of the self. We accept the
real and supposed character of those in the
group. Gender, age, employment, political,
and fraternal groups may each give some of
the self-picture. As mature adults, we also accept certain ethical and moral principles.
These principles set another dimension to our
self-image and our consequent acts. Peter
Marsh, Elisabeth Rosser, and Rom Harré
(1978) describe the situation of British foot-

ball hooligans, gangs of young men following a team and fighting with similar gangs representing another team, in terms of the moral careers that each develops. They write of each moral career as "a continuous summing up of his life in terms of what sort of person he is supposed by his fellows to be" (p. 19).

Aggressive acts become one possibility in defending the self-picture. Some people or events may challenge our personal identity. The challenge to our identity may be neutralized by aggressive acts aimed at asserting real and important existence. Failure to be recognized is quickly reversed by aggressive attack that diminishes the self of the other. Anne Campbell (1982) studied groups of 16-year-old girls in a British working-class school. She examined the accounts they gave of their fighting, including the causes and the consequences. The majority of the fights were described as being about personal integrity. Countering common belief, she concluded that "the need to prove one's worth may well turn out to be much more a human quality than a male one" (p. 148).

In a similar way, the instigation of aggressive acts may be attacks on what we see as our personal worth. The aggressive response reasserts our worth. Poor parenting, academic failure, or unusual physique may be at the heart of the original self-picture of inadequate worth. Aggressive acts may then be a purposeful attempt to gain the acknowledgment of others, if not their respect. The aggressive acts are likely to continue as long as the fundamental problems remain unchanged and the aggressive acts give results.

Aggressive acts are most likely to come from people at times when they feel most devalued and feel the need to defend their selves. Aggressive acts, by being successful in social situations of self-development, may become a consistent part of self-expression. An aggressive style can become habitual.

Social Sources of Aggression

Aggressive acts and acts of violence are found embedded in human social relations, but, at the same time, they are actually rare and fleeting events. As complex patterns of acts with complicated and changing causes, they are built on past experiences, feelings, and present interpretations of the whole situation. It is overly simplistic to ascribe aggressive acts to drives, instincts, or similar dispositions and fail to account for the normal life in which they play an interacting role. The total complex of influences, however, is very difficult to study. One approach is to examine descriptions we use for aggressive situations.

Those descriptions show we sometimes act aggressively in settings of conflict or competition; sometimes we act for ourselves against others, and sometimes we physically injure others. Aggression descriptions can be found and interpreted in their natural social contexts. As Peter Marsh (1982) put it,

> At a practical level, there is no substitute for the general strategy of listening to individuals talk, witnessing them in action, and examining the day-to-day features of the social worlds they inhabit. . . . It is only after such a strategy has been pursued . . . that social science is possible. . . . We need to know what it is that needs to be explained. (p. 115)

Marsh and many others have proposed and demonstrated how to analyze aggression and violence in talk, using the accounts that people make of social happenings.

In part, this strategy of examining talk is forced on us because of the difficulty of observing actual violence. Aggressive acts are not as common or as easily observed as their interest value suggests. Marsh calls it the "It-never-quite-happens" phenomenon. But people do talk a great deal about aggression. Studying talk produces accounts. But we can't stop there. The accounts themselves must not be taken as statements of what actually happened, but as one primary source of evidence of the social rules that may then be submitted to experiment to understand their causes.

Accounts from participants will be shaped by conventions of local cultures. Each has its specific form of language, including special meanings for terms, stylized manners of description, and certain glosses or "spin" (artfully misleading interpretations) to account for the events. Some of the group talk and action is uninterpretable or judged senseless by outsiders. That was found by a team of scientists (Marsh et al., 1978) studying groups of British "football hooligans" in some depth. They published their work under the informative title *The Rules of Disorder.*

Marsh and his colleagues found that some rules of such groups are in apparent contradiction. A football hooligan's social status is derived from evidence of his aggressive acts, yet other rules of what they do in an actual confrontation minimize if not prevent any actual violence. Thus, in the group, there is a need for aggressive acts that are actually forbidden. The solution is provided by the talk. Descriptions of what happened in an encounter restore the violence that is needed for affirming status. It becomes clear that the rhetoric has more social importance than the acts. Therefore, the social scientist must dig beneath the accounts for the meaning of the talk as it relates to the action patterns that actually take place.

Aggressive acts are social episodes of high predictability. Joseph Forgas (1986) writes of the sophisticated cognitive strategies that are required for appraising aggression, and these are commonplace matters in daily human affairs. Richard Felson (1984) outlines several perspectives in which aggressive acts have social meaning. People see aggression as retaliation to save face, as coercion, and as punishment.

Aggression is permitted and expected when we perceive we have been attacked. The retaliation is more likely or stronger if there are others present to whom the face-saving is communicated. This is a social display of defense of our self. Its intention is communication to others of our worth, an act of impression management.

James Tedeschi and his colleagues (Tedeschi, Gaes, & Rivera, 1977) believe that aggressive acts (they prefer the term *harm-doing*) are used to influence others. Just one of many ways that people can be coerced, aggression is more likely when other techniques of persuasion have failed to achieve personal rewards. We weigh rewards and costs before deciding to attack.

Richard Felson's (1984) preferred view is that aggression is an actual or threatened punishment. We do it in response to a perception of misbehavior by others. The wrongdoing of others justifies the aggressive act. Legitimate offenses are described as those of violations of norms (something a person has already done) and those of violations of orders (where a person will not comply with our wishes).

A somewhat different approach is that of Robin Fox (1982). He defends the thesis that violent acts are natural and necessary. Violence is a normal part of life, necessary to simple acts like getting food. Aggressive acts are rational, calculated responses. In some common human social interactions, aggression is an expected expression of frustration. The violence in these actions is both satisfying and fascinating. But Fox goes further. Not just the violence is normal, but so is its regulation. That is so because he assumes that human society is essentially and naturally bound by rules. Violence regulation is natural, and people are equally fascinated by its rules.

> I venture a rough-hewn hypothesis: where 'pure dominance' is involved—a simple matter of who is top nation, tribe, or kingdom—the rules, negotiations, and displays proliferate; where 'real interests' (territory, population, women) are involved, the rules break down and we approach mayhem. The basic hypothesis behind this one [is] that [people] are as attached to rules as to the killing, and that other things being equal they will minimize the killing in favour of the display. (p. 26)

Fox (1982) also claims that the idea of violence becomes a social problem when human imagination gives new, unnatural meaning to violent acts in changed social contexts. Some animal-rights promoters and some vegetarians, for example, believe that killing animals for food is unacceptable violent aggression. Fox argues that the violence remains a natural event. He argues that romantic human interpretations of normal violence makes the problem.

Aggression as a Stable Trait

There is little direct evidence about how aggressive acts develop in children, but there are several good studies relating aggressive acts at different life stages. The general conclusion is that aggressiveness is a somewhat stable style of act. Some have suggested that the basic inclination toward aggression is formed by the time a child is 3 years old. Few studies have examined those crucial early years to see how children acquire the social and cultural rules. Most study begins with observations of the more available populations in nursery school or elementary grades.

Robert Sears and colleagues (Sears, Maccoby, & Lewin, 1957) studied 379 children and their families. He showed that aggressive tendencies are formed early in childhood. The level of aggressive acts shown by preschoolers correlates well with their extent of aggressive acts as young adults. Looking at their parenting and family setting, the strongest evidence is that aggression in children is associated with heavy use of punishment and other aggressive treatments in the family. Aggression begets aggression. Aggressive children grew up in families that made liberal use of physical punishment, that were permissive toward aggression, and that witnessed parental battles.

Dan Olweus (1979) surveyed a set of studies from America and Western Europe and found strong correlations over time using a variety of measures of aggressive acts. The longer the time elapsed, the weaker the relation, but they were quite strong nonetheless. For example, David Farrington (1989) continued a project begun by David West on 400 boys from a working-class London area. Although most of the boys changed somewhat between measures at ages 8, 13, 17, and 21, many violent 21-year-olds had also been aggressive earlier. Or to say it differently, those who were highly aggressive as young men were much more likely to have also been aggressive at the intervening ages.

Leonard Eron (1987) studied 870 boys and girls at age 8, also interviewing their parents. These upstate New York youngsters were again sought out and interviewed at ages 21 and 30. Again, those found to be aggressive in their early years were those judged aggressive later in life. It is interesting to see that those consistently aggressive people, at age 30, used more punishment to discipline their own children than did the less aggressive. Robert Sears's observations are supported.

Men's and Women's Aggression

As we make more sophisticated studies of how men and women experience different aspects of culture, we learn that the focus on men of the past led us astray. That becomes very important in matters of what aggression means. In her recent book *Men, Women, and Aggression*, Anne Campbell (1993) asserts,

> For women aggression is the failure of self control, while for men it is the imposing of control over others. Women's aggression emerges from their inability to check the disruptive and frightening force of their own anger. For men, it is a legitimate means of assuming authority over the disruptive and frightening forces in the world around them. (p. 1)

Later, Campbell labels these ideas by noting that women's approach to aggression is expressive, whereas men's is instrumental (p. 7). We will outline her analysis of the causes and consequences of these differences.

Expressive and instrumental roles are embedded in learned gender roles. Infants are treated alike by mothers. By preschool years, mothers continue to show relative equality of role directions, but fathers strongly discourage boys from doing girl things. From early preschool years, girls and boys know their gender roles and are happy to follow them. Both girls and boys spend most of their time with their mothers, but boys do not learn feminine ways. Instead, they look for masculine roles, defining themselves negatively as "not feminine." If the father is not present, boys adopt stereotypical media images such as GI Joe or Batman. These have a double impact of being parodies of masculinity and also devoid of attachments to other men. Boys reject female roles and see no overlap with male roles. Control by fathers emphasizes avoiding of feminine things, including their style of social control of aggression. Men encourage the opposite, instrumental use of aggression. The taboo of doing women's things leads boys to look for evidence in culture for what men do. They have no trouble finding it. Movies, television dramas, and even children's cartoon shows are heavily biased toward stereotyped gender differences. And these masculine culture images are heavily loaded with aggression as a style of being.

Girls learn feminine styles of relationships and control through mutual social obligations. In these social interactions, aggression is a mistake that hurts others. Angry aggression is an error that is selfish and inconsiderate. Social control of their aggression is built on guilt and empathy. Campbell (1993) believes each girl extends this to other relationships and "she learns it is better to swallow hard and bottle up her anger than to risk the ugly words and blows that might cast her out into the cold world of social rejection" (p. 28).

The outcome, according to Campbell, is that a woman may periodically erupt with anger born of frustration. The resulting acts may be violent but are not directed at causes. In its purest form, her aggressive violence is evidence of losing control in a situation where the usual feminine rules and styles don't work. They are expressions with only accidental instrumental effects. They are often private violence (such as throwing things in a tantrum, but not hurting anyone), crying, or privately sharing her frustrations and anger with other women. She does not want her lost control to be publicly known. The angry woman is caught in a trap where being aggressive cannot work. If she attacks the frustration source in order to change it, she is not acting as a (feminine) woman should, and she loses. If she does nothing, the frustration continues, and she loses. Violent outbursts can and often do end a frustrating situation, as in a marriage, but this is a last resort that is intended to signal not a solution, but an escape to a different life.

For men, in Campbell's presentation, the nature of aggression is a matter of a fair fight and defense of all aspects of self-esteem. Men hold to a morality in fighting but see nothing wrong or immoral about the fighting itself. Men fight in physical and stylized ways to constantly place themselves in dominance over others. Although they may be angry at the time of the fighting, it is not a building anger that led to the aggression. For a man, aggression is a coldly acceptable way to control others and to show them who he is. In all of these battles, there are complicated rules to ensure that the fight is fair. The fight must be "fair and square." Men don't pick a fight with those dramatically weaker or those who by other characteristics are weaker. They don't act aggressively toward old people, women, children, men much smaller than they, those deranged, and so on. Men also feel comfortable fighting in public and expect audience approval. Emotional aggression for many men is just one way of being effective in living.

Campbell's view is an analysis of the stereotypical gender differences in modern Western society. Of course, these differences don't apply to all individuals, and there are cultural trends forcing moderation of the cultural training aspects of gender differences in using aggression. However we may strive to change the way we have been, the reality is that there is not an equality of the sexes in matters of aggression and, for certain biological reasons, perhaps never will be.

SECTION SUMMARY: INSTRUMENTAL AGGRESSIVE ACTS

Continuing the inheritance idea, one of aggression's important uses is in defining and elaborating who we are, making others acknowledge and respond to us. Aggression is one way of establishing our self-worth. We also can use aggression and threats of aggression to coerce others and to punish them.

Because we naturally pay attention to aggression, we tend to overemphasize its frequency in social life. Thus, talking about aggression tends to take the place of actual aggressive acts, especially where being destructive is counterproductive, dangerous, or against the situation rules. When we follow the rules, being aggressive is satisfying. Both aggression and the rules are fascinating to us.

The evidence suggests that our tendencies toward using aggression are set from an early age, whether a natural variation or acquired in early experiences. Family influence is implicated, but genetic sources have not yet been ruled out.

In recent Western cultural history, women have refrained from aggression until they lose self-control, whereas men have tended to use aggression instrumentally, following rules of fair fighting. The sources of these differences lie in part in aspects of teaching girls cooperative social styles and teaching boys individualist and self-defense social styles. Again, certain genetic adaptations are likely but have not been adequately examined.

LEARNING ANGER AND AGGRESSION

Psychology's traditional thesis is that all human performance is learned. Aggression is assumed to be among these learned performances.

Modeling and Imitation

Albert Bandura proposed that understanding aggressive acts depends on knowing how they were learned. What are the cues and what are the rewards for acting aggressively? Bandura proposed several sources for aggressive acts, but the most studied is that of modeling or imitation. In a classic example, nursery-school children were shown a film of adults entering a room and attacking a life-size, inflated, clown doll (Bobo) using several specific actions. Later, the children were allowed in a room with a similar doll; they acted in a similar manner. Without clear reasons or specific drives, children imitate aggressive acts. A child sees an adult do something and copies the action (Bandura, 1973; Bandura, Ross, & Ross; 1963).

The modeling notion has been elaborated as a likely mechanism determining the frequent me-too crimes that follow publicity of a major event. A film of an airliner with a bomb set to go off as it descended below 5,000 feet was matched by a real-life mimic. Other examples have included mass murders, serial murders, setting derelicts afire, kidnappings, and acts of terrorism including hijacking airplanes. The showing of the *Wizard of Oz* often leads to preschool children playing the role of the flying monkeys, the harpies, the next day. Furthermore, Jeffrey Goldstein (1986) noted from his studies that "witnessing violence on the playing field increases proneness to aggression among observers" (p. 252).

All of these might be seen as instances of Leonard Berkowitz's priming mechanism, which we discussed earlier. Learning the specific aggressive acts of others primes the emotional complex of anger. When later events evoke unpleasant anger, the dormant model of what to do is activated.

The importance of modeling becomes political when we ask whether violence in movies and television makes watchers more likely to be aggressive. The simple answer is yes, but it matters who the watchers are and what they are experiencing and thinking. A study in a Belgian reformatory demonstrated that a week of evening movies with a high violence content evoked much higher levels of physical aggressive activity, especially for those already inclined toward aggressiveness. A week of low violence movies had no such effect (Leyens, Camino, Parke, & Berkowitz, 1975; Parke, Berkowitz, Leyens, West, & Sebastian, 1977). A summary of many such experiments is given by Wendy Wood and her colleagues, and she concluded the influence of media violence was on the average a significant effect (Wood, Wong, & Chachere, 1991). These viewings primed the watchers with aggressive thinking and feelings of anger, which dissipate with time.

Rewards and Punishments

The notion that aggressive acts may be rewarded and thus strengthened is directly obvious. Like any acts, those that lead to more pleasant consequences, that remove discomfort, or that add excitement are likely to be continued. Aggression often becomes an instrument to further social goals. After learning that it is permitted to strike the Bobo doll, a child may strike another who is ahead in the lunch line. If the child gets served faster, the aggressive strategy will be strengthened.

Being aggressive can also be reinforced by other rewards and satisfactions. Rewards take the form of approval of aggression by caregivers, whether parents or others respon-

sible for what we do. Our peers can influence specific acts or provide a code of behavior that must be followed to retain their companionship.

Physical punishment has been noted in several studies of aggressiveness among children; however, its effect depends on how it is used. Punishment appears to lead to an aggressive style when parents use it impulsively, inconsistently, severely, and without communicating its purpose. Gerald Patterson (1986) believes that the key is that punishment was used by these parents in an ineffective way; it was not the use of punishment itself that led to learning to use aggressive acts.

Acquiring Social Rules

From the view of constructivist theory, it is not the aggressive acts that are learned, but the social rules in which anger and aggression are appropriate and required. Thus, the formation of these rules will be closely tied with the development of other major representations of social acts, such as language. Children learn the social rules through experiencing instances of aggression in others around them. Some of these events are clearer, better examples than are others. James Averill (1982) writes of these special learning situations as prototypic examples that are presented in paradigm scenarios. These special instances produce a powerful learning of the social rules at an early age.

A **paradigm scenario** is a uniquely important event to a specific child. Being physically punished for an improper act is an example. The event may be rehearsed later by reminders from parents, and still later, it may appear in a similar form in stories on television. The child learns both the appropriate feelings of anger in response to the situation and the socially expected punishment. More study is needed of prototypic learning experiences of very young children, including the possibility that we are evolutionarily adapted to use anger and associated physical acts to correct social errors.

TABLE 5.4　A Rough Summary of Four Centuries of Western Social Changes in the Use of Anger

Historical Anger	
1600s	open anger; used for power and obedience
1700s	some restraint; excess called tantrums
early 1800s	used in work life; women restrained but conflict in home life
late 1800s	anger as a trait; boys channel it, girls repress it
early 1900s	anger control in work; avoid it in family
middle 1900s	less gender difference; cool the anger

Historical Emotionology of Anger

Carol and Peter Stearns (Stearns, 1988; Stearns & Stearns, 1986) have argued that there have been systematic changes in the social rules for anger and in their experienced consequences in child rearing, family life, and work. They use the term *emotionology* to collect the conventions, standards, and institutions used to evaluate anger. We will briefly sketch their views of some historical changes in American ideas and experiences of anger and its control (see Table 5.4).

Before the eighteenth century, anger was not viewed as a problem, and emotionology was minimal and variable. Methods to break the will of children often used force, but the intent was to get obedience, not to reduce anger. Social life was openly angry, usually in a downward direction from those holding power. Thus, servants, employees, wives, and children were commonly treated with anger. Except in extreme physical abuse, no one saw anything wrong with this. It was just the way things were. Groups of all kinds—religious, national, local—were routinely abusive to others from the outside, and there was no guilt over unrestrained angry attacks.

During the eighteenth century, anger was beginning to be restrained, especially in the family. Bursts of anger were disapprovingly called *tantrums*. Building conscience and guilt came to replace punishments and breaking children's will. Family order became valued, perhaps reflecting the pressures of smoother relations required outside the home (made necessary by more people to deal with and increased business competition).

In the first half of the nineteenth century, the emotionology of marriage pictured a contrast between the stress and strife of work with the peace and quiet of the home. The home as a refuge was to be free of anger. Books of advice and fiction alike celebrated the good wife and her obedient home life versus the mistaken mate who quarrels with her husband and ventures into the world. Children were to be taught control of their anger. Physical abuse and punishment were reduced. The heavier load was on women, who were to entirely remove or repress their anger. Men still had limited competitive anger in their work world. New anger sources appeared in failures of the expectation of better marriages, in reduced support from community and extended family, and in uncontrolled frustrations from the outside world. Anger in the home perhaps actually increased in this time, or at least the home became an appropriate place for expressing anger.

In the second half of the nineteenth century, from about 1860 through about 1940, two new ideas about anger developed. Anger was thought to be a natural trait of personality, and it was believed to have some usefulness. With this in mind, child rearing changed from removing anger to channeling it. For boys, this meant competitive sports, including organized fighting such as boxing. Girls were still implicitly trained to become keepers of a peaceful and cheerful home, learning to restrain their anger. Anger in the family was still to be controlled and moderated by joking about it.

As the twentieth century got under way, changed emotionology began to enter the workplace, with less tolerance for using anger. By the 1930s and later, managers were expected to suppress their own feelings and handle angry workers by skillful understanding of causes. Personnel tests were designed to select managers and workers who fit the new model.

The new managerial style of emotionology of the workplace spread into child rearing. Children were to be taught that their natural anger gave no advantage. Children were taught to avoid angering situations. Children's anger was not returned by parents but was instead talked away. The goal was to make children embarrassed with their show of anger and intolerant of straightforward aggression acts.

Beginning in about the 1960s, the dual standards of gender began to weaken. Masculine rights to anger and aggressive strategies were questioned. Media images portrayed less angry aggression. Violence and aggression remained, but now in less heated, dispassionate ways. The ideal was to act "cool." In marriage, increased equality of roles removed much of the emotion-control burden from women. Couples were told it is normal to have conflict and work out their troubles rather than one-sidedly repress and accept them. Even in quarreling, the managerial approach set rules, techniques, and time limits. The success of a marriage was based partly on how hard the partners worked on it.

Are we changing again in the 1990s? Stories and news in public media show a tolerance for more vivid depictions of details of violence. Will this promote more public violence, or will there be a return to increased control over public expression?

SECTION SUMMARY: LEARNING ANGER AND AGGRESSION

Ample evidence shows that children model others' aggression, suggesting that aggression themes in media will affect them if they have no other instruction. Aggressive acts that are rewarded are adopted as new instrumental means to achieve desired situations. Punishing aggressive acts shows children both the consequences of their acts and that punishing is acceptable. Consequently, poorly used punishment may increase children's aggressive tendencies. In both reward and punishment scenes, the optimal outcome is to show children the consequences of their actions. Thus, often repeated, simple cause-and-effect stories teach children about aggression in social life.

The historical study of anger and aggression shows us that standards have changed dramatically over the past few hundred years in Western society. Before the 1700s, public displays of anger were commonplace, aimed from those in power to subordinates. Through the 1700s and early 1800s, increasing restraint was demanded, especially in the home. At the end of the 1800s, men's and boys' anger was thought to be normal and to be channeled into sports and work. Into the 1900s, ideas changed again toward minimal anger by all, except where prescribed for punishing rule breaking. The cultural influence on anger's expression seems obvious in this recent history.

◈

CHAPTER CONCLUSIONS

Anger and aggression are intensely important to us because they seem destructive to the social life we would like to live. It is both disturbing and fascinating that we could intend to hurt one another. Still, few topics seem to have as much potential for being inherited adaptations as using aggression in attack and in defense (except perhaps sex). That makes the biology of aggressive acts especially important to examine. Although aggression has clear physiological elements, we have tended to presume too much of its cause is in brain and brain chemical elements. Being a complex set of actions evoked by an even more complex set of interpreted situations, anger and aggression should never be thought of as just a mechanical brain response.

Study of the social and cultural dimensions of learning and being aggressive illustrates more of its complexity. We act aggressively, for example, when we feel bad, when we are provoked to defend ourselves, when we want to show others who we are, and when we coerce and punish others. Whatever our natural heritage might be, our personal anger and aggression are malleable. We learn aggressive strategies at an early age by examples of aggressive others and by observing life consequences. Cultural history shows that anger and aggression can be enhanced and can be inhibited, as the conditions and rules of social living make demands.

Study and Review Questions

1. What conditions in a situation make you believe an act is aggressive?

2. Do you have to *do* something to be aggressive?

3. What is passive aggression?

4. In what sense is there an aggression center in the limbic system?

5. What is the relationship between the presence of testosterone and aggressive acts?

6. Does alcohol or low levels of blood sugar cause people to act aggressively?

7. For what reasons do animals use threats and aggressive acts?

8. Do people have a slowly filling reservoir of fighting energy that must be emptied?

9. What genetic evidence do we have for variations in individual human aggression?

10. What is an evolutionarily stable strategy (ESS)?

11. What ESSs of aggression are likely?

12. What mixture of strategies have computer simulations shown likely to be stable?

13. Why and how did aggression likely aid our ancestral fitness?

14. What are the traditional theories that worked with aggressive "drive"?

15. What is needed besides arousal to produce aggressive acts?

16. How can we keep Leonard Berkowitz's "feeling bad" from making us aggressive?

17. What are the situations in which we *should* be angry?

18. With what rules and principles is anger applied to others?

19. How may aggression be a part of one's self-picture?

20. Is human aggressive violence as common as it seems?

21. How do we commonly use aggression for normal social purposes?

22. How do rules keep us from being aggressive?

23. Why do we like aggression, according to Robin Fox?

24. Is aggression a stable trait, that is, "once a fighter always a fighter"?

25. How do girls and boys learn different gender aggression styles?

26. How do women traditionally differ from men in using aggression?

27. When can TV violence lead watchers to increase their own aggressive acts?

28. What kind of physical punishment yields aggressive children?

29. How should we teach children about appropriate and improper aggression?

30. In what ways have we changed our rules about anger from the 1600s to the present?

CHAPTER 6

Pain, Fear, and Stress

Pain protects us from damage, yet pain does more than that and has puzzling elements. Pain comes from many body places, but why does it not always match tissue damage? How can what we feel depend on what the experience means to us and how we interpret those events in our personal and cultural lives?

Fear is a classic emotion category, having obvious themes of danger and avoidance. Anxiety labels a vague, non-specific fear that accumulates with some kinds of life events. Stress became fashionable more recently, encompassing acute and chronic states of emergency as we react to life's threats.

Fear, anxiety, and stress have consequences that derive from life changes and from crowding and result in heart disease and mental disorders. Coping with these conditions involves perceiving control of life situations.

Experiencing Pain

Pain Physiology

Managing Pain

Fear

Anxiety

Stress

Physical Bases of Stress

Life Applications of Stress

Control and Coping With Stress

An air of negativity surrounds the topics of this chapter. Pain, fear, anxiety, stress, helplessness, and depression designate undesirable states of being ineffective, unhappy, and in need of help. Part of that is true. These are directions of life we don't willingly choose. In fact, a substantial business has formed to aid people with the more serious forms of these conditions. But these states are also normal, often useful parts of our lives. Knowing their nature may spare some of the unpleasantness and short-circuit some of the fear of the fear, as it were.

TABLE 6.1   Some Ways We Understand and Use Pain (inspired by Wall, 1979)

	External Stimulus	Internal Event
Ability to describe the nature, location, and strength	STRONG	WEAK
Effects of distraction, suggestion, and culture	WEAK	STRONG
Association with emotion, learning, and predictable acts	MAYBE	STRONG

EXPERIENCING PAIN

Pain is an unpleasant sensory and emotional experience associated with actual or potential tissue damage, or described in terms of such damage. (Merskey et al., 1979, p. 250)

That is how a committee of pain experts agreed to clarify the definition of *pain.* Their words are adequate but tell us little we don't already know. In further comments, they gave some nourishment to the definition, outlining some of the phenomena and ideas we will document.

Pain is always subjective. Each individual learns the application of the word through experiences related to injury in early life. Biologists recognize that those stimuli which cause pain are liable to damage tissue. Accordingly, pain is that experience which we associate with actual or potential tissue damage. It is unquestionably a sensation in a part or parts of the body but it is also always unpleasant and therefore also an emotional experience.

Many people report pain in the absence of tissue damage or any pathophysiological cause; usually this happens for psychological reasons. There is no way to distinguish their experience from that due to tissue damage, if we take the subjective report. If they regard their experience as pain and if they report it in the same ways as pain caused by tissue damage, it should be accepted as pain. This definition avoids tying pain to the stimulus. Activity induced in the nociceptor and nociceptive pathways by a noxious stimulus is not pain, which is always a psychological state, even though we may well

appreciate that pain most often has a proximate physical cause. (Merskey et al., 1979, p. 250)

Pain is an absolutely necessary function, protecting the body from increasing damage. We must feel many types and sources of pain because pain protects us. But if signaling damage were all there is to it, we would not spend much time with pain in describing motivation. A few necessary facts of physiology would satisfy. But pain is not straightforward sensory physiology. Much of it is indirect and modified.

We must consider pain as it functions in the broad range of life experiences. Patrick Wall (1979) compared some aspects of sensory experiences to show how pain grows in complexity. Lights, sounds, and touches have experiences different from internal events of hunger, nausea, and fatigue. Outside stimulation sources are easily described, are not much altered by distracting ideas, and are not necessarily affected by what we have learned and what we do about them. Internal disturbances are difficult to describe, are manipulated by mental states, and can be readily attached to other feelings and activities (see Table 6.1).

Pain is part of living, but there is more to pain than feeling it each moment. The pains we feel are products of lifelong experience, coming from our learning as well as from damaged tissue. Those feelings and what we expect to feel will motivate what we do. We think, we remember, and we plan, and that all makes part of pain. There are many examples. Pain from damaged tissue may not arise until minutes, hours, or days have passed. Some people express great anguish with their pain and tell everyone around them of their suffering; others are stoic and deny being in pain. People use pain and threat of pain to force their will on others. Some use their experience of and talk about pain to manipulate others' feelings. Pain is an important part of the way we live. As we will see in the next chapter, pain's roots reach deep into human affairs.

We begin with pain's obvious function. Whatever else it is, pain plays the adaptive role of communicating about damage and danger. In this sense, pain is vital. Prime examples of that vital communication begin with situations causing injury and lead to acts correcting it. Twisting an ankle, overusing a muscle, leaning against a hot pipe, and grasping a thorny branch are examples. Pain informs us of damage and guides our response to the situation. Those rare people who are born with no sense of pain at all typically do not live long; death comes from some injury or accumulation of damage that pain normally signals (Chapman, 1984).

On the other hand, pain appears when there seems to be no clinically valid reason for it. This is part of what Melzack and Wall (1982) call the puzzle of pain: Why are pain and injury not always related? Pain sometimes appears to come from amputated limbs and from areas of the body that no longer have neural connection. Intense burning pain is sometimes felt at the location of a modest injury, and that pain persists after the tissue damage has apparently healed. These examples of unwanted and apparently useless pain provide part of the challenge for our understanding the many aspects of pain.

One obvious source of pain information is the clinic. Clinical experience is the collected facts, observations, and wisdom of those who observe the variety of a phenomenon. The clinical experience of pain is a good beginning because it shows the breadth of the problem and reveals the inadequacy of simple definitions. In particular, we must see that (a)

there is a great variety of types and intensities of pain, (b) pain comes from tissue damage but is not limited to that source, (c) pain reports from similar sources vary in different people, and (d) the psychological circumstances of an event modify pain experience.

Describing Pain

We use *pain* as a word for a variety of experiences from different causes. A direct cause of pain is localized tissue damage to body surfaces. Two kinds of pain from such sources are common: fast pains and slow pains. **Fast pains** appear in a fraction of a second from punctures, cuts, and shocks. These feel sharp and prickly. **Slow pains** arise from pressures, pulls, burns, and inflammations. Throbbing, aching, burning, and sometimes nauseous painful feelings result. Longer experiences with these are **chronic pains.**

Our personal experience is that each of these gives a qualitatively different pain. We can usually identify the kind and location of the damage. We also know that the greater the damage, the more intense or long-lasting the pain. These are common experiences building our mental pictures of pain.

Localized surface pain is common and easily identified, but it makes only part of the variety of pain causes and experience. Some internal tissues give different messages. Cuts in a portion of the stomach or intestine tissues give no pain, but stretched tissues or inadequate blood supply over a wide area can be severely painful. Stopping blood supply to nearly any tissue eventually forces pain. This condition is called **ischemia** and can be hastened by working the muscles. Brain tissue gives no pressure or pain sensations at all, but the tissue walls of the brain's blood supply tolerate no abuse.

Some causes of pain hide. **Referred pains** are felt from incorrect locations. Many sources of internal damage refer pain. Pain in the shoulder may arise from an inflamed diaphragm. The appendix, which is low on the right side of the abdomen, produces pain appearing to be in the body center just below the rib cage. Angina pectoris, a condition of inadequate blood to the heart, feels like a tightened band around the upper chest with pains down the left arm. Pains from the roots of infected back teeth may seem like earache; pains of front teeth are often mislocated. Many referred pains have neurological explanations. We know that the afflicted organ and the referred location share sensory nerve central endpoints. Although damage in the organs is often mislocated, disturbances to their surfaces are usually felt directly over the organ. See Melzack and Wall (1982) and Guyton (1991) for detailed examples.

Pain without appropriate tissue damage is of several types. **Phantom limb pain** is one form, which is rare. A few amputees feel sensations in their missing limb. Similar sensations remain in patients who have a complete block of actual neural connection to parts of the body. Melzack and Wall (1982) describe four properties of phantom limb pains. First, the pain continues after the tissue damage heals. Some report that the kind of pain is like that of damage existing at the time of amputation or nerve blockage. Second, stimulation to other areas of the body may trigger the phantom pain. Third, desensitizing those trigger points for a short time may stop the phantom limb pain for long periods of time. Finally, stimulation of the nerves related to the phantom limb may give long relief from the pain.

Another pain without obvious cause is **causalgia.** This burning pain appears where a brief trauma to nerves has healed. Gunshot wounds and punctures are typical sources. In most cases, the pain disappears after several months, but for some, it reappears with a variety of gentle stimuli quite unrelated to the injury. Noises and startle stimuli, for example, often worsen the causalgia.

A related sort of pain is **neuralgia.** The original sources are damage to large peripheral nerves caused by viral infections, poor blood circulation, vitamin deficiencies, and some poisons. After healing, pain is sometimes felt along the originally affected nerve.

Collectively, the phenomena of referred pain, phantom limb pain, causalgia, and neuralgia illustrate the puzzle of pain at a physical level. Reported pain does not match tissue damage. More of the puzzle appears in how we interpret our pains.

Interpreting Pain

Pain is a personal and a social experience. Our interpretations affect the pain we feel. Experiences of physical pain depend on the culture we accept and the company we keep.

Suppose that someone asks you to judge your sensations to a small piece of metal placed on your forearm. That metal pad gradually heats, and you report when the first feeling of heat appears, Threshold 1; then when it first becomes painful, Threshold 2; then when it is all you can tolerate, Threshold 3; and then the highest pain you can tolerate when encouraged to take more, Threshold 4. These four temperatures show aspects of the experience. People do not differ substantially in the temperature they can first detect, Threshold 1. People do report different Threshold 2 times at which they first call it pain, and when they can tolerate no more, Threshold 3 and Threshold 4. These differences reflect psychological pain modification. An illustration of hypothetical individual reports is shown in Figure 6.1. Of course, similar patterns would result from any of the many different sources of pain.

Culture Sources

One broad influence on pain experience comes from culture. Different ethnic groups, on the average, report different pain values in experiments structured like the threshold example. Most of the studies are several decades old, but they remain valid sources that have not been altered by more recent study. (Such research was more easily done before

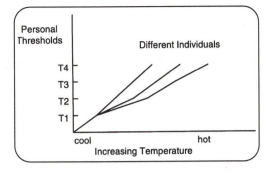

Figure 6.1. A hypothetical experiment showing diverging individual differences in judging pain. As a probe on the skin is heated, people judge it differently.

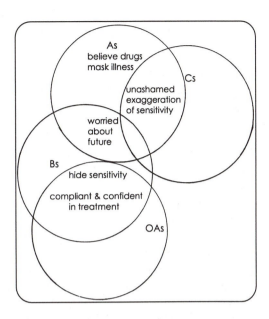

Figure 6.2. Schematic of shared and different attitudes about pain in four groups having different cultural background, based on Zborowski (1952, 1969).

NOTE: Groups A, B, and C are groups of recent immigrants of different ethnicities. Group OA is long-established Americans.

recent standards of human subject review boards.) Researchers, for example, found that women of one ethnic culture tolerated lower levels of electric shock than did women of another group, even when encouraged to accept more (Sternbach & Tursky, 1965). These experimental studies established that differences in pain tolerance thresholds appear to be formed through general cultural experience. The idea for the studies came from earlier and less formal inquiries about experiencing pain.

Mark Zborowski (1952, 1969) studied hospitalized people having pain from herniated disks and similar neurological sources. He compared people in four cultural groups. We will not identify them because nothing is served by reinforcing stereotypes. The first three groups were composed of recent immigrants and the fourth was long-established Americans. The point of studying the immigrant groups was that they had grown up in different cultures but were now in a common testing situation, an American hospital. Zborowski interviewed patients, discussed records with their physicians, and observed them in pain. He also asked other members of each culture about their pain attitudes. He found consistent differences in feelings and expressions of pain. Patients in Groups A and C appeared more sensitive to pain and were

not ashamed to exaggerate their expression of it. Those in Group C focused on the feelings of the moment and expected their doctors to give pain relief. The Group A patients looked for the pain's meaning for the future and disliked drugs because they believed medication masks the basic illness. Those in Group B and Old Americans hid their pain, both in their expression and in delaying medical treatment. Group B members and Old Americans expressed more confidence in physicians than Group A and C patients, and they quietly complied once hospitalization began. Group B patients were like the Group A patients in expressing worry about the consequences of the pain for their future. Most of these attitudes and expressions diminished in the children of the immigrants. With time in American culture, American values were accepted. (See Figure 6.2)

Another illustration of how we embed pain in culture comes from histories of how groups view the pain of other groups. As a general rule, dominant groups see those dominated as less sensitive to pain, and if the group difference is strong enough, the dominated are seen to have no pain at all. Native Americans and indigenous cultures around the world have been described as having less sensitivity to pain than those of Western writers describing them. Slaves were thought to suffer less pain than their masters. Women in nineteenth-century Western cultures were described as feeling less pain. The pain of laborers was valued less highly than pain of elite classes. These are not all historical curiosities. There are still traces of these attitudes, particularly in some physicians' views of women patients, and wherever some degree of dominance exists. Read David Morris's (1991) *The Culture of Pain* for elaboration.

Apparent Meaning

Pain is modified by the interpretation we give to the situation causing pain. Examples come from men injured on the battlefield. Henry Beecher (1946) observed that only one in three men carried into the field hospitals at the Anzio battle in World War II felt enough pain to ask for pain-deadening morphine, yet four of five civilian patients with similar injuries requested morphine. He suggested that the meaning of the injuries may cause the difference. Battlefield injury meant that the war was over for the soldiers and marked an escape from further danger. Injured civilians see their injuries as the beginning of a troubled period, including loss of freedom and perhaps a bleak future. Beecher thought the meaning of the injury modified the resulting experience of pain.

Patrick Wall questioned these conclusions. He asked wounded Israeli soldiers in the Yom Kippur War about their pains and thoughts. They too expressed little feeling of pain, but they talked more of anxiety and guilt than relief. All had intense pain 24 hr later.

Wall (1979) believes that pain often does not appear immediately after injuries when "treatment of the injury does not have the highest biological priority. . . . The three obvious high priority behaviors are fighting, escaping, and obtaining aid" (p. 260).

There is another sense of apparent meaning influencing the pain we feel. Our ideas may prepare us for stronger feelings of pain. We commonly feel pain more intensely when we believe that it may reveal something. After reading in a magazine that a sign of bone disease is pain in certain joints, we may exaggerate feelings of a sore elbow. A slight toothache becomes more painful as we read of cancer of the jaw. A friend's lung cancer makes every chest pain sharper. The meanings we hold of these events affect our feeling of pain.

The flow of information in the situation may also influence pain feeling. Distractions, placebos, and suggestions are examples. Dental work has been done relatively painlessly by allowing the patient to control loud music or noise in a headset. In uncontrived, natural situations, athletes and others may feel no pain from an injury during the remainder of intense activity; the pain comes later when the event finishes. Performing artists find their chronic pain disappears while they are on stage but returns immediately when the performance concludes. Some of this may involve physiological processes, but psychological situations are causing pain reduction nonetheless. These fit Wall's (1979) criteria of highest priorities, although not obviously biological necessities.

The effect of a placebo on felt pain is particularly interesting. A **placebo** is a treatment that has no effect but is given as if it did. Postsurgical pain relief happens for about one third of patients given only a placebo medication under double-blind conditions (where neither patient nor physician is aware that the medication is a placebo). Study with placebos shows that they are more effective against strong pain than mild pain, that injections are more effective than pills, that two placebo pills are more effective than one, that the effectiveness of a placebo weakens with repeated administrations, that they work better with chronically anxious patients, and that they usually have about 50% of the pain reduction of the drug against which they are being compared (Evans, 1974; Lasagna, Mostellar, von Felsinger, & Beecher, 1954). The common theme of these conditions is that stronger perceived treatment yields greater placebo effect. The more it *should* do, the more it does. People who are placebo responders also tend to have greater pain relief from real medications. Placebos fail with young children, showing that placebo effects depend on social and cultural conditioning (Wall, 1979).

The list of interpretations we have reviewed highlights the complexity of pain experience. We know that pain is more than just a direct response to tissue damage. Pain is a complex of information with a physiological origin that can be modified in extensive ways by psychological states. Now we must look at the mechanics of pain and its control.

SECTION SUMMARY: EXPERIENCING PAIN

Pain is a subjective warning of damage and danger, and we cannot live without it. It comes in a variety of qualities, intensities, and durations, yet it is not always truthful. Pains sometimes appear referred to incorrect locations. They can appear where there is no longer any damage, or even any body part.

We differ in how we feel the same external stimulation, some calling it pain when others do not. Pain interpretation is partially conditioned by cultural expectations. Experienced pain is also intensified or weakened by the life meaning it holds; some pains indicate relief from problems, whereas others mean the beginning of troubles. Our pain feelings can also change with our beliefs about pain relief, as in placebo treatments.

These make up the puzzle of pain that can be partially resolved by looking at pain's physiology.

PAIN PHYSIOLOGY

Nociception

At the site of tissue damage, pain begins as **nociceptive stimulation.** Nociception sources are mechanical, thermal, or chemical changes. Stretching, temperature changes, or chemical actions stimulate the endings of certain sensory fibers that are called simply **free nerve endings.** Fast pain is usually rooted in mechanical or thermal changes; slow pain in any of them.

Special among nociceptive sources are chemicals. The effective chemicals, called **alogenics,** come from local tissue processes and include bradykinin, histamine, serotonin, acids, acetylcholine, and potassium ions. Bradykinin is the most potent and is sometimes suggested to be the most involved in nociception.

Nociception does not adapt. Instead, as the pain continues, sensitivity usually increases over time. That result is called **hyperalgesia.** Much of the hyperalgesia comes from inflammation and swelling of tissue by the action of prostaglandins. Prostaglandin

SELECTED NEUROTRANSMITTERS		
Group	*Family*	*Specifics*
Fast-acting, small molecule types	Acetylcholine	acetylcholine
	Amines	norepinephrine epinephrine dopamine **serotonin** histamine
	Amino acids	GABA
Slow-acting neuropeptides	Pituitary peptides	ACTH **β-endorphin**
	Gut and brain peptides	**leucine enkephalin** **methionine enkephalin** **substance P**
	Other tissues	**bradykinin**

Figure 6.3. Some neurotransmitter chemicals and their groups. Those in bold type have important roles in pain

reduction is part of the pain-relief system of aspirin we will examine later.

Neural Complexities

Part of the mechanism of pain control involves systems of neurotransmitter chemicals. Some neurotransmitters involved in pain are highlighted in Figure 6.3.

Three neurotransmitters have roles in slowing or blocking nociceptive stimulation. These are the **leu-enkephalins, met-enkephalins,** and **β-endorphins.** They are called the opiate peptides because they resemble in structure and function the opiate drugs morphin and heroin. Because these neuropeptides are endogenous (made inside the body), the label *endorphin* was constructed by shortening endogenous morphine. **Substance *P*** and **bradykinin** facilitate nociception. The pain role of each of these substances is a combination of what it does, where it does it, and how much is there.

Our common and traditional idea of pain follows the experience of having a cut. Some-

thing specific happens, it stimulates receptors, and pain is signaled along special nerves to the brain. This has been called the **specificity theory** and is a reasonable first draft of a model. After all, this is how we receive other specific bits of vision, audition, taste, smell, touch, and so on. We can't deny that those kinds of events happen. The problem with the specificity model is its simplicity. A variety of this idea is the **pattern theory,** in which there are no special pain nerves; a particular pattern of activity on sensory nerves describes pain.

A more inclusive model of pain describes the product of an active nervous system specially stimulated. Pain experience comes from certain neural activity in the brain. The usual beginning of pain is some kind of tissue damage, but contributing neural activity comes from mental states, from other pains, and from damage unrelated to the current events. The specificity and pattern models suggest quiet message tubes through which pain information flows to a waiting receiver in the brain. Perhaps a better picture of pain is a messenger traveling across a town in heavy traffic to deliver a message to a chaotically busy office. The major point of that image is the context of helping and interfering activity. The nervous system is always active, stimulation from damaged tissue adds to that activity, and one result is what we call pain. Existing nervous activity may suppress, exaggerate, or delay the feelings. The nervous system may also produce pain feelings without apparent external cause. Thus, the idea of pain is not one of a single communication line from stimulation to brain event. The better model uses nervous system complexity, which we are just beginning to understand in details and effects.

The study of pain is a vigorous field. Even the simplest ideas are subject to debate. Hence, it is not possible to proceed in simple efficiency. No single model organizes the facts and principles. We will draw on chapters in a major summary of recent work, Wall and Melzack's (1989) edited compilation *Textbook of Pain*. Some of the established highlights will help us see how pain comes about and how it can be managed. These are the bases for knowing pain as a motivator and the motivation for seeking pain relief.

Free nerve endings stimulate neurons in two pathways. Fast-sharp pains travel to the spinal cord along fast-conducting **A-delta** fibers, following long fibers going across the cord to the other side and then up to specific areas of the thalamus, with some ending in the reticular formation. From there, they are relayed to other brain areas, finally reaching the sensory cortex. When combined with touch receptors, A-delta fibers report the event as sharp and localized.

Slow or chronic pains reach the spinal cord in slow-conducting **C fibers.** C fibers release the neuropeptide **substance-P,** a neurotransmitter chemical that forms and disappears slowly. Slow substance-P action may be part of the reason pain fades slowly and suffering increases slowly over time. These fibers project the signals up the same spinal tracts as the A-deltas to the brain stem, where they end in a broad area involved in suffering, primarily the reticular formation. The consequence is a general feeling of aching and dull pain rather than sensory-like experiences, but they also arouse the brain, making it harder to sleep with pain.

Spinal Cord Pain Gating

Pain is typically a perception of nociceptive stimulation, and it happens when a certain kind of neural activity reaches critical brain areas. Pain from this basic source can therefore be controlled by exciting or inhibiting that information flow. One location of control is the dorsal horn gates of the spinal cord. Melzack and Wall presented a theory of this called gate control theory (Melzack & Wall, 1965). The theory takes its name from a critical part of the system, the modulation or gatekeeping of neural activity passing through the dorsal horns of the spinal cord. Like a gate or valve that ranges from being open to closed, it is a neural control of what is allowed to pass.

Pain is facilitated and inhibited by different parts of the nervous system, but gate control theory pays particular attention to acute pain as it is controlled by sensory and nociceptive stimulation from the damage site and by inhibiting activity coming down from the brain to the dorsal horns.

The gate control theory can be paraphrased in three propositions from Melzack (1986, p. 4).

(1) When the signals from certain spinal cord neurons exceed a certain level, they produce in the brain the complex, sequential patterns of function characteristic of pain.

This first proposition states that specific neural transmission to the brain produces pain.

(2) A gating mechanism in the dorsal horns modulates nociceptive signals passing through the spinal cord. The gating depends on the relative amount of activity in small-diameter fibers (A-delta fiber and C fiber-pain signals) and large-diameter (A-beta fiber sensory information of touch). Small-fiber activity opens the gate and large-fiber activity closes the gate.

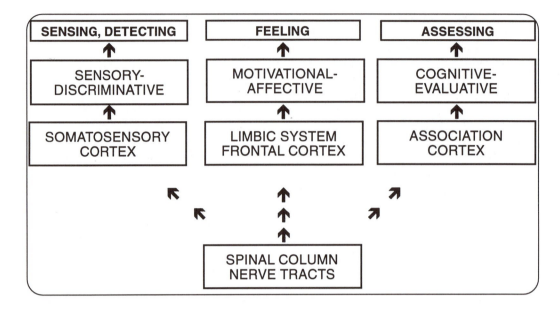

Figure 6.4. An outline of cerebral cortex processing of pain nerve excitations.

Their second idea presents the means of controlling that neural transmission by gates in the spinal cord.

> (3) Brain signals also affect the gating mechanism. A system of large-diameter, fast-conducting fibers sends information to brain areas that then return signals to the gating mechanism.

This third proposition argues that some control of the gates comes from higher centers.

The dorsal horn gating mechanism seems to be one of duration of activity of relaying neurons. Repeated stimulation to large-diameter fibers (A-beta sensory) leads them to increase the time between the pulses in the bursts of activity that they emit. Thus, nociceptive stimulation slows down the large-diameter fiber transmission and purely sensory information of what is happening and where. Nociception in the small-diameter fibers makes them increase the intensity of their bursts of activity, called a "wind-up" effect. Before the pain stimulus appears, both large-diameter and small-diameter fibers have a resting level of firing. They balance so

that the brain gets no pain signals. With nociception, the large-diameter fibers slow their rate and the small-diameter fibers increase theirs. That opens the gate and pain signals flow to the brain.

But there is more. Higher centers along the spinal cord appear to directly inhibit the transmission up the spinal cord. Parts of the brain stem at the top of the spinal cord seem to influence the dorsal horn gates directly.

Although complex, these neural events are the foundations of what we know of pain control in terms of the gate control theory. Cognitive states of the brain affect the arrival of pain mechanisms partly through these brain-stem centers and partly through fast fibers leading directly to the dorsal horn gates of the spine. We know considerably less about the brain's operations that lead to these controls of pain.

Brain Dimensions of Pain

Brain control of pain is most important, but we don't understand how many of the important higher centers function. Simple tracking of fibers and neural messages gives way to fantastic complexity and diffusion. Because we know so little about the detail of human brain function, we resort to generalities. However, even in broad sweeps, there are useful ideas. Quite some time ago, Melzack and Casey (1968) proposed three brain systems, identified partly by pain experience. They suggested sensory-discriminative, motivational-affective, and cognitive-evaluative systems (see Figure 6.4).

The **sensory-discriminative** dimension is the primary focus of much thought and work on pain. This system shows pain as a channel of information like any other sensory experience, telling location, timing, and intensity. Melzack and Casey proposed three fast-fiber routes of A-delta and A-beta fibers projecting sensory detail, each reaching a different brain area. These channels carry touch, heat, and pain information, but their control is different. The channels may be blocked separately by brain process, leading to different kinds of pain perceptions.

The **motivational-affective** dimension of pain appears controlled by limbic system as well as brain-stem areas at the top of the spinal column. These areas receive a convergence of C fiber information from wide areas of the body without detail of where or when it originated. This system makes the feeling of pain, the suffering that people avoid and relieve. Involvement of the frontal cortex is assumed in the feeling process as well. Disturbing this area, as in a lobotomy, reduces aversion to pain; it still hurts, but the concern is gone.

The third, the **cognitive-evaluative** brain dimension of pain, adds context and interpretation to experiences. These are accomplished in the cerebrum. Cerebral cortex control may block pain's other dimensions completely or modify their extent in essentially unlimited ways. Patterns of experience with pain, expectations about pain sources, cultural habits, and so on translate into pain control mechanisms in the cortex. The fast neuron routes to the brain and back to the dorsal horns and other areas are known. The actual processing in the cortex remains a mystery.

Mechanisms of Chronic Pain

Some pains last longer than the causing damage. After the cut, burn, or other damage heals, pain persists or begins again. Other chronic pains may have no history of damage, or the connection to the past is vague, as in headaches and lower back pain. These long-lingering pains are called chronic pains and seem to bring out new complexities of neural action.

After tissue has been damaged and free nerve endings have been stimulated by movement, heat, or chemicals, new forms of nociceptive stimulation appear. C fibers by nature have high threshold receptors; it takes a great deal to set them firing. With damage, C fiber thresholds are lowered a great deal, even to the point of the nerves firing on their own, thus producing the lingering pain and tenderness at an injury site. Different causes are suggested. The terminals may be changed by the injury, their sensitivity may be changed by products from the damaged tissue, or sensitizing chemicals may be leaked from the fibers themselves (Wall, 1989).

Nerve fibers not only transmit impulses of excitement, they also contain and transport chemicals. With damage, C fibers send impulses to the central nervous system and also release chemicals such as **prostaglandins** at the damage site. They thereby dilate blood vessels, accumulate by-product fluids, and sensitize the nerve endings. Chemicals also move centrally along C fibers to inform the system of the nature of the continuing damage. Both the fact of their firing and the chemicals they release over time at the spinal ends affect the central relaying circuits and their sensitivities.

In later stages of repairing damaged tissues, nerve ends may be affected by the forming of scar tissue, by the release of healing by-products, and by new nerve endings sprouting into the healing areas. Sprouts may grow into a neural tumor and continue to stimulate the nerve, they may be unusually sensitive to mechanical stimulation, or they be especially vulnerable to changes in general adrenaline flow. In each case, the sprouts generate continued, chronic pain.

SECTION SUMMARY: PAIN PHYSIOLOGY

Pain stimulation, called nociception, can come from nearly any kind of assault and destruction of tissue. It continues via body chemicals from the damaged and healing tissue. Several different kinds of information are passed through neurons up different tracts of the spinal cord for brain interpretation. A-delta fibers quickly pass information of sharp, acute pain. C fibers move aching, chronic pain signals more slowly. Levels of neurotransmitters play their roles: substance P and bradykinin facilitating nociception, and met-enkephalins and β-endorphins moderating pain stimulation.

The gate control theory proposes that pain is controlled at spinal cord levels by moderating the flow of information along the different neural tracts. All fibers have a normal level that is in balance, but nociception increases A-delta and C fiber activity, tending to open the gates to the brain. With no pain stimulation, the gates are held closed by A-beta sensory stimulation. Pain causes an imbalance that tends to increase as the pain source continues. Also moderating the gates are neural signals coming down from the brain.

At the brain, different systems use nociceptive stimulation. Sensory-discriminative parts of the brain interpret the sensory detail telling where and what the pain is. Motivational-affective areas tell us that it hurts and lead us to avoid more. Cognitive-evaluative systems tell us what it means in the light of experience and the future.

Chronic, long-lingering pain shows various physiological accommodations including lowered pain neural thresholds, accumulation of chemicals at the healing sites and along the neural tracts, and changes in receptors at the healing site.

MANAGING PAIN

Pain is a necessary and persistent aspect of life, and its essential nature is motivating. We avoid pain, and we try to stop it. These are part of broader strategies of managing pain that can mold our personal motives and present motivation.

Wall (1989) points to three conditions of pain treatment and implies a fourth. We have pains where we know the causes and where we do not know the causes. We have pains where we can give adequate treatment and where we cannot yet give adequate treatment. These are sorted in Table 6.2.

Medical Treatment

Traditional medical treatment of pain uses drugs and surgery. Neither is universally effective. Each has its many uses and limitations.

Drug Treatment of Pain

Drugs for pain control are of three basic varieties: the aspirin types, the opium type, and local anesthetics. Each of these pain relievers or analgesics is available under a very large number of trade names and mixtures, giving the appearance that there are different kinds of treatment effects.

TABLE 6.2 Varying Conditions of Known Causes and Treatments of Pain

	Known Cause	*Unknown Cause*
Known Treatment	Sprained Ankle Laceration	Tension Headaches
Unknown Treatment	Rheumatoid Arthritis Angina	Migraine Many Back Pains

The **aspirin** forms of pain medication include aspirin, acetaminophen, (e.g., trade-named Tylenol), ibuprofen, (e.g., trade-named Nuprin or Advil), and many others. All work directly on damaged tissues by blocking the formation of prostaglandins (although the exact mechanism of acetaminophen is unknown). We saw that prostaglandins, along with bradykinin, are chemical enhancers of nociception. Prostaglandins dilate blood vessels, produce swelling, and sensitize nerves (Sunshine & Olson, 1989).

These analgesics reduce prostaglandin effects and consequently reduce the neural sources of pain, largely at the damage site. Aspirin-type agents have no effect on pains of other origins; pains not mediated by prostaglandins will not be reduced. (For example, no drug has been found to block the more potent bradykinin at the damage site.) Aspirin types will be effective against pain from slowly healing tissue, caused by such damage as strains, bruises, and bone breaks. Side effects are several, but the most common are reduced blood clotting and digestive system upsets.

The **opioids** or narcotics operate in the central nervous system by mimicking the effects of the endorphins and enkephalins. Their role there is to modulate the flow of nervous activity downward to the gate control in the dorsal horns. The opiates are also known to act in the periaqueductal gray and below through the spinal cord, directly affecting the flow of peripheral nerve transmission upward. These drugs traditionally have been given to the entire system orally or by injection into the blood. Recently, they have been put directly at certain spinal areas with good results. A common weak opioid is codeine; a strong opioid is morphine (Twycross & McQuay, 1989).

Opiates give a reduction of pain, not a complete blocking, unless the level is high enough to force unconsciousness. There are pains that do not respond to opioids, some that respond only weakly, and some for which opioids work but should not be used. Further complicating the use of opioids is a well-established but unfounded belief that opiates are dangerous to use because they are always addicting. This belief is not supported in the vast majority of medical uses for pain relief. We will develop the addiction issue in Chapter 11, "Addiction."

Local anesthetics prevent neuron communication by blocking normal triggering stimulation. More than 100 years ago, cocaine was found to be an effective local anesthetic. Derivatives of cocaine were refined, and now any of a family of related drugs, most with the name ending -*caine,* can be injected near nerves to reduce function. They vary in how quickly they act, how deeply they penetrate, and how long they last. A serious problem with some is the possibility of permanent damage to the neurons from overuse. On the other hand, there is evidence that pain reduction may last longer than the drug's blocking effect and that successive treatments have longer and longer effects. These lingering effects perhaps result from interrupting self-sustaining neural circuits believed to be part of chronic pain (Bonica, 1989).

Pain Surgery

Surgery for pain relief followed the course of theory about pain. The early notion that pain follows a specific sensory route from the peripheral area through the spinal cord to brain areas fostered attempts to eliminate it by cutting the chain. Peripheral nerves were cut. Spinal nerves and nuclei were sectioned or removed. Brain areas were disconnected from others or destroyed. Many of these forms of surgery gave temporary or partial relief, but not without serious side effects or the eventual return of the same or greater pain.

It appears that the control of pain is too complex for the simple point-source attack of surgery. We are learning that pain is developed in new ways during healing, varying from regrowth of nerve fibers to sensitizing areas with released neurochemicals (Wall, 1989). The surgical cut doesn't just block one route. It adds new possibilities of its own in the healing.

Stimulation Control

Recent treatments apply nondestructive stimulation to nerves to control the system rather than eliminate it. The idea developed from the gate control theory of balanced stimulation from sensory and nociceptor nerves. **Transcutaneous electrical nerve stimulation (TENS)** is applied to the skin surface, to electrodes placed beneath the skin, to electrodes placed on or next to nerves, or to other inputs to the spinal cord gates. Vibrating the skin is also effective. All of these are ways of treating chronic pain. The goal is to deliver sufficient stimulation to the sensory system feeding the dorsal gates but without causing lost sensation or tissue damage. The best site is not usually predictable, and considerable time and practical skill are involved in finding just the right treatment for a patient. TENS gives relief after an average of about 20 min, and if continued, the pain relief increases with time. Many details are variable. For some, the stimulation is best when intermittent; for others, it must be continuous. Some find relief only during the stimulation. Others experience an aftereffect of pain relief (Woolf, 1989).

TENS and a variety of more intense pain relief procedures are sometimes called **hyperstimulation analgesia.** Hyperstimulation is overstimulation, or intentionally applying nociceptive stimulation. Hyperstimulation analgesia can be in any sense modality. Besides electricity and vibration, there have been many traditional pain remedies using heat, cold, pressure, and painful stimulation. Folk medicine has long recommended that irritants such as blistering be applied to parts of the body. These methods are alike in reducing pain by adding some form of stimulation. Skin has been bruised, cut, punctured, and burned in some of these procedures. All seem to work better than placebos and depend on using milder, brief pain to relieve chronic pain (Melzack, 1989).

A certain mystique has surrounded one of these methods, Chinese **acupuncture.** The ancient Chinese traditions placed acupuncture in an elaborate system of energy harmony and used body *meridians* to precisely locate the points of puncture. It is most helpful for patients long accustomed to it, but its effectiveness has been ensured in many experiments with people and animals. Research studies have shown that brief and intense stimulation of certain places on the body called trigger points can remove chronic pain for long periods of time. The Chinese practice of acupuncture is one colorful example. Studies comparing trigger points and acupuncture locations show they are similar, but precise locations of stimulation are not necessary for pain reduction (MacDonald, 1989).

The use of heat, cold, and massage have each demonstrated pain relief beyond that of placebos. The pain relief of heat may be from several mechanisms. Heat may dilate the blood vessels and thus remove the waste products of the tissue damage that produce painful tissue aftereffects. Heat may also be strong enough to add to the sensory stimulation to the dorsal horns and affect the gate control. Cold pain therapy slows nerve response, reduces swelling, and, if done with painful ice packs, may deliver additional sensory stimulation to dorsal gates as well (Lehmann & de Lateur, 1989). Touching and massage are among the oldest natural pain treatments. Modern therapies include a variety of surface and deeper massages, passive and active movements, and chiropractic manipulation of the body. Their effectiveness varies, perhaps a consequence of the variety of pain relief mechanisms being recruited. Muscle tension, sensory stimulation to the dorsal horn gates, improved blood circulation, and reduced swelling are some likely possibilities (Haldeman, 1989).

Psychological Control

Psychotherapy

That the cortex can influence the condition of the gate controls of pain underwrites the psychological treatments that provide pain relief. We reviewed how pain is partly a matter of psychological state. The mental conditions leading to body damage can affect the level of pain felt. We know that our past experience with pain, our cultural style, and the consequences we see of the damaging pain are all psychological factors that help to form the experience. Some of these same conditions may be changed through psychological treatments. Chronic and long-term healing pains may be made more bearable by psychotherapy, making the most of our ability to think the pain to be weak and unimportant rather than strong and debilitating.

Several specific strategies form a collection of cognitive skills for coping with acute pain (Druckman & Bjork, 1991; Turk, Meichenbaum, & Genest, 1983). We can imagine being somewhere else and doing something more pleasant. Pain can be transformed to another sensation, as in Lamaze childbirth training's substitution of pressure for pain. We can focus attention on some perceptual experience, such as the number of

grate holes in the light fixture above the dentist's chair. We can play mental games that are challenging, like trying to think of words beginning and ending with same letter. We can imagine the pain as coming from some heroic experience in which we are acting. Finally, we can see the pained body area as not ours, but rather as belonging to someone else.

Symptom Therapy

Some of the more common psychological strategies of pain reduction are relaxation training, biofeedback, hypnosis, and behavior modification, along with the different kinds of attention focusing just mentioned. None will usually remove the pain experience, but each helps some people, and often a combination of them along with other therapy provides a relief greater than the sum of the individual effects. Few controlled studies support symptom therapies, but lack of research support has not dimmed the enthusiasm of their proponents.

Relaxation training is a component of many therapies but also may be practiced directly. The essential components are a purposeful attitude of rest but not sleep, including maintaining a relaxed state of all the muscles and keeping a content-free, passive mental state for about 15 min a couple of times a day. Simple muscle tension pains will ease, but little research has been done with more extensive, chronic pain.

Biofeedback training uses the idea that we can control a body function if we have more precise information. Biofeedback of brain-wave alpha rhythms, muscle tension, pulse rate, and blood pressure is typical. There are some apparent successes, but close analysis of the mechanisms leaves considerable doubt. For example, most biofeedback training sessions also include the basics of relaxation training. Studies separating these components show that biofeedback does not add significantly to the pain reduction effect. Mental state and belief in biofeedback effectiveness seem to contribute as well, suggesting a placebo or psychotherapy effect may be mediating the biofeedback pain reduction. The case is far from closed on biofeedback, but sufferers should be wary of the often exaggerated promises of pain relief. (See, e.g., Jessup, 1989; Silver & Blanchard, 1978; Turk, Meichenbaum, & Berman, 1979)

Hypnosis of a sort has been used against pain since the first shaman applied incantations and music to patients. Hypnosis was popular with physicians in the 1800s as a tool for controlling pain and has been used in a variety of surgery procedures and dentistry in recent times (Orne & Dinges, 1989). Apparently hypnotized sufferers have sometimes achieved large amounts of pain reduction for extended periods, but that is not typical. It seems most effective for acute and medical pains rather than for those involved with functioning, such as migraines and back pains. The pain reduction also depends on the effectiveness of the hypnosis itself. Some people conform easily and others not at all. Less than one third of people tested report pain reduction. The effect is most likely related to cortex control over the pain experience. Hypnosis appears to involve focusing attention according to suggestions of the hypnotist. The hypnotized person, instructed to disregard the feelings of pain, puts them out of awareness. We will explore the reality of hypnosis in Chapter 10, "Motivated Cognition."

A psychological treatment having enthusiastic but single-minded proponents is **behavior modification.** The varieties of strategies under this label have developed and matured over the past 20 years, but certain basics remain. The core concept is that complex human action can be influenced by the rewards it produces. Applied to pain, the thought is that people get certain rewards from suffering chronic pain and that pain may be reduced or eliminated by removing those rewards. Pain brings sympathy, attention, and relief from work, among other benefits. The treatment is to place the sufferer in an environment in which these rewards are denied; complaints are ignored, and normal movement and work are rewarded. The feelings of pain are of no consequence to the most radical behavior therapists, because those feelings are not observable (Fordyce, 1976).

Disregarding the negative and naive philosophy, the behavioral treatment effectively reduces pain-supporting lifestyles. The efficiency of the procedures is not attractive, however. Long-term changes are not great, and the procedures typically involve lengthy stays in a hospital environment. A serious criticism may be lack of comparison with control populations on the important factors of constant attention and care that the treatment also gives. Nonetheless, attention to removing the benefits of pain should be a part of any treatment program.

Pain Clinics

The best pain therapy strategy appears to be a combination of different procedures appropriate to a patient. Studies suggest that combinations of techniques combine to magnify their individual effects. Thus, hyperstimulation analgesia combined with attention focusing followed by relaxation practice may give more pain relief than each of them applied separately. A program of cognitive reinterpretation along with massage and medication may work. Given that there are no sure cures for pain—no treatment removes all pain—the best therapy must come from applying a battery of those that are partially effective.

In recent years, many pain clinics have appeared, combining contributions from a variety of medical, rehabilitation, and psychological professionals. There is no set structure, but their popularity comes from the success in applying a pattern of treatments simultaneously to chronic sufferers (Newman & Seres, 1986). Along with the synergy of several treatments adding up to more than the sum of their individual effects, pain relief specialists themselves become aware of treatments beyond their specific specialties.

SECTION SUMMARY: MANAGING PAIN

Medical treatments for pain include drugs, surgery, and stimulation. Drug categories are prostaglandin-reducing aspirin types, endorphin-mimicking opioid pain moderators, and neuron-blocking local anesthetics. Each has beneficial applications and liabilities. Surgical intervention, once popular, now is uncommon because long-term aftereffects can be negative. Stimulation therapies add neural activity, perhaps to shut spinal gates, and give lasting relief. Other applications of heat, cold, pressure, massage, and the like perhaps also affect circulation and dissipation of tissue damage by-products.

Psychological treatments address control of the symptoms and how we think about the pain. Psychotherapy works on the interpretation of the pain stimulation and putting pain feelings in a more bearable context. Relaxation training, biofeedback, and hypnosis share a goal of reducing pain feelings by taking mental focus away from pain toward another challenging mental task. Behavior modification supposes that pain's implicit rewards may be minimized by nonreinforcement.

Some of the best relief for chronically and severely pained people has come from pain clinic teams of various health care specialists, each contributing expertise to help the individual sufferer.

FEAR

Fear needs little introduction. Fear is one of the classical emotion labels, and, in the traditional view of many, fear is the clearest example of human emotion. Fear is marked by well-defined elements of mental content, physiological disturbance, and functional actions. Some theorists have used these elements to define fear as a model of all emotion.

Fear Phenomena

In common experience, fear is a mental state of apprehension about dangerous and threatening events. Apprehensions are linked with fear feelings and body conditions. Body sensations include cold and clammy hands, blanched skin, and a pounding heart. These experiences lead us to acts of avoidance. The most likely fear response is fleeing, but hiding and other methods of avoiding may be optimal alternatives. This conventional view of three parts to fear is quite serviceable for specific, typical events. The exemplary model of fear is the approach of a large, threatening animal. The mental states, body events, and appropriate acts all occur, and we conclude correctly that we are afraid.

Implicit in fear events are their objects. Each fear is fear of some thing or event. (This connection with an object separates fear from its cousin, anxiety.) The object of true fear may be real, or it may be an imagined condition or anticipation. The phenomena of fear respond to that object, and usually, we have little difficulty knowing the sources of our fears.

Fear's adaptive theme is avoidance. Fear motivates us to avoid events that might cause damage. To motivate us, fear responds to and anticipates dangerous events. The key to human fear, then, is the evaluation of events for their possibilities. The fearsome animal's approach presents immediate possibilities of harm, based on natural reflex and some acquired knowledge. Other fears are founded primarily in personal experiences of direct harm or perceived harm. After having painful dental surgery, anticipation of more calls up fear. Any pain-producing event adds to our store of knowledge of possible harm agents. These obvious life happenings become the lessons that develop fears.

Fear situations also have social contexts. A social basis for fear is less apparent than in the conflictive emotion of anger or the self-reflection of love, but it is an important developmental aspect of events. Few of our fears are untouched by our life of social experiences. Fears are based on collected experiences of actual harm agents, but how we get those experiences, elaborate them, and express them involve the social community. By communications, we inform one another of fearful events. No person acquires a normal human repertoire of fear without social learning.

Life situations unfold a complex of socially acquired, socially elaborated, and socially expressed states of fear. A pilot sees a large thunderstorm line ahead and lands the airplane to wait its passage. The pilot built a thought of fear by learning that the storms are dangerous, and, to be safe, they must be avoided. The pilot then carries out an orderly avoidance by landing and securing the airplane. A firefighter climbs a ladder to enter a burning building through a third-floor window. Later reports to colleagues about being terrified communicate the mental state. Fear is normally shown by appearance of distress and acts of avoidance, yet the firefighter's fear is displayed only after the necessary acts of extinguishing the fire.

Elicitors of Fear

We have a rich literature of evidence of natural fears in animals. The extent and depth of these facts leave little doubt of their ex-

istence, although details may be argued and refined (Gray, 1987). From young chickens fleeing from hawk-shaped forms (Tinbergen, 1951) to chimpanzees terrorized at seeing a model of a headless chimpanzee (Hebb, 1946), there is ample evidence of animal behavior patterns similar to human fear that suggest a strong biological heritage. These studies give us clues but not direct evidence of specific human fears.

Pursuit of evidence that there are innate human fears is attractive but difficult, partly because no one is without massive cultural exposure. Certain fears seem sufficiently elementary to have natural roots, for example, babies' responses to loud noises and loss of support. Other kinds of elicitors, perhaps including the approach of predator animals, response to strangers, and approach to a drop-off, would seem to have good arguments supporting their functional role in human fitness. The natural bases of other human fears are likely found in broad kinds and families of elicitors. We will consider some aspects of certain likely elicitors.

Fears of the unknown take two logical forms. Either the presence of unfamiliar events or the absence of familiar ones may be fearsome. Strangers evoke fear in infants and adults. Uncertainties about their behaviors appear to be the source of fear, and the more that strangers are different, the greater the fear that they may produce harm. Unfamiliar objects and situations are likewise effective. Many fears of animals are logically in this same class, although there may be some other natural dynamics at work as well. For example, there is an inordinate fear of snakes, lizards, and certain large insects that appears to persist in the face of knowledge that they are harmless. The underlying dimension of these fears is what we don't know. We do know ourselves best, so things like ourselves and that give pleasure to our senses become anchors we hold. Differences—cold rather than warm, slithering or jerky movements rather than smooth walking, hard and damp rather than soft and fuzzy, distorted heads and eyes rather than humanlike shapes, and so on—are fearsome. Things that look like humans look safe; things that look unlike humans appear scary.

The absence of the familiar is a different twist of the frightening unknown. Darkness removes the comfortable cues of the visual world; the cues that inform us that there is no harm in store. When the lights are removed at night, when we enter a darkened room, or when we travel into a dense, dark woods with little range of vision, fear arises. Few people are unafraid of swimming in deep water at night; the mere thought of diving off the dark pier brings shivers to many. Except during sleep, being without normal cues of the world provides a strong basis for fear.

Heights bring fear to many people. We saw that toddlers show strong avoidance of apparent drop-offs presented in laboratory tests. The harm potential of a fall is direct and intuitively obvious, after we have a mature view of the dimensions and forces of our world environment. These provide a solid foundation for elaborating possibilities of falls. Leaning over cliffs, hanging out windows in tall buildings, and seeing others climbing precariously at a great height are all reliable fear stimuli. Those few who show no such fear of heights provide an interesting curiosity to the majority of us.

Fear of evaluation is distinctly social in its form, but it may have roots in natural defense. The result is fear of being examined, of being stared at. Large, staring eyes are part of fear rituals in numerous human cultures, and they are also effective with many animals, especially primates. Perhaps on this base, we are led to fear any sign of evaluation. Socially, being examined presents a direct threat to our self-image.

A paradox appears in our motivations about fear. We often choose to be scared. We submit to a variety of amusements in which we are asking to be terrified. Films delight us with fright. Science fiction stories are typically filled with entertaining distortions of the familiar. Perhaps, the key is the social context of safety and control. We willingly sample frightening experiences when they are matters of choice and under our control. We will soon see this matter of control is a large factor in the varieties of anxiety and stress applications.

Response to Fear

The root of fear responses is sometimes thought to be in the **startle.** An unexpected, loud, sharp noise will force a typical startle pattern: eye blink, specific facial expression, head jerked forward, shoulders raised and pushed forward, upper arms moved outward, elbows bent, trunk moved forward, abdomen contracted, and knees bent. This classical description was accompanied by the suggestion that the startle happens before the brain integrates the stimulus, and thus, it reflects a fundamental pattern that is pre-emotional. The startle response pattern has many elements in common with an initial response to a fear stimulus (Landis & Hunt, 1939).

The function of response to fear is avoidance. Fear is an interaction with potential harm-causing agents. The things we do can separate us from harmful possibilities we perceive. Our interpretations of the situation lead to doing things that keep us at a safe distance. As we keep ourselves effectively separated from the feared, harmful situation, our perception of potential damage weakens. Fear thereby weakens and may eventually disappear.

We avoid harm by fleeing. Flight from the situation removes direct perceptions of potential harm. There are many ways to leave the scene of the feared perceptions. In addition to obvious physical movements away from scary situations, we may also flee by mentally distancing ourselves. At a zoo, the approaching tiger makes a small child try to run away, but we see the strong fence and moat of the zoo enclosure as sufficient to prevent harm. Knowledge of the effective barrier provides a sufficient distance, requiring no further flight. Our imagination may defuse fear. Classic advice to a nervous public speaker is to reduce fear when in front of the audience by imagining them to be less threatening—

naked or dressed as monkeys (unless you are afraid of naked people or monkeys).

We shield ourselves from harmful possibilities by hiding. Remaining unmoving, covered, or embedded in a mass of similar others are some of the possibilities. The human analog of some animal's "freeze" response is purposeful hiding. In our social lives, we commonly shield ourselves by being with others. We hide by being in an audience, a large lecture class, a street-corner gang, or a club. Each person in the group has less personal exposure. Being so hidden, we perceive less possibility of harm, and fear does not develop. But then some people have social fears of being in crowds. The possibilities go on and on.

SECTION SUMMARY: FEAR

Fear is an emotional apprehension of dangerous and threatening events. Fear's adaptive purpose is avoidance. Basic elicitors of fear include uncertainty and what we don't know in events. We also seem to naturally fear potential damage presented by heights. Being evaluated, too, is a common fear cause. We respond to fear by avoiding, including both fleeing and hiding.

ANXIETY

Anxiety Phenomena

Anxiety has a long history as a word for a collection of vague and little understood feelings. Anxiety is often thought of as the experience of fear but without a feared object. Everyone agrees that anxiety includes feelings of uneasiness or distress, often associated with apprehension of misfortune or danger. Sigmund Freud (1926/1959) used and developed the anxiety concept, giving much of its popularity. He wrote of it this way:

> Anxiety, then, is in the first place something that is felt. We call it an affective state, although we are ignorant of what an affect is. As a feeling, anxiety has a very marked character of unpleasure. . . .
> . . . not every unpleasure can be called anxiety, for there are other feelings, such as tension, pain, or mourning, which have the character of unpleasure. Thus, anxiety must have other distinctive features. . . .

> Analysis of anxiety states, therefore, reveals the existence of (1) a specific character of unpleasure, (2) acts of discharge, and (3) perceptions of these acts. (pp. 132-133)

Different theoretical perspectives form the kinds and causes of those feelings. Psychological and psychiatric theories have also viewed anxiety as a cause for mental problems as well as a major symptom of mental disorder.

Anxiety Theories

One of the better ways to grasp the diverse ideas about anxiety is through theories of it. We will look at five examples. Each has a somewhat different philosophical point of view and purpose. Description of the first four was adapted from George Mandler (1975).

Existential Theory

Soren Kierkegaard (1844/1957), in the early 1800s, believed that anxiety is a part of being human. Being free to choose, without knowing the correct choice, causes anxiety. He saw choice as a burden. The more choices we have, the greater the anxiety.

The central concept of existential philosophy is freedom. Freedom is awareness of the possibilities faced in life, possibilities that each person creates and develops. Thus, freedom includes the existence and awareness of choices. Anxiety results from this potential freedom. The very consideration of choices of action brings with it the experience of anxiety. As we attempt to carry any possibility into action, anxiety is a necessary accompaniment. "Therefore, for the existentialist, the antecedents of anxiety are, in a sense, [our] very existence in a world in which choice exists" (Mandler, 1975, p. 184). Without exception, anxiety will be encountered in life. "Growth toward freedom means the ability to experience and tolerate the anxiety that necessarily comes with the consideration of possibility" (Mandler, 1975, p. 184).

Psychoanalytic Theory

Sigmund Freud struggled to build an adequate theory of anxiety. In the course of his work he changed his view to present two theories. Freud's (1917/1963) early theory was a simple derivation of his system of psychic energy. Anxiety came from blocked libido. Whenever we are unable to carry out a sexual urge, there are feelings of anxiety. The anxiety motivates a symptom like repression, which in turn functions to terminate or prevent the subsequent occurrence of anxiety.

Freud's (1926/1959) later theory proposed that anxiety is a signal from the ego. Whenever the ego detects danger, defensive apparatus is mobilized, including repression. If those defenses are inadequate, the ego produces anxiety. Freud bases anxiety process on avoidance of overstimulation. "Anxiety anticipates an impending situation for which no adequate coping mechanism is available. The ultimate unpleasantness is overstimulation, including pain" (Mandler, 1975, p. 179).

In his later writings, Freud also described various kinds of anxieties, which differ by the conditions that produce them. **Reality anxiety** is essentially normal fear and comes from real external threats. **Moral anxiety** comes from the interaction of the ego and the superego, producing guilt or shame. Three forms of **neurotic anxiety** show the failure of the ego's defenses to deal with the id's instincts: focus on a specific phobic symptom, unattached and free-floating unpleasant states, and panic. Some of these are part of recognized clinical anxieties we will meet below.

Learning Theory

Anxiety is a composite of many learned fear responses, according to the perspective of the learning theorists, particularly the people following Clark Hull's behaviorist drive school (most influential during the 1940s and 1950s). For example, O. Hobart Mowrer (1939) and Neal Miller (1948) showed that an internal state they called anxiety could be acquired by classical conditioning of fear responses. In each experience, fear is conditioned to the cues in a painful situation. The collection of these conditioned fears makes up an anxiety condition.

The anxiety concept of learning theory was used to explain avoidance acts. Painful events inhibit responses. Anxiety is conditioned to the cues of a situation, and the resulting learned anxiety motivates avoidance. According to the learning theories, anxiety acts like drive to motivate performance, its reduction reinforces performance, and the conditioned anxiety may interfere with and suppress performance.

Some learning theorists have suggested that there is a continuing level of anxiety that can be measured. Anxiety was thought to be a learned or acquired drive that becomes a permanent part of an individual's personality. Chronic anxiety is thought to be a relatively stable trait and different between people. The Manifest Anxiety Scale (MAS; Taylor, 1953) has been the most widely used test of such chronic anxiety. Its original intent was to measure a drive-like personality trait of people. This test came from the school of behavior theorists led by Clark Hull in the 1940s and 1950s, following their logic that motivation was primarily a matter of one's quantity of drive. Using the MAS test scores, people were separated into groups having high drive (high MAS scores) and low drive (low MAS scores) and then tested on tasks. High MAS-score people performed better on simpler, uncomplicated tasks than low MAS-score people, but on complicated tasks, those in which there are strong interfering initial responses, high MAS-score people initially performed more poorly (e.g., Spence, 1956, 1958).

Cognitive Interruption Theory

George Mandler (1975) sees anxiety as a natural part of certain mental processes serving normal roles in life. For example, anxiety can come from the interruption or threat of interruption of well-planned actions when no alternative acts are available. Inability to complete plans with no other choices available produces anxiety. Once under way, cognitive interruption theory holds that anxiety disrupts other acts as well. Anxiety-dominated activity becomes disorganized. The anxious person begins a search for appropriate actions. As long as that search is unsuccessful, the anxiety continues. The mark of anxiety is helplessness and disorganization.

The life goals we learn from our society reflect an important source of cognitive interruption anxiety. Western culture expects a high level of achievement. It is best to climb the ladder of success, but real society offers only a limited number of positions on that ladder. We are led to construct plans that, for most, are doomed to be interrupted, and being interrupted, we experience anxiety. Achieving success is an appropriate motivator as a life ideal, but the interrupted individual is left with few alternatives and much anxiety.

Cognitive Expectancy Theory

Cognitive expectancy theories are also based in learning, but in learned expectations rather than conditioned fears. The emphasis is on the collected mental events of anticipating dangers, threats, and even the conditions of fear and anxiety. Steven Reiss (1991) lists several contributors to fear and anxiety states.

Expectancies of danger

Sensitivity to injury

Anxiety expectancy

Anxiety sensitivity

Social evaluation expectancy

Social evaluation sensitivity

These contributions to anxiety come not only from direct experiences but also from observation of others' experiences as models and from social communications. The conditions of being afraid and of experiencing anxiety may themselves be part of the aversive complex and contribute to the conditions.

SECTION SUMMARY:
ANXIETY

Anxiety is fear, but without an object, a nonspecific fear that builds with time. Existential theorists assumed that anxiety accumulates in a life of making choices among possibilities. Sigmund Freud first saw anxiety coming from blocked urges but later pictured it coming from failures of ego defenses. Learning theorists assumed anxiety to be accumulated conditioned fear responses, measurable as a stable trait with the MAS and acting to motivate performance. Cognitive interruption theorists think anxiety arises from blocked goals when no alternative exists. Cognitive expectancy theorists believe anxiety is the collection of learned dangers and fearing. Common to these approaches is an idea of unpleasant vagueness. Severe anxiety will be one of several applications of stress considered below.

STRESS

Although ideas such as tension, anxiety, and conflict had been a part of psychological thought for a long time, Hans Selye coined and developed the specific term *stress* in 1936. Thereafter, it was rapidly promoted into an important research and theory concept (e.g., Selye, 1976). The stress idea rapidly resonated with popular culture and became an icon of the modern Western world.

Stress Concept Origins

Selye, a physician turned endocrinologist, published work in 1936 on the effects of physical stressors in a journal article titled "A Syndrome Produced by Diverse Nocuous Agents." He observed that in addition to the body's specific defenses against the treatments, some other responses also occurred no matter what the treatment. He called these the "nonspecific responses to a demand." His experiments seemed clear. There were responses that were not specific in the sense of being unique to a kind of stressor. Particularly, Selye noted three changes in his animal subjects: The adrenal glands were enlarged, the spleen and lymph structures were shrunken, and the stomach and gut formed ulcers.

Selye went on to describe a time pattern of these symptoms. He saw this as a syndrome of response to injury as such. As he developed the idea, he saw it as a model of the larger picture of injury and recovery. Selye called the pattern the **General Adaptation Syndrome** and described it as made up of three stages.

1. An **alarm** stage is marked by general mobilization of body resources to resist the stressor; the general "call to arms."

2. The **resistance** stage is then begun, in which the body's adaptation to the stressor is developed.

3. The stage of **exhaustion** follows continued stressor action, after the adaptation and resistance resources are depleted.

This basic model was widely adopted to organize ideas about stress.

At about the same time, psychologists were becoming interested in tests of the limits of people. Questions of sensory deprivation, tolerance of unusual environments, and response to disasters were posed. These, too, were seen as forms of stress and were expected to affect the physiological systems outlined by Selye. As more study was made, the picture began to get murky. There was no easy definition of what was a stressor, of what the stress response would be, or of which individuals might be most stressed and under what conditions. Even in medical matters, the Selye model was too simple to handle the complexity of the findings, as we will see below.

Thought about psychological stress has continued to have broad development with little real consensus. Among some common research topics of stress are these from Mortimer Appley and Richard Trumbull (1986):

Stress vulnerability of the individual

Perceived risk versus controllability of the stressor

Experience with the stressor

Feedback of consequences at any part of the process

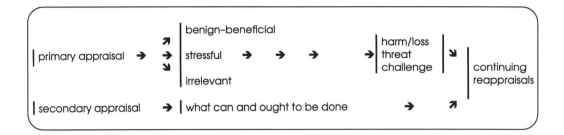

Figure 6.5. Lazarus and Folkman's (1984) outline of primary and secondary appraisals defining stress.

Resources for coping, including wealth and social support

These ideas of stress focus on some of the content. No obvious way is apparent to cover all of the subject of stress. We will continue with some ideas of the phenomena of stress followed by notions of conditions that set it off.

Outlines of Stress

The fundamental dimension underlying stress phenomena is change. The normal events of our lives are a series of changes, but most are of no real consequence. We respond to them as necessary. Stress begins when the changes demand more than can be delivered. Psychological stress arises from a discrepancy between two perceptions: perception of the requirements of a change and perception of resources to handle it. That casual definition merely marks the broad outlines of a stress condition. It would take an inventory of life itself to account for all of the possible changes, all of the individual interpretations of them, all of the resource conditions, and all of the related factors that moderate those many changes, interpretations, and resources. It is more practical to examine specific situations and parts of ideas to grasp the development of personal stress. Some regularities, rules of thumb, and theory emerge.

Richard Lazarus and Susan Folkman (1984) describe what they call the cognitive appraisal processes, illustrated in Figure 6.5. At the beginning of an encounter we simulta-

neously make primary and secondary appraisals. **Primary appraisals** label a situation as benign-beneficial, stressful, or irrelevant. If it is stressful, it can be of several forms: harm or loss (existing damage), threat (anticipated harm or loss), or challenge (anticipated mastery or gain). **Secondary appraisals** note what can and ought to be done. These are assessments of our resources and what effects they might have. As the encounter continues, constant **reappraisals** are made with changing information. We are aware of some but not all of these appraisals.

Factors of Stress

Lazarus and Folkman (1984) believe that among the important cognitions brought into the appraisals are commitments and beliefs. Commitment describes the factors that are important to people. These are the motivational directions of various strengths that push or pull us to make certain choices and seek certain situations over others. You may be committed to have a piece of scenic land for your home. Beliefs reflect how we structure what is happening. One person may have a stronger belief than another about the control that is possible over events. You may hold a general belief in the power of money to sway any person. These beliefs may be subtle and unnoticed until they rapidly change. Commitment to have that scenic land interacts with your belief that its owner will sell it to you if you offer enough money.

Two clusters of aspects of event changes affect appraisals of stress. One has to do with the ambiguity we perceive. The ambiguity cluster includes novelty, predictability, and event uncertainty. Each of these reflects our knowledge of events and their probable impact. Stress arises from thinking of things we don't know well enough. Entirely new objects or social settings yield stress. Many people feel ill at ease on going to the first meeting of a new group, the first day at class, or the first encounter with relatives of an intended spouse. Unpredictable people and events are stressful. The man babbling religious incantations on the street corner is given a wide berth. Just not knowing whether something will happen or not is stressing. Will there be a damaging earthquake? After exposure to carcinogens, will we get cancer? If I smoke, will I get lung cancer? Many procedures of coping with stress center on changing some of this cluster of ambiguity.

Another cluster of stress situation factors involves time: imminence, duration, and time uncertainty. We are most stressed as an expected event draws near. Stress rises before the examination, the first airplane flight, the first dive from the high board, or the first time on the "black diamond" ski slope. The time course of indicators before some stressful events has been well documented. Some events are stressful because they are prolonged, perhaps without any end. Living next to a freeway and its noise, facing a lifetime of being chronically ill, or caring for someone who is permanently disabled are each cases of prolonged events. It is the duration rather than the intensity of the event that is stressful. Time-uncertain events are those that we know will occur at some unpredictable time. They will happen, but when? Earthquakes in California may fit this category. Better examples are the cracks of thunder in a developing thunderstorm or the noise of jets directly under the major flight path of a nearby airport. Stress mounts with the assurance that the event may soon occur.

SECTION SUMMARY: STRESS

Stress was first identified in animals as a physiological nonspecific response to a demand, marked by enlarged adrenals, shrunken spleen, and ulcerated digestive systems. Hans Selye described a pattern of change he called the General Adaptation Syndrome of alarm, resistance, and exhaustion stages. The ideas and concepts transferred easily to psychological situations.

Appraisal of change is the fundamental element of stress. Stress results from perceiving events and demands that we have insufficient resources to handle. Stress events often include aspects of ambiguity and timing. Some psychological factors include commitments and beliefs we have about what is important and what is happening.

PHYSICAL BASES OF STRESS

Body response to fear, anxiety, stress, and the like is based in natural mechanisms that deal with emergencies and respond to continuing threats. From Claude Bernard's *vital pro-* *cesses* to Walter Cannon's *emergency reaction* to Hans Selye's General Adaptation Syndrome, physiologists have observed and speculated about what fearing does to us. The descriptions overlap, and they tie to other physical activity mechanisms. Our view of these will necessarily be simplified and smoothed. (See Asterita, 1985; Gray, 1987; Sapolsky, 1994; as well as physiology texts and current research reports for more details.)

Emergency Physiology

In the middle 1800s, Claude Bernard described a balance of vital processes of the body. A similar concept of homeostatic balances of body systems was developed by Walter Cannon in the 1930s. Together, these ideas provide one controlling aspect of the fear response of the body. Systems respond to change to keep the body essentially unchanged. Fear upsets those balances.

In his classic books (Cannon, 1915, 1929, 1932), Walter Cannon described a diffuse reaction of the sympathetic nervous system and the adrenal gland to pain and strong emotion. To flee or to fight, the body must rapidly prepare for action when needed, so his logic went. He saw the emergency reaction to be a dominance of sympathetic nervous system activity over that of the cranial and sacral divisions of the autonomic nervous system (these latter divisions we now name the parasympathetic nervous system). The eye pupils dilate, and the heart pumps more blood, carrying increased oxygen to cells. Skin arteries and abdominal viscera muscles are tightened. Muscles raise hair erect, and sweat glands activate. Digestion is inhibited, but the bladder muscles are relaxed. Some genital muscles tighten, and the liver releases stored material to the bloodstream. Most important is release of epinephrine from the adrenal gland. All of these are involuntary and diffuse activities of the activated sympathetic nervous system.

Evidence of a pattern of change specific to fear has been elusive. Cannon (1929) saw no autonomic difference between anger and fear, arguing that there should not be any. He said any differences "are not noteworthy" and "are of little significance" (p. 343). Modern study has shown different patterns in processes of fear and of anger (Ax, 1953; Funkenstein, 1956), although later studies failed to find the same differences (Levi, 1965; Pátkai, 1971).

A negative argument is that a specific fear pattern, different from general emotion excitement, does not exist, and the small differences in that direction may be attributed to socially conditioned communication mechanisms. This learning idea is that we notice a pounding heart more readily when we are fearful because we expect it. Blanched white skin is a physical component of fearing that can be noticed. When we are afraid, we become especially aware of body changes that have become culturally associated with that condition. These are real perceptions that feed back into the ongoing assessment of the fear experience.

Arguing for positive physiological differences are several physiologists who note the specific ways our body prepares us for specific acts depending on the situation demands. When fearfully running, energy reserves are diverted to the leg muscles and not spread evenly to all the skeletal muscles. Subtle internal management like this occurs, but as yet, we don't know how (Sapolsky, 1994, pp. 63-64). Our gross measures of the autonomic system are not able to reflect these details.

As we saw in Chapter 4, "Emotion," brain origins of fear are probably among the most primitive reflexes of the older layers of the brain, but these are overlaid with adaptations in the unique heritage of each species, including cognitive interpretation and control. Panksepp (1982) sees fear as one of four major classes of situations that demand of the brain a rapid adjustment. Pain and threat of destruction produce anxiety, alarm, and foreboding, contributing to fear. Panksepp and his colleagues later described a "fear command system" in the brain that

> is thought to actively inhibit competing behavior patterns (such as feeding, reproduction and "pain" responsivity) so that the relevant species-typical defense behaviors can be exhibited. At the same time, memory systems are concurrently engaged to promote the learning of stimulus characteristics that predict threat, which can help organisms avoid dangers in the future. (Panksepp, Sacks, Crepeau, & Abbott, 1991, pp. 18-19)

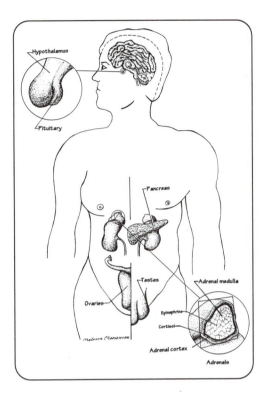

Figure 6.6. Location of glands having a role in stress physiology.

They saw this command system acting on three integrated levels. (a) Perceptual knowledge forms about what is dangerous in the world. (b) Arousal and affective intensity come from hypothalamic influences on hormones, viscera, and somatic preparations for adaptive behavior. (c) Brain stem areas switch on species-typical defenses and inhibit competing acts. Aspects of this command system form naturally in response to pain and threats; others develop with the complexities of life experiences and acquired interpretations.

The need to deal adaptively with threat must be a part of the designed functions of each species. There is no reason to see ourselves as exceptions, although there is good reason to expect that fear has been elaborated in our evolved design and in our cultural overlay. That suggests caution in looking for causes solely in physiology, especially by extrapolating from similar acts of other species.

Stress Physiology

We have already noted the variety of changes coming from some kind of emergency exciting the sympathetic nervous system. For the past several decades, the physical focus to stress has been on the hormones of the endocrine glands. It all comes down to the pattern of secretions. The complexity of this system continues to amaze, and we are fairly close to understanding some of its consequences. The keys are in knowing feedback and regulatory systems, accumulations of hormones, and timing and duration factors. A place to begin is with a quick look at where the major glands are located and their important parts. Then, we will examine the somewhat central role of the pituitary gland.

A picture does it best. The glands having roles in the body's fearing and stress reactions include the pituitary, thyroid, and adrenal glands; the pancreas; and the ovaries and testes. Other areas and functions affected by secretions are also shown in Figure 6.6.

The two adrenal glands are located atop the kidneys and are each made of two different organs closely integrated. One part is the **adrenal medulla,** an internal core, and the other part is the **adrenal cortex,** surrounding the medulla. These organs react to different events and with different effects.

The adrenal medulla directly and rapidly responds to sympathetic nervous system stimulation from the brain, probably by way of the hypothalamus, producing epinephrine (the British term is *adrenaline*). From the same sympathetic stimulation, norepinephrine (*noradrenaline* in Britain) is secreted all through the body. Their effect is to jump-start some organs and to shut others down for the coming emergency need for action. Among the most obvious effects are our speeded heart and raised blood pressure. A curious fact to consider later is that our norepinephrine levels are higher when we are depressed (Gruen, 1993; Siever, 1987).

Each adrenal cortex is composed of three layers—three shells, each fitting over the other, with the medulla at the center, four parts in all. The major stress reaction is release from the middle adrenal cortex layer of glucocorticoids, 95% being cortisol. Glucocorticoids control metabolism throughout the body. Stress levels of cortisol affect production and retention of glycogen in the liver and release of amino acids from various body tissues to circulate in the blood. The glycogen store gives a ready energy resource, and the amino acids are used for tissue repair where needed. Sustained high levels of cortisol will lead to weakened muscles and inhibited inflammation and immune systems. Stress levels of cortisol are stimulated by the hypothalamus via the pituitary gland's ACTH (corticotropin). High levels of cortisol are believed to produce feelings of anxiety and uncertainty.

The inner layer of the adrenal cortex produces small amounts of androgens under the influence of ACTH from the pituitary. The androgen produced here is androstenedione, not testosterone, and men secrete about 20 times as much as women. The outer layer produces mineralocorticoids, principally aldosterone. **Aldosterone** from the outer shell controls levels of sodium, potassium, and other vital electrolytes in the cells. Stress increases the aldosterone directly through the central nervous system and indirectly from the sympathetic nervous system and from greater than normal levels of ACTH from the pituitary gland. The results of stress-level aldosterone are decreased potassium and increased sodium. The greater sodium leads to body water retention, necessary for preserving electrolytic balance.

From the earliest studies, endocrinologists knew that the hormones of the pituitary affect the secretions and functions of other body glands in more remote locations, much like a puppet pulling strings. One of the major stress reactions, as we just noted, is secreting the hormone ACTH (corticotropin), which releases glucocorticoids and other hormones from the adrenal glands. Pituitary hormones stimulate the pancreas to release glucagon, which checks insulin and aids glucocorticoids in raising glucose levels. Glucocorticoids, glucagon, and the sympathetic hormones epinephrine and norepinephrine release stored energy in stress emergencies.

Protein is broken into usable amino acids, glycogen is converted to glucose, and fat (triglycerides) is transformed into fatty acids and glycerol.

Prolactin from the pituitary affects fertility during periods of sustained stress. Endorphins and similar hormones from both the pituitary and other parts of the nervous system diminish pain. Vasopressin from the pituitary stops urine formation and signals retaining water. Finally, several hormones under pituitary control are reduced or stopped, including the reproduction hormones testosterone, estrogen, and progesterone. The case for growth hormones is unusual in having first an increase and then a decrease with continued stress.

Of course, the pituitary does not decide all of this on its own. Pituitary secretions are directed by hormones from the hypothalamus, an integral part of the brain. Brain interpretation of situations and body conditions is what determines the specific stress reactions in the body and how they are orchestrated.

Lack of consistency and uniformity across stressors is an important aspect of these physical responses. We have listed the possibilities. Many of them tend to go together for a variety of happenings that alarm us. Yet, there are major differences for specific situations. Here the salient factors are the following: what emergency? what response? and how long? These are the puzzles we are beginning to solve.

In this area of psychology, the pattern of the physical reaction will be extremely important and will likely sort out the generalities and inconsistencies we are finding. But the reverse has been true as well. The physiologists could not predict and were surprised by the moderation of stress reactions of purely psychological factors, such as social support or a friend's touch. There are many kinds of stress situations, and each is likely to have its unique body reaction using the pieces we have outlined. For one example of how we might picture some of that uniqueness, we look briefly at the global effects of the two parts of the adrenal glands.

Marianne Frankenhaeuser (1986) has proposed that the two systems of the adrenal glands are differentially activated by environ-

TABLE 6.3 Adrenal Hormone Reaction to Different Situations (adapted from Frankenhaeuser, 1986)

	Adrenal Medulla Epinephrine	Adrenal Cortex Cortisol
Effort and Distress	↑	↗
Effort Alone	↑	↓
Distress Alone	↗	↑

ment events. Conditions of effort and of distress combine in special ways, as shown in Table 6.3.

Situations of effort and distress increase both the catecholamines (medulla) and cortisol (cortex), but with perhaps more of the former. This is typical of what we think of as high-stress normal work life. Effort without stress increases only the catecholamines and may decrease the cortisol. The feelings are positive in these situations of successful coping and personal control. Finally, distress without effort increases cortisol greatly with only a modest increase in catecholamines. These are conditions of passivity and helplessness that give feelings of anxiety and depression.

SECTION SUMMARY: PHYSICAL BASES OF STRESS

In the 1800s and early 1900s, physiologists saw the sympathetic nervous system seem to act in a coordinated way to underwrite action: fleeing or fighting. Modern theory and research have elaborated this view, describing, for example, the fear command system. Stress physiology is tied to the adrenal glands. Each central adrenal medulla produces epinephrine, which accelerates and maintains intensity of sympathetic nervous system efforts. One layer of each adrenal cortex produces cortisol, directing energy resources and producing feelings of anxiety and stress. The relative balance of epinephrine and cortisol correlates with combinations of activities having effort, distress, or both.

LIFE APPLICATIONS OF STRESS

To bring out further principles, we will look briefly at some applications of fearing and stress that have been highlighted in research. Each has been popular with researchers and the public.

Life Change Stress

A popular research strategy is that of listing happenings of life and trying to construct a scale of their contributions to stress. One productive research approach uses a Social Readjustment Rating Scale that assesses the stress potential of 43 common major events. The 43 events have been scaled in terms of how stressful each is in Life Change Units (LCUs; Holmes & Rahe, 1967). (Some typical events and their LCUs are shown in Table 6.4.)

The sum of recent Life Change Units predicted future health problems (Rahe, 1975). One study of a population of young adults showed a high incidence of illness dur-

TABLE 6.4	Some Items From the Social Readjustment Rating Scale Assessing Magnitude of Change in Certain Life Events

Life Event	Assumed Value of Life Change Units
Death of a spouse	100
Divorce	73
Jail term	63
Personal injury	53
Marriage	50
Fired	47
Vacation	13
Christmas	12

ing the 9 months after the measure was made for those with LCUs greater than 300. Almost half had significant illness, compared with less than 1 in 10 of those with LCUs less than 200. In other studies, LCU measures were related to injuries in athletes, to heart disease, and to stomach ulcers.

Crowding

Crowding is usually thought to be stressful. Some of this idea comes from general feelings of need for privacy and distance, and it is also seen in animal species that function in ways to keep themselves separated. There is no simple relationship in humans. Physical density may be a necessary condition for crowding stress, but it is not sufficient. Crowding is a subjective state of feeling that is rooted in our experiences and expectations.

Cultural norms and adaptation also set some limits on crowding stress. Many people in Tokyo, Jakarta, and Hong Kong live under incredibly dense conditions, yet seem to have no more stress than those in less dense places. People come to expect crowding in some places and not in others. The close seating at a ball game is tolerated, whereas the same density of seating in our living room is not acceptable.

One hypothesis is that crowding stress appears when the density of others restricts our possible acts. At a performance event, we are seated in great density without normally feeling crowded, but at the conclusion, when the flow of people exiting restricts everyone's movement, we are stressed by the same density of people.

A second idea is that we feel crowded by the stimulus overload of too many others. The stress may arise from not being able to deal with the amount of social information that the many others present. Underlying this view is the arguable assumption that we are naturally autonomous individuals and continuously dealing with others as competing rather than as complementing and supporting us. A different assumption is that we normally are accustomed to a limited set of individuals; family members and those we know well. In the crowd, we face people whom we don't know, and we fear them because they are unfamiliar.

A third view is that crowding effects are rare unless there are distinct and usually negative aspects of those others. Crowding makes other dimensions of people more important. If an aspect of people is annoying, say, they have unclean body odor or they are smoking, then more of them will be troublesome. Crowding does little more than magnify those other mental or physical dimensions of stress. The density of others, pure crowding, is neutral (Freedman, 1975).

Coronary-Prone Acts

Some years ago, research scientists described a pattern of actions of people who had a higher risk of heart disease (Friedman & Rosenman, 1974). This became famous as the Type A pattern. Type A people have a high level of competitive striving for achievement, an exaggerated sense of time, and abnormally strong hostility and aggressiveness. They described Type A as an

> action-emotion complex that can be observed in any person who is *aggressively* involved in a *chronic, incessant* struggle to achieve more and more in less and less time,

and, if required to do so, against the opposing efforts of other persons. (p. 67)

The alternative personality was called Type B. Type Bs tend to be more relaxed and freer from time-imposed pressures. These Types A and B are the extremes on a dimension of such activities. The most important element of difference is likely the Type A's proneness to hostility. This is the element that makes them react to each challenge as a threat that activates their emergency systems. Type A people have been shown to have a higher physiological arousal in stressful competitive situations, and they have a twofold higher risk of coronary heart disease.

Clinical Anxiety Disorders

Perhaps listing psychiatric anxiety conditions as a form of stress is stretching the text organization a bit, but in a sense, they fit here. Anxiety, in some measure, is a mildly stressing part of life. It can also come to dominate and interfere with life. Under certain conditions, anxiety becomes a clinical condition. A standard reference for psychiatric disorders, the *Diagnostic and Statistical Manual of Mental Disorders* or *DSM-IV* (American Psychiatric Association, 1994) lists 12 conditions of anxiety disorders. Two examples will serve to outline the conditions of psychopathology. In addition, we will start with two conditions, formerly among the variety of anxiety disorders, that now are a part of listed disorders. These extreme forms will help us to form ideas about fear, anxiety, and stress and note the normal limits.

Panic Attack

A panic attack is an experience marked by sudden and intense fear, anxiety, or abnormal body sensations. According to the *DSM-IV,* the essential features of a panic attack are

intense fear or discomfort, in which four (or more) of the following symptoms developed abruptly and reached a peak within 10 minutes:

(1) palpitations, pounding heart, or accelerated heart rate
(2) sweating
(3) trembling or shaking
(4) sensations of shortness of breath or smothering
(5) feeling of choking
(6) chest pain or discomfort
(7) nausea or abdominal distress
(8) feeling dizzy, unsteady, light-headed, or faint
(9) derealization (feelings of unreality) or depersonalization (being detached from oneself)
(10) fear of losing control or going crazy
(11) fear of dying
(12) paresthesias (numbness or tingling sensations)
(13) chills or hot flashes. (APA, 1994, p. 395)

Agoraphobia

Agoraphobia involves fear or anxiety about being in places where escape is difficult or help may not be available. The *DSM-IV* criteria for agoraphobia include anxiety or phobic avoidance that isn't part of another disorder, and

A. Anxiety about being in places or situations from which escape might be difficult (or embarrassing) or in which help is not available in the event of having an unexpected or situationally predisposed Panic Attack or panic-like symptoms. Agoraphobic fears typically involve characteristic clusters of situations that include being outside the home alone; being in a crowd or standing in a line; being on a bridge; and traveling in a bus, train, or automobile.
B. The situations are avoided (e.g., travel is restricted) or else are endured with marked distress or with anxiety about having a Panic Attack or panic-like symptoms, or require the presence of a companion. (APA, 1994, p. 396)

When agoraphobia is tied in with panic attacks to become a full-blown disorder, agoraphobics usually have a period of stressful life events some months before a first incident of panic in a public place. Following that initial panic, the individual will retreat to known safe places like the home. They appear to have learned that their panic is caused by those other places, and they attribute their physical evidence of panic to being exposed in public. The result is a vicious circle, called by some a "fear of fear." They believe that the symptoms of panic will lead to some dire state that they may not survive. To escape those symptoms, they avoid any situation in which they might not get immediate help or relief. They have come to fear the features of their fear.

Social Phobia

The essential features of a social phobia, according to the *DSM-IV* include

a marked and persistent fear of one or more social or performance situations in which the person is exposed to unfamiliar people or to possible scrutiny by others. The individual fears that he or she will act in a way (or show anxiety symptoms) that will be humiliating or embarrassing. (p. 416)

and

Exposure to the feared social situation almost invariably provokes anxiety, which may take the form of a situationally bound or situationally predisposed Panic Attack. (p. 417)

Examples of common social phobias include fears of speaking or performing in public. Less common are anxiety over using public lavatories, eating in public, and writing in the presence of others.

Common mild forms of social anxiety include distress about talking to authorities or others of the opposite sex. The trait of shyness comes to mind, but the social phobic has a more serious response, including physiological symptoms, extreme feelings of discomfort, and very negative self-evaluations. Some writers emphasize social phobia as a disorder of evaluative threat.

Generalized Anxiety Disorder

The *DSM-IV* describes a person having a generalized anxiety disorder as showing excessive uncontrollable worry for 6 months about different things, where the anxiety is excessive as judged by the real impact of the events. The diagnostic criteria include

A. Excessive anxiety and worry (apprehensive expectation), occurring more days than not for at least 6 months, about a number of events or activities (such as work or school performance).

B. The person finds it difficult to control the worry.

C. The anxiety and worry are associated with three (or more) of the following six symptoms (with at least some symptoms present for more days than not for the past 6 months)
   (1) restlessness or feeling keyed up or on edge
   (2) being easily fatigued
   (3) difficulty in concentrating or mind going blank
   (4) irritability
   (5) muscle tension
   (6) sleep disturbance (difficulty falling or staying asleep, or restless unsatisfying sleep) (pp. 435-436)

Aaron Beck and Gary Emery (1985) listed a number of predisposing and precipitating factors of anxiety disorders. Each individual may have a unique combination of these factors. The predisposing factors include: hereditary disposition, physical diseases having lasting effects, past traumas, inadequate experience to develop coping, and counterproductive thoughts, unrealistic goals, and so on. The precipitating factors listed are physical disease, severe acute stress, chronic insidious stress, and conditions of specific stress for vulnerable people.

The most common reported symptoms of people with generalized anxiety disorders are inability to relax, tenseness, difficulty in concentration, fright, and fear of losing control.

Depression

Life does not usually run a smooth and even course. There are periods of increased arousal and energy, times of normalcy, and sessions in which things in general aren't worth doing. This section is focused on those periods of being down. Sometimes, these periods are low enough to be called states of depression. Depression can be a debilitating pathology arising from a variety of causes. We believe some depression comes from heredity. Conditions of the brain are involved. Psychological causes are legendary. Putting this together into a simple, coherent description may not be possible.

The symptoms and phenomena of depression are several and not always obvious.

1. Most common is loss of pleasure in any aspect of living. None of the little acts or even major events are enjoyed. Instead, there is nothing at all, with slight tinges of deprecation.

2. A pattern of negative thinking emerges, sometimes with delusions. The happenings of living are distorted to fit a negative picture. Events are seen in their worst light and as getting worse.

3. All acts are done slowly or not at all, even necessary ones. Depressed people eat less, sleep poorly, and are uninterested in sex. Daily chores are kept to a minimum. Planning new activities is nearly nonexistent, even scheduling professional help.

4. Yet, the depressed person's body is not without available energy. Glucocorticoids, for example, may be flowing heavily. Signs of active stress are there. The body, and often the mind, is in a state of tensed opposition. It's like a standoff in a mental battle that does not allow the body to act.

Depression is not an equal opportunity condition (Gruen, 1993). Women are 1.2 to 2 times more likely than men to experience depressive symptoms. Younger people have a higher incidence of depression. Having major negative life events makes us more depression-prone. Even a period of consistent daily hassles can set it off. There is good reason to believe that some of us are biologically less able to overcome negative stress experiences, a kind of physical predisposition to become severely depressed if the right triggers appear.

Biological Depression

We know that the neurochemistry of depressed people is disordered. We have many ideas about what the problem is, but we don't as yet have a complete picture. Most theorists believe that depression involves either too much or too little norepinephrine, and that serotonin and endorphin levels are involved, but the various facts haven't yet clicked together. We suspect the role of some enzymes and other intricate mechanisms of producing and breaking down norepinephrine. There may even be a Factor X, some component, perhaps a neurotransmitter, that has eluded detection. With this complexity, we don't pretend to have good answers. For a readable discussion of the theories to date, see Robert Sapolsky's (1994) *Why Zebras Don't Get Ulcers.*

We will not discuss medical depression further. Common periods of mild depression have enough of a direct bearing on motivation. The causes are many, but the condition is very difficult to pin down.

Learned Helplessness as Depression

If we have been exposed to repeated experiences in which the outcomes could not be controlled, those learned beliefs may be generalized to new situations. That is, we may learn to be helpless. With such a belief, we will not be able to learn, or at least we will not try to learn new tasks.

There is a long history of this kind of thing from studies with animals in which the motive for learning is aversive. Ivan Pavlov called it *experimental neurosis* when his dogs were given more and more difficult discriminations to make. They eventually refused to respond to anything. Norman Maier (1949) found that rats given problems that could not be solved would adopt defensive acts that looked like a motor fit and a temporary break with the world.

More recently, some systematic experiments by Martin Seligman (1975) with dogs and other animals have illustrated the strength of the result, and the label applied to them is *learned helplessness.* A series of inescapable shocks in what had been an avoidance learning situation led to the dogs being apparently unable to learn to avoid shock. They seemed to give up and make no further attempts to do more than accept the shock. In each arrangement, it is a response to inescapable punishment.

Three things seemed to happen in learned helplessness in animals and then in studies with people. First, there appeared to be a decrease in motivation; the incentives seemed to lose their value. Second, there was a reduced capacity to work with information in the situation. Third, there was a distinctive emotion pattern, starting with a stage of fear and anxiety and giving way to apathy and depression, with some occasional anger.

Some people appear to be naturally more immune than others to helplessness-causing events. Those who have a personality style of relying primarily on themselves for sources of information and reward appear to have this immunity. It is logical that people who depend more on others for the validity of their actions will be more affected when that external information is withheld.

This relationship may develop in the reverse direction as well. Following a pattern of life experiences of inconsistent information and rewards for correct performance, we may come to rely more on the internal and less on external sources (or we may develop a self-perception of being generally incompetent).

Depression From Cognitive Distortion

Aaron Beck (1976) has developed a description of depression based on a stable but pathological self-picture of having failed, especially in comparison with others. The depressed person believes that most events of the world have negative implications, that life is a source of defeat and despair. The thinking of chronically depressed persons becomes biased. They alter their perceptions of events to be negative, ignoring any positive news. They go even further to misrepresent or selectively focus their perceptions to make it even worse.

These are global perceptions in that the depressed person sees no positive future. Mistakes or criticism are interpreted in a general way, showing how defective one is as a person. Depressed people are certain that nothing will turn out right. Thus, they see little point in doing anything, and they often give up on the routine tasks of life. They claim to have no energy for doing these things and see no use in trying.

SECTION SUMMARY:
LIFE APPLICATIONS OF STRESS

A commonly told research discovery showed that people with an accumulation of life change events tend to have consequent health problems and injuries. Crowding is not always a stressing situation, but when it is, we propose that it is stressing because it limits our action choices, gives us too many others to relate to socially, or makes unpleasant aspects of others more

important. Type A styles of acting are nearly synonymous with stress, following early research tying Type A striving to more frequent heart diseases.

Clinical anxiety disorders range from panic attack to agoraphobia to social phobia to generalized anxiety disorder and others. Panic attack disorders are relatively brief but very intense mental and physical fear symptoms. Agoraphobics develop strong fear of having panic symptoms where they cannot get help, and thus they avoid such places, literally being afraid of being afraid. Social phobics have intense fear of being evaluated in some aspect of their actions. Generalized anxiety disorder is a long-lasting pattern of anxiety symptoms that interfere with valued living.

Depression seems to be opposite to the excitement of stress, fear, and anxiety, but it shares the negativity and similar physiological patterns of energy. Although some depression is or becomes essentially a medical disorder, much experienced depression arises from negative experiences, such as learned helplessness, with its decreased motivation, incapacity to use information, and negative emotionality. Chronically depressed people tend to see and interpret the events around them in negative terms.

CONTROL AND COPING WITH STRESS

Life changes do not necessarily lead to physical illnesses when they reach some critical mass. We are not always passive victims of change. We can make adjustments and can act to break the stress–illness connection. The ways to deal with stress and anxiety are many and complex. The common term for the active efforts is *coping*.

Following the work of Lazarus and Folkman (1984), coping may be defined as "constantly changing cognitive and behavioral efforts to manage specific external and internal demands or both that are appraised as taxing or exceeding the resources of the person" (p. 141). This definition of coping emphasizes not the outcome but the process—the process of thinking and doing, changing with time and the stressors. Coping does not include automatic adaptive activity but refers to effortful and directed acts that attack the situation of stress and its effects. Coping then is constantly changing effort to manage stressful demands.

The process of coping may be described in terms of certain components similar to those of the General Adaptation Syndrome. First, the situation is perceived and appraised for its stress content, as we described earlier. The level of stress perceived will depend on many factors, such as whether this is the first time or whether it has been experienced before and whether we are facing it alone or are being supported by others. Second, defenses are marshaled to handle the stress effects. These may be any of a large collection of acts, including cognitions. Finally, these processes may be inadequate or may fail, perhaps leading us to consult others for help. Improvements in coping with stress may be applied at each of these three components: appraisal, defense, and reporting. Coping strategies are all matters of getting and maintaining some kind of control over what is happening.

Some forms of coping address the stress problem, and others are directed to the resulting emotion and experience (Folkman & Lazarus, 1980). Problem-focused coping attempts to change the situation to make it appear less stressful. Students often become stressed and anxious as they anticipate periods of examinations. Problem-focused coping may include making adequate preparation by using study tools that ensure mastery of the materials or taking practice examinations. The coping tasks focus on altering either oneself, the situation, or one's interpretation of the situation so that less stress is appraised.

Emotion-focused coping is most likely when there is little to be done about the stress situation. For example, stress and anxiety come from learning you have a high likelihood of hereditary heart disease. That stress may be reduced by immersion in work and hobbies to be distracted from the situation. These tasks focus on removing the emotional feelings component of the stress.

These two kinds of coping may be at odds in some situations. Attempts to change the problem may increase the emotion, or ways of reducing the emotion may increase the stress appraised in the situation. As we get near to taking an important examination, the stress builds. We may choose to reduce those emotional feelings by stopping preparation and doing something else to get it out of mind. That in turn increases the perception of being unprepared and results in increased stress. Or, we may have reached a high level of mastery of the material for the examination, but continue to study and review and thus continue to be exposed to the stress of anticipation. The continued work prevents other stress-reducing acts from being performed. The trick is to find the point of adequate preparation and then turn away from the situation.

Coping Resources

There are many basic resources for dealing with stress. Lazarus and Folkman (1984) provided this list. First are health and energy. Illness and weakness leave little with which to fight. Up to a point, the greater our strength, the more effective the coping.

Second are positive beliefs. There are many examples of the value of a belief in making one's coping effective. The art of medical healing assumes that the will of the patient is a large component of the success. Inspirational literature and programs of positive thinking are widely acclaimed. To be sure, excessive morbidity and negative thinking can work against our coping with stress effectively. However, it is likely that some kinds of strong beliefs can run counter to effective coping. Putting on a happy face may take the place of a more effective emotion-focused coping action. Some theological beliefs in the inevitability of "God's will" may prevent some people from trying problem-focused coping strategies.

Third are problem-solving skills. As we have more experience and skill at solving problems, those that cause stress are likely to

be readily handled. These skills accumulate with successful life events, and they can also develop from specific instruction and passive observation of others' lives.

Fourth and fifth are social skills and social support. A great amount of stress involves our relations with others, directly or indirectly. Thus, the skill we have in personal interactions will determine a large part of the felt stress and anxiety in situations. Coping often depends on relying on others. Coping may use the presence of others willing to listen, to help, or to provide needed professional therapy.

Sixth are material resources. Those with money are more able to buy a change of the stressful environment, help of professionals, or whatever else is needed. Without such resources, often itself a component of the stress, the situation does not change and may be viewed as unchangeable.

Coping Acts

Stress sometimes can be reduced by choosing the situations. By taking charge of the where and when of troublesome events, people can tolerate larger amounts of stress with fewer costs. Studies have shown that such a process works with pain and with very loud noise. People tolerate more when they can choose where and when they receive stress. People who were asked to look at pictures of accident victims had fewer physiological stress signs if they had the option of turning off each picture when they wanted, even though they didn't do it (Geer & Maisel, 1972). A similar effect was found with bursts of aversive noise. Although both groups received exactly the same noise bursts, those who had an option of controlling a stressor reported fewer symptoms such as racing of the heart, ringing in the ears, sweating palms, chest pain, flushing, and dizziness (Pennebaker, Burnham, Schaeffer, & Harper, 1977).

Some other studies suggest that the act of doing something is a critical factor (Gal & Lazarus, 1975). Stress effects are reduced by making some attempt to change it, whether it is partly effective or not. Sometimes students do a poor job of studying, but because they are doing something and believe it to be proper, feelings of stress are reduced.

A popular prescription for coping in some situations is becoming more assertive (Alberti & Emmons, 1990; Wolpe, 1958). Assertive acts do something in the face of risks. Assertiveness training assumes that taking such action is a learnable skill. Experience in doing will weaken the stress and anxiety attendant on the act. There are four assertiveness training assumptions:

1. Effective skills to act must be learned.

2. Our self-concept must be changed toward the positive.

3. Inhibiting states such as anxiety are due to weak assertive skills.

4. Assertiveness training will give us an enduring change in action style or personality.

Cognitive control of stress banks on the idea that fear of the unknown is a powerful motivator. Acts leading to knowing more should reduce the feelings and hence affect the perceived stress. Gaining information may reduce stress. One kind of helpful information is knowing the certainty of the stressor happening. Another is detail. Information about the details of a sensory experience with a stressor will moderate its effects. Knowing that the cold water treatment we are about to receive to the arm will produce numbness and other sensations of the fingers, for example, is more effective in reducing the stress than knowing the nature of the refrigeration equipment and the procedures of the experiment. But there is one kind of information that may actually increase felt stress: mention of the pain of the stressor (Leventhal, Brown, Shacham, & Enquist, 1979). The difference is one of what to expect. If an expectation is built of sensory experiences excluding pain, the focus will be on that. If pain is expected, the focus is on pain. Thus, stress will be reduced if it can be interpreted as less threatening and more informative.

We tell stories to ourselves and others as one way of making stability in our lives. We can construct stories that make stress effects unlikely, working like the mechanism of a medical inoculation, or we can build stories of events after they have happened to reduce stress effects. We can recall the picture of the lives of flight attendants described in Chapter 4. "Emotion," about "managing their hearts" in dealing with their job stresses (Hochschild, 1983). What we are doing is putting a coherent meaning on life events that have broken the usual patterns and rules. These stories put back what stress events may have damaged. We repair certain beliefs that we need, including that we are relatively invulnerable and worthy and that the world is predictable, benevolent, and meaningful, among others. In a variety of ways, we can rebuild our views to bring back these qualities (Meichenbaum & Fitzpatrick, 1993).

Symptom Therapies

Biofeedback has been in use as one of the major treatments of stress symptoms since the 1960s. There are many claims of its successes, but it falls short of promises in careful testing (Raskin, Bali, & Peeke, 1980; Rice & Blanchard, 1982). Biofeedback is a way of informing us in clear sensory form of body changes that normally cannot be sensed. In each case, appropriate sensors can be easily attached and a machine converts physiological changes to visual or auditory signals. In stress relief applications, the body changes most used are muscle tension, heart rate, and temperature.

Both heart rate and temperature biofeedback have disappointing effects. Although some changes are found, we can question whether the biofeedback produces more than just the instructions and setting alone. The same kind of effects usually come from simple relaxation procedures. Muscle control by biofeedback gives larger changes, but little research has been done to show that it works outside of the controlled laboratory room and, relatedly, whether we have learned something that continues to control the stress symptoms in the absence of the machines. A final concern is the obvious one: that biofeedback does not address the source of the stress, just some of its symptoms. Although there may be some long-term benefits for the stressed person, these have not been described as yet.

Another symptom therapy is training to relax. The several relaxation techniques share four basic components: a quiet setting, reduced muscle action, attention focusing, and a passive attitude. The techniques have been clinically useful in treating several stress disorders, including high blood pressure, tension headache, and insomnia. The process that makes the effect may be the focus of attention on the relaxation procedures and hence away from the stress situations. The reported effects include increased feelings of mental calmness.

There have been three methods of relaxation training in general use. The progressive relaxation program consists of tightening of the skeletal muscles of a part of the body to feel their tension and then relaxing them completely (Jacobson, 1938). The purposes are to clearly distinguish the difference and to train our control over the two states. Then, another set of muscles is tensed and relaxed, and so on up, down, or around the body. The formal training requires a long-term effort. Its original proponents suggested 1 to 2 hr per day for weeks to learn control. More recent users have a much abbreviated program. When the training is completed, we are trained to relax completely in a few minutes. Relaxation of mental activities is theoretically assumed to follow naturally from relaxation of the muscles of speech and the eyes.

A second form of relaxation training is that of meditation. The elements of meditation are a quiet place, a comfortable position, repetitive mental stimulation, and a controlled, passive attitude. We will examine meditation more deeply in Chapter 10, "Motivated Cognition."

The third form of relaxation therapy uses mental imagery. With the same kind of quiet environment as the other techniques, mental imagery relives in the mind a particularly restful experience. The depth of the relaxation achieved depends on concentration and ability to imagine. The more vivid the relaxing image, the greater the resulting relaxation.

SECTION SUMMARY: CONTROL AND COPING WITH STRESS

Efforts to manage stress are called coping and hinge on perceptions of control. Coping may be directed toward the problem source or toward the emotional aspects that result. We bring to the process certain resources of positive beliefs and attitudes, skills in solving personal problems and dealing with other people, and assets of social and material support.

Coping activities involve getting some kind of control or perception of control. Stress is lessened when we can decide some dimension of the events, such as when and where they take place. Just making some purposeful act or telling stories to ourselves and others about it tends to help. By doing these things, we become involved and tend to know more about the situation, moderating some aspects of fears of the unknowns.

Symptom therapies for stress include biofeedback, relaxation training, and meditation. There is no magic cure in these activities; they all work by changing the mental scene for the stressed person from focusing on the stressor to focusing on the difficult mental control of the program. The consequence is to break some links and moderate the perceptions of the stress events.

◈

CHAPTER CONCLUSIONS

The capacity of negatives to motivate much of our lives is literally inescapable. Pain is vital to survival, and perhaps in a less directly medical form, so too are fear, anxiety, and stress. All have basic dimensions of suffering, and we might ask why that must be. Could not the nociception, fear stimuli, and major life changes be simply information without the feelings of hurting? Perhaps that is logical, but how then would they make us change? If it didn't hurt, would we really stop doing it or plan to not have it happen again? The essential motivation element of these pieces of life is the power that their hurting has over us.

Pain is becoming known as an intricately designed capacity of the nervous system to manage damage, something much more complicated than a one-direction flow of information from a damaged body place. The puzzle of pain is approaching solution by our new views of how nociception is controlled as it flows toward the brain and is treated there. Age-old and modern pain therapies are beginning to come together in the new views.

Fear and anxiety are obvious and regular pieces of living. Being afraid is one foundation of childhood living, and for many of us, it is just below the socially constructed surface all through life. More study is needed of the evolutionary psychology roots of these phenomena, because they are obviously part of human and animal nature. What are the limits and what are the detailed functions beyond the obvious?

Stress has become a cliché of modern life, perhaps overdrawn and substituted as an excuse for other ailments and incompetencies, but it is also a bona fide condition in the sense of being a useful descriptor of some of the negative aspects of life. We do have limits, and when we exceed them, physically or mentally, the body has built-in responses. Perhaps stress is reacting to attempts at living that we were not designed to carry out. The tie between stressful patterns of living and medical disorders is clear, even if the details of the influences are still under study. Techniques of moderating stress effects, the coping strategies, perhaps are just stopgap measures that await a more mature view of how we are designed to live our lives.

Study and Review Questions

1. How do we define pain?

2. What are some varieties of pain?

3. What have phantom limb pain, causalgia, and neuralgia in common?

4. At what levels of increasing-intensity stimulation do people agree?

5. What evidence have we that experienced pain is affected by cultural background?

6. How does apparent meaning of painful events affect the resulting experience?

7. How do placebos reduce felt pain?

8. What is the puzzle of pain?

9. What are the technical pain words?

10. Which nerve fibers reduce pain?

11. Which nerve fibers facilitate pain?

12. Which neurotransmitters reduce pain?

13. Which neurotransmitters facilitate pain?

14. What are the rules of the spinal gating theory of pain?

15. In the gate control theory of pain, which nerve fibers close the gates for pain?

16. In the gate control theory of pain, which nerve fibers open the gates for pain?

17. What are the three general brain systems of pain?

18. What are the three kinds of painkiller drugs, and what do they do?

19. Can we relieve pain by just cutting the sensory fibers from the source?

20. What kind of added sources of pain reduces chronic pain?

21. How can psychotherapy reduce pain?

22. How are relaxation training and biofeedback similar?

23. Will hypnosis work for everybody?

24. Is behavior modification efficient?

25. What is the basic idea of pain clinics?

26. What is the adaptive theme of fear?

27. What are the general sources of human fear?

28. What does fear make us do?

29. How is anxiety different from fear?

30. According to existentialist philosophy, from what life conditions do we get anxiety?

31. How did Sigmund Freud see anxiety working in psychoanalytic theory?

32. In the view of behaviorists, how does high anxiety make us act?

33. According to cognitive interruption theory, what makes anxiety?

34. According to cognitive expectancy theory, what is mentally collected to build anxiety?

35. What did Hans Selye see in his laboratory animals when he defined stress?

36. What are the stages of Hans Selye's General Adaptation Syndrome?

37. What simple life condition or event underlies all stress?

38. What are primary and secondary stress appraisals?

39. What nervous system is most active in stress?

40. What are the stress-controlling products of the adrenal glands?

41. How do epinephrine and cortisol affect stress?

42. What results when a person accumulates too much life change?

43. Why and when is crowding a stress?

44. What are the key Type A behaviors?

45. Is a panic attack mental or physical?

46. What do agoraphobics fear?

47. What do social phobics fear?

48. How long must anxiety last to be a generalized anxiety disorder?

49. How is depression different from being sleepy?

50. What are the components of learned helplessness?

51. What is the nature of the distorted thinking of depressed people?

52. What is the key mental factor in coping?

53. What are the six categories of mental coping resources?

54. Why does doing something moderate stress?

55. What changes after assertiveness training?

56. What is shared between biofeedback and relaxation training?

57. What are the three forms of relaxation training?

CHAPTER 7

Sexual Motivation: Politics and Biology

Before we could be, there was sex. Certainly, love and sex are parts of our emotional and social lives. Looking at our human history shows how ideals change and how fragile our present beliefs really are. Along came science, but scientific sexologists remain bound to culture, typically defending current gender roles, beliefs, and politics.

We will describe sensual sexual motivation, the essential or biological stimulation for sexual acts. That opens the complex and politically sensitive questions of gender differences in sexual interest, attraction, arousal, feelings, and orgasm. Gender politics, evolution theory mechanisms, physiology, and social learning concepts are intertwined.

Western Social History of Sex and Love

Scientific Studies of Love and Sex

Politics of Sex

Dissecting the Sexual Acts

Sensual Arousal

Gender Differences

In every age, people believe that their own ways of thinking are the most natural and correct. The ways of the past or the practices of different cultures appear to be more primitive or misguided. A social history of human love and sex in Western civilization, even from rather recent times, reveals some of that fascinating diversity. Sex is inseparable from social traditions. Beliefs and social rules about sexual acts have been embedded in the ways of people in all times and societies. Thus, to understand loving and sexuality requires that we know some patterns of the social history of humanity.

Especially in modern Western society, histories of love and sex intertwine. Our late

TABLE 7.1 Partial Summary of Historical Changes in Western Rules and Attitudes About Men's and Women's Love and Sexuality

Era	Women	Men
Greek state	as property raise children run efficient house	family procreation passionate sexuality as amusement
Early Christian	submit to husband love to God	avoid passion
1700s America	pleasurable sex a duty bear children	pleasurable sex a duty control immoral acts
Mid-1800s America	bear and raise children feminine love no sexual "passion"	support family sex as biological force
1900 America	same as mid-1800s + increased individuality double standard	same as mid-1800s + immoral acts by "deviant" individuals
1970 America	sex = pleasure good sex means love weaker double standard	sex = pleasure separate from marriage
1990s America	sex = a right with costs very weak double standard	sex = a right with costs

twentieth-century beliefs about love and sex are rather new and unique, particularly so for those not born to a life of wealth and privilege. These sketches of love and sex are informed by histories of different breadths and points of view provided by Aries (1985), Banes, Frank, and Horwitz (1976), Birken (1988), Branden (1980), Bullough (1976), Cancian (1989), D'Emilio and Freedman (1988), Giddens, (1992), Hunt (1960), Murstein (1974), Seidman (1991), and Weeks (1981).

Our historical survey of ideas of love and sex has valuable lessons. That is why we are examining love's roots in a separate, orienting section. Among the many messages, we will find that present Western standards are not free from the past. That idea reveals how political ideas of morality drive our sexuality. We will also discover that whatever there is of a "natural" human sexuality is accommodated and controlled by society's influence. And as scientists try to scientifically study our existing sexuality, legal and moral rules of society (and needs to maintain those morals) influence their work.

WESTERN SOCIAL HISTORY OF SEX AND LOVE

Greek, Roman, and Christian Ideals

A look at the past reveals two sets of ideas about love in elite, classical Greek culture of the times of Plato and Aristotle through pagan Roman times to the establishment of Christian influence. The first form of love described the relationship in a lifelong family arrangement. Marriage was a matter of practical necessity, often arranged for political reasons, filling the roles of housekeeping and child raising. Love developed in marriage and was marked by the modesty and stability of the relationship. The best marriage was one in which many children were raised and the domestic enterprise was thriving. A statement attributed to Seneca by Aries (1985) relates this proper relationship in the marriage and contrasts it against the second form of love:

Any love for another's wife is scandalous; so is too much love for one's own wife. A prudent man should love his wife with discretion, and so control his desire and not be led into copulation. Nothing is more impure than to love one's wife as if she were a mistress. . . . Men should appear before their wives not as lovers but as husbands. (p. 134)

The second form of love in these times was passionate, typically sexual. This kind of love was most associated with affairs outside of marriage or with certain wives in polygamous marriages. Love of this kind could be an amusement having no lasting significance (Hunt, 1960), or it could often be a deeply romantic, spiritual, and not necessarily sexual relationship (Aries, 1985). Some intellectual discourse of the time claimed that passionate sexual acts were undesirable, a form of madness. The Stoic Romans, for example, saw passion as something sought outside of marriage. Passionate sex in historical myth became a sport connected with the decadence of the Roman era.

In either form of love, women had markedly different status and roles from men. Women were subordinate in both body and mind. They had little or no legal status except as property, and their roles were bearing and raising children and running an efficient household.

In Christian theology, spiritual love was to be directed to God. The ideal was sexual abstinence. The church rulers were hostile to earthly pleasure in any form, and particularly to sexual pleasure. The body, in its quest for sinful sexual pleasures, was said to trap the soul. Bodily pleasure was associated with the devil. At the most, marriage was the prescription to minimize the immorality, but the sexual desire should not be consummated beyond the purpose of procreation. Love of others was seen in Christian dogma as a competition that interferes with one's love of God and the ecstatic pleasures that produces. A man who spiritually loves his wife commits a sin as bad as adultery. The link of sex and love was a serious error. It was better for a priest to take random sexual partners than to keep a mistress, but a mistress was better than marriage. The worst was to actually love one's sexual partner.

The two forms of love compared by Seneca became the moral law of early Christianity but with a deemphasis of the passionate. Being unclean, fornicating, and loving outside of marriage were condemned together. Inside marriage, the goal was a union that was not to increase passion but to suppress it. The union in marriage was a binding together, the two becoming one in the sense of trust and identification with one another. This kind of fondness is like a possession of the other, a bond that does not exist before the marriage. Instead of appearing suddenly, the relationship grows as the marriage continues. It was not, however, a relationship of equals. Husbands were asked to love their wives, and women were asked to obey their husbands. Women were to submit to men as men were to submit to God—without questioning.

The basis of marriage was in religion. Although the practices and rules were complicated by class differences, one important principle was that monogamous marriages were permanent. Dissolution was not possible in the views of the churches. Changes came only with death, and that was not an infrequent event among women in those premedicine times.

Sexuality and Feelings

Through the ensuing centuries, accounts of marriage practices and procedures inform us about how and why people were married and how and why they sought passion (Gillis, 1988). Language of mental feelings was not yet common. The passions were viewed as bodily events. Love relationships in this period were identified by the ways people acted rather than as a spiritual or emotional state. Often the love acts were rough, intended to make the other feel pleasure or pain. They did not appear to reflect on their feelings of attachment toward the other.

Marriages among the elite classes continued to be arranged for practical reasons, but among common folk, it was more a matter of magic-based customs and happenstance choice. Among rituals of pairings, the betrothal was an important beginning of a period of public acknowledgment, signifying attachment and culminating in a formal wedding ceremony. As love began to be defined as a feeling (the plays of Shakespeare, for example, began to celebrate the cause of love), the common elements of magic and ritual declined. Rituals also suffered at the hands of leaders of the church, who viewed some of the bawdy old ways as obscene and irreligious.

In what is called the 1700s' Age of Reason, new ideas appeared in philosophy. Sex was described in those new views as a materialistic act without spiritualistic consequences. These ideas used mechanistic, scientific views of processes of the body. The new philosophers' conclusion was that whatever gives pleasure is appropriate. At the same time, these philosophers still held reason in high regard and continued to believe that it must be clearly separated from passion. The passions were intellectually discounted but at the same time became an obsession. These body-pleasure passions were often sought outside the marriage. The mental stage was being set for the nineteenth-century development of love as a spiritual, almost abstract feeling, disconnected from the passionate pleasures of sexuality.

Yet, sexuality itself was not condemned. In the religious context of the Western social order of eighteenth-century America, sexual acts were duties that were pleasurable parts of a good Protestant marriage. "Mainstream Puritans did not see marital sexuality as a threat to moral constancy; in fact, they saw it as a remarkable and happy harmony of carnal, moral, and spiritual bonds" (Leites, 1986, p. 76). This was a culture of intimacy built on love that was prescribed by religion. Sexual acts were, of course, the means of fulfillment in marriage of procreation. That is, sexual acts were a necessary part of the church ideal to produce children.

Sexual acts outside of marriage, such as masturbation, extramarital sex, or sodomy, were immoral, sinful choices that were pun-

ished by society and by God, but they were not the mark of a kind of person. It was the immoral acts, not the people doing them, that were sinful and deviant. Doing such things did not make one a "pervert" or immoral as a person. Late eighteenth-century scandals arose over the apparent debilitating effects of the aristocrats' sexual excesses. The view was that these activities had moral bases, that they were essentially voluntary acts. The stigma was attached to the acts, and everyone was thought able to act correctly as an exercise of their will. Immoral acts were at worst a sign of needing some strengthening of one's faith.

Gendering Love

In the nineteenth century, there was a gradual alteration of the ideal of the husband and wife loving each other in passionate ways. This came about through a growing apart of the traditional gender roles of family life and a change in the conception of love, moving toward feminine dependency. The new romantic love ideal was built on a view of attachment as a narrative outlining possibilities for the relationship.

Earlier daily life was based on family and economic life activities in common. The partners were together for most of the day in the shared life of producing food, raising children, and providing for their common welfare. On the farm, children's labor remained necessary for the family to prosper. In all of this common life, parents were instructed by their church to be loving toward one another, including in their sexual life.

In modern Western society, the new order was one of men working away from the home in a setting that was increasingly cold and competitive compared with a family life of warmth and care. The result for love was a separation of gender roles and attitudes. Men in the working world became more impersonal, competitively amoral, and individualistic. Women were left to care for the children and home and changed toward being more personal, dependent on emotion, and intimate with the lives of their children and husbands. Women's work became the work of love.

Increases in city-dwelling, industrial-based, middle-class families led to a changed role for children as well. Applications of science and diversified work into specialties continued to provide more comfortable living. But in nineteenth-century city families, fewer children were desired. Children needed support and education in the new city life. These new arrangements had effects on views of sexuality. Among them was attempted birth control. Men were encouraged to restrain themselves, and women were asked to be passionless. Concerns grew about the morality of the working classes and their higher birth rates.

To middle-class working men, the home became the respite from the cold world, offering the warmth of women's emotional love. These diverging gender roles were strengthened by the growing belief that they were innate. With evolutionary answers being applied to every question, women were thought to be *naturally* dependent and emotional, and men were viewed as *naturally* competitive individuals.

Love was seen as an innate feminine quality. Francesca Cancian (1989) writes, "The ideal family was portrayed as a harmonious, stable, nuclear household with an economically successful father and an angelic mother" (p. 17). Love images in literature of the times showed themes of feminine tenderness, weakness, and affectionate feelings. Love was a private experience found and realized in the marriage and family.

These productive mid-1800s years yielded a large and unified middle class. In all but the very rich and the underclass, there were shared ideals about the family that we call the Victorian culture. The model was housewife and provider-husband making a home and family life. Jessie Bernard (1990) pictures the Victorian model with five ground rules. First, woman's place is in the home. Second, the husband is head of the household. Third, the marital bond is permanent. Fourth, the couple shall maintain lifelong fidelity and sexual exclusivity. And fifth, they shall bear and raise children. Each of these rules gradually eroded.

Individualism and Romanticism

A period of slow changes in gender relations and roles marked the later decades of the nineteenth century. The dominant social standard remained the monogamous family. There was no question that had to be protected. Changes stemmed from increased freedom from work for both men and women. The industrial society provided more wealth and leisure time with its attendant freedoms. With developing freedom, there came more opportunity for smaller family groups, for identity as an individual apart from family, and for romantic ideals of association with others.

All of these led to potential changes in the moral code, and the concern was with gaining control over the changes. And how were the changes to be explained? Specifically, how can sexual acts be held to conform with the traditional ideal social order? The answers were to be sought with the new tool of social development—science.

By the end of the nineteenth century, different changes in politics, economics, and control by religion all fostered the concept of individuality at the expense of eighteenth-century social groupings of family and community. Political rights were developed founded on the ideal of the emancipated individual (at least for White men). Free-enterprise capitalism flourished, and standards of living rose dramatically. Americans in particular developed traditions of mobility, and part of that was freedom to move into different social groups.

The productivity and luxury of the new industrial society partially freed women. It was no longer necessary that they spend all of their time housekeeping and child raising. The daily activities of men and women once again became more similar, and with lessening role differences, there was less reason to continue the old structure of gender role-based feelings and personalities. Many individuals, men and women, had time and resources to pursue their individual pleasures, activities open only to the elite in the past. In political changes, the prescriptions of the church were divorced from the rules of the state, and one's conduct became a matter of personal choice. More broadly, in America and a few other Western societies, personal choice and individual identity became the highest social values.

With these attitudes, new forms of relationships could emerge. Ideas pictured the individual as a free, self-determined person, but the practice of individuality separated each person from constant exposure to specific others. The family or tribal nature of a shared existence was replaced by being separated and autonomous. Separation denies a fundamental part of social existence, the intimacy of a shared identity with others. That loss has consequences. The ideal of individuality came with a price—loneliness.

The continuing rules of social life kept young people free from sexual life before formal marriage. Whether or not honored strictly, public social morality was one of constrained sexual activities. Perhaps the sexual urges did not change during this time, and perhaps there was little that was different in how young men and women found ways of consummating those urges. But what had changed was the way those urges were viewed in relation to their new loneliness, focusing on personal feelings.

The excitement of sexual frustration, arousal, and relief were combined with the imagined and idealized pleasures of intimacy. Romantic love combined that intimacy and sex into a personal feeling of exceptional influence. No one felt these emotions more than young adults, delayed in assuming adult roles by extended education and social rules. The focus of romantic love was on its feelings, emphasizing their powers over the lovers.

The possibilities of romantic love were displayed in literature. The Romantic movement in literature at the turn of this century relied on the ideal of individualism plus the idea of choosing one's own values. Romantic love was among the factors in the choices. The Romantic ideal emerged to be an uncontrolled fall into a relationship of passionate love between equals. Above all, Romanticism reflected the view that life is pursuing one's chosen purposes—and choice is fundamental to human existence. Romantic love was the clearest and most exciting example of freedom, especially in America.

Sexual acts took on a new burden of meaning in romantic love. They were judged by the depth of love they reflected, and love was judged by the success of the sexual acts. These ideals, although a serious misreading of actuality, were to blossom in the twentieth century.

SECTION SUMMARY:
WESTERN SOCIAL HISTORY OF SEX AND LOVE

Two complexes of ideas, roughly similar to what we call love and sex, have been common in Western history. Until recent times, we consistently viewed these from the dominant men's position, women being mere property or at best subservient. In earliest times, sex with one's wife was a household duty intended to procreate children. Love was an amusement in Greek and Roman times, transformed in Christian theology to a spiritual bond with God. Under later philosophy, the passion of sex was seen as an important body function but separated from one's pure and noble reason.

Sexuality was an important part of a good marriage in early America, and disapproved sexual practices were sinful, immoral choices, not works of an immoral person. Life in the nineteenth century increasingly found men working away from the home and women caring for the household and their children. A subtle but vital part of women's work became that of love. Love was feminized and seen, according to the thinking habits of the times, as an innate capacity of women.

By the end of the nineteenth century, several forces, conditions, and beliefs came together. There were separate gender roles in love. Individual freedom and smaller families came from increasing middle-class wealth. Control by theology was weakening in favor of rules of political laws and of science. Emerging from this was strengthening of the ideal of romantic love.

SCIENTIFIC STUDIES OF LOVE AND SEX

Social change and progressive reform marked the nineteenth century. Some changes were overt, and some had hidden and largely unspoken bases in sexuality and its consequences. Throughout the century, social movements of purity were launched. American social philosophers assumed that there was opportunity for progress toward perfection of humanity in the new world, and that this was (the Christian, Protestant) God's will. Steady growth toward perfection was the theological plan. Reform was the message. Among the social ills needing change were alcoholism, slavery, prostitution, divorce, and generally poor public health.

From about 1830 to 1890, the Western culture was labeled Victorian, perhaps most clearly seen in all but the very rich and the underclass of America. The Victorian era began with essentially the same Puritan ideas of love, marriage, and sexuality. But by the end of that period, love lost some of its spiritual meaning by becoming identified more closely with the sensual and erotic pleasures of sex. At the start of the modern era at the turn of the present century, aspects of sexuality became a primary element defining and maintaining love. The deteriorating Victorian culture gradually changed to view sexuality more openly, especially its sensual and erotic aspects.

By the end of the nineteenth century, middle-class concerns focused on population change, race, and ethnicity, all stimulated by heavy immigration of those decades. There were fears of increasing feeblemindedness, the general term for a variety of conditions thought to reflect genetic inferiority. Through this period, there was a shift from the ideals of the eighteenth century, which became a reversal. By the turn of the century, social ills were thought to be reflections of a kind of person, not just a poor choice of acts. That put the proper treatment of those ills in the hands of the politicians and scientists rather than the clergy.

Affirming Social Beliefs

Charles Darwin's theory of evolution simply overwhelmed the thought and theory of biology in the last half of the nineteenth century. Evolution theory applications to humanity gave greater force to the thought of sex as a biological rather than moral topic. As a part of biology, sexuality resided in the domain of science and medicine rather than theology.

Beginning in the late eighteenth and early nineteenth centuries, science began to show that causes can be found inside of people. In this view, biological causes show part of what a person is and also what will become of that person. Sexual acts slowly became a part of scientists' thoughts, if not their direct study. Thus, sexual urges were thought of by scientists as something inside a person, rather than habitual acts or moral choices as pictured by the church. From there, scientists made prescriptions based on inference but in accord with the general politics of the day. For example, acts of self-stimulation were commonly believed to be evidence of a wasting of the person. Masturbation was described as directly causing feebleminded-ness, laziness, and ruin.

Sexuality's proper place in a loving, re-ligious marriage also changed. The sensual and erotic aspects of sexual acts were valued in their own right and came to be the defini-tion of what is love. Participating in sexual acts was evidence of love. The pleasure of sexual acts was their primary justification. When love was defined in terms of sexuality, the pleasure of sex became legitimate in its own right.

As a biological process, sex was logi-cally thought to be a matter of physiological force. The metaphors scientists used were of sex as uncontrollable spasms, as dammed water, or as some material thing that could be retained or spent. The common view was of a kind of hydraulics of building pressure and release. That image was retained through the drives of Sigmund Freud and the mid-twentieth-century behaviorists to modern sociobiolo-gists. But if society's customs were to be maintained, social rules must oppose the bio-logical force. Sexuality became a matter of biology's driving us in competition with so-ciety's constraining us.

Medicine gave sexology a home and the respectability of science, but the physicians also housed and protected social beliefs and ideals. Physician-scientists did not find new information about sex; they looked only at evidence for what they and their society al-ready believed. The new sexologists used sci-ence to affirm general social beliefs, but society did not openly welcome the sexolo-gists' efforts. Studies of sexual acts were never completely acceptable. People merely tolerated them if they presented the right ideas. Each of the pioneers studying sexuality gave a scientific dressing to ideas that already prevailed. Where their studies conflicted with society's ideas, the researchers suffered the political consequences. The point is that ap-plication of science to sexuality served to de-fend existing social and political beliefs. Sexology maintained the standards of social movements (Weeks, 1985). It did not look be-yond them in an objective manner.

The attitudes of physicians in the late nineteenth and early twentieth centuries were uniformly male-oriented. The biological problem and the models proposed to account for it were all from the male perspective. Sex-ual acts were described as essentially male functions, following the earlier nineteenth-century notion that women had no sexuality. Women, for the most part, were seen as merely receptacles for male sexual acts, and their biological role was that of breeding and child care. Descriptions and theory of sexual-ity were made to conform to those dominating assumptions. We can see the force of these views in late nineteenth-century arguments about sex and gender differences.

Sexuality and Gender Differences

The words *sex* and *gender* can be used loosely, but there seems to be some agree-ment that the phrase ***sex differences*** refers to physical differences between men and women, whereas the term ***gender differ-ences*** is the cultural elaboration of the physi-cal differences. Sex differences include matters of size, strength, metabolism, repro-duction physiology, and evolutionary adapta-tions. Gender differences are social and political constructions, sometimes founded on sex differences but more often not. Sexu-ality is a matter of both sex differences and gender differences. In earlier writing, all of this was called sex differences. More detail and references for ideas and arguments can be found in Russett (1989).

Late nineteenth-century scientists pic-tured women as inferior in most but not all aspects of sexuality. Women were thought to be mentally influenced by their periodic sex-ual hormones and thus not capable of rational thought at the level of men. Men were thought to be civilized, reasonable, cultured, and re-sponsible. All of these reflected men's supe-rior mind functions, but they nonetheless tended toward depravity in sexuality. Women followed instincts instead of reason, nature instead of culture. They had less personal re-sponsibility, being ruled by their bodies. Yet, in sexuality, women were seen to have a contrasting morality that countered and controlled men's depravity. Later, we will see some of these tendencies (minus the judgmental language) to be founded on ancient evolutionary adaptations.

Four sets of ideas were argued in the nineteenth century that separately and collectively placed women as different and inferior to men. The arguments were given by many different people in different contexts, and we will summarize them in four labeled sets. The first of these was the **biogenetic law,** outlined in the phrase *ontogeny recapitulates phylogeny.* The idea was that the development of individuals and the differences among different kinds of people can be explained by the presumed evolution of humanity. White men in Western society were seen as the furthest evolved; all others were somewhat inferior. The slogan was also interpreted as *anthropology recapitulates biology,* wherein "savages" are not as far evolved. Children too are not yet complete in their development and show an incomplete form. Thus, savages are childlike and immature. Savages also were believed to be people of greater endurance and less sensitivity to pain. All of this was presented to show that women are also not completely evolved, showing childlike immaturity and emotionality, with savage-like endurance and insensitivity to pain. The best they could get is education for motherhood, a development of their intuition rather than their intellect.

The second idea used to argue women's inferiority was that of **Darwin's thesis of sexual selection,** which predicted greater male variability. Darwin defended the theory that at least in the higher species, the males battle and the females choose. Thus, males evolved features that maximize female choice, within the limits of their surviving other forces of natural selection. The corollary to this is that men are more variable in their traits than are women. There are more men in the genius categories and among the imbeciles. There are more men who are deviant in any naturally based character. Thus, women do not have potential to greatness equal to men in any social endeavor. Evidence was that few women were great writers, artists, musicians, and the like. Cultural factors were ignored because it seemed so obvious to men (and some women) that the real cause was biological.

A third thesis was a compound of ideas of **conservation of energy and of force** with those of limited personal resources. With its principles of energy conservation, the new physics viewed the human body as an engine with limits. Nervous function was pictured with electrical metaphors of limited available power. Intellect consumed that power, taking away from one's emotional energy, and vice versa. In overextending oneself, in pushing the limits of the resources, one flirted with neurasthenia, a kind of nerve exhaustion. The key was to conserve resources to avoid that exhaustion, especially in the light of the increasing demands made by the new industrial and business society. Women had a special problem with their reproductive organs, which used large amounts of energy. Education of women's intellect would seriously compete with and retard reproductive organ maturation in the crucial years of adolescence. These were the issues debated in the "books versus babies" wars. Some psychologists showed that women who attended college had fewer children. Society would surely suffer.

The fourth principle argued was that of the **physiological division of labor.** The status of women was an important indicator of how far a society had developed in the evolutionary hierarchy. Women in primitive societies worked alongside men, essentially as their slaves. Women of the most advanced and morally progressive societies were exempt from productive labor (except the bearing and rearing of children). That was seen as the consequence of evolution and hence was biologically determined. The best society was one in which the work was divided into specialties, and the kind of work women were to do was biologically ordained. To do men's work was to threaten women's health and shorten their lives.

In Grace Shirley's (1901) *Lovers' Guide,* she codified the traditional nineteenth-century views:

> Man's proper sphere is that of provider and caretaker, and it is for him to maintain, with his wife's assistance, the dignity of the establishment.
>
> His position as "head of the family" reflects no discredit upon his wife, but only establishes her reputation as a sensible woman in having married a man whom she could look up to as her protector. (p. 63)

> Woman was not created to endure the extreme hardships of life, and should therefore be content with less arduous duties. That she has the ability to perform all that man has performed does not mean that she is fitted or intended for such performance. (p. 64)

> Convince your husband that you look upon him as the head of his household, and you will be spared many anxieties and perhaps much hard labor, for it will give him an incentive to provide more lavishly. (pp. 64-65)

The overall picture was fairly clear and thought to be scientifically derived: Women are immature, modest in ability, limited in energy partially sapped by reproductive hormone periodicity, and designed primarily for bearing and raising children. All of these ideas were defended by scientists, especially those in the new sexology. The hidden and largely unexamined social goal of the sexologists was to defend this structure of relationships and gender roles that underlay the existing society. Their scientific knowledge complemented the political protection of those ideas and roles. Physicians dominated the science of sexuality. Only they held the biological keys to unlock sexual secrets and the political and moral authority to do it. We will take up a sampling of the sexologists and their work.

Through the middle and late twentieth century, marriage and concepts of love also followed further social change. Individuality became more and more of a reality in practical affairs as well as philosophy. Increasingly similar gender roles followed. Much of the eighteenth-century model of love as an intimate, dependent, emotional, feminine experience remains, but the new image is one of life companions of similar if not entirely equal obligations and responsibilities in love and sex.

SECTION SUMMARY: SCIENTIFIC STUDIES OF LOVE AND SEX

Applying science to human sex was socially and politically dangerous and thought to be appropriate, at best, if done by medical scientists. But they were only willing to find evidence for what they already believed to be proper and true. They focused on perversions, and, in line with the biological science of the day, believed them to be internally caused. They were marks of perverted people, not just immoral choices.

Scientists also saw the late nineteenth-century gender roles to be natural ones and marshaled evidence to prove that women were childlike and immature, rarely having exceptional ability, handicapped because their limited energy was needed for childbearing, and suited through evolution for leisurely housekeeping.

◈

POLITICS OF SEX

We saw that in the late nineteenth century, sex was turned over to scientists for limited study. The new view was of sex as a biological force and in the domain of physiological scientists, especially physicians. But each investigator brought specific biases and general cultural rules to the study. The implication was that science would find the truth of sexuality, but the political filters each person wore were the product of changing cultural history. More examples and detail can be found in *Science in the Bedroom* (Bullough, 1994).

Sexology Studies

Richard von Krafft-Ebing published a description of sexual perversities in 1887 under the title *Psychopathia Sexualis*. His classification was little more than illustrations of the social system of the times, thereby giving scientific descriptions to legal sexual offenses, such as sadomasochism (using pain in arousal), fetishism (arousal from objects), bestiality (using animals), and intercourse with the dead. The details in the work were printed in Latin so that only physicians would understand. The book was reprinted many times, but it was not until editions in the 1960s that a full English version was offered. His work stimulated hundreds of medical publications over the next several decades. Because he followed the prevailing social morals, his work was accepted.

Sigmund Freud, also a physician, published *Three Theories of Sexuality* in 1905, one of several books presenting his psychoanalysis theory. Freud's theory placed sex in a central motivational position wherein experiences with sex were responsible for the development of an individual's unique adult personality. Freud, like Krafft-Ebing, focused on the perversities of sexuality, but he was less interested in their nature than the psychic dynamics he thought they reflected. Freud's agreement with the conventional ideas of the status of women is revealed in some of his offhand comments. He maintained that clitoral sexuality was a mark of immaturity because he saw the clitoris to be but an undeveloped penis. After women's sexuality was acknowledged as real, he maintained that only vaginal orgasm was true sexual response. If a woman could not climax to vaginal stimulation, she was labeled frigid.

Just a few studies of sex appeared at the beginning of modern psychology near the turn of the century. Psychologist G. Stanley Hall, then president of Clark University, prepared a sex activity questionnaire in his studies of adolescence, but little notice was taken of it. Later, on the twentieth anniversary of his university, he brought Sigmund Freud to America to speak. Freud was an immediate sensation because of his openness in discussing sexuality as well as the part sexuality played in his psychoanalysis. But neither Hall nor Freud was looking for biological facts or sexual act descriptions. Hall was a staunch defender of the traditional gender roles in which women were intellectually inferior, biologically and sociologically suited entirely for producing children and family life.

In 1919, John B. Watson, psychology's promoter of behaviorism, did some survey and interview studies with Karl Lashley, a biological science colleague. Inspired by World War I army programs about sex and disease, and funded by appropriate government medical entities, they targeted physicians' attitudes toward teaching sex education. Watson believed in the need for informed study about sex, and he later carried out a series of sex observation studies in his laboratory. He was forced to resign from the Johns Hopkins University when a scandal ensued. (Of course, there was a little more to it than that. He and his graduate assistant were the subjects in the research, and his wife was distinctly displeased and divorced him.)

The lesson of Watson's fate and that of a few others who dared study human sex was not lost on academic researchers. Open studies of sexuality, especially by those not authorized in the medical community, were not acceptable to society. In the first half of the twentieth century, psychologists and physiologists more typically focused their sex research on animals and, from that base, constructed a picture of sexual events and of the operation of sexual motivation. They built theory and description on what they observed in animals (e.g., Beach, 1969).

More than with other acts, there has been a long-standing belief that sex acts are essentially reflexive, animal-like responses. From the hidden assumption that sexuality is essentially biological, it is easy to accept studies of sex by animals as the same, at least physiologically, as that of humans. Although scientists were aware of the patterns of species differences, and nowhere are species differences as obvious as in the specifics of sex, they nonetheless generalized liberally from studies of rats and dogs to humans. Again, it is likely that the goal of finding evidence for the prevailing assumptions took precedence over looking for what is really there. To justify the compelling nature of sexual motivation, sex was identified as fundamentally driven by animal-like biological processes. Some specific facts and ideas from these studies are widely assumed but are very misleading when applied to human sexual motivation. We will note those later.

Among the few studies of human sexual acts was that of one of Karl Lashley's students. Alfred Kinsey led a large-scale interview project to determine the normal frequency of sex attitudes and activities. He and his colleagues interviewed 5,300 men and 5,950 women, and the results were published in two volumes. *Sexual Behavior in the Human Male* (Kinsey, Pomeroy, & Martin) appeared in 1948, and *Sexual Behavior in the Human Female* (Kinsey, Pomeroy, Martin, & Genhard) in 1953. These volumes were judged notorious, and the political backlash led to the researchers' loss of funding support. Although far from perfect and subject to much hindsight criticism, Kinsey's works were scientifically valuable in providing data of the kinds of common sexual acts. They included important statistics about sexual acts reported by people of different ages, education, and social class. Kinsey's work has been continued in the Institute for Sex Research in Indiana.

Direct study of human sexual act physiology once again appeared in public 35 years after Watson's attempts. Beginning in 1954 and from the refuge of a prominent medical school, William Masters, a physician, with Virginia Johnson, conducted observational studies of the biological actions of human sexual intercourse. Hundreds of people and thousands of orgasms were measured. From these records came their elaborate but technically written physiological details of sexual acts. They published the first edition of *Human Sexual Response* in 1966, and that work has been the basis for sexual activity descriptions that are found in textbooks.

From their research laboratory base, Masters and Johnson also developed theory and practice of treating sexual dysfunctions. Here again was medical sexology at work to justify common beliefs about sexual acts. Defining dysfunctions followed a political model of what they thought ought to be normal. Masters and Johnson's therapeutic work, and that of many others who came later, followed the social changes of the times. Individual freedoms, and, particularly, gender equality ideas combined with an openness to sexuality ideas. The general acceptance of sex study was a part of those social goals. Definitions of what was normal and what was a dysfunction came from the current politics of gender equality. To have less than full sexual interest and performance was identified as a disorder to be treated. The sexually normal person was one whose sexual experiences were attained in the manner currently described by the sexologists.

Beginning about 1960 in the contemporary period and through the 1970s to the present, there have been journals, texts, sources of funding, and organizations of researchers devoted exclusively to sex study and presumed sexual dysfunctions. By the end of the modern period, study of the sensual and erotic aspects of sex had become essentially legitimate. Psychological dimensions, especially eroticism, desire, and personal meanings, have been late arrivals in these studies. Formal research of all aspects of sexual acts is now more open and common, but it is wrong to believe that there is not still a social taint involved.

A definitive, modern survey of sexual activities of Americans was planned beginning in 1987, to be funded by the National Institute of Child Health and Human Development. Politicians intervened, forcing the planned survey to be funded privately. Sampling was finally begun in 1992 and results published in 1994 as the National Health and Social Life Survey. As always, scientists must abide by the social beliefs of the day; the successful researchers are aware of those beliefs and work with and around them as they can.

Ideology of Sex

Beliefs in a society involve politics. Ideals about sexuality amount to scripts that change as society has changed. Some sexual politics are matters of asserting what is permitted. Images of sexual politics are brought out by labels such as degeneracy, vice, permissiveness, Victorian morality, and monogamous marriage.

Some form of sexual propriety always exists, and there has always been dissent (Weeks, 1985). Sexuality is one of many themes in politics. We will outline a few different, somewhat broad dimensions.

In one political classification, the various sexual politics strategies of the Christian West can be seen as absolutism, liberal-pluralism, or libertarianism. Absolutists hold a clear ideal of morality based on the monogamous family. Through the nineteenth and early twentieth centuries, there was general agreement that social purity followed from strong laws that prohibited permissiveness and vice. The family was protected by outlawing sex outside of marriage, especially by women. Prostitution ranked along with alcoholism as a social problem to be eliminated.

Liberalist-pluralists base their ideals on the rights of the individual and maintaining social order. They appear to reflect the manner of operations if not the ideals in contemporary Western politics. Sexuality was part of this as the newest phase of Western individualism, but sexuality was a special problem because it was not just a matter of one person. Interests of individuals conflicted in matters of sexuality. As concepts of individual rights were put into practice for women, more complexity appeared. Women's individual rights challenged, potentially, the system of male-dominated, monogamous family morality. At the same time, the ideal was that sexual acts were to be judged by general social acceptability, not on absolute standards. Varieties of sexuality were possible and permitted but still had to be politically negotiated.

Libertarians believe the ideal society allows complete freedom of individuals. They object to denial of freedom in sexuality and envision idyllic, unrestricted sexual settings. Individual freedom runs into practical conflicts because sexual acts require others. Commonly, libertarian goals have been based narrowly on men's ideas of sexuality and its pleasures. That women have equal rights but perhaps different interests is at the root of the difficulty many see in libertarianism.

Similar categories were abstracted from the answers to questions in the National Health and Social Life Survey in the United States in 1992. In this comprehensive sample of the population, 3,432 people ages 18 to 59 were interviewed, face-to-face, to complete the 90 min questionnaire (Michael, Gagnon, Laumann, & Kolata, 1994).

Based on their attitudes about sex matters, the answers of the respondents were clustered into three groups with subtypes. Shown in Table 7.2 are the resulting clusters and some representative questions marking differences in the attitude clusters. In these data, about 30% of the population expressed traditional values, about 45% expressed relational ones, and 25% viewed sex as recreational. The percentage of the whole sample agreeing with each question is in the far right column.

More men than women tend to have recreational attitudes about sex, the difference made up in women's slightly stronger traditional and relational attitudes. With age, both men and women agree more with traditional

TABLE 7.2 Seven Attitudes Toward Sexuality Inferred From Patterns of Responses to Nine Questions

	Frequency of Agreement With Five Statements (Percentage)							
			Relational					
	Traditional				*Contemporary*	*Recreational*		
	Conservative	*Pro-Choice*	*Religious*	*Conventional*	*Religious*	*Pro-Life*	*Libertarian*	*Σ*
Statement 1	100	24	0	0	1	6	0	20
Statement 3	98	91	92	94	52	59	32	77
Statement 6	88	66	98	84	65	10	20	66
Statement 7	91	73	75	9	100	25	0	52
Statement 9	0	100	0	87	85	9	89	52
All 9	15	15	19	16	9	9	16	

NOTE: The following five statements were selected from nine probing attitudes about sex. 1 = Premarital sex is always wrong. 3 = Extramarital sex is always wrong. 6 = I would not have sex with someone unless I was in love with them. 7 = My religious beliefs have guided my sexual behavior. 9 = A woman should be able to obtain a legal abortion if she wants it for any reason.
SOURCE: Constructed from data in Table 14.1 in Laumann, Gagnon, Michael, and Michaels, 1994, p. 514. © 1994 by Edward O. Laumann, Robert T. Michael, CSG Enterprises, Inc., and Stuart Michaels. Reprinted by permission of the University of Chicago Press.

attitudes about sex; the difference made up in lesser relational and recreational views (see Figures 7.1, 7.2, 7.3, and Table 7.3).

Modern Western Sexual Culture

The dimensions of Western sexual culture in the last half of the twentieth century are unique in history. Consider this compari-

son. In the middle nineteenth century, women were denied sexuality. In the view of the men who wrote the laws and the textbooks, women's roles were child bearing and housekeeping. In the increasingly protected home-as-fortress, women were thought to have no need for sexual feelings and interests beyond the needs that served procreation. Authors of marriage advice books insisted this was a

TABLE 7.3 Differences in Attitudes Toward Sexuality by Men and Women at Different Ages (in percent)

	Traditional	*Relational*	*Recreational*
Men	27	40	33
Age 18 to 29	19	47	34
Age 30 to 44	28	38	34
Age 45 to 59	37	34	29
Women	34	47	19
Age 18 to 29	25	53	22
Age 30 to 44	34	47	19
Age 45 to 59	44	42	14
Total	30	45	25

NOTE: Classifications are based on a set of nine questions.
SOURCE: Constructed from data in Table 14.2 in Laumann, Gagnon, Michael, and Michaels, 1994, p. 519. © 1994 by Edward O. Laumann, Robert T. Michael, CSG Enterprises, Inc., and Stuart Michaels. Reprinted by permission of the University of Chicago Press.

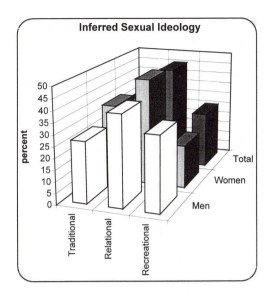

Figure 7.1. Attitudes toward sexuality by men and women, using data in Table 7.3.

From Laumann, Gagnon, Michael, and Michaels, 1994. © 1994 by Edward O. Laumann, Robert T. Michael, CSG Enterprises, Inc., and Stuart Michaels. Reprinted by permission of the University of Chicago Press.

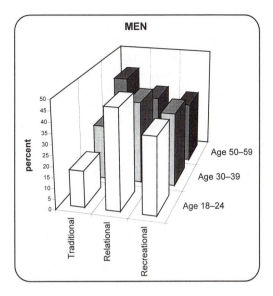

Figure 7.2. Attitudes toward sexuality by men of different ages, using data in Table 7.3.

From Laumann, Gagnon, Michael, and Michaels, 1994. © 1994 by Edward O. Laumann, Robert T. Michael, CSG Enterprises, Inc., and Stuart Michaels. Reprinted by permission of the University of Chicago Press.

truth of nature with roots in evolution, and England's Queen Victoria was said to advise a newlywed woman to "Lie still and think of England." Contrast that with our contemporary period extending from the 1960s, wherein women's sexuality has been glorified. Some major features of that change are in publicity and selling of sexuality, in gender interrelations, in legal regulation, and in political repercussions.

In the contemporary period, sexuality has been increasingly discussed and sold. The generally liberal climate in the late 1960s was illustrated by talk of a "sexual revolution" and permissiveness. The theme underneath that talk was an absolute separation of procreation and recreation missions of sexual relations. Sensual sexuality was promoted, if not demanded, as a criterion of personal happiness and life success. To meet that need, there was an increased selling of aspects of sexuality.

Sexuality emerged as something to be marketed, as society shifted from production values of the first half of the twentieth century

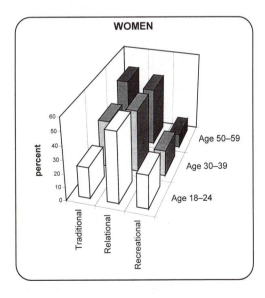

Figure 7.3. Attitudes toward sexuality by women of different ages, using data in Table 7.3.

From Laumann, Gagnon, Michael, and Michaels, 1994. © 1994 by Edward O. Laumann, Robert T. Michael, CSG Enterprises, Inc., and Stuart Michaels. Reprinted by permission of the University of Chicago Press.

to consumer values of the second half. Aspects of sexuality could be offered and bought. Sexual fantasy was easily sold to men in new picture magazines offered openly on newsstands. The magazine publishers included a self-justifying philosophy to aid their sales. Video and film pornography and telephone contacts were new techniques added to the older subcultures that aided masturbation. On the open market, sexual aids, erotic clothing, and sex advice have been displayed freely. There is little doubt about the availability of sources for learning the importance of being sexual and the many cultural scripts of sexuality.

Some of the most interesting history of cultural ideas of sexuality in this century are found in changing gender relations. Two social facts are relevant. First, society continues to be structured by marriage. It can be argued that marriage survives as the dominant social coupling because it is forced by elements of economics, tradition, and systems of morality. Second, sexuality has always been and continues to be defined from men's perspective. Nevertheless, there has been acceptance of new ideas.

One major shift has been toward recognition of women's interest in sexual acts and their rights to sexuality. But other changes in Western culture, particularly in the United States, altered some supporting structures such as extended family groupings, neighborhoods, and coherent communities. That left only couples in marriage. In the new view, marriage offers equal sexual rights and opportunities for women. The quality of a marriage was now judged in part by mutual sexual harmony. Rights to sexuality were developed by gender politics into insistence that women must experience no less sexual arousal and orgasm than men. Women who were not experiencing the sensual aspects of sexuality equal to that of men were thought to be in need of therapy for their sexual dysfunctions. This was developed as another selling of sex, illustrated by if not following the programs of Masters and Johnson.

Legal regulation of sexual acts has concurred with the changing openness, mercantilism, and gender politics. Laws tend to be based increasingly on what is practiced rather than on moral or theological foundations. The liberalist-pluralist position dominates, in which rights of individuals and maintaining the public order have become the criteria in setting legal codes. However, these changes have not gone unnoticed or free from dissent. The views of the self-styled "moral right" have found it easy to play on old fears that sexuality is a danger that must be controlled. Liberalized sexuality has been challenged as weakening family values in which women have economic, social, and sexual stability. The hidden fear is that free and open sexuality will likely weaken men's ties to women in marriage. Thus, programs of laws to protect the monogamous family are periodically promoted with new fervor.

SECTION SUMMARY: POLITICS OF SEX

Early European sexologists described perversions, but Americans tried to examine sexual acts and beliefs. Social pressure was negative at first, turning most researchers' efforts toward animals. As the social climate liberalized, survey studies were done in the late 1940s and detailed physiological studies of sexual acts were published by the mid 1950s. Extreme gender myths of women's lack of sexuality reversed to assuming women's equality of sexual interest and experience. The 1960s and beyond saw an increasing research attention toward sexual matters and a corresponding weakening of negative social pressure.

Wide variance of opinion about sexual matters still exists. Absolutists see the late nineteenth-century monogamous family as the ideal. Liberalists-pluralists want individual choice within a framework of social order. Libertarians want unfettered personal choice of sexuality. One modern survey shows similar categories under the respective labels of traditional, relational, and recreational attitudes about sexual choices.

Our present sexual culture is marked by considerable openness to sexual topics, nearly equal gender rights and opportunities, and heavy commercial marketing and use of sexuality. Still the dominant social form of sexual bonding remains the monogamous family protected by social laws and agreement. There are good physiological reasons, we will see, why this is likely and satisfying.

DISSECTING THE SEXUAL ACTS

Sexual acts are obviously biological. The biological events are the primary focus of a large part of sexology, because it seems apparent that body changes are themselves a major source of the content of sexuality. But biological conditions are intertwined with the psychological and social to make up the sexual environment. Therefore, biological facts have a great importance, but they don't stand alone as a sufficient description of sex motivation. Without an understanding of the personal and social ends, it is hard to grasp the organization and subtle features of sexuality. Thus, we approach the biological facts from the vantage of their purposeful design—meaning, of course, the successful evolutionary adaptations we each carry.

The foundations of enjoying sexuality are in the original purpose of it all: fertility and conceiving children. Our bodies are designed to enjoy frequent sexual intercourse with a regular partner. Only in the past few years of sexual physiology study has this become apparent, and it is changing our picture of sexuality in fundamental ways. Some of the roots of importance are in the interacting hormones as they ebb and flow. **Hormones** is a common name for sexual feelings, and that is a well-founded belief, but there is much more to it. The what, when, and how much of hormone change is vitally important.

Hormone coordination has recently supplanted sex organ physiology in the attention of many physiological sexologists. The physiological patterns of sexual organ activities were described in detail in the 1950s and 1960s. Those facts somewhat demystified sex organ events and served perhaps too well in giving a biological finality to certain ideas of sexual experience. The politics of equality then suggested that everyone must have the full range of sexual experiences and enjoyment described in these studies. To not be fully sexual was to suffer a dysfunction needing therapy.

Stages of Sexual Acts

Masters and Johnson (1966) measured physiological actions during sexual acts and constructed a four-stage model entirely from those changes. It was intended as a beginning or outline. Their extensive research led them to identify essentially the same cycles—excitement, plateau, orgasm, and resolution—but with different detail in men and women. For each change in men, they found a comparable change in women. Their implicit intent may have been in line with the social philosophy of the times: that of demonstrating equality in sexuality. Their work seemed to be aimed at reducing the strength of the prevailing idea that women are less sexual than men.

Briefly, the Masters and Johnson stages are these. In the **excitement stage** there are increased erotic feelings, penile erection in men and vaginal lubrication in women, changes in position of women's sexual organs, and excitement of the sympathetic nervous system. The **plateau phase** is a substantial and distinct peaking in intensity of these changes.

Orgasm is the phase of the most intense pleasure sensations, with men's emission followed by ejaculation of semen in a rapid rhythm. A similar rhythm of pelvic muscles appears in women. Orgasmic reflexes differ in speed in men and women. Cutler (1991) likens men's orgasm to a sneeze and women's to a yawn. In both cases, once begun, they carry through to their natural completion.

The **resolution phase** is a return of the body to resting state, a detumescence (reduction of swelling and erection), during which most men do not respond to unchanged sexual contact.

Subsequent researchers acknowledge the quality and importance of the Masters and Johnson work, but many take issue with their interpretations. The emphasis on stages perhaps places too much emphasis on differences at the expense of the continuity of changes that takes place. Particularly, the separation of the buildup of sexual activity into excitement and plateau stages may not be meaningful beyond the purposes of detailed physiological study.

A modification of Masters and Johnson's physiological pattern by Helen Kaplan (1974, 1979) may be more useful in describing the different psychological experiences of sexual acts. Kaplan's model is composed of three stages: desire, excitement, and orgasm.

Before the Masters and Johnson physiological measurement usually begins, Kaplan's **desire stage** or libido includes specific sensations that move the individual to seek out, or become receptive to, sexual experiences. These sensations are probably produced by the activation of specific neural systems in the brain, perhaps by the presence of greater

amounts of the hormone testosterone. When this system is active, a person feels vaguely sexy, interested in sex, open to sex, or even just restless. These sensations diminish after sexual gratification.

In Kaplan's scheme the **excitement stage** includes both the excitement and plateau phases of Masters and Johnson. The argument is that both involve the same physiological systems, and the distinction is a physiological one of degree rather than a noticeable qualitative change.

The **orgasm stage** is the same as that in Masters and Johnson's description. Masters and Johnson's resolution phase is omitted because it is really just a period of recovery, not a part of the sexual act.

One of the values of Kaplan's scheme of three stages is that it emphasizes a closer correspondence of psychological and physiological systems. Particularly, Kaplan's first stage of desire provides a location for the psychologically interesting components of sex motivation. The three-stage model also fits the general classes of sexual dysfunction that have been identified. That is, the sexologists and sex therapists have claimed that there are separate disorders of desire, excitement, and orgasm.

Neural Mechanisms

Sexual excitement and orgasm are caused and maintained by tactile stimulation to parts of the body, and those events have some degree of local neural control. Mechanisms of arousal, ejaculation, and orgasm can be fully formed through nerves in the lower spinal cord. In normal use, however, those mechanisms are influenced by messages to and from the brain and can therefore be either facilitated or inhibited by states of the brain.

Several of the 32 pairs of spinal nerves integrate sexual action. Parasympathetic nervous system impulses from sacral nerves form the male erection and female lubrication responses to direct contact with the genitals. Ejaculation and orgasm are reflexes from sympathetic nervous system action in the lumbar portion of the spinal cord.

Studies of selective damage to the spinal cord show that these two kinds of functions may be complete in those different locations. Men whose spinal cord is severed will ejaculate from manipulation of the penis, although they feel no sensation when this occurs. That is, ejaculation *can* occur without erection, as can erection without ejaculation, and either or both can occur without mental awareness or the brain's normal control.

Although there is evidence that sexual responses are possible from local stimulation alone, that is not the normal course of events. It is unlikely that those mechanisms ever operate in undamaged people without some monitoring and control. Areas along the spinal cord are involved in the normal response mechanisms, relaying and perhaps filtering the neural information. It is not questioned that brain activity modifies all sexual activity. Brain control can facilitate sexual acts (by, for example, erotic fantasies), or it can inhibit them (by conditions of stress or thoughts of pain or danger). Natural sexual reflexes occur at spinal levels, but similar natural operations take place in the rest of the nervous system. All areas are in it together to enable or inhibit appropriate sexual acts.

Hormone Foundations

Hormones are materials that circulate in body fluids and often affect body functions remote from where they were produced. The essential psychological role of hormones in sexual acts is sensitization. Until recently, male hormones were the primary focus of study, following the slow-to-fade idea that sexuality is something that men experience, women being merely receptacles. In this view, certain sex hormones have been shown to increase sexual feelings and interests or libido during what we will call the desire stage. A system maintains a quantity of certain sensitizing hormones circulating in the bloodstream. The brain and nervous system, the endocrine glands, and the sexual organs each are necessary parts of the system. Sexual hormones are different in women and men, but perhaps there is much less difference than often assumed.

Bases of Fertility

We will turn around the usual picture built on men's sexuality, exploring instead women's much more complicated system of hormone variation, assuming that it is women's fertility that regulates both men's and women's sexuality. How this works is buried in the hormonal system and the effects of specific hormones. We will have to be brief, but you may wish to consult Winnifred Cutler's (1991) *Love Cycles: The Science of Intimacy* for a readable source of more detailed information.

Six kinds of hormones function in women's fertility. **Estrogen** and **progesterone** are the general names for the feminizing sex hormones that are formed in the ovaries and the adrenal glands in women. Estrogen produces feminine features of hair, skin, fat deposits, breast development, and curved hips. Progesterone counters some of the excesses of unchecked estrogen. Two other hormones come from the pituitary gland. These two are gonadotrophic hormones, meaning they are gonad-seeking after their release into the bloodstream, stimulating the ovaries. **Follicle-stimulating hormone (FSH)** controls women's ovarian follicle maturation. **Luteinizing hormone (LH)** stimulates women to ovulate. Women's ovaries also produce small amounts of the androgens **androstenedione** and **testosterone.** These are responsible for masculine characteristics, but their potency is perhaps 5% of that in men. Androgens affect energy, muscle strength, and libido.

Women's hormones are in a dynamic interaction. The four ovary hormones enter the bloodstream to reach the brain and pituitary gland. The pituitary secretes its gonadotrophic hormones that stimulate the ovaries. Estrogen and progesterone also stimulate fluid protection for the walls of the uterus and vagina and stimulate cervical glands to make prostaglandin, which regulates the cyclic period of the ovaries. Bone metabolism is also affected by ovary hormones reaching the thyroid and parathyroid. Variations in these hormones in different phases of life add to the complex picture.

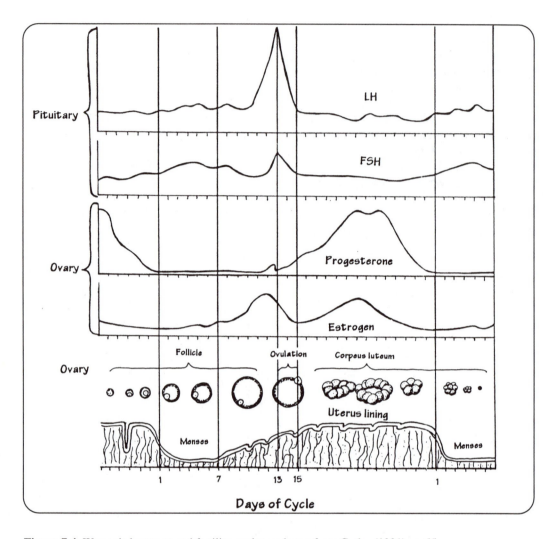

Figure 7.4. Women's hormone and fertility cycles, redrawn from Cutler (1991), p. 65.

The key structure in fertility is the follicle, an ovarian egg covered with a sheet of cells. This is the source of estrogen and progesterone. One egg ovulates each period, and several others also grow somewhat in size. Estrogen is formed in the swollen follicles of the chosen eggs and in the corpus luteum, the follicle that has released its egg. Estrogen rises to a peak twice in each periodic cycle.

Beginning at the onset of menses, estrogen is at its lowest. It steadily rises until just before ovulation, the release of the chosen egg into the fallopian tube. Estrogen levels reduce somewhat and then rise to a second peak before falling to the low level at onset of menses again. This second fall in estrogen level is associated with less cheerful feelings known as premenstrual syndrome (PMS). Cutler (1991) believes PMS effects are often exaggerated and that "the percentage of women with this debility is probably less than the percentage of men with similar inhibiting debilities of personality" (p. 86).

Progesterone rises to a single peak coincident with the second estrogen peak. Progesterone is formed only in the corpus luteum. Progesterone also affects general well-being, often making a pleasant sleepiness as it rises.

A letdown follows as it falls along with the estrogen in the days approaching menses.

The lining of the uterus grows each cycle from a flat lining to a thick nest for the released egg. At the end of the cycle, lowering estrogen causes the endometrial nest to get less blood supply. Cells die, and the lining breaks off, causing the bleeding of menses.

The region connecting the uterus to the vagina is the cervix, a collection of glands and nerves. Those nerves are pressure sensitive only in the presence of estrogen and are one important basis of sensations during sexual intercourse. Depending on estrogen condition, cervix sensitivity to a stroking penis may be absent, a source of pleasure, or verging on pain.

Sexual activity in tune with hormone fertility cycles aids that hormonal function and leads to ensuring fertility, good health, and slowed aging. Although it sounds like moralizing, there is strong physiological evidence that regular sex in a monogamous bond is good for both partners' health and sexuality. The required sexual activity is not just a matter of orgasm; the effect requires a partner. We will show why that is so.

Part of the evidence starts with the fact that women with regular cycles of about 29.5 days are nearly always fertile, and fertility reflects the best health, at least in the childbearing years. The physiological basis for the optimal cycle length is in the time required for hormones to stimulate the growth of the endometrial nest. This **luteal phase** is optimal at 14 to 16 days.

In the 1970s, Winnifred Cutler noted that women who had sex at least once a week had the greatest likelihood of a fertile cycle length. Women who were not sexually active or whose sex lives were sporadic included mainly women with cycles longer or shorter than the fertile optimum (Cutler, Garcia, & Krieger, 1979, 1980; Cutler et al., 1985). The connection is with estrogen. Estrogen was much greater for women having weekly sex than for those without it. No differences were found in their progesterone or testosterone. Further support is seen in women approaching menopause. They show a slower decline in estrogen and fewer hot flashes if they have weekly sex.

In addition to aging or to sporadic sex, estrogen levels may fall to menopausal levels from excessive loss of fat tissue due to dieting or athletic conditioning. Fat is one of the storage places for estrogen. Associated with drastically lowered estrogen is depression, loss of bone mass, and heart disease. When corrected early, the estrogen loss and its effects can be readily reversed. However, persisting conditions can produce a premature menopause. With less estrogen, the vagina lining is less thick, of poorer muscle tone, and slower to lubricate.

Bases of Sexual Desire

Androgen is the general name for the masculinizing sex hormones. The most prevalent androgen is testosterone. In men, most of the androgen production takes place in the testes, with about 5% being produced by the adrenal glands. The adrenal glands, positioned on top of the kidneys, secrete large amounts of androgens but of a form that is less potent than that from the gonads. A given unit of androgen lasts about 15 to 30 min before it is used or changed in the body; thus, a constant production at some level may be necessary to sustain whatever functions it moderates.

The pituitary gonadotrophic hormones have a complementary function in men to that in women. LH affects the testes' production of androgens. FSH activates sperm production in the testes.

Testosterone can be identified in three components, and it makes a difference which is being measured. Some (about 5%) is called free testosterone because it is not bound to a protein molecule as it travels in the blood. Some is bound to albumin protein molecules, and some is bound to other proteins. Biologically active testosterone includes both the free and the albumin-bound, making about 60% of the total in the blood (Nankin & Calkins, 1986). Studies before 1989 measured only the small amounts of free testosterone and thus underestimated the testosterone potential.

Testosterone has a circadian or daily cycle (Rubin, Govin, Lubin, Poland, & Pirke, 1975). Testosterone levels rise to a peak on wakening in the morning, perhaps carrying through midmorning. Levels fall during the afternoon. Curiously, at the time most people report that they have sexual intercourse, testosterone levels are approaching their lowest levels. The second most-reported time of sexual activity, however, is the early morning, when testosterone is highest. There is also some evidence for an annual cycle of testosterone levels, with the highest in October (Reinberg & Lagoguey, 1978; Reinberg, Smolensky, & Hallek, 1988). Smoking reduces it by about 5% (Deslypere & Vermeulen, 1984).

Greater testosterone is associated with faster and stronger sexual arousal. Young men with high levels of testosterone have more frequent sexual thoughts, unwanted penile erections, a tendency to quick ejaculation, and slower reduction in arousal after orgasm.

In testosterone's absence, some physiological basis for sexual desire is lost. A great deal of research with males of many species has confirmed this. Loss of testosterone sources eliminates sexual acts in many male mammals. Men with lost testosterone production generally experience a waning sexual appetite that returns with testosterone replacement (Bagatell, Heiman, Rivier, & Bremner, 1994; Burris, Banks, Carter, Davidson, & Sherins, 1992). The amount of testosterone is not great, and experimental studies reducing levels within the normal range have no inhibition effects (Buena et al., 1993). This also makes intuitive sense. Loss of male sex hormones should reduce male sexual functioning.

The testosterone influence on men's sexual interest is limited, however. Therapeutic replacement of androgens to hypogonadal (underactive gonads) men increases sexual appetite and interest, but it is not needed to produce penile erections or sexual excitement to direct visual or physical contact. In experimental studies, testosterone was given to hypogonadal men to bring them to a normal level, or antiandrogen drugs were given to normal men to reduce their testosterone levels. Without normal levels of testosterone, the

men continue to respond with erections to sexually provocative films, but they reduce or lose their normal sexual response to sexual fantasies, and they have less of the sexual feelings normally associated with penile erection. In the absence of direct sexual provocation, testosterone apparently forms the basis for sexual responses and feelings (Bancroft & Wu, 1983; Bancroft, Tennant, Loucas, & Cass, 1974; Davidson & Myers, 1988). Testosterone in the blood seems to be most necessary for becoming excited through sexual thoughts. With adequate testosterone, men think more about sex and are more interested in sexual contacts.

Androgens determine women's sexual interest, desire, and thoughts as well (Alexander & Sherwin, 1993). Information comes from study of hormone replacements to women who have had surgical removal of their ovaries. Replacement of estrogen has no direct effects on sexual interest (Bellerose & Binik, 1993; Sherwin & Gelfand, 1987). Doses of estrogen, in fact, appear to reduce sexual desire in both men and women (Persky et al., 1978). Although estrogen appears to influence sexual attraction and receptivity in many studied female mammals, the level of estrogen does *not* appear to affect sexual desire in human females. In women, estrogens play a supporting role in sexual acts by maintaining the elasticity and lubrication of the vagina and the texture and function of the breasts. This is a clear example of a major error in generalizing from animal mechanisms to infer human mechanisms.

Therapeutic additions of testosterone, however, increase women's reported sexual desires and fantasies, as well as their feelings of arousal during sexual acts (Sherwin & Gelfand, 1987; Sherwin, Gelfand, & Brender, 1985). In normal women living in a coresidential college, levels of androgens correlated with their number of sexual partners and with their own judgments of self-regard (Cashdan, 1995). The role of testosterone in producing women's sexual appetite is counterintuitive. Why should masculinizing sex hormones affect women's sexual desire? That may not be the right question, but one answer leans on the notion that interest in experiencing sex comes before the sexual acts. It seems not to matter whether we are man or woman. Testosterone regulates the brain's intensity of sexual desire. The male-female differences in later performance may not be relevant to that basic desire. Testosterone presence prepares each person for sexual activity of some kind. The question then shifts to what those sexual acts are and to what partners our sexual desire is drawn.

Testosterone is not a magic potion. It does not turn sex on and off, although it plays a strong enabling role for some dimensions of sexual interaction. In the reverse direction, sexual activity does not turn testosterone production on and off (Carani et al., 1990). Yet, there is an interaction pattern that develops over time between testosterone and specific sexual experience. Regular sexual intercourse raises testosterone levels before, during, and after (Knussmann, Christiansen, & Couwenbergs, 1986). Self-stimulation and irregular activity do not alter the testosterone levels. Furthermore, men's testosterone tends to adopt a cycle following their regular partner's ovulation (Persky, Lief, O'Brien, & Strauss, 1977). Even the quality of sperm produced in regular sexual intercourse is better in sperm count, motility, and other measures (Zavos & Goodpasture, 1989). Monogamy produces endocrine harmony. We will explore one idea of how this comes about as we consider the mechanism of pheromones.

In the last few years, more and finer details of brain chemistry of sexual motivation have been uncovered. There is evidence that neuropeptides, possibly regulated in part by testosterone, stimulate or inhibit sexual activity. Among the stimulants are oxytocin and substance P; the inhibitors include CRF, beta-endorphin, and prolactin. These inhibitors are typically released during stress, possibly accounting for lowered sexual interest with conditions of depression (Dornan & Malsbury, 1989). Oxytocin has been targeted by several researchers in studies of sexual activity. For both men and women, levels of oxytocin in the blood increase during sexual arousal and reach a high during the orgasm (Carmichael et al., 1987; Carmichael, Warburton, Dixen, & Davidson, 1994; Murphy, Checkley, Seckl, & Lightman, 1990).

SECTION SUMMARY: DISSECTING THE SEXUAL ACTS

Since the 1950s, several stages of sexual acts have been described in physiological terms, modified according to definitional points of view, including desire, excitement, plateau, orgasm, and resolution. A rudimentary neural physiology underwrites essential body part arousal and orgasm at the spinal cord level, but normal sexuality follows an intricate brain control via hormones.

Sexuality is founded on fertility, making women's reproductive systems the essential research focus. Optimal timing of women's hormone cycles permits fertility. Regular sexuality controls that optimal timing, improves women's hormonal and general health, and maximizes the possibility of conception.

Men's sexual desire and the magnitude and speed of their sexual arousal are moderated by magnitudes of testosterone. In its absence, sexual arousal and orgasm are possible via direct stimulation, but little unstimulated interest can exist. A man having regular sexuality with the same woman will have raised testosterone levels and improved sperm quality. For women, too, their (smaller quantity of) testosterone builds sexual desire.

SENSUAL AROUSAL

An old cliché of literature refers to three fundamental drives of life: hunger, pain, and sex. The message is that they are biological imperatives—each of unquestionable power. Sex is powerfully attractive and necessary. As some see it, "Sex is a misdemeanor: The more you miss it, the meaner you get." At best, that message is trivial, and at worst, it assumes a simple theory of sexual acts. As we found in hunger and pain, we will see compelling physiological elements in sexual acts, but the question is what role those elements have. The cliché suggests that sexual acts are biologically driven and hence inevitable.

The biological message is inadequate, but there are perhaps things in common among hunger, pain, and sex that don't appear on the surface. In earlier chapters, we saw eating motivated by much more than hunger, and we learned pain has many social controls. So too, motivation for sexual acts is perhaps founded as much on mental states and social conditions as on body need.

Aspects of sexual motivation may be usefully divided and labeled the sensual, the erotic, and the social (see Table 7.4). Natural physical mechanisms that constitute sexual acts are described as the sensual aspects of sex motivation. Sensual arousal is composed of a general readiness, or libido, and of responses to touch of erogenous body areas. Sensual aspects include the events that directly produce sexual acts and their controlling physiology. Erotic factors are learned, serving to evoke sexual interest and prepare for sexual acts. Erotic sources of sexual motivation come from personal experience in a culture, with theoretical undertones of innate inclinations. The social constitution and regulation of sexual motivation work through sexual scripts, self-definition, and social purposes. The erotic and social aspects are considered in the next chapter.

Adequate sensual events are those that naturally evoke sexual excitement. Sensual cues evoke sexual reflexes. They are fundamental in a structural sense. Other sexual arousal, that of the erotic, comes from learning and cultural experience. Erotic cues may be typical, but they are not necessarily so. We will examine that issue later.

Purely sensual arousal is based on our physiological state and direct stimulation. Libido is a term for our general level of interest in being sexually aroused. Erogenous touch is the most assured sensual form of direct sexual stimulation.

Libido

Feelings and thoughts that make one more likely to be sexually aroused constitute **libido.** Evidence from the past 10 years supports a connection between libido and adequate testosterone. Reports of frequency of sexual thoughts and measures of men's spontaneous erections depend on amount of testosterone.

Sexual Stimulation

Human bodies are richly endowed with receptors for pressure and touch. These receptors are distributed unevenly, which means that some areas of the body are more sensitive than are others. The more sensitive sensual areas are called the **erogenous zones.** The sexual organs are the clear leaders. Men's penis tips are their most sensitive sensual areas. That sensitivity declines with age and with infrequent sexual intercourse. In women, the clitoris and cervix in the vagina are the most sensually sensitive, but they are subject to hormone conditions of the fertility cycle as we noted earlier.

Many areas besides the genitals can be sensually sensitive to touch, including the breasts, mouth, ears, buttocks, palms of the hands, fingers, abdomen, inner surfaces of the thighs, soles of the feet, and toes. All of these have been shown to have some sensual sensitivity, but there are great differences among people.

TABLE 7.4 Some Convenient Labels for Aspects of Sexual Motivation

Sensual	Erotic	Social
libido	learned cues	self-definition
sexual reflexes	cultural training	social purposes

Touch appears to be the only source of reflexive sexual action that *can* be directly shown to be independent of higher brain centers. The physical evidence appears clear. Men with spinal cord injuries that prevent impulses from reaching the brain, but that leave the sexual centers in the lower spinal cord intact, are able to have an erection when their genitals or inner thighs are touched. Touch effectively arouses sexual action without brain-moderated experience.

No other sensory channel but touch has been shown (or perhaps can be shown) to have sensuality that is not influenced by experiences. Evidence of physical reflexes similar to that of touch is not possible because vision, audition, and olfaction nerves project directly to the brain. There is no neural circuitry from the eyes, ears, or nose to sexual reflexes of the spinal cord that can be separated from that to the brain. These senses are mediated by the brain. It is possible that innate sensual arousal may exist to sights, sounds, and smells, but those effects will have to be shown by other means.

Despite the difficulty in showing the physiology, it seems clear that men have sexual arousal to sufficient visual stimulation, even in the absence of adequate levels of testosterone. Some kind of primitive sexual reflex to seeing fertile women and sexual activity seems to be there. Culture moderates it, but a reaction appears whenever the right sights appear.

The sense of smell is also sensually involved. Sexually potent chemicals are called **pheromones.** Unlearned sexual arousal from smell is a part of the mating pattern of many species. These species rely heavily on chemical attractants in their sexual interactions. The pheromone influence, however, seems to be weaker in species with more developed brain systems. Effective pheromones have been hard to locate in monkeys and don't always work. The pheromone picture illustrates the general comparative finding that the more complex the brain of a species, the less that the sex depends on simple factors.

Although there don't seem to be chemical switches in humans for sexual activity as there are for moths, rats, and others, evidence suggests a chemical source of sexual harmony. In 1971, Martha McClintock first showed that women who live together cycle together. Their fertility cycles come to operate in synchrony. Other studies have verified this menstrual synchrony (Graham & McGrew, 1980; Quadagno, Shubeita, Deck, & Francoer, 1981; Russell, Switz, & Thompson, 1980).

A decade later, intrigued by her own discovery that sexual activity with a man produces a more fertile and regular cycle, Winnifred Cutler teamed with George Petri to develop a double-blind pheromone study using underarm essences applied to the upper lip disguised by a light alcohol smell (Cutler et al., 1986). They found female essence produced menstrual synchrony in women, supporting McClintock's finding. In a separate group of women, male essence was used. Two thirds of the women who were not having regular sex with a man and had aberrant-length cycles adopted a normal-length cycle after 14 weeks of receiving male essence. The critical element in both groups was not a detectable odor, and it is not likely that deodorants or artificial odorants will have positive effects.

The pheromone power here seems to be one of harmonizing and regularizing hormone patterns. Fertility likelihood is maximized. And so it appears that fertility is optimized by regular sexuality.

SECTION SUMMARY: SENSUAL AROUSAL

Sensual reflexes are the natural, unlearned physical mechanisms underwriting sexuality. Prior to stimulation, testosterone-primed individuals have sexual feelings and thoughts that make up the desire stage or libido. The most sensually sensitive areas of touch are the erogenous zones, primarily the sexual organs but including many others. Men experience some sensual arousal from sights of fertile women and sexual activity, but little else is proven to be sensual as opposed to erotically learned. Sexually arousing chemicals, called pheromones, although common in animals, have been elusive in men and women. A recent variety of evidence converges on the idea of some chemical sensitivity and communication between women that synchronizes their fertility cycles and between men and women that regularizes women's fertility cycles.

GENDER DIFFERENCES

Sexuality is a blending of psychology and physiology with politics. Both the theory and the realities of sexual acts are partly the ideas of the participants. Nowhere is this more apparent than in the subject of gender differences. The political positions are the obvious standpoints of men and of women but also of the scientific philosophies of evolutionary mechanism and of environmentalism. In these theories and positions, a common theme of **essentialism** is prominent (Blumstein & Schwartz, 1989). The essentialist idea is that there is a true, biologically given sexuality to each person. The idea is that each of us is really, or essentially, of a certain sexuality. Essentialism can be a bias leading to oversimplified pictures of individual sexuality.

Evolution Theories of Sexuality

In 1979, two books presented the thesis that gender differences in sexual motivation have evolutionary origins. The case presented by Richard Hagen in his *The Bio-Sexual Factor* is based on observations that women appear to be sexually aroused less easily and by different factors and may be less orgasmic, and that these differences have biological causes that training can't erase. A somewhat less strident and more complete evolutionary theory argument of sexual motivation came from Donald Symons in his book, *The Evolution of Human Sexuality.* Symons outlined a number of implications of some logical differences in men's and women's strategies for maximizing their genetic survival. These were not new ideas; in fact, Charles Darwin presented many of them in his 1871 *Descent of Man.* The important evolution theme is that gender differences in sexuality are part of our biological heritage. But what are the specifics?

Symons based his ideas of gender differences in sexuality on some logical facts of reproductive biology. He began with the different roles that men and women have in producing children that survive to pass on their genetic material. The major gender differences have to do with number of children carrying one's genes and the necessity of sexual arousal and orgasm. Men have nearly unlimited sperm and possibilities of transmitting their genes, and sexual arousal and orgasm are necessary to deliver their sperm. Women have a limited number of occasions to transmit their genes (because they are likely to produce only a few children), and it is not necessary that they be sexually aroused or experience orgasm.

From these beginnings, it follows that men may genetically profit from impregnating as many women as possible, and men are more likely than women to desire sexual acts with many different partners. Women have a much larger stake in ensuring the development of their few children to mating maturity and are likely to desire mates who assist them. From those role differences, evolution theorists believe they can deduce women's characteristics attractive to men, men's characteristics attractive to women, and differences in sexual interest and orgasm. But we will see that the evolutionary adaptations are more complicated than that when we add coherent assumptions about the social and survival facts of living of our breeding ancestors.

Before examining the evidence of gender differences in sexuality, we must note the historical roles of politics and philosophy in evolutionary theories. In light of the political influence on ideas in science, an extremely important criticism and caution emerges. Specific pieces of evolution logic can be and are chosen because they conform to what is thought to be patterns of functioning. The specific observations of experience that are used to inspire the theory are not evidence that validates the theory. As we noted in Chapter 1, we must make predictions from each evolutionary theory plank and then validate them independently.

Evolution theories are possibilities. They provide reasons that are in accord with what appears to be true in modern Western civilization. Even if they predict our current acts well, they are not proven in that way. Proper evolutionary theory rests on a coherent system of ideas of adaptations of the past. In this sense, it is reasonable to suggest that, for example, men have biological structures that tune them to sights of fertile women. Support for this idea is built on how such an adaptation could have been naturally selected in human or prehuman history. We nourish this proposal on factors of how more surviving offspring would have been produced, were it true. Secondary, but not necessary, evidence may come from illustrations of how it is a possibility of expression across different human population groups. Not pertinent at all is evidence of how it serves reproductive success now. An evolutionary adaptation is a performance potential that was formed in the past. Whether it still "works" is not relevant. Even during the period they were being selected, only very weak tendencies were needed to accumulate an advantage in fitness. The message is that they were not all-powerful or even a part of all of the breeding population then. They surely are not necessarily so now.

Some of these theory ideas are part of long-standing battles between instinct-versus-learning and nature-versus-nurture points of view. In this fashion, evolutionary adaptation theories, as well as competing feminist social learning theories, have sometimes been ways of justifying what the proponents want to believe.

Judging from the flood of new books summarizing and extending human evolutionary theory in the past 15 years, there is no longer any question about the significance of adaptations (Allman, 1994; Barkow, Cosmides, & Tooby, 1992; Buss, 1994; Dawkins, 1982, 1986, 1989, 1995; Dennett, 1995; Leakey, 1994; Morgan, 1982, 1990; Wright, 1994; and others). It now remains to sort among the various ideas for the most coherent picture.

We will consider a variety of complications of the pattern that Symons outlined as we present some of the patterns of sexual motivation.

Sexual Attraction

Sexual attraction is a qualitative gender difference. Of course, men are sexually focused on women, and women are sexually focused on men, and men and women are qualitatively different in many ways. The question is which qualities attract the other gender.

In the evolution theories, men are attracted to women who give visual evidence of high "mate value." High mate value means high probability of successfully bearing children, thus improving the men's gene survival. Successful childbearing is shown by health and age. Health is seen in general condition of the potential mate, and especially revealing is the skin. Clues of appearance also tell about women of childbearing age. Age of optimal child bearing is about 23 to 28 years, although the optimal fertility range begins at about 17 years. Men should be most attuned to visual cues that tell age. Sexual attraction arises in men when they see signs of a woman able to bear children.

Women, on the other hand, have a larger stake in each child. With few opportunities for gene survival, women must form social bonds for care and nurturing of their children. Thus, the theory predicts that a woman is attracted to men who are able and willing to provide for her and her children. Character, status, and caring head the list. These are not given by sight but through time in social relationships. Sexually attractive men provide food, shelter, and defense of women, but also, each woman is attracted to a man who shows interest in her. The process of attracting and "capturing" a mate will likely be more exciting than the sex act of impregnation.

A recent study by Russell Clark and Elaine Hatfield (1989) illustrates some of these gender differences in an audacious study. On a college campus, experimenters asked opposite-sex students one of three questions after commenting that the student had been noticed and seemed attractive: "Would you go to bed with me tonight?" "Would you come over to my apartment tonight?" "Would you go out with me tonight?" Men agreed most strongly in that order. From two thirds to three quarters said yes to bedding, but fewer would go to the apartment, and even fewer wanted to date. No woman accepted the bedding, just a few would go to the apartment, but about half would accept the date.

Katherine and Kermit Hoyenga (1993) assembled the many studies on mating pref-erences in their recent book, *Gender-Related Differences.* They found that there are many qualities that both men and women seek in a mate, but men give higher value to attractiveness and women value status. David Buss (1989, 1994), with a number of colleagues, found this same difference across 37 different cultures.

These ideas of men seeking attractive women and women seeking supportive men apply most readily to long-term mate selection. But is that the only mating that is likely? The reality of most species including ourselves is that there is also a strong pattern of short-term mating. This is most often shown for men, with the idea that men have little to lose in trying. Additional genetic transmission can be had by seeking other women. Mating with new women carries little risk and a high genetic value to a man. Not only does it provide a potential for more children, the children will have a different mother, whose genetic material, being different, decreases the risk of nonviability. Because of his unlimited sperm, there is little cost and some potential benefits in trying.

Following this adaptation idea, a man is attracted to many different women. Sexual variety goes together with number and survivability of potential children. Little else about a woman is sexually important to a man beyond that she is capable of successfully bearing his child. In these situations, other standards tend to be relaxed or even contrary to what is desired in a long-term mate. Buss (summarized in 1994) found men will accept less charm, education, honesty, intelligence, kindness, emotional stability, and the like, but they look for increased sexiness and physical attractiveness.

The value to a woman of short-term mating is not so obvious. How might a woman's offspring have had some advantage by her mating with someone who is not going to help ensure the child's survival to breeding age? In answering this, we may deduce what kind of man is attractive to her. (a) Women could have benefited from mating with men who

TABLE 7.5 How Many Sex Partners Do We Have?

	Reported Number of Sexual Partners in the Past Year (in percent)			
	0	*1*	*2 to 4*	*5+*
All	12	71	14	3
Men	10	67	18	5
Women	14	75	10	2
Age 18 to 24	11	57	24	9
Age 35 to 39	10	77	11	2
Age 55 to 59	32	65	4	0
Married	2	94	3	1
Cohabiting	1	76	18	5

SOURCE: Constructed from data in Table 5.1A in Laumann, Gagnon, Michael, and Michaels, 1994, p. 177. © 1994 by Edward O. Laumann, Robert T. Michael, CSG Enterprises, Inc., and Stuart Michaels. Reprinted by permission of the University of Chicago Press.

satisfied their immediate and longer needs for resources. Consequently, men showing evidence of power and wealth would be most attractive. And a variety of such liaisons would also be sought. (b) Women may mate with men of superior genetic qualities compared with the mate she was able to attract. This would not indicate a different selection criterion but would allow strengthening those features already attractive. (c) Like men, women increase their offspring's viability by having some diversity of genetic contribution from the mate. Men sought in short-term mating would likely be of different genetic background, but strength of commitment would not be as strong as his tendency to give resources to her. Buss (1994) found the latter to be true. (d) Women may hedge against losing their mate by having another ready and willing to step in. These liaisons would likely be with men of the same qualities as are sought in permanent mates. (e) Finally, women may choose to mate with sexy men in order to have sexy sons, who will thus likely have more offspring. Thus, evidence of virility would be attractive.

There are also costs to be counted in short-term mating. Women are protected by their kin and current mates. The costs of attempting or succeeding in a liaison may range from social reprisal to ostracism to death. Women also may be punished by rejection by their mates, social harassment, or death of themselves or the child of the liaison.

There being evolutionary logic and evidence for attraction to others for monogamous pairing and for short-term mating, it is reasonable to suggest that there is a stable balance of these two in human populations. As we saw in Chapter 5 regarding aggression, there may be Evolutionary Stable Strategies in a balance. If so, there is another problem to be worked out. Do these two strategies exist in the same individuals, to be used as opportunities are presented? Or are there some people who are essentially inclined toward just one or the other and remain consistent in that strategy?

Before we leave this, it is useful to see just what degree of casual or short-term pairing is common in the United States now, as shown in the National Health and Social Life Survey described above. Of all respondents, 17% reported two or more sex partners in the previous year. Among marrieds, about 4% in a year reported two or more partners, and, among those living together, it was 25%. Among those neither married nor cohabiting,

TABLE 7.6   How Often Do We Think About Sex?

	Reported Frequency (in percent)	
	Men	Women
Every day	54	19
A few times a week or month	43	67
Less than once a month or never	4	14

SOURCE: Constructed from data in Table 3.9 in Laumann, Gagnon, Michael, and Michaels, 1994, p. 135. © 1994 by Edward O. Laumann, Robert T. Michael, CSG Enterprises, Inc., and Stuart Michaels. Reprinted by permission of the University of Chicago Press.

34% reported multiple partners, but note too that 26% reported no partners at all. (See Table 7.5.)

Sexual Interest and Orgasm

Evolutionary theory about gender differences in sexual interest and orgasm experiences is varied and inconclusive. Essentially, no one finds difficulty in understanding the fitness advantage to men of being interested in sex and having orgasm. In a puckish phrase, sex without interest for men is like trying "to push a wagon up a hill with a rope." Men who have no interest have no children, and men without orgasm likewise cannot ejaculate their sperm into the vagina. For women, there are no comparable necessities. Why then should women have sexual interest, and why do they need orgasm at all?

The variety of evidence suggests that women's sexual interest and orgasm experiences are different from those of men. In describing gender differences in sexuality, both Hagen and Symons in their 1979 books seemed to believe that there is ample evidence that women express less intense sexual interest than men. And from his survey work,

Kinsey et al. (1953) say, "The average younger male is constantly being aroused. . . . Many females may go for days and weeks and months without ever being stimulated unless they have actual physical contact with a sex partner" (p. 682).

Other surveys verify the simple fact that men express a desire for sex more often than do women. Ann Landers, an advice columnist in many newspapers, once questioned her women readers, and a majority preferred closeness and hugging to "the act," although of course this was far from an informative sample. Blumstein and Schwartz (1983, reported in 1989) reported that men and women agree that men more often initiate sex. Hagen (1979) claims that no study has ever shown equality of sexual desire in comparable populations of men and women. Of course, no argument is intended to imply that this direction of difference is always true of individuals. The gender distributions of sexual desire overlap such that there are many women with stronger sexual desire than many men. The NHSLS addressed Kinsey's question of thinking about sex and how often we have it (see Tables 7.6 and 7.7, and Figure 7.5 and 7.6).

Surveys of sexual feelings support the thesis that men are more likely to enjoy sex. About 90% of husbands but only 56% of wives enjoy regular sex. Many women report that they don't relish it. In Shere Hite's (1976) book, *The Hite Report,* women respondents stated more interest in the expression of love and intimacy of sexual acts than in orgasm. These women rated orgasm less important as a sensation than the act of penetration.

Evidence on orgasm gender differences has been closely dissected. Surveys show that men more frequently have orgasm than women, and some women never do (Fisher, 1973; Hite, 1974, 1976). Again, the recent NHSLS survey documented this (See Table 7.8).

This has not changed, Hagen (1979) states, because the revolution led to open "how-to" manuals. Critics ask, Is it poor male technique? Sometimes it may be. Marital

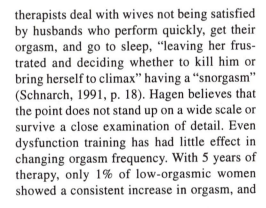

Figure 7.5. Mens and women's reports of frequency of having sex, using data from Table 7.7.

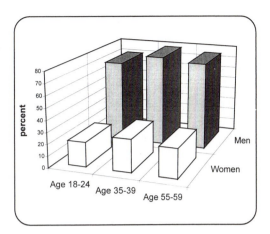

Figure 7.6. Mens's and women's reports of frequency of experiencing orgasm, using data from Table 7.8.

therapists deal with wives not being satisfied by husbands who perform quickly, get their orgasm, and go to sleep, "leaving her frustrated and deciding whether to kill him or bring herself to climax" having a "snorgasm" (Schnarch, 1991, p. 18). Hagen believes that the point does not stand up on a wide scale or survive a close examination of detail. Even dysfunction training has had little effect in changing orgasm frequency. With 5 years of therapy, only 1% of low-orgasmic women showed a consistent increase in orgasm, and

only 8% of nonorgasmic women now had an occasional orgasm, according to Hagen's citing of Fisher (1973).

With more sophisticated understanding of harmonious hormone cycles and the virtues of regular monogamous sexual life, Hagen's and Fisher's evidence may soften. There is indeed better technique for achieving mutual sexual success, but it depends on willingness to cooperate rather than an attitude of one partner being dysfunctional. Optimal sexual intercourse is a matter that must be de-

TABLE 7.7 How Often Do We Have Sex?

	Frequency of Sex Experiences in the Past Year (in percent)				
	None	*A few/year*	*A few/month*	*2 or 3/week*	*4 or more/week*
Men	10	18	35	29	8
Age 18 to 24	15	21	24	28	12
Age 35 to 39	7	13	40	35	5
Age 55 to 59	16	25	42	17	1
Women	14	16	37	26	7
Age 18 to 24	11	16	32	29	12
Age 35 to 39	11	16	38	32	3
Age 55 to 59	41	22	30	5	2

SOURCE: Constructed from data in Table 3.4 in Laumann, Gagnon, Michael, and Michaels, 1994, p. 89. © 1994 by Edward O. Laumann, Robert T. Michael, CSG Enterprises, Inc., and Stuart Michaels. Reprinted by permission of the University of Chicago Press.

TABLE 7.8 How Often Do We Have
Orgasm With Our Partner?
(in percent)

	Men	Women
Age 18 to 24	70	21
Age 35-39	78	28
Age 55-59	75	25

SOURCE: Constructed from data in Table 3.7 in Laumann, Gagnon, Michael, and Michaels, 1994, p. 116. © 1994 by Edward O. Laumann, Robert T. Michael, CSG Enterprises, Inc., and Stuart Michaels. Reprinted by permission of the University of Chicago Press.

veloped and changed to meet life circumstances. Research in 1981 showed that there are two different neural routes to a woman's orgasm: One comes from clitoral stimulation, and the other from vaginal or cervical stimulation (Perry & Whipple, 1981). Later study showed that it is the rhythm of stimulation that is most important (Alzate, 1989, 1990; Alzate & Hoch, 1986). Each woman needs a particular kind of thrusting that varies from time to time, often in cycle with her hormone patterns. Nerves yielding the orgasm depend on a pattern of thrusting that recruits increased neural intensity. The rhythm is the important thing. With patience and exploration, just the right position and pattern will be found. The NHSLS data above suggest that may be the case. The number of women never having orgasm is less in the older age groups. It is likely that being in a stable and caring monogamous sexual relationship, the couple will develop mutually supporting techniques. Such care is less likely from men (or women) in casual sexual affairs.

Orgasm for women has usually been described as a less likely event having no specific purpose. Again, with finer study of mechanisms, it appears that there are specific functions of orgasm that involve retention of sperm. On average, about one third of men's sperm are ejected during the 30 min after their insemination. But much less is rejected if the woman experienced orgasm within the time period of 1 min before and 45 min after the ejaculation. Further control over sperm retention and the effectiveness of competition of new sperm depends on the occurrence of orgasm over the next week. These kinds of fine control over reproduction are complemented by similarly complex patterns of amounts of sperm ejaculated by men that depend on time away from the woman. See the pair of articles by Robin Baker and Mark Bellis (1993a, 1993b) for more details. An account written for a general audience by Robin Baker (1996) is entitled *Sperm Wars: The Science of Sex.*

There are some good critical arguments that can be applied to both evolutionary theory and the interpretation given to the survey of evidence of gender differences in sexual attraction, arousal, and orgasm. Most fundamental are (a) inadequate and historically male-based knowledge of sexual physiology, and (b) minimizing of the means and extent of cultural influence on sexual acts. Viewing sexuality as serving fertility rather than male experience has helped to deal with the first, although there is still a great deal to learn. We turn in the next chapter to the second of these two. Although few informed readers now doubt whether there are gender differences in tendencies toward sexuality, there are still important differences in expression that are set by the culture and cannot be erased from everyone's personal deep structure. Women experience a distinctly different culture than do men. These differences have changed in some ways following the politicizing of gender roles in the United States and Canada in recent years, but cultural influences on girls and boys are still fundamentally different. To reduce gender differences in sexual activity to absolute determination by evolutionary adaptations is to miss the important cultural roles that shape those natural reactions, forming sexual motivation.

SECTION SUMMARY: GENDER DIFFERENCES

Personal political views are common in examining gender sexuality, represented by extremes in environmentalist or biological essentialism. Evolutionary psychologists approach gender differences in sexuality from the necessary roles women and men have in conceiving and raising children. Women have few offspring; men can have many. Arousal and orgasm are necessary for men; for women, they are not. On these bases, and with assumptions about the social order of our ancestors, we can hypothesize gender differences in sexuality.

Men are attracted to and aroused by women having visual appearance of fertility. Women are attracted to sexual acts with men who show interest in caring for her and their children. Although there are interest-ing complications of short-term versus long-term mating conditions, a variety of evidence of modern sexual life supports those basic principles.

Men will always have arousal and orgasm in successful (i.e., potentially reproductive) sexual acts. Women do not need these conditions and may bear children without either. Evidence of these gender differences comes from reported frequencies of thinking about sex and of who initiates sexual acts. Women report fewer orgasmic experiences, but the usual men's lead in sexual activity complicates pinning down causes. Although not fundamentally necessary, women's orgasm does play a role in accepting and rejecting men's sperm, depending on recent events.

CHAPTER CONCLUSIONS

Love and sex seem so well established that it is surprising to find that they have a complicated and changing history. Following social and political history, the very essence of being attracted, aroused, and attached to another person has evolved. There is not and never has been a right and natural form of love and sexuality. The important features of sexual motivation developed around reproductive fitness—successes in producing offspring and raising them to breeding maturity. The history of applying science to sexuality is a re-cord of looking for what people want to find, and there are many more chapters to the story yet to be opened.

After recent modern science tools were directed to our sexuality, we began to learn of the bodily changes during sexual acts, the dependence of sexual arousal on specific body chemistry, and the fundamental differences in roles played by men and women, with women's fertility being primary. The interesting, although tentative, conclusion seems to be that our bodies are designed to have regular, monogamous sexual experiences. Men are attracted to fertile women and, to have offspring, must be aroused and have orgasm. Women are attracted to bonding with caring and supporting men but need not be aroused or have orgasm. Mechanisms of sexual motivation seem to be in tune with these principles. But there is more to the pattern of sexual motivation, and the complicated topic of emotional and lifelong love remains. These are the next chapter's focus.

Study and Review Questions

1. What were the two sets of ideas about love and sex in classical Greek culture?

2. What was a woman's love and sexual role according to early Christian theology?

3. What was the attitude about sexual acts in early American Puritan society?

4. How was deviant sexuality treated in early 1700s America?

5. In 1800s middle-class industrial America, what were women's roles in love and sexuality?

6. What were the ground rules of Victorian-era family life?

7. How was deviant sexuality treated in 1900 scientific thinking?

8. What views did scientist-physicians of 1900 promote regarding sexuality?

9. What did pre-1900 science say about gender differences in sexuality?

10. What were the four sets of late-1800s arguments that placed women as inferior to men?

11. What did Sigmund Freud contribute to sexology?

12. What did academics learn from John Watson's studies of sexual acts?

13. What therapeutic treatment came from the Masters and Johnson sexual act studies?

14. What are the three traditional political views on sexuality?

15. What age and gender groups express the strongest support for recreational sexuality?

16. What age and gender groups express the strongest support for traditional sexuality?

17. What was the primary theme beneath the 1960s sexual revolution?

18. How did Helen Kaplan modify the Masters and Johnson stages of sexual acts?

19. Why is the study of sexual motivation interested in women's fertility?

20. How does sexual activity affect fertility?

21. Is there a hormone affecting human sexual desire?

22. What factors determine testosterone production?

23. What does testosterone do for women's sexuality?

24. What neurochemical affects libido?

25. How do pheromone effects differ from testosterone's effects?

26. What does transmission of women's underarm chemical secretions do for the recipient?

27. What does transmission of men's underarm chemical secretions do for the recipient?

28. In evolution theory, how do men's and women's roles in reproductive fitness differ?

29. What features of women sexually arouse men?

30. What do men look for in short-term as opposed to long-term sexual mates?

31. What attracts women to sexual activity with men?

32. How might women's reproductive fitness benefit from short-term sexual encounters?

33. How many sex partners do we have in a typical year?

34. How often do men and women think about sex?

35. Which partner usually initiates sex?

36. How often do we have sex?

37. What gender and age effects appear in reports of having an orgasm with our partners?

38. Why might women's orgasm experiences not reflect their potential?

39. What physiological role might orgasm play for women?

CHAPTER 8

Eros, Love, and Commitment

We become sexually attracted in a variety of ways. Erotic sexual arousal, based on sensuality, is formed through specific cultural and personal experiences. Sexual arousal is accomplished in fantasy and by various erotica. We define ourselves in part by forming and carrying out sexual acts with specific others, using sexual scripts in social roles.

Ideas of romantic love and realities of pragmatic love may be founded on evolutionary adaptations triggered by resources available to raise children.

Love relationships begin with attraction to another, move into communications, and develop into sharing of life. Love may be a way for individuals to reflect themselves, or love may be that of mature, differentiated persons sharing periods of intense intimacy from which both grow and further refine their selves, or both.

Erotic Sexual Arousal

Images of Love

Attraction to Others

Relationship Development

Functioning of Love Relationships

EROTIC SEXUAL AROUSAL

Erotic arousal is based on physical sensitivity, but its power is formed and released in each of us by cultural standards and customs. The capacity for sexual arousal is inborn, perhaps like the capacity for language. However, the specific language we speak is learned, and likewise the specific objects and acts we find sexually arousing appear to be, for the most part, conditioned by culture and personal experiences.

Ultimate Arousal Origins

Sexual erotica builds from what our bodies offer. Experience and context shape our erotic arousal using sensual stimulation and evolutionary gender-specific tendencies. Everyone has touch-sensitive areas of the body that are at least somewhat sensual, and these develop to be erotic cues. Erotic experiences form in sexual contexts of lust, affection, security, or love. Physical touch will be erotic as it is joined with positive feelings, strong levels of desire, a cultural script of sexual acts, or all of these. Without that context, there is no erotic arousal. Genital touch by a physician during a medical examination will generally yield no sexual arousal. In other settings, even sexually intended stroking may have no effect if the receiver has strong nonsexual feelings of fear or anger. Nonsensual events and conflicting mental states inhibit erotic arousal.

Just a casual survey of social and personal life will reveal that there are variations of what is erotic and what is not. Not all events appear to have an equal chance of developing erotic power. Even among skin areas, there are preferences. Erotic touches focus largely on sensitive areas and on those that relate to distinct male-female differences. People are usually not consistently aroused by touching just knuckles, elbows, or knees. The question this raises is more typically illustrated in another erotic mode, vision.

Visual images are strong stimuli of sexual desire and excitement in men. This commonplace observation is easily shown in controlled studies. Men are most effectively aroused by viewing women's genitals and surrounding areas. In Western culture, women's buttocks and breasts are rather universal erotic cues. An underlying question is whether there is evolutionary predisposition to attach erotic excitement to these and other areas, or whether it is simply a pervasive cultural standard that no individual can really escape. The evolutionary adaptation ideas we reviewed earlier suggest that sights of fertile partners and sexual acts yield natural arousal in men.

A casual survey reveals that features as unnatural as clothing and toiletry fashions have erotic powers. Each hairstyle and clothing fashion may seem to be sexy at the moment. The effects are temporary, lasting until overtaken by the next fad. Of course, those styles and fashions are unlikely to be based on any real biological pressure. However, at the roots of it all, there may be a natural erotic arousal to sights of genitals, especially as they suggest sexual intercourse. Does this suggest a potentiality for erotic learning? Can perceptions and images be placed on a dimension of ease of being attached to sexual arousal? There seems to be no method to directly test these questions. The origins of erotica must be studied indirectly, eventually building sound theory.

Scripts of Love and Sex

Sexual acts involve a great deal more than mechanics and plumbing. The sexologists' emphasis on physiology and technique is incomplete. A major source of sex's power to motivate (to affect our energy, choices, and feelings) lies in its social nature. Each sexual act, despite its physiology and its roots in evolutionary function, is primarily the consequence of an interaction with another person. That sexual act is always the culmination of lifelong learning, however long or short that may be, about sexuality and about oneself. The physical and sensual pieces of it notwithstanding, the role of sex in our lives is carried out socially.

The literature of the social dimensions of sexuality is scattered. Almost none of it is in standard motivation writings; those usually focus on animal models with a reluctant nod to the physiological descriptions of Masters and Johnson. A newer set of studies and writings has been developing in social psychology, gender psychology, and sociology, along with a few good observations from professional philosophers. Others interested in contributing have been looking at sex from the practice of family therapy and counseling psychology. Course textbooks aimed at human sexuality have generally used a more biological style, covering the physiology of reproduction and the sex act in great detail and then moving on to perversions and deviance, homosexuality, self-stimulation, and potential therapies for dysfunctions. The culture-bound nature of normal sexuality development is not presented clearly. Thus, the organization and content array of this section is somewhat unique and tentative. A much better description will be written as we have experience putting these things together coherently.

William Simon and John Gagnon (1987) have promoted the concept of scripting to outline social and personal dimensions of sexuality. Sexual scripting implies that there is much more to determining a sexual act than what appears at the moment. Each person brings a complex background of images and ideas from culture, adapted to personal feelings of the moment and to the perceived needs of others. These come together in particular patterns of sexual acts or sexual scripts. Scripting is a perspective that emphasizes the cultural learning and communication bases of human activity.

Our sexual scripts are based on models of what sexuality is and how it is done, on ideas about sexual politics we absorb from our culture, and on general attitudes that prevail about sexuality in our society. On top of that, sexual acts are part of the way we express what is unique about ourselves. Sexual scripts are formed to get pleasure, meaning, and satisfying relationships with others. All of this is a pretty big burden to put on short periods of heated interaction with someone.

Cultural Sources

Cultural models give us basic information about sexuality. We acquire a fairly consistent collection of information about what is sexual among the objects, characteristics, and qualities of the cultural environment. Included are the forms of sexual acts, the patterns of preparation, the feelings of the participants, and the details about appropriate times and places. We learn from culture what, when, where, and with whom sexual acts can be accomplished. These often-repeated scenarios are the beginnings of our scripts, and they give meaning about sexual acts.

Cultural sources are everywhere. Cultural scripts of sex are learned from observing the actions of others, from media in all forms, and from relatively formal instruction in the family, school, or church. Cultural scripts range from the desired to the usual to the prohibited forms of sexual activity. The cultural models exist as the likely possibilities.

Until they are tried, models are merely hypothetical. Each individual must personally confirm sexual scripts. Some may be used in relationships with partners, and other scripts may need only an exercise of imagination. Some forms will fit easily with one's self-image, working fairly well with little adjustment. Others will need modification to be satisfactory.

Interpersonal Scripts

Interpersonal scripts use cultural models as a base from which to deal with the world and to establish successful relationships with others. Interpersonal scripts account for the other people in the sexual acts. Developed scripts are those that move an encounter toward a sexual act, generate appropriate erotic and sensual communication, and provide bases for satisfactions beyond the sexual act itself. These are the ways one accomplishes a mutually successful sexual experience with another person.

Intrapsychic Scripts

Intrapsychic scripts lead each person to sexual acts. A pattern of sexually meaningful bits and pieces of activity produce each individual's sexual arousal. Intrapsychic scripts are those necessary acts and thoughts that both define a person as an individual and lead to being interested, to being aroused, and to experiencing orgasm and other feelings of completion. Intrapsychic scripts are the means used by an agent as an actor to make a self-presentation. We connect interpersonal scripts in cultural settings, the public sexual culture, with private sexual realities.

Modes of Erotic Arousal

Contact is made with sexual thoughts through all sorts of cues. One can be sexually aroused by bits of sensory and cognitive events. It may be a certain smile, a twist of a body, a phrase, a sentence of reading, or a familiar smell. The list is nearly endless and partially personal. Erotica of different kinds are one basis of sexual motivation. Purely mental sources of arousal can be formed and elaborated in fantasies. An important aspect of erotic arousal is its apparent gender variation.

Sexual Fantasy

One of the most intriguing aspects of being human is the ability to have fantasies. In the world of personal awareness, we can recall and redesign past experiences, anticipate and rehearse future events, and create unique scenes that are neither likely nor perhaps desired in reality. Fantasies appear spontaneously and frequently in testosterone-primed individuals and can aid in developing potent sexual motivation.

Based on personal and cultural experiences, sexual fantasies can assist, arouse, or substitute for sexual acts. Some fantasies are developed into elaborate scripts that are employed to take up time, to avoid thinking about unpleasant things, or to improve the depth of sexual interactions with others. Such fantasies can easily be more sexually arousing than external sources in a person's life. Erotic fantasies can both begin and give direction to sexual activity and may be a major influence on sexual identity and preference.

A variety of studies have provided information about sexual fantasies. Although these studies are not directly comparable, they do give hints of the extent and kind of sexual fantasizing people do. A recent summary (Leitenberg & Henning, 1995) examined the methods typically used, their shortcomings, and the sort of evidence we have.

Gender differences of sexual fantasy occurrence are complicated. Part of a study of Danish married couples revealed that 63% of the men had sexual fantasies, compared with just 37% of the women (Hesselund, 1976). Compared with women, college student men reported more than twice as many sexual urges evoked by external stimuli, but they did not differ from women in frequency of spontaneous fantasies of sex. Data were recorded by each student over a 3-day period (Jones & Barlow, 1990). Generally, men will report more daily sexual fantasies than women, but during actual sexual activity, there is no clear evidence that either men or women are more likely to employ fantasy.

More gender differences appear in the themes and contents of fantasies. Researchers in New York City asked graduate students for their most frequent sexual fantasy during the previous 3 months, in daydreaming and, separately, during sexual activity with another (Mednick, 1977). In both daydreaming and sexual activity, men had more fantasy themes of giving sexual experience and women had more themes of receiving it. Their experiences are shown in Figures 8.1 and 8.2.

College students at privileged eastern U.S. schools were asked about their fantasies during sexual activity. Men reported more fantasies regarding past sexual activity; women had an emphasis on exciting fantasies of new situations (McCauley & Swann, 1978). Their reports are shown in Figure 8.3.

In the summary study of sexual fantasy mentioned above (Leitenberg & Henning, 1995), familiar gender-based themes in content were described. Women's fantasies tended toward narratives of feelings of love and attachment, including men's interest in their bodies. Men's fantasies were filled with visual anatomical details of women's bodies and performing sexual acts with them.

Midwest college students were asked about their fantasies during sexual activity (Sue, 1979). They were given 13 categories; their reports of five kinds of sexual fantasies are shown in Table 8.1.

There is little doubt about the existence of sexual fantasies, and it is quite likely that they have a major role for many people in

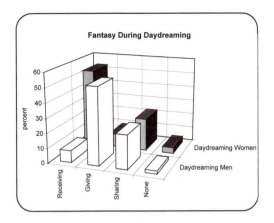

Figure 8.1. Percentage of specific reported fantasies by men and by women during daydreaming, with data from Mednick (1977).

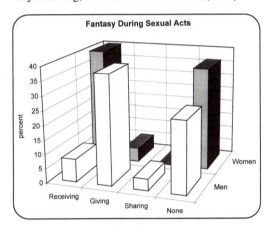

Figure 8.2. Percentage of specific reported fantasies by men and by women during sexual acts, with data from Mednick (1977).

developing and maintaining a high level of sexual enjoyment. Their use appears to be pervasive, but it must be noted that most studies have been done with relatively educated and privileged groups. These are populations of people most likely to develop and report their personal mental experiences.

Erotica, Pornography,
Gothic Romances

It has long been claimed that there are major differences in the sensory modes of

TABLE 8.1 Types of Sexual Fantasies During Sexual Acts Reported by College Men and Women, Abstracted From Sue (1979)

	Percentage	
	Men	*Women*
Being irresistible	55	53
Imaginary lover	44	24
Being watched	15	20
Being forced	21	36
Forcing others	24	16

erotic arousal of men and women. For example, Kinsey's surveys (Kinsey et al., 1948, 1953) revealed that women are less likely than men to be sexually aroused by nude pictures of the other, and pornography is provided primarily for a male audience.

In recent years, many psychologists, following the equality hypothesis of social science ideology or ideas of feminist politics, have tried to show that gender differences in visual sexual arousal are not valid. Using physiological indicators as well as more tra-

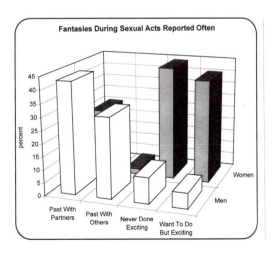

Figure 8.3. Reported fantasies by men and women during sexual acts, with data from McCauley & Swann, 1978.

NOTE: Percentage of time each occurred "often."

ditional ratings and interview techniques, sexual arousal has been measured in men and women volunteers watching a variety of sexually oriented visual material. When examined closely, the traditional differences remain. Women are less interested in seeking views of men than are men of women, and they are less aroused when exposed to them; but women do show an intriguing positive response to views of other women.

This last finding suggests an interesting gender difference in what is sexually arousing. Both men and women are aroused by seeing sexually suggestive poses of women, but perhaps for quite different reasons. Men see the women as sexual objects. On this everyone agrees. But in viewing other women in sexually oriented situations, women appear to identify with those women as objects to whom men respond. The idea is that women are romantically aroused by looking at a sexy woman role model (Money & Ehrhardt, 1972). Thus, women as well as men respond to advertisements using sexy women models (unless they have adopted overriding political beliefs against such tactics). The men see a sex partner; the women see themselves in the role portrayed by the model.

Laboratory studies of sexual arousal to film depictions of sexual acts show a supporting set of evidence. Mosher and Abramson (1977) found men to be highly aroused to a film of women masturbating but not to that of men masturbating. Women had lower but equal arousal levels to films of either women or men masturbating. Steinman, Wincze, Sakheim, Barlow, and Mavissakalian (1981) presented films of male-female, male-male, female-female, and group sexual acts to heterosexual viewers. Men's physiological and subjective arousal was highest to male-female and group sexual acts and somewhat less to female-female. Women were physiologically aroused only by the male-female and group sexual depictions. They were subjectively aroused by female-female films and less so by male-male. Male-male films did not arouse any of the men. Following Money and Erhardt's (1972) role model-

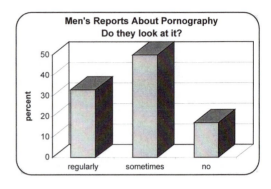

Figure 8.4. Men's reports regarding frequency of looking at pornography, from Hite (1981).

ing view, women had some arousal to male masturbation because they could project themselves as the object of the acts, a thought that was not possible in viewing the male-male films.

Strip shows in Western culture give more evidence of gender arousal differences. Women exposing themselves to men for money is an old trade and is often marked by unskilled dancing and simulated sex. The goal is to expose as much as the law permits. Men are quiet, often masturbating (Boles & Garbin, 1974; McCaghy & Skipper, 1972). There have been recent, although infrequent, strip shows exhibiting men using considerable dancing skill to a largely exuberant and celebrating audience of women. Women show strong social activities among themselves during the performance with overtones of liberating politics. Most women attendees seem not to have arousal and sexual experience as their goal (Petersen & Dressel, 1982).

The studies of the bases of erotic arousal we have reviewed show that men are potently aroused by sights of women in nearly any form of sexual act. Visual forms of sexual stimulation were clearly different if not more effective for men than for women. In her study of men's sexuality, Shere Hite (1981) reported that more than a third of the men respondents said that they look at pornography regularly. Almost half said they view pornography sometimes or infrequently, and

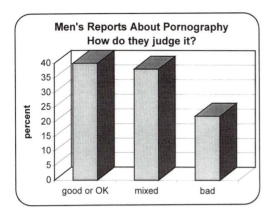

Figure 8.5. Men's reports regarding the value of pornography, from Hite (1981).

TABLE 8.2   Sex Purchases

	Reported frequency (in percent)	
	Men	Women
X-rated videos or movies	23	11
Visit place of nude dancers	22	4
Sex books or magazines	16	4
Sex devices	3	4
Phone sex	1	0
Any of the above	41	16

From Laumann, Gagnon, Michael, and Michaels, 1994. © 1994 by Edward O. Laumann, Robert T. Michael, CSG Enterprises, Inc., and Stuart Michaels. Reprinted by permission of the University of Chicago Press.

only 17% said they did not look at it or no longer do (see Figure 8.4).

Politics on matters of gender equality are not one-sided. Men's preferences for seeing pornography vary from positive to negative, depending on each man's view of its social meaning. About 40% of Hite's sample of men said they thought pornography was good or OK, 38% had a mixed reaction, and the remaining 22% thought it was poor, disgusting, bad, sexist, or ridiculous (see Figure 8.5). Almost 50% of the men thought pornography does not represent truths of sexual reality. Many commented on the degradation wrought by pornography—that it is basically demeaning to women.

The National Health and Social Life Survey reported a good trade in aids to sexual activity and fantasy (Laumann et al., 1994), as shown in Table 8.2. In her later study of women and love, Hite (1987) asked women about their views of pornography, but she did not report those results, presumably because they reported few experiences. Others, like Helen Hazen (1983), are convinced that women are not aroused by sights of slippery bodies, sexual acts, and genitalia of the opposite sex. She believes that those promoting gender equality politics have tried to force an equality of sources of sexual stimulation that does not have a sound basis. Attempts to market magazine pornography to women compa-

rable to that for men (e.g., *Playboy*) have not succeeded. There is argument and evidence that male-nudity magazines (e.g., *Playgirl*) were sold largely to homosexual men. The NHSLS data above, however, show that some women do seek sexual depictions, although the mode of choice seems to be in the new video technology.

Helen Hazen believes that women respond to romance novels in a way analogous to men's interest in pornography. The volume of their sales and the nearly total appeal to women rather than men gives a good foundation to her belief. The appeal of these romance stories is as unappreciated by men as the appeal of naked women is to women. Her thesis is that there is a formula to them that is changed only at the peril of decreasing sales. Abbreviated mercilessly, that plot is a third-person view of a young woman who is a misunderstood or underestimated virgin. She is better than every man except one, who is handsome and experienced and aloof from her. Complications and thrills abound, often with elements of violence through rape and torture, until the final scene of seduction that ends with a passionate kiss signifying she has seduced him into loving her. These themes are supported by an early study of women's fantasies. The most popular themes were of an imaginary romantic lover, being overpowered and forced to surrender, and doing something forbidden (Hariton & Singer, 1974).

Personal Sexual Motivation

What we believe about what is being done is what determines the function of that act. In the general human scheme of sexual acts, there is nothing that can be claimed to be natural outside of each person's ideas of those functions and the social order in which they exist. The most obvious personal reason for seeking sexual acts is the pleasure they bring. But pleasure is not the simple idea that it first appears to be. The nature of what gives pleasure has much to with philosophy, timing, duration, and long-term interpretations of what is happening. Sexuality is also valued because it allows a person to find meaning and personal expression by being with and being recognized by another person.

Pleasure

There has been a change in some of our worldviews about the role of pleasure, illustrated perhaps with some theoretical descriptions by psychological theorists at the beginning of the twentieth century. Sexual pleasures became a part of that changing view (Solomon, 1987). These new views emphasized the build up of tensions and the therapeutic value of tension release. The new view became one of permitting and seeking tension-release forms of pleasures. The emphasis was on the pleasures of attaining the goal rather than in the process of reaching it.

In sexual acts, seeking tension-release pleasure has at least two aspects that may not be truly satisfying. First, personal pleasure is sought without accommodation of the other person in the acts. The partner is treated as an object of pleasure, having no other value. Thus, sexual pleasures may conflict with anxiety over unsatisfying social interaction. Second, the focus of a pleasure model tends to be on the end release of tension. More tra-

ditional, and perhaps more developed views of pleasure hold that it be an accompaniment to an action, not an end in itself. Greater pleasure in sexual acts is found in doing them interactively with partners as a complete process including the end experiences. The personal, orgasmic release is just a part of the pleasure that can be obtained.

Finding Meaning and Expression

The conventional sayings of society attempt to mask the purposes of sexual acts. People try to find justifications for their sexual actions in terms of conventional practical outcomes. Thus, sexual acts are said to be carried out for nonsexual reasons, such as personal pleasure, good health, sleep promotion, or family happiness. Although there may be bits of truth in some of these, the context is one of making excuses for sexual acts rather than seeing their intrinsic positive contribution to being a person.

Sexual functioning contributes to a structure of meaning and purpose. In mature sexual acts, people find and express meanings. Susan Sprecher and Kathleen McKinney (1993) outline sex in a close relationship as an act of self-disclosure, intimacy, love, interdependence, maintenance, and exchange. These meanings give sexual acts a purpose different from the obvious biology of it all. Meanings are given by these interpersonal acts of sex and the intrapsychic feelings of the whole process that we noted above. Individuals operate within their culture, with others, and with full awareness of the unique people they have become and are becoming. Sexual acts are an important part of establishing that kind of personal meaning, both when they occur and when they do not occur.

Sexual acts are complex matters of identification, expression, and defense of one's self. Bodies are the means through which sensual ideas of sexuality become meaningful, but the most important meanings of sexual acts are related to personal goals and social relationships. In one sense, sexual acts are a matter of interpersonal politics where the doing and the outcome are intended primarily to enhance each person's selfhood to oneself and to others.

Sexual Identity

Robert Solomon (1987) considered the different ways people view their unique sexual identity. He distinguished four dimensions: biological sex, gender identity, sexual orientation, and sexual ethics. **Biological sex** is usually not an identification problem. Male and female differentiation is easy to accomplish, although there are subtle, infrequent complications of a biological origin. **Gender identity** is composed of the cultural roles each person has learned. The roles of boy or girl, woman or man, are infused into each individual as they are structurally embedded in society. The gender role is one fundamental part of each person's sexual identity.

Sexual orientation has to do with whom one chooses as a sexual partner. At one extreme, sexual orientation is toward a partner having the most clear characteristics of the opposite gender. At the other extreme, sexual orientation may be toward people of the same gender. It is not just a matter of the partner's body structure; displays of gender roles are important, too. There are many possibilities. A man might prefer a woman who displays very little feminine social style. A woman may prefer a dependent man. The kind of person toward whom one orients sexually is an important dimension of each person's self-identity.

Sexual ethics concerns how each person treats others in sexual encounters. There are conventional rules of sexual acts such as those of marriage, but Solomon also notes that there are interesting alterations of the normal rules for dealing with others that appear in sexual encounters. Notions of privacy and of respect are commonplace. Masochism, which is pain or degradation inflicted on oneself by a sexual partner, is an extreme case.

These variations in sexual identity illustrate that there is much that is personal and unique in sexual acts. What one does depends on what one has come to believe in sexual matters. Those beliefs will structure the meaning of sexual acts, which are in turn an expression of one's self.

Social Roles of Love and Sex

The social roles of sex might be put into the question, What are the cultural patterns of sexual acts? The answers are several and complicated. Another question turns this around and asks, What other social purposes are causes of sexual acts? There are some logical categories.

Sex for Offspring

Sex is necessary for the continuation of the human species. This social function may be fundamental in a logical sense but probably does not matter in the heat of the moment. Few do it for the glory of the human species.

Nonetheless, couples typically plan to have children, and this purpose may affect the frequency and timing of their sexual acts. Sexual acts at other times may be thought to be a form of practice for the reproductive act. Couples with mutually low sexual desire or strong theological principles, or both, may not have sexual acts for any reason except procreation. Other couples, for reason of family planning, may refrain from sexual acts for long periods of time. These beliefs control their sexual acts.

Sex for Bonding

Sexual opportunity is often said to be among the strongest reasons individuals make a lasting commitment to each other in a pair bond. Sexual acts strengthen intimacy, commitment, and love. Once people have formed such a bond, sex becomes a sort of emotional glue that holds a couple together in the family unit, which serves the additional role of successfully rearing the children.

However, there are some apparent gender differences that work against continued pairing. Men have traditionally been thought to be more promiscuous and women more faithful in their relationships, the famous double standard. Despite this variation, the overall facts seem to be in favor of an overall mutually beneficial pair-bonding and maintenance function of sexual acts. For both partners, this gives a regular opportunity for sex as often as they both wish, and if there is a difference in desire, a compromise of sorts is worked out that is better for each than the alternative of an unpaired situation. We saw in Chapter 7 that there is also a physiological reward for monogamy.

Sex for Sale

Selling sex is allegedly the oldest profession on record, a major social structure in society with varying degrees of official and unofficial sanction. Prostitution exists because there is a need and a solution to that need that can be offered for a price. Like many commercial arrangements, some of the actual service deliverers are treated poorly or become trapped in the web of the arrangements. From the sex motivation perspective, it is easy to see why this activity is difficult to remove from any society.

Sex for Status

Sexual activity is used for enhancing status. Men in some social groups use records of sexual conquests to develop and enhance their esteem. Young men confirm their masculinity to themselves and their peers through sex. For some, it becomes a game beyond the need; the continued success is the important thing, as it was for the Sam Malone character in the long-running and often rerun television show *Cheers*. The motivation pattern is illustrated by the ultramillionaires who were asked why they continued to try to increase their wealth. Their answer was something like this, "We don't care about the money. It's just a way of keeping score."

Women too use sex for status. Although for women it may be a matter of total score, women also use sex to raise their social position. Status, according to traditional society rules, has been determined by the man's position. Thus, either by marriage to the properly selected socially prominent person, or by being associated with such people, the woman's status is elevated. It isn't usually so crassly described as sex for status, but the underlying principle, seen in the once-common arranged marriages, essentially has this pattern.

SECTION SUMMARY:
EROTIC SEXUAL AROUSAL

The foundations on which erotic excitement builds are sensual stimulation of touch and perhaps vision, but the outcome is moderated and developed by acquired experiences. Our sexual education comes partly from cultural scripts giving us guides about what, when, where, and with whom. Scripts become personal erotica if they work in forming a sexual identity, taking into account our sexual partner.

Fantasy is a common way of building sexual excitement. Men report more sexual fantasies than women, but both use them in and outside of sexual encounters. Themes of men's sexual fantasies tend toward past adventures and giving sexual experiences; women fantasize exciting possibilities and receiving sexual experiences.

Pornography in all its forms remains primarily attractive and sexually arousing to men. Most men report having some experience with it but also know of its potential for distorting sexual reality. Analogous excitement for women has been suggested to come from romance novels.

The motivational power of sex lies in its obvious emotional excitements and body pleasures, although we tend to focus too much on the personal orgasmic end rather than the developing interpersonal contact. Sexuality has less obvious motivational power in what it says about each individual. The successes and failures of sexual acts establish who we are, motivating us to develop or hide that image. In a more categorizing way, our biological sex, our gender identity, our sexual orientation, and the ethics of our sexual encounters all help build the picture of who we are.

Sexual acts can be a part of motivation toward other ends. Sex is necessary to produce children. Sexual acts can be sold, and accomplishments in sexual activities are one way social status can be displayed. Sexual activity helps bond people, and this role seems an obvious part of what we have come to call a love relationship.

IMAGES OF LOVE

What is love? That is more than a poet's question, and more than just the usual problem of defining a common word, because some fairly clear choices can be made. As we saw in our brief cultural history of love in the last chapter, love can be a lustful amusement of no lasting meaning, it can be a spiritual surrender to a deity or a person, it can be a product of loneliness and sexual urges in adolescence, or it can be a developing attachment to another based on mutual needs. And perhaps, it can be all of these things to each of us, if we are careful to keep their conditions and consequences separated in our minds. The different perspectives are partly due to the convenient habits of social science research and partly from biases in our recent common culture.

Most research and discussion have focused on the experiences at the beginning of a love relationship. The reasons are practical: College students are the most available populations for most researchers. Thus, passionate or romantic love has been most typically researched using college students, few of whom have experienced the development and maintenance of a love relationship. Much less attention has been given to lasting, mature love relationships. Mature love doesn't make as good a story. That is, it is not a unique and intense experience, nor is it an excuse for temporary mental conditions or irregular acts.

Mature love is also more difficult to study, there being few large and willing samples available to the academic research communities.

Another factor influencing the bias toward romantic love is media worship of youth. Television, movies, magazines, stage shows, and essentially every other form of conveying cultural roles are focused on youth. The exceptions are so rare as to be noteworthy. A partial explanation can be found in the age of those responsible for determining the programming filling the media. Advertisers, being in their twenties and early thirties, demand programming and content aimed at what they know, which is the experiences of turbulent attachments and dissolution at the beginning of life. However we might account for the causes, the fact remains that ours is a youth-centered public culture. The effect is to make the problems and experiences of adolescence and early adult years the standards. Mature adult love has come to be judged by those standards. In our common-sense view of things, disruption of life by mysterious, emotional excitement is the mark of true love.

Romantic and Pragmatic Love

Following traditional thought and some research, two different kinds of love relationships have been proposed. The labels have varied, but the common core is apparent. We saw their roots in our sketch of love history. Elaine Hatfield and G. William Walster

TABLE 8.3   A Comparison of Experiences and Dynamics of Romantic and Pragmatic Love

	Romantic Love	Pragmatic Love
Based on:	unmet affiliative and sexual need	successful interactions
Develops:	suddenly with encounter	slowly with satisfactions
Thrives on:	idealization, fantasy, hope	trust, respect, sharing, loyalty
Experiences of:	obsession, weakness, clumsiness	differentiation, support
Consequences:	quick disappearance	coordination in living

(1978) describe them as passionate and companionate love, and Hatfield (1988) lists earlier views of romantic and conjugal love, unreasonable and reasonable love, and of deficiency love and being loved. Not everyone agrees to a simple division. Some writers, like Nathaniel Branden (1980), mix the two and call it all romantic love. Others take one or the other and view that as the "real" love with the other being something else.

The descriptions of love show a fairly clear dichotomy. Romantic or passionate love begins suddenly, arouses intense physiological events, and fades rapidly. This is love between people with unmet sexual needs and others they find to be attractive. It also has aspects of affiliative and dependent needs, predisposition to help, and feelings of exclusion and absorption. Others have added that it thrives on idealization of the partner. It makes liberal use of fantasy and is renewed by adversity. Passionate love alone is sometimes said to be an insecure foundation for a lasting marriage.

The second kind is companionate, conjugal, or pragmatic love, the love found between mature adults. Pragmatic love builds slowly on the satisfactions of successful interactions. Trust, respect, sharing, and loyalty are some of its characteristics. Each of the lovers gets satisfaction of personal needs, and they both grow into mutual interdependence. Feelings, thoughts, and acts of love are reciprocated. Table 8.3 highlights these differences.

These two psychologists' models of love relationships reflect the strategy of analysis and looking for differences among the pieces.

Too much can be made of forced differences. Perhaps, a blend is more appropriate. Is there evidence and reason to consider love relationships as evolving processes with, at most, different features emphasized under certain conditions? The questions then become what conditions maximize the romantic feelings of love, what is the nature of continuing personal experiences of love, and so on.

Romantic Passion's Role

Taking the blending approach, one theory strategy proposes that selection and movement from one of these two general forms of love to the other is determined by events in early life. These interesting ideas take us back to the kinds of fitness strategies we may have inherited. The theory's value is enhanced by successful predictions of the form and duration of different love relationships. James Chisolm (1995) has presented this case, building on attachment theory of love (Bowlby, 1969, 1973, 1980) in which love's roots are in the mother-child relationship of our ancestors.

Chisolm suggests that childhood environments of insecure attachments make us more likely to have experiences of passionate romantic love. This tendency is founded on one evolved option of fitness, an evolutionary reproductive strategy maximizing mating. A mating strategy stresses producing a large number of offspring with minimal effort toward ensuring their survival or quality. Such a strategy would be most successful in a competitive environment of insufficient resources. Chisolm argues that the guiding factor in the

TABLE 8.4 Life Conditions Evoking Romantic Versus Pragmatic Love, based on Chisolm (1995)

	Romantic Passion	*Committed Love*
Conditions	stressful	stable
Adult-child relationship	insecure attachment	secure attachment
Fitness option	mating strategy	parenting strategy
Pairing	lustful attraction	similarity
Children	maximum quantity	few of quality
Age of pairing	early	late
Duration	short	long

ancestral environment producing this strategy is a pattern of early mortality. With death likely at an early age, the most genetic material would survive for parents who bred early and had many offspring. Motivating the pairings is early romantic passion; passion results in more children. Attachment theory predicts that stressful and anxious life conditions produce insecure attachments to children, and insecure attachments bias the offspring toward more lustful or passionate romantic love styles.

The other fitness option is a parenting strategy in which the primary effort is ensuring that a few children of quality survive to reproductive maturity. Given stable conditions of resources and little likelihood of early death, parents produce secure attachments to their children. With parental investment in few offspring, those children have resources to select similar marriage partners and continue the pattern of competitively effective children. These early advantages and secure attachments bias children toward commitment and interest in long-term pairing with mates.

These two styles are not genetically separate populations but are rather two strategies that are set off by the conditions of childhood attachment. Anyone can have a strong tendency to romantic passion, evoked by childhood conditions. The different love styles are conditions that may be developed, not genetic certainties, one kind to each person.

In this view, the possibility of passionate, romantic love is present for all people, not just those in the individualistic West. If romantic love is more than just a piece of European culture, we should find widespread evidence for it among cultures. William Jankowiak and Edward Fischer (1992) did just that. They searched the ethnographic records of 186 cultures and found instances of passionate love in 147 of the 166 cultures having appropriate records. The authors believe that in the remaining 19 cultures, for which the evidence was inconclusive, it was a matter of definition and oversight of the ethnographers. They also note that not everyone in a culture experiences romantic love, and some cultures specifically try to suppress it.

From the study of twins comes a different kind of evidence for this model of different genetic programs in each of us, ready to be activated by live events. In twin populations, genetic similarity predicted none of the variance in love styles (Waller & Shaver, 1994). Their similarities and differences in love styles were set off by their life conditions, not by their genetic material.

There is considerable evidence that fits well with the "insecurity equals passion" theory. If life conditions in childhood are insecure, more romantic styles of love will emerge. These relationships will be formed earlier in life and produce children rapidly. The parents will also be more prone to extra-pair passionate mating, events favoring greater numbers of children. Marriages will be dissolved earlier, the breakup motivated by loss or transfer of passion. (See Table 8.4)

If we can assume that insecurity in childhood produces insecure adults, we can examine the patterns of their pairings. Secure adults have love relationships of about 10 years, insecure adults about 4 to 6 years (Hazan & Shaver, 1987). Chisolm cites not-yet-published data by others that insecure adults who married did so when younger and more rapidly after meeting. Among secure adults, men's love relationships lasted longer, and women courted longer and married when older.

Speculation about the physical bases enabling romantic passion have been suggested by Liebowitz (1983) and by Fisher (1992, 1995). They argue that passionate love is built on the action in the brain of phenylethylamine, or PEA. PEA begins to flow on perception of an appropriate sexual mate, producing infatuation and emotional excitement. They suggest that eventually the passionate infatuation ends, after sufficient exposure and the resulting habituation of receptors to PEA. If the relationship endures, other brain chemicals begin to flow, the endorphin family. Endorphins are stimulated by the presence of the partner, producing positive feelings of contentment and safety, bonding the pair. With the absence or loss of the partner, the lowering of endorphins makes negative feelings and depression. Fisher adds a third normal stage of the relationship, detachment, perhaps caused by habituation to the endorphins or a weakening of the production of endorphins by the partner. To prevent this third stage of dissolution of the love relationship, participants must work to keep it together. All of these ideas remain speculation in that we do not know whether the named chemicals are triggers or consequences, and if they are triggers, what exactly determines their timing and levels.

There have been many other attempts to analyze varieties of love relationships. We will outline two popular systems to illustrate some of the forms into which the variety of love experiences has been sorted.

John Lee's Styles of Love

John Lee (1988) proposed nine love styles to describe different kinds of love rela-

tionships. He intended that love be thought of in analogy with color. There are different colors and combinations of them; so also there are different love styles and their combinations. He suggests that we can use these different styles of love to purposefully make compatible matches.

Lee believes that love is an ideology that is acquired as a personal explanation. We are influenced to accept a love style, in the same way that we acquire a political ideology. Life experience builds part of it. Some of the style comes from learning that is purposefully directed toward changes and variety. Styles are learned by watching others and by listening to what they say. Cultural media of songs, novels, and movies all help build this repertoire of love styles.

Lee has given esoteric names to his nine styles of love. As in color description, there are three primaries: eros, storge, and ludus. The secondary love styles he labels mania, pragma, and agape. The remaining three are combinations: storgic eros, ludic eros, and storgic ludus. Lee pictures love styles something like this.

Eros is love of appearance. Having this love style, the lover holds a clearly defined ideal of a partner, primarily a visual image. The erotic lover is strongly attracted to individuals close to this ideal and can easily describe the preferred type. Erotic lovers move to become physically close to their beloved quickly. Ideas of love at first sight probably arise from observing the eros love style. Eros lovers express frequent appreciation to their beloved of those ideal qualities and hold their love relationship to be a most important life component.

Storge (pronounced STOR-gay) is a slowly developing affection. Love builds with time together, and there is little evidence of passion or romance. The storgic lovers share interests rather than feelings. Love and sexual relations are not goals for them but just parts of their relationship. The very idea of romantic love is somewhat embarrassing to storgic lovers and perhaps uninteresting to them.

Ludus is love as play or a game. Ludic lovers seek many interesting relationships.

They hold no ideal, like the erotic lover, and they are not interested in building a life relationship, as is the storgic lover. Ludic lovers do not hold feelings of love for a partner, and they consort with any one person only sparingly to prevent developing commitment or involvement. They have no experience of jealousy and can openly love several partners over the same period of time. Love is not primarily a life focus; relationships are for fun.

Mania is intense love. Manic lovers are obsessed with their lovers and feel intense jealousy at the threat of loss. They have a strong need for love, and they protect the intensity of the relationship by whatever means available. They insist on being together constantly and on receiving assurances of the love. Manic lovers often hold love relationships with people they don't really like, and thus if the love fails, they don't remain friendly. They brood over a lost love for a long time.

Pragma is a practical love style. Pragma is opposite to eros and between storge and ludus. A compatible lover is sought, one who is similar in attitudes, interests, and beliefs. Pragmatic lovers reflect a mature analysis of their partners. They are more inclined toward displays of commitment than of emotion, thoughtfulness rather than jealousy. Sexual relations are matters of skills to improve rather than of passion. A suitable love relationship is sought but is not an essential element of life for the follower of the pragma love style.

Agape (pronounced ah-GAH-pay) is one-direction, altruistic love. This last of the secondary love styles is rare and is associated more closely with religious experience than with human pairing. Agape is a selfless and giving love style, a duty to love even when there is no return.

Ludic erotic lovers look for and enjoy a variety of others and see their loves in an artful fashion, as if they were just acting a role in one scene of life. Ludic eros holds the same relative position as mania, between eros and ludus, but without the emotional intensity of the manic. Ludic erotic love is a creative, non-possessive love that is ended when the enjoyment stops.

Storgic erotic lovers believe the process of loving is essential in life but the particular partner is less important. Storgic eros fits between the same primaries as does agape. These lovers don't have a preferred type, as do the erotic, and they show little sexual intimacy with any particular partner. They value loving feelings over commitment. They are not concerned when their love is not returned, and they move on when their partner finds another lover.

Finally, the **storgic ludus** love style has the same primary position as pragma but with less concern with permanent love rather than passing affairs. It is more of a mating style than a matter of love. Storgic ludic lovers enjoy a discreet, restrained relationship, usually while continuing normal life affairs, perhaps including a happy marriage to another. They will tolerate no possessive attachment, and there are no strong expressions of feelings or commitment to a future together.

Some researchers have used parts of Lee's analysis in further work (Hendrick & Hendrick, 1992).

Robert Sternberg's Three-Component Love

A different approach to understanding the diversity of apparent types of love relationships is that of Robert Sternberg (1986, 1988), presented to the popular book market as *The Triangle of Love*. He pictures his three components of love as the corners of a triangle. Intimacy, passion, and decision-commitment are the components that make up seven kinds of love plus their absence in nonlove.

The labels of the components perhaps make much further explanation unnecessary. **Intimacy** refers to close, warm feelings. **Passion** is the primarily sexual urge or drive to love. **Decision-commitment** is the short-term decision to love and the long-term commitment to maintain the love. Sternberg's three components are logically combined to define love types.

Liking is having only intimacy, without decision-commitment or passion. Relationships characterized by liking are true friendships with long-term feelings of closeness and warmth for another.

Infatuation comes from having passion without intimacy or decision/commitment. Often seen as love at first sight, infatuations appear quickly and disappear almost as fast. While under way, the lover experiences a high degree of physical and mental arousal, often becoming obsessive. The infatuation is typically not reciprocal.

Empty love is Sternberg's label for holding the decision/commitment component without intimacy or passion. Sternberg holds empty love as the residual in a love relationship when the other elements have faded. It may also be present in the beginnings of arranged marriages.

Romantic love is the combination of intimacy and passion. There is both liking and physical desire. It may develop out of an infatuation when an interest in the other also forms. Conversely, it may begin as liking with the passion component emerging later.

Companionate love combines the decision/commitment and intimacy components. Sternberg sees companionate love as the later stage of a love relationship in which the passion has faded. Their love is a committed friendship.

Fatuous love lacks intimacy but has sufficient passion and decision/commitment. Fatuous love relationships appear when passion is the primary basis for a marriage. With the fading of the passion, the remaining decision/commitment may not be sufficient.

Consummate love combines all three components: passion, intimacy, and decision/commitment. This is society's ideal of a love relationship, and thus, it is what most individuals hope to achieve. Close friendship and satisfied physical urges are combined in a long-term commitment to love.

Finally, the absence of the three components is called **nonlove.** Nonlove in Sternberg's system is a label for the many interpersonal relations people have with others.

SECTION SUMMARY:
IMAGES OF LOVE

We recognize two quite different mental pictures of love. Romantic love, prized in stories and the media, forms suddenly on unmet needs, ideals, fantasies, and hopes. It displays obsession, weakness, and clumsiness, and it tends to rapidly fade. Pragmatic love, the most common bonding of adults, builds slowly through successful interaction and is marked by trust, respect, sharing, and loyalty. It is a long-term experience of mutual support by differentiated people who coordinate their living.

These two forms of love may each be an optimal fitness strategy under specific life conditions. If life conditions are hazardous for children and parents, optimal fitness may thrive on a mating strategy—early and frequent mating. Thus, an emotional, lustful attraction will produce more children. But if conditions are stable, optimal fitness may come from a parenting strategy—raising a few children of quality to maturity. Here the bond is based on similarity and evidence of security.

Different systems have been used to categorize the variety of ways people seem to be attracted and bond with others. John Lee proposed nine styles that people adopt, much as they assume political or religious views. Although these styles are stable, they also may change over time and with experiences. Robert Sternberg hypothesized three components forming love, pictured as the corners of a triangle. Seven love forms are made of combinations of these, located on the resulting surface. However we view the variety, we still must address the question of how and why we (a) are attracted to others, (b) develop the relationship, and (c) make that relationship work. These are our next topics.

◈

ATTRACTION TO OTHERS

Love relationships necessarily depend on people first being attracted to each other. Love forms after a measure of personal contact, but to whom are we attracted? What characteristics and events lead to us becoming close? One answer is statistical: From 57% to 80% of people report that they were introduced to their partner by a mutual friend who thought they might like one another (reported in Duck, 1991, p. 32). The National Health and Social Life Survey (described in Chapter 7) showed that about 60% of people married or cohabiting were introduced by family, friends, or others who knew the two (Michael et al., 1994, p. 71).

Another answer comes from certain gender differences in presentation. Men tend to feature their status, height, and emotional openness and seek younger women when they make overtures to women in public advertisements; women feature their physical attractiveness and seek older men (Hoyenga & Hoyenga, 1993; Koestner & Wheeler, 1988). A later study examined responses to ads. Men who were older got more replies, women who were younger got more. Men's wealth and education were important to women, but these attributes in women were not important to men. Mention of attractiveness was important for all, but moreso for women (Baize & Schroeder, 1995).

To begin in another way, we can ask what is attractive in people we already like. One feature that we can abstract from our thoughts about those we like, or are attracted to, is the simple notion that they reward us in some way. They provide something that satisfies us; they make us feel better. Rewards, however, are personal, and there will be no absolute rules that are reliable. We will examine three categories of attraction ideas: familiarity, physical beauty, and positive regard.

Familiarity

Liking follows knowing. We get to know people in many different ways. An important source of familiarity is the amount of time we are with others. Just spending time with someone increases positive feelings of attraction, or perhaps it decreases feelings of aversion. Either way, there are increased feelings of closeness.

Some researchers have suggested that just exposure to someone, or anything, is enough to increase feelings of attraction. The more we experience others, the more positive the feelings we have for them. Positive feelings are formed for neighbors we pass often but with whom we have never interacted. People in a classroom group appear to be more attractive than strangers who are met on other grounds. One explanation poses the idea that we naturally fear what we don't know. Mere contact with others reduces some of this ignorance and makes possible a relatively stronger attraction.

Part of familiarity involves closeness. Liking follows closeness. In this manner, people who are physically closer to others will have more positive relationships; a remote existence reduces feelings of attraction. One aspect of closeness is that of the cultural norms by which we live. Each social situation has rules for how close we are allowed to approach others. Social scientists have proposed that there is a zone of intimacy, a personal distance for close friends, a social distance for interpersonal relationships, and a public zone for formal settings or passing strangers. Positive feelings are developed for those who respect these rules of distance and are often in the closest zone that is appropriate.

Physical Features

Beauty attracts. Of course, cultures have different standards of beauty, but with common factors. Generally, men are more swayed than women are by physical features indicating mating readiness. Cultural stereotypes appear in many populations. For example, college-age American men see women as most attractive if they are blond with blue eyes and light skin. In the same population, women prefer darker complexioned men (Feinman &

Gill, 1978). Across many cultures, attractive others have good complexion and are clean (Fisher, 1992). The matter of figure shows some interesting variations. Men are obviously attracted to evidence of a women's sexuality, and in a short-term mating scene, they focus on exemplary characteristics. Large busts, with narrow waists, and generous hips displayed in revealing clothing catch men's eyes and blatant stares when they are contemplating casual sex. But in a mate selection frame of mind, men find women most attractive when they show close-to-average torso proportions. Although overall weight standards vary with time and fashion, men are most attracted to women whose hips are one third larger than their waists (Singh, 1993). Men are not attracted to the very thin, nearly figureless women prized by women as fashion models.

Women are more attracted by evidence of resources. Wealthy men are attractive to women (Fisher, 1992). College-age men describe and use their appearance to show their resources. The clothes they wear, the material things they show, and the stories they tell of their success and ambition all attract women. Based on examining photographs, women were not willing to date or become involved with men wearing clothes of low status, but the same men in expensive sport or business clothes were attractive to them (Townsend & Levy, 1990).

We tend to think that most people like others who have striking beauty and somewhat exemplary attributes, but our actual preferences run toward averages of people similar to ourselves. Some research studies have averaged the features of many people, yielding a composite picture of the average man and woman. These composite averages tend to be selected as most attractive (Bowen, 1990). Further advantage in long-term mate selection for both men and women is evidence of brightness and intelligence in their partners' actions.

We are also swayed by the other extreme. Non-beauty repels. We link extreme ugliness and deformity with misdeeds and de-

viant personalities. Given a choice, people pick the normal-looking person as less likely to have committed a crime, or better behaving, or more deserving of rewards. Outrageous as these ideas seem in a cold light, they are easy to demonstrate. A simple survey of media villains or cartoon characters is a start.

But mere appearance is limited, particularly after the first blush of the encounter. People try to choose relationships with those who are likely to be similar to themselves. Men are not likely to approach very attractive women if those men view themselves as much less attractive or if they have a low opinion of themselves. Very confident men, however, seem able to approach very attractive women successfully, regardless of their own excellence (Stroebe, 1977). There is evidence that each person approaches others only after taking into account certain aspects of themselves.

These initial tendencies may affect our opportunities, but they have little to do with formation of love. The forces of physical attraction may not always lead to closeness. The first glance and contact merely provides the opportunity.

Positive Regard

Attraction follows positive regard, which comes from others' attention. Positive regard is a friendly look, a smile, a comforting touch, or kind words. These contacts may be the strongest attractive forces. In the vast majority of situations, positive regard determines positive social relations. Attraction follows the reward of others' attentions, and such relationships tend to be sincere and may develop further.

In a few cases, however, what appears to be positive regard may be ingratiation. Such a situation is one of intent to manipulate or to gain something besides friendship. We tend to want to believe in others' sincerity, but it is hard to know true intentions. The only defense is an open attention to cues as to what is really meant. Evidence of ulterior motives usually cools attraction feelings quickly.

The key word for women in positive regard is commitment. Men indicate commitment by showing persistent, interested attention; by expressing concern and kindness; and by claiming love (Buss, 1994). A man shows persistence by spending time with her, calling often, dating her rather than others, and writing to her. In conjunction with acting kindly and doing things for her, the most clearly attractive thing for a man to do is to express love for the woman.

SECTION SUMMARY: ATTRACTION TO OTHERS

We are attracted to others who are familiar to us in some way. Being close to others, however accidental, provides an opportunity and enhanced positive feelings for them. We are somewhat influenced by physical beauty, although the intent and gender of the beholder make a difference. Men are attracted to sexuality, moreso when expecting a short-term encounter, but they are likely to restrict their choices to those with whom they feel likely to succeed. Women look for men showing evidence of being able and willing to care for them. Population averages seem most attractive to all, and everyone seems repelled from ugliness. Overriding the modest effects of familiarity and physical features is the powerful attraction to others who indicate that they like us. Positive regard, if genuine, is the most potent attractant.

RELATIONSHIP DEVELOPMENT

There are certain basics that each relationship requires. A firm foundation is made of mature and successful personalities that share certain essentials. With these beginnings, an encounter has a chance of being formed into a love relationship. How that happens can be complicated. These are the matters of love we consider next.

Personality Patterns

Development of a love relationship requires some common ground of patterns of personality. A continuing romantic love relationship requires that both people have maturity of personality, including a developed and stable self-esteem. Furthermore, each must seek in the loved other a degree of similarity to oneself and valued, complementary differences.

Maturity

Maturity of personality broadly refers to our general success in developing a stable and successful self-image. Conflicts of childhood have been resolved in favor of productive adult roles.

Immature people often attempt to make up for specific deficiencies in their relationships. For example, the lack of love from a parent is sought from a parent-like lover. Maturity is always a matter of degree and usually involves some but not other aspects of oneself. Often, people have certain very immature features buried in an otherwise normal adult personality. Others have a rather mild but more diffuse, childlike approach to most of life. Aspects of immaturity often interrupt the development of love relationships.

Self-Esteem

Self-esteem is a matter of confidence in one's self-worth. It usually comes with development in the sense of being formed over time. Self-esteem is found at the root of most pleasure. The deepest positive feelings come from instances of experiencing who we are and what we can do. Self-esteem comes from within. Others cannot create our self-esteem, although they may perceive it and reflect it back. We get pleasure from that reflection. Thus, we are attracted to form love relationships with people who are aware of and respond positively to our self-esteem and mature self-regard. This factor is fundamental to love relationships, and we will describe more of it below.

Similarities and Differences

What of the similarities and differences between people in love relationships? Do opposites attract, as one piece of colloquial wisdom holds, or can we only love people like ourselves? The overview is that lasting love relationships are formed with others who share a great deal of likeness but who also possess a degree of valued, complementary difference. This amounts to saying that we do not remain close to those who are opposite to what we value in ourselves. Again, there is a matter of degree, and the tolerance we hold for differences depends on the breadth of our self-image.

Antagonistic differences are not tolerated for long. At the beginning, certain exotic differences may seem attractive. As their newness and excitement moderates, we are left with the conflicts they form in what we wish to share and integrate. Consider general energy level. A somewhat phlegmatic person may be attracted to another who is continuously energetic and moving on to new things in a never-ending stream. Soon that difference presents conflicts. Neither can easily moderate his or her energy level to the other;

no lasting relationship develops. Or consider general ethical maturity. A socially responsible person may be fascinated by the deviant and risky actions of another. Some amount of thrill may be felt from living a contrary life pattern for a time. Unless one person changes, however, that thrill wears off, and the antagonistic ethics remain. According to Grace Shirley, in her 1901 book, *Twentieth-Century Lovers' Guide of Love, Courtship and Marriage*:

> It is wise to conclude that robust men will soon tire of frail women, and that the merry nature will soon be soured by contact with the hypochondriac. The sage should not marry the frivolous or empty-pated, nor should the world-worn pessimist wed the innocent, unsophisticated lambkin, for in each case the interest is apt to wane when the novelty of the new plaything has become familiar. (p. 32)

Long-term love relationships form between people who share a core of common values and expectations. They have a strong affinity of likes and dislikes of feelings, thoughts, and actions. There is something more, however. Others are sought who bring to a shared experience some unique but valued aspects of life. Part of the attraction to a lover is what that person adds to you. The addition complements one's self. The artistic values you have not developed are attractive as they are shared in a relationship with another. Another person's logical style may complement your more intuitive imaginative style. It is not simply a matter of one having and the other not having. Love builds on seeing in the other a part of oneself that is valued but not yet actualized, but there must usually be a deeper sharing than mere summation of capacities or traits.

Forming the Relationship

> *To suggest that one simply starts a friendship, courtship, romantic partnership or marriage and "off it goes" is simple-minded.* (p. 3)

That observation is part of Steve Duck's (1991) thesis on *Understanding Relationships*. Duck notes the absolute need for skillfully managing relationships, especially in their earliest stages. Although there appear to be elements of magic and mystery in a beginning love, it won't survive beyond being a fleeting experience unless it is given attention—and perhaps there is a measure of luck as well. "Friendships do not start until people do friendly things in friendly places" (p. 64), Duck said.

There are several ways that skill in managing relationships can be listed. Established love reflects caring for the other, supporting that person, showing appropriate loyalty, and valuing the other's interests. Lovers' interactions have affection, communication, trust, and reciprocation. These are the topics that require management skills. Argyle and Henderson (1984, 1985) suggest that the rules of a relationship are clear: Give emotional support, trust and confide in the other, converse, don't publicly criticize or reveal confidences, and repay favors.

Among the skills supporting love are seeing the other's needs, communicating correctly, acting interested, satisfying mutual needs, adapting to the other, presenting a part of oneself, and building trust. The core dimensions of love skills are attending, presenting, and pacing. For many people, the necessary skills just happen and are good enough. For others, the promising love fades because one or both partners did the wrong things. Many other relationships are in between, being a fragile partnership without the participants quite knowing why it often flounders.

Emergence of functioning love has dimensions of opportunity, encouragement, growth, and maintenance. Opportunities are regulated by the principles of attraction to others that we discussed in the section above. Encouraging the other to continue contains the most delicate range of skills and processes. Moving an encounter toward continuance requires craft. Growth, too, requires careful and capable social moves to deepen the love toward shared intimacy. The process

is never done; maintenance and repair must be faithfully performed.

Encouragement

The strategies of encouraging love center on learning about each other, acting on feelings for each other, and building a system of intimate communication.

The critical elements at the beginning of an encounter are things that are done. The encounter generally is judged as promising or not within the first 30 seconds (Berg & Piner, 1990). In that time, we can see enough from the other to know whether the encounter should continue. What is important at the start are the crucial skills of presentation of oneself in a manner that is appropriate in the situation. It is perhaps more likely that an error will be made to end the association rather than that something will spark a beginning love where there has been none. It is very hard to recover from a disaster in those first critical moments.

Social skills needed are those of assessing what kind of self-presentation is appropriate in the setting. This is a matter of knowing whether and how to approach someone. In some settings, it is best to do nothing but be seen by the other, saving any direct action until a better time. It is perhaps easier to give examples of what typically fails than to prescribe what will encourage a relationship. Success will not come from trying to "come on" to someone who is preoccupied with an important task. Men do not like to begin a relationship when they are under public scrutiny. And weird conversation openings rarely have the intended effect. These examples and others like them show an insensitivity to the ecology of the encounter setting.

What is appropriate? Helen Fisher (1992) put together some ideas from different observational studies of the singles bar scene (Givens, 1983; Perper, 1985). The acts fall into a pattern of five stages: getting attention, recognition, grooming talk, touching, and synchronizing.

Getting attention combines positioning yourself to be seen and making movements to attract attention. You enter the room in a noticeable way, move to an appropriate position, and carry out appropriate but slightly exaggerated acts. Matters of appearance are important, emphasizing your mating potential in obvious yet suitable ways. The point is to be noticed and judged attractive.

Recognition is the process of making contact and moving together. Eye contacts and smiles are the primary cues. Not all smiles mean come hither. A "simple," mouth-closed smile is a greeting without further intention. A "nervous" smile exposes the back teeth in a clenched position and implies a hostile politeness. An "uppers" smile exposes the upper teeth and, combined with a wide-eyed gaze and an eyebrow raise, shows interest and flirting. An "open" smile shows all teeth and suggests more of a courting come-on and openness.

The pattern of a woman's flirtation is to begin with an uppers smile, raise the eyebrows, fix the man with a wide-eyed gaze for a few seconds, then drop the eyelids, tilt the head down and to one side, and look away, perhaps with a hand raised to cover the face and some giggling. Men tend to smile and "stand tall" with the chest out (and stomach sucked in) giving a simulated but subtle strength display. Beyond personal control is the size of our eye pupils; opening of the pupil during the gaze reflects our interest.

Who does the flirting? Women initiate a flirting contact at least two thirds of the time.

Grooming talk develops an interaction by its form more than its contact. Both people speak in a softer tone, pitched higher than normal, much as they would to gentle a child or animal. As long as it is respectable and something they can share, the content does not much matter: exchanges of useful information, comments on the surroundings, talk of the weather, or whatever. Encouragement also comes from the expressions on their faces, the ways they orient their bodies, and the hand and head gestures they make. Each of these should show interest in the other, openness to the person, and the pleasure they have in being with him or her. The next stage shows a physical contact.

Touching is a signaled request for continuing and deepening the relationship. Women typically make the first gesture in some form of subtle and gentle grazing motion of contact. A light brief touch on the arm is offered. The response to that can be critical. With any shrinking away from the touching, or with a failure to return it in an appropriate time, the message is "Stay away!" Further reciprocal touches mark the progress of the contact until there appears a different feature of pairing.

Synchronizing of the form and rhythm of their acts shows the pair is forming well. Couples now have oriented more directly to one another and appear to observers as if they were mimicking each other. One moves a shoulder and so does the other. A leg is crossed and the partner follows suit, and so on it goes, one mirroring the other. The rhythm of their shared conversation is also noticeable. Formal acts of synchrony appear in dancing, but also in just walking together.

Men tend to class these flirting acts of the ritualized "pickup" as sexual, but women often see them, at first, as friendly. They are tests, in a sense, of what the other might permit. Flirting directs the new relationship toward personal feelings, a form that has potential for building further encounters and love. Women usually begin the encounters but then leave it to the men to make the later moves.

These matters are fairly recent standards. About a hundred years ago, Grace Shirley (1901) asserted firm rules on making contacts.

> Nothing is more vulgar or more dangerous than the besetting sin of youth which is known as Flirting.
>
> To attract the attention of a person of the opposite sex without any introduction, and in public places, is an offense which carries with it its own just punishment in far more cases than we care to chronicle. (p. 43)

Growth

Conversation encourages a growing relationship. New encounter conversations often contain questions about one another. The best are questions that provide opportunities for revealing parts of oneself, that have potential for answers that allow the other to relate as little or as much as is comfortable. The idea is to solicit sharing from the other and for that person to reply in kind. Each person needs to affirm that the other shares certain attitudes, especially interest and feelings toward one another.

Part of the developing relationship is a sharing of what is understood. Getting that understanding takes time and careful exploration. Revealing what we believe or tolerate is a delicate matter that must be carefully coordinated with revelations from the other. We differ in how open we are to sharing, and that must be worked out. Being frank and open is not always appealing. Saying too much without getting similar replies may be seen as indiscreet. Timing is important. Growth of love may hinge on the success of the process as well as its results.

Men and women have different styles of sharing about themselves. There is, however, one preferred direction. Both women and men prefer women as partners with whom to share casual intimacy (Hays, 1989). For reasons that are not yet apparent, even physical health is better for those who talk more to women (Reis, 1986).

The format of intimate conversations varies with the speaker. Women tend to lead conversation by the example of their own conversation; men ask direct questions. Women express attention with frequent utterances during another's talking; men tend to respond primarily as a matter of agreement with the content. Thus, men say less when women are talking, and women sometimes interpret men's silence as not paying close attention.

Women present more intimate information and in a more open manner than men. Explanations of this conduct include the ideas that women are more relationship-oriented, less competitive, and more likely to take the initiative in conversation. When it is over, women define the intimacy of an interaction in terms of what was talked about; men think in terms of what was done (Helgeson, Shaver, & Dyer, 1987). These gender differences reflect cultural norms that most people hold,

and even if they complain about them, they see breaking them as social errors.

The more alike a couple's attitudes and values, especially those they believe to be unshakable, the smoother the growth of the relationship. Serious differences, or failures to reveal to one another, will block or end it. This process and its success is a major measure each person has of the value to them of continuing to be with the other. Susan Sprecher (1987) found that a romantic relationship's success can be best predicted by the amount of early disclosure by the couple.

The growth of the budding love is further set by what is done. Relationships are supported by what couples do together. Meeting at a place and eating together gives more to a relationship than equal time at a place of work. Food plays another role also; wooing with food is nearly universal. Offered food and shared food convey a variety of messages that each person cares for and supports the other. Meeting for recreation sends a different message, that of positive feelings and enjoyment. These settings suggest that they are friends, being together by their choice. Growth of their relationship will be seen in elaboration of the kinds of things done together. Each accepts and coordinates activities to account for the interests of the other. Together, they mark out what it is that they do as a couple. That pattern of activity itself grows and thereby strengthens the pairing.

With time, a couple will develop a shared, private meaning of their common interests and experiences. They construct a private, coded language of terms and other kinds of communications. As the relationship develops, they focus more on what they have together. Their shared past becomes more important than their separate individual pasts. Like the pattern of activities that is theirs, the shared experience also strengthens their bond.

Sharing love with another reforms and supports the personality. A relationship gives a consistent and stable reassurance of who we are, what we are thinking, and how we are acting. Some of the ways this happens are elaborated in the next section.

SECTION SUMMARY:
RELATIONSHIP DEVELOPMENT

Certain basic personality features underwrite a developing relationship. Each person must have sufficient maturity and self-esteem. Uniqueness in personality is important both in its absence and its presence. Similarity of attitudes and the various life choices each makes are necessary, but complementary differences provide some of the continuing interest each has in the other.

Critical to forming a relationship is personal attention to managing it. Self-presentation is crucial. This is done through acting normal at the first encounter, being noticed, making appropriate recognition of the other, and showing interest in continuing. Once begun, the relationship grows through balanced conversations of sharing. With increased time together in public and private activities, the couple constructs a special, common world.

FUNCTIONING OF
LOVE RELATIONSHIPS

First, we will re-enter the domain of trying to describe love. The diversity of love makes it hard to summarize. Attempts to do that are many and unrelenting. Philosophers, creative writers, scientists, and people in no special category have all tried to specify what it is to love and be loved. Such descriptions have value, although their quantity can be overwhelming. We should be ready to accept that there may be in fact very few generalities that we can uncover.

Next, we will return to the mechanisms of love as it is maintained over time. Love relationships are assuredly regulated by the belief systems and social constructions that each person holds individually and collectively. That makes love partly personal and partly a common social condition. We learn by listening to individuals with functioning love. How do they describe and construct their experiences, past and present? What are their accounts of love that is going well? The idea of mutual visibility provides one interesting model. Another model builds on the premise that we must recognize our separateness and loneliness to truly connect with another in love.

We can also learn from relationships that are challenged and failing. What do people tell about themselves and their loves when they are experiencing difficulties?

Experiences in Love Relationships

A developed love relationship is one of exceptional feelings, communications, mutual admiration, and shared acts. These characters are found in the routine as well as the unusual experiences lovers describe. Mark Fisher (1990) writes of love as something that happens to people; it becomes a narrative in which they participate, which yields feelings of humble benevolence. Added to those feelings is a partial fusion of identities that leads the lovers to share their lives.

Using standard methods of analysis, psychologists have sought the elements that constitute the existence of a love relationship. Specifically, they have examined the feelings, thoughts, and acts reported by those in love. Their assumption has been that these language elements may reveal some of the essence of what people believe about love. Harold Kelley (1983) believes that different expressions of love may be sorted into a few categories: caring, needing, trusting, and tolerating. Those expressions are found in the thoughts and acts of people reporting their love.

Reported Thoughts of Love

We begin with the methods of social scientists. There continue to be many new and improved attempts to measure the reality of a person's love. To illustrate them, we turn to one of the first. In this early and popular study, thoughts of love were studied in an attempt to develop a Love Scale, as distinguished from a scale of liking, by Zick Rubin (1970). A collection of statements about loving and liking were gathered from various authors. They were separated by various judges into the two categories and given to college-age people to sort with respect to someone they loved and with respect to someone who was just a friend. The results validated two scales of 13 items each. Statistical analysis of the Love Scale showed three components: affiliative and dependent need, predisposition to help, and exclusiveness and absorption. These are Rubin's Love-Scale items:

If ____ were feeling badly, my first duty would be to cheer him/her up.

I feel that I can confide in ____ about virtually everything.

I find it easy to ignore ____'s faults.

I would do almost anything for ____.

I feel very possessive toward ____.

If I could never be with ____, I would feel miserable.

If I were lonely, my first thought would be to seek ____ out.

One of my primary concerns is ____'s welfare.

I would forgive ____ for practically anything.

I feel responsible for ____'s well-being.

When I am with ____, I spend a great deal of time just looking at him/her.

I would greatly enjoy being confided in by ____.

It would be hard for me to get along without ____.

Verbalized Acts of Love

Studies by social scientists of the acts expressing love have a much stronger base of observations. Starting with reports of the ways people act toward others they have loved, these hundreds of statements were classified into several rational categories. They were then given to many other groups of people of different ages and further analyzed. Seven dimensions of acts of love were found (Swensen, 1972). These are

Verbal expression of affection

Disclosure of intimate facts

Giving emotional and moral support

Having feelings for the loved one that are not verbally expressed

Physical expressions of love

Giving material aid as evidence of love

Toleration of the less pleasant aspects of the loved one

Kelley's four categories are evident in both Zubin's scale of love thoughts and Swenson's reports of love acts.

Patterns of Intimacy

We move now to looking at some ideas about how an ongoing love relationship functions. What are the dynamics and mechanisms that make it work and keep it together? In examining two complementary approaches, we will see dimensions of reciprocity, differentiation, communication, and sexuality.

Developed Reciprocity

An interesting model of love relationships was described by Nathaniel Branden (1980) as **mutual visibility,** seeing in others a reflection of oneself. That visibility is one aspect of the special world that the pair has constructed in sharing their lives. He describes a literal giving over to the other a part of oneself and a simultaneous acceptance of comparable parts of the other. To understand mutual visibility, we must put it in the context of each person's self-perception.

The operation of mutual visibility depends on each person's need to construct and maintain a self-picture. We construct our self-pictures in different ways. An indirect kind of evidence comes from our meaningful acts. We can each observe the totality of what has happened and form a subjective picture from that. The basic nature of a self-picture, however, is judged in relation to others. Without others, a single being would have no need for such a concept. The reactions of others must be involved in forming our personal image.

A primary and direct reflection of our self-picture is seen in the mirror of the consciousness of another person. Mirror reflections of oneself take place in many different features or aspects of life. A simple two-person chat with someone in an informal setting gives each personal visibility. At the least, that simple reflection verifies that we are being seen as a similar conscious being. Two people who are alike in mental ability, belief system, and values and who interact for a period of time will develop a deeper visibility, both of themselves and of each other.

We appear to need such experiences to verify our existence as conscious beings and to maintain ourselves in our social order. Close interaction with another person shows us how we are doing. The self is most directly seen through perceptions of other people. Visibility includes a desire to be seen as well as to see; to be explored as well as to explore. Overall, it is willingness to be known as well as to know.

But there are personal requirements that enter. The foundation for a successful love relationship is our own self-esteem. The confidence we have in our separate worth is the basis for reaching out and connecting with others. Our love is based on the self-esteem values we each hold. Love is the joy felt in

seeing parts of our own valued self reflected by another person. It is in this sense that there is a mutual visibility—visibility of our valued self in another.

Another of the major and most important marks of a lasting love relationship is the admiration each holds for the other. This is the feature that holds a couple together in the face of a lifetime of difficulties. The admiration that each receives is a part of the visibility process with the other. We are reinforced by feelings of pride from the other, and the resulting pleasure feeds the positive feelings we have for the other.

Note that there is a selfishness implied by the self-esteem basis for love relationships. Love is based on our self-interest, but including the other. Love relationships are a special depth of mutual visibility with the addition of a constructed, shared world. This shared world is more than that of either lover. There is an overlapping of what exists plus something new that they have formed in their interaction. That special construction serves to support the love relationship. As the love relationship develops, so too the shared world reflects those changes.

Differentiation

Perhaps contrasting with Branden's reciprocity model, perhaps working beyond it is David Schnarch's (1991) view of developed, monogamous relationships. Schnarch builds sexual and marital therapy on a model of differentiated people periodically experiencing deep intimacy, especially during their sexual interactions. He borrows a chemistry metaphor to describe the couple's dynamics as being in a "sexual crucible."

The key concept in Schnarch's model of love is differentiation. **Differentiation** is our ability to be close to others yet retain a separate identity, to interact with them without conforming to and reciprocating their emotional reactivity, and to tolerate pain and aloneness in order to grow. A high level of differentiation is a life direction of development that moves beyond and away from the useful intimacy of earlier stages. Differentiation requires new skills of self-soothing rather than reflected, shared comforting. As it is formed, differentiation makes periods of intimate sharing more profound, exciting, and a celebration of differences. Periods of sexual intimacy are especially exhilarating with a self in contact with another, reflecting intense maleness and femaleness.

Traditional intimacy models take unconditional positive regard and unrestrained sharing as the ideal of love. Differentiation moves beyond that. Achieving differentiation may be stormy, and the differing successes in achieving greater differentiation of each person are traditionally thought to be a mark of a relationship heading for failure. But differentiation, instead of being a mark of a troubled relationship, is the primary necessity in a developed and successful one. The goal is a new foundation of love in begrudging respect for the separateness and integrity of the other. In this love, each person truly *wants* the other, integrating the aloneness of differentiation with the attachment of intimacy. Lovers are at the same time individuals and together.

Communication

Communication is the primary vehicle for maintaining the love relationship. A breakdown in communication is the surest sign of trouble. As in relationship development, there is no other way to maintain a shared world and interact with a differentiated other than through meaningful and continuous communication. Talk is the most common way to communicate. What is said and how it is said carries messages to the other. But actions and acts also suggest love. Unexpected smiles, winks, and touches are important and meaningful communications. Much of this communication is unnecessary in a strictly informational sense but is used to keep up the relationship.

Communication is even more vital when the couple faces troubling problems. If one or both are suffering in some way, the kind and form of communication must be regulated to help the other and protect the relationship. There are times when the best communication

is a protective silence that respects individuality. Other problems require a review and an intimate sharing of the plans and feelings of each person. Knowing which is needed may require a trial and error process.

Sexual Acts

Among the most intensely pleasurable parts of a love relationship are shared sexual acts. The pleasures of the physical union combine with the satisfactions of personal communication. This is the most intense of the experiences of a shared world. Each brings an intense interest in pleasing and being pleased by the other. Sexual acts are the ideal and perhaps the peak experience of many love relationships.

Nevertheless, sexual acts alone do not constitute and will not sustain a love relationship. Sexual acts are merely pleasurable physical events if there is not appropriate self-esteem or differentiation in both people, if there is not respect for the other, and if there is not a pattern of successful communication. The sexual acts are periods of peak intensity of the love relationship. They are not necessary nor are they sufficient to develop or maintain it. Idealists believe that if there is love, good sex will follow. The flip side to that is that if the sex is not good, the love is not "real." Neither is true.

A complementary idea is that working at making good sex will establish or reestablish love. The simple truth is that sexual acts are but one kind of interaction with another person. Sex holds no special key to love, but it can be a major vehicle for working through good and bad aspects of a monogamous relationship. Sexual and marital therapy are typically intertwined for couples who are not satisfied with their relationship.

Challenges to Love Relationships

As they have been described, love relationships are special experiences that grow from self-interests. They may be shared and mutually reflected, or they may mark a developed separateness with periods of intense intimacy. Of course, not all interactions work out. Many problems and challenges impair continuation of an initial attraction into a lasting love relationship. There are barriers to development, including unrealistic views of the other, fears of losing the other, looking to the other for one's self-esteem, and avoiding happiness.

Unrealistic Views

The foundation to a mature relationship is one of a shared acceptance of the uniqueness of the other. Love will not build on an immature perception or use of the other. One person may see the other in terms of attachments that are not appropriate. Neither person will likely develop a differentiated identity, and both remain in the dependency of early development of the relationship. Each denies that the other has a separate life, and both want that other to "belong" to oneself.

One practical consequence of denying the other's separateness is that a person judges personal reality by what is seen in the other and by what that other person does. Each disliked action of the other becomes a battleground because it is reflecting oneself. If a man engages in deep and intimate platonic communication with another woman, his mate may see that as a mark of the inadequacy of herself as a partner. Without a mature separation, these acts escalate into challenges to continuing the relationship. When the points of difference are in sexual matters, the damage soon becomes entrenched.

Fear of Loss

A love relationship may be blocked by one or both people holding a fear of losing the other. That fear is not openly recognized but is instead reflected in a defensive breaking off of the relationship. In the face of a problem, one becomes hostile and moves toward erecting a barrier as a protection from facing the fear of losing the other. Instead of admitting "I am afraid of losing you," the response becomes "Maybe I don't really love you."

Using the Other to Build Oneself

The love relationship will not in itself build one person's mature, differentiated self. If it is used in this way, the interaction becomes one of receiving and not of sharing, of clinging rather than sharing periods of deep intimacy.

Soon, the giving one begins to sense that there is no real duality. The receiving one may continue to be supported by the attention, but there is no maturing of the relationship. The partners do not establish their separate selves or a meaningful shared world, being focused instead in the inadequate world of the undeveloped person.

Avoiding Emotional Extremes

In a well-formed mature love, we can have occasional intense negative feelings directed at the other. Life can't be all head-over-heels rapture, nor should it be.

There will be times when one gets truly angry at the other. Differentiated selves can carry that out without breaking apart. Such periods are opportunities for growth. It permits going beyond the common beliefs of "If you love me, you can't hate me." Shared anger and hate directed at the other is as natural as love and sexual intimacy with the other, or shared sorrow at a loss, or fear of a danger. The key to maturity is accepting these periods as further definitions of who each person is and what the love pairing is all about. There is nothing wrong with periods of difference. Conflicts destroy love only when they are believed to be evidence of lost love.

Both participants must recognize that it is appropriate and necessary to experience happiness in the love relationship. That seems to be an obvious statement, but its failure marks many undeveloped interactions. There is a deep-seated piece of culture that surfaces strongly in some people. The belief is that there is something wrong with being happy. One can find theological bases for it, including the Calvinistic maxims of finding happiness only in the next world by rejecting all pleasures in this one. Carried into a relationship, the avoidance of happiness runs counter to the maturation of love.

Genetic Pressures

Following the tendencies toward mating and parenting we described from evolutionary theory, a lifelong relationship may not be easy to maintain. Although mating and caring for offspring to a survivable age, if not breeding maturity, is almost a definition of fitness, there may be no comparable fitness advantage to staying with the same partner beyond that point. We noted in Chapter 7 the possible fitness advantages to extra-pair mating for both males and females. On the whole, however, such affairs can never supplant the dominant pattern of two parents caring for the young during the early years.

At some point, however, two parents are not needed, nor is it necessary that the same individuals mate again. Diversity in genetic material results from changing partners. Over a period of time, this pattern is called serial monogamy. If this pattern has had some fitness advantage in our ancestry, it may underwrite the tendency for pairings to break up at about 4 years. Fisher (1995) proposes this reasoning to account for the most frequent time of divorce at about 4 years, and it most likely for couples with one or no children. Furthermore, these divorces occur in the prime reproductive years of life and are followed by remarriages within about 3 years. Dissolution of marriage becomes less likely as the mates age, as they have more children,

and as the length of the marriage increases. Clearly, these things run together; they all depend on time together.

Finally, our capacity to make and change social rules and traditions influences these tendencies in complicated ways. Our biological core tendencies may be set off by the social conditions we have learned, and they may be enhanced by supporting rules. Some theological beliefs encourage unlimited numbers of children and permanent mates. Conversely, if our rules discourage and sanction certain acts and feelings, we may be inhibited and acquire negative and active reinterpretation. Our theologies may also discourage passionate sex and require love focused to a deity. The people we become are conditioned on not just the biology and not just the social learning, but a mix of the two. In all likelihood, that result can be modified by continuing life experiences.

Most interesting are the concepts of mating and sexuality in old age. We may speculate that life beyond the fertile years is required because children must be provided resources and nurtured for several years after their birth. Perhaps, our genetic heritage includes a period of menopause, shutting down of women's ovary egg production, that has a fitness advantage of supporting the last children to breeding maturity. We continue to use the attachment and sexual mechanisms designed for fertility even though they no longer yield children. They do, however, continue the useful social bonding of those supporting parents.

SECTION SUMMARY:
FUNCTIONING OF LOVE RELATIONSHIPS

Studies of established love relationships reveal common themes of needing, trusting, caring, and tolerating the other. Two complementary views of developed intimacy reveal the dynamics of long-term love. Nathaniel Branden describes a mutual visibility in which each mature person is re-

flected, as it were, through the actions of the other in relationships. We are attracted to others who show that they like us, and we show pleasure in that and mirror similar feelings back. David Schnarch adds the necessity of being a separate person having important differences that are respected by the other. This differentiation allows some conflict within the bounds of reflected visibility. Critical to both views is a managed flow of communication in all forms. Sexual activity, although not vital, adds considerably to the successful love relationship.

Love relationships dissolve for many reasons. Some are founded on unrealistic views of the other, breaking the mutual visibility dynamics. Some turn a fear of losing the other into a rejection of that person.

Love relationships cannot be used to make up for wide differences. Some couples part on the belief that their periodic emotional differences mean there is no love. Sometimes, one or both believe that they should not have such happiness. From genetic heritage ideas is the thesis that lifelong love serves no fitness goal, and there need be no pressure to continue a relationship past the breeding maturity of one's offspring.

CHAPTER CONCLUSIONS

Sexuality is not synonymous with love, but these two concepts share a great deal of motivational space. Love and erotic aspects of sexuality share origins in social encounters that develop who we are and how we function toward others. Erotic arousal may be elicited with unreality as in fantasy, pornography, and romance imagery, but it needs social experiences and cultural images to develop and thrive. Successes and failures shape sexual motivation, even if those encounters are based on needs to make children, make money, or mark social status.

Accurate ideas of forms of love are distorted by our natural fascination with what is irregular. So we savor the emotional disturbance of youthful romantic encounters, and we notice unusual patterns of loving and the breakup of couples later in life. We ignore the stable and developed mature love as boring, perhaps believing that it is not really love. In this picture, the unusual romantic love becomes real, and the commonplace pragmatic love disappears from view.

Another fictional view of love relationships assumes that mere fate lies behind success. In reality, each relationship must be managed with careful attention to presenting oneself as an attractive, sharing person interested in developing that love. It isn't a spark that somehow welds people together, but rather a continuous process of gentle massage of one another and what is shared. Breakdowns come from failure of one or both to persist in that or to value what is shared.

Study and Review Questions

1. On what kinds of sensual stimulation does erotic arousal build?

2. What role do sexual scripts play in sexual motivation?

3. From what are sexual scripts formed?

4. What is the role of interpersonal sexual scripts?

5. What do intrapsychic sexual scripts do for us?

6. About what kinds of sex do men fantasize?

7. About what kinds of sex do women fantasize?

8. What form of erotica arouses men?

9. Do most men view pornography, and how do they judge it?

10. In Helen Hazen's view, what form of erotica arouses women?

11. What kind of meanings do lovers develop in a mature sexual relationship?

12. With what are sexual ethics concerned? . . . gender identities? . . . sexual orientations?

13. What kinds of nonsexual social motivations can be satisfied by sexual acts?

14. Why is more research attention paid to romantic love?

15. What are the characteristics of romantic love?

16. What are the characteristics of pragmatic love?

17. What overall life conditions lead us to romantic versus committed love?

18. What is the source and nature of one of John Lee's love styles?

19. What are the three triangle elements of Sternberg's view of love?

20. What is it about people that attracts us to them?

21. How should we treat others to make them like us?

22. What personality patterns must we have to attract others?

23. What kind of personality differences do we tolerate long-term?

24. What skills are needed to form and develop a love relationship?

25. What is critical at the beginning of a relationship?

26. How should you encourage a new relationship?

27. In Helen Fisher's summary of mating contacts, who makes the recognition contact?

28. In Helen Fisher's summary of mating contacts, who is usually first to touch the other?

29. In Helen Fisher's summary of mating contacts, what is the final stage of acts?

30. With what actions does the relationship grow?

31. With what descriptive categories do we describe a mature love relationship?

32. What are the dynamics of mutual visibility in a love relationship?

33. What does differentiation in a love relationship entail?

34. What activity is most vital to maintaining a love relationship?

35. Will good sex repair or hold together a weakening relationship?

36. What beliefs and acts impair love relationships?

37. Why might we not be designed to stay together until death?

CHAPTER 9

Social Interactions

We all follow some form of social order, conforming to social patterns. To keep a smooth flow of social events, our potential errors and incidents are managed by accounts, using facework, motive talk, and attributions. Disruptions of social order show our underlying social motivation strategies. Why do we fail to help others, and why do we act in special ways when in a crowd? Social majorities easily influence us. Dissenters, a normal part of social groups, are at first marked as deviants, but if they persist, their arguments influence the majority group agenda and their thoughts. We are influenced by and can influence others through social mechanisms of authority, attraction, conformity, commitment, and reciprocation.

Social Order

Accounts of Conduct

Social Order Disruption

Bound to the Majority

Practical Social Influences

We have to be orderly. The alternative is chaos, and chaos is not a logical possibility for the world or for any of its inhabitants. Without order, there can be no survival. In this extreme context, it is perhaps trite to say that we are orderly. At the least, without order, there is no possibility of studies such as psychology or physics or music, or even communications at all. Given the necessity of world regularity and of some degree of social order, we can still ask questions about the nature of that social order.

Social order is the mark of all human societies and appears also in our nearest primate relatives. How much of the social order is founded on evolutionary adaptations that underwrite the form that culture takes? What is unique to specific societies?

In this chapter, we first focus on social order and how it determines our choices, intensities, and feelings. Our view will first be of patterns of social conduct and the ways people account for them. These ideas give the foundations on which the processes of social influence are built. In a sense, this is a subtle distinction of convenience rather than a major demarcation of real substance. Social order facts and influence processes are intertwined. Influence is both a matter of being obliged to conform to social order and of being changed to a new or different order. Geneviève Paicheler (1988) views these issues of influence as being on several dimensions. She contrasts gentle persuasion versus strong suggestion, conformity to the normal majority versus innovation by deviant minority, and public versus private acceptance. The social conduct topics of this chapter are usually matters of gentle persuasion to the style of a majority in our public acts.

SOCIAL ORDER

The most obvious, but easily overlooked, feature of any group of people is the orderliness of acts of its individuals. Each person follows a pattern of actions that is remarkably similar to that of every other. In public places, we dress in similar ways, walk in the same places, interact in standard fashion, and perform uncounted acts with the same rules. In this section, we illustrate the forms of general social order and some of the justifications that seem obvious if an explanation is called for.

Manners and Propriety

All human societies have specific rules of conduct that their members are expected to obey. Examples are drawn from modern Western society, but the principles of order are no different in any others. A complete analysis should examine the sources, purposes, and evolution of each specific rule of social action. An analyst might borrow the methods of zoologists, who examine each specific act of a species for its value to individual members and to others of that species. That kind of study has rarely been applied to Western human society; it may not be profitable work, however. In its place, we can begin

with a rational sketch of how and why we are orderly.

We can approach the underlying rules of proper action and manners in different ways. One route is through common patterns of acts described with psychologists' concepts, such as reciprocation, ritual, logic, legal rules, and feelings. These are ways of describing the psychological activities that have been proposed as causes of specific social acts. A second avenue to describing manners and propriety puts them in topic classes. Classes of concerns such as health, safety, personal rights, gender norms, and personal defense are among the obvious motives for acting in concert with others. It seems more convenient to illustrate social order by presenting examples in these latter motive classes.

Health-Derived Concerns

Manners formed because of health concerns, which follow customs, which are in turn justified by knowledge and acceptance of specific principles. Germ theory of disease is one such principle. Germs must not be allowed to reach other people. Rather recently in human history, we learned that disease-causing germs exist in body fluids and are carried in any form of dirt. Thus, we bathe and present ourselves in clean clothes. We offer only clean parts of our bodies for contact by others. Body wastes are not placed in public areas. Spitting is not a cultivated public activity (except in baseball games). Noses and mouths are covered when sneezing or coughing, and we refrain from probing body cavities when others are watching. These are among the most direct and crude examples.

Other derivations from germ theory are more subtle. As acts of cleanliness have become widely practiced, sensibilities of related things are refined. We demand that there be no odors associated with being unclean. It is appropriate not just to smell clean but also to add acceptable perfumes to ensure that no offense is given to others. We are repelled by odors from processes of the farm and nature, perhaps because they imply a lack of the cleanliness standard. Thus, societies insist that farm animal areas are kept some distance from concentrations of population, that septic fields have no odor, that organic gardening compost piles are suitably controlled, and that pets do not leave their wastes in public areas. All such wastes are believed to be dangerous and hence their odors have come to be unpleasant. To control these sources is proper action.

Specific manners related to health are produced in part through reciprocation. We do what we view as the correct thing and expect that others will do the same. Add to that the forces of logic and law. The conclusion has been formed that germs are dangerous, and that has been written into laws requiring cleanliness. Social habits have been formed around these conclusions and laws. The logic and the law are implicit behind the patterns of germ-avoidance acts.

Safety-Based Proper Social Action

Social acts that preserve safety also depend on some logic and law that evolved into habit. The simplest of these are those regulating movements, whether in or out of vehicles. We obey traffic regulation signs and signals. We internalize the principles of keeping to the right when meeting others on a common path and yielding to those coming from the right (change that to the left in Great Britain). We yield to those having difficulty in their movement. Of course, the necessity behind these safety-based orderly acts is prevention of collision and injury, and everyone can understand that intuitively.

Manners Respecting Personal Rights

Many Western-world manners reflect understanding of the personal rights of others. We are quiet in an audience so that others may hear. We listen to the views of others, even if we believe they are hopelessly misguided. Property is honored. These are again matters of logical derivation using everyone's understanding of reciprocation, and they have been codified in laws. To ensure that no one's rights are violated, each must protect the rights

of others. The appropriate acts have become matters of habit that need no thought for their execution. We have become accustomed to honoring the rights of others.

Manners Reflecting Gender Norms

Some of the most highly developed manners and principles of proper activity have concerned the ways that men and women treat those of the other kind. Gender differences in manners have obscure origins but likely reflect some long-held rituals of pair formation practices. The customs of earlier societies, perhaps those that were smaller and bound by strict principles of acceptable mates, dictated rules of treating others to encourage only the permitted contacts. All other social interactions were prescribed to maintain proper social respect and distance. Western social history provides a clear picture of recent custom that we reviewed in Chapter 7. Middle and late nineteenth-century women were sequestered at home as child bearers and housekeepers, with supplies and protection provided by their husbands. Styles of deference to the "weaker" sex became proper manners.

Gender manners have been changing, however, and the standards of 100 hundred years ago or even 20 years ago are not those of today. Not too many years ago, men were expected to provide a high degree of protection and deference to women. Women were properly submissive with no evidence of being too "forward." This was evidenced in such simple matters as holding doors open and more complex interactions such as extending invitations and paying for shared social events. The gender was the important factor, ignoring practical matters of strength, position at the doorway, opportunity, and wealth. Following some changes in principles of social equality, increasing numbers of people view these as "sexist" acts, and these "diversity" and equity attitudes are slowly changing the standard of normal action. Eventually it will reshape what is the official and proper action.

Manners Based on Defense

We protect ourselves, our families, and our property. From this fundamental motive, conventions have been established to ensure that protection is maintained with a minimum of aggression. We greet others with a raised open hand or a handshake to show mutual respect and perhaps to reveal that a weapon is not being carried. In one movement, both aggressive and defensive feelings are neutralized. There are elements of reciprocation in the acts, and standardized greetings seem to be based on rituals of society of ancient origins.

Other examples of propriety present defense or non-threat messages. We place ourselves with others, either in seating or other situations, so as to be no closer than the space and our relationship with those others suggests. To move closer (or too far away) is perceived as a threat. It is less threatening to speak with someone on equal terms. That is, both parties are to be in the same body position, standing or sitting, so that neither has any perceived advantage. We are most comfortable speaking with others when we face at a slight angle to one another, looking primarily to one side rather than facing the other directly.

Fads and Fashions

A powerful social pressure comes from the ideas we assume about a personal style of living. We follow fads. We act according to fashion. We follow fads and fashions in appearance, in styles of action, and even in ideas.

Fashions of Appearance

Appearance fashions are easy to document. Fashions are apparent as we look around and compare what we see with pictures and memories of earlier days. Habits of personal hygiene are part of it. Long hair or short hair, beards or no beards, tanned skin or blanched, straight hair or curled and wavy hair, faces covered with makeup or scrubbed clean. There are general, overall trends of these and many specific variations that enjoy a very brief time in the limelight.

Modes of dress are perhaps the most institutionalized fashions of appearance. Clothing and shoe types and styles show major trends and minor variations of style in a never-ending progression. Experts can pinpoint the exact period of a piece of clothing. Individuals find it compelling to follow the pattern of what others are wearing. In the world of high fashion and in the workday world, we feel comfortable appearing like others. We may have feelings of fear of being out of style. Even those who purposefully choose to go against the prevailing fashion usually adopt a conforming style of nonconformity.

Fashionable Styles of Action

Like personal appearance and clothing, we also have some broad patterns of social conformity in our activity styles. Examples of style can be seen in the ways we eat, in personal habits of consumption, and in forms of recreation.

Eating a large percentage of meals outside of the home is a recent fashion. Fast food, pizza, and soft ice cream are recently developed choices in eating. As these eating styles become established by advertising and their success is widespread, they have a stronger social power.

Smoking, drinking coffee or alcohol, and taking other mood-altering drugs have a long history. Each step in this social history is one of fashionable style that attracts adherents. These are particularly powerful motivators because they do several things for the users. First, they are stylish acts by which we join and conform to groups. Second, they change personal affect. They make us feel better at the moment. Third, they supply action structure. Smoking and drinking in particular provide something for us to do while we interact socially. We will discuss these and other addiction factors in Chapter 11, "Addiction."

Recreations are many and varied. These too we will discuss later. Each has a power to attract, and this power comes from involvement with others. We do what others are doing and enjoy what we see others enjoying. Sports, dances, parties, and watching television and movies all fit this pattern. Each perhaps has other rewards for us, but we are led to do what others are doing because others are doing it.

Fashions of Thought

Fads and fashions of thought are somewhat harder to know because we cannot easily stand apart from them and compare them with the past. Ways of thinking are part of oneself in a more fundamental sense. Yet, as we look for the evidence, thought is not seen to be different from observable actions in following the lead of others. We will consider examples of several types. We have learned certain patterns of beliefs. Our thinking is subtly influenced by the prevailing structure of the world and the things we have fashioned. Even the ways we learn to solve problems impose a fashionable structure over all of thought.

Some patterns of belief have been directly learned. Religion is an easy example because it is typically a separated life segment. There is clear evidence that religion is taught and becomes reinforced by social ritual. Our political beliefs also tend to be founded on learning in the company of others. If our family was populist or socialist, we begin with that structure but may later modify it after experiencing a social group expressing different views. Even some of the phrases for the process of changing beliefs reflect verbal fashions; for example, consciousness raising.

A century and a half ago the ideas of progressive biologists centered on the nature of the diversity of life forms. The concept of evolution was gathering support and found great strength in the mechanisms proposed by Charles Darwin in his 1859 *Origin of Species*. There followed a major revolution of thought in the wide field of the sciences and the humanities. After a period in which evolution was used to explain and think about nearly everything, the general idea became a part of the background of thought that few people seriously challenged. For a time it was high

fashion of thought, and it now is quietly assimilated, affecting everyone.

The modern world has been a mechanical one and is becoming an electronic information-unit world. Ways of thinking were fashioned on the machines that came to dominate society more than 100 years ago. Machines are structures made up of pieces, and people have learned to study the pieces to know the machine and how it works. This method of thought has become part of culture. It predicts that we can know anything by examining its pieces. Systems that don't fall to this form of intellectual attack (like mind experience) are often ignored or discredited. These, too, are powerful fashions of thought. If the mechanical worldview is changing in a fundamental way toward a new kind of thought process based on structures of information, there also may be significant alterations in the structures of sciences and humanities. At the least, the complexity of computing machines will complicate the mechanical model that has been used. Can anyone resist the trend of these collective thoughts?

Another example of fashionable thinking is science. Scienctific thinking has been enormously successful in understanding the physical world. Scientific ideas have made human lives comfortable and convenient. That success has bred a fashion of thinking that some specific methods of science are the only proper ways to answer questions or supply knowledge. This narrow view is called **scientism.** Scientism thought dominates culture, and it can be resisted only with great effort. Many important human social questions, however, find no answers in narrow science methods. For example, when a social group wants to know what ought to be done about pollution, scientism can tell nothing about what is the proper thing to do. It can give facts of mechanisms and statistics of events, but it cannot tell what should be done. A question of what should be done about pollution must be answered from a perspective of values and ethics. Science has nothing to say to that domain. At best it can give reliable evidence to reach valued goals decided by broader human judgment.

Following the scientism fashion of thinking, we try to make the scientific methods think for us. The logical assumption is made that if scientific methods do not yield an answer, there is no answer to be found. Any nonscience attempt must be just personal opinion or nonsense. From a broader perspective, the arrogance of the scientism conclusion is seen to devalue rational thought, which includes an attempt to develop personal and public values based on ethical standards. The social pressure of the dominant scientism view tends to force the rejection of such other ways of thinking. Can we resist scientism? Perhaps, but not without great effort.

SECTION SUMMARY: SOCIAL ORDER

We have little choice about being orderly, at least at some level. Chaos is avoided by social conventions of manners and propriety. Examples come from our concern with doing what maintains our health, keeps us safe, and respects our individual rights. Other manners flow from the ways men and women treat each other. Significant parts of our manners involve styles of aggression and self-protection.

Similarly, we operate according to fads and fashions. Appearance fashions are among the most obvious, constituting an industry in itself. We also follow socially fashionable styles of doing things, the ways we eat, adopt personal habits, and engage in recreation. Most subtle are our fashions of thought. Both broad and narrow ideas structure our minds, becoming in essence the nature of our minds. We will explore this principle again in Chapter 10.

ACCOUNTS OF CONDUCT

Social conduct is orderly in its general patterns and by way of its influence on the acts of individuals. The flow of detailed actions of individuals, however, is a balance involving the presenting of oneself and understanding the self-presentations of others. The way we present ourselves in a situation is called, following Goffman, our **face.** Sociologist Erving Goffman (1959) wrote of face in various interactions he called public performances, and he used the purposeful metaphors of actors and audience. His perspective of social interaction is based on the ways we establish and maintain our understandings of our own and others' individual identities or faces.

Social order or balance is threatened when someone acts inconsistently. When such errors are made in self-presentation, the identities of that person and all of the others in the situation, the "audience," are threatened. Thus, each social interaction is regulated by the need to restore the balance. This need is a potent form of social motivation.

Restoration is accomplished by both the performance of the actor (the person in error) and by the audience (everyone else in the social situation). Actors prevent errors by adopting certain roles or styles of acts, called by Goffman **defensive practices.** The members of the audience also do things to prevent their noticing potential errors, called **protective practices.** Together, these strategies are called **facework** by Goffman (1955). After an incident or error has occurred, there are many ways of correcting the social interpretation of the situation to restore order. These have been called **motive talk.**

TABLE 9.1 A Taxonomy of Accounts of Conduct

Facework
- defensive practices
- protective practices

Motive Talk
- requests
- disclaimers
  - hedging
  - credentialing
  - sin license
  - cognitive disclaimer
  - suspension of judgment
- apologies
- accounts
  - excuse
  - justification
  - concession
  - refusal

Attributions of Responsibility
- global association
- impersonal causation
- foreseeability
- personal causation
- justifiability

Following our description of facework and motive talk, we will consider an analysis of the application of this general process to **attribution of responsibility** (see Table 9.1).

Facework

When someone's face is threatened by the happenings in a scene, it amounts to questioning this person's identity and, thus, credibility. But there are different needs that make up each person's face. Brown and Levinson (1987) found evidence of two kinds in their study of politeness in several cultures. One sort of face need is founded on positive desires to be known, respected, and liked. Another, which they called negative face, reflects desire for individuality and freedom in actions. Being a part of most social groups usually puts these needs in conflict. Wanting

to be liked and included conflicts with wanting to make our own choices about what to do and when to do it. When conflicts arise, we do what we can to defend the face most appropriate to the setting.

When we must act differently from our face needs, Goffman's defensive practices generally protect our self from the somewhat different role we are playing in that situation. At the extreme, we may project the image of our real self being detached from the role, and we subtly communicate to others that we are not taking it seriously. This **role distance,** as it is called, gives the audience the message that incidents and our errors are a part of the role we are playing, and we should not be held responsible for them. Discrepancies of identity can thus be ignored as a nonthreat to each person's understanding of the social setting.

Using role distance, we show, for example, that we are acting as part of a specific social group, such as being a football fan. Acting according to the demands of that group may be discrepant from the actions that the audience normally expects of us. As football fans, we may become very excited and yell cheers, wear extreme forms of clothing, and wave garish decorations on game days. None of these unusual acts form our identity as college professors, students, real-estate agents, barbers, or whatever, except when we are in the football-fan role.

Some defensive practices involve adopting a role that communicates that we may not be able to respond to discrepancies from our typical self-identity. Salesclerks assume an impassive role; everyone knows that customers are to be dealt with kindly and with the understanding that salesclerk actions are not to be taken as measures of personality. When they do not become angry during a customer's verbal attack, salesclerks are not judged to be passive but are seen to have self-identities hidden and defended by the employment role.

More elaborate formal preparations may also be undertaken as defensive practices. We may present an elaborately complex and detailed performance, reducing the ability of the audience to detect errors of self-presentation. We can control the likelihood of confrontation in a potentially hostile formal meeting by using a detailed agenda. The formal structure reduces the likelihood of unexpected events. Or in a carefully planned physical arrangement, we may stay distant from the audience, as in a recent president's feigning inability to hear reporters' questions as he boarded his helicopter.

The protective practices of audiences are generally those of politeness and tact. Members of the audience avoid being perceived as observing. Both we and the audience judge the deviant acts as being overlooked or ignored. By feigning inattention, the audience prevents an incident by protecting its privacy. Audience members may act as if they did not hear a social disturbance near them. Another protective practice protects the social interaction by the audience members clearly marking their presence or absence in the social interaction. On entering too quietly a room where two people are engaged in deeply personal interactions, we may quietly retire, and then approach again making considerable noise before entering. As audience members, we are giving notice to the actors to revise how they appear to us.

Motive Talk

We try to present a self that is evaluated positively by others. If there is some event that places that positive evaluation in jeopardy, a question is raised and some corrective actions are necessary. The corrective actions to answer self-evaluation questions are some form of motive talk. Writers have proposed four forms of motive talk: requests, disclaimers, apologies, and accounts (Semin & Manstead, 1983).

A **request** as a bit of motive talk is a solicitation to the audience to ignore some act we are about to do. We admit that a rule is to be broken and that it may have offensive consequences. The intent of the request is to receive an offer from the audience, thereby changing a broken rule into a charitable gesture from the audience. The request may be, "Do you mind if I go first? I'm in a hurry." The

gracious responding offer is "Of course. Go right ahead." Without the request, the act of moving ahead of another in line would be a serious rule transgression. After the request and the offer, it becomes a social exchange of generosity by the audience.

The several kinds of **disclaimers** are intended to discredit in advance a likely evaluation of poor performance. John Hewitt and R. Stokes (1975) illustrated five forms of disclaimer. **Hedging** uses statements that claim we have no expertise, and errors are to be judged as those of the class to be expected from the novice.

I'm not a doctor, but I think you have a skin cancer. (Sorry, I didn't know you had a tattoo.)

This is my first time at a baseball game; how many hits do you need for a field goal?

In **credentialing,** we proclaim personal fact or principle that is in opposition to what may be inferred in the acts that are to follow.

I like dogs, but it is not pleasant to have that beagle around.

I don't eat heavy meals at noon; but those ribs and dumplings look great and they are free.

The **sin license** has the effect of suspending the rules for the exception that is to follow, thereby supposing that the rules don't always hold.

I know the speed limit is 55, but I want to get there early.

Broken cookies don't have calories; they have all leaked out.

Cognitive disclaimers justify what is to follow by proclaiming that our thinking is normal, but what follows may not seem so.

This may appear weird, but I think the world may end next week.

Sometimes I think about strange things. I wonder whether Elvis really is alive.

Finally, we make appeals for the **suspension of judgment** to hold off the audience's evaluation until some specific time or event has ended.

Don't say anything until you see all of the pieces put together.

I have 3 more days to get this done; I'm still just trying possibilities.

Apologies come after some act. By apologizing, we acknowledge responsibility and thereby admit that some rule has been violated but that it will not be done again. We are presenting the act as an unrepresentative part of ourselves, thereby protecting our general image. Goffman (1959) speaks of "splitting of the self into a blameworthy part and a part that stands back and sympathizes with the blame giving" (p. 144).

An apology has elements of guilt, remorse, and embarrassment, each having a different focus. Guilt focuses on the rule violation, remorse centers on the harm to a victim, and embarrassment highlights the actor's public image.

M. B. Scott and S. Lyman (1968) made a systematic study of **accounts**: statements "made by a social actor to explain unanticipated or untoward behavior" (p. 46). They describe two fundamental kinds of accounts, those used to excuse the error and those that justify it. In using the **excuse,** we deny responsibility for the error. Comedian Flip Wilson's famous line was "The devil made me do it." Another traditional oldie is "The dog ate my homework." **Justifications** try to minimize the seriousness or offensiveness of the act. "Its just a little scratch on the fender." "Hey, in a few years we'll all laugh about this."

Stephen Read (1992), relaying the recent work of others, outlined four kinds of accounts with different purposes. Besides excuses and justifications, there are also concessions and refusals. In making a **concession,** we admit the offense but deflect attention from the act toward offers of restitution. Our **refusals** are blunt denials that the act happened, that the interpretation as an offense is accurate, or that the complaining person has a role in the matter.

Working from a variety of research ideas of story comprehension, social narratives, and modeling close relationships, Read suggests we build our accounts to be (a) coherent and (b) in accordance with others' perspectives. Our accounts aim toward pragmatic goals somewhere between accurate, true descriptions and narratives that will make sense and be honored by others. We take into account what those others know and how they view the situation. Putting these into analytic terms, we use a narrative form to portray the situation, our goals, the instigating factors, the sequence of acts, and how it came out. To do this, when we construct our account we must bear in mind:

1. The kind of account we wish to construct (excuse, justification, concession, or refusal)

2. Our desire to have the account honored

3. What we know of the facts of the case

4. What the reproacher knows of the facts (or is likely to learn)

5. The reproacher's beliefs about social and physical causality

6. Our own beliefs about physical and social causality. (Read, 1992, p. 9)

There have not been many empirical studies of accounts. A common methodology has been to present the details of an incident in a brief written vignette and then to ask people to indicate the adequacy of different responses. A major problem centers around whether we tell what we would do or tell what we believe to be the most socially acceptable actions. Either response gives useful information but of a different kind. Thus, children chose the more elaborate and complete apologies if the social error was stronger (Schlenker & Darby, 1981). Actions of penitence were chosen over other accounts when the social error was most clear (Mehrabian, 1967).

An experimental study found that requests made before minor social transgressions led to positive offers in reply, even if there was no real content or information in the request. An actor approached people about to use a copy machine and asked to use it first. When just a few pages were to be copied, the simple request without an excuse was honored, a "mindless" social form according to the authors. If the request was for many pages, then an informative excuse ("I'm in a rush!") was more likely to yield a compliance offer (Langer, Blank, & Chanowitz, 1978).

Field studies have been done observing preschool children (Much & Shweder, 1978) and accounts of crimes by imprisoned felons (Felson & Ribner, 1981). In the latter, justifications were more frequent than excuses. Those who denied their crimes were likely to get more severe sentences if the nature of the crime was one apparently high in intent.

Attributions of Responsibility

Attributions of responsibility are another way we categorize the nature of unfortunate social events. Levels of increasing personal responsibility are given as global association, impersonal causation, foreseeability, personal causation, and justifiability. We judge our responsibility in terms of information about being connected to the actions and our capacity to understand the situation.

Assignments or attributions of responsibility for blameworthy actions are primary and commonplace means of maintaining social order according to rules. They have also become a basis for society's formal and legal processes of keeping order. Legal responsibility follows the current and common practices of people making attributions of responsibility for the consequences of their actions in daily affairs.

Attributions of responsibility depend on three important elements. First, attributions occur in a particular and specific social setting that is a part of a progression of social events having rules and expectations of its

participants. Second, the actions focused in attributions are perceived as coming from people in a social role and having authority for their actions. Third, there is a particular audience having a direct relationship to the social interaction. Thus, the responsibility attribution cannot be isolated from its social context. Attribution is not a concept or process to be studied apart from these constituting elements: social rules, authored acts, and relevant audience.

Attribution of responsibility became an attractive topic in psychology following Fritz Heider's work. He used responsibility to distinguish personal, impersonal, and mixed causation as these ways of thinking are employed in commonplace, naive psychology to explain general actions. His paper in 1944 and his book in 1958 attempted to consider a broader scope than did the volumes of research in social psychology that ensued. These others focused on locating the responsibility for faulty actions.

Heider described five different kinds of conditions in which a person may be thought to have caused an action. He did not intend these to be more than a list of possibilities. Under the principle of **global association,** there is responsibility for any actions that are in any way associated with an actor. For example, all citizens are responsible for the acid rain produced by their country, or all hunters are responsible for the poaching acts of a few.

Second, **impersonal causation** gives responsibility for acts when the actor was instrumental in the performance even if the ends were not foreseen. The landowner burning a ditch is impersonally responsible for the destruction of wildlife in the ditch and the neighbor's woods that were ignited by a wind-blown burning leaf. In closing the car door, the parent is impersonally responsible for squeezing the child's fingers in the jamb.

Third, **foreseeability** is a label others have applied to Heider's idea that an actor is responsible for acts that may have been foreseen. In applying excess pesticides, the farmer could have foreseen that the water in aquifers below the fields would be polluted. Owners of businesses can foresee that holding employees to minimum-wage, part-time work prevents them from earning sufficient money to afford the very products and services the businesses offer.

Fourth, **personal causation** holds actors responsible for the actions they intend. This is the strongest personal form of causation, the attribution most closely tied to each person's self as an agent.

Finally, **justifiability** refers to past and present events that conditioned the intention. Thus, our acts are justified by the happenings, and there is personal responsibility only to the extent that the actions went beyond the justifications. We are justified in making known the polluting acts of a specific person or company, but we become personally responsible if we destroy property in doing so. Or, facing acts of insubordination by an employee, we are justified in becoming angry and taking appropriate sanctions; those responses are conditioned by the situation and expected. But we go beyond justifiability and are personally responsible if we physically attack that person.

In an ongoing social setting, an attribution of responsibility is a part of the continuous process of **reflexivity.** We all monitor our actions and those of others to continuously affirm definitions of ourselves and others, as well as the stability of the social rules. In this normal situation, we can account for actions because it is assumed that all participants have responsibility for their actions. Each of us is an agent who can cause action. As participants in a social order, we are assumed to know that order and to know how to act in accordance with its rules and our self-knowledge. Attributions of responsibility are thus fundamental to social and moral order and at the same time are derived from it.

Responsibility rules infer that there is a justification for punishments or sanctions against breaking those rules. In making judgments about the appropriateness of sanctions, there are two aspects of the responsibility to be considered. **Connection rules** establish our causal link to the actions. These are the rules of objective facts of what was done and by whom. Peter was seen hitting George with the stick. But responsibility in many contexts also hinges on capacity rules. **Capacity rules** consider our subjective state relating to understanding the situation and the action, having the reasoning necessary to carry out the intended act, and having the control to carry out or prevent the action. Peter is just 11 months old, and George is his father.

SECTION SUMMARY:
ACCOUNTS OF CONDUCT

We are motivated to rectify social errors, those happenings that disrupt the flow of normal order. Some such events are handled with defensive practices by the one potentially viewed as the offender. Defensive practices include making the acts seem not what we normally do, perhaps by appearing detached from the role, taking on an obvious identity as one who does do those things, or erecting a barrier of complex rules that we pretend to be following. Other facework includes protective practices by those in attendance, who tactfully pretend they did not notice the offense.

Four categories of motive talk attempt to establish that our true self is not represented by the ongoing actions. We make requests that serve to change the act from an offense to the assent of a charitable offer by those observing. Our disclaimers are another way of putting a different light on what is about to happen. Examples of disclaimers are hedging, credentialing, the sin license, cognitive disclaimers, and suspensions of judgment. Apologies as motive talk come after the event. Finally, accounts attempt to excuse, justify, deny, or deflect attention to restitution.

Attributions of responsibility are another way we categorize the nature of unfortunate social events. Levels of increasing personal responsibility are given as global association, impersonal causation, foreseeability, personal causation, and justifiability. We judge our responsibility in terms of information about being connected to the actions and our capacity to understand the situation.

SOCIAL ORDER DISRUPTION

The ideal by which social order is defined, a perfect flow of meaningful social interactions without mistakes, conflicts of selfhood, or other disruptions, is a fiction. However, this ideal represents a model by which socially based motivation can be understood. But even as a model, the ideal is meaningless until used to compare and describe the nature of specific disruptions of the social order. Our motivation interest arises in studying the interplay between social order, disruptions, and modes of reestablishment of social order. Two topics of disrupted social order are bystander apathy and mob acts.

Altruism and Helping

Altruism refers to acts intended to aid others without obvious return benefit to the actor. Helping acts are common, yet they present both philosophical and logical problems for traditional thought about how people are motivated to act. The common view is that we are selfish. It makes no logical, mechanical sense to expend effort if there is no obvious personal reward. Yet, we do often help others. On what mechanisms may an explanation of helping acts be founded? Answers to this question require good descriptions of helping acts and their conditions. Under what conditions are we more or less likely to help someone else?

Bystander Apathy

A starting point for a mass of research on helping was the news story of a young woman's public murder. In 1964, a young woman was returning from work at about 3 a.m. to her home in Queens in New York City when she was attacked by a man with a knife. She was stabbed repeatedly, and she screamed. Some 38 neighbors heard her cries and some watched from their windows, but none of them came to help or called the police as she was murdered.

This scene is described in virtually every discussion of helping and altruism because of the dramatic failure of anyone to help a person obviously in need. An immediate interpretation was that people in big eastern cities have become callous and indifferent to the plight of others. That may be partly true, but it is not the whole cause.

Research was quickly formed around the model of that incident, concluding, contrary to common wisdom, that the presence of others makes it less likely that any specific individual will help. Researchers used contrived psychology lab studies, and they staged events elsewhere. They had smoke pour into a room where students were working (Darley & Latané, 1968), arranged for them to hear an apparent accident over an intercom (Latané & Rodin, 1969), staged an epileptic seizure (Darley & Latané, 1968; Schwartz & Clausen, 1970), and played a fake robbery in a liquor store (Latané & Darley, 1970). Bystanders were more likely to help if they were alone than if someone else was present.

When *are* we likely to help? If we feel competent, we are more likely to help, even if this feeling was just recently developed in an experiment by, say, success at a task. Also, if we have low self-esteem, we may be more likely to help under conditions where we can thereby raise our self-esteem. And, we may be more ready to help if we are in a good mood. Christmas music and decorations produce charity in the holiday season. Experiments show that being offered food or letting us find money increases the chance that we will then help someone (Isen & Leven, 1972).

When are we likely to remain a victim without help? A reputable-appearing victim generally has a better chance of getting help, but we are also more likely to be helped by people like ourselves. One study had both informally dressed and more formally dressed people solicit money on the street from people who were also dressed each way. The passersby were more likely to help the solicitor who was dressed more like they were (Emswiller, Deaux, & Willits, 1971).

Apathy Analyses

Many reasons were proposed by researchers for failing to help others, using diverse theoretical ideas. One reason, **audience inhibition,** suggests that if others are present, we are slower to act because of concern about evaluation of our acts. The audience of others keeps us from venturing any unusual acts. Perhaps, we may think, the smoke is not really an emergency. What would others think if we caused a great excitement without cause? Wouldn't we look foolish to act rashly?

A second, related reason is **social influence.** We watch others to see how they are acting. Each of us follows the lead of the others around us. The result may be that everyone tries to be cool and nonchalant, and the whole group will fool itself into believing that there is no emergency, no need to help.

Diffusion of responsibility is a third reason for failing to help others. Psychologically, we may feel a need to help if there is no other person present at the scene of need. If other people are present, however, there is less pressure for any single individual to act. The responsibility is spread among everyone. Hence, we each feel less pressure, creating the possibility that nobody will act.

Some theorists have also proposed that people weigh the relative costs and benefits of getting involved. Helping others carries the potential costs of inconvenience, unpleasantness, and actual danger. The cost of not helping may be one's feelings of guilt and possible scorn from others. Some first aid instructors recommend you ask conscious victims if they want help before you give assistance, lest you be sued later. Benefits of helping may be a feeling of greater self-esteem, praise from others, or thanks.

Another idea psychologists have used to understand victim characteristics is called the **just-world hypothesis** (Lerner, 1977). Some people believe we bring our problems on ourselves and so judge the world as fair, with the result that they think people get what they deserve. Thus, if we share this notion, we are unwilling to help others because we think that people in trouble are getting what they have earned.

Victims who are clearly dependent on the helper get more help. An extreme case is a baby in distress; almost everyone feels a need to help. Or if a boat has capsized and those in the water are crying for help, they are likely to get it. On the other hand, victims without obvious dependency are not likely to be helped.

Another view of victims uses the norm of reciprocity. If a person is known to have given help to others in the past, then this person is more likely to get help in the future. Tests have shown that if persons are seen refusing to help others, others will subsequently not help them (Regan, cited in Freeman, Sears, & Carlsmith, 1978). If the victims have given help to others, they are even more likely to be helped if it is apparent that their help to others was voluntary rather than forced.

Other people's influence contributes to the result of helping. One such factor in a situation is modeling. Having an example of helping produces help. In one study, two disabled cars with women drivers were positioned along the side of a busy street. Someone was helping the first driver part of the time. Some 58 people stopped to help the second woman after they saw the first being helped; only 35 stopped when neither woman was being helped (Bryan & Text, 1967). A similar effect can be demonstrated with charitable giving. Seeing others give promotes generosity.

General ideas about the setting and circumstances provide a general context for one's likelihood of helping. The big city setting discourages helping, because we believe the social norm is to keep a distance from others and not trust them. This attitude is reinforced by the prevailing belief in frequent crime, suggesting a high potential risk and cost to any social interaction with strangers.

The city also has a dominant pattern of a great deal of activity, which makes any one event masked or even unnoticed. A personal style of moving quickly and disregarding the surrounds keeps us from helping. One study showed that people told to hurry to another place were less likely to help someone who was apparently in need of aid. Those people in a hurry were theology students who were going to another building to deliver a lecture on Good Samaritanism (Darley & Bateson, 1973).

Of course, the most curious situation factor is the presence of bystanders. The more of us in the situation, the less any one of us will help.

One logical approach to the nature of helping others (Latané & Darley, 1970) is to describe it as a perception-cognition problem having a chain of several identifiable steps: perception, interpretation, analysis, decision, and action. Helping will occur only if the complete chain is unbroken. First, there must be a perception that something noteworthy has happened. If we don't hear the gunshots, we will not act to help someone who might be shot. Second, the perception must be interpreted. Having heard several loud sharp sounds, we might interpret them as gunshots or a car backfiring. Only if the perception is interpreted as a real danger are we likely to help someone. Next, if there is a correct interpretation that someone needs help, there must then be an analysis of the situation. Whose responsibility is it to help? We must see the situation as requiring our personal at-

tention. Then we must make a decision about what to do. Should we call for others to aid, perform some act, or what? Finally, we must act in what has been decided to be the best manner.

Crowd Acts and Mobs

Why do people in groups sometimes do things in common and in concert with one another, things they might not do themselves? The question regards our collective acts in crowds. The title of this section is biased and may be part of the problem. Our focus has been on socially disruptive and often violent crowds. One of the oldest spirited questions of social psychology asks what makes up the acts of a crowd. Two views have arisen from different philosophical (and political) assumptions. Is a crowd and its actions merely the sum of individuals, each acting according to individual principles, or does the crowd constitute a new reality including some sort of group mind that suppresses the collective minds of those making it up?

In the last century, Gustav LeBon (1895/1960) described crowd acts in terms of an emerging group mind. To him, the crowd produced a group mind that was qualitatively different from the minds of those making it up. His real concern was with the destructive, primitive acts committed by people in crowds. LeBon emphasized the instinctual and emotional causes of those crowd acts. He believed that individuals in a crowd were subjected to three basic alterations of their personal control: deindividuation, contagion, and suggestibility. Being a part of the crowd leads us to feel free from our usual personal responsibilities. We are freed from part of our self-control, and this is **deindividuation.** As deindividuated people, we act out our more primitive impulses. The **contagion** of the crowd is a kind of sameness of interests and urges through a mutual imitation. One way that contagion spreads is by suggestions from others, and being in crowds, we take suggestions more readily.

Many others have kept these deindividuation ideas alive (e.g., Festinger, Pepitone, & Newcomb, 1952; Moscovici, 1985; Zimbardo, 1969). When we try to understand social order and disorder, such views of common madness are satisfying and shift blame. Even though we see ourselves as well-formed individuals, we all have predispositions waiting for an opportunity. Our unconscious frustrations, bigotry, or childlike irresponsibility are waiting to be released. Presence in a crowd is the opportunity that we cannot resist. That is the way we excuse what we have done or might do. The blame is then shifted to the circumstances forming our predispositions or to the setting of opportunity.

Our usual thought about crowd and mob acts concerns antisocial acts, but do the same principles seem to describe many religious services, community sandbagging to control flooding, and military acts of battle? In these acts, the collective mind forms the cultural traditions of a people. Included in this collective mind are our common ways of thinking, feeling, and acting, producing positive functioning groups. Such positive groups attend to common activities with similar feelings, respond to the expressed thoughts of others,

and have an awareness of the whole group. Thus, the sense of mental continuity or group mind also produces the finer acts of humanity. But we steer away from language of deindividuation, contagion, and suggestion in describing such gatherings. Instead, we talk of commitment and sacrifice to the common good. The social values are different, but are the underlying causes any different?

In all studies of groups in action, it is important to begin with solid information of exactly what is happening. Recent study of specific events has questioned some of the common assumptions we have (such as those we reviewed above) about what is done in civil disruption (McPhail & Wohlstein, 1983; Wright, 1978). Modern studies show that people do not lose control, there is no evidence of a psychological state different from that of observers, and most of what members of a group do is not extraordinary (McPhail, 1991). Explanation must build from a solid base of what actually happens and from a wider range of evidence (Gaskell, 1990), rather than from assumptions designed to separate mob acts politically from the socially preferred order.

SECTION SUMMARY: SOCIAL ORDER DISRUPTION

Two patterns of disrupted social order are bystander apathy and acts of crowds. Bystander apathy is the flip side of altruism, in which we fail to help people in seeming need. Several sets of explanations have been proposed, including being influenced by others present, feeling less responsible because others are there, considering costs and benefits of helping, believing people get what they deserve or do not need to be

helped, having models of helping or not helping, and seeing whether the overall circumstances are ones of helping or ignoring others. Acts of mobs have been thought to be partly a matter of losing one's individual self-image and control, being responsive to what others are doing, and following an example of what to do. Crowd acts can be either negative or constructive.

BOUND TO THE MAJORITY

On the face of it, everyone is bound to the majority. The ways of social conduct described above document what is obvious. Much of our majority conduct is useful and necessary, although some appears contrary to the general good and welfare of individuals or the group. Certainly, no one can escape entirely the majority influence. The next step is to discover the workings of that social influence. Some good ideas have come from studying influences of majorities in social psychology laboratories.

Influence Experiments and Analyses

Conformity to what a majority is doing is perhaps the primary feature of our social acts. The psychologists' questions are of how conformity is evidenced, its strengths, its limits, and its exceptions. A large bundle of research papers has been produced in answering these questions, and some of the findings have been shocking to our collective human self-image. It is disturbing to find how easily we are led to conform to what others are doing, especially in view of our Western world social image of personal freedom and individuality.

Among the best known of the studies of **conformity** are those that presented a simple perceptual judgment to people in a setting in which others had already made public their choices. Solomon Asch (1952) began those studies intending to show that we will not be socially influenced against the evidence of our senses. In his studies, he asked people to tell which of three lines was equal in length to a fourth. The perceptual task was not difficult, but everyone else in a small group in the laboratory made the same, apparently wrong, choice. These other people were actually confederates of the experimenter but appeared to be just other volunteers. Over the 12 opportunities in the experimental sessions, four in five people agreed with that majority at least once; conformity was 33% overall. Such conformity was found with as few as three other judges. Perceptual judgments of control observers working alone were in error only 7% of the time.

The reference studies of **compliance** or **obedience** come from the work of Stanley Milgram. Milgram (1974) recruited volunteers from college classes and from public settings to aid in his research, advertised to be the effect of punishment on learning. Everyone in the setting except the volunteer was a confederate of the experimenter, although they were presented as and appeared also to be volunteers. One person was to be the learner and was placed in another room, and all watched while shock electrodes were applied. A second person presented the learning material, and a third tested the learner's memory of it. The real volunteer was to deliver the shock that was the lowest that the three trainers had specified. The machine could deliver different shock levels, ranging upward at 15 volt intervals to 450 v. Of course, no shocks were actually delivered, but the learner responded with appropriate complaints and cries as the shock level was increased. If there were signs of faltering, the shock-delivering volunteer was instructed with messages to the effect that the experiment requires that they continue. The measure of compliance was the strongest shock that was delivered.

About 60% of college undergraduates gave the full range of voltage. In various populations, full compliance with the demands of the experiment ranged up to 83%. Various details of the setting were changed in different tests. Compliance was greater if the research was sponsored by a more prestigious institution, if the instructing experimenter was seated close to the volunteer, or if the learner was remote from the real volunteer.

Psychologists have proposed a variety of theory mechanisms to account for social conformity. One is **social comparison.** Social comparison is the idea that we use the acts of others to guide our own. Allen Funt's *Candid Camera* television show often had a group of people doing the same, unusual thing such as standing in an elevator facing the rear. The victim also would face the rear of the car, yielding to the example of the others as the standard for what one is to do. Such social comparison is especially strong when those others are believed to be similar to oneself.

A related idea about conformity is self-awareness. We are uncomfortable when we are made aware of our acts and at that point are most likely to do what others are doing. Self-awareness discomfort is eased by reducing our uniqueness.

There are many details that have been worked out in related studies of conformity and compliance. Some factors increase and some decrease the effects, but the conformity and compliance are there. We do conform, and we do comply with the actions and wishes of others. The majority does bind.

Mechanisms of Influence

Some analyses have been proposed for why we conform to groups. For example, if we are alone, we need help in understanding the surroundings. When cues are weak in the world about what to do, we form our acts on what others are doing. Social reality becomes the standard and the model. Asch, Milgram, Funt, and others have made that unmistakable. Furthermore, the less clearly we see the world, the stronger is the social influence from others. Groups of others are assumed to be correct. They are stable and powerful forces. To think otherwise is to question the fact of stability and the necessity of rules of order. The greater the uncertainty that we have, the more likely that social influence will be effective.

Social control within each group comes from its members knowing and following group norms. Dependence on the group follows from each individual's needs for information, especially about and from others. Even the idea of having clear information and ideas is part of the social norm of influence. These principles are the foundation of traditional descriptions of social functioning of groups and their influence on individuals. This perspective is heavily biased toward the stability and correctness of the group and its leaders.

In shifting to social reality in order to know the world environment, collective truths of groups are established and defended (Festinger, 1950). Social groups and their acts don't just spontaneously happen, nor are they capricious. The ways of a people form over time and in complex ways. In part, social norms evolve by democratic process and by consensus, but a major part comes also from the interests of the leaders. Groups, leaders, and their interests define normality.

An individual always has less power than the social group. That is seen in attempts by one or a few to be different or to change something. Any individual or dissenting group will have little such influence and will be devalued by the majority. If the dissenting members persist, their views will be seen as deviant and in error. Furthermore, that opposition is a mark of their inferiority. Resistance to group influence by low-power dissenters is not seen as legitimate interest in change but instead as maladaptation. Those dissenting must give up and conform or get out.

Changes do happen in group norms. Change by the majority is assumed to be an evolutionary process within its functioning, but that remains an unspecified mystery that is rarely directly examined. Innovative change is valued, but it can only be done by those in power. Nonconformity is always unpopular unless it is judged by other norms as also elitist—that is, in some way better or more powerful. Leaders and those judged to be of higher social station can hold different ideas and be judged eccentric and creative. Low-power and low-class people are said to be out of line and deviant. We will see this working in the social and political history of addictive substances in Chapter 11, "Addiction."

The politics of social scientists emerge as we examine these questions. The direction of social science questions has consistently favored the powerful; those in power want no views that see dissenters any way but in error. Resistance by groups and their leaders, pressuring for change, is ignored in the bulk of social science. The interests of most social scientists have remained with that of the power group and its preservation, and each topic is viewed from that perspective, both in evaluating the issues and in constructing theory.

Seductions of Dissent

The overview at the beginning of the chapter stated that influence is both a matter of being obliged to conform to social order and of being changed to a new or different order. Geneviève Paicheler (1988) views these issues of influence as being on several dimensions. She contrasts gentle persuasion versus strong suggestion, conformity to the normal majority versus innovation by deviant dissenters, and public versus private acceptance. The usual flow of social conduct is formed of gentle persuasion of public acts to the style of a majority. Added to this are the dynamics of dissenting people and their ideas.

Social influence is founded on two themes: avoiding the ambiguity of information and conforming to the social group. Individuals who attempt nonconforming acts or suggest change to the group are thought to be generating conflict. Conflict is abhorred. Conflict is thought to be unnatural, undesirable, and in need of elimination. Conflict or any of the differences that brought it about are seen as marks of deviance. Deviance itself also must be removed or controlled. The difficulty in these views of conflict and deviance is that they describe change as it is idealized, not as it is likely to happen. Conflict is really part of the way that groups function.

Conflict

In traditional social psychology study of groups, the major responsibility for everything is with the individual. Each person is assumed to desire a stable place in the several social groups he or she encounters, and this desire is formed on needs that are assumed but not clearly explained. When conflict happens, it is repaired by changes in individuals. Conflict is thought to be caused by nonconforming acts and can be removed only by changing those acts to be in accord with the public acts of the group.

Another view is that social order is always just a temporary balance of competing interests. Conflict is a natural part of social reality. Change in each system comes from conflict's tensions. Conflict is a part of the structure to which individuals respond with changed judgments and acts. The process is not just aimed at prevention or reconciliation of the conflict but also at accommodating it. All members of the group and the challenging dissenters are changed in their thoughts about what is the new social reality (Simmel, 1955). This model is one of constant change in which social order and balance are just labels for one position within that process.

Those holding a dissenter's social position, however, face the general view of the leaders of the majority, that only the dissenters will change or be excluded. Leaders do not want to have their supporting reality questioned. But by insisting on their position, members of the dissenting group make themselves even more visible. If they are to be dealt with by the majority, the dissenting group's views must be part of the majority's agenda.

Deviance

One way that dissenters' views are eliminated is making those holding them appear deviant and thus separate. "This has been a hunter's lodge for 20 years. Those two with their environmental ideas even wear funny T-shirts. We don't want their kind here." Deviation is without doubt a logical concept of fact, but it also has strong connotative meaning of being undesirable. To be deviant is to be in an uncomfortable position with negative connotations (Moscovici, 1976). From the perspective of the group, a deviant must be changed or removed (Festinger, 1950).

Yet, from the individual perspective of each group member, these general ideas about deviance apply only to others, never to the self. Group members prize their own uniqueness but see that of others as deserving of rejection. They put those deviants in an inferior class but at the same time see them as responsible for their acts and for their being rejected from the group. "Those tree-huggers brought it on themselves. We better not let any more like them in the lodge." For all that the deviance is said to threaten the group, it tends also to force the majority group members to be even more closely joined (Paicheler, 1988; Schachter, 1951).

If the dissenters from the majority group resist being changed and attempts to reject them as undesirable deviants will not work, the only alternative is to deal with the issues that they propose. The agenda is now controlled at least partly by the dissenters. "Mike and Pat want us to listen to their idea of keeping that swamp by the industrial park. We're a hunting group and it's none of our business, but let's let 'em talk about it for awhile." It is from the conflict of these interactions that change is enabled. Even if their intent is just to eliminate the dissent, the majority must now consider the merits and possibly the foundation beliefs on which the dissent is based. For their part, those presenting the dissent must establish that they are involved in the dissent, that they have a different position of which they are certain, and that they will not be changed in it. That strength of individual position in fact reflects the individual autonomy each group member implicitly holds, and that is attractive.

At this point, it becomes clear that there are factors in group influence that are on the surface and others that are unrealized potentials. Going along with the social majority is a matter of influence on the surface. We can easily act as others do and profess to believe what they say without actually having personal agreement with them. "We've voted down Mike and Pat's petition. Now let's hear no more about it in the lodge." These are public acts of imitation rather than real influence, and they need not have effects that persist outside that situation.

The influence potential of a dissenting position can reach beneath the surface to change our private potential. By presenting a problem, the dissent invites further study and the potential for change. The new view becomes a matter of curiosity and can be operating a long time after the stimulating situation has passed. As a dissenter, if we are in conflict with a majority, the conflict passes as soon as the required acts in the situation are made and forgotten. As a majority group member in conflict with a credible dissent, however, we are left with a nagging problem. The problem and conflict remain and motivate change that continues to collectively alter the majority. "I'm not so sure Mike and Pat didn't have a good idea last month. Now those developers want to build in the Barton tract where we've all hunted for years. Let's see if we can get a petition drive going to stop it. Where're Mike and Pat?"

SECTION SUMMARY:
BOUND TO THE MAJORITY

The focus of most social science has been on goals of keeping the order while minimizing conflict. We are surprised how strongly we are led to conform to what others are doing, to defer obediently to their requests, and to guide our actions in ambiguous situations according to what others are doing. These are factors in keeping order, but they also make it difficult to account for the changes that do happen.

Conflicting intentions and actions are handled by the majority attempting to marginalize or expel the offending dissenters. Change comes from credible dissenters holding their position yet giving in to majority order. The ideas and logic of the dissent will remain to influence individuals and eventually build to successful change. Thus, to make effective changes, present a credible dissenting view while remaining a part of the group.

TABLE 9.2 Summary of Mechanisms of Influence

	Being Influenced	*Influencing Others*
Authority	Follow the power signs	Use "experts" and power signs
Attraction	Be like attractive others	Show how they can be attractive
Conformity	Do what others do	Display others/everyone "doing it"
Commitment	Show consistency	Lead them in positive steps
Reciprocation	Appear to be fair	Make them feel obligated

PRACTICAL SOCIAL INFLUENCES

The practice of social influence includes both the ideas of conformity to a group and the more subtle effects of dissent. We have considered the many ways that people are influenced by the groups of which they are a part. Now we examine some ways that people intentionally influence others to behave according to a plan. The means of influence typically take advantage of our adherence to group order and standards, although the forces of dissent can also be harnessed.

We look at five mechanisms of influence in this section: authority, attraction, conformity, commitment, and reciprocation (see Table 9.2). The basic pattern of topics and ideas follows Robert Cialdini's (1984) popular book of applied social psychology, *Influence*. Many possible arenas of influence use these mechanisms, including political manipulation and changing of personal attitudes, but the topics of consumer influence, being so common and important in Western society, make the best illustrations.

Authority

We obey and defer to authority. Authority is a broad concept with many facets and features. Influence comes from the many ways we have come to accept the lead of others whom we presume to have something better than we have. The influence comes in part from having accepted our position. It may be involved with feelings of inferiority or help-lessness. We may have simply learned that rewards come from those in authority. Whatever the mechanisms, authority works to influence.

Power Sources of Authority

Everyone starts in the world in a helpless condition. Caregivers have powers of giving life and comfort. As we mature, we come to associate our well-being and comfort with being rewarded by these caregivers. That is, the caregivers' natural power is reinforced in countless ways. The power of authority applies broadly to the many other elders we meet while still young. By the time we reach adulthood, we are thoroughly indoctrinated. We defer to the authority of those who communicate the appropriate, natural power signs.

This is a plausible account of the origin of the power forms of authority. The exact signs of authority that we have learned will be somewhat different, yet, there are many in common. There are great numbers of signals of authority and power that function in the normal affairs of society. We respond to size, looks, dress, titles, degrees, wealth, position, expertise, and all similar cues. Anything that indicates greater power gives authority.

Advertisers select appropriate experts and professionals to present their products. A famous test pilot promotes automobile engine-care products. Athletes proclaim the invigorating benefits of a soft drink. Most often, the expertise is simulated by the model. A person appearing to be a plumber promotes a drain cleaner. The scientist presents the charts showing the speed of action of different pain medications. Sometimes, the connection is even more remote but no less effective because of prior association. The actor Robert Young reminded viewers of his longtime starring role as *Marcus Welby, M.D.* as he appeared in countless ads for decaffeinated coffee. He noted that he was an actor, but he used the medical doctor image associated with him from years of acting.

Compliance

We reviewed the Milgram compliance-obedience studies. These are a clear measure of the motivational pressure to defer to authority. Little more than the prestige of research scientists and their statement that the plan is to continue was sufficient to lead people to comply with torturing another person. Compliance is the carrying out of actions directed by an authority.

We are unaware of much of our compliance. We respond automatically in a manner of deference and obedience to the authority signs. It is the nature of this mechanism of social influence that makes it unnecessary to think through and logically decide the proper acts in each encounter. It is one way that the cognitive involvement of social relationships is simplified. Most of the time such compliance serves personal ends. It keeps order and allows us to make rapid social decisions.

Problems arise in those infrequent instances when we should not defer to the authority signals. When should we not comply? How can we learn to make rapid distinctions between legitimate and suspect power signals? These, too, are some of the topics of becoming an adult and being educated. As we learn to respond to authority, so, too, we acquire experiences that give clues to false authority. One domain of suspicion is contexts in which, by definition, some people are attempting to influence others. Advertising, recruiting, selling, politics, and religious outreach are all such domains. With experience and education, we begin to understand the methods of these social activities and look for indications that authority might be used to get automatic, unthinking compliance.

Attraction

We try to be like those we admire. Underlying attraction is the subtlety of identifying ourselves with others and trying to model them. We all hold several models of who and what we would like to be. Admired people are those who fit those models. The models change with the images of current fashion, with momentary experiences of others, with changing life ideals, and with spontaneous ideas acquired. There are three ideas here. First, we will always have an idea of what we would prefer to be like. Second, there are multiple and overlapping models ready in mind that can be called out with appropriate cues. Third, we will do things that make ourselves more like those models.

We can be influenced by suggestions from our models. Of course, there are some general models that everyone shares. Most people would prefer to be attractive in appearance by cultural standards, healthy, in the company of similar others, powerful, and capable of the most current fashionable ideas and activities. Any of these features influence.

Consumers will be influenced by showing appropriate models using a product. Attractive, likable people are employed to endorse the product. Use of an attractive endorser can be particularly effective for issues or products that are relatively low in personal relevance or for issues and products about which the consumer has little prior information. We form our opinion on the basis of the kind of others we see associated with the product. As consumers, we like the endorser, so we also like the product.

Soft drink television ads frequently show a series of rapid images of attractive people doing exciting things and consuming the product. Print media ads for tobacco products have a great precision in selecting images of attractive people displaying an admired style or flair of behavior. In political contests where other factors are not dominant, attractive candidates usually win (to the point where objection has been raised to using only pictures without other messages).

Another influence of attraction is presentation of the message that purchasing the product will make us more attractive or desirable. Blatant ads show people enhancing their social lives dramatically with a breath mint or a bath soap. More subtle ads convey hints of an image that we would like to project to others—the Marlboro man was very successful. A related but subtle use of attraction involves autonomy and uniqueness. A particularly effective ad makes a product appear to be desired by almost everyone but indicates that only a few can have it. Sometimes this is done by showing a product as desirable but too expensive for the average person. In other ads, the product is made to appear to be scarce, and thus owning it makes one unique.

Attraction has also been used effectively in an active sense. Trading on the fact that attraction is based on positive regard, we can be influenced by expressions of positive regard. Salespeople who project an image of liking their customers do very well in influencing them to buy. One highly successful car salesperson regularly sent out postcards to past customers and potential customers he never met, saying nothing more than that he liked them and that he sells cars (Cialdini, 1984). The short duration of the sales encounter is well suited to a well-acted role of positive regard.

Conformity

We do what others are doing. Conformity is the fundamental concept of public influence. It is a social rule that normally serves very well. We follow the cues of others' acts to guide our own. Logically, conformity is a necessary convenience to aid a limited cognitive capacity. Conforming to the model of others' acts frees us from having to think through the exact details of what to do in each situation. We can see that others are doing all right, and their acts become our model. Conformity by the many also prevents social chaos. It is effectively used in crowd control in well-managed amusement parks and related situations. With gentle suggestions to the first people to arrive, the pattern is set that is followed by all those to follow. In short, there are many good reasons for conforming.

Influencing others with conforming is similar to mechanisms of authority and following the lead of attractive models. We can be led by what others are doing. A common theme of advertising is to use testimonials from people portrayed as average users of the product. Hidden cameras and direct interviews are simulated to appear natural, and average-looking people give their endorsements.

The mechanism of conformity is also used by associating a product with a large number of endorsers. This gives the consumer the message that everyone is buying the product. Crowds of people are shown demanding a product in television ads.

Entertainment media provide simulation of audience reaction (laugh tracks) to lead viewers to know that the program is to be enjoyed. Fashionable talk-show hosts have audiences selected for their enthusiasm or prepare them in warm-up sessions to be responsive to the program's content, or both. Historically, this practice dates to the early 1800s in Italian operas, where people were paid by performers to clap, cheer, and so on, according to a fee schedule. Related, too, is the use of the "salted" tip dish. Indications of the expected tip are placed in view for arriving customers. If a dollar is expected, the dish is partially filled with ones with a few fives, and any coins offered are immediately removed from view. People will conform to what others are doing and what others have apparently done.

An interesting use of conformity is aimed in the apparently reverse direction. Advertisements for a bathroom tissue suggested that people were not to squeeze the product in the store. Of course, the pitch was that everyone wanted to do just that. Once a package is touched, it is also likely to be purchased.

Commitment

We honor our commitments to others. Promises are kept. Actions are completed in a manner consistent with past actions and self-images. We try to keep the appearance of being consistent in our thoughts and acts. These consistencies have been socially rewarded. Society rules state that promises are to be kept and lies are wrong. Inconsistent actions are the performance equivalent of lying. Everyone is expected to carry through in the direction that their past acts have indicated.

Once we make a statement or complete an act, we are strongly motivated to continue in that direction. Thus, we can be influenced by getting us started. Initiation rites are an initial commitment to a group and serve to strengthen bonds to it. Simple agreement with a statement, or beginning the first step in a chain, is often enough to motivate and direct the flow of later acts. Salespeople often lead customers to make a beginning commitment to buying a product through a very attractive offer. That commitment to buy is strengthened by a series of preparation activities like filling in sales contracts, selecting color, choosing style of features of the product, setting up delivery arrangements, and the like. At this point, the customer has a strong psychological commitment to buy and is vulnerable to changes toward products that would not have been attractive initially. The "low-ball" sale is essentially a scheme of denying the availability of the promoted product at the agreed price because, for example, "the manager wouldn't approve it." The committed customer is led to accept a somewhat higher price. In "bait-and-switch" sales, the advertised product is not available ("Just sold the last one a few minutes ago") and the customer is switched to a more expensive one.

An interesting variation is the salesperson who greets a customer with the information that there are no more of the advertised products left but says there just may be one hidden somewhere in the warehouse and asks if the customer would buy it if it could be found. The agreement is made and, of course, after a suitable wait, the "last one" is discovered (among the dozens yet to be sold with the same ruse during the day).

Reciprocation

We balance our actions with those of others. We want to appear to be fair. If something is done for us, we want to return an action of equal value. This equity is a part of the social structure. We have learned that we can only have those rights that we also give to others. Automatically, a standard of fairness is applied to social dealings. If someone offers something, something is given in return. The pattern is seen in holiday seasonal giving. People who offer a gift must be given an appropriate return.

Reciprocation takes many forms in consumer influence. Small samples are offered in grocery stores to place an obligation on the customer. The social face of the event is to sample the flavor or quality, but the effect is to make the customer obligated to reciprocate, and the only action open is purchase of the product. Even when the purchase is not made immediately, there is a residual obligation of "owing something" to that product in future decisions. Companies making sales directly to the home often have salespeople leave packages of products as free gifts. In later visits, the customer is reminded of the gifts and asked how they were liked. Again, the samples become a social obligation to reciprocate by making a purchase.

Salespeople can also build an obligation by working hard to aid the customer and giving good service. It is much more difficult to leave a store empty-handed when the salesperson has tried hard to find what was wanted and has demonstrated various possibilities. The more information and aid one has received, the greater is the obligation to find something to buy to balance it. At the least, we will return to that store regularly.

SECTION SUMMARY:
PRACTICAL SOCIAL INFLUENCES

We conclude the social influence chapter by examining three typical vehicles of social influence. In each case, there is a personal motivational principle or rule. We obey and defer to authority. We try to be like those we admire. We do what others are doing. We honor our commitments to others. We balance our actions with those of others. These make up the mechanisms of authority, attraction, conformity, commitment, and reciprocation.

CHAPTER CONCLUSIONS

The overriding principle of social motivation is order. We think, make rules, and act so as to keep social order. That order extends to ourselves. We treat our own social disorder, potential disorder, and defense of selfhood with an elaborate set of rules of presentation and accounting for those events. Still, most social life has elements of disorder. In the cases of bystander apathy and mob actions, we see the rules seemingly being broken, at least at the high level of what abstract society should be like. Yet, at the individual level, those same actions can be reckoned as personally consistent and orderly. We disdain conflict when it appears in our social groups, leading us to eject or set aside those who dissent. At the same time, a credible position presented within the rules is admired and remembered. From these seeds, there is an eventual change of thought and group rules. Influencing others and being influenced by them builds on a number of basic principles that reduce to each of us trying to build an attractive and consistent self-picture.

Study and Review Questions

1. What is the basic principle on which influence is founded?

2. Where do we get our rules, manners, and fashions of social acting?

3. Why do we follow these rules, manners, and fashions of social acting?

4. What motivating mechanism guides these rules, manners, and fashions of social acting?

5. What are the two facework types, and what form of social problems do they solve?

6. For what purpose do we use defensive practices of facework?

7. How do we accomplish defensive practices of facework?

8. Who initiates protective practices of facework?

9. How do we accomplish protective practices of facework?

10. What are the four kinds of motive talk?

11. What is the motive talk called a request asking for?

12. When is a disclaimer given?

13. How do each of the motive talk disclaimers differ?

14. What is the key element of the apology form of motive talk?

15. What is the purpose of the account form of motive talk?

16. What is the theme of an excuse form of motive talk?

17. What is the theme of a justification form of motive talk?

18. What is the theme of a concession form of motive talk?

19. What is the theme of a refusal form of motive talk?

20. What are the varieties/degrees of attributions of responsibility?

21. What is the key situation element of bystander apathy?

22. What are the nine or so different proposed reasons for failing to help?

23. What are LeBon's classic elements of mob acts?

24. What are the three classic experimental demonstrations of influence?

25. Why is it often practical to follow social influence?

26. Who normally makes changes in what a group does?

27. How does the group typically treat dissenters proposing new ideas?

28. With what strategy can the dissenters influence the group?

29. On what common personal history do power cues build their social influence power?

30. On what motivational basis does attraction influence us?

31. How can conformity be used to influence others?

32. What is the social motivation power behind using strategies of commitment?

33. What is the social motivation power behind using strategies of reciprocation?

34. How do we respond to gifts?

CHAPTER 10

Motivated Cognition

From the simple commonsense truth that everyone is conscious, we note that conscious awareness seems to each of us what is most real; it appears in a continuous flow, yet it is packaged in episodes of attention focused on ourselves and others in our social life.

What are the biological bases of consciousness? How can we make things happen with our mind? Current theories of these old puzzles of mind and body attempt to picture answers in the domain of natural science.

Some other aspects of awareness appear at its margins, in varieties of meditation and hypnosis. Are these really different mind states and abilities?

Solving puzzles and other kinds of active thinking are based on adaptations designed to solve consistent social puzzles. Limitations on our thinking and the errors we make reflect the brain's finite capacity to direct a few things at a time.

Experiencing Consciousness

Theorizing Mind

Controlling Awareness

Thinking

Awareness is personal conscious experience. We perceive our surrounds with an awareness of certain important and changing features. Most important to us are (a) objects and events necessary for personal care and (b) the acts of other people. Awareness also includes (c) our own acts, our self-acting-in-the-world; and (d) awareness of potential for acting in worlds-to-be (see Figure 10.1). Furthermore, we know (e) that other people have similar awareness; we assume that water and sticks do not, and deciding whether there is similar awareness in other life forms that move about is a problem. These are some basic phenomena of human folk psychology with which any compe-

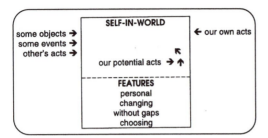

Figure 10.1. A representation of elements of our phenomenal world.

tent and complete natural science of mental life must deal. The view we have of these common happenings is one important foundation to understanding motivated cognition.

EXPERIENCING CONSCIOUSNESS

According to those building psychology 100 years ago, reliable and valid mental observations can be made. They can be verified by each person's repeated observation, verifiable in principle by others willing to follow the same protocol, and reported in standard communications. We can search our personal experience for regularly occurring features and communicate those observations to others. These were thought to make up a part of the unique subject matter of psychology.

In such a manner, William James began the substance of his 1890 *Principles of Psychology* with descriptions of the experience of consciousness as a stream of thought. James's stream of thought was a metaphor for the continuous flow of awareness. James followed his compelling picture of stream-of-contents awareness with an account of the attention choices we seem to make in that stream, the essential selectivity of awareness. As real as these observations appear to us, there are legitimate questions about the ultimate source of consciousness awareness and its relations with our bodies.

Stream of Consciousness

The major features of conscious awareness are the same for everyone, although perhaps with some personal differences. We describe primary features in fairly consistent language. William James (1890) put it this way in his chapter "The Stream of Thought":

> How does it go on? We notice immediately five important characters in the process, of which it shall be the duty of the present chapter to treat in a general way:
> 1) Every thought tends to be a part of a personal consciousness.
> 2) Within each personal consciousness thought is always changing.
> 3) Within each personal consciousness thought is sensibly continuous.
> 4) It always appears to deal with objects independent of itself.
> 5) It is interested in some parts of these objects to the exclusion of others, and welcomes or rejects—chooses from among them, in a word—all the while. (Vol. 1, p. 225)

James's description is that consciousness is personal, changing, without break, and choosing among objects other than itself.

After discussing each of these points at length, James presented a theoretical analogy to illustrate the observation that consciousness depends upon a sifting of information and selection of bits and pieces from a multitude of possibilities. As a sculptor works on a stone to bring out a statue, and as other sculptors may make other statues from the same block, one mind brings out one of many possible formations of consciousness. Other minds produce other formations from a similar world of experience.

Our minds have a great amount of stuff in common. We are alike in what we attend to, name, and relate. This fact is probably given by our common biological and cultural heritage. James (1890) writes, "The human race as a whole largely agrees as to what it shall notice and name, and what not" (Vol. 1, p. 289). He also notes one great difference between all minds: the distinction that each person makes between what is "me" and what is "not-me." We all focus our primary attention on our personal me. From this beginning, James elaborates the nature of the self and his treatment of many of the subjects of this chapter.

Personal Awareness

Attention labels a pattern of mental functioning. In common language, the word **attention** has two aspects complementing one another. Attention describes the awareness making up experienced perception and also labels the observable focus of perception. William James included both of these aspects of attention in his analysis of personal awareness.

His comments provide an overview. Again, James's (1890) words have a content that can't easily be expressed in a paraphrase.

> Millions of items of the outward order are present to my senses which never properly enter into my experience. Why? Because they have no interest for me. My experience is what I agree to attend to. Only those items that I notice shape my mind—without selective interest, experience is an utter chaos. (Vol. 1, p. 402)

> Everyone knows what attention is. It is the taking possession by the mind in clear and vivid form, of one out of what seem several simultaneous possible objects or trains of thought. Focalization, concentration, of consciousness are of its essence. It implies withdrawal from some things in order to deal effectively with others. (Vol. 1, pp. 403-404)

> Attention may be divided into kinds in various ways. It is either to
> a) Objects of sense (sensorial attention); or
> b) Ideal or represented objects (intellectual attention).

> It is either
> c) Immediate; or
> d) Derived: immediate, when the topic or stimulus is interesting in itself, without relation to anything else; derived, when it owes its interest to association with some other immediately interesting thing. What I call derived attention has been named "apperceptive" attention. Furthermore, Attention may be either
> e) Passive, reflex, non-voluntary, effortless; or
> f) Active and voluntary. (Vol. 1, p. 416)

We may use some examples to help clarify James's concepts. A sudden sound, sight, or touch would excite passive, immediate, sensorial attention. The quiet whistle of a friend trying to contact you would yield passive, derived, sensorial attention. Thinking of things you could do if you had a new car is passive, immediate, intellectual attention. Truly active or voluntary attention is difficult to hold for more than a few seconds before it lapses into a passive train of images, especially if the object does not change.

James's motivational dimension of attention is based on interest. He thus related the range of attentive acts to each person's structure of beliefs and experiences. Attention is focused by what one has come to believe. Personal interest is the summary of what each individual brings to the encounter. The uniqueness of the person is a necessary part of attention. Personal interest is a matter of being ready to perceive certain things and events. James (1890) writes of the power of the image in the mind being the perception. The images come from existing mental workings.

> The only things which we commonly see are those which we preperceive[,] and the only things which we preperceive are those which have been labeled for us, and the labels stamped in the mind. If we lost our stock of labels we should be intellectually lost in the midst of the world. (Vol. 1, p. 444)

```
┌─────────────────────────────────────────────┐
│   JAMES'S VIEW OF COMMON MENTAL EXPERIENCE    │
│  we know our stream of awareness in consciousness │
│             personal, changing, continuous, choosing │
│                          me versus not-me     │
│  we attend to what is interesting based on our personal beliefs │
└─────────────────────────────────────────────┘
```

Figure 10.2. William James's classical analysis

Not only is our attention formed by our interests, it depends on the labels we have acquired. We focus on things that connect with our experience. These are the ideas that William James gave us to introduce some of the general phenomena of consciousness (see Figure 10.2).

The nature of what is personally interesting is likely founded on our history as social beings. Some examples can be found in our common human attention to gossip.

Social Attention to Gossip

Being social beings, it seems likely that we would be naturally tuned to be aware of other people and their doings. Jerome Barkow's (1992) interesting thesis, which we will explore in this section, is that our attention to certain aspects of other people and their actions is a likely adaptation at the root of our mental interests. Communicating is one way that we reflect and elaborate our attentive interest. Communicating about others, to use a hard-line label, is **gossip,** a common human phenomenon.

Why do we gossip? The simple answer is to get information about other people. In our ancestry, this helped solve certain persistent problems of predicting and influencing the acts of (a) potential rivals for resources, (b) present and potential allies, (c) possible mates, (d) close kin (Barkow, 1992).

These ancestors acquired adaptations to use whatever information they had and could glean to build useful models of others who would have affected their breeding success. They would need to know about relatives, rivals, mates, partners in social exchanges, and very high-ranking people. They would need

to know their own and others' relative standing and anything that affects it, including information about control over resources, sexual activities, births and deaths, current alliances, friendships, political involvement, health, and reputation of reliability in social exchanges.

Comparable adaptations involve the reliability of the gossip. We favor information that makes us look good and our rivals look bad. Thus, we develop biases about what we say as well as what we like to listen to.

We remain interested in gossip about those same things. That interest is based on the adaptations that affected our ancestors' breeding success in a Pleistocene environment. How soundly someone is sleeping is not interesting; who they are sleeping with *is* interesting. Activities of people with whom we have no business are not interesting; those of relatives, business partners, and leaders *are* interesting. (See Figure 10.3.)

So why do we gossip about strangers on television screens with whom we are not kin nor who are likely in any way to affect us? Before mass media, a very recent condition, gossip was about real people, not strangers. Now, we build elaborate film, video, and printed stories about people who do not exist or do not really matter to us at all.

The answer appears from what we have just proposed. The media mimic the cues that trigger the Pleistocene adaptations. Strangers on the video or large screen or in the printed story are mistaken for people important to us. We had no reason to evolve mechanisms that sort among those people constantly close to us. Media personalities are in our bedrooms, our dining rooms, and throughout our daily activities, so we treat them as kin, friends, and rivals. Automatically, we are interested in the relevant information about them.

We may be embarrassed by this interest, but knowing of this natural interest is more likely to lead us to build systems to mask it rather than ignore it. This tendency becomes the basis for our "news" and "entertainment" industries, in which the importance of specific people and specific activities is magnified

OTHERS	ACTS	ARE INTERESTING
rivals allies mates kin leaders	wealth alliances sexual activity births/deaths health reputation power politics	
		makes us or mates or allies or kin look good or rivals look bad

Figure 10.3. Our adaptations to social information: Who and what is interesting?

and deemed of great value. We justify the interest by calling it a philosophical good named "current events."

We are interested in people with high rank, including politicians and leaders such as Bill Clinton, Newt Gingrich, and Queen Elizabeth; people who are wealthy such as Donald Trump and Bill Gates; media news personalities such as Connie Chung, Barbara Walters, and Tom Brokaw; and entertainment people such as David Letterman, Elizabeth Taylor, and Rush Limbaugh. Some people carry double value by appearing as potential mates, for example, Elvis, Madonna, Cindy Crawford, and Tom Selleck.

We find interesting their wealth, sexual activity, alliances, pairings, births and deaths, health, reputation, politics, and whatever else might affect our breeding success if they were a part of the group with which we shared resources and living space in ancestral times, the times when these factors influenced our ancestors' adaptations. These items become even more potent as they take the form of the information units of brains called memes that we will discuss later in the chapter.

Agency

We know that we do cause things to happen. Experiencing our mental life, combined with the acts that result, eventually produces the idea of our personal causal agency. We accept as patently true that we can make

things happen and that we do make things happen as a matter of our will. Personal assurance of our agency and personal causation is repeated in each voluntary act that we perform, ranging from a simple physical act of reaching out to grasp one object from among others to purely mental excursions, such as thinking of a blue unicorn. The many repetitions of similar experience under different conditions are no different in principle from experiments performed by laboratory scientists in, say, biochemistry. Based on these personal experiences, we each believe in our personal agency.

Explaining mental events such as these presents problems. As a matter of fact, we have our individual and collective beliefs in agency, and as facts, they cannot be disproved by evidence. But no matter how real our agency seems to us, we have no way of knowing its source in natural causes. The experience of causing things to happen is not valid evidence (or perhaps even a very good picture) of how they are caused. This seems to be an apparent standoff, but a resolvable one. We cannot grant priority to common experience as evidence of the causes of agency. Still, the very concept of agency rests in those informal experiments we each have performed in countless ways.

Some of our complex of ideas about agency concern that old problem we have visited before: the role of language. We all have mental experiences that are labeled by language agreement. More specific labels for some of those experiences can be collected into categories such as feeling, remembering, making decisions, and producing actions. These and other mind functions are real to everyone as experiences, and their word labels are fairly clear. There is no evidence to doubt that. The question is whether they are accurate descriptors of what is actually happening and if they are part of the cause of a motivated act.

Part of the sense we share is the appearance of our words causing some of our acts. It appears in how we describe ourselves and others. Standing in a line to purchase tickets, you see a person walk to the line, scowl, and push in. The events may be sufficient to produce anger. Labeling yourself as an angered person further defines the ways you will interpret the unfolding events and what may be done. The label feeds back into the situation as a new element of focus. You may then take direct action to confront the violator and correct the improper social action. If you had represented that happening as one calling up fear, then a different set of acts, like withdrawing or remaining quiet, would be justified as the situation is played out. The labeling with specific words may at least be partly causing the ongoing acts.

In that sense, pieces of our language are parts of situations and can be examined as evidence. Their functional role is a matter of empirical fact to be established. For example, they may really be causes or they may be just a description to ourselves afterward to justify what we did. It is important that we not make hasty judgments of causes.

We must also not methodically exclude language elements of personal description, as was commonly done by many theorists in the long era of behaviorism. The reason that individuals' accounts in language were purposefully ignored in much of psychology can be traced to the early period of psychology's history. Psychologists of 100 years ago, most clearly the structuralists and early functionalists, used reports of mental experiences improperly. They believed that our descriptions could (only) be used as direct and unimpeachable knowledge, if not statements of causes, of psychological states. In this thinking, if you reported that because you felt anger, you formed an intention to hurt the person blocking your path, then there were mental states of anger and intention that caused that aggressive action. The agent's account was viewed by these psychologists as a true statement of causes, verified by having others report experiences in similar situations.

Later behaviorists and modern psychologists alike object to that sort of introspective psychology of causes on many grounds. We can see some objections by looking at the pos-

sibilities in this example. First, the presence of the act is not determined by the agent's classifying it as such. Saying that one is angry does not make it so. The agent may be retrospectively justifying the acts or purposefully lying. Furthermore, to assume that our experiences are part of an act does not imply that they are causally sufficient or even necessary for it. Feeling that you were angry does not prove that your anger state caused the aggressive act. Accounts of mind are evidence to be considered and explained, not statements of causes.

Agent accounts have also been questioned because of the possibility of their being in error. Can people actually observe, use, and report their mental states? By answering no, some if not most psychologists, following the lead of behaviorists, rejected, for a long time, the entire idea of mental states and their use. We can see now that this position denies the obvious. It is possible to have valid observations of psychological states, and the prime evidence for that assertion is their successful use in our daily social interchange. It is absurd and incomprehensible to suggest that we are regularly mistaken about our psychological states and our verbal descriptions of them. On the other hand, mental experiences are neither complete nor without some error. Personal accounts of psychological states are likely to be partial at best, and of course, any assertion of true causality in which they play a role must be verified by further study just as any other natural dimension of events.

There are no philosophical problems in using psychological states in an objective manner. The practical difficulties are ones of verification rather than of the kind of observation. There are no special instruments to detect valid psychological states (although there is a long history of efforts to use physiological events such as brain waves and gland secretions to do it). What we have are people's acts and their accounts of themselves. One kind of verification or corroboration can come through plausible statements by others of the states they would have as they see the context and know something of the personal

WHAT DO WE KNOW ABOUT CAUSES?	
personal accounts tell "how-it-seems-to-me"	natural science requires "the outsider's view"
we believe in our personal agency because we experience doing things we seem to produce some thoughts we experience these over and over	we discover valid causes by impartial observations of conditions reliable correlations of events experimentation in likely situations
personal accounts of experiences use words words become post hoc theories "I was 'angry', so I hit..."	naturalistic theory built on patterns of valid causes explaining common mental experiences
personal accounts are evidence to be explained, not principles of mental cause	

Figure 10.4. A summary of what we experience versus what we need to discover to explain our mental functioning.

history of the other person. We can easily grasp what "rings true" and what is not probable. Like any other data, these are accumulated across different settings and conditions to estimate their truth.

A last part of the agency problem we must consider, the issue we have been leading up to, is knowing what stimulates any specific event in the flow of our awareness. We believe that an act or thought was made through our personal agency, but what were the causes natural to the physical world of that event? The romantic solution has been to introduce an inner being in which the real agency resides. Early psychological description was of the "I" or "me" who collects the essence of

one's real self and produces caused acts. Our common thought is also like this. Western society's rules are formed by assuming unique selves to be the causal agents of acts. No matter how widespread such views may be (and they *are* quite satisfactory in the workings of social life), they are not satisfactory for natural science. We have here pitted "how-it-seems-to-me" against "how it actually works" (see Figure 10.4).

The practical goal of natural science remains (a) discovering the role of such expressions of experience in accounting for our agency and (b) explaining how and why that experience is caused. We will examine some approaches to answers in the next section.

SECTION SUMMARY:
EXPERIENCING CONSCIOUSNESS

Following William James, we picture our experience as a continuous stream that is personal, changing, without breaks and choosing. We attend to what is of importance to us, following the ways we divide up (or preperceive) the potential material. Some of what is interesting about others, material we call gossip, may be rooted in natural adaptations based on advantages to knowing

about others whose activities may affect our reproductive fitness.

Agency is the name we give to the power we seem to have to cause thoughts and actions. Agency, an obvious part of what we call motivation, is a challenge to explain. Our reports of agency experiences come after the events and tend to embellish or make sense of what has happened. These "how-it-seems-to-me" statements are valid evidence to be considered, but they are not adequate accounts by themselves. Such self-reports are part of what we need to explain.

THEORIZING MIND

We are somewhat ready now to turn to the many and contentious ideas of how we have tried to account for the phenomena of consciousness, explaining "how it seems to me" with "how it actually works." We can appreciate some of the wonder and complexity of understanding mind in this piece from Diane Ackerman's (1992) *The Moon by Whale Light.*

> After all, mind is such an odd predicament for matter to get into. I often marvel how something like hydrogen, the simplest atom, forged in some early chaos of the universe, could lead to us and the gorgeous fever we call consciousness. If a mind is just a few pounds of blood, dream, and electric, how does it manage to contemplate itself, worry about its soul, do time-and-motion studies, admire the shy hooves of a goat, know that it will die, enjoy all the grand and lesser mayhems of the heart? What is mind that one can be "out of one's"? How can a neuron feel compassion? What is a self? Why did automatic, hand-me-down mammals like our ancestors somehow evolve brains with the ability to consider, imagine, project, compare, abstract, think of the future? If our experience of mind is really just the simmering of an easily alterable chemical stew, then what does it mean to *know* something, to *want* something, to *be*? How do you begin with hydrogen and end up with prom dresses, jealousy, chamber music. (p. 131)

Consciousness: A Persistent Problem

Philosophers of psychology, some psychologists, and a sprinkling of others have been wrestling with the tough problems of psychology for a long time. The center of interest always turns out to be some approach to the toughest of all nuts to crack: What is the nature of consciousness? We won't pretend to put all of the arguments into some neat summary. Even grouping them is dangerous because it makes bed partners of estranged and combative people. In studying this, it is very difficult to avoid being seduced by the ideas being read at that moment. The major challenge is to find what is being assumed, where there is more hand waving than clear statement, and where there are points in which the only possible bridge is like the one illustrated in a famous cartoon, wherein two collections of mathematical formulae on a blackboard are connected with the statement "and then a miracle happens." The miracles are often easy to spot. It is in the beginning assumptions and in the chosen paths of the guide that it is easiest to lose one's critical way.

Consciousness remains at the core of psychology's philosophical soul because it is at once a given and an unreality that logic tries to take away. If we assume we are biological beings that are totally open to natural law, then much of the mystery of consciousness seems elusive, somewhat ephemeral, perhaps merely a set of tricks the brain plays. Consciousness seems to be entirely personal, yet, at the same time, it appears not accessible to materialistic scientists. Some see it as a problem of **intimacy:** What makes the difference between observing the density of water vapor in the air as it is revealed in the diffraction of sunlight and seeing the beauty of the sunset? Others see the problem of consciousness in its intrinsic qualities or **qualia:** How can mere material process account for the pleasure I am feeling, the imagining I can do about green people, or the way a tune is to me? If we assume that there is a certain reality of awareness, then we must find the mechanics of that.

A little background is in order. One of our most persistent bad ideas dates from at least René Descartes' explanations in the early seventeenth century. Descartes described us as essentially body machines with a separate and independent soul. Body and soul are of different essence and follow different laws, yet they somehow give us the appearance of being together. Descartes began his program by looking for what seemed to him absolutely beyond doubt. He concluded that at the least, he could not doubt that he was thinking, that he was a thinking thing. On that, he built a philosophy of separate mind and body. Then, he had to face the big questions of accounting for the correspondence between awareness and the real world and how the mind could move the body, lumped together as the mind-body problem. His answer was that the soul and body interacted in a part of the center of the brain. The physiology was naive, but it was not the solution that is the bad idea.

The real trouble came from the earlier step of assuming the different body and soul. He assumed at the outset that mental experience was not in the realm of natural body machinery. This separation we have labeled **mind-body dualism.** By assuming a difference, he was also foreclosing a natural science approach. But of course, we can't blame Descartes for not knowing what the tools and ideas would be hundreds of years later. Still, for whatever reasons, the mind and body separation has remained and gets in the way of our clear thinking about other solutions.

The strongest surviving opponent of dualism comes from the modern natural science assumption of **physical monism.** This view proposes no soul or mind essence at all, believing that everything is material and material process. But what then are these pieces of consciousness we all have? No easy answer comes to mind, so in practical affairs we all

tend toward the easier description of dualism, the bad idea. To find a better perspective, we must back up much further in our assumptions and question even what we have traditionally taken to be sacred, the continuity and accuracy of our awareness.

The challenge, particularly to motivation psychology, is to account for the apparent reality of conscious awareness and then to describe the role of that awareness in human events. At the outset, we must agree to follow natural science. That means that at some elementary level, people are biological machinery, however complex it may appear. Both body and mind functions are at root the events of structures of the body. With this agreement is a simple rule: Only natural processes are considered. We must rule out all ideas of spirits and mysterious, unknowable mind forces. But the problem remains. What is conscious awareness, what roles does it have, and how did it come to be? There are no agreed-to solutions as yet, but there are good reasons why that is so. Still, some of the theories tendered are worthy of brief study to clarify the issues that underlie this problem of motivation (see Figure 10.5).

Eliminative Materialism

One form of physical monism (e.g., Churchland, 1981, 1986) dwells on the physiological events. Because, in principle, mental events are physiological, some physical monists believe the solution is in just knowing more physiology. Eventually, the awareness will be described in physiological terms. Some call this idea **eliminative materialism** because the physical terms eliminate the need for the psychological description. Another label is **promissory materialism,** because the answer is promised at some point with physiology details.

One fault of physical monism is that it automatically refers any real comprehension to some distant physiological knowledge. Perhaps a more serious problem is seeing psychological experiences of awareness themselves as unnecessary and unscien-

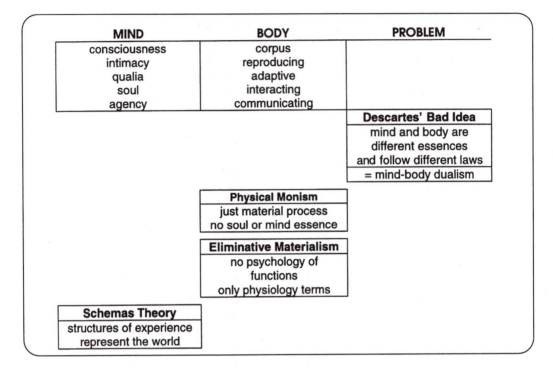

Figure 10.5. The mind-body problem and approaches to solving it.

tific observations, leading to rejection of awareness study. The first fault leaves us waiting indefinitely for any description of human functioning, and the second denies the reality of the consistent mental experience that we want to have explained. Strict physical monism may be correct as our ultimate goal but impractical to reach. We want an explanation in terms of natural, physical units, but that is not likely to cause the experience to change in any fundamental, functional way.

Among the theories sidestepping the first fault are those trying to put together mind function from physical pieces. In this view, pieces of very simple mental operations are assembled so that their collective functions can be seen to be machine-like. Thus, if each mental piece acts like a machine, mental functions must be just those kinds of machines, and if enough small machine-like functions are put together, all of mind will thereby be explained (Fodor, 1983). The issue here is of the size and organization of those units. How do the bits, of whatever size, work together to make our acts and experiences?

Cognitive Closure

Not everyone thinks the problems of knowing how minds work are solvable. Some philosophers focusing on the problem of consciousness conclude that there is no way of understanding conscious awareness and its properties in physiological or any other physical terms (e.g., Hannay, 1990; McGinn, 1991). It is not a question of whether conscious awareness has physiological roots—everyone who seriously addresses the problem from a natural science assumption assumes that— but of how can we understand awareness.

In the way these philosophers set up the issues, they prevent finding answers. They claim physical facts describe brain states, and phenomena and narrative language terms describe conscious awareness. They see these separate realms of knowing as not connecting. No brain observations or physical terms make up a description of any conscious events. The terms of brain events do not describe mental awareness.

Colin McGinn (1991) believes that humans are not able to comprehend that link for reasons that follow from the way human functions have evolved. As conscious awareness evolved, McGinn reasons, its primary use was to deal with the physical world, including other humans in social life. There was and is no survival benefit for that awareness to have access to its own workings. Stated in metaphor, humans are designed to deal with pictures of the world and its events but not with the ways their own pictures are made. McGinn describes this as the principle of **cognitive closure** to properties of the world. Just as some perceptual properties of the world are closed to our direct human observation (X-rays, for example) and humans cannot perform some mental functions (echo location of flying objects, for example), so too there are links of physical perception and conscious awareness that humans cannot make. Humans are not evolved to "see" consciousness in living brains, and they cannot directly perceive the mechanisms by which they can think. These are cognitively closed to the limited mentality of humanity.

The mind-body and mind-mind problems exist, McGinn asserts, because of conflicts between the assumptions of naturalism, the inaccessibility of certain mental phenomena in physical terms (mind-body problem), and the human belief that everything that can be conceived can be understood by human mentality. It is this last assumption that has remained largely hidden and is his key to making the problems understandable although not solvable.

McGinn's working conclusion is that the mind-body problem is closed to human solution. It remains unknown whether that closure is absolute or will eventually fall to some insights of the future. Whichever is true, this conclusion liberates the naturalist from having to resort to spiritualism or to ignore all but studies of physical mechanisms in the brain. He suggests that the best strategy of the moment is to carry studies of awareness phenomena to their limits without the impossible goal of describing them with physical mechanisms. George Mandler's work, which we review next, is in that vein.

Representing Reality

George Mandler (1985) presents a cognitive perspective about representation, operations of the mind, and the role of consciousness. He uses the idea of mental representations of events as patterns of knowledge called **schemas.** Mandler states that the mind is an agency responsible for human thought and action. The contents of mind are about **representations** of meanings and knowledge. Representations make it possible to generate consequences relating to commonsense notions of meaning and knowledge. The usefulness of our representations depend on their fit to perceived situations. Representation is accomplished by schemas; schemas are representational systems.

The term *schema* has had wide use in cognitive psychology as a general label for one form of a cognitive structure. Schemas are organizers of experience. They represent simple features of perception and general categories. There are schemas of fingernails, schemas of tissue, and schemas of life processes. The number and variety of schemas are essentially unlimited. Mandler (1985) defines a schema as "a category of mental structures that stores and organizes past experience and guides . . . subsequent perception and experience" (p. 36).

Conscious experience is composed of a construction of activated schemas. Mental events are continuous processes of activating and elaborating schemas, according to certain needs of the situations faced. Mandler's rule is that "conscious constructions represent the most general interpretation that is appropriate to the current scene in keeping with both the intentions of the individual and the demands of the environment" (p. 58). Schemas are brought from preconscious states as they are needed to make as much sense of the happenings as possible.

In many common experiences, there is little change needed in the schemas brought into awareness. They represent the events adequately. However, there is new conscious construction of schemas under certain circumstances. Mandler notes that this happens most certainly when we are acquiring new knowledge. New or changed schemas are built to represent the new materials. New schemas are also constructed when we make a choice or judgment or when we face a problem or are troubleshooting. Mandler (1985) summarizes these conditions in general with this rule: "When current conscious constructions do not account for the state of the world, then a new conscious state will be initiated" (p. 60).

Mandler's theory presents a summary of considerable thought. It is not without problems, but those will not be addressed here. It is one version of state-of-the-science cognitive theory trying to organize the structure of mental experiences. We conclude this section with an outline of a solution that defies McGinn's pessimism, using natural brain processes to account for consciousness.

Dennett's Parallel Brain Machine

From the most ancient writing, philosophers have begun with the contents of our consciousness to state what we know and believe. We picture it like this. External and internal sensations are pure and personal events that combine with memories of others and are brought together in a central processing. That makes up our experienced stream of consciousness. Planning and intentional choice are among the processing activities. That stream and its history are what we know as our self.

What if we demote our experience to being just an illusion of our natural brain and body operation? We must challenge other assumptions as well. That stream of consciousness is not from a central processing; there is no central processing. The personal qualia (personal qualities of experience) are myths coming from complexes of dispositions. Self (the me or I) is not an active controller at all but just a kind of floating summary of narratives, sensation sequences referenced to our body. Experiences are not direct contacts, personal intimacy is a construction, and personality is the result of chaotic competition among existing reflexes and habitual ideas.

Is nothing of our common personal experience sacred? In a word, no. The point is that we must go beyond our personal experience to construct a scientific psychology. We cannot test our theories by assuming and using the mechanism we are trying to study, particularly if it is already loaded with a set of bad ideas about how it really works. The first step is to chisel away at assumptions to discard problems that are trivial. Then, a constructive process forms a new model. We will look at a few of the major structures Daniel Dennett (1991) outlines in his book, with its pretentious title *Consciousness Explained.*

We begin with the reality of our consciousness. We all know how-it-seems-to-me. That conscious awareness is what we must explain with brain machinery. We must build explanation with facts and observations that are different from how-it-seems-to-me or else we get in a circle with no escape. Dennett says we can approach that explanation by examining what we know of how the brain works and by discarding some of our cherished assumptions about how it *must* work. Those assumptions were built on our how-it-seems-to-me, and that gets in the way.

We don't have the space for a complete study, but let us look at two illustrations of how the brain works. Suppose we watch a red ball fly across the room. We know that different parts of our brain process features of that visual experience. Motion detection is done separately from color perception, for example. We also know that how-it-seems-to-me is perception of a colored moving object. Now, consider a color demonstration of the apparent movement of the phi phenomenon. A red light flashes followed closely by a flash of green light next to it. We experience movement of the red light and its becoming a green light, midway. Now think about how you will explain that. The red light seems to become a green light even before the green light comes on. If you see a problem of "filling in" the color before it actually appears, you are assuming the how-it-seems-to-me view, which Dennett calls the Cartesian Theater, the place where all of the elements are brought together to make a picture of the world as it is for us to see.

We can expand the point with a second illustration: the "blind spot" in vision. With the left eye closed, any small object a modest distance to the right and slightly below focus in the right eye is not seen. We know the blind spot only by seeing a small object disappear as it crosses that part of the retina. But in normal vision, we don't see anything different there from what surrounds it. If we are looking at a picture of the world that the brain is presenting in our Cartesian Theater, why don't we see a "hole" or blank spot there all the time? Does the brain "fill in" the hole here also? In both cases, we are assuming that there must be a central brain process that corresponds in structure and time to how-it-seems-to-me, and that is the persistent bad idea we must discard.

Dennett reminds us that we have a massively parallel-processing brain, and these color, motion, and location items are just a few pieces of the vast array of processing going on at each moment. We use the results of that processing whenever they are needed without ever having to bring them together into a Cartesian Theater. Timing and location information can be anywhere in the brain to be used when it is essential for results such as answering questions about what color something was or noticing or not noticing a blind spot object. (See Dennett's 1991 Chapters 5 and 6 for elaboration.)

Another important feature of how the brain works is its ready stock of functions. Our brains are the product of a long evolution, leaving us with adaptations that were designed to meet specific problems in our ancestral history, such as moving away from a rapidly approaching object, knowing the faces of our caregivers, and spotting red berries on green bushes. These adaptations that evolved for specific chores of life were enlisted into new uses as our nature and environment became complex. The brain machinery

that gives consciousness is an elaboration of those elements that served our ancestors in their moment-to-moment survival activities.

Language added another layer of complexity of functioning, and the resulting patterns of culture influence us through what Richard Dawkins (1989) called *memes,* microhabits of thought that parasitize our brains. Memes are knowledge units, large (such as democracy), intermediate (such as being "cool"), and small (such as answering a question, "Not"). Patterns of memes are the functioning structures of thinking; the way the brain translates the sensory information of the world.

Next, Dennett addresses the single channel or stream illusion of how-it-seems-to-me. Again, our personal experience is hard to set aside. Our awareness being along a narrow channel makes any other parallel channels unavailable to our direct inspection. Knowing that our brains are massively parallel in functioning, we have to explain how that results in our awareness as a narrow channel of essentially one thought at a time. The idea Dennett uses is that our brains have many patterns or streams of thought under way all the time. They are in a chaotic competition, each writing its own "draft" of potential function. Drafts enlist the evolutionary mechanisms and functions of the brain combined with the large population of memes that populate it.

Now, Dennett must account for how the functioning of one of the drafts is promoted and succeeded by another to give the experience of a single continuous channel of thought. A central controller won't work; that creates the never-ending problem of explaining how the controller "thinks." Dennett dips into computer metaphor for the idea of virtual machinery. A virtual machine is an organization of functions that puts together a systematic, coherent, yet unreal presentation. A word-processing program gives its users a virtual reality of functioning on the electronic hardware. More exotic virtual reality machinery can allow users to explore a computer-generated space by seeming to actually manipulate objects in that image. Dennett proposes that our brain is designed as a comparable virtual reality, which sorts and patterns the many drafts into a virtual mind.

Dennett describes brain functioning as making simultaneous drafts of possibilities that come together into patterns by using its predesigned virtual machinery. Those resulting drafts appear in our consciousness as narratives. Over time, each of us in our separate brain and body builds a memory of our narratives. A **self** is the history of consciousness referenced to a body. Looked at with another word, the **mind** is our label for the actions of that historical self, but it is no thing or force-causing agent. It is how we describe how-it-seems-to-me.

In Dennett's (1991) colorful words and phrases,

There is no single, definitive "stream of consciousness," because there is no central Headquarters, no Cartesian Theater where "it all comes together" for the perusal of a Central Meaner. Instead of such a single stream (however wide), there are multiple channels in which specialist circuits try, in parallel pandemoniums, to do their various things, creating Multiple Drafts as they go. Most of these fragmentary drafts of "narrative" play short-lived roles in the modulation of current activity but some get promoted to further functional roles, in swift succession, by the activity of a virtual machine in the brain. The seriality of this machine (its "von Neumannesque" character) is not a "hard-wired" design feature, but rather the upshot of a succession of coalitions of these specialists.

The basic specialists are part of our animal heritage. They were not developed to perform peculiarly human actions, such as reading and writing, but ducking, predator-avoiding, face-recognizing, grasping, throwing, berry-picking, and other essential tasks. They are often opportunistically enlisted in new roles, for which their native talents more or less suit them. The result is not bedlam only because the trends that are imposed on all this activity are themselves the product of design. Some of this design is innate, and is shared with other animals. But it is augmented, and sometimes overwhelmed in importance, by microhabits of

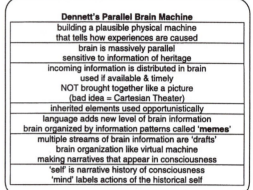

Figure 10.6. Dennett's Parallel Brain Machine.

thought that are developed in the individual, partly idiosyncratic results of self-exploration and partly the predesigned gifts of culture. Thousands of memes, mostly borne by language, but also by wordless "images" and other data structures, take up residence in an individual brain, shaping its tendencies and thereby turning it into a mind. (pp. 253-254)

The last step is to review this abbreviated picture of our brain functioning in order to grasp what exactly is consciousness. This is the hardest step for many readers of Dennett, because they want to put the explanation for consciousness in simple images of their personal how-it-seems-to-me. We want to fall back on our own pictures of the narrative stream, our own poignant qualia, and our cherished illusion that our self is controlling all our experience as it is pictured together in the Cartesian Theater. Although Dennett has systematically shown each of these to be poor models and put alternatives in their places, we still resist. What is consciousness? Just the stream of narratives, and Dennett has proposed a coherent scheme of the brain mechanisms making them (see Figure 10.6).

Why have we tried to engage this apparently complicated set of ideas? What is so interesting in Dennett's approach? A big part of it is where it begins and the limits Dennett has assumed. Most of our current philosophy of psychology makes one or another unsatisfying assumption. The extreme materialists want to find everything in tissue change, do away with all of culture, and pretend that experience does not exist (Churchland, 1986; Stich, 1983). Others want to avoid the physical side. Certain social constructionists deny that there is anything of human functioning that follows universal laws beyond the social interactions of the moment, and even those interactions continuously change (Coulter, 1979). Some mentalist philosopher-psychologists want to ignore body function (although acknowledging that somehow it is really responsible for all that happens), because they believe that there is no way to connect the realm of brain tissue change and experiences of awareness (McGinn, 1991). Still others want to stay entirely at the mental phenomena level, ignoring the physical side completely, and importing wonder processes as needed to account for our conscious phenomena (Searle, 1980, 1988). The battles among these and their variants have been our recent history of philosophy of psychology.

Dennett's ideas are clearly in the naturalist, mechanist camp, but they also account for mental experiences in a physical way. He does so without the excesses of denial of the tough cases and extrapolations from easy cases to hard ones as an act of faith. Neither does he have a place hiding where "a miracle happens." Dennett's are among a new breed of ideas, presented not as a finished program but as a kind of sampler to open up fresh possibilities. By questioning traditional assumptions, we may be able to think more clearly. The toughest problems may melt away when we approach the topic from a different base. The trick is to be open to those approaches.

SECTION SUMMARY: THEORIZING MIND

Explaining our mental experience presents the peculiar problem of trying to get outside of the very thing we use to construct the account. Since the time of René Descartes, we have acknowledged that our bodies are physical machinery, but our intuition tells us that our minds are something different. This is mind-body dualism and presents the mind-body problem of accounting for how they work together. Early materialist philosophers, as well as modern natural scientists, suppose physical monism, seeing mind as a property of the body machinery at the most. Eliminative materialists propose the most raw physical monism in suggesting that we confine our study to the physical processes that will eventually explain away or eliminate accounts using mental experience. A middle ground proposes that the gap between physical and mental accounts cannot be closed because there was no reason for our mentality to have evolved to know that. Some cognitive scientists attempt to explain mind's functioning in terms of psychological functions such as storing and using information about events in patterns of knowledge called schemas.

Philosopher Daniel Dennett presented the outlines of a change in scientific thinking in which consciousness might be explained in purely natural science terms. He insists on taking an "outsider's" view, treating how-it-seems-to-me as the phenomenon to be explained. He puts together a number of new pictures of brain function to help us out of unproductive thinking. Among these are a massively parallel processing brain in which there is no need for information to come together in a Cartesian Theater. That brain comes stocked with many functional adaptations that are put together opportunistically. Language is a vital addition to brain function in that it allows dramatic expansion in function by using microhabits of thought called memes. The complexity of the parallel brain is organized by a system of those memes analogous to a virtual machine in which the many inputs to the brain are processed in patterns called drafts. Collections of drafts sort themselves out by the complex pandemonium of the virtual machinery and produce narratives that appear in our consciousness. We identify our self as that stream of narratives, taking into account its recent history. Dennett's ideas are a valuable attempt to break the hold of Decartes's mind-body dualism and downgrade the evidence we find comfort in falling back on, the how-it-seems-to-me.

CONTROLLING AWARENESS

Awareness of mentality is incomplete and has variations in clarity. We sometimes feel moments of peak focal attention, but most of the time, we just routinely follow life events. As we get drowsy, we lose most awareness. Attention slides further away as we fall asleep. We have no sensations of mental control as we enter deeper sleep. But awareness even in sleep has variety; dreaming and partial awakenings appear through the night, as we described in Chapter 2.

At the other extreme of control of awareness, we can command sharper awareness when needed. William James assumed that a person can control attention, although he believed that such voluntary forms of attention are very difficult to hold for long before attention passively follows routine external and internal events. Such voluntary awareness control is the goal of meditation practice and, in a contrary way, hypnosis.

Meditating

In meditating, we learn to have more control of our awareness than normal—we prolong the active, voluntary attention that William James said was so hard to do. Anyone can choose to attend to specific things or choose to not attend to them. The duration and depth of that focal attention is an ability that can be developed with practice. This is the primary psychological skill underlying the developed study and practice of meditation.

Meditation is an unusual, cultivated control of attention that was developed in cultures of the East and hence has been rarely understood in Western thought. Many psychologists and others have dismissed meditation as a religion and disparaged the showy performances of some of the most accomplished practitioners. Acts of lying on beds of nails, walking on live coals, and slowing the heart to a stop are commonly portrayed in Western culture as curiosities of the East. We need to look beyond the show to what we can learn about attention control.

Four common forms of meditation are Zen, yoga, transcendental meditation (TM), and Sufism. The first three are now common in the West; Sufism is a collection of practices that are surrounded by pledges to secrecy and hence are little known. Yoga, Zen, and TM have roots in Hinduism and Buddhism. Written descriptions of meditation appear in fifth-century Buddhist writings as a means of purification. This record described eight levels of jhana, or breaking away from normal consciousness, leading to an altered state called *nirvana*. From Hinduism has come an emphasis on the *mantram*, an utterance on which one concentrates.

Zen, the classical Buddhist meditation, is a set of acts of personal control. Instruction is begun with counting breaths from 1 to 10 and over again until that concentration is mastered. Then, we are to concentrate on the process of breathing as air is inhaled and expired. This gives a regular, unvarying pattern to permit the addition of a meditation *koan*, a question that is intended to transcend rational thought. Common examples are "What is the sound of one hand clapping?" or "Show me your face before your mother and father met. Certain specific physical postures are also maintained, such as the lotus position: being seated with the legs crossed and toes on opposite thighs, back straight, and hands on the bent knees (Ornstein, 1977).

Yoga also employs the lotus position but often uses a visual stimulus, a *mandala,* instead of the utterance of sound. There are several common geometric forms of mandala, and focus is systematically moved over their parts. An alternate to the mandala is steady focus on most any object, called a *trakakam.* A mantram is chanted, serving a similar function to the Zen breath counting. Finally, the yoga practitioners also make repetitive physical movements of the limbs called *mudra.* These yoga elements (mandalas, trakakams, and mudras) are all means of learning to control awareness and prevent a shifting of awareness to distracting events.

Transcendental meditation (TM) is like yoga but uses only a mantram, with practice twice a day for about a half hour to maintain control over awareness. Commercial promotion of TM has become prominent recently. Although the methods and teaching of meditation skills may be satisfactory, the promises of solving life's problems are unproved and generally inaccurate. We should be skeptical of commercial promises of levitation or of major social changes resulting from having a threshold number of meditators.

Meditators experience attention control and relative absence of other mind content. Following the exercise, meditators describe a natural high. They tell of a kind of rebound of attention, a sharper awareness described as "opening up." A variety of positive therapeutic results have been reported including, among others, enhancing self-esteem, reducing anxieties, and lowering high blood pressure (Wallace & Fisher, 1987, pp. 148-149).

Experiencing Hypnosis

The experience of control over conscious awareness becomes most interesting in demonstrations of hypnosis. With little more than a willingness to relinquish control, a phenomenon we call hypnosis appears. Under hypnosis, we experience a purposeful selection of mind content. We focus specific mind content or perhaps block it out. Few psychological topics have been so intriguing, and so misrepresented, as hypnosis. People identify it as a kind of trance in which mysterious powers appear and the hypnotized can be made to do and think anything the hypnotist chooses. Our media image suggests we will bring back lost memories, cure our mental weaknesses and afflictions, endure extreme pain, or contact our deep or lost unconscious. We can be made to forget the experience, and media hypnotism stories have us carry out a suggested act years later with the right suggested cue. None of these images is factual; all are patently incorrect.

Hypnosis is no more than relaxing and doing what is suggested by a hypnotist. Hypnosis is not a special state of mind. We can focus on our imagination, calling it daydreaming, and we can fall asleep, calling it dreaming. We all dream and daydream, and with a similar power we all can be "hypnotized" if we want to be, and *only* if we want to be. It's nothing more than agreeing or not agreeing to follow someone else's instructions. Rather than some not usually accessed state of mind, hypnosis is only unusual exercise of the imagination. With considerable justification, Robert Baker (1990) calls hypnosis a game we play with a hypnotist.

Definition of hypnosis experience, like that of other states of awareness, is handicapped by lack of words precisely distinguishing consciousness levels. We use general terms such as *alert, drowsy,* and *sleep,* but we have much more difficulty communicating our consciousness, for example, when we are almost awake early in the morning or when lost in the reveries of a pleasant daydream. Without adequate language, these conditions are difficult to describe. Thus, we look at performances instead. And in performances we can be tricked and misled.

A few, very few, researchers believe in hypnotism as a special mental state. Characteristic effects under hypnosis (according to a researcher, Ernest Hilgard, 1965, who appears to believe in a real hypnotism state), are these: (a) personal planning done by the hypnotist, (b) directed and sharply focused attention, (c) increased facility for producing fantasy, (d) toleration of distortion of reality, (e) increased suggestibility, (f) capacity to perform in new roles, (g) selective and directed amnesia for events. Each characteristic may be present but need not be. Collectively, this has been a much-used list of the acts of a hypnotized person.

Hilgard (1965) also gives these examples of verbal recollections, each from a different person who experienced hypnosis.

> My thoughts were an echo of what you were saying.

> My head sunk into my body like a dark sponge.

> Your voice came in my ear and filled my head.

> When I felt deepest, I was down in the bottom of a dark hole. I turned over and over on the way down. Now and then I would float up toward the top.

> I was completely unaware of any other part of my body. I felt as though I were inside of myself; none of my body was touching anything.

> My eyes were unfocused, even when closed.

> I felt I was being squeezed in a closed place—like a tube perhaps—but it wasn't unpleasant. (p. 13)

These are representative fragments of awareness that people have reported when they were hypnotized. One theme across these reports is that of distortions of sensory attention and control.

As we noted, everyone who is willing to cooperate can be hypnotized, but only if they cooperate. Mentally alert people cannot be hypnotized against their will. In another meaning, the "Who can?" question is also asking for the characteristics of people who would be good hypnotism subjects. No reliable measures have been found of how easily a person may be hypnotized except trying the hypnosis game itself. The conditions of willingness have more to do with the social situation than with enduring properties of personality. With the right scene, most people will comply with another person's wishes and use their imagination as they believe a hypnotized person should.

Shiny, swinging objects and deep, relaxing voice tones are stereotypes of hypnotic procedures. It certainly is helpful to ease induction if the subject is made to focus attention on an object and other conditions are suitable for concentration and relaxation. The reality may be that many procedures and icons that symbolize hypnotic induction become social excuses for entering the hypnotist's game. There has been a long history of popular gadgets and techniques, but there are no absolutely necessary objects or procedures other than a willing subject and a serious hypnotist.

Again, a bit of history is helpful. Anton Mesmer in the 1780s believed that magnetism from the planets could cure the sick. He focused these forces by touching people with magnets or having them touch the outside of a fancy container of magnetized water. The occasional cures were probably placebo effects and spontaneous remissions. Some patients seemed to respond to his showy routine and his calls for them to focus on the magnetic powers. In doing so, they entered states of inactivity that look like hypnosis. His attractive procedures were soon called Mesmerism, and we still talk of being *mesmerized*. Mesmer was later discredited by the French government through the efforts of the medical profession. The prestigious commissioners correctly said his apparent results were nothing but imagination.

Nevertheless, similar techniques reemerge periodically. In the middle of the 1800s, they were named hypnotism. They enjoyed the attention of several reputable teaching physicians in France in the late 1800s, including Jean Charcot, who artfully developed dramatic hypnosis cures of hysterics. Among many others, Sigmund Freud was attracted to study hypnosis as a therapy tool for a period of time, although he later gave it up in favor of his method of free association. William James included a chapter on hypnosis in his famous *Principles of Psychology* in 1890. Clark Hull, later renowned for his behaviorist drive-reduction learning and motivation theory, researched hypnosis in the 1920s, producing *Hypnosis and Suggestibility* in 1933. During World War II, there was expanded medical use of hypnotism on casualties. Medical use has also included applications to dentistry and obstetrics. All in all, hypnosis has a long history (See, e.g., Gauld, 1992; Inglis, 1989; Moss, 1965)

Hypnosis proponents have gathered around three poles: medical practice, experimental research, and entertainment. We have sketched instances of the first two. As to the third, hypnotism's reputation has always been clouded by sensationalist claims, largely from entertainers. Stage hypnotists reinforce the myths of mysterious powers and often include trickery or extravagant therapeutic claims in their advertisements and performances. Several accounts of stage hypnotism are described by Kreskin (1973) and Baker (1990).

Hypnosis-like acts are within the power of anyone, even when not hypnotized. That is, prepared people can fake the same effects. This presents a problem for studying hypnosis, but it also gives a valuable insight. Hypnosis gives no new powers. There are no mysterious forces, just normal mental and body functions under unusual control.

Hypnotized people can stop their body movement, remain rigid, or repetitively perform an act beyond their normal inclination to do so. They react with surprise to the extreme acts they perform. Hypnotized people do things that we think to be impossible. Almost anyone can lift 200 to 300 pounds under the right conditions, but few are aware that they can or are they willing to try. A person can be made to take off clothes in front of strangers, tell deep secrets, or commit acts of violence. The key to these events is a carefully constructed deception in which the person agrees to believe that events are different than they are. They may disrobe if they are given the excuse that they are alone in their shower and are hot and dirty. They may tell secrets to those whom they are told are supposed to receive the messages. They may shoot a gun at someone if they believe that it is loaded with blanks or if they believe that another person is dangerous and about to kill a friend. However, each of these examples is very difficult to stage and must be something that person would normally do. A casual hypnosis demonstration will not produce acts that the person believes to be out of bounds.

For an extended presentation of the critical evidence about hypnosis, including the medical, research, and stage versions, see Robert Baker's (1990) *They Call It Hypnosis*. Another earlier critique (which is harder to find) is from the stage magician Kreskin (1973), *The Amazing World of Kreskin*.

The important motivation principle that both meditation and hypnosis illustrate is the unrealized potential we have to control our awareness. With practice and with the right conditions, mental experience can follow unusual patterns.

SECTION SUMMARY: CONTROLLING AWARENESS

Meditation and hypnosis teach us that we can exercise a great range of control over our consciousness. Meditation trains a sharper control, with extended regular practice reaching extremes of focusing on or rejecting sensory and mind content at will. Hypnosis is also learnable, giving us the opportunity to turn control of perception and mind content over to another person. Neither meditation nor hypnosis introduces any mysterious process or gives any unusual powers to us beyond the obvious facts of a different degree of mental awareness control.

THINKING

My thinking is first and last and always for the sake of my doing, and I can only do one thing at a time.

James (1890, Vol. 2, p. 333)

William James believed thinking to be the way that each person chooses self-maintaining acts. Material of our mental life is tied to causes both outside and inside. At the all-inclusive extreme, thinking provides foundations for all aspects of being a functioning person, including motivation. Taking this extreme, a study of motivation would include essentially all of the aspects of mental functioning, such as perception, memory, decision making, judgment, and so on. Each of these is a major topic of study in psychology, so we must make choices.

With the necessity of brevity, we will look at mental functioning that in itself directly motivates acts, broadly speaking. That narrows our focus to the limitations and directions of mental functioning. In what ways is our thinking a natural product of our heritage? What motivated acts are formed by principles and rules of our thinking? To answer, we will explore how some mental operations, by their own ways of functioning, directly structure our choices, intensities, and feelings.

We begin by noting that mental activities have roughly three levels of awareness and intentionality. First, a great amount of apparent mental functioning goes on without difficulty. Along with natural mental mechanisms, it uses the many experiences we have acquired about world events in the course of life, and our performances flow without interruption. We follow a path as we walk across the university campus. The operations of thought proceed, and we are typically not aware of them. Perhaps there are limitations and foibles of such thinking, but the outcomes are without conflict or consequences of which we are aware.

We passively follow a second sort of general mental functioning in awareness; it just appears to unfold automatically. We are inactive observers of pieces of thought operations. We pause at the curb to allow a car to pass. This is a step closer to an aware involvement because pieces of the processing itself are consciously available as the actions get under way, but still, there is no interruption. We have no sense of intentional agency.

The third category is that of full intentional involvement. We are actively reasoning and, of course, aware of the situation. We believe ourselves to formulate, choose, and direct our acts. Most of the interesting mental operations fall into this category. The path turns a corner and enters a building; not where we thought we were going. Full awareness typically occurs when the automatic flow of thought operations and skills fails to provide the appropriate result. Then, more intentional reasoning is applied, a decision is made, or a problem is solved. These happenings bring with themselves some experiences of awareness of mental functioning.

Traditional study of mental operations in awareness, such as that of William James, relied on the third kind: thoughts we seem to be controlling as well as experiencing. Focus is on the operation of actually reasoning, deciding, or solving problems and, by default, ignoring those many mental functions that are unproblematic. Laboratory science methods, too, have been applied to situations requiring reasoning, deciding, and solving problems. We gather evidence of our capabilities in situations that test limits and tell what may be happening between the presentations and the acts.

Reasoning

If we form a general idea from what we observe, we are using inductive reasoning. In **deductive** reasoning, we use a general rule to think about a specific case. We will look at a few interesting forms, motivationally interesting because they don't give perfect conclusions.

Finding Rules

Often, we form rules from a very few experiences. Such decisions follow the **law of small numbers.** Just a few pieces of information lead us to make a conclusion. We had two trips to the lake during which the weather turned out to be much better than forecast. Today the forecast is again poor with evidence that it will deteriorate. We decide that again the weather will be better than forecast. According to the law of small numbers, those few experiences are powerful elements in a decision.

Once made, we don't like to change our minds. The biases stretch over time. In many life experiences, a flow of observations is common. After a short time, we form models and make judgments. But then, as we get more recent information, we tend to discount it, even when it indicates a revision of our first model. One account is that we hold a conservative bias, reluctant to change for several different possible reasons. We don't see the new information as equal to the old but instead as somewhat less important. We discount it because we don't want to think again about the issue. We may also see the later data as dependent on or biased by the earlier data and for that reason regard it as not as important or as pure.

Labeling Causes

The philosophy and mathematics of deductive reasoning logic are venerable topics of education (and literary mysteries) having become one of the qualities by which proper thought is judged. The varieties of forms and errors make up a language unto itself. Those rational and intellectual topics of mental function surely bear close study, but the more typical deductions of people also include the nonrational and sometimes utterly emotional. These are the forms of practical deduction we address here.

One deductive deception of the mind is **causal fantasy,** our way of finding reasonable causes for events, particularly our feelings. It also seems to be part of the mechanism behind placebo pills and other nonfunctional treatments, and it may be part of how we bias our acts unintentionally to meet the expectations of others.

We are willing to learn of the things that influence our feelings. We readily associate what we have done with what happens to us. The extra game of tennis played yesterday is what made today's sore knee. The end of the exams this morning gives a lighthearted lift to the afternoon. The celebrating tonight will produce a headache tomorrow morning. Sometimes, this learning is in error. The upset stomach yesterday was attributed to the fried clams eaten the previous night, when it was really just a touch of the flu. The cure of the upset was thought to be the stomach-coating medicine taken before sleep, but it more likely came about because of the time spent asleep during the night. Many such mistakes are made in attributing causes because of the confusions of experience.

The astute physician and the knowledgeable experimenter have long known that we will change when we believe that we ought to, especially when a good reason is available. Physicians can make us feel better by prescribing physically inactive sugar pills. As patients, we think that the pill ought to work, we wait patiently for its effects, and the passage of time, plus perhaps the tranquillity it instills, makes the cure. For some, the pill reduces chronic pain or fear, as we noted in Chapter 6. A substance having no direct medicinal action is given and a change comes about just because something was given, a placebo effect.

Experimenters use the same placebo operation as a control for the effects of having a treatment. A placebo control is a group of people given everything that the experimental group gets except that its pill, injection, or other treatment is known to have no effect. In some experiments, neither the volunteers nor the experimenter knows who is getting the real treatment and who the placebo, a method called **double blind.** The double blind method can be necessary to prevent the volunteer from learning from the experimenter the performances being sought. These methods try to account for our unfailing deductive interest.

Deciding

We begin with the analyses of making decisions by William James and Edmund Husserl. James gives us a study of the feelings in the process. We follow that with a modern perspective on the rational ideal of making choices. Then, we look at Husserl's focus on the consequences for mental change.

Making Decisions

William James (1890) saw the making of decisions as a function of the operation of the will. In his analysis of awareness, indecision is a matter of "inward unrest." It is being aware of

> the existence of the whole set of motives and their conflict. . . . Of this object, the totality of which is realized more or less dimly all the while, certain parts stand out more or less sharply at one moment in the foreground, and at another moment other parts, in consequence of the oscillations of our attention, and of the "associative" flow of our ideas. (Vol. 2, pp. 528-529)

James described five kinds of processes in overcoming the indecision. Three pro-cesses of deciding involve suddenly dropping or diminishing all alternatives but the chosen one. This may occur by accident of events (the other candidates have all dropped out), by an impulse of feeling to get it over with (I can't stand the indecision any longer), or a motivational shift that makes one choice most important (It's time to stop enjoying the choosing and get down to business). The fourth resolution of indecision focuses on the active process of willing a choice through the feeling of effort but agonizing over the alternatives all the while. James (1890) speaks of holding the alternatives in view, "and in the very act of murdering the vanquished possibility the chooser realizes how much in that instant he is making himself lose" (Vol. 2, p. 534).

The fifth means of resolving indecision is actually that which James lists first, and it is a common theme in the literature of decision. This is the reasonable, calm, uncoerced, and rational balancing of alternatives. It is the ideal and abstractly logical mental act. It becomes the prescription for thought operations, and by being desirably rational, it becomes the model by which human judgment is said to operate. More often than not, the ideal is impossible. Ultimately, pure rationality is not possible—choice always means feeling.

The modern rational ideal in making decisions is summarized by Janis and Mann (1977, p. 11). They outlined seven criteria that they believed to be essential to avoid decision defects.

- Examine a wide range of alternatives.

- Consider the objective and values of the choice.

- Weigh costs and benefits of alternatives.

- Seek evidence about alternatives.

- Use information and expertise of other viewpoints.

- Review evidence for all alternatives.

- Provide a plan to execute the choice.

These criteria not only suggest what we believe to be best for formal decisions, failure to follow them is considered an error that may evoke postdecisional regret. The reality of life, however, is that such a plan is usually neither possible nor needed. Life choices come too fast, and we face too many of them to afford the luxury of contemplating alternatives. The consequence is that we adopt shortcuts and strategies that work with our limited range of awareness. Furthermore, our emotions are always involved in what we do. Pure rationality of thought, if that is intended to mean free of emotion, is impossible. Or, rather, it is not the way we function.

The philosopher most noted for his emphasis on describing phenomenon of experience, Edmund Husserl (1859-1938), believed that deciding is a flowing process of questions and answers. His focus was on those conscious situations of indecision that James thought bring mental unrest. The goal of our conscious deciding is to know what to do in the face of the possibilities, taking into account assumptions about our personal identity. He saw that negative consequences of choosing, such as alienation and estrangement, may come from failing to include a clear picture of the self in the knowledge of possibilities of the choice. To accept a career choice as a banker, for example, based on its being a family tradition may ignore the lack of interest we hold for that indoor life and overlook our need for a physical lifestyle. Alienation from life may result. Or, an entirely different result may ensue. The life of banking may open new directions of personal challenge and development. There are no simple rules for outcomes.

Husserl (1973) suggested that we make decisions based on broad rules and unquestioned ideas from social training.

I always buy cars from that dealer.

A college education is necessary to get a good job.

It is necessary to fight forest fires.

He calls these "empty judgments," and in using them one avoids dwelling on the process of deciding and the consequent feelings of indecision.

Taking Shortcuts

Husserl's suggestion of simple rules and ideas that underlie decisions banks on the known limitations of human mental functioning. At least at the level of awareness, there are but a few ideas that may be carried at one time, and a complex task must be sorted out over time. Thus, it follows that the simplest, shortest, most efficient patterns of thinking will prevail. Decision styles will follow those patterns. Some examples of styles are easily identified and named.

Practical decisions often are handled almost automatically by **rules of thumb.** Things are simplified and coded. A pilot's rule may be to not fly unless the visibility is greater than 5 miles. The rule may depend on cues in the situation. The colors, shapes, and markings of traffic signs are rules of thumb of sorts that allow quick reference to make specific adjustments.

Other simple rules are from a more general set of biases. **Availability bias** is one of these. We make decisions based on the most available information, whether right or wrong. Officeholders are surrounded by those who have the same views, giving no account to other thoughts and desires of the population being served.

We tend to believe that there is a fairness principle in events that are really only chance. This is the **gambler's fallacy.** If a coin is flipped, and it comes up heads seven times in a row, we may strongly believe that there is a better than even chance that the next throw will show a tail. We then have assumed there is some law that says that an equal number of heads and tails will occur on the average, so there are some tails to make up. But chance doesn't keep score, people do. Each toss has exactly the same probability, no matter what other tosses have shown. So, too, with lottery numbers.

People become caught in a decision process. A good label is **entrapment.** Once we have gone part way into something, we feel compelled to continue. We go ahead in the face of information that would have been enough to keep us from starting at all had we known it before. Without firm rules, we are led at an auction to spend more for an item through this kind of entrapment. After we reach our personal bid limit, we feel that having gone this far, we ought to continue bidding just a bit further, and on it goes. Drivers and airplane pilots are led by entrapment to continue trips that ought to be ended. Some call it *get-home-itis.* The trip has been started and now there are signs of fatigue and worsening conditions, but it is only another 150 miles to home. Once started, the investment of time, resources, and effort is protected by continuing. Major government policy decisions follow a similar pattern. Sometimes, it is a matter of political strategy to get a small decision to plan and initiate a project that would never have been approved in total at the outset. Once begun, the canal, weapons system, dam, or housing development is then promoted as an effort to protect the investment already made. Critics call it "throwing good money after bad."

Natural Detections

Considerable evidence informs us that our remarkable general thinking power is built on or around a set of natural, specialized solutions to unique and often-encountered problems. We like to think that we have essentially pure computational brain power limited only by the quality of our education, but evolutionary psychology informs us otherwise. The complicated social life of our ancestors dictated some efficient solutions to common problems, and general purpose rules are likely to be slower and less accurate than specialized ones in those situations (Cosmides & Tooby, 1992). We will look at three illustrations.

An example begun 30 years ago showed that people do not follow the rules of formal logic. Peter Wason (1966) presented a simple task, asking people to show how they would verify that a rule had been followed. His classic problem used this scene.

Suppose you have a new clerical job and you must verify that records have been correctly handled. The task is this: If a person's card has a D on one side, then the other side must be marked code 3. Each card record is for one person, and you must decide which of these cards you must turn over to know all violations of the rule:

D	F	3	7

About one quarter of college students answered correctly. Before revealing the answer, we should consider this second problem.

You are responsible for serving drinks to a group of students and the enforcement of the legal age is severe. The rule is this: If a student is drinking beer, then that person must be over 21 years old. With the same card format, which of these four cards must you turn over to be sure the rule has not been violated?

drinking beer	drinking coke	25 years old	16 years old

In this problem, of exactly the same logical form, three quarters of college students get it right (Griggs & Cox, 1982). In both cases the first and last card must be examined. Why the difference in correct responses? It appears from a variety of other forms of this problem that we are not as able to find errors in descriptions or in causes as we are able to detect cheaters (Cosmides & Tooby, 1992). There is a fitness advantage to have natural facility in knowing when someone is taking unfair advantage.

In a further illustration, the definition of cheating depends in some settings on where you fit into the scene. Let us try this variety of the Wason task.

The rule is if an employee gets a pension, then that employee must have worked for the firm for at least 10 years. If you are the employer, which of these cards must you see to know if the rule is applied correctly?

pension	no pension	worked 10 years	worked 8 years

From the employer's perspective, the correct cards are also the formal logic ones, pension and worked 8 years. These are the ones we need to check to be sure we are not being cheated. If workers are not getting a pension or if they worked 10 years, it doesn't matter. We look now at the same cards from the worker's perspective. Now the cheating is to be found with no pension and worked 10 years. This is just the results pattern that has been found (Gigerenzer & Hug, reported in Cosmides & Tooby, 1992). Again, we see that we are sensitive to evidence of cheating in social scenes, overriding rules of formal logic.

Another form of our natural thinking appears in our reasoning about numbers of things and events. In this case, we do much better when we think in terms of frequencies as we deal with statistics.

Medical disorder D happens to 1 out of every 1,000 people. A test exists for it, but the test also incorrectly shows the disorder 5% of the time in healthy people. What is the chance of a person actually having the disorder when the test result says so?

In this form, few people accurately calculate the chances, including medical faculty. But they are just responding as they can to a difficult and unnatural format of the problem. With a change of wording to frequencies, most people do very well.

Medical disorder D happens to 1 out of every 1,000 people. A test exists for it, but the test also incorrectly shows the disorder in 50 out of every 1,000 healthy people.

Now we can easily count the positive tests, get 51, and see that only one actually has the disorder, so the chance of having the disorder when the test says so is 1 in 51.

If the problem were drug use and the incidence was known to be 1 in 10 and the test had false positive indication of 1% or 1 in 100, we could count 10 in 100 drug users and one false indication, so the success of the test will be 10 in 11 tests. But if drug use was really just 1 in 100 and the test had a 5% false positive rate, that seems to be saying that the test is only wrong with 5% of the positive tests, but actually only 1 in 6 positive testing people would have really been using drugs.

A third example of specialized, natural thinking concerns the well-documented differences in spatial abilities between women and men. In essence, women do better in tasks using memory for items and specific locations; men do better with directions and mental mapping. Men do not remember as well as women what specific things are in an area and where they were placed. Women do not function as well in orientation when location cues are altered. Thus, women will become confused if the old landmarks are altered; men will be disoriented when they lose track of the pattern or time they have traveled a certain distance.

The evolutionary adaptation thought to be responsible for these differences is based on assuming that Pleistocene ancestors were hunters and gatherers with those functions most commonly separated as roles for men and for women. The hunting men survived better when they knew their way in their excursions to get food and return. Women thrived when they were able to detect the correct pattern of food plant materials in specific locations. Thus, remnants of these abilities in our modern environment are responsible for the gender differences in spatial ability.

Solving Problems

A problem exists if the way to a goal is not clear. Solving problems is finding successful paths. This spatial metaphor of paths illustrates the nature of a problem. We face hundreds of minor problems daily where the form of their solution is a matter of using our inclinations and our experience; we easily see the alternative paths to the goals.

More difficult problems take up significant mental time. Psychologists analyze these into stages of preparation, production, evaluation, and verification. In preparation, we put the elements of the problem in manageable form, perhaps using notation devices such as tables or pictures. In the production stage, we produce possible solutions or paths to the goal. Each production is evaluated and verified.

The heart of solving problems is the production of solutions. There are different strategies. The strategy of representation is a matter of putting a problem into terms of another sort. Pieces and relationships may be translated into a visual form or into mathematics. The visual form may be a table of data, a diagram, a schematic drawing, a matrix, a hierarchy, or a model. A good representation will make it easy to see which are good solutions and which are not.

Solutions may be found by the strategy of trial and error. When there is a small number of possible solutions, as in a five-letter anagram, the easiest strategy is to just try each possibility systematically. Other problems are best solved with the strategy of working backward from the goal. The common visual maze problem is most easily solved by beginning at the goal and tracing backward to the start. Solutions are also produced by applying common rules, by applying decision trees, by using metaphors and analogies, or by brainstorming.

Some blocks to problem solving are ways of thinking that prevent the production of the appropriate solution path. Solutions may be blocked because the elements available must be used in an unusual fashion. Psychologists called this **functional fixedness.** It is illustrated in the two-string problem. Two strings are suspended from the ceiling just far enough apart that we cannot grasp one while holding the other. They are to be tied together, and the materials available in the room include a screwdriver. A screwdriver is not usu-

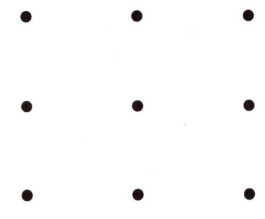

Figure 10.7. The nine-dot problem: Connect all dots with four straight lines without lifting pencil from paper.

clude a screwdriver. A screwdriver is not usually thought of as a simple weight, but the solution uses it as a means of getting one string to swing toward the other.

Another block to thought comes from assuming more than the problem solution requires. The classic illustration is the nine-dot problem in which dots are placed in a square with three dots to a side and one in the middle (see Figure 10.7). The task is to connect all of the dots with four straight lines without lifting the pen from the paper. We have difficulty because we tend to assume that we cannot make lines outside the boundaries of the square. We assume too much.

Finally, some problems impede solutions because the solver knows too much. Misleading additional information and data appear to be a part of the problem but are not. An old favorite is the sequence of information regarding a bus trip. The listener is proposed to be a bus driver making a series of many stops. The exact number of passengers getting off and on at each stop is related. At the end, the question is either "What is the bus driver's name?" or "How many stops did the bus make?"

Another example is this. There are black and brown socks in a drawer in the ratio of one black for every brown, and it is totally dark. The question is "How many socks must you pull out before you are sure of having a matching pair?" The ratio of socks is irrelevant and with three socks there will be at least two of the same color.

Acting Absentminded

Acting absentminded is common. We all do it, not just old professors, as the cultural stereotype suggests. There are some specific categories into which absentminded acts may be sorted, and conditions promoting absentmindedness have been identified. It illustrates well some limitations in our thinking and how motives can disrupt.

Actions in a sequence are often repeated. In preparing a cup of tea, I take a bag from the package, and place a water pot on the stove. As the water begins to boil, I open the package again and remove another tea bag. Sometimes the repeated act presents a problem. I take a special pair of socks from a drawer and put them on. After doing a few things in the bathroom, I return to the drawer looking for the socks and, of course, now can't find them. One variant is carrying a sequence beyond its intended stopping point. I intend to change into work clothes and find that the act of undressing stimulates the ritual of putting on sleeping clothes and nearly getting into bed.

Actions are performed to the wrong object. After many vain attempts, I discover that it is the house key I am trying to put into the car door. More severe lapses are legendary.

The philosopher deep in conversation with another while walking along a river, picks up a flat stone and is holding it when reminded to check the time. He removes his pocket watch and glances at it. He continues talking and then flings it across the river, placing the stone in his watch pocket.

Actions are omitted from a sequence. Daily rituals of toiletry and dressing provide a number of examples. I forget an intended item of clothing like a belt. Tooth brushing or applying deodorant are missed in the sequence. It is common to carry an object beyond the point of intended deposit: failing to mail a letter or carrying the garbage bag to work.

The conditions that promote these common acts of absentmindedness include at least these three, according to a recent analysis. First, we are in a familiar environment with nothing particularly new or changed that might promote specific attention. Second, we are engaged in routine, rather automatic actions of some sequence that require little attention control or decision. Third, we have a mental preoccupation on or distraction from some topic unrelated to the actions under way. These conditions have in common an involvement in intentionally directed mental activity that perhaps subtracts too much of the normally available awareness for monitoring routine actions (Reason & Mycielska, 1982).

Producing Consistent Thought

Consistency is a fundamental principle of nature. Mental consistency mirrors nature's consistency, and it also reflects an economy of operating design of people. Events happen in much the same way, time after time. We can abstract regulatory principles in all dimensions of things and events of human experience and describe their specific principles with the language of science. No one versed in modern studies will seriously hold that everything happens by chance and that there is no order in the world. But even before the laws of science were understood, people observed regularities of the world's objects and events, formed rules and principles about them, and regulated their lives accordingly. Some of those rules concerned the acts of other people and even their own acts. Our mental functions and regulation must conform to that consistency in world reality.

Consistency is necessarily the mark of our mental life; it can be no other way. Mental consistency takes a different twist in considering the nature of cognitive operations. Our cognitive operations are limited. We can see that in several ways. Sensory channels are restricted. Information is simplified and coded. Just a few coded elements can be handled at a time. Cognitive operations thrive on patterns. Redundancy and repetitions of consistent information are sought and used to generate conclusions of certainty.

In the complicated scheme of mental operations, inconsistent elements stand out and must be handled in special ways. Fundamentally, all consistencies and inconsistencies are mental. Mental consistency is the operational rule, and mental inconsistency motivates an additional complexity of mental operations. The regulatory principle is that mental consistency must be maintained. In psychological language systems, we have labeled this a need for consistency or a cognitive dissonance drive. In all views, the inconsistency is thought to motivate changes toward the purpose of achieving less inconsistency.

At a very fundamental level, a great deal of human life appears to follow the consistency regulation. For example, science is a way of thinking and doing things to satisfy mental inconsistencies. Looking at the moon, we wonder why it appears to change shape over time, and picking up a host of other questions, we begin a search for astronomical laws. Each question's answer brings out new discrepancies to be answered. A history of science could be formed around the inconsistencies that individual scientists tried to resolve.

Some information is a part of existing knowledge, and some arises directly from perceptions, including those of our own acts. Some information is uncertain, even imagined or projected happenings, but it is all important to the resulting mental events of relative consistency. Motivationally, it is the relative consistency that matters. The regulatory principle is that changes will be made to achieve, protect, or reestablish a greater degree of mental consistency.

Research on mental consistency has focused on provocative theories (themselves an illustration of inconsistency generating motivation in others). The two major theories are Fritz Heider's proposal of need for a balance of mental states and Leo Festinger's description of need to reduce dissonance of cognitions.

Keeping Ideas Balanced

Fritz Heider proposed the prototype of balance theories in a 1946 article entitled, "Attitudes and Cognitive Organization." Heider was a Gestalt psychologist, and the mark of that viewpoint was apparent in his choice of analogies and mechanisms. He purposefully modeled the dynamics of his larger cognitive theory upon the Gestalt ideas of perception of objects. Thus, he applied consistency ideas to perception of social events. He proposed that social motivations are social perceptions (Heider, 1944).

Perception of objects in Gestalt theory follows four principles of unit formation: proximity, similarity, good continuity, and common fate. These are static laws in the sense that they do not change in the situation. Once a collection of images is first organized by these laws, we see a perceptual unit. The laws themselves don't influence the stability of a perception. Heider looked for similar laws in social perception processes. He examined the relationships involved in a simple setting of a person (p), another person (o), and some impersonal entity (x). He found that some social perceptions are balanced, and some are imbalanced. Balance is preferred—it reflects simplicity through consistency.

Heider saw two sorts of relations between ps, os, and xs. Unit relations describe possession (as in o owns x), proximity (as in p is in situation x), similarity, causality, membership, or belonging. These are dissimilar elements but are roughly of the class of things that are together in some unit of cognition. Heider symbolizes these relationships by U and $\sim U$ for having or not having a unit. The second relation between ps, os, and xs are attitudes. Attitudes include liking, loving, valuing, and having esteem. Heider uses L and $\sim L$ for positive and negative attitudes. The relation *pLo* may mean *p* loves or likes *o*. The relation *p~Lx* means *p* does not like or value *x*. *U* and *L* are positive dynamic relationships and ~U and ~*L* are negatives.

A balanced state is one in which there is a consistency in all aspects of the relationship, for both *Ls* and *Us*. For example, *p* likes and values *o,* who is a roommate. According to Heider, people are in a balanced state if they like what they are united with or dislike what they are separated from:

$$(pLx) + (pUx) \text{ and } (p{\sim}Lx) + (p{\sim}Ux)$$

Bringing in the *x* makes a three-entity situation that must balance, meaning all three relationships must be positive or if just two (not one or three) are negative. A *p* wants his son (*o*) to like what he likes,

$$(pLx) + (oLx) + (pUo)$$

Or *p* dislikes o and his friend (*o*) dislikes it,

$$(p{\sim}Lx) + (o{\sim}Lx) + (pLo).$$

According to Heider (1946),

> If no balanced state exists, then forces toward this state will arise. Either the dynamic characters will change, or the unit relations will be changed through action or cognitive reorganization. If a change is not possible, the state of imbalance will produce tension. (pp. 107-108)

These principles give balance theory their motivational character. Imbalance motivates thought or acts or both to restore balance.

Reducing Dissonance

Leon Festinger's 1957 book *A Theory of Cognitive Dissonance* marked the beginning of one of the most intensively researched topics in the history of social psychology. Cognitive dissonance theory is not fundamentally different from other consistency theories, but it became much more popular. It was studied because it was attractive and provoked psychologists to consider its possibilities. Part of the attraction of the theory was its application to a wider scope of cognition than the personal relationships of Heider's more modest formulation, and part of cognitive dissonance theory's success followed the genius of Festinger in devising appealing research and implications.

The essential hypothesis is familiar: Having cognitive elements that don't fit with others leads to efforts toward consistency. Festinger chose to speak of nonfitting cognitive elements producing **cognitive dissonance.** Cognitive dissonance motivates us to make changes because having dissonance is psychologically uncomfortable. Thus, we will try to reduce dissonance and prevent its increase.

Cognitive elements are pieces of knowledge of our psychological world. The elements of content correspond to our experiences. Relations among these elements can be irrelevant, consonant, or dissonant. Elements having no relationship are said to be irrelevant and do not bear on the motivation to consistency. Consonance is the description of elements that fit together and present no aspects of discord. The focus of the theory is on dissonant relations among elements. Elements are in a dissonant relation when they are in opposition, when holding one is not consistent with holding the other.

Festinger suggested four sources of such dissonant relations. Some dissonance arises from expectations of logical consistency. In visiting a botanical greenhouse, we would not expect to see a collection of plastic plants. Cultural mores may be violated. Dissonance is produced when a dinner partner begins to slurp up soup with a straw. Dissonance arises when a general opinion is contradicted by a specific act. A political conservative should not propose an increase in public welfare. And dissonance follows from cognitive elements that are different from knowledge based on past experience. There has always been a newspaper machine on this corner, and now it is missing. These four forms are noteworthy examples; they do not exhaust the possibilities of dissonance.

In elaborating theory, Festinger directly addressed the magnitude of dissonance, holding that the degree of cognitive dissonance from any two elements follows the importance of those cognitive elements and their degree of difference. In typical life experience, there are many cognitive elements composing a situation, and the actual dissonance will reflect the proportion of elements contrary to a given cognitive element, weighted according to their individual importance.

Dissonance may be reduced by changing cognitions. Dissonance in cognitions is reduced in three ways: adding new cognitive elements, changing an environmental cognitive element, or changing an act-based cognitive element. Suppose that I have built a stone and concrete wall that has begun to show many cracks. The new cracks are dissonant with my general belief that a wall should be sound and strong. Dissonance may be reduced by adding new cognitive elements that suggest that the cracks imply flexibility and that normal ground movements make it impossible for any wall to be perfectly rigid. The environmental cognitive elements may be directly changed by denying that there are significant cracks or that any concrete wall is without them. An act-based element may be changed by taking down the wall and rebuilding it, or by denying responsibility for the design. The theory does not predict what kind or magnitude of change will be selected. It just holds that some dissonance reduction is very likely.

Part of the stimulation of Festinger's cognitive dissonance theory has been the several specific experimental paradigms that he and others have presented in illustration. Four such situations are postdecisional acts, forced compliance, selective exposure to information, and selection of social support.

Making decisions necessarily produces dissonance because in selecting one alternative, we must reject others. The dissonance comes from rejecting the valued alternatives. Dissonance is stronger when the decision is of greater personal importance and the decision is difficult to make because the alternatives are attractive. Festinger claimed that after making a decision, we have greater difficulty in reversing the decision the more difficult it was to make, that we actively look for information in accord with the decision, and that the alternatives not chosen grow to appear more unattractive, making the decision appear to be a good one.

The forced compliance paradigm has been difficult to demonstrate to the satisfaction of critics. It requires that a person publicly act contrary to privately held opinion. The compliance is accomplished through threats or promises. Greater dissonance comes from a situation of larger difference between public act and private belief or from smaller degrees of threat or promise used to accomplish the compliance or both. The dissonance is reduced by later change of belief in the direction of the public acts or by believing that the threats or rewards were larger than they actually were.

We will seek out cognitions that remove dissonance and look for support for them. This may be a matter of selecting only supporting information and listening only to those who will not provide dissonant cognitive elements. Having chosen computer Model D over E after a long indecision, we will tend to avoid any advertisements for E, focusing on those for D, talking only with other D owners, and subscribing to special magazines for D owners. Heavy smokers will not seek out the Surgeon General's reports on smoking and disease links. That information is misinterpreted or rejected as invalid.

Selective exposure doesn't always happen, however. Selective exposure is most likely when the set of cognitions is unstable; if the overall system is stable, dissonant information is integrated (Frey, 1986).

Some dissonance comes from knowing that others hold different ideas. Dissonance builds from lack of social support. Large numbers of attractive others who agree on other matters but who disagree on the target cognitive element make for a high degree of dissonance. Of course, dissonance also increases with the importance of the issue and the relevance of the others to the issue. A near-alcoholic couple may decide to take up square dancing. After they are well into the lessons and enjoying the fun, they discover that there is no drinking associated with the dances. They like the people and have committed themselves to the dancing, but their attitudes about alcohol are at variance with the dance club's. Dissonance may be reduced by changing their opinions, trying to change the ideas of the others, or by separating themselves from the comparison others. The new dancers are not going to change the beliefs of the others, because it is clear that drinking and square dancing don't go together. Their dissonance may be reduced by modifying their own opinion or by compartmentalizing their thoughts about drinking and alcohol or both. They continue to drink but have no expectation of drinking at the square dances or with any members of that social group.

Cognitive dissonance theory and research was intensely followed for many years, and as might be expected, many problems were found and necessary modifications were made. It was a rough theory that formalized what amounted to logical guesses and general truths about the relations among mental elements and consequent actions. Like the other consistency theories, it simplified the complexity of a slice of life. It has problems of definition of components and of predicting the form of change that will be chosen to reduce the inconsistency or dissonance. Nonetheless, the core idea remains an attractive and practical description of one class of mental causes of motivated actions.

Staying Happy

When we feel good, we think in different ways. Positive feelings bring more positive memories to mind, perhaps excluding unpleasant ones. We tend to protect that enjoyable state in the tasks we choose to do, and

we solve problems more efficiently, perhaps adding creativity. These are some of the general conclusions of Alice Isen (1993), following a long series of studies with her colleagues on positive affect. Contrary to the established philosophical fashion that emotion destroys rational, quality thought, we are now convinced that, for positive emotion at least, feelings alter our thought in ways that are more productive of life success. The comparable case for negative feeling still needs thorough study. Following Isen, we will look at three categories of evidence.

Feeling good affects the materials we bring to mind and thus the organization of them in later thoughts. We seem to be able to bring more positive ideas from memory because there are more of them and they have greater variety. Hence, being happy tends to introduce unlike materials in the mind, leading to new associations and complexes of ideas. From there, it follows that we will be more flexible in our decisions and judgments.

A second feature of feeling happy is our tendency to maintain that happiness in what we choose to do. We tend to select tasks that maintain our feeling good and turn away from those suggesting negativity or boredom. So, not surprisingly, we do things we enjoy doing and things that will expand the variety that feeds that enjoyment. Behind this is an apparent strategy of protecting our positive feelings by actively seeking activities that we expect to be fun or challenging. Negative tasks or consideration of negative ideas will be done, but only if they are presented as necessary.

Happy people usually make the same decisions and choices when faced with complex problems, but they do so in less time and with higher quality in the process. Some of the additional time taken by less happy people was in refocusing ideas already considered and paying undue attention to things of no importance (Isen & Means, 1983). In a diagnosis problem, happier medical students came to the conclusion earlier with less confusion and then added other ideas about treatments (Isen, Rosenzweig, & Young, 1991).

SECTION SUMMARY: THINKING

Active and fully aware mental processing of events rests on a collection of relatively automatic and minimally conscious operations. Formal thinking tends to be influenced by those existing adaptations and habits. We find biases of our reasoning in which decision rules we make follow the law of small numbers and causal fantasy. Making decisions has been rationalized into normally correct rules, but we still are led by systematic biases. We follow simple rules of thumb and take shortcuts such as the availability bias, the gambler's fallacy, and entrapment. We seem naturally inclined to be sensitive to detecting cheating and to deal with proportions rather than abstract statistics. Men do better at mapping directions, whereas women excel at knowing where items are placed. In solving problems, we simplify the elements and relationships, leading us to fail to see new uses for old items and to be misled by tracking surplus information. Being absentminded is founded on being in a familiar place, doing familiar things, but having a distracting mental preoccupation.

Another aspect of keeping mental things simple is keeping them consistent. We are motivated to achieve and maintain consistency. Fritz Heider pictured relationships between people in different conditions of consistency, which he called balance. An unbalanced situation causes mental unrest, and that motivates changes toward restoring balance. Leon Festinger described mental inconsistency as a state of cognitive dissonance that is aversive. He proposed a variety of sources and cures that cleverly account for some of our common and seemingly illogical patterns of thinking and acting.

Opposite to inconsistency's unpleasant state, Alice Isen shows the power of feeling good on our thinking. In addition to perpetuating that happiness, we are more creative and productive, and we take less time to choose and decide.

CHAPTER CONCLUSIONS

Our consciousness, the capacity to experience our separate beings, is not difficult to describe, but we bow to William James for his most elegant presentation of most of it. We know, too, that much of it is self-centered and self-directed. What we experience of the world depends in large measure on what we have come to expect is there. Our mentality has an active part also, expressed as our agency. How can we explain these phenomena and these powers?

From earliest times, our natural tendency has been to believe that we could understand our mind's causes if we would just attend more closely and logically to our experiences. This how-it-seems-to-me stance gave us mind-body dualism, the mind-body problem of accounting for how one affects the other, and varieties of other dualism and monism. A natural monism, one that assumes that our experience can be explained by an appropriate understanding of our body material, depends on working out how we think about the problem. Dennett proposes a massively parallel brain, furnished with some natural functions and infected with an organized array of informative memes, producing narrative drafts that are our conscious experiences.

Meditation and hypnosis appear to us as mysterious processes precisely because we have assumed that controlling what is in our awareness is not possible. That fatalism of our age is a particularly virulent meme that leads us to see these as secrets unlocking fantastic powers. In truth, they are merely seldom-practiced skills, with powers available to any who choose to make the efforts.

We pride ourselves on logical thought and decisions, but we are easily able to see how we make mistakes. Some thought bias comes from natural adaptations to solving specific problems such as detecting cheating and finding directions and physical things. Other biases rest on the tendency to simplify and keep consistent our mental contents. New directions lie in using positive mental states to enhance the quality of our thinking.

Study and Review Questions

1. What is William James's idea at the base of what is most interesting to each of us?

2. What did William James mean by "the only things which we commonly see are those which we preperceive"?

3. About who and what do we find gossip naturally interesting?

4. What is agency?

5. What evidence should we accept for mental causes of agency?

6. What are problematic phenomena of intimacy and qualia?

7. What are the mind-body problem and mind-body dualism?

8. What is the physical monist approach to understanding mental phenomena?

9. What do eliminative materialists assume?

10. What are George Mandler's schemas, and what do they do?

11. What does Daniel Dennett mean by saying our brains are massively parallel-processing?

12. Where is the Cartesian Theater in Daniel Dennett's theory of consciousness?

13. What are memes in Daniel Dennett's theory of consciousness?

14. How does Daniel Dennett describe "simultaneous narrative drafts" using "virtual machinery"?

15. What are minds in Daniel Dennett's theory of consciousness?

16. Why is it improper to judge a theory of mentality by our personal how-it-seems-to-me?

17. What do we learn in meditating?

18. Who can be hypnotized?

19. What new mental powers emerge under hypnosis?

20. What can a hypnotized person do?

21. To what did William James tie thinking?

22. What is the law of small numbers?

23. How are we misled by causal fantasy?

24. What is the availability bias?

25. What is the gambler's fallacy?

26. What is entrapment?

27. What natural facility do we have in simple logic problems such as those of Peter Wason?

28. In dealing with numbers, do we find it more natural to use frequencies or percentages?

29. How do men and women differ in natural spatial abilities?

30. What are some common impediments to solving problems?

31. What three elements are needed to act absentmindedly?

32. What does inconsistency motivate?

33. What mental state results from Fritz Heider's mental imbalance of perceptions?

34. What makes Leon Festinger's state of cognitive dissonance, and how does it feel?

35. In what different ways do we reduce cognitive dissonance?

36. What are the features of thinking when a person is happy?

CHAPTER 11

Addiction

Our common ideas about addiction are social and political constructions largely based on mythical medical pictures. A useful concept of addiction shows causes in physiological effects and psychological dependence, habitual actions, and cultural roots. Addiction acts can be social reactions, efficient ways to minimize pain and suffering, and essential parts of how we picture ourselves.

Taking drugs, drinking alcohol, and using tobacco each has a social history of pleasure in use and later political control based on allegations of social disorder and disease. In those histories, political interests nearly always overrode sociological, psychological, and biological facts. A different example of addiction appears in obsessive dieting, where personal compulsion comes from internalized cultural pictures of ideal body shape.

Components of Addictive Acts

Addiction Theory and Change

Taking Drugs

Drinking

Smoking

Dieting

What does it mean to be addicted? We have a shared cultural picture of addiction that is really quite new by historical standards, perhaps 75 years old. In our political view, the meaning of addiction seems to be rooted in the commonly accepted disease metaphor of how drugs such as morphine, heroin, alcohol, and barbiturates work. Our model assumes that an addict has a disease made up of an acquired or inherited physiological need for a substance or both, that the physical need controls specific addiction-maintaining acts, and that the only possibilities of change are medical therapy and complete abstinence.

This addiction model was and is defined politically, not medically, and now it is enshrined in society's laws, treatment pro-

329

grams, and research strategies. Addiction was labeled a medical disease, and the disease label spread to other things we do. In turn, it has become its own metaphor, and as a metaphor, it is now employed widely through the literary device of adding *oholic* or *addict* to any activity that seems difficult to resist or that someone dislikes. Moving back to real addictions, our treatments, research, and laws have all had poor success in dealing with specific addictions. The reasons for the failures may lie in having assumed the disease theory of addictions and its implication that people cannot control their addictive acts. These ideas we will explore.

We begin with a bold assertion. With just a few physiological exceptions, there are no physical indicators of addiction; addicted persons are those who act addicted. The only reliable indication of addiction is what a person says and does. We will assume acting addicted to mean habitual, motivated acting that dominates parts of an individual's life and is perceived by the person or by others to be interfering with valued aspects of living.

Our goal is to outline principles for understanding the motivation of addictive acts, with particular attention to some hidden and less popular concepts. We will not make an exhaustive study of addiction. References are given to more complete information about psychopharmacological action and fuller accounts of other addictive acts. In this chapter, we first outline some principal components of addiction, and then we describe addiction theories and principles of how to change addictive acts. Finally, we outline historical patterns and experiences regarding the use of prohibited drugs, alcohol, smoking, and dieting.

COMPONENTS OF ADDICTIVE ACTS

Specific addictive acts are maintained from a variety of causes and conditions. This section outlines the possibilities. Addicted acts are potentially composed of physiological effect,

TABLE 11.1 Listing of Addiction Components

Physiological effect
Psychological dependence
Habitual action
Cultural origins
Social response
Economical affect maintenance
Self-representation

psychological dependence, habitual action, cultural origins, social response, economical affect maintenance, and self-representation (see Table 11.1).

Physiological Effect

Cocaine can cause sleeplessness, loss of appetite, and heart stoppage. Alcohol slows some nerve functioning, destroys brain cells, and can produce death by liver failure. Tobacco smoke alters lung tissue toward cancers and emphysema. Overeating produces body fat, setting the stage for artery and heart function disorders. All of these well-known effects suggest the physical nature of addictions and their medical treatment. The common idea is that addictions are diseases.

The disease model of addiction is a seductive metaphor borrowed from medical successes. People catch an infectious agent, experience symptoms, and submit to medical treatment to cure the disease. A part of the body is exposed to fire, becomes burned, and is treated by specific medical acts. The model is simple and the implications are unequivocal. Specific drugs, treatments, and physical changes remove the offending symptoms by attacking their causes.

Although the disease model is satisfying and has had remarkable success for some aspects of medicine, it is not always a suitable description, even of medical facts. The disease model often fails. Many afflictions are not easily defined. At what point, for example, does high blood pressure or a partially clogged artery become a disease? What are their causes, and what makes a cure? The symptoms are physical events, but many nonphysical causes control them. Similarly, there are physical aspects to addiction, but that is not all there is to them or perhaps even what is very important.

Physical dependence rests on changes in the body that come from repeatedly using a substance. Physical dependence is thought of as a disease, and that way of conceiving addiction has become common and unquestioned. Drugs do have effects on the body, but physical dependency is defined by some lasting changes: tolerance and withdrawal.

Tolerance is a measure of the increased amounts of a drug that are taken over time to achieve a constant effect. At first, a few mild drinks give a pleasant feeling of relaxation. With continued regular use, more alcohol is needed to get the same psychological state. There is evidence that some drugs accumulate and have moderating effects. Barbiturates, alcohol, and opiates all show tolerance effects. Alcohol and the barbiturates are also described as cross-tolerant—tolerance to one increases tolerance for the other—but these two are not cross-tolerant with the opiates. Tolerance increases to a limit set by the nature of the specific action of that drug on the body.

Withdrawal names the negative reaction experienced when the drug is no longer received. Some reported symptoms of withdrawal include anxiety, inability to sleep, nausea, seizures, disorientation, and convulsions. Specific patterns of withdrawal symptoms depend on the drug, the amount of drug typically taken, and the length of time it was taken.

Physical dependence is not the only direct physical basis for addiction to be considered. At the roots of many addictions are strong physiologically based experiences of changed feelings. The addictive action makes the person feel different, often better. Amphetamines and cocaine produce feelings of alertness and energy, neutralizing fatigue. Morphine deadens pain. Barbiturates produce states of relaxation. With many strong drugs, the user rapidly learns to expect changes in affect. Similar changes in affect come from acts of smoking, eating, sex, and exercise.

Less direct, or perhaps just less well-understood, physiologically based changes may underlie experienced feelings in gambling, acquiring objects, dominating others, and an essentially unlimited domain of psychological and social acts. In these acts, a complex of emotional systems is in action. This extension of physiologically based feeling to other sources is not intended to minimize their force, but instead it shows that such changes in feelings are a primary component of any addicted act. They are, of course, a part of human life. Acting addicted includes an unusual dependence on drugs or specific acts to supply expected feelings.

Psychological Dependence

Psychological dependence is defined by the properties of tolerance and withdrawal, but a third is added, craving. We commonly assume a physical basis for each of these properties, but we can proceed with equal ease as if there is not. In the absence of a complete explanation in physical terms, the case for physical dependence forcing use of a specific drug use must be suspect, especially in light of the variety of evidence for psychological dependence underlying addictions.

The idea of tolerance is based on the model of physical changes from repeated use, but it is measured by drug-taking acts. Causes of those acts lie partly in general habituation. Any repeated stimulus has a weaker effect. Consider these instructive comparisons. We look at the scenic view with strong interest, but after a few moments much of that attraction has weakened. After a few mouthfuls of ice cream, we become partly sated on the flavor, and it is no longer as attractive. The faces of friends, although desired for many reasons, hold little fascination over time. The effect is psychologically less with repeated dosage, and more is taken to get a constant effect. So, too, it is with the effects of specific drugs.

Withdrawal is the collection of feelings or suffering expressed upon failing to get the drug. Again, a physical cause is usually assumed, but psychological accounts abound. If we expect to suffer from withdrawal symptoms, that becomes part of the negative motivational basis for continuing to use the drug. The script of withdrawal pain is learned by users, and some perform it because it is expected. Thus, withdrawal, like tolerance, can be psychologically developed.

Craving is a great desire to have more of the drug or experience, building as the time for normal dosage or activity comes near. This, too, is thought of as physically determined, but there is no way to know except through psychological actions. Craving, too, is part of the script of actions that addicts learn and perform.

Habitual Action

Regular and often repeated addictive acts are habitual, but there are more subtle meanings to be described. Part of the essential nature of some addictions is the pattern of actions involved. The ritual-like character of the acts provides some motivational substance to the act, perhaps in the sense of deepening the psychological expectation of changed affect. The very doing itself also may be a large component of the complex of feelings. Eventually, the ritual of the addictive act becomes a part of a self-picture and image of being consistent.

It is the nature of life that something must always be happening. Patterns of actions form meaningful acts. Certain of these actions and acts are performed over and over because they have consequences that are valued. They become habits that are pleasant, at least relative to doing other things or not doing anything at all. If these habitual acts are attached to expected feelings, a strong motivation to continue is forged. In this fashion, the ritual acts that are part of smoking, taking drugs, drinking alcohol, or eating become firmly established and are a foundation component of the addiction. A great deal of pleasure is attached to the habitual rituals.

Smoking a pipe requires preparation and practice. Various tools and materials must be assembled and time set aside to carry out the acts. A pipe is selected and inspected for potential cleaning. Perhaps it must be scraped or reamed and the mouthpiece augured with a special pipe cleaner. A few puffs through it verify that it is ready. The tobacco is selected and the pipe is loaded by special hand movements in a pouch, tamping the material to just the right depth and compression with the finger. The pipe is then placed in the mouth and a flame brought to it. Lighting and holding matches or special lighters have ritual forms all their own. The tobacco is lit and thus is begun a set of special ways of adjusting the pipe in the mouth and holding it in hand during the smoking.

Habitual acts themselves become part of the pleasure of the addiction. Smoking gives a good illustration. Its acts are stylish and satisfying in themselves. Pipes require special tools and close attention in ritualistic acts of cleaning and filling. The manner of holding and lighting cigarettes becomes important and satisfying. In another addiction, the styles of drinking, whether socially or alone, become established and part of the complex of changed affect coming from the acts. The ritual of eating is important in itself; just eating anything becomes a compulsive act, without relation to the consequence.

Habitual patterns of actions can be more than just a part of an addiction. They can be the major substance of an addiction, if not the addiction itself. Running, having sex, and maintaining extremely close personal relationships, when they are carried out to pathological excess, have been suggested to be addictions. They are no longer acts for the sake of other pleasures and states. Addicted runners run only to run. Lovers have sexual relations just to perform those ritual-like acts. The complexities of being closely tied to the life of another become the end in itself for one addicted to a close relationship.

Addictions become part of one's self-definition. In general, we see the composite of personal action styles as definitions of our self. As components of addictive acts become established, they are accepted as part of the normal self, and they are further embedded as habits supporting addiction. Having several cups of coffee in the morning, cigarettes at breaks, and drinks before and after dinner are marks of a personal style made stylish. They become the things that one does and thus define to oneself and to others a consistent picture. These styles make the underlying addictions to caffeine, nicotine, and alcohol stronger. To break the addictions, a valued part of the habit-based self-picture must be changed.

Cultural Origins

Tendencies toward addictions are set by one's culture. The scripts of one's culture are followed. Some of those scripts are cultural rules about addiction. There are scripts of more or less detail for every set of meaningful acts to be performed. Scripts exist for eating, sleeping, loving, and fighting, and the list goes on. Scripted actions and thoughts that form addictions are included among each culture's scripts. There are rules about how much self-control is expected in performing potentially addicting actions.

For someone living in a small, isolated farm town, things are not easily done in unique ways. There are rather specific expectations that we will act as others do, and even our eccentricities must conform to prescription. We may attend either of the churches, usually a decision forced by family tradition, or we may choose not to go at all and accept the community disdain, but we may not deny the authority of the church people and their core beliefs in running the affairs of the town. The cultural standards are those of "God-fearing Christians," whether a person is one or not.

A culture's scripts may define standards of social drinking in moderation, for example, and include the expectation that no one will exceed a certain limit of alcohol consumption. If we think addictive, excessive drinking is under our personal agency, it is expected to be controlled, and we do so. On the other hand, if we think alcoholism to be a medical disease that has no permanent cure, being labeled an alcoholic will lead us to accept that fatalism and assume that there is no possibility of controlling our drinking by any effort of personal will. We will conform to that cultural script by drinking to excess. Cultural mores of fatalism produce addicts, whereas those of personal responsibility do not. In either case, the scripts of our society are followed.

One of the strongest collections of evidence for a fundamental cultural component to addiction is the fact that some groups have high rates of substance addiction and others are moderate users of those substances. The clearest examples concern alcoholism. People immersed in Irish culture have more alcoholics than those in Italian or in Jewish cultures (Vaillant, 1983). Fewer women than men are alcoholics (Ferrence, 1980; Helzer et al., 1988; Robins, Helzer, Przybeck, & Regier, 1988). Asians have very little alcoholism, and many Native Americans have very high alcoholism rates, although both groups have a somewhat stronger physical response to consuming alcohol (Peele, 1986). Low socioeconomic-scale people have more alcoholism and more substance abuse of all kinds. A core city sample studied at length had three times as many alcoholics as a comparable Harvard-educated group (Vaillant, 1983), although ethnic differences also existed in these samples, and alcohol abuse is more frequent in people with less education (Robins et al., 1988).

In each of these cases, the difference appears to be the expectations toward performance that are set by each culture. Out-of-control alcoholism is prevalent in cultures where there are beliefs that alcohol is a disease that cannot be prevented or that a person need not have self-control while drinking or both. The principle of addiction in general is extremely important and may underlie much of the failure to reform those judged to be addicts. The expectations and ways of our local culture as well as those of the legal and scientific society are assumed. We conform to our culture's beliefs.

Social Response

Powerful expectations are set by other people. The social setting dictates the acceptable acts of the moment. To avoid being different, we do what is suggested by others. Addictive styles of action may be commonplace among groups facing special circumstances.

The bottle of bourbon is passed around a group of teens. It was taken from someone's parents' home with the intent of having a "party." None of the partygoers can easily resist the social pressure to drink. All eyes are on each, as turns are taken. Years later, the social equivalent is an offered drink at a gathering at a friend's home. Few will refuse a toast to the speaker at a formal dinner party. Social conformity is a powerful source of individual motivation, as we discussed earlier. Mere presence with others is a sufficient stimulus. Conformity to what others are doing also reflects a fashionable microcosm of culture. The acts with which we conform are those we learned from social experience. A young person involved with others joins their party and comes to conform to what is accepted by everyone to be appropriate partying acts. If members of the social group have learned that it is good style to experiment with alcohol, drugs, or other addictive substances, each individual feels even more social pressure to conform.

Another remarkable feature of social influence is its time or place limits. Socially motivated, addictive acts are carried out while in those specific social settings but are dropped when the social forces change. A strong example, discussed below, is that of the military personnel who used drugs heavily in Vietnam but abruptly quit on return to the United States. Those who continued drug use were largely those who returned to social groups expecting drug use.

Addictive acts tend to be interchangeable, linked with social patterns of nonconformity. The specific acts of addiction in social groups of nonconforming people tend to be variable. A variety of substances are used, often depending on what is most available. The important social fact in the group is that some sort of substance is used, appearing as a mark of the group's style of nonconformity. The social pattern of nonconformity often is a combination of substance abuse and other roles. Members "act out" in a variety of styles, including acts of rejection of achievement values of the larger society, acts of aggression, and actions designed to alienate and thus insulate them from society expectations. Specific addictions are motivated by this larger pattern of social forces of nonconformity.

Economical Affect Maintenance

From the psychological base of an addicted person, maintaining an addicted pattern of action may be the most efficient way to minimize discomfort. It hurts emotionally to be fat and see the disrespect of others. But those hurts are not as important when the tasty food is there, and acts of eating will produce good feelings. During the eating the other pains of life aren't important, including those judgments coming from others. Eating can be a break from depression and that break has pleasure.

An addiction can be an escape from aspects of life. The sources of negative life experiences that enable an addiction are as varied as life itself. They also vary in severity or in duration. The events may range from the temporary, severe stress of losing a loved one to relatively permanent but mild situations of career boredom or unhappy marriage. The addictive act may provide temporary relief, or it may in the long run simply be less painful.

The prime motivator of acts is expectation of affect, but many expectations are not of positive affect. A pattern of fear and anxiety will set the stage for expecting more. If an act postpones those expected experiences, it becomes a more desirable alternative. The addiction acts may actually give positive feelings, or they may just postpone the beginning of the negative. The effect is the same. Potential pain is set aside.

The addictive acts themselves may come to lose some of their initial stigma in our mind. The addiction is seen to be an efficient solution to the pressures of life. In our expectations, there are worse states than maintaining the pattern of addictive acts. The addiction thus becomes insulated. The potentially negative affect from self-evaluation is removed and that adds further to the complex of positive feeling ascribed to maintaining the addiction.

Once the benefits of being addicted are accepted, it is easy for a person to shift from one pattern to another. It is the style and attitudes about self-control that have been assimilated. Excessive substance use becomes the life pattern. Specific addictions can run together, even though there is no similarity among the substances. Addicted people tend to engage in a pattern of negative health and safety acts. Furthermore, people who have been heavy substance abusers can shift to being compulsive in other ways, perhaps addicted to eating, exercise, religion, or other nondrug activities (Peele, 1988).

Self-Representation

A part of the complex of addiction is the view that the agent has of being an addict. Society's labels and expectations are easily internalized and become self-fulfilling prophecies. It is perhaps this aspect of addiction that gives vital importance to the theoretical ideas that we accept.

Many of the components underlying addictive acts come together in the set of beliefs the addict has constructed. As a result of assuming society's theories about physical dependence, conforming to the performance style of a social group, adopting a comfortable set of habits, and feeling somewhat better during those acts, a person accepts an addict identity and plays that role.

The ideas that each person has assumed about the acts will carry a heavy influence. It is a matter of the philosophy that each person has accepted about personal control over life. The extremes may be labeled fatalism and personal efficacy. In holding to fatalism, we believe that forces from outside our control produce the addiction and make futile any attempt at change. If we assume a fatalistic model, we will keep our addictions because we will make no effort to change what we do. The fatalistic, loss-of-control model is a popular explanation, especially with the majority of addiction therapists (whose personal interest is obviously served by this stance). It is also a convenient excuse for failing to reform an addictive lifestyle.

The personal efficacy view is that we can change our acts by personal effort. Ideas of agency and person-generated change have been unpopular in behaviorist psychology and physicalist philosophy. The reasons for that general bias are not valid, but they are historically rooted and are widely assumed. It is curious that some variety of fatalism is the typical view of addiction theorists and is often cited in failures of personal reform, yet these theorists believe that the vast bulk of their personal actions are under their personal control and choice. We will look at evidence below showing that most often the lasting change away from addictive acts is to moderation, not abstinence, and that change appears to have come about as a matter of personal choice largely unaided by, and frequently in spite of, specific therapy from others.

SECTION SUMMARY:
COMPONENTS OF ADDICTIVE ACTS

What makes up our habituated, motivated acting in ways that dominate part of our lives and interfere with our values in living? There is no single or simple cause.

Addictive acts come from a complex of components.

Physiological effects are part of addiction, both in their direct alteration of body function and the changes in feelings they enable. Physical dependence is assessed by tolerance and withdrawal. Tolerance makes us do more to get the same effect, whereas withdrawal is the complex of symptoms resulting from not getting a substance to which we have been accustomed. Analogous psychological dependence is based on mentally derived forms of tolerance and withdrawal, plus cravings based on learning to expect the addicted acts.

Habits are powerful aspects of some addicted acts. Doing those things is preferred to other possible activities, they become pleasurable in their performance, and they become part of the observable structure of one's personality, defining who one is by what one does.

Culture scripts are followed, in which some acts are viewed as beyond control or as part of the important criteria of being of that culture. Of shorter term are forces of social conformity to doing what others are doing. These time- or place-limited influences may be to perform specific acts or to move toward a style of social nonconformity.

Addicted acts may be unhelpful or even dangerous in the long term or larger picture of life, but at the moment, they make one feel better than if they weren't done. Gradually, these periods of lesser unpleasantness are viewed as good solutions to life's troubles. People assume an addict identity and may come to believe that they have no power to change it. This fatalism contrasts with the personal efficacy view that we can be successful on our own to change what we do.

ADDICTION THEORY AND CHANGE

Addiction is commonly pictured to be a moral evil founded on a physical necessity. The prevailing model of addiction contains many assumptions:

> The physical causes of the addiction are overwhelmingly powerful.
>
> Once the requisite acts are begun, no one can return to pre-addiction without help.
>
> Choosing addiction is a moral transgression, made knowingly and in the face of the dire consequences.
>
> The only possibility of redemption is through complete abstinence achieved and maintained with outside help.

All of these ideas, typical and common, are fundamentally unsupported and contradicted by ample evidence.

Models of Addiction

Theories of addiction are of more practical importance than evidence. Only through the principles we have accepted is addiction defined, maintained, and cured.

The dominating medical model is based on the subtle and common metaphor of disease. Having a disease implies that there is a specific physically based fault and a program of treatment that will remove that physical fault. As a consequence, the disease theory of addiction assumes fatalism and one-slip return to addiction. Fatalism is the belief that there is nothing one can do to prevent the disease if the supposed causes are present. If we "catch" the virus, we will get the flu. Control may be accomplished by complete separation from the addiction causes. Wash your hands often, and stay away from sick people. Even a single encounter with the causes reverses the cure and the addiction disease returns full-blown. Cure is thought to come from study of the disease itself and eventual discovery of a medicinal "magic bullet," often

TABLE 11.2 Models Based on Assumptions of Responsibilities for Addiction, Based on Brickman et al. (1982)

	For getting it	For not getting it
For changing it	moral	compensatory
For not changing it	enlightenment	medical

conceived as some sort of counteracting drug. Medical science will soon find a cure for flu.

The medical model of addiction developed historically to justify the politics of controlling opium use (discussed below). We assumed that opium and other narcotic drugs were physically addicting and thus produce a form of disease. Consequently, the existence of nonnarcotic drug addiction has been confusing to medical model theorists. Nicotine, caffeine, cocaine, and amphetamines are stimulants and thus don't fit with the category of opiates and their properties. In particular, there is no physical evidence for withdrawal with amphetamines and cocaine. Yet, individuals heavily using these drugs give evidence of withdrawal.

A parallel problem comes from alcohol, widely known to be used in a controlled manner by many, although drinking is an addicted act for some. That has generated a variety of revised disease theories. Some believe that certain individuals are genetically predisposed to alcoholic addiction. Others hold that after a certain intensity of alcohol drinking, addiction becomes physically inevitable. Almost no one seriously questions the validity of the medical model itself.

Furthermore, heavy dependence on ideas of disease sources of addiction leads theorists to suppose that there are yet-to-be-discovered physical bases for any pattern of intense acts, such as running, overeating, and love relationships.

One useful analysis of possibilities of thought about addiction separates beliefs about personal responsibility for causes from beliefs about changes. Philip Brickman and his associates (1982) proposed four logical possibilities, defined by belief that one is or is not responsible for forming the addiction

and is or is not responsible for changing the addiction (see Table 11.2).

The **medical model** assumes the least personal responsibility for both. The addiction is conceived as a disease process without fault to the person, a disease that can be arrested only by actions directed at its physical causes. The addicted person accepts the illness and expects to be treated by experts.

The **moral model** assumes the highest personal responsibility for both forming and changing the addiction. The addicted person strives to overcome the self-image of being of low willpower or lazy and expects strong supportive urgings from peers. The prospect of change must come from personal will.

The **enlightenment model** is one of strong responsibility for forming the addiction but low responsibility for changing it. These addicted people feel guilty and submit to the discipline of authorities. The programs of alcoholism treatment administered by the Alcoholics Anonymous groups preach guilt for being addicted and the need to give over personal control to a higher power and follow the dictated narrow path of total abstinence.

Finally, those holding the **compensatory model** assume little responsibility for forming the addiction but strong responsibility for changing it. These addicts feel that they have been deprived and need to assert themselves. Therapists are believed to be servants helping to mobilize the resources of the addicted persons. The addiction is something that has just happened to them for whatever reason, and now it is necessary to focus on change.

Abstinence Versus Moderation

One of the most contentious issues of addiction change is that of the existence and possibility of change from acting addicted to moderation rather than to complete abstinence. Those holding the medical and enlightenment models typically believe that only total abstinence is effective, whether achieved by disease therapy or the substitution of allegiance to another authority. The issue has become clouded by a failure to examine the evidence from the population as a whole rather than samples of people who have failed at self-help and thus presented themselves for professional treatment.

Most of the ideas about drug addiction have come from study of people who have experienced an inability to control their habits. The clinical population on which the theories have been based does not include those who are successful in self-control over long periods of time. The medical profession has ignored, or perhaps has been largely unaware of, the casual, controlled users who experience little of the withdrawal and cravings that are emphasized by the medical model. It is unlikely that controlled users will reveal their use to addiction professionals because of embarrassment or legal liabilities to themselves and thus little has been told of their self-regulation story.

As the addiction medical model became entrenched and widely known, those individuals who were not able to control their use followed the pattern prescribed by the model, feeding back to and fulfilling the theory prophecies. A major theme of change in Western culture has been toward loss of belief in personal control. From a pattern of technical successes and biological theory, we have come to expect that there are causes beyond our control and experts who will fix things. So the reasoning follows that addiction too can be fixed. No self-control is necessary or possible.

Evidence from systematic study shows that many former addicts, perhaps the majority, have made changes by assuming personal responsibility. Many people, once addicted, have moderated their own acts. Remission of addictive acts is common when the addicted people intentionally use coping strategies or face environmental change. These changes happen outside of the province of official therapy, and so they must be discovered by special effort.

Stanley Schachter (1982) reported a study of two specific populations. These were not intended to be representative of society as a whole, but because they were exhaustive studies of all members of those populations, they give some idea of the natural history of different personal experiences with addiction. He selected a group of educated people in an academic department at a city university, Columbia University, and a small resort community on Long Island, New York. Schachter found that more than half of the population trying to stop smoking or lose weight did so on their own.

Other studies of populations also show a high rate of giving up drinking alcohol to excess. Most typically, young men are likely to take up heavy drinking but give it up as they become older (Fillmore, 1988).

Patrick Biernacki (1986) purposefully sought a sample of self-recovered heroin addicts through a method of chain referrals. Recovered addicts contacted those they knew and asked them to cooperate; eventually a sample of "hidden" former users was studied under assurances of anonymity. The intent of this study was not to discover relative numbers but instead to examine facts of their recovery from addiction. A summary of those facts shows some principles of recovery from addictive acts. Biernacki found two sorts of recovery patterns. One was that of the addict who was living apart from a normal life and deeply in the drug culture. The process of change for these addicts was a traumatic shift, often toward an opposite, drug-free society such as religious commitment. The second recovery process was that of addicts who had been balancing a normal and addict life. Their change was more rational, responding to a kind of burnout from the difficulty of trying to maintain both worlds.

On withdrawal from heroin, most addicts reported being able to manage two kinds of cravings: one based on avoidance of the pain of withdrawal and one reflecting the desire of wanting the drug. Cravings were managed by finding ways to separate themselves from the heroin and viewing it in a negative way, occasionally by resorting to periods of using alcohol or other drugs. A continuing problem was the social stigma of having once been an addict.

Studies of physicians using narcotics over long periods of time showed there was little evidence of diminished abilities, and they appeared to have integrated their narcotic use into a normal life. No withdrawal or craving was evident in the periods when they abstained from the narcotic (Zinberg & Jacobson, 1976). These controlled users and others stop their drug use whenever they have things to do that they value more highly. Patterns of use vary over a person's lifetime. People take up controlled use, sometimes increasing to intense levels of addiction, and yet return to a moderate controlled use. Such

individuals are unlikely to come to the attention of addiction therapists.

Research studying veterans' drug use showed that only 14% were readdicted, after their return home, to the narcotics that they had used heavily in Vietnam. Perhaps half of the veterans had used some heroin after their return, but that use did not continue into an addiction. They displayed controlled use. Only those who returned to social settings in which they were expected to use drugs continued in the addiction (Robins et al., 1980).

The findings of controlled use are largely absent in the popular conceptions held about drug addiction. The thesis of controlled use is regularly attacked by professional addiction researchers. Theirs is an entrenched belief having strong political overtones and reflecting their own dependence on maintaining the simplistic medical model we noted at the start of this section.

SECTION SUMMARY: ADDICTION THEORY AND CHANGE

The current Western cultural beliefs about addiction follow a fatalistic medical model. Our laws, treatment programs, and research strategies treat addiction as a disease one catches and then needs medical expertise to cure. Part of the cure requires abstinence.

Thus, we find it hard to accept that large numbers of people have changed their acts toward moderation or personal control without outside help and without danger of sliding back into addiction.

TAKING DRUGS

Some insights about the "drug problem" come from entertaining some provocative questions.

Which is the greater danger to us: users of drugs or the "war on drugs"?

We will keep this question in mind as we review the evidence and history of "narcotic" drugs. Now for a check on our national rationality.

Which drugs should we control?

1. Those that in moderate use kill thousands of people a year and shorten the lives of thousands more?

2. Those that kill or debilitate a few hundred people a year, people who have seriously overused them, even though the same drugs have been known to make life more pleasant for countless users in moderate and occasional low dosages?

3. Those that have no significant verifiable lasting damage and have strong evidence of beneficial medical use for a few rare conditions?

As we can easily see, if we are willing to look at evidence, we openly promote the sale and use of the most dangerous in the first alternative: alcohol and nicotine. But we forbid the use of those in the second and third alternatives: cocaine and opium, and marijuana. How can this be true? Is it true?

Using opiates and cocaine is the model on which the modern political concepts of addiction and its presumed evils were formed, and it continues to be the reference of comparison. That makes it especially important for us to know what these drugs are, what they do, where they came from, who uses them, and why they are now controlled by politicians rather than physicians or ourselves.

Narcotic Drugs

The term *narcotic* is a loose label of convenience covering opioids, stimulants, depressants, and some drugs with other forms of experience-altering effects. The label has mostly political roots and refers to whatever substance is both legally controlled and presumed to have addicting potential. Exact definition varies.

Opiates are drugs that come from the opium poppy. Some are different forms of the natural product, and others come from processing and chemical alterations. Opium is the dried liquid that seeps from poppy plant seed heads that have been lightly cut just after dropping their flower petals. In this form, it has been eaten or smoked for more than 6,000 years. The primary active chemicals are **morphine** and **codeine,** both of which are extracted by chemical process. Other alkaloid chemicals in the opium have been separated for their medicinal value or as starting materials for synthesizing other opiates. **Heroin** was first synthesized from morphine in 1879, making a chemical with 10 times greater potency and much more rapid uptake to the brain. For much of medical history, opiates were the only effective drugs for pain relief. That use continues, primarily in morphine form. Opiates also give euphoria, a pleasant feeling of tranquillity and passivity. In the 1800s, this was called opium's stimulant effect. With these properties, we can understand why the Sumerians of 4000 B.C. called poppies the "plant of joy" (Berridge & Edwards, 1981).

The opiates—opium, morphine, and heroin—make people happy and relieve their pain. The physical means by which this is done is still being studied, and it is a matter of educated conjecture rather than specification of exact physiological causes. The general agreement is that opiates intercede in the normal action of communication between cells in the central nervous system. Their role in moderating pain of many kinds is generally acknowledged, although dosage and effect can be determined only by trial and observation. Repeated and continued moderate use of the opiates causes no organic damage. Unlike alcohol, aspirin, and many other medications in general use, the opiates, in casual and low doses, have not been shown to cause physical injury. Some researchers describe the opiates under these conditions as nearly neutral and benign substances.

Cocaine is a stimulant extracted from leaves of the coca shrub. A paste is formed that is chemically processed to cocaine hydrochloride salt. The natural leaves have been chewed and processed in other ways by natives of South America for at least 1,000 years, but cocaine's present processed form was introduced to the West in the 1880s as a medicine for a long list of complaints. It was soon supplied in soft drinks and in over-the-counter medicines. Taken slowly as a food, cocaine increases alertness, energy, and general feelings of well-being. Introduced rapidly by injection, smoking, or snorting, cocaine gives a rush of intense euphoria with positive feelings of sociability and competence. Physicians recommended cocaine as an antispasmodic, a local anesthetic, a specific remedy for hay fever and asthma, a cure for alcohol and opiate addiction, a general blues tonic, and an antidepressant. Cocaine is a short-acting stimulant to the sympathetic nervous system, but it also has local anesthetic effects. Its pleasant feelings of alertness and raised mood are strongly reinforcing properties that are thought to alter the normal reward or pleasure operations of the nervous system (Dunwiddie, 1988).

Marijuana and hashish are products of the hemp plant, which has long been cultivated for other reasons, including making rope, paper, paint, and soap. Marijuana comes from the processed leaves and is usually smoked, although it can be placed in food and beverages. Hashish is the refined resin secreted from the flowering tops of the female plant, making a product five times as potent. The primary psychoactive compound is called THC and has variable but small effects on the cardiovascular system. Its mechanism in the brain is not understood. It is reported to be one of the few effective treatments for the nausea and discomfort of cancer chemotherapy, effective because it can be taken in a form that operates quickly when it is needed.

Psychological effects are not entirely predictable. Most common are feelings of relaxation and well-being, but emotions of all kinds may be exaggerated. Perceptions may be distorted in a variety of ways. Some find little effect at all beyond the social influence of others in the setting. Large doses increase some of these effects into states of mental pathology, although usually of short duration. A few heavy users report flashbacks of druglike phenomena during later periods when no drug is being taken.

Varieties of other mind-altering drugs are many and seem also to have power to physically alter brain function, often in a permanent manner. The nature of addiction to such substances may be similar, but their abuse has other aspects beyond our present purpose of understanding the motivation principles of addiction. Neglecting these other drugs is a choice we must make to con-

serve time and space. We will also not take up the most common state-altering drug of modern times, caffeine.

Social History of Drug Use

Opiates, cocaine, and related drugs have a long past. Since the beginning of this century, there has been movement toward making addicting drugs illegal. Under the guidance of medical and political theory, using certain drugs has been thought to be a major evil in society. Concepts of opiate drug addiction have been developed and spread to account for other habitual actions. Those theoretical myths now perform as explanations that deserve a more critical analysis. To understand our cultural concepts of addiction, we must examine our political history of opiate use and control.

We noted that opium poppy plants were a source of pleasure in records 6,000 years old. Further evidence of use appears in later writings of Greeks, Romans, and Arabs. Arab invasions into the West and the resulting crusades to the East spread opium knowledge and materials to Europe. By the 1500s, it was generally in use there as a medicine. An alcohol-based opium medicine called laudanum was developed in 1660s' England.

Arab traders probably introduced opium to Persia, India, and China. Opium in China appeared first as a medicine, beginning in the 700s. In the early 1600s, the British brought India opium to China, and it was smoked along with tobacco. Authorities were more concerned with the tobacco than the opium. Official Chinese prohibition in 1729 had no effect. Soon, the opium was smoked alone and in a rather pure form.

For the next 100 years, the British developed an effective smuggling operation that took advantage of local politics. British opium was bought in India by private dealers and shipped to China, where it was smuggled up the rivers. At first, it just offset the trade in silk and tea, but the value of the opium increased and payment was now in silver. Combined with considerable corruption of the cultural and political system, the economic

TABLE 11.3 Basic History of Opium Users, Uses, and Controls

Time Period	Users	Use	Control
Earliest history to roughly 1500s	all civilizations, most likely by elite	pleasure	unknown
1500s and 1600s	general European population, elite in China	medicine and pleasure	some taxation
1700s and 1800s	general American, European, and Far East populations	medicine and pleasure	prohibited in China
mid-1800s	American Civil War soldiers	general medicine; ease pain	none
	middle-class women and physicians	cure aches and pains	none
1906 to 1914	primarily underclass and Chinese American laborers	cure aches and pains; pleasure	labeling required
1914 on	underclass and addicted	habit and pleasure	use forbidden

threat led China's emperor in 1839 to take police action against the opium-smuggling trade. Britain replied with force that the Chinese could not match, and by 1842, the first of the Opium Wars was over. The effect on China was forceful opening to freer trade, colonialism, and missionary penetration into China's social order. Missionaries shared the riverboats with opium.

Opium continued to be banned by the emperors, but there was no hope of control. The Chinese developed their own production in the 1850s. Renewed fighting with the British at the end of this decade led to another defeat. A provision of their 1860 treaty was legalizing opium. A secondary consequence of these battles was a permanent change in the Chinese culture that weakened the central government in favor of local military powers. Opium taxes and fees financed the local rulers.

Other nations, including the United States, joined in the trade. Reform-minded forces began to appear, perhaps sparked by missionaries who blamed opium for their lack of success. Traffic was intense. One fourth of China was now smoking opium and thereby enriching local and international govern-

ments. America banned opium trade by its citizens in 1880. England was reluctant to follow, being more involved in the trade. Reform within China was sparked by Chinese students returning from abroad. Britain and China agreed in 1907 to reduce the trade by a small amount and to control the smuggling. Local effort succeeded in returning four fifths of opium land in China to food crops. International opium meetings were held in 1907, 1909, and 1912. The last was in The Hague, Netherlands, and amounted to a penalty-free agreement for each nation to do its best to reduce the traffic in prepared opium. Nevertheless, that was the goal that motivated drug controls in the following decades. (More detail can be found in Walker, 1991, *Opium and Foreign Policy*.)

Opium and similar drugs were in general use in the West beginning in the 1600s (see Table 11.3 for a social history). Their primary effects were to dull or remove pain, but they were also often used to control sleep, insanity, coughing, alcohol intoxication, diarrhea, and communicable disease. People at all social levels used opium in its simple and patent medicine forms in an open and unremarkable manner. Overuse was most often noticed officially in accidental poisoning. But opium was one of the most effective medicines that physicians used. By some accounts, opium was the singly most widely prescribed drug in the United States, but it also was openly available to anyone from any merchant (Berridge & Edwards, 1981). Opium use increased steadily through the 1800s to a peak in 1896.

Patent medicines often included opium or alcohol or both. Laudanum had a long history. Another popular concoction was chlorodyne, made of hydrochlorate of morphine, chloroform, and often some hemp. Paregoric was a camphorated preparation of opium. Others were proprietary compounds of sweet or bitter, tasty or repulsive materials mixed with opium. Ironically, a few medications made primarily of opiates were labeled to imply that they were effective in curing opiate addiction. Mild preparations were sold for quieting babies.

Civil War use of opium and morphine, primarily in powders and by nonhypodermic administration, was responsible for introducing many soldiers to continued heavy use. Opiates were frequently given to soldiers for diarrhea, malaria, and the like. Some was used for pain from injury. Those who became heavy users during the Civil War tended to die of old age at about the turn of the century, contributing to the decline of opiate use in general.

The majority of the users in the 1880s and 1890s were middle class and in middle life, and about two thirds were women (Terry & Pellens, 1928). Their most frequent occupation was housewife. Among the men, most were physicians. Opiates were used in about 15% of several samples of prescriptions in the 1880s. Most women acquired their opiates from a physician, having been treated with the drug for some disorder. Opium and morphine were prescribed for nervous disorders, headaches, varieties of "female complaints," rheumatism, and arthritis. Middle-aged women most commonly presented these symptoms, and the doctors prescribed opium and morphine for them. Historians estimate that about 3% of the U.S. population was addicted in the middle 1890s (Duster, 1970). In general,

populations whose members frequented physicians tended to have the highest addiction rates.

Although doctors were beginning to be aware of some problems, it wasn't until around 1900 that suitable alternatives for opium and morphine were available. The discovery of the salicylates in the 1880s, and the analgesic properties of aspirin in 1899, led to better treatments for aches and pains. Some American states were beginning to pass limits on the sale of narcotics, including cocaine, except to those who held medical prescriptions. Heavy use of opium drugs in the United States lessened in the late 1890s.

By the 1900s, there were fewer prescriptions being written for opium and morphine. In 1906, the U.S. Pure Food and Drug Act required that foods, drugs, and patent medicines state any narcotic content. These controls led to less opiate use and were one of the principal reasons for the reduction in both numbers of heavy users and amount of imported opiates in the first decade of the twentieth century. Patent medicine use reached its high point just before passage of this federal law (Duster, 1970).

As the medical source of heavy users declined in numbers, a proportionately greater share of the drug using was by more disreputable parts of the population. Among the nonmedical addicts were Chinese opium smokers, laborers brought to America beginning about 1870. Another underclass group using opium were women prostitutes. For these users, opium had multiple effects, one being simply to make life more bearable. Opium also disrupts fertility and was used essentially as a contraceptive, a practice that was borrowed by some women in more elite society.

By the early 1920s, after drug use became illegal, heavy users were harder to identify, but the population seen in clinics had changed in age, in socioeconomic status, and in sex. The addicts were now young men of the underclass. Only one in four was a woman (Duster, 1970).

Heroin, the semisynthetic derivative of morphine, was introduced as a cough suppressant in 1898. That led to its being another iatragenic (caused by medical treatment) source of addiction, although not on the scale of the other opiates that were prescribed widely for different disorders. Many thought that heroin might even be a cure for addiction to the other drugs. Nearly all of the heroin use centered in New York City and the immediately adjacent areas, because heroin was developed by two major German pharmaceutical companies, Bayer and Merck, with local manufacturing in New York. Druggists were well supplied. About the time opium smoking and cocaine were beginning to be suppressed by law and discouraged by medical opinion, some users turned to heroin. Most of the new users were lower-middle-class and youthful males.

Heroin can be eaten, taken by snorting, smoked, or injected into a muscle, the skin, or a vein. The preferred method of taking heroin became intravenous injection for its rapid and intense effect. Eastern and Mideast heroin users tend to smoke it, a method commonly adopted by American soldiers in Vietnam. Heroin use grew dramatically during the 1960s and 1970s but stabilized during the 1980s at an estimated half million users in the United States.

Cocaine was introduced to Europe and North America in the mid 1800s, following procedures developed to extract it from coca leaves. A series of glowing reports from physicians followed early research. Most notably, it was an effective local anesthetic. Counterreports showed that many of the benefits of use, except that of pain relief, were false claims; the reports also argued that cocaine was addicting, and heavy use had undesirable effects. Other specific pain relief -caine drugs (for example, Tropocaine and Novocain) were developed in the early 1900s, and physicians turned away from cocaine. However, it continued to be widely available. It soon found its way into patent medicines, wines, and other drinks, notably Coca-Cola. Other cocaine products were cigarettes and cigars, tablets, injections, ointments, and sprays (Musto, 1973).

Restrictions on cocaine came from the states and from federal laws passed just be-

fore World War I. It was briefly popular in the 1920s, but then it again fell from favor. The recent explosion of use began in the late 1970s (Winger, Hofmann, & Woods, 1992). Because it was high-priced, cocaine came to be primarily the choice of the wealthy and the upwardly mobile, for recreational use. Beginning in the middle 1980s, cocaine was again declining in popularity, especially among the middle class (Karan, Haller, & Schnoll, 1991). But a new form of cheaper, quick-acting, smokable cocaine, known as crack, appeared on the market for the underclass.

Politics of Illegality

In describing the social history of drug use, we noted some legal and political elements affecting drug availability. By far the most important of these was the passage in late 1914 of the Harrison Narcotic Act. Complicated politics and social attitude changes led to this. We will outline the most important. From about the turn of the century, research by physicians showed some major liabilities to even moderate continuous use of certain drugs. Addiction was one of the most important and increasingly feared consequences. Because opium, morphine, cocaine, and other drugs were hidden in patent medicines, the 1906 Pure Food and Drug Act was designed partially to handle this problem. We saw that it had the intended effect in reducing casual use.

We noted also some history of U.S. involvement in controlling international traffic in opium. Although the United States was not a major part of that traffic, it was important that it be seen in a strong legal position. Considerable legislation existed in the states, where it belonged under the Constitution, but there was no federal control. Leading the cause was a moral reformer, Bishop Charles Brent, and a nearly fanatical State Department official, Dr. Hamilton Wright.

To support legal restriction, Wright supplied a campaign of inaccurate and misleading statistics and outright lies. He emphasized the evil of opium by exaggerating the danger of addiction and presenting the idea that there were vastly more addicts than there were and that the numbers of heavy users were increasing. However, usage was actually decreasing at this time. Wright played on fears of minorities, including Chinese and Blacks. The best he could manage was 1909 legislation outlawing the import of smoking opium, a law that did little that wasn't already handled by the 1906 act.

The 1909 international conference was little more than discussions, but Wright again planned federal legislation to control drug traffic. The problem was how to make it constitutional. He proposed the mechanism of taxation, requiring registration of those selling drugs and of the drug transactions and application of a revenue stamp to all drug containers. The legislation was introduced in 1910 by Representative Foster. Again, Wright supplied a campaign of exaggerated dangers, misleading statistics, racial fears, and now derogation of physicians and pharmacists by noting some of them were addicts. He focused on the dangers of cocaine, particularly as used by blacks in the South, alleging that it might be the direct cause of rape or stimulate uprisings there. Debate in Congress in 1911 featured counterarguments, including objections to the financial burden of the record keeping, the severity of the penalties, and the intrusion into personal liberties of the proposed bill. The bill failed.

Although Wright's arguments failed to get the Foster law passed, they were rerun when attitudes had changed, and some of the provisions were moderated. The 1912 Hague international conference on controlling drug traffic once again specified that participants must control all phases of opium, cocaine, and similar drugs. To that end, Representative Harrison proposed legislation of control that would not upset the pharmacists, physicians, and manufacturers. Better prepared, these groups essentially agreed to registration of producers and distributors, taxation of drug transfers, and, what became the key element, prescription from a physician based on a legitimate medical use required for purchase. The Harrison Narcotic Act was passed, and it was signed by the president in December 1914. The law restricted opium, cocaine, and

their derivatives, and it required registration and bookkeeping by those dispensing the drugs. Small amounts were still permitted in patent medicines.

The immediate effect was to flood physicians' offices with habitual users seeking prescriptions. Many complied, believing that maintenance was necessary. That was judged not "in good faith" by enforcing Treasury officials, and court cases ensued. At first, the doctors won on grounds that the "good faith" section was not needed to fulfill treaty obligations, a major constitutional argument justifying the Narcotics Act. This was reversed by two Supreme Court rulings in 1919. The reversal reflected changing attitudes of the people during the course of World War I, which had just ended, and some real insecurities about anarchy and fears of revolution in the United States similar to what had just happened in Russia. This was a time of suppressing all dissent—note that the prohibition of alcohol amendment had also just been passed (Musto, 1973).

After the Harrison Act, physicians lost control over prescription of narcotics, but they gained another kind of practice in the treatment of the new medically defined addiction. At first, the Harrison Act sent many addicts to prisons. The overcrowding led to establishment in 1928 of Public Health Service treatment centers in Lexington, Kentucky, and Fort Worth, Texas. Treatment was essentially ineffective, but it offered an opportunity to study addiction.

Marijuana was similarly prohibited in 1937 after a campaign of inflammatory, lurid stories in the media about how it was at the root of just about every kind of evil. An example was the wildly inaccurate but powerful movie *Reefer Madness,* which invented the ideas that marijuana made people sexually promiscuous, moved them to kill people, and drove them insane. The source of all of this was nothing more than a power play by government bureaucrats with a moral crusade. Specifically, officials of the Federal Bureau of Narcotics, particularly Harry Anslinger, saw this to be in their domain and proposed legislation and gave their "facts" to the media. Marijuana had never before been a noticeable problem, and its use was by small numbers of urban African Americans, southwestern Mexican Americans, jazz musicians in New Orleans, and a scattering of working class and "artsy" people—in short, a small population of users who would have no political power to resist (Becker, 1963).

During World War II, in the early 1940s, there was a significant reduction in drug use, essentially because production and transport were nearly impossible, but federal officials feared a return. Stiffer penalties were part of the 1951 Boggs Act, and following the fear of internal subversion in the McCarthy Un-American Activity hearings in the early 1950s, the penalties were increased further in 1956. In the 1960s, opinion was spreading that addicts were diseased rather than criminals. A 1966 act stipulated opiate abuse a disease. But drug abuse was growing. A series of changes were made leading to the 1970 Comprehensive Drug Abuse and Control Act, which limited import, manufacture, prescription, and distribution of drugs with abuse potential. Drugs were placed in one of four schedules with different rules. Schedule I listed drugs of no medical use and high abuse potential, including opiates, marijuana, and LSD (Winger et al., 1992).

The 1970s marked the beginning of a series of "wars on drugs," including formation of the Drug Enforcement Administration and the National Institute on Drug Abuse. The 1986 Anti-Drug Abuse Act again changed some of the rules and organizations and increased the weapons and zeal of drug fighting. The 1990 Crime Control Act added a few more pieces, including a hopeful direction of education.

The pattern of control in Great Britain has been different from that in the United States, and it is worthy of a look because it is often referred to in argument. England started earlier in registration laws for pharmacies, following the lead of a strong professional association (a group with no counterpart in the United States then). In that 1868 Act, opium was given little restriction except sale through the pharmacists. In the 1890s, patent medicines with opiates were included. In 1908, opium and cocaine in greater than 1% mixtures were placed on the poisons list, but control was left to the professional discretion of the pharmacists. Britain's response to The Hague conference report was to leave it to the pharmacy and medical professions to act responsibly.

World War I in England saw an Undersecretary of the Home Office take up the cause similar to Wright's in the United States. With inflammatory rhetoric and statistics and aided by an overexcited press, he made the case for increased drug control, and the Dangerous Drugs Act of 1920 was passed. In the next few years, the Home Office attempted a penal approach like that of the United States. The pharmacists and physicians rallied against the restrictions of their professional prerogative. The key elements were the problems of maintenance prescribing and the doctor addict. The Home Office needed medical expertise in administering the act, and after a period of negotiations, a committee was set up in 1924 to study the issue of addiction, particularly the medical basis of refusing maintenance. Chaired by Sir Humphrey Rolleston, the final report appeared in 1926, essentially giving physicians the authority they desired. This became the British system, which identified addiction as a disease that must be treated according to the physician's discretion. Addicts were not to be reported, nor was there to be compulsory treatment. Maintenance, but not escalation, was permitted. The medical association would police its own members.

An important fact to note is that Britain's addicts during this time were primarily middle class and respectable. There were few of them, and they posed no real social problems. The British Rolleston system did not produce fewer addicts, and it was possible because there were few addicts. In the 1960s, England along with most of the West, was met with a change in youth culture. The junkie underclass appeared and did not fit with the system, after which Britain moved increasingly toward repression and penal control (Berridge, 1984).

U.S. medical theory about addiction was first begun in the 1870s, in a movement supporting the view labeled *inebriety,* a disease that proponents believed was triggered by an underlying mental disturbance. The common view at this time was that addiction was little more than a habit or vice, a moral problem. Those in the inebriety movement proposed and popularized the idea of an actual disease based on predisposition. The addiction came to be thought of as a nervous disease.

It was at the time of the change from middle-class opium use to lower-class heroin use that physicians began to develop the disease concept in earnest. As several theories were developed, there was some battle between physicians who believed that addiction was a disease caused by specific events, for example, medical treatment, and those who believed that it was rooted in some sort of hereditary disturbance or personality disorder. The former assumed that nearly anyone can be addicted under the right conditions. The latter believed that certain individuals were more likely to be addicts.

Those who held the specific-events theory had hypotheses such as one proposing antitoxins. Taking the drug leads the body to produce antitoxins. The presence of the antitoxins accounts for the tolerance effects. The antitoxins also have properties such that, without the drug, they would produce the symptoms of withdrawal. These were popular sets of ideas at the same time as the germ and antibody theories were also prevalent and successful in medical theory.

The hereditary or personality theories ranged from a neurasthenic model, which held that there was a fundamentally inadequate nervous system impaired further by opiates, to the psychopathic theory, in which it was believed that the individual's moral sense was hopelessly perverted and unable to be affected by any ethical standards. Among the believers of the latter view was Lawrence Kolb, a psychiatrist at the U.S. Public Health Service Hygienic Laboratory in Washington, who undertook a major study of narcotic addiction (Kolb, 1925). He saw the addicts as having a true mental disease requiring extended treatment and indefinite maintenance. After serving as the first medical director of the Lexington Narcotic Farm, he came to see addicts as mentally sick people needing help and not as dangerous criminals. Largely through his work, the psychopathic theory became the dominant position by the 1930s and beyond.

SECTION SUMMARY: TAKING DRUGS

Narcotic is a loose political label covering substances derived from opium poppies, coca shrubs, and hemp plants. Psychoactive substances in each have been refined for human use, giving a variety of mental and physiological effects.

Each substance has a long social history of common use, culminating in politically based legal control. Bartering drugs as international commodities has been a common theme in that social history. Institution of legal proscription in the beginning of this century was founded on power politics, either aggrandizement of certain individuals and their bureaucratic control or suppression of weaker people's cultural interests or all three. When the majority of users was no longer of the middle-class, respectable sector of the population, absolute control was easily instituted. As that control became increasingly difficult to maintain in the light of illicit trade, escalation in regulation reached a crescendo in metaphors of wars on drugs with consequential erosion in civil order and liberty.

TABLE 11.4 Basic History of Alcohol Users, Uses, Estimated Consumption, and Controls

Time Period	Users	Use	Amount (per person/year)	Control
Earliest history to late 1700s	all civilizations; all people	pleasure and sanitary beverage	5-8 gal	none
Early to mid-1800s	most American, European, and Far Eastern populations	pleasure and social custom	7.1 gal	local temperance

Focusing on U.S. alcohol use:

Time Period	Users	Use	Amount (per person/year)	Control
mid-1800s to 1920	heaviest among urbanites and immigrants	pleasure, social custom, and contests		increasing temperance
1920-1933	wealthy, underclass, and remote populations	habit, pleasure, and social custom	0.9	manufacture, sale, and transport forbidden
1933 on	gradually increasing general population	habit, pleasure, and social custom	~3.0	forbidden to minors

DRINKING

Alcohol is rapidly absorbed from the digestive tract, although the rate of absorption is slowed by the presence of food in the stomach. The alcohol is spread evenly throughout body tissues, and thus people with larger body mass will take a larger amount of alcohol in order to get the same effect on the brain as someone with smaller body mass. The alcohol is metabolized and excreted through the liver at a constant rate of about 10 milliliters of ethyl alcohol (roughly equal to 12 ounces of beer) per hour.

Alcohol's effect is to depress all of the neurons in the brain, forcing a sedating effect, particularly on brain efficiency. There is disorientation and clouding of mental awareness, poorer memory and judgment, and a loss of inhibition. The loss of inhibition produces feelings of euphoria and is often misinterpreted as stimulation. These physical changes lead users to perform otherwise unexpected actions. Because aspects of cognitive control appear to be removed, the results are not predictable. It is not uncommon for an alcohol-poisoned person to have a lowered threshold for being aggressive and violent, to more readily perform morally substandard acts, or to be unable to respond in a normal manner to sensory events with motor actions, or all of the foregoing.

Alcohol causes organic injury of various kinds following extended use. Brain cells are damaged, and certain cancers are known to be formed.

Early American Alcohol Drinking

Alcohol has been a part of civilized life throughout recorded history. We will focus on drinking in America because the major elements for understanding drinking too much are present in that social history (see Table 11.4). In overview, American cultural forces have been complicated and changing. Drinking too much is intertwined with other bad social habits and subject to commercial interests. Drinking mild alcoholic beverages was common at first, with society dictating moderation. With some loss of that influence, perhaps arising from aspects of individualism, attempts to manage problem drinking began. Drinking was increasingly allied with other underclass vices. Control of alcohol became law before the 1920s, but social change, based in a reversal of what people believed to be respectable, forced repeal of that legislation (Burnham, 1993; Lender & Martin, 1982).

Alcohol was commonly consumed by the early settlers as the most common liquid drink. The European societies from which they emigrated had come to distrust the local polluted waters and found that beers and wines were more healthful. The common belief was that modest amounts of alcohol were necessary to maintain health. Every aspect of society involved drinking, from ordination of ministers to town meetings to funerals. Among the most important functions of the small towns was to ensure that there were adequate amounts of alcohol beverages for the citizenry.

As their numbers became too large to rely on obtaining imported beers and wine, colonists began to brew their own. Local conditions dictated the kind of brew that was possible. For a time in the 1700s, the Americas became noted for their making of rum from the molasses by-product of West Indies' sugar production. Away from the coasts, grains were the plentiful sources, leading to concentrated, distilled alcohol products, such as rye and bourbon whiskeys.

Drinking remained largely under close social control in the towns of the colonial period. Drunkenness was periodic and was treated like any other social infraction. Repeated offenders were treated as people who must and would change their ways. There was no concept of an addiction to alcohol; drinking too much was a personal moral failing. Alcohol tended to be abused by some individuals living apart from the social structures. Traders,

trappers, and others on the frontier had less social control and apparently had more periods of heavy drinking. These more remote areas were also the locations where the distilled spirits of much higher alcohol content were produced and used. A small amount of whiskey had much more potential to produce drunkenness than beer or applejack.

At the end of the colonial period, alcohol was still thought to be generally a good and necessary material to sustain a healthy life. The dissenters were few and aimed their attacks at excessive use of the distilled spirits. Social life and attitudes were slowly changing as a result of the new ideology of personal freedom brought on by the revolutionary war and its enabling rhetoric. The championing of the individual and freedoms also weakened some measure of social control upon each person. There was less pressure to conform to the moderation and common goals of one's local society.

The early 1800s were times of increasing divergence in styles and reasons for drinking. New populations of immigrants brought their traditions to America. Large groups of poor Irish were not assimilated into American culture, and they tended toward drinking bouts of distilled alcohol as a mark of their imported culture. German immigrants had a more favorable reception, but they too carried with them traditions of heavy drinking as well as exceptional skills in brewing beers. America became a land of regional and local forms of drinking, and drinking to excess was reaching notice. Estimates are that the early 1800s were the time of the heaviest alcohol consumption in America's history. Average consumption in 1830 was about 7.1 gallons per adult per year, up from the 5.8 gallons of 1790. The 7.1 gallons translates to more than 50 ounces of beer or 5 ounces of whiskey per day every day of the year.

Politics and Consumerism

By the 1850s, the national consumption was down to less than 3 gallons of alcohol per person per year. That reduction was the culmination of a period of various alcohol temperance and abstinence movements. Beginning after the late 1700s' American Revolution, with Dr. Benjamin Rush's thesis that drunkenness was a disease, a movement for temperance grew. The temperance thesis of Dr. Rush was taken up as a mission by the Presbyterian church leadership, and its excitement quickly spread. The thesis was that America could become the finest development of humanity, a tribute to God's work, if its people would eliminate the handicaps of intoxication and inefficiency brought on by excessive alcohol use. Alcohol was the premier reform, among many others, that excited people in the early 1800s. The hidden politics of these reforms were many; for example, some issues were aimed at controlling both the recent immigrants, who found alcoholic beverages uncommonly cheap, and the growth of taverns and saloons, which had become centers of other vices like gambling, swearing, and fighting.

Soon, the thesis of the reformers shifted from temperance to complete abstinence. The "drys" were set against the "wets." Resisting alcohol control were, of course, the tavern and saloon owners and their suppliers, but also many recent heavy-drinking immigrants from middle-class Germany and working-class Ireland. Both commercial profits and cultural differences were involved. By the mid-nineteenth century, drinking had changed from modest home consumption to frequent binges at commercial drinking establishments. The wets opposing control were the lower classes who were not part of the reform evangelism, the ethnic groups who wanted to continue their culture of drinking, the upper-class wealthy who demanded freedom to do what they pleased, and the producers and sellers of alcohol (Burnham, 1993).

Among the drys, many different fraternal orders proclaiming abstinence were popular, and some of those turned toward politics. One group, the Washingtonians, focused on bringing to abstinence those who had become drunkards. In reformers' politics, the drys saw the only cure for society to be legal removal of the source. In 1851, Maine passed the first dry law, and soon, 13 other states and two Canadian provinces followed suit. The effect on alcohol consumption was dramatic, but it was not to last. Certainly the wets fought with a well-financed countercampaign, but other politics also moderated temperance. Alcohol prohibition was closely associated politically with abolition of slavery, and those politics became of overriding importance in the late 1850s and the early 1860s. The alcohol issues were thought to dilute those of slavery abolition, and the political power of alcohol temperance faded for a time. The dry laws were quickly repealed or simply not enforced.

The decades after the Civil War were times of major social change. Industrialization and technical developments, population expansion, and development of westward lands were among the many forces to be accommodated. People felt a need to impose a stability on the country. The earlier middle-class reformers' dreams of achieving a more perfect society were still alive, but the problems were now becoming more complicated. The temperance movement attempted to regain its strength, and it soon had new examples to fuel the issue.

Immigration once again became a major factor, but this time, the new Americans were also coming from southern and eastern European countries. Italians, Jews, and Poles brought their drinking culture with them. Their preference for wines led to development of wineries. Social traditions of controlled drinking were maintained, and despite the fears of many, liberal use of alcohol in these groups did not produce significant instances of abuse. Drinking to excess was prevented within the Italian and Jewish cultures particularly. Yet, these immigrants were in favor of drinking; they did not support the drys.

In the urban population, in general, however, a new wave of drinking styles developed. Saloons and other drinking establishments, usually owned by the alcohol producers, became popular at all levels of society. Mixed drinks were invented, partially to soften the harshness of the distilled alcohol. Competition became heavy, encouraging more drinking and providing a haven for anyone who brought in more drinkers. Social standards became those of the underclass, and heavy drinking was promoted as a mark of masculinity. The worst of these bars and dives became centers for illicit and immoral activities, reaching the point of being fearsome places for respectable people to approach. Public drunkenness and chronic drunks were becoming commonplace.

The Women's Christian Temperance Movement (WCTU) was formed in the 1870s precisely to attack the danger that the saloons presented to families and to women. Among their efforts was introducing temperance instruction into the schools, aimed at eliminating the next generation of drunkards. Their direct political action, along with other temperance groups, did not have significant immediate success, although the seeds were being sown for growing doubts about the wisdom of drinking.

Since Dr. Rush, before the Civil War, there had been ideas, with no factual basis, that drunkenness was a progressively debilitating disease, alcoholism. A few reformer physicians accepted this as dogma and proposed that special "inebriate asylums" be built for treatment of the afflicted. Institutions were formed, and the idea spread. Some 50 were constructed before the end of the century, often combining alcoholics with opium addicts. Asylumists organized as a scientific group and became another force in the general temperance movement.

Marginal treatment ideas and outright frauds took advantage of the growing public sentiment for special medical treatment of alcoholics. One example was the Keeley Cure, briefly famous in the 1890s. Keeley applied a mysterious substance at short intervals to effect his cures. His quackery was not especially less successful than orthodox medical treatment in general. There being no cure for drunkenness, a political elimination of the source became most important.

Among the more effective political groups was the Anti-Saloon League, formed as a coalition of dry forces in the mid 1890s. It was skillfully guided by Wayne Wheeler, and his political lobbying efforts were famous. The idea of Prohibition was successful in election after election, demonstrating that the people were willing to take a chance on the promises of the temperance movement and were unwilling to support the alcohol "traffic" with its increasing corruption and destruction. In 1916, the idea of a constitutional amendment was pushed by all of the temperance groups, and it easily won the support of Congress. Sufficient states ratified it by 1919, and it went into effect in January 1920, following a 1-year grace period to allow an orderly drying up of the nation. Actually, the nation had pretty well dried up before this by federal restrictions intended to use grains for food during the World War of 1914 to 1918 rather than for alcohol production. These restrictions were continued until a set of regulations and enforcement penalties for the amendment were passed in 1919 as the Volstead Act. The great experiment had begun.

Actually, the prohibition was not absolute. The amendment only forbade the manufacture, sale, or transportation of intoxicating liquors, defined as more than one half of 1% alcohol. Possessing or drinking alcoholic beverages was not restricted. Wealthy people with foresight had laid in a good supply. Home brewing for personal consumption was allowed. Only the low-income drinkers who always relied on the taverns and saloons were seriously inconvenienced, and of course the alcohol industry (Burnham, 1993).

Cutting the supply of alcohol did have many of the results foreseen by its proponents, but the outcome never developed to the degree that they desired. Taverns and saloons were closed or converted to clandestine operations that no longer threatened the public order. Alcohol consumption declined to a value near 1 gallon per person per year. Many areas turned completely dry, yet others continued illicit operations largely in the open. Alcoholism also declined along with related health and social problems. Consumers spent alcohol money on other products, giving a boost to such businesses as the automobile industry. These facts were not enough to carry along the movement.

The wets continued to campaign against the restrictions, but their efforts were disorganized at first. Those repeal campaigners included the alcohol industry, a few individuals opposing the restrictions of personal rights, and a few sophisticates who were able to keep their views in the public eye. New York, which had serious problems in compliance, gave up trying and repealed its state dry laws in 1923. That signaled a change and encouraged other campaigns. The media, dominated by New Yorkers, painted a negative picture of Prohibition. Organization and money were funneled into the Association Against the Prohibition Amendment. One of the champions and major financiers was Pierre DuPont, with a strong interest in countering certain of the drys who had socially snubbed him for profiting in munitions manufacture during the war. DuPont and others among the very rich also saw alcohol revenue as a way to prevent or reduce taxes on their wealth. They used national advertising, subversion of journalists, and injections of drinking into the popular media, especially the movies. Their messages were many, including portraying Prohibition as responsible for apparent criminality, emphasizing the failure of enforcement, and making the drys appear to be unattractive and fanatical. Even the temperance label was taken over by the wets to put the Prohibition drys in an extreme position.

Image was a major part of this campaign, and it had a far-reaching significance. Drinking was pictured as respectable, something that was mandatory in sophisticated society. No longer was proper action set by middle-class morality based in the church. Joining this campaign was the increased respectability of using tobacco, gambling, swearing, and engaging in nonmarital sexual activity. This collection of vices became the mark of sophisticated respectability that was portrayed in movies and popular literature. The vices appeared in advertisements in different combinations. Sometime during the 1920s, this inversion of values became the new reality. The habits of the underclass, the acts of the Victorian underworld, became, and have remained, our common media standards.

So, too, the fervor for reform in general was cooling. Society was becoming more stable. Many of the financial ills of the late 1800s seemed to be reduced. Women's suffrage was accomplished by a 1920 amendment, and fears of immigrants were easing due to legislation restricting the flow. Americans were becoming more used to the variety of life in America, reducing the earlier motivation to simplify and purify social ills. Business was encouraging less saving and more buying, reflecting a shift to a consumer economy. Tolerance for a variety of forms of drinking fit into this pattern.

Enforcement of alcohol prohibition was more of a problem than the drys envisaged. The federal bureau was stretched very thin, and state and local support was marginal if not hostile. People were beginning to speak of personal liberty, and these ideas were supported by some excesses in enforcement that had come to light. Temperance leaders were beginning to sense failure, moving toward more extreme positions rather than accommodation. Still having political power in Congress, the temperance leaders passed the Jones Act, which greatly increased the harshness of enforcement and penalties. More social turmoil was generated by this act.

Alcohol advocates were unintentionally aided by these extreme acts and the situation of the drys. The wets were more effective in presenting their case than the drys had ever been, painting the latter as naive and fanatical. There was little fight left in the drys because they had no money or strong leadership. Public sentiment rapidly moved toward a repeal of Prohibition. In much the same way that World War I had provided a sort of catalyst for the passage of the prohibition amendment, the appearance of the Depression of the early 1930s aided its repeal. The general elections of 1932 also became a referendum on Prohibition, and the drys lost. The amendment was soon repealed.

With alcohol once again legal and taxed, funds were made available for financing recovery from the Depression, fulfilling one argument of the wets. The alcohol industry adopted a more moderate strategy of promotion than they had in the days of the company-owned saloons and displays of heavy drinking. The worst of the image problems were avoided. Drinking did not quickly return to the pre-Prohibition levels. People who did not drink during the 1920s remained dry, and the years of alcohol education must have had some effect on younger people. Consumption rose to only 1 gallon in 1934 and 1½ gallons by 1941. Change was slow over the next 30 years, reaching a level still under 3 gallons per person per year in the 1980s.

Military leaders during World War II were in favor of alcohol. Beer manufacturers were permitted to continue in business, although distillers were converted to making other war products. Brewers even managed to get draft deferments for their workers and used the collection of young men in the military as an opportunity for introducing them to their products. So a generation of young men began drinking, even if their home locality was essentially dry.

Alcohol manufacturers learned from their failures and their successes how to make even greater profits. Large-scale advertising and systems of wholesalers combined to pressure drinkers to consume specific products. Small brewers merged with the large or disappeared entirely. Sales were aimed at home consumption and the respectability of suburbia. Alcohol products were aligned with other foods and with popular events to further develop the image that drinking is normal. Increased pressure was put on the youth market, with the idea of getting a customer for decades of purchases. Sexuality and masculine images were easily and effectively tied to drinking. Stories in the different media continued the theme of drinking as the one activity that is always appropriate, whatever the happening.

With alcohol once again widely available, problem drinking again became an issue. Producers had to deal with the problems of excessive drinking and of alcoholism. They did so by committing themselves to advertising moderate drinking, thus appearing to be providing a solution to a growing social problem. They dealt with alcoholism by supporting the disease view, making alcoholism rather than drinking the deviant condition. Producers described the problem as solely in the alcoholic individual, never in the alcohol.

The treatment of alcoholics, which had been largely suspended during Prohibition, was resumed with repeal. Alcoholics Anonymous was formed in the mid 1930s and became the most popular program of recovery. In some ways, this group's methods brought back some of the elements of social control over excessive drinking that had existed during the colonial period. Another program followed a resurgence of the disease model of alcoholism by E. M. Jellinek of the Yale University Center of Alcohol Studies. These and others were ideas supported by the alcohol industry as they separated the blame from the product. By the 1970s, alcoholics and treatment professionals successfully lobbied for a separate National Institute on Alcoholic Abuse and Alcoholism.

SECTION SUMMARY: DRINKING

Alcohol use throughout history was more pervasive and common than that of other drugs. Weak alcoholic beverages have been common, sometimes even necessary for health. Stronger alcoholic products led to increased problem drinking in the 1800s, followed by calls for temperance. At the end of World War I, shortly after narcotic drug control, there began a decade of Prohibition in the United States of alcohol manufacture,

TABLE 11.5 Basic History of Tobacco Users, Uses, Dominant Forms, and Controls

Time Period	Users	Use	Dominant Form	Control
Late 1500s through 1600s	sailors, general population, primarily the elite	pleasure and medicinal	pipe	taxation
1700s	fashionable general population	pleasure and social custom	snuff	taxation
1800s	fashionable general population	pleasure and social custom	chewing; cigars	taxation
Late 1800s; early 1900s	fashionable general population	pleasure, social custom, and style	cigarette	taxation
Early 1900s to late 1900s	gradually increasing general population	pleasure, social custom, and style	cigarette	forbidden to minors
Late 1900s on	gradually decreasing in American population	habit, pleasure, and social custom	cigarette	advertising venue; prohibited locations

sale, and transport. Media campaigns favoring alcohol use as glamorous and then political arguments in the early 1930s about Depression relief led to Prohibition's repeal.

Problem drinking subsequently returned, and it was theorized to be a problem of weak individuals.

SMOKING

The psychoactive drug in tobacco smoke is nicotine. Between 0.1 and 0.4 milligrams of nicotine reach a smoker's bloodstream from each cigarette. The nicotine bonds with carbon monoxide, which enters the blood and is rapidly distributed to the tissues of the body. Nicotine reaches the brain almost immediately, but it has a short effective time. It is reduced to half strength in about 10 to 15 min.

Nicotine affects the brain, other nervous tissue, and other organs indirectly by making receptors abnormally sensitive to the neurotransmitter acetylcholine. Thus, the central nervous system is stimulated, heart rate and

blood pressure are increased, and adrenaline is released. Nicotine users report mental alertness, muscle relaxation, improvement in memory and attention, and decreases in appetite and irritation. Additional positive experience comes from the taste and smell of the tobacco.

Social History of Smoking

Tobacco has roots in American soil and the practices of Native Americans. Sixteenth-century explorers brought it to Europe and promoted its use but without much initial success. Sir Walter Raleigh was most enthused among the English, and M. Jean Nicot was the

French advocate. By the late 1500s, tobacco had been introduced to most areas of the world by sailors.

There was official resistance, and import duties were intended to slow its sale. England's leaders at the time, successively James I, Charles I, and Oliver Cromwell, were all against allowing tobacco. James I wrote against it in 1604, calling it "loathsome to the eye, hateful to the Nose, harmful to the braine, dangerous to the Lungs." He believed it would also impair health and make workers unfit for their labor.

This campaign was not effective. Smoking began to develop into a major business on the strength of its obvious pleasure and of claims that it enhanced sexual powers and cured a variety of diseases, including kidney ills, wounds, and ulcers. Although it began as a commercial enterprise of private companies and governments in the American West Indies, English colonies in the Chesapeake were exporting more than a million pounds of tobacco by 1640. By the time of the American Revolution, annual trade had grown to more than 100 million pounds (Goodman, 1993). Tobacco became one form of international currency for trade. The import taxes continued and were becoming a major revenue source for the British government. By the time of Charles II in the 1660s and 1670s, tobacco was no longer being officially persecuted. Some of the moralistic attack was now being diluted toward the newly introduced coffee and tea.

Attempts to discourage smoking tobacco were not limited to England and its colonies. Severe penalties were delivered by other governments. In 1916, Japanese smokers were imprisoned and their property taken away. Russia's first czar flogged smokers and sent them to Siberia. Turkey's Murad the Cruel had smokers beheaded, hung, or quartered. Smoking persisted, and these countries' new leaders also came to discover the financial advantages of tobacco trade.

The form of using tobacco also has a varied cultural history. The most general form of use by the late 1600s was pipe smoking. Taking of snuff was fashionable in many areas following the lead of French royalty. Keeping tobacco in a snuff box was high fashion in the mid 1700s. Tobacco chewing had its major popularity in the 1800s, when spittoons became mandatory parlor furniture. The 1800s also saw increasing attraction to cigar smoking. The large cigar came to symbolize wealth and power in the late nineteenth century.

Cigarettes had their origins in Aztec tobacco-filled reeds, developed by the Spanish into paper tubes. Cigarette use grew slowly in the late 1800s following its fashionable use by women in France, England, and New York and by men returning from the Crimean war, bringing tobaccos from Turkey. Virginia tobaccos were prepared in a different way that made them milder and more suited for inhaling, and these were placed into better papers by new machines at the turn of the century. Sales of cigarettes dominated the tobacco market in the first decades of the twentieth century, being the most-used form of taking tobacco during World War I (Ashton & Stepney, 1982; Mangan & Golding, 1984). In the 1920s through the 1960s, some of the cleverest, most effective advertisements programs of all time were delivered. Maturity, glamour, sex, individuality, and every other icon of society were used as enticements to buy and smoke tobacco (Goodman, 1993).

Health and Politics

Anti-smoking arguments began to once again accumulate in the 1930s, this time based on science rather than morality. In 1937, laboratory studies showed that animal cancers were produced by tobacco tars. In 1938, statistical studies showed that nonsmokers lived longer than smokers. In the 1950s, more evidence was found for cancer of the lung resulting from cigarette smoking. In the early 1960s, both British and American governments released official reports on smoking and health. Advertising of cigarettes was banned in certain media, and health warning labels were required for product packages. Most recently, a growing intolerance of public smoking in confined spaces has developed.

The proportion of smokers has declined in the "developed" world, largely as a result of these government health campaigns. The greater decline has been in numbers of men smokers; women, never as great a proportion of smokers, now approach equality in proportion with men. The Surgeon General's Report of 1988 described men's smoking at a peak in the middle 1950s at about 54% and slowly declining to a 1985 level of about 30%. The level of women who smoke reached an earlier but lower peak, 36% in 1944, fell to 28% in 1985. Tobacco merchants have turned their efforts toward Third World countries that have no effective regulation or official health information. They have shown considerable success.

SECTION SUMMARY: SMOKING

Tobacco use, after some initial governmental resistance, spread widely throughout the world. Fashionable styles of use were successively pipes, chewing tobacco, cigars, and cigarettes. By the midpoint of this century, medical evidence accumulated against smoking, followed by heavy taxation and restrictions in the United States on its advertisement and where it can be used.

DIETING

Addictions to overeating, with its consequent obesity, are major problems for many. A substantial part of the population is significantly overweight. Dieting also has marks of being an addictive pattern of acts. Both are serious problems for individuals and for society. The weight loss industry, combined with the effects of excessive weight, amounts to a multibillion-dollar annual cost to society. The cost to the well-being of individuals is also great, but there is no numerical measure of that.

Overeating and dieting show different patterns of addiction. Some obese people make no serious attempt to change their weight, either being satisfied with their overeating or having reached a compromise in their lives such that overeating is the preferred alternative. Many other obese people spend their lives searching for ways to decrease their body fat. In that quest, they become periodically involved in dieting. The result is that they spend their lives in alternation. Periods of addictive overeating are interspersed with periods of attachment to programs of dieting. (See also Chapter 3.)

A third group includes those who have no real obesity but nonetheless have become addicted to dieting. Anorexia nervosa and bulimia sufferers are no less driven than the dissatisfied obese by concerns for being thin. These disorders are less widespread, but they have morbid consequences. The word *anorexia* means loss of appetite and consequent unwillingness to eat. Many different sources of anorexia exist. One form comes from certain cancers that alter one's taste sensitivity. Some drugs also affect the appetite. The form that is most common, anorexia nervosa, is an unwillingness to eat but not because of a lack of appetite. This disorder most often afflicts white, financially secure women in their teen years through their thirties. Estimates put the occurrence at about 1 in 1,000, with prevalence increasing. Mortality may be as high as 20%.

Anorexics are not at all indifferent to food. On the contrary, they are totally involved with food and eating control. They believe themselves to be larger and heavier than others see them to be. Anorexics restrict what they eat and may exercise vigorously. They appear to be motivated by avoidance; they seem to have a fear of looking fat. Consequently, they lose a large percentage of their ideal weight. Loss of 25% of ideal weight is sufficient to suspect anorexia; some patients lose as much as 50%. In severe cases, some body processes are interrupted because of lack of essential nutrients. Women often stop menstruating because hormone production and storage in body fat are disrupted.

Treatment for anorexia combines an adequate diet to gain weight and get needed nutrients with some sort of psychotherapy or reeducation program. Success has been shown for cognitive and behavior therapy forms of psychotherapy. Cognitive therapy is aimed at changing the self-image of anorexics to make them see their actual weight. Behavior therapy controls the patient's environment so that the desired eating must be completed to receive other rewards and pleasant experiences.

A disorder with close ties to anorexia is bulimia. **Bulimia** is the impulsive, unpredictable, episodic, and rapid ingestion of large amounts of food in short periods of time. The binges are usually made up of "junk" food loaded with sweet or salty carbohydrates. Most bulimics then physically force vomiting or take emetics and purgatives to rid themselves of the food. A variety of serious physical disorders occur as a result of the frequent vomiting—from tooth decay to kidney failure. Bulimia is like anorexia in many respects, including prevalence, type of person, and treatment success.

SECTION SUMMARY: DIETING

Dieting addictions include psychologically driven medical problems of anorexia nervosa and bulimia based on individuals' false perceptions of having too much weight or fat.

CHAPTER CONCLUSIONS

Addictions and the control of addictions have become a primary force if not an economic industry in the United States, shared to a lesser degree in the rest of the Western world. We have built a political box around addictions that keeps us gagged and ignorant. We build drug control bureaucracies without restraints; respond with knee-jerk emotion to addiction icons; and agree that we must not ask questions, experiment, or fail to follow the rules of designated experts. We have extended drug addiction control as a metaphor to control medicinal materials and even some

foods. The exceptions are commercially favored processed drugs that actually do us the most harm, even in modest use: alcohol, nicotine, and caffeine.

The irony in this is that we are harming ourselves in a vicious circle of being ignorant and unquestioning. We got started in the circle by fear-mongering politics, not medical facts. Control by drug wars has become an unimpeachable political symbol because "everyone knows" how dangerous it would be to relent. Our media are filled with every aspect of fighting drug wars but rarely picture drug use accurately or question the validity or effectiveness of those wars. Forgive the media, for distortions and extremes are its substance, but the sad consequence is we see the distortions as truth.

Most drug study is a part of the problem, by assuming the myths and refusing to leave the box. In this text, we have tried to present a broader perspective and analyze some of the individual components that underlie addictive acts. Many styles and activities of our lives fit the loose definition we made for addiction. We can see the origins and continuance of these styles and acts through physiological effects, psychological dependence, habitual action, cultural and social influences, mini-

mizing pain, and presenting our self-pictures.

We can also note that many if not all of those proclaiming the universal requirement of medical therapy or other outside help to break addictions have themselves stopped smoking, reduced their weight, stopped getting drunk, and even rejected narcotics *without* help. The curious anomaly is that the self-control they found in themselves they believe to be missing in those others. The best prescription here may be more study, unfettered by politics, of the nature of addiction, of drugs, and of the actual consequences of a gradual decriminalization.

Study and Review Questions

1. In addiction theory, how is physical dependency defined?

2. What is drug tolerance?

3. How is drug withdrawal defined?

4. How are drug cravings defined?

5. In what three ways do habitual acts become part of the addiction motivation?

6. What are some cultural scripts regarding alcohol addiction?

7. When can taking drugs just be doing what is socially expected?

8. In what way can a life of addiction feel satisfying?

9. Distinguish fatalism and self-efficacy as views of self-control.

10. Compare the moral and medical models of addiction.

11. Can we and do we change from heavy addiction to moderation?

12. What addictive drugs are derived from opium?

13. What lasting body damage comes from casual low doses of opiates?

14. Who were the opiate users in 1870 compared with 1910?

15. Why was the Harrison Narcotic Act passed?

16. When and why was marijuana use prohibited?

17. What are the two theoretical views on causes of drug addiction?

18. How and when did the early American colonists use alcohol?

19. When in history did Americans drink the most, per person?

20. What late 1800s problems did alcohol use pose in America?

21. Why did Americans vote to ratify Prohibition?

22. Why did Americans vote Prohibition out?

23. How long do tobacco's psychoactive chemical effects last?

24. How and by whom was tobacco use first promoted?

25. When was the medical danger of tobacco first shown?

26. How do anorexia nervosa and bulimia dieters view food and eating?

CHAPTER 12

Work

We commonly say that we don't like to work, but we really do. We try to choose work we like, and we find enjoyment and self-definition through it. In some ways, we are motivated by our needs, but the work itself keeps us on a job. What is attractive in work? What makes it more so?

Can the organization of work and its management enhance our work motivation? Do meeting goals and participating in decisions increase our motivation to work at a job? Are we really motivated primarily by money and other external rewards?

Images of Work

Worker Character

Conditions of Work

Work Organization Systems

Work, as we use that term, is perhaps the most important of life activities. Western society is structured in a fashion so that the many necessary functions are divided up and completed by different individuals. This plan is so natural to Western people that it seems strange to state it. Yet, a broader perspective, from philosophy or from cultural anthropology, may show that the activities of life called work are fabrications. The point to consider is that there is not something different about us when we undertake work activities, and we should not expect to find a qualitatively different set of ideas to account for working.

Part of the illusion that there is something special about Western work roles flows from the fact that work has been separated from other parts of our lives. The forms of separation are as varied as the work roles. For most middle-class Western societies, work is defined by clock hours, such as 8 to 5, combined with being in a particular place. In that setting, certain acts are completed that are the substance of work. There are clear boundaries between being at work and not being at work. In comparison, traditional life roles such as farming or crafting products at home have almost no boundaries between work and nonwork acts. In these settings, there is a flow of daily acts of different kinds in which it is difficult to believe that there are special work motivational factors. Are there important differences introduced by bounded work settings?

We can find one answer in observing work as a bounded activity. We believe it to be set apart from other life, and we give it special status. Because it is apart from other life, we must account to ourselves and others for why we do it. Beyond the obvious features of providing for life needs, we have also come to identify and categorize ourselves socially by our work roles and by how diligently or slothfully we do them. Work has become a means of social exchange to provide for our mutual lives. But work also is one of our primary vehicles for social opportunities. It marks our position in social life and thus becomes a primary part of our personal identity.

We need to begin by describing the images we commonly hold about work and how they drive our thoughts about work motivation. Later, we will look at work motivation as a characteristic of each worker, as an attractive or unattractive activity, and as a special management arrangement.

IMAGES OF WORK

Reluctant Producing

Work, according to a dictionary, is "effort directed to produce or accomplish something." Work's synonyms are "drudgery," "labor," and "toil." Something is done not for the doing, but for the ends. The product is of the greatest importance. This image of work is the common prototype in Western society. The varieties of our real work are extensive, and many do not fit this model, yet the implicit image remains. Psychologists' ideas and theories of work address the problems suggested by this model.

The state of mind that fits with our society's image of work is that of reluctance. We may know that we must work, and we may want to achieve the goals of the work, but yet, we will not do the work without other prodding and reasons. Using ideas of mechanical things, we are like machines that perform work when some energy source is provided to stir them into action. Believing that machines are a good example of life processes leads directly to believing that our normal state is that of rest. Doing nothing is the goal condition of life and is naturally preferred to working. The costs of applying energy are to be avoided. These models predict that no one truly wants to work and everyone must be motivated to do so.

Whether or not these common ideas about work are justified by the separate nature of the work itself or are built on poor theories of human nature, they have become a part of culture. "Everyone knows" that rest is preferred to work, that a life of doing nothing in a friendly climate is universally desired, and that people who work hard when they "don't have to" are a curiosity for the news. People who continue to work and resist retirement are thought to be merely exercising strong old habits; with a little retraining, they will be cured of their abnormality.

Following this view, the motivation aspects of work are ones of pushing people to do things. We assume reluctant, lazy people must be motivated to work. Douglas McGregor (1960) called this *Theory X*. Managers see their employees as lazy, unable to discipline or control themselves, and led by irrational feelings. Managers using Theory X supervise workers closely, using external rewards and punishments. In this kind of work setting, workers quickly learn the manager's model and come to see themselves in the same way. They play the role expected of them. The theory becomes widely assumed and thus proven by being commonplace.

Contrary to the banal rhetoric, it is easily apparent that activity, not rest, is the fundamental human state. Casual observation and detailed laboratory study alike show that people are always engaged in some acts and move in a succession to other activities. Indeed, understanding those choices of new tasks and the persistence at each are fundamental goals of motivation psychology.

There are other, better models of human activities than the machine. For example, a biological model of continuously active, evolving substances may be better than the mechanics of inert physical objects. The biological idea suggests that activity is our normal state, and work is just one form of the succession of our activities. The goal of work motivation managers is not getting us to choose to be active rather than to rest, but guiding us to choose a particular set of acts rather than others. We will always be doing something. Work managers must specify what those activities will be.

Work is a label placed on sets of activities as they are socially related to others. We may clean a car to earn money, to maintain the car's appearance for the sake of personal reputation in the community, or to perform an act of pleasure based on long habit. Doing something for money is a clear case of socially defined work. Doing the same thing only for pleasure is not. Doing that task for social maintenance is ambiguous but probably falls more on the work side. The arbitrariness of the labeling becomes apparent.

This car-washing example reveals a number of facets of work motivation. Any activity may be perceived as work or nonwork, and that perception depends on our experience history, present situation, and the social setting of the activity. The meaning of work labels becomes muted by personal views. Consider the person who gets great pleasure from teaching children or from programming computers and who would do it regardless of the work label and rewards. Is this activity no longer work, or does the example suggest a fundamental work motivation factor, a rough outline of an intrinsic cause of selection of tasks and persistence in specific work situations?

Work Motivation Theory

The many psychological theories applied to work are at once trying to do many things. A traditional goal of work motivation theories is to find the inner triggers producing work. Traditional ideas of human needs provide the foundations to these studies, and they have led to ideas of work that run counter to the fundamental premise of Theory X. Accumulated evidence shows that, when given the chance, we work because we enjoy the doing. Psychologists recognize that workers will decide what they will do, taking into account their abilities, needs, and goals. That leads to another application of work motivation theories: showing how we can be made to overcome any reluctance to work by suitable structuring of the work environment. Such structuring ranges from subtle studies of social comparisons one worker makes with another, through plans that supply performance goals for workers, to blunt applications of rewards for desired pieces of work.

Theories of work motivation have typically been pitted against one another and summarized in a serial fashion, weighing their various merits and deficiencies. Psychologists search for the one best model of work. Each theory, promoted with something like religious fervor, becomes the only correct way to think about all aspects of work motivation. Ideas borrowed from many parts of social and psychological science are dressed up for the work scene. Part of the rhetoric outlines the many forms of empirical tests of each theory, tests that usually give weak support. Summaries of work motivation have settled on a rough pattern of models but with little synthesis (Campbell & Pritchard, 1976; Steers & Porter, 1975, 1979, 1983, 1987, 1991).

It is more or less clear that these many different models deal with different aspects of work or with different perspectives on the same work. The focus of one is on the needs that workers bring to the tasks. Another treats the means of increasing the frequency of a certain unit of production. A third discusses the means of setting a worker's personal production goals. Work is perhaps too large and diverse a topic to be covered by a single, all-inclusive theory. What is shared by the daily, common work of the majority of blue collar or clerical people and the creative production of the top 5% of those in various professions? Is there a set of principles that guides the daily work of these different groups and those in other situations? We can easily see differences in their work settings and acts, but the question is of similarities. Are there some common psychological elements of working? In the actual doing, are there some fundamental motivation principles? Answers to these questions are the hopes and goals of work motivation theorists.

SECTION SUMMARY: IMAGES OF WORK

We say people don't want to work, yet we value our own work and measure ourselves with it. The paradox of work motivation psychology is that we seem to be searching for reasons to make ourselves do what we all really want to do. Work comes in many varieties, and so do the forms of theorizing about why we do it.

Workers are not alike in what they can do, want to do, and value, and few work environments are just like others. Thus, there may be no single way to picture worker motivation. Work motivation is the product of many forces. Some are in the individual worker, some are in the work setting, and others are in the work system environment. This chapter is organized according to these three kinds of perspective, and the various specific work motivation ideas are sorted among them as they illustrate work motivation values.

WORKER CHARACTER

Certain aspects of work motivation are brought to the work setting by the circumstances and intrinsic nature of the worker. This is both a hypothesis and a traditional perspective of psychologists, particularly those who focus on the importance of individual differences.

Fulfilling Needs

An old and venerable model of human activity assumes that we are driven to satisfy our needs. Lists of needs have been formed that are almost as long as the lists of performances that they are intended to explain. From these collections, two theories of needs have remained popular: Abraham Maslow's system of needs in an ordered hierarchy and Henry Murray's list of 20 human needs used to account for personality. We will look at three forms of work motivation theory coming from these systems.

Maslow's Need Hierarchy

Maslow (1970) assumed that healthy people are motivated to grow, and part of that growth is expressed in an ordered set of needs, as illustrated in Figure 12.1. In steps from most basic to most rare, those needs were labeled physiological, safety, belongingness and love, self-esteem, and self-actualization.

Applying Maslow's hierarchy of needs to work motivation is at once obvious but lacking in precision. The basic rule is that we will be motivated to work to satisfy our needs in the order of the hierarchy. In a condition of poverty, work provides the substances for satisfying our physiological needs. If a tolerable level of physiological comfort has been attained, then we will seek to prevent threats to safety. Companionship with others will be the

MASLOW'S NEED LEVEL	AVERAGE SATISFACTION	NEED-FULFILLING JOB FACTORS	ALDERFER'S ERG NEEDS
SELF–ACTUALIZATION	10%	Creative Work Challenging Work Advancement Opportunity	GROWTH
SELF–ESTEEM	40%	Recognition Important Work Job Status and Title	
BELONGINGNESS, LOVE	50%	Benevolent Supervisors Compatible Coworkers Job-Related Organizations	RELATEDNESS
SAFETY	70%	Benefits Job Security Safe Working Conditions	EXISTENCE
PHYSIOLOGICAL	85%	Adequate Rest Food and Other Body Needs Comfortable Working Conditions	

Figure 12.1. Maslow's need levels, their average satisfaction, how they are satisfied in working, and their correspondence to Alderfer's ERG components.

work goal as the two lower needs are reasonably satisfied.

Maslow's two highest levels of needs propose a basis for doing acts of work for their own sake. Attempting challenging work satisfies our self-esteem and provides some of the substance for those self-actualizing moments of doing our utmost. The intrinsic values of the work help to satisfy these needs. Maslow was one of the pioneers in developing the idea that we are motivated by needs to work toward our highest potential and in the service of developing our positive self-picture.

Using Maslow's ideas, work motivation may be managed in the light of knowing the strongest needs or combinations of needs. But given the partial satisfaction of needs at each level at any one time, it will not be easy to clearly tie specific work acts to particular active needs.

Tests of the theory have foundered on the problem of measuring the needs while respecting the complex determination of each person's work acts. Some support for the hierarchy has been found when workers in different groups are compared, for example, assembly line workers and design engineers. The few attempts to measure changes in workers over a period of time have not given support to Maslow's theory. None of these tests, however, have solved the test problem of measuring the total motivational determinants of the workers, accounting for life activities outside of the workplace. The general assessment by work motivation psychologists of applying Maslow's need hierarchy theory is negative, reflecting their frustration in trying to make adequate tests with the resources available (Campbell & Pritchard, 1976). Nonetheless, the theory contains good ideas, an interesting construction with ample intuitive appeal. Key components of it are implicit or developed in other ideas of work motivation.

Alderfer's ERG Needs

A simpler form of need hierarchy theory directed specifically to the question of work motivation is that of Clayton Alderfer (1972). Alderfer collapsed Maslow's five need levels into three: existence, relatedness, and growth (ERG theory). The translation from Maslow to Alderfer is roughly like this. Maslow's physiological and safety needs are labeled existence needs in ERG theory. Belongingness and love are roughly the same as ERG's relatedness. Maslow's self-esteem and self-actualization are what Alderfer calls growth. There is little in the ERG list that solves the frustrations in testing the Maslow theory. It should be noted, too, that the ERG theory has less of the richness and extent of description that was provided by Maslow and that made the ideas so attractive in many different psychological contexts.

ERG theory has provided some special attention to one fairly common feature of work motivation. If a particular level of need cannot be satisfied for whatever reasons, what then shall the worker do? A simple application of Maslow's hierarchy leads to the suggestion that the need remains potent and unsatisfied. Alderfer proposes that in such a case, the worker would return to a lower level and focus more strongly on satisfying those lower needs. Thus, the ERG theory proposes that in the face of frustration of a higher need, we will regress to a lower level and concentrate energy there. An engineer, for example, who has not found satisfying challenges in the projects to be completed, or who has not been able to solve them well, may instead look for satisfactions in personal relationships in the workplace and value highly the friendships maintained there. A postal worker who dislikes the people in the work setting may look instead to the pay and benefits that accompany the job, seeing these as the source of energy for doing the job well.

Another component proposed in ERG theory is that higher level needs may actually become stronger as they are regularly satisfied. With repeated success in presenting creative advertising campaigns, the motivation to do more becomes stronger. Finding and repairing troubles in automobiles makes a mechanic more strongly inclined to solve tougher problems. This, too, appears to be different from Maslow's formulation, although it is not at all clear that he proposed that higher needs, once satisfied, were forever reduced in strength. Maslow instead suggested that it is not likely that a person ever satisfies more than a portion of the highest level of needs, those called growth needs in the ERG theory. (Note the second column in Figure 12.1.)

Personality Styles

Three of the 20 needs in Henry Murray's theory (1938) have been given special atten-

tion and development by work theorists. The greatest attention has been directed toward the need to achieve. The focus of that research has been on what determines choosing tasks. Using similar methods of motive measurement, the needs for power and for affiliation have been measured alongside the need for achievement in sets of people. The relative balance of these needs has been used to predict their success in jobs having different requirements for the three motivations.

Need to Achieve

It was more or less unplanned that one part of Henry Murray's attempt in the 1930s to form an understanding of personality was given much closer development. The **need to achieve** was 1 of 20 needs he proposed to be measured in a variety of ways. One of his many tests evaluated stories we invent about pictures. His psychological theory suggested that we will put ourselves into our fantasies, indirectly revealing our needs. Those fantasies were scored for achievement themes. The resulting scores of achievement need were combined with some rational analysis of the nature of tasks and their difficulty. The result was a good prediction of the ways in which people select tasks.

After World War II, a decade of concern with measuring achievement needs led to a succeeding period in which John Atkinson and others developed a model of task choice. In his 1957 paper, Atkinson defended a rather simple and elegant theory that can be stated with a few terms in an equation. The tendency for success is a product of the motive for success, the probability of succeeding, and the incentive value of that success. Or,

$$T_s = M_s \times P_s \times I_s$$

where

T_s is the tendency to choose to choose a particular task that will lead to success

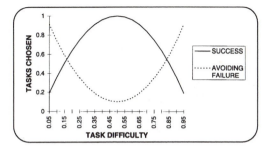

Figure 12.2. Theoretical picture of difficulty of tasks chosen by people with high achievement motivation or with high motivation to avoid failure.

M_s is the measured level of achievement motivation

P_s is the person's estimate of the probability of succeeding with that task

I_s is the incentive value of succeeding in that task

Atkinson and his colleagues assumed by logic that as the probability of success increases, the incentive value of that success decreases. That is, easier tasks are valued less and difficult tasks are valued more. Thus,

$$P_s = 1 - I_s$$

These formulas predict the difficulty of tasks that we will select. With a strong achievement motivation, or motive for success (M_s), the theory predicts that people with a high achievement need will choose tasks that are intermediate in difficulty, avoiding those that they believe are too hard or too easy.

(Calculating a few points makes that clear—M_s does not change. The terms P_s and I_s are probabilities having values ranging between zero and one. The greatest value of P_s multiplied by I_s will be when both are 0.5; the product is 0.25. If either value is 0.6, the other is 0.4 and the product is 0.24. If either is 0.3, the product is 0.21; and with either at 0.1, the product is 0.09. The curve relating the strength of the task choice and the perceived difficulty of the task will be an inverted-U shape.)

A complementary motive to avoid failing at tasks was also theorized and was found to be stronger in some people, and these people (showing a need to avoid failing) are predicted to choose tasks according to a similar set of theory assumptions. The analogous formula for the tendency to avoid failure is

$$T_A = M_F \times P_F \times I_F$$

The preferences of such people are for very easy or very difficult tasks, avoiding most strongly those in the middle that are selected by people with high achievement motive. These ideas appear in Figure 12.2.

Achievement, Power, and Affiliation

Another branch of work from Murray's assessment of personality also developed from the use of measured achievement needs, this time to predict work motivation. In the 1960s, David McClelland (1961, 1965) applied measurements of need to achieve in many work settings and in different cultures. Need to achieve scores predicted level of activity in a variety of business settings, academics, and domains of creativity. Furthermore, he found that achievement patterns could be developed in individuals so that their business activities improved.

Needs for power and for affiliation were assessed in similar ways and found to be important in the work setting also. **Need for power** reflects a desire to control events and influence other people. Wanting reassurance and companionship marks the **need for affiliation,** and it is shown by acts of conforming to the pressures of friends and being interested in their feelings. This trio of needs were thought to be the foundation for work performance. The underlying theory was that these are relatively stable aspects of personality that affect our success in specific work. Some possibilities may exist for modifying the strengths of the needs, but those details were to be worked out in further research. The current wisdom is that achievement patterns may be modified but that power needs cannot be trained (Stahl, 1986).

Examples of the need trio abound. People with high needs for power and affiliation may do well in religious ministerial work, nursing, or organizing community service projects. Political dictators are thought to have high power and low affiliation needs. High power and achievement needs but low affiliation needs describe people successful in managerial positions. A shop manager with a high need for affiliation and a low need for power may find it difficult to command the performance that is required of the subordinates. Similarly, an excellent salesperson with a high need to achieve but low power needs may be unable to handle the requirements of a promotion to sales manager.

In practice, these ideas may be used to guide people in making career choices in which their needs will be satisfied. In some applications, workers are made aware of the structure of their personal needs so that they may build on their strengths and compensate for the deficiencies in light of their current positions.

One limitation of the scheme lies in the original method of assessing the needs. The Thematic Apperception Test procedures of scoring stories of fantasy has been shown to have problems of reliability. Thus, other measures have been developed with some success (Stahl, 1986).

SECTION SUMMARY: WORKER CHARACTER

In work, we may satisfy our various needs: physical, social, and psychological. Maslow and Alderfer saw those needs in that priority of importance. Working to keep our physical existence is no surprise, but the psychological satisfactions of working are an important theme buried in many work motivation theories. From personality descriptions, others have matched people and jobs in terms of needs for achievement, power, and affiliation.

CONDITIONS OF WORK

Motivation can come from the work itself and its setting. Fundamental to interest in doing work is the intrinsic nature of work activities and its significance to the worker. Important, too, are the surrounds in which the person does the work. Physiological, physical, and social conditions have a lot to do with getting a person to a workplace and with assuming work responsibility.

Work conditions include all those physical and social aspects of the work environment that are related to the work, including the nature of the work itself. We begin with an influential and provocative theory that addressed both structural conditions of work and the elements of work that motivate.

Hygiene and Motivator Factors

Frederick Herzberg (Herzberg, 1966; Herzberg, Mausner, & Snyderman, 1959) proposed two sets of factors of work motivation: hygiene factors and motivator factors. Following an intense analysis of 200 accountants and engineers in different companies, he grouped their satisfactions and dissatisfactions about working into those two categories. Hygiene factors include attitudes about the job context and were typically related to feeling bad about working there. Motivator factors are satisfying job experiences having positive feelings. We focus first on the hygiene factors.

Hygiene factors were identified as aspects of job context. They do not motivate us to work harder if they are satisfied but have the potential, if unsatisfactory, to reduce our performance by making us dissatisfied with the employment. This component of Herzberg's theory was novel and interesting. Hygiene factors include job security, working conditions, company policy and its administration, technical supervision, peer relationships, and relationships with supervisors. As Herzberg saw these factors, none of them will make us work harder. They do not improve our work motivation, but instead, they must be at an adequate level to keep us from being dissatisfied and leaving the job. In later versions of the theory, pay and salary were listed also as hygiene factors, but the earlier study showed those items divided equally by workers between the motivator and hygiene categories.

Satisfying experiences of employment in Herzberg's studies were what he called **motivator factors.** As the label implies, work motivation comes from the motivator elements, and these are aspects of the work itself. This part of Herzberg's theory is not different from many others. It is similar to the implications of the higher-level needs in Maslow's hierarchy and Alderfer's ERG theory. It is related to aspects of intrinsic motivation theory and to ideas of goal setting and participation described below. The emphasis is on the internal satisfactions of doing the work, the challenges and rewards of the doing. Factors contributing largely to the motivator category in Herzberg's lists are achievement on important tasks, recognition for doing good work, the nature of the work itself, responsibility for the work, and advancement on the basis of work. Focus on motivators led directly to management recommendations, particu-

HYGIENE FACTORS	MOTIVATOR FACTORS
job security	achievement on tasks
working conditions	work recognition
company policy	challenges in work
technical supervision	responsibility for work
peer relationships	advancement at work
supervisor relationships	

Figure 12.3. Herzberg's (1966) reported components making up the hygiene and motivator factors.

larly job enhancement, which we will consider below. (See Figure 12.3.)

Two-factor theory has been a controversial proposal, but to its credit, it had an important historical role in stimulating psychologists to consider work motivation questions more seriously. Consequently, other work motivation proposals were also given increased attention. For their part, Herzberg and his colleagues presented their ideas in an attractive manner to managers and sold their system to many on its logical merits.

Research tests of Herzberg's two-factor scheme have not been supportive, in part because of ambiguities in the theory itself. One critic found five different versions that Herzberg presented and claimed that Herzberg's own data did not fully support any of them (King, 1970). Are hygiene factors never sources of motivation, or are they just less likely to be so, and what of individual differences in workers and in kinds of employment situations (Maidini, 1991)? The bare theory assumes the same scheme works for all. In general, the distinction between the motivator and hygiene factors is not clear-cut, making it difficult for exact test predictions or even for consistent application.

Perhaps most important to consider is that measuring satisfactions and dissatisfactions in the job is not the same as measuring motivation in the sense of energetic and quality performance. A happy worker is not necessarily doing good work. Satisfaction keeps a worker committed to the job and the work institution, but that satisfaction does not automatically cause motivated performance. Satisfaction may be the result, not the cause, of high performance (Henne & Latham, 1985), and workers' reports may reflect their personal expectations about the work. We shall illustrate these ideas later. Still, the value of the theory is in the recommended applications and how they affect workplace activities.

Job Enhancement

A common theme we have seen in work motivation is focus on the nature of the job itself. What is there in work that draws people to it, and what keeps them working? What can be done with the work to entice workers to approach it and continue doing it with more enthusiasm? Not everyone will respond to the same puzzle, and a challenging change to one person may be avoided by another. The major intention of job enhancement practices has been to create optimally attractive work (see Figure 12.4).

One of the means of reducing the boredom believed to be a part of repetitive work is the technique of job enlargement. **Job enlargement** is simply repackaging a worker's tasks to increase the variety of tasks to be done. In the regimented work environment of factory assembly, for example, it may be necessary to first enlarge the job by adding new elements. Positive benefits of enhancement may be gained through adding the sort of challenge that allows one to identify and "own" more of the product and satisfy mastery needs. These forms of job enhancement can be described as *horizontal* increases in activities at the same level, compared with *vertical* enhancements to new levels of job skills using job enrichment strategies.

Job enlargement has intuitive support, but it likely has limited use. In the work environment, for example, of an engineer, lawyer, architect, or professor, job enlargement is likely to merely add to the many different pieces of the work. Little increase in work motivation will be possible because variety is part of the job. A limit is already achieved, and motivation will not be gained by simply asking that more work be done.

JOB ENHANCEMENT
make optimally attractive work
JOB ENLARGEMENT = increase variety of tasks
JOB ENRICHMENT = increase intrinsic challenges

Figure 12.4. Job enhancement as ways to make optimally attractive work.

Further problems have appeared in applications to different kinds of worker populations. Urban worker populations have sometimes been found to respond differently than rural workers. One key suggestion is that job enlargement is effective with those workers who have accepted the middle-class social norms of work.

Job enrichment is intended to increase the intrinsic challenges and satisfactions of the work itself. As such, job enrichment can be seen as a prescription from Herzberg's two-factor theory, from Maslow's growth needs, and from several other theories. Proponents of two-factor theory developed job enrichment, but the idea fits equally well with any orientation in which growth needs or intrinsic motivation sources of work motivation are present.

Job enrichment in its simplest form is a set of changes to work that satisfy one's needs for mastery and personal growth. The focus is on the challenge of the task as a source of motivation. Among the elements of job enrichment are these: demanding content, opportunity to learn, autonomy or discretion in decisions, social support and recognition, and worker feelings that the work leads to a valued future. There are several principles of job enrichment that have been used: forming the work in natural units, combining tasks, establishing relationships between the worker and the product users, and improving feedback of work success.

One analysis and extension of job enrichment (Hackman & Oldham, 1976) appears in the Job Characteristics Model. The model's authors identified five job dimensions that feed three critical psychological states of

JOB DIMENSIONS		COGNITIVE STATES	OUTCOMES
SKILL VARIETY	↘		INTERNAL MOTIVATION
TASK IDENTITY	→	MEANINGFUL WORK	QUALITY WORK
TASK SIGNIFICANCE	↗		SATISFACTION
AUTONOMY	→	RESPONSIBILITY	SATISFACTION
FEEDBACK	→	KNOWLEDGE OF RESULTS	WORK ATTENDANCE

Figure 12.5. Outline of theory for work design to improve motivation by J. Richard Hackman (1991).

work, which in turn combine to produce four work-quality outcomes (see Figure 12.5).

Three job dimensions—skill variety, task identity, and task significance—add together to produce the psychological experience of meaningfulness of the work. **Skill variety** is "the degree to which a job requires a variety of different activities that involve the use of a number of different skills and talents" (Hackman & Oldham, 1975, p. 161). **Task identity** is "the degree to which the job requires completion of a whole and identifiable piece of work—that is, doing a job from beginning to end with a visible outcome" (p. 161). **Task significance** is "the degree to which the job has a substantial impact on the lives or work of other people, whether in the immediate organization or in the external environment" (p. 161). The result is experienced meaningfulness in which "the person must experience the work as generally important, valuable, and worthwhile" (p. 161).

The job dimension of autonomy produces experiences of responsibility for outcomes of the work. **Autonomy** is "the degree to which the job provides substantial freedom, independence, and discretion to the individual in scheduling the work and in determining the procedures to be used in carrying it out" (Hackman & Oldham, 1975, p. 162). With experienced responsibility, "the individual must feel personally responsible and accountable for the results of the work" (p. 162).

The job dimension of feedback produces knowledge of actual results of work activities. **Feedback** is "the degree to which carrying out the work activities required by the job results in the individual obtaining direct and clear information about the effectiveness of . . . performance" (Hackman & Oldham, 1975, p. 162). With knowledge of results, the worker "must have an understanding, on a fairly regular basis, of how effectively . . . [he or she] is performing the job" (p. 162).

The three psychological states (meaningful work, responsibility, and knowledge of results) together produce outcomes of high internal work motivation, high-quality work, high satisfaction with the work, and low absenteeism and turnover.

These psychologists (Hackman & Oldham, 1975, 1976) used the same system to identify jobs that have motivating potential. Their Motivating Potential Score (MPS) is used to determine how workers view their job. They calculate the motivating potential score by averaging the first three job dimensions—skill variety, task identity, and task significance—and multiplying that sum by the other two job dimensions: autonomy and feedback. These are the job dimensions of their job characteristics model. Their next step is to find those people for whom that motivating potential is actualized. Their Growth Need Strength (GNS) measure identified such workers. These people are motivated by changes in any of the factors of the MPS. In this scheme, Hackman and Oldham have put together several aspects of different motivation theories.

In applying this system, the authors illustrate five principles of enriching jobs (Hackman, 1991). First, we must form work in natural units, referenced to the worker, not the "system." The worker is the judge of what fits together as a unit. By respecting task iden-

372 ◈ CHAPTER 12

tity and significance to the worker, the meaningfulness of the work is enhanced. Second, we can combine tasks to get greater identity and use a greater variety of worker skills. Third, we may develop client relationships in which workers see the consequences of their work and its social value. Fourth, we can vertically load the job to give workers more autonomy in managing their work and thereby promoting their sense of personal responsibility for it. Fifth, we must open feedback channels to give workers increased information about how well they are doing. Some of the best feedback is that coming directly from the work itself. Work design must be done with care to ensure that quality and quantity measures are delivered promptly; it is best if that feedback provides for correction before notice or recording by others.

Intrinsic Motivation and Rewards

The concept of intrinsic motivation for work requires us to build some theory ideas. We will explore their origins here to give us the necessary foundation, and they will be useful for topics of the last chapter as well.

There have been three general ways that psychologists have tried to account for curiosity, exploration, and related information-seeking acts. The first of these was a defensive attempt to account for these acts with the once-popular drive and arousal theories. The second group of theories tried to model the acts with some concept of optimal level of body stimulation. The third set of theory ideas introduced the concept of intrinsic motivation. Intrinsic motivation ideas about curiosity rest on the agreement that some activities are done strictly for internal consequences. We can say it in different ways.

The activities are internally rewarding.

They have no consequences other than for the central nervous system.

They are not related to external rewards.

Each of these statements reflects theory ideas that individuals have used in proposing intrinsic motivation, and collectively they provide orientation to the basic notion.

Robert White (1959) pointed out a class of actions that seems to have the purpose of dealing with the environment effectively, and he labeled it **competence**. The motivation to competence was also given a special name, **effectance,** representing "what the neuromuscular system wants to do when it is otherwise unoccupied or is gently stimulated by the environment." This urge toward competence does not produce random or aimless acts. It directs actions that are focused and persisting. Its essence is exploration, curiosity, and experimentation.

There are three interesting features in White's theory. One aspect is that he proposed no goal state for the motive in the usual sense. The motive and its satisfaction are the action. A second intriguing feature is referred to in the definition of effectance. Effectance motivation is latent, and it becomes dominant only when body needs are not pressing. Strong biological urges usually overshadow effectance. This feature of the theory is a familiar idea in psychology, for example, in Maslow's need hierarchy we just outlined.

White's third notion is that competence acts tend to be carried out in a continuous stream that builds greater effectance once begun. When under way, competence actions will resist the influence of minor physiological and psychological pressures. A related idea is that of **flow**, which we will elaborate in the last chapter. Flow is an intense form of effectance, the experience of being totally involved in an activity and unaware of or resistant to whatever else may be happening. Flow is accompanied or followed by feelings of pleasure in the doing.

Robert deCharms (1968) has proposed that intrinsic motivation is based on a need for controlling our acts. We experience that self-determination by doing things and being aware of actually causing changes. Competence acts are based on our need to be actually

Figure 12.6. Staw's (1979) outline of the four possible mixtures of high and low intrinsic and extrinsic reinforcements.

making a difference, of being in control of the doing.

Edward Deci (1975; Deci & Ryan, 1985) combined these two kinds of intrinsic motivation. He added to competence and self-determination an emphasis on the feelings we have of being able to choose what to do. It is not just the feeling of doing, but also the feeling of being able to choose to do it. **Intrinsic motivation** is the need for self-determined competence.

Deci further developed the concept of intrinsic motivation for working and supplied another twist. Deci's evidence showed that adding extrinsic reward to people doing an intrinsically rewarding task could decrease task performance. The practical idea for work motivation was that intrinsic and extrinsic sources of reward do not simply add together. It may be possible that being paid too much to do an interesting task, for example, will reduce rather than add to our motivation. This suggestion is one of the more provocative of a class of ideas that may be conceptually confusing.

Deci's proposals put the concept of intrinsic motivation in direct competition with the commonly accepted idea of work being controlled by external rewards. In almost all work settings, extrinsic reinforcement is believed to be the foundation for motivation, and any form of intrinsic motivation is thought to add to that. Deci concluded that money, an extrinsic reinforcement, could decrease intrinsic motivation. The idea led to a focus on the ways those two factors combine.

Barry Staw (1979) outlined the four possible mixtures of high and low intrinsic and extrinsic reinforcements (see Figure 12.6).

Staw saw no problem with two mixtures: high extrinsic added to low intrinsic reinforcement, and low extrinsic added to high intrinsic motivation. The third work setting, where both are low, is one of insufficient justification for continuing the work. The worker will solve that problem by increasing the perceived intrinsic value of the task (perhaps following Festinger's 1957 cognitive dissonance principles, which we saw at the end of Chapter 10). The fourth mixture is Deci's example of both intrinsic and extrinsic reinforcement being high, a case called **overjustification.** A likely solution for a worker facing overjustification is to decrease the perceived intrinsic value of the work. The intrinsic value is weakened because it is not as strong, not as clear or obvious, as the extrinsic reinforcers. A summary of this work appeared under the title, *The Hidden Costs of Rewards* (Lepper & Greene, 1978), in which some authors maintained that the addition of the money reward overjustifies the work. Overjustification is a cognitive inconsistency that must be removed. The most likely action is to alter the motivation over which one has the clearest control, the intrinsic.

Criticism of both the original laboratory demonstrations and the theory (Thierry, 1990) have appeared. At this time, there is no convincing demonstration or refutation of the Deci proposal based on field study, but it remains a possibility that may apply to some forms of work. An additional note is that there is a need to clarify the concepts and ideas of intrinsic and extrinsic reinforcement and intrinsic and extrinsic motivation. It does not directly follow, for example, that extrinsic reinforcement just produces extrinsic motivation. The fact of the reinforcement may also provide information about worker competence and thus add to the intrinsic motivation for doing the task (Deci & Porac, 1978). Similarly, being rewarded may be seen as coercion and control, distorting the worker's natural view of the work. We will explore the nature of rewards later in the chapter.

Equity Theory

Equity theory of work motivation comes from the social psychology theory tradition of cognitive consistency or balance theories. Balance theories assume that people hold sets of beliefs and that they strive to maintain consistency among them. Inconsistency is a source of motivation to achieve consistency. Inequity produces distress. A form of these ideas was developed for work settings by J. Stacy Adams (1963, 1965).

Adams's equity theory deals with cognitive consistency as it relates to social exchange of workers. The cognitive data for each worker are presented as a ratio of outcomes to inputs. **Outcomes** are all the valued results one perceives in working at the job. Satisfactions of accomplishment, pay and benefits, social status of the job, and the like are perceived outcomes (see Table 12.1). **Inputs** are those factors that we perceive as being brought to the job. Inputs include effort, skills, education or training, experience, seniority, and in Adams's list of 1963, age, sex, and ethnic background. The perception of combined outcomes and combined inputs is given in an **equity ratio,** outcomes over inputs. Note the consistent use of the word *perceived*. No reality matters except our perceptions.

We compare our perceived equity ratios against what we perceive of others. Equity arises from seeing equal ratios. Inequity motivates change to reestablish equity. The theory proposes that change comes in different ways. We may change the outcomes, change the inputs, cognitively distort the inputs or

TABLE 12.1	Adams's (1963, 1965) Equity Theory of Inputs and Outcomes

Inputs	Outcomes
Effort	Feelings of accomplishment
Skills	Pay and benefits
Education	Social status of the job
Training	
Experience	
Seniority	

outputs, quit the situation, get the other person to change, or change to a different comparison standard.

A commonly experienced inequity comes from perceived underpayment. We may believe that similar inputs are being made to the job but that we are receiving too little pay compared with what we perceive others are getting. The inequity produces dissatisfaction, and that motivates attempts to change the ratio. We may change the outcome by directly requesting an increase in pay, citing the inequity. That failing, we may change our input by putting less effort into working, reasoning that being paid too little, less work is required, and the equity ratios are made more equal. We may cognitively change the inputs or outcomes of either party, perhaps reasoning that pay is not as important as the satisfaction in doing the job. We may simply quit, terminating the comparison and its inequity, or try to get the other person to increase inputs toward equity. We may shift comparison to another person or group, perhaps looking at similar workers in another setting.

Equity theory also predicts that being overpaid will yield inequity motivating dissatisfaction. Psychologists have been quite interested in this counterintuitive prediction of the theory. Although we are more tolerant of overpayment than of underpayment, the resulting perceived inequity should also lead to performance changes. Equity could be reestablished by changing the perceived inputs. We could apply more effort to the work, we could increase the value of our qualifications, or we could put a greater emphasis on our experience. Changes could also be made in outcomes such as reducing our perceived status of the job or seeing less personal satisfaction in the work's accomplishments.

Another common form of perceived inequity involves job qualifications. A worker with years of experience in the work may be dissatisfied when a newer worker with a higher degree is given the same or higher rate of pay. That same new worker may also see inequity, believing that the education producing the degree is more important than years of experience.

One of the important variables of equity theory is choice of comparison. There are many targets with which you may compare yourself. Coworkers are the most common and available, but we also have models of expectation in work settings. A laborer with experience expects to get more than the minimum wage. An engineer expects to have work that provides for creative and novel solutions. Pilots expect to have coworkers with equivalent professional training. Physicians and professors expect to get a high degree of social respect. We compare our equity with an ideal comparison standard.

Writers have provided several other possible reference standards against which we can make equity comparisons, including other workers outside of the area of employment, our own past job experience, and our own internal model of worth (Goodman, 1974).

Not all of the possible changes to achieve equity are equally likely (see Table 12.2). In real work settings, some principles of strategy are more typical. We tend to try for the greatest possible positive outcomes, those with the highest value. We prefer changes that keep the input effort low. We will protect our self-picture and avoid doing things that appear unlike our typical ways. Cognitive distortions of inputs and outcomes are more easily made regarding the comparison worker than oneself. Quitting is likely only when there is a very strong inequity and alternative jobs are available; the more likely strategy is

TABLE 12.2 Possible Changes to Achieve Balance in Equity Theory

Theoretical Changes	Typical Changes
Change outcomes	Maximize positive
Change inputs	Keep effort low
Distort inputs	Protect self-picture
Distort outcomes	Distort comparison
Quit the job	Absenteeism
Get other to change	Change comparison

partial quitting, such as absenteeism. Once we establish a comparison standard, we will strongly resist changing to another (Adams, 1965).

Fatigue

The last of the topics of "Conditions of Work" is considerably more intensive and in a little different direction, the consequences of doing work. A great deal of the picture we have of working is influenced by how we expect to feel while we are working and how we will feel after some work is done. Fatigue is an obvious part of those feelings. We will see that fatigue has various aspects that make it troublesome to bring together in a single definition, not a novel problem in motivation. Yet, there is a general theme of fatigue: Fatigue protects us.

Fatigue is a warning to us, restraining our action. If we engage in heavy and rapid work, our performance will be reduced. We will feel lost muscle energy and sensations of heat and discomfort. We can use muscles until they have exhausted their resources, but that can be dangerous and our bodies are designed to protect us from that. Body limits are expressed as fatigue, and through experience, we build mental expectations of fatigue feelings that directly affect what we do. If we engage in prolonged, low-energy work or have a vigilance task, fatigue shows up in a different, psychological way. Generally, our fatigue results from events of a certain kind inserted into a stream of experience, and we are more or less prepared for it. Our specific and general body and mental conditions will have a lot to do with the results.

Fatigue seems to be very similar to being sleepy. We often talk of being "tired of doing something." Being fatigued, however, is different from being sleep-deprived, even though one effect of some fatigue conditions is feeling sleepy. As we noted in Chapter 2, being sleep-deprived has some elements of fatigue, but many conditions of fatigue have no elements of sleep deprivation.

Fatigue Ideas

Although we all intuitively agree that what we do is strongly influenced by its presence, we struggle in defining what we mean by the word *fatigue*. One tradition of study breaks fatigue into three different pieces: physiological change, objective decrements in work performance, and subjective reports of being tired (Bills, 1943). Another major approach collapses all the sources into one psychological state, the summation of mental events of feeling tired (Bartley & Chute, 1947). Although other definitions add variety and subtlety, these two approaches remain a good general summary.

The basic prerequisites of fatigue are time and activity. Without activity over a period of time, there can be no fatigue. The kind and intensity of activity form the nature of reported fatigue. Our typical fatigue has two kinds of consequences. We have (a) reduced potential for performance with (b) parallel mental states of discomfort or aversion to continuing that action.

There are both physical and psychological dimensions in fatigue. Examples will illustrate these two major aspects of fatigue.

> In building a roof on a conventional house without lifting machinery, a roofer must typically carry an 80-pound bundle of shingles 12 feet up a ladder. If the worker takes no rest, performance will change after a few bundles. The work conditions force a slower pace or a period of complete rest after a few trips.

> Piloting an airplane takes very little physical effort, and the times of mental concentration are widely separated by periods of a few important events. After several hours of flying, fatigue is apparent, and fatigue becomes important after 10 hours or more.

> A 10-year-old may play a running game with the family cat after supper. Dragging a piece of foil attached to a string, the child is having a good time. The child's mother then calls, asking that the evening chores be done. The child abruptly changes from showing vitality to being limp in arms and legs. The 10-year-old claims extreme tiredness and inability to do anything at all.

In looking at these three examples of fatigue, we recognize that the general use of the word includes both physical and psychological activity. Fatigue is a label for mechanisms decreasing performance possibilities *and* for involvement in a task for long periods *and* for subjective unwillingness to continue acts. In some settings, these come together, and in others, there is a preponderance of one over the others. The roofing example of heavy physical demand combines primarily muscle-based sources with some sensitivity to the feelings from that use. Pilots feel the effort of remaining seated for long periods and a sense of boredom with little to do. The child's fatigue comes from feelings anticipated in changing from self-directed play to other-directed work. We separate these two sources—physical and psychological—for our convenience in presenting some principles of fatigue.

Physical Fatigue

Objective fatigue, championed by early researchers, is reduction in performance that accumulates with continued work of a muscle system. Consider raising a weight attached to your finger. Measurements reflect how much you can do, how long before you can do no more, or how your movements reduce to some defined level. The facts of sources and conditions of objective fatigue of this sort are useful for work designers and other applications, such as like sports.

We know a great deal about the conditions of muscle work. Muscle-based fatigue arises from relatively high work demands on the body. The production of action and the return of the body to a ready state underlie conditions of muscle-based fatigue. Muscle fatigue is easily demonstrated by demanding a high level of action at a fast pace. Any of the traditional exercise regimes such as push-ups, chin-ups, sit-ups, running, and speed swimming are effective fatiguing tasks. Such tasks require the rapid use of stored energy. The key idea is that the demands of work exceed the capacity to maintain resources. Obviously there are metabolic and perhaps other factors that underlie such fatigue.

In part, fatigue exists because there is a limited physical capacity for movements of muscles. Rarely are muscle resources totally exhausted. Physical performance declines at a rate short of complete depletion. Awareness of fatigue typically signals or forces a slower physical pace. Fatigue is an effective warning. The source of the muscle-based performance decline may lie in the muscle tissues themselves and perhaps also in the nervous tissue that directs them to action, but the fatigue anticipates exhaustion of energy resources. We slow or stop before we are damaged or put at risk by being unable to act.

Muscle-based fatigue is physiological. The tissue changes of muscle action and fatigue have been researched by physiologists for more than 100 years, and we know a great deal, but some mysteries still exist.

The primary flow of action energy is in glucose, some being chained together to make glycogen. Use of that energy in the cells involves, first, releasing some energy in a reaction that converts it to pyruvic acid, and then changing the pyruvic acid to carbon dioxide and more energy. Molecules of adenosine triphospate (ATP) store most of the energy; the rest becomes heat. ATP is the energy source stored in cells. When there is not sufficient glucose for energy needs, fats and proteins convert in similar processes.

A muscle contraction is begun by neural impulses releasing calcium ions that activate muscle contraction. The energy for contraction comes when phosphate ions split from ATP, producing adenosine diphosphate (ADP) and adenosine monophosphate (AMP) successively. Stores of ATP in the muscles are sufficient for 5 seconds or so of muscle action, so ATP must be replenished. About 10 more seconds of muscle action come from release of phosphate ions and energy from phosphocreatine recharging of ATP. Together, these make up the phosphagen energy system.

Another 30 to 40 seconds of muscle endurance arises from the glycogen-lactic acid system. In the absence of oxygen, glycogen, the primary carbohydrate storage material in the body, is split into glucose. Glucose molecules are split into pyruvic acids plus energy to form ATP. Without sufficient oxygen, the pyruvic acids convert to lactic acids. Lactic acid in the muscles produces some of the sensations of fatigue, and these acids slowly diffuse to the blood with a half-life of about 30 minutes.

Longer periods of muscle action are supported by energy from other energy deposits in the body combined with oxygen. Those reactions replenish phosphate into the AMP to ADP to ATP systems. Oxygen from these changes is stored in muscle and other body tissues. Using this resource produces an oxygen debt, but that is only about one sixth of the oxygen that is needed to bring the body to a resting normal. Another one sixth is needed to replenish the phosphagen system, and two thirds will be consumed by the glycogen-lactic acid system. About an hour may be needed to bring oxygen levels back from near-exhaustion levels. Table 12.3 summarizes these muscle processes.

In addition to the work produced by the muscle, the reaction also produces heat. Under the best conditions, no more than one quarter of the energy is used in muscle action. The rest of the energy is released as heat. The energy used in direct muscle action is also

TABLE 12.3 Energy Supplies Available to Muscles to Do Sustained Work

Use Time in Seconds	Muscle Energy Source
0 to 5	ATP in muscles
5 to 15	Phosphocreatine recharge of ATP
15 to 50	Glycogen-glucose conversion
50 or more	Oxygen plus nutrients replenishment

converted primarily to heat through friction within the muscle system and blood supply. Very little energy powers external work; nearly all goes to heat in one way or another.

Body changes during and following heavy physical work produce a pattern of fatigue feelings. During hard work, we feel increasingly uncomfortable. Muscles produce sensations of ache, tremor, twitch, and cramp. Body heat from the muscle energy system dissipates by evaporation of moisture. Thus, perspiration joins heat, making skin sensations of dampness. Oxygen demand increases the speed of breathing and heart action. Sensations of gasping, shortness of breath, and pounding heart result. We feel these changes during extended effort. Sore and tender muscles are noticed later. Collectively, these physiological conditions and their sensations make up our physical feelings of fatigue.

Other fatigue feelings arise from specific health problems. **Hypothyroidism** is reduced functioning of the thyroid gland that slows metabolism and weakens muscles, slows thoughts, and makes less tolerance of minor discomforts. **Emphysema** is damage to the lungs that reduces oxygen intake and lowers the upper limit of tolerable energy expenditure. **Diabetes** changes metabolism in ways that limit performance. **Arthritis** is painful inflammation of joints that limits movement. Fatigue may be a part of the nonspecific symptom collection of any disease or physical stress. The body response to the disease or stress depletes resources and produces feelings of fatigue. Fatigue is also a part of the clinical pattern of certain psychological pathologies. The hypochondriac focuses great attention on body functioning and hence is likely to exaggerate the body symptoms underlying normal feelings of fatigue. Depression is a general condition that resembles great fatigue. In a depressed state, any effort is too unimportant and tiring. In summary, being tired is a major symptom of health problems.

The simplicity and ease of understanding the idea of muscle-based physical fatigue leads us to use this as our model of fatigue. The focus is on tissue change and performance decrement, as if they were the only things of importance. Of course, fatigue always results from extreme situations of energy depletion, but there are other sources of fatigue that may be more important in common work and are more psychologically interesting.

Psychological Fatigue

Part of our self-picture is a personal impression of habitual responses to fatigue factors. Classic extremes come to mind of stoically refusing to acknowledge the weakness of fatigue versus weakly giving in to the first feelings and ideas suggesting it. Experiences are important in forming those general ideas of fatigue style. We come to accept different levels of fatigue as normal in certain tasks. For example, we may accept a strong collection of body discomfort while exercising. Much less of the same discomfort may be accepted when laboring to rake the fallen leaves in the yard. Only minimal discomfort is acceptable when watching television. Each person's exact level of tolerance will be different. Experiences and style set the limits of what we feel to be fatiguing.

Psychological conditions producing fatigue are many and varied, leading to concern about what fatigue actually is, beyond its role as a collective label in the human condition. Thought in the Bartley and Shute (1947) tradition has focused on fatigue as a central state or condition that broadly affects all subsequent actions. In this view, fatigue closely resembles sleep deprivation. An alternative hypothesis is that psychological fatigue is an accumulating reduction in motivation to perform a task. That reduced motivation has external elements, as in the influence of rewards and task-irrelevant psychological conditions. More interesting are apparent reductions in task-generated motivations. Psychological fatigue, such as a decline in interest in doing the task, is related to the psychological phenomena observed in habituation, boredom, reduced cognitive arousal, and weakened intrinsic motivation for that task. The theme is of reduced motivation and perhaps cognitive capacity for continuing that task. Tasks having variety will not be affected. Thus, fatigue, in this tradition, may be pictured as a task-specific consequence, not a general psychological inhibition.

If fatigue is conceived as coming primarily from energy-consuming tasks, it is hard to understand why we get tired in jobs that use little physical energy. After 3 or 4 hours of driving a car, little physical energy has been used, we have been comfortably supported in a seated position, and the mental requirements on the average are very low. Still, most drivers begin to feel tired, beyond just feeling sleepy. After 8 hours or more, they are noticeably fatigued, and performance may worsen. This problem has been addressed by many interest groups. Specific tasks are examined in detail, and that may be the most effective way to study fatigue. Driving, air crew performance, power plant control, industrial process control, and a miscellany of government and military jobs have had and still receive research attention. In each case, many of the same apparent causes of fatigue are found.

In a study during World War II, British psychologists made intensive study of pilots "flying" a Spitfire simulator for long durations and under difficult conditions. Accuracy of timing and skill slowly worsened over the test period. Pilots failed to integrate the instrument displays, suggesting a narrowing of attention and the forgetting of some of the information sources. The investigators concluded that the pilots seemed to accept lower standards for their coordinated actions. They performed more poorly, making an increased number of errors at the end of the simulated flight (Bartlett, 1943).

Another example of specific task study was an analysis of air crew fatigue, done at a time when airline flights were slower and often longer. Ross McFarland in 1953 published an impressive study titled *Human Factors in Air Transportation,* in which one chapter was devoted to "Operational Aspects of Fatigue." First, McFarland noted the absence of physical demands for work in the airline pilot job. Muscle movements required are very light in both intensity and frequency. The pilot is comfortably seated and the environmental conditions are reasonable, although typically not as good as for the passengers in the cabin.

McFarland found total duty time to be one important determinant of the pilot's fatigue. Schedules of flights determine this: specifically, the number of hours in one flight and the total amount of flying in a month. Early rules stipulated no more than 8 actual flying hours in a day and no more than 100 hours in a month. These limits were not an easy guarantee of being safely fatigue-free, because the total daily time could easily double the 8-hour limit. Delays caused by traffic, weather, and mechanical problems add up quickly. Layovers frequently did not provide adequate rest.

Mental unrest was another label McFarland applied to a set of factors. Some of the schedule problems and their causes produce mental unrest as well as direct fatigue. Uncertainties from severe weather, eroded confidence from mechanical problems, difficulties from terrain and night flying, skill requirements of instrument flying, and boredom all contribute to that mental unrest. Additional sources of anxiety remain in mind from outside of flying. Family discords are often caused by flying schedules. Pilot versus management problems also weigh on pilots.

Even less demanding of physical action are tasks of **vigilance**. In these situations, one has only to wait for a very infrequent event to happen and make a brief response to it. From studies of military jobs, psychologists have noted some evidence of very rapid decline of task-specific performance. After a short time, observers miss a very large proportion of the events. The worker's best performance is in the first few minutes of the task. Poor vigilance appears faster and with greater error when the signals are more infrequent or the conditions of observing are physically or mentally uncomfortable (Mackworth, 1970).

Apparent fatigue in vigilance is reduced by rest and frequent distractions. In these jobs, it has also been useful to alter the situation by introducing more targets to be detected. There is an optimal frequency of successful detection that appears to reduce the inactivity and boredom that perhaps underlies errors of fatigue.

Work Conditions That Cause Fatigue

States that we call fatigue can be caused by work conditions. The nature of the task may appear to be too demanding on our mental resources, or the task may require different mental resources than we are willing to give. The work may not have satisfying end points or goals. Rewards for doing a task may not be adequate. Whether accurately based on reality or not, our ideas of work conditions will form the basis for claiming fatigue. Following are some facts about fatiguing conditions.

Judgments of fatigue are affected by pacing. Repetitive work is often thought to be tiring. Assembly line work is one example of a paced task that is fatiguing for many. The production speed may not be great, but it is unrelenting. In these conditions, freedom to work at one's own pace or at a variable speed

of one's own choosing is limited. Feeding material to a machine or receiving products from one can be very demanding. Scheduled inspection work was found to suffer in quality after 30 minutes at an unrelenting, moderate pace. However, that performance decrement did not appear if the workers expected and received a 5-minute break after the first 30 minutes (Colquhoun, 1959). Fatigue from paced activities is not always objectionable; sports and dancing are paced activities that we enjoy. The key to fatigue is likely to be in the context we use for interpretation.

If given the opportunity, workers will take breaks at times and of such lengths that reduce their fatigue and keep their performance at effective levels. Self-chosen work breaks yield higher production than standardized breaks. This is most effective on repetitive, monotonous work; work requiring significant muscle energy; and tasks requiring a constant posture, such as standing at a machine or sitting at a computer or typing keyboard (Chambers, 1961).

We expect to have points of completion in work. Goals are approached and reached. Without meaningful end points, the routine of doing things loses some of its attraction. Knowing that there will be adequate rest will change the fatigue component. Volunteers asked to make regular pulls on a machine measuring their strength pulled stronger from the first try when they knew they were to get a longer rest (100 seconds as opposed to 25 seconds). If a task presents challenges that are frustrated or goals that are delayed too far in the future, there is mental discomfort. We label part of that discomfort fatigue (Caldwell & Lyddan, 1971).

The rewards we expect for doing a task shape our ideas of fatigue. People who volunteered to see how long they could hang from a bar with their hand muscles were able to hang on almost twice as long if they were offered a sizable sum of money ($5 in 1953). Personal reward can be a major part of staving off fatigue and ensuring willingness to continue work. Rewards and tasks must be considered together in determining best performance. The key is the perception that the worker holds of them (Schwab, 1953).

Fatigue Consequences

Fatigue worsens aspects of judgment. This psychological effect of fatigue may be somewhat more difficult to detect, but not impossible. For example, fatigued drivers are more likely to take chances in passing other vehicles (Brown, Tickner, & Simmons, 1970). More investigation is needed on this and related fatigue effects on complex mental functioning.

Some fatigue can only be seen when we look at overall performance. Single pieces of action may be performed adequately when viewed out of context, but when compared against the whole, we see them as imprecise, at the wrong time, or to the wrong events. Not only do many fatigue effects appear only in the integrated performance, tests that periodically look at another, different action to examine fatigue fail to show effects. Among the more interesting and surprising results of study of fatigue conditions is the difficulty of finding evidence that doing a certain thing makes one fatigued on other things as well. The label **transfer of fatigue** is analogous to **transfer of training** as studied in motor skills learning. It makes some sense to suppose that being fatigued on one job will make one perform more poorly on others as well. However, evidence for this is hard to find.

Periods of violent exercise had no real effects on tracking skills or linguistic skills (Hammerton, 1971; Hammerton & Tickner, 1968). In extreme conditions of studies in the Spitfire tradition, when pilots were so tired that they had to be helped out of the machine to another test apparatus, they still performed adequately on that new test. Continuous work for more than 2 days in an aircraft simulator had no effect on skills on a separate tracking task, although some volunteers had to be physically helped to get to the tracking test station (Chiles, 1955). Fatigue accumulates to the actions under way and does not always

transfer to others. In prolonged work settings, muscle-based fatigue appears to be specific to that work. Those few instances where some transfer of fatigue was demonstrated involved a new task essentially identical to that on which the volunteer had been fatigued.

Two sorts of explanations have been given for the failure of transfer of fatigue (Holding, 1983). One is described by the notion that a change is as good as a rest. Industrial work studies have found that regular job switches yield higher levels of performance than sticking to one task (Chambers, 1961). A second idea is that of compensation by changing or revising the task to minimize those parts most subject to fatigue. Indirect evidence for that was found in studying long-term pilot skills.

Managing Fatigue

A list of ways to control fatigue comes directly from principles we discussed. The body sources of fatigue sensations may be controlled by the rate of work. Rest periods can be placed so that muscles have sufficient time to recover. From the early studies of heavy industrial work, which came to be known as Scientific Management (discussed below), managers established exact patterns to be followed in specific skills. Both timing of work and rest, as well as elimination of extra movements, were important in increasing productivity of bricklayers, stevedores, and selected others while actually decreasing their fatigue during the job and at the end of the day. Rest periods and length of work sessions are important, and rest periods from work are best when controlled by the worker.

Body sources of fatigue can be managed indirectly by maintaining optimum physiological conditions. Oxygen and food resources must be adequate. Temperature and humidity may be controlled to give optimum comfort levels. The feelings from muscle exertion may also be attacked by drugs. Discomfort may be removed by analgesics or the topical application of heat or cooling.

Among the psychological conditions of fatigue, prolonged work must be broken by periods of freedom from the demands and cognitions of the task. The rest must change one's mental set away from the work and its related worries. Tasks may be redefined into more manageable subgoals, increasing the number and frequency of ideas of completion. The worker will be assured by frequent knowledge of attainment of goals and reward. In total, there is a great deal that could be done to minimize fatigue. It demands a careful design of the activity in relation to the events of life and the environment.

But do we want to eliminate all fatigue? What will it mean to be rested, if we do not have regular experience of being tired? As we will discuss in the last chapter, perhaps a life of nothing to do, or a life of just doing easy work, is not healthy, physically or psychologically. Fatigue provides some of the meaning underlying positive and negative affect change. It is one of the regular changes that form life. In addition, there are many pleasant aspects of being tired that reflect other values and goals in life. In these several senses, fatigue may be a psychological necessity as well as a bodily warning system.

SECTION SUMMARY: CONDITIONS OF WORK

Herzberg divided workers' reported satisfactions and dissatisfactions into collections he called hygiene and motivator factors. Hygiene factors can only be satisfied or fail to be satisfied; they don't motivate actual work. Motivators, such as Maslow's growth and self-actualization needs, are what make us interested in our work. That interest can be improved by attention to job enhancement: enlarging the variety of tasks or enriching the challenges of the work.

Intrinsic motivation of work is thought to be of a fragile sort but, once established, develops strength based on our need for self-determined competence. Argument continues over whether extrinsic rewards destroy intrinsic motivation for tasks. We do seem to change our perceived value for tasks to balance the intrinsic and extrinsic rewards.

Some personal motivation comes from social comparisons we make based on perceived equity. We consider our ratio of outcomes to inputs with those of others. Perceived inequity motivates us to change, but

we usually protect our self-picture and efforts while maximizing positive outcomes and are absent from work if it is necessary to escape the comparison.

Fatigue is a warning conceptualized as muscular exhaustion. Work decrements with time are termed objective fatigue. Real physical sources of fatigue are based on energy losses when muscles work faster than they can be replenished. Discomfort associated with fatigue comes from heat, moisture, increased breathing rate, and muscle soreness.

Fatigue is more commonly based in psychological events in most work situations. Tasks requiring sustained attention, vigilance, or repetition are quickly fatiguing. Contributors to that fatigue are forms of mental unrest from extraneous life situations, unrelenting requirements of timing, and absence of clear end points. Fatigue can be controlled by periodic rewards, worker-chosen break times, change in tasks, and change in manner of doing tasks.

◈

WORK ORGANIZATION SYSTEMS

Work motivation is more than our needs and values, more than the working conditions, and even more than the nature of the work itself. These elements must be brought together. Sustained motivation is a product of working in a system where we have a place if not part ownership. We focus now on some ideas of motivating systems. We examine the organization of the elements of the work environment, often in a system of activity in which the workers participate. In each case, the work system in itself is thought to motivate our work actions. We begin with an early system that became notorious, not because it didn't work, but because of labor politics and misapplications.

Frederick W. Taylor entered the ranks of industry in the late 1800s as a machinist's apprentice and eventually acquired knowledge and skills in engineering, having many important patents to his credit. His early experience as a worker, supervisor, and eventually as plant manager led him to the concept of totally redesigning the work situation to achieve both a higher work output and a higher wage. Taylor (1911) assumed at the outset that

> the majority of [employees] believe that the fundamental interests of employees and employers are necessarily antagonistic. Scientific management, on the contrary, has for its very foundation the firm conviction that the true interests of the two are one and the same; that prosperity for the employer cannot exist through a long term of years unless it is accompanied by prosperity for the employee, and vice versa; and that it is possible to give the workman what he wants—high wages—and the employer what he wants—a low labor cost—for his manufactures. (p. 10)

Taylor's system, called Scientific Management, was based on four principles:

1. Scientifically designing the methods of work for efficiency

2. Selecting the best workers and training them in the new methods

3. Fostering a cooperative spirit between managers and workers so that they work together and recognize each other's value

4. Sharing the responsibility of the design and work process between management and worker (a change from the practice of leaving the work to the devices of the workers with no instruction and little interference from management)

These principles gave important early successes in increased production. The pieces of scientific management—work design, selection and training, worker relations, and management participation—persist in modern systems.

Many elements of what Taylor established are now commonplace. What was overlooked was the importance of these elements staying together as a system. Since Taylor's time, many different systems have appeared, and they share the elements of making workers know and be a part of the work goals. The titles in the sections below are good descriptors of the focus of each one.

Management Participation

Stronger motivation may be produced in workers who have personally participated in the work decisions. This is both an empirical finding and a conclusion of a number of philosophical positions. Humanists, socialists, and pragmatists alike see an advantage to allowing workers a say in what they do. Humanists see that as a basic human right. Socialists believe it partially frees workers from dominance by employers. Pragmatists accept the idea that people will work harder to realize their own decisions. Worker participation in decisions has a long, if spotty, past, and these early applications varied in effect on worker motivation. These ideas we will address first. Then, we will discuss a recent development in participation, Quality Circles, and its varieties.

Given the principle of participation, there is a wide range of possible applications. Participation in making work decisions can vary in content and degree. The content of decisions can involve aspects of doing the actual work, the physical conditions in which the work is accomplished, and personnel and training policies. The degree of participation can range from mere attendance at some decision-making meetings to complete participation and voting rights in all aspects of the work.

The functions and values of participation in decision making are both informational and social. Participating workers better know and understand what is being done. They identify with the decision and thus may work harder to justify their agreement with it. They are more aware of precisely what needs to be done and the rewards that will come from meeting the goals. Other benefits of the process are more general. Better use is made of the knowledge and abilities of the workers. The cooperative social environment pressures each individual to reach the goals. Social relationships among workers and with managers are improved, and communication is improved.

There are also some liabilities of the process in some settings. Workers may want to be involved in decision-making processes to an extended degree and take significant time away from actually working. Some workers view the process as a sign of the managers' weakness or inability. Instead of increased involvement, there may be a diffusion of responsibility and lessened motivation. Workers with little ability may dilute the quality of the decisions (Yukl, 1981).

General conclusions about the effectiveness of participative management in these early studies are rather weak and reflect the complexity of the situations. There are many variables of the kind of decisions, the people involved, and the work structure in which it is placed. Simple rules are not available. Research analysts suggest that participation does usually improve the attitudes of workers; yet, the effects on actual work performance are sometimes negative and sometimes positive, but most often unchanged (Locke & Schweiger, 1979).

Schemes of worker participation became fashion as **Quality Circles**. The typical Quality Circle gathers volunteers from different work groups to form a structure without management hierarchy. Most applications of Quality Circles have immediate positive benefits, but there is a trend toward losing those advances after the "honeymoon" period is over. The positive changes are like those of older participative management applications: employee involvement, development of worker skills in solving problems and working with others, and production of good ideas for increasing efficiency. These changes lead toward real participation in and ownership of the work. All of this is assumed to be positively motivating.

Separated from regular management, Quality Circle members are free to provide suggestions for change. They have no real authority except permission to think and discuss together. Their only power tool is persuasion. Such groups usually provide some good ideas that are implemented, and similar groups are begun in other areas of the larger work institutions. Soon, the work institution's management comes to fashionably value the number of Quality Circles, perhaps more than their contributions.

As the Quality Circle becomes commonplace, backlash appears. After the first blush of excitement, the easy ideas for improvement are exhausted. Some groups become unproductive, although they are using company resources and time. Implemented ideas don't pan out. In the original work groups, the Quality Circle volunteers are seen as getting special treatment. Work group managers, being left out of the decisions, resist the system and its changes (Lawler & Mohrman, 1987).

For some work institutions, the system is ended, but some others develop a work team approach that preserves the values of basic participation, Quality Circles, and job enrichment. The idea in a work team is to make all members of the work group part of the decision making, with responsibility for that work; Quality Circles are a parallel advisory team. Each work team is structured to be responsible for a whole product or service, and members of the team make all the decisions about how it is done. Typically team members share or rotate different aspects of the work so that cross-training and opportunities for growth are built in. More advanced work teams are given information about their place and function in the entire work institution and are allowed to participate in its higher levels of operations, design, and strategy. Systems of evaluation and rewards reflect the successes of the work group and of the work institution. **Gainsharing** is a label for allocating to workers a part of the profits from improvements or performance above expected costs.

The varieties of these systems follow the diversity of forms of work and the history of work in an institution. As with simple forms of participation in decisions, some activities work and some don't.

Outcome Expectancies

VIE theory is a form of the time-honored expectancy theory of psychology. Expectancy theories hold performance to be a product of our mental anticipation and our values. It was first presented to work motivation by Victor Vroom (1964) and has been modified by many others since then (e.g., Lawler, 1973). The theory assumes that we think about what we are doing, what we are getting, and the worth of it to us. From different points of view, it can be a rational, economic, or cognitive theory of work acts. The three elements are valence, instrumentality, and expectancy, forming the VIE acronym for the theory.

Valence or attractiveness is a measure of the value of the product or outcome of work. Pay, promotion, and recognition are among the common outcomes. The value of these contribute to our motivation to begin and continue working. A youngster may hold a high valence for the pay to be received and subsequently used for a trip to the amusement park. These valued outcomes provide a part of the cognitive structure motivating the work of cleaning the garage and spading the garden.

Instrumentality is our view of the relationship between two outcomes in the work situation: our work itself and another outcome, such as the expected reward. It is a performance–outcome expectation. In a simple contractual agreement, the relationship is direct and high. The youngster will get a specific amount of money for doing the work. The work is the performance, and the money is the outcome. Other situations have weaker perceived instrumentality. A writer is not at all sure that the time spent in producing a magazine article will lead to its being accepted by the editor. An insurance agent does not know if greater service in satisfying customers will produce greater monetary commissions. Students are not always convinced that knowing the material in greater depth will yield a higher grade for the course.

Expectancy is our assessment of whether effort will produce increased performance. This is an effort–performance expectation. Will putting out greater motivation lead to a higher level of productivity? In feeding materials to an automatic machine, a worker can easily see that increased effort beyond a certain adequate level will yield no greater performance. A gardener does see an immediate relationship between the amount of effort in trimming, watering, and feeding shrubs and the beauty they display.

Motivation to work is determined by combining these three components. The accepted form of combining is simple multiplication: $V \times I \times E$. Each worker thus considers three cognitions and combines them to guide acts. Each work situation usually has more than one set of instrumentalities and associated valences, however, so the actual motivation will be the E times the sum of the V and I products of each set.

These examples put together the theory components. A self-employed carpenter has accepted the belief that greater effort will produce a house more rapidly (E), that the more rapidly the house is built, the higher will be the

```
┌──────────────────────────────────────────────────────────────┐
│   EFFORT↘                                                      │
│      EXPECTANCY↘                                               │
│          PERFORMANCE↘                                          │
│              INSTRUMENTALITY↘                                  │
│                  OUTCOME↘                                      │
│                      VALENCE↘                                  │
│                          SATISFACTION                         │
└──────────────────────────────────────────────────────────────┘
```

Figure 12.7. The chain of likely thinking about work pictured by the VIE theory.

net profit (I), and that the financial rewards from that increased profit are valued because they provide life comforts (V). Students generally believe that effort in learning produces higher course grades (E), that higher grades give better employment possibilities (I), and that a better job will give a more satisfying lifestyle (V). (See Figure 12.7.)

Managers have proposed using the VIE ideas in these rules to motivate increases in work. First, identify what the workers want and value as outcomes. Second, determine what is good performance that is attainable. Third, link the workers' valued outcomes to the attainable performance. Fourth, be alert for conflicting expectancies and be mindful of equity among workers.

General criticism of VIE theory rests on its assumption that workers make rational decisions based on evaluations of expectations. The complexity of many simultaneous decision elements strains human ability even in the clearest of situations. In the rush of changing life events and under the influence of many pressures, workers will resort to a simpler view. As such, the theory presents more of an idea of a mechanism underlying work motivation than a practical description of how work is motivated.

Accepting Goals

Accepting a harder goal leads to higher job performance. That simple relationship was established in studies and forms the basis for goal-setting theories of work motivation. A specific, hard goal will lead to more work than easy goals or rules like "do your best."

Of course, the worker must be capable of doing the work set by the goal, but it is not necessary that the worker be the one to set the goal or even take part in establishing the goal. The critical factor is that the goal be accepted. Edwin Locke and his colleagues (e.g., Latham & Locke, 1979; Locke & Latham, 1994), who established and developed many of the principles of goal setting, believe that the most direct source of a worker's motivation is the acceptance by that worker of specific performance goals and intentions.

In an illustration of goal setting (Latham & Yukl, 1975), two groups of drivers were given instructions about loading logs to be delivered to a lumber mill. One group's drivers were told to do their best. The others were told to load as close to 94% of the legal limit as they could manage. The latter group loaded close to that goal, higher than the 60% or so under the "do your best" instructions. The goal was clearly the guide, directing the drivers' attention to feedback of their success and leading them to compete over who was doing it better.

A popular goal-setting system devised by Peter Drucker in the 1950s was management by objectives or MBO (Carroll & Tosi, 1973). As the title implies, the goals are those of managerial-level tasks. Typically, each department manager's goals are derived from long-term company goals. Managers then develop their plan of action to meet their goals. The goal-setting system's success or failure hinges on personal acceptance of their assigned goals by lower managers and the workers. Where managers are committed and enthusiastic, MBO has been productive.

Figure 12.8. The high performance cycle.

SOURCE: Locke & Latham (1990a, p. 244). Reprinted with permission of Cambridge University Press.

In determining work motivation, Locke and his colleagues noted three ways that the goals may function. First, the goals indicate how much effort the worker must provide. The statement of the amount of work to be done establishes just how much the worker needs to put into tasks. It suggests the speed and the quality that is required. Goals do more for the worker than just affect motivation.

A second function of goals is guidance. Goals guide and direct the worker in performing the correct work activities. They tell the worker what must be done, and they set a standard of performance for those acts. The stated goals may form the structure of the work itself, serving to give it legitimacy and a place in the work organization. Specifications of goals set out clearly what must be done and, along with regular feedback, provide a running check of progress. By stating what must be done, the goals cue the worker as to whether the current acts are appropriate and what might be done next. The goals give choice and structure to the many possible acts on the job.

Third, job goals establish the persistence workers use in working. When there is no time pressure, the goals keep the worker from quitting early when problems are encountered. Delayed success is accommodated. The worker perseveres until the goal is met.

Motivation-Performance-Satisfaction Cycle

Edwin Locke and Gary Latham (1990a, 1990b) recently proposed a model of high performance that presents a cycle of several factors leading through motivation to work and satisfaction. Although there is some variation in their presentations, basically, they propose two sets of factors producing work performance (Locke & Latham, 1990b). First, mediators of that performance include effort, persistence, direction, and task strategies. These mediating mechanisms are in turn influenced by levels of expectancy (of success) and of self-efficacy (confidence) and by specific high goals. Second, moderators of performance include ability, goal commitment (acceptance or work goals), feedback (about performance), task complexity, and situational constraints (needs, motives, values). Performance leads to rewards that are contingent on that performance (pay raises, promotion, recognition) and those that are not contingent (base pay, benefits, job security). These rewards produce satisfaction. Satisfaction yields commitment to the organization and its goals, which feeds back in the cycle to the specific high goals and commitment to them.

Locke and Latham propose that satisfaction is the result and not the cause of high performance and that it feeds back into the cycle only indirectly. Satisfaction maintains commitment. Commitment is slow to change and joins with the other factors moderating and mediating high performance. Management for high performance rests on this collection of factors. Key to management is expecting high performance in workers who have been trained to accept what they must do and to know that they are competent. Consequent rewards feed satisfactions that build commitment to the work, and the cycle is rejoined.

Reward Systems

The concept of reward is a familiar one in psychology. We will do what has in the past been rewarded. Using rewards to change acts goes back a long way in human history, but the refined idea became a high fashion tool of reinforcement learning theories in the 1930s and 1940s. Rewards strengthen actions, the primary principle of B. F. Skinner's operant conditioning. His underlying assumption is that behavior is a function of its consequences. According to other theorists, reinforcements strengthen habits in small steps or protect learning bonds between stimuli and responses.

A unit of learning was thought by the behaviorists to be a building block that forms performance. Volumes of experimental work with animals built a lore of procedures. Applying those ideas is labeled **behavior modification.** The sophisticated techniques and the details of the reinforcement strategy are based on three elements: definition of the rewarded act, specification of the reward, and connecting the two in an effective relationship. None of these elements is trivial or without difficulties in application to human work life.

Behavior modification requires that defined units or standards of performance be identified by the manager. Widgets produced in the shop, customers approached in the store, and packages delivered to homes are all easily defined. They can be noted and counted. The best units are those that appear frequently, so that the opportunities for rewards are many. They are direct indicators of job performance. Some work, however, does not easily break into such pieces. There are tough challenges in finding units or standards of work of a college teacher, a police officer, or an airline pilot. Acts like smiling, coming to work on time, or wearing the proper clothing may be easily defined and controlled, but these are not primary aspects of the jobs.

In reinforcement theories, rewards are defined by their effects. This may be logically circular as an ultimate theory of learning, but it is not a concern in use. The practical problem is to know what works in a job setting. Some rewards are easy to find. Pay, praise, encouragement, and tokens redeemable for valued things are the most typically used in work settings.

The contingency between specific work acts and rewards is of the utmost importance. According to behavior modification principles, each action to be strengthened must be surely and quickly followed by reinforcement. The technology of operant conditioning is applied. Schedules of reinforcement have specific effects on rate and permanence of sustained performances. Performance may be made to reach goals by a process called **shaping.** Work is shaped toward the goal by first rewarding changes in the required direction and gradually increasing the standard as the goals are approached.

Criticism of simple reward systems in the workplace is at once obvious and complicated. No one argues that rewards are not effective. They do change what we do. The issue is what they change and whether optimal work and satisfactory living are the results. The case against rewards (in work or any life activity) lists many negatives. Rewards

are time- and place-limited

devalue work

implicitly punish

break relationships

avoid reasons for performances

limit looking for improvements

undermine interest

Rewards also demand performance evaluations that focus on past rather than future work, on counting successes and failures rather than seeking help from managers. Each of these criticisms is focused on the relatively uncomplicated system of rewarding people (with money, awards, recognition, etc.) for work that they have done, whether that work was specified beforehand or not. We will examine each of these arguments somewhat.

Rewards are effective as long as they last, but when they stop coming there may be no lasting change. Workers given a unit of money beyond their base salary for doing certain things will focus on just those activities. When that special incentive is removed, performance is likely to revert to what it was. There is little if any new motivation from the rewards for doing those things. All of the incentive is invested in the pay, not in the specific work.

Rewards are effective in making people comply, but in that compliance, we are also being taught that what we must do is not something we want to do. We must do this to get that. *This* must not be as good as *that* or rewarding that would not be necessary. The reward is informative, teaching subtly that the work wouldn't otherwise be done.

Rewards show the power rule of who is in control and from where the worker's motivation comes. Rewards are always exercises of power. A reward system is no different than a threatened punishment. In both cases, bad things will happen to the worker unless the specified work is done. Whether it is a threat of harm or a failure to get what is wanted is an unimportant difference.

In work settings normally having advantages to cooperation, or in settings where each individual does much the same thing, rewards given to individuals for their work minimize mutual helping. Why should a worker collaborate with another when that person's success may diminish his or her own reward? Assuming the rewards are limited, one person succeeding must mean others will not do as well. Awards and rewards to the best or top few always mean most others are not rewarded. Workers who recognize that they are not able to reach those performance levels are not likely to help those who do; no one is likely to be motivated in specific work for such occasional and uncertain recognition.

Reward systems for a schedule of performances is an easy and lazy managerial solution, but it is not likely to gain the greatest overall worker performance. By ignoring workers' needs for aid, training, job redesign, temporary support, and even kindly encouragement, the manager avoids the hard work of improving performance. Performance gains from simple reward systems are often effective in the short run and reflect easy changes from imposing power, but all of the structural elements of work problems are left to the worker, who in turn will focus on doing only what gets rewards.

Workers will do exactly what they must do to get the rewards, and no more. Few work settings cannot be improved or are so unchanging that there are no other possibilities. (If they are that boringly stagnant, the need for that job should be rethought.) Any such exploration of new ideas or taking of risks to get better production will be ignored because that is not rewarded. Workers become experts at the "game" set up by management. They "play" the work to get the best score. It is against their interests to do the work in any way other than the one specified.

Implicit and fundamental to most specific criticism of simple reward-for-work systems are that such plans destroy or minimize the natural interest each worker has in the work. The work is less important than the extrinsic reward. Motivational focus is on the reward.

The essence of this fact is also part of our common (non)sense about what we want in our work. Each of us values interesting work more strongly than pay and other rewards, both when we are speculating about what we want and when we are contemplating the work we have. Yet, we will also believe that other people select their jobs for the pay and rewards (Jurgensen, 1978; Kovach, 1987). Applying the nature of human projection as a general rule in a work setting, managers will view workers as most wanting rewards, whereas workers are more naturally inclined to wanting interesting work. After managers apply reward systems, the workers' natural interest goes dormant. Pay or rewards rarely cause people to change their work style (Csikszentmihalhyi, 1990; Gruenberg, 1980). Instead they look for better kinds of work, better working conditions, or better management conditions.

The broader view of reward systems is that they can be made to work and satisfy workers. Instead of simplified pay for performance schemes, broader reward systems put together a system in which intrinsic motivation, social factors, job support, and even pay have parts. Two sets of these ideas will conclude the chapter.

Alfie Kohn (1993), one of most radical critics of rewards systems, outlined his ideas in *Punished by Rewards.* He begins with the pay issue by stating, "Abolish incentives!" He says, "Pay people generously and equitably. Do your best to make sure they don't feel exploited. Then *do everything in your power to help them put money out of their minds*" (p. 182, italics in original).

His second step is changing evaluations to be continuous sessions for helping workers do better work. The managers interact with workers to solve problems and identify work directions. Evaluations are not about measuring performance or determining pay.

Kohn's third step presents a way of building authentic worker motivation by way of managers who watch, listen, talk, and think. Management's role is to work with rather than apart from the workers. Some good management practices include his three Cs: collaboration, content, and choice. Where managers encourage collaborative work,

workers build on each other's strengths and add a contagion of excitement to the work. Following Herzberg, Kohn believes motivated workers need good work to do. Work content must be meaningful, challenging, and open to showing each worker's competence. Workers must have some personal choice in their work. Kohn notes that most work systems allow the least choice and decision making to those whose work is least interesting and valued. We manage the lowest paid job carefully while giving large latitude to those highest in the hierarchy.

Thomas Wilson presents less of a revolution than an intelligent broadening of reward system ideas with other work motivation concepts we have discussed. In his 1994 *Innovative Reward Systems for the Changing Workplace,* he arranges reinforcers into four categories: verbal-social, monetary, work-related, and tangible-symbolic. The first two seem clear. By work-related, Wilson means better work content, increased control and decision making, and promotions. In his tangible-symbolic category, he lists awards, special equipment and tools, and nonpay material gifts where the value is more emotional than monetary.

These rewards must be delivered in a system that meets five self-explanatory criteria labeled by the acronym SMART: Specific, Meaningful, Achievable, Reliable, and Timely. Although he avoids some of the liabilities of the simplest pay-for-performance schemes and adds recognition of some intrinsic motivation elements of doing work, Wilson does not see Kohn's comprehensive removal of rewards for work as a practical alternative in all workplaces.

SECTION SUMMARY:
WORK ORGANIZATION SYSTEMS

From the days of Scientific Management 100 years ago, workers have been placed in systems intended to improve their work.

Participation in management decisions can instruct workers in the requirements of their work and what they must do. It uses their talents to improve the work and builds productive workplace relationships. It may also subtract work time and dilute the quality of work decisions accepted. Quality Circles and work teams are special forms of participative management.

Workers implicitly judge their work situations in terms of how their effort produces performance (expectancy), whether those performance outcomes yield expected rewards (instrumentality), and how attractive those rewards are (valence). Workers are also motivated to reach specific hard goals. The goal instructs them on what they must do, how much effort they must supply to reach the goal, and how persistent they need to be.

Ongoing work flows in a cycle of motivation yielding performance yielding satisfaction yielding commitment to goals and around again. In this view, satisfaction results from continued effective performance; it is not the direct motivating cause of the work.

Rewards effectively dictate expected performance but are unlikely to build lasting motivation to work. Use of rewards can devalue the work itself in favor of the reward, reflect power relationships over effective managerial assistance, discourage creativity and cooperation, and perhaps destroy intrinsic interest in the job.

CHAPTER CONCLUSIONS

We work because we like to do those things, because it becomes a part of who we are, and only incidentally because it provides for our physical needs. Yet, our common discourse is that everyone else works primarily for their pay and only because they have to. Work managers typically assume workers have to be coerced, and they look at motivation psychology for tricks for their trade.

The reality is that motivation to work is right there in the workers all the time, needing only supportive conditions to bring it out. By giving us challenging, satisfying work in ways we understand, and by providing us the tools, authority, and work conditions to do it, motivated work will happen. Managerial actions should set goals and interact with us to guide us into greater productivity. Our worker satisfaction will come from seeing our effective performance, leading us to commitment and continued high effort in the work.

Study and Review Questions

1. What is our common cultural image of working?

2. What is Theory X and how do we respond to it?

3. Are there criteria that clearly identify a task as work?

4. What are the steps of Abraham Maslow's hierarchy of needs?

5. What are the rules of Abraham Maslow's hierarchy of needs?

6. What are Clayton Alderfer's ERG categories of work needs?

7. How did Henry Murray measure need to achieve?

8. How is measured need to achieve used to determine which tasks we will select?

9. Which three of Henry Murray's needs are used in career selection?

10. What is the function of Frederick Herzberg's hygiene factors?

11. What items make up Frederick Herzberg's motivator factors?

12. What makes up job enrichment?

13. Compare job enrichment and job enlargement.

14. What job dimensions make up meaningful work in the Job Characteristics Model?

15. What conditions in a situation are necessary for intrinsic motivation to build?

16. What are Robert White's definitions of competence and effectance?

17. What is overjustification, and how is it most likely to be resolved?

18. What goes into J. Stacey Adams's equity ratio?

19. What leads a worker to experience inequity?

20. In what ways are experienced inequities likely to be resolved in practice?

21. Compare physical and psychological sources of fatigue.

22. How is objective fatigue defined?

23. What is the role of adenosine triphosphate (ATP) in muscle action?

24. How long may a muscle work in the absence of oxygen?

25. What sensations result from prolonged, intensive physical work?

26. How much time passes in a boring vigilance task before signals are missed?

27. What makes a paced work task fatiguing?

28. What kind of breaks are best for monotonous work?

29. Do frequent end points increase or decrease fatigue?

30. How can low transfer of fatigue be used in management?

31. What are advantages and disadvantages of participative management?

32. Why are most Quality Circles judged successful at first?

33. What are the VIE theory components: instrumentalities, expectancies, and valences?

34. Describe the flow of events proposed in the VIE theory.

35. What characteristics of goals motivate best?

36. What three functions do accepted goals have in worker performance?

37. Is satisfaction a cause or a consequence of high performance?

38. Will performance be changed by reward?

39. Why do rewards fail to build sustained work motivation?

40. Without rewards, how can work be managed?

41. What are the elements of the reward-delivery system with the acronym SMART?

CHAPTER 13

Play and Leisure

Playing is part of our nature, but we commonly discount and trivialize it. We are designed to be curious, preferring modestly changed stimulation, following our accumulated life experiences. In play, we may become absorbed, captured in the flow of the activity.

Few theories attempt to view play beyond childhood, but fundamental ideas of play tie it to protective social rules and to what we believe we are doing. We play with others in countless varieties of language, games, and sports.

Study of leisure shows us how diverse and commonplace it is and how poorly we function without it. We end by examining touring as an elaborate example of motivation principles underlying one form of leisure.

Foundations of Play

Looking for Experience

Theories of Ritual, Play, and Leisure

Forms of Playing

Forms of Leisure

Should playing be taken seriously? Working is serious, but isn't play trivial, mere spare-time-filler typical of children? Even if it is common, is there anything motivational in it? Can we know anything different about ourselves by studying our playing and leisure?

Some have suggested that play is a frivolous subject. It seems paradoxical to speak of a scientific study of playing. The features of play reflect an unreality of sorts. Its very un-reality seems to remove play from the domain of rational science. Leisure studies are often ridiculed by other academics. That, however, is not a legitimate objection, partly because the study of play and leisure is being confused with the phenomena of play and leisure. It isn't the study that is unreal. A science of play no more requires play and frivolity than a study of schizophrenics requires unreal and disordered thinking.

The nature of the criticism of studying play is important because it illustrates the fundamental submission of play to work ideals and the resulting bias with which nonwork topics are evaluated. Play and leisure are typically identified in their cultural contexts, but it is worth speculating also about possible natural origins.

FOUNDATIONS OF PLAY

Why do adults play? A few writers have suggested a fitness advantage to childhood play through the developing and practicing of skills for life work, but that leaves the problem of adult play unsolved. Play and related derivations are part of all peoples' lives. Why should that be? Does any evolutionary mechanism lie behind it? A good beginning is to consider the ways play and leisure might be by-products of other aspects of the nature of our species. We can begin with the way we form and develop our brain functions to "process information" about the world.

Natural Bases

We develop very slowly. Compared with most other species, we spend more time in gestation, in childhood, in periods of reproductive fertility, and, somewhat unique among species, in a significant period of life after our reproductive years. Most relevant to understanding human play may be the implication of the extended period of development in childhood. Rough comparisons among species suggest that development time is related to brain programming. An obvious observation is that the developing childhood years are spent in acquiring the ways of adult functioning. This is not just a matter of storing experiences, of course. Details of physical brain development require and follow patterns of specific and general experiences.

Consider our place among the species. We are not all alike. Each species has a reproductive fitness history in which many survival factors were trade-offs. For some nonhuman species, it was and is great numbers of offspring with a small degree of brain function formed from experiences. At some point in the rapid development period for members of these species, the fully developed brain is no longer open to important change in function as a result of experience. It has matured, and the individual is an adult. Adult brains for most nonhuman species typically continue to allow for learning, behavior changes tied to specific environmental experiences, but we have assumed there is little possibility that later learning will influence the design of other brain functioning. We believe that the developmental program that shapes brain functions has shut down.

For other species, especially those like ours whose fitness depended on versatility, fewer young are protected as they develop appropriate brain functions from their experiences. A brain that is most versatile will require more experience and hence longer periods of development. During that longer development is the prospect of malleability, the potential for experiences to fine-tune the brain functions. The brain initially must be tuned to certain appropriate kinds of stimulation, sensitivities in tune with the species' environment and needs. Within that environment and respecting those needs, there must also be brain design that seeks out and digests experiences of considerable variety.

Capacity for play may be a leftover of that longer development program. If, in slow-maturing species, openness to certain varieties of stimulation is prolonged, could not parts of the usual brain design-fixing program remain operating, never completely reaching an end? If so, that continuing program could be part of the structural basis of curiosity, play, and leisure.

New situations are typically greeted with some part of the species' or individual's repertoire of acts. The appearance is one of playing with the new situation. Konrad Lorenz and others in the ethology tradition, those who comprehensively study behaviors of individual animal species, have listed specific sequences of acts that some species will attempt with something new they have encountered. Working with broader abstractions, some general functions are common among the simian or apelike species, including movements of all kinds, manipulation, repetitions of sequences, and putting things together in various ways, sometimes called **relational** play. For many species, that playful trying of its repertoire on new situations is much of what we value as its intelligence.

In our species, children's brain development makes use of symbols and ideas of make-believe along with rules. Across all cultures, children play in the same ways (manipulation, repetition, relational, make-believe, and rule-governed). These are also apt descriptions for adult play. Along with that of a few close simian relatives, our play remains a useful function of a brain that has not finished its design work, in the sense of remaining potentially able to change. Play, then, is both a leftover piece of brain development design and an important component of change in neverending brain development. For some species, it is the former; for us, it is both. Again, each situation reflects brain design based on the unique fitness history of the species.

As cognitive scientists sensitive to evolutionary mechanisms, we need to look at this more carefully, but that is the future. For now, how can we describe our playful functioning?

Social and Cognitive Concepts

We fill time with more than just productive work or just functions that directly relate to survival. That simple statement reflects our cultural bias. Playing is being compared to work. Our usual assumption is that playing is surplus activity. We believe that playing need not be done, perhaps even should not be done, at least until all work has been completed. But we do play, and we ask why. Social answers have been sought in the context of work. Theorists have searched for reasons and justifications that show how playing aids each person in necessary life functions.

The primary analogies and examples of play add another dimension to understanding common beliefs about play. Play is thought of as something that children do. Children are growing toward being adults. Thus, this line of thinking goes, play must have the function of preparing the child for adult roles. Adult play, it follows, is either acting childish, something remaining from childhood, or yet another learning experience for "real" adult life.

How do adults play? Games come quickly to mind; we play games. That being so, they are our most common model. Games have formal structure including rules, time factors, and end products or goals. Following that model, all play can be analyzed for its structure and end products. Play comes to be thought of as a formal organized entity, more like work. Games, too, are a culturally biased form of thought about play.

Some recent study of play, leisure, and the like has gone beyond those cultural models of nonwork, life preparation, and structured games. Play and leisure acts are constituted of various personal and social actions, and like all such actions, they are motivated. In the analysis we will make, ritual is added to the list for various historical and theoretical reasons. Play, ritual, games, and leisure share certain structure elements. They each can be seen as finite-length segments of human action, making up discrete, motivated periods of human life. Each occupies a place in a chain of ongoing social acts and has causes that must be discovered. The best account of them and their causes may lie not in what is done but in our view of why we do them.

Formal thinking about play and leisure brought out several themes (Barrett, 1989). Play and leisure (a) occupy "free time," (b) give us pleasure, (c) are done by choice, (d) are what we want to do, (e) are done for their own sake, and (f) are marked by rest and relief from work. Each of these ideas seems to describe play or leisure, yet with close inspection is ambiguous. Free time implies freedom from something else, and what is that other activity? Work comes to mind, but nonwork free time might also be taken up in necessary life chores and other activities we are obliged to do. Pleasure is often a part of it, but many forms of play and leisure may actually be painful and severely challenging; and aspects of work can be filled with pleasures. Likewise, choice and "what we want to do" are not restricted to play and leisure acts. Rest and relief from work better describes sleep and doing nothing than it does play and leisure.

That leaves "done for their own sake" as a descriptor that is the hardest to criticize. Play and leisure serve no apparent purposes or goals but their doing. If consequences are attached, the activity usually becomes a form of work. More than anything, these kinds of analyses point out the fuzzy boundaries and arbitrariness of dividing the different things we do with language labels. We will come back to some of these ideas below.

Life segments of work, play, ritual, leisure, and the like are identified by their boundaries. Each unit has some clues marking that it has begun, that it is continuing, and that it has ended. Social scientists speak of the segment being "framed." The means of communicating those boundaries vary from obvious to extremely subtle and complex. Knowing and using boundaries allow us to move into and out of different segments and identify the purposes of activities of others. We label and categorize what we are doing partly by those bounds.

Boundaries are an important part of defining some life segments. Touring boundaries are obvious. We begin by moving away from home territory. Our touring lasts as long as we stay away and ends on our return home. In other life segments, the cues are not obvious parts of the action but are still relatively easy to find by anyone trained in that piece of culture. A game of poker, for example, is marked by assuming playing positions at a playing table, handling cards, and talking a specific language. The continuation of the game is shown by these same signs, and its end is given by either moving away from the positions or by stopping the card handling and associated talk. In a different setting, a ritual of worship is marked both by being in a special place and by including a series of rigidly structured actions and talk that is relatively unresponsive to outside influences.

The exact bounds of a playful act are more difficult to state in some informal social settings. A man is seen to walk up behind another, tip his cap down over his eyes, and then quickly turn around to imply he didn't do it. We judge this a playful greeting between friends, but the markers are subtle cues that require a sophisticated experience with social interaction. In a similar vein, people agree that some acts of their pets and other animals are acts of play, but specifying exactly what was used to make those judgments is difficult.

Boundedness can be an important property of life segments, although the exact boundaries may be left unspecified. The causal role of the bounds also ranges from the obvious, as in touring and religious worship, to the very subtle, as in the cap tipping.

SECTION SUMMARY:
FOUNDATIONS OF PLAY

Human brains are not born with all of their adult capacities, having instead development programs that build mentality from experiences. We are forever curious and wanting to interact with the world in novel ways because those information-seeking programs do not reach a closure state.

Although we acknowledge that we are information seekers, our cultural habits put a serious face on play, making it something children do, something that is made of rule-bound games. Leisure seems best defined as what we do for its own sake. Play and leisure are seen to be separate from work as separate life segments with boundaries between. We turn next to the nature of experience within those boundaries.

LOOKING FOR EXPERIENCE

"All people naturally want to know" is Aristotle's opening line of his *Metaphysics,* in modern paraphrase. His statement is a good summary of our looking for experience or, simply, curiosity. There is no doubt that our species is consumed with knowing, and our fashionable language is enamored with ideas of information and its handling through cognition. We will begin by examining our overall patterns of seeking or avoiding information.

Curiosity

A common, perhaps banal part of human life is being curious: having a desire to know, an attraction to things and doings for their own sake. We begin by noting that curiosity is so fundamental to human ways that it becomes nearly invisible. Nearly all human acts, from the small routines that fill time to the major structures used to organize lives, reflect the property of curiosity.

Try to imagine a people devoid of any curiosity, people who pay no attention to newness and spend no time examining the materials and events around them. I get an image of a monotonous world populated by some form of zombie, or robotic machine. The view is of an automated factory composed entirely of robots doing their specialized tasks, unable and surely unwilling to consider any unprogrammed object or event. What sort of programming would those incurious objects require to have human curiosity? There must be regulating structures that direct the senses toward objects and events and classify them as new or old. This in itself is a major programmer's challenge. The mechanism must then direct available processing resources to events that are new or different. But how new and how different? What choices are to be made in a field of new and strange happenings? How strongly shall the machine be directed to pursue those new materials relative to other programmed functions? How can it decide whether to continue a line of exploration and when it shall be terminated? Using this mind experiment, it perhaps becomes clearer that curiosity is not merely another function added to a working robot. The capacity for curiosity must be a part of fundamental design structure, and we have that design.

Curiosity is, of course, only a word we use for a special feature of how we act. Like many of the word labels we have discussed, curiosity is not a thing or separate function we can take aside for study. At best, we use the term in thought about one aspect of our lives. But as such, curiosity aspects are common pervasive features.

Modalities

Curiosity is usually thought of as a total act; a kind of act we do. We can think of those acts as constituted by different actions, and those actions suggest different kinds of cognitive function. In this vein, we may find it useful to distinguish three modes of curiosity acts: sensory, manipulative, and cognitive.

The easiest evidence of curiosity comes from sensory acts. Sensory curiosity shows what a thing appears to be. Vision is unique in the ease by which we can observe what a person is attending. The direction of focus of the eyes tells a great deal about the information that a person is seeking and receiving. Under many circumstances, curiosity is revealed by the eyes. We can note what is being examined and for how long. Less public but no less obvious to oneself are the other channels of sensory curiosity. We hear something that attracts attention, and we stay tuned to that novel sound. We smell an unexpected odor, touch an unusual surface, or taste a novel food. Uncounted and often unnoticed experiences of common curiosity are primarily sensory.

We focus each sensory event for as long as it remains interesting. When the novelty wears off or disappears, we attend something else. The effect is primarily a sensory one. We are attracted to the event by its sensory cues and continue in contact with it as long as that attraction remains. Other factors may also be brought in, but in their simplest form, these can be simply sensory experiences of curiosity.

Manipulation modes of curiosity reveal what a thing is and how it works. The functional key to manipulation is moving or changing an object or event. The prototype manipulation is that of physical contact with the hands. We grasp an object, perhaps remove it from its context, move its parts, disassemble it, and maybe even destroy it in the process. Each aspect of manipulation permits us to know the object in a different way. We want to experience the operation of a driving machine, becoming familiar with the way it responds to controls and the ways it feeds back information of its movements.

Experience with manipulation allows many actions to be carried through without actually touching an object. We can observe the construction of a machine and gain the same kind of information that we would receive by direct contact. For example, we can see what moves by noting the location of levers, pivots, gears, and springs of a mechanical timepiece. The manipulative mode of curiosity uses sensory channels; however, the curiosity is not about its appearance but about its function, broadly considered. Sensory information is the vehicle for curiosity but not its purpose.

If sensory curiosity looks for what a thing appears to be, and manipulative curiosity finds what it is and how it works, **cognitive** curiosity tries to find what it is for. These are mental acts, cognitive functions of which

we are only partly aware. Others cannot directly know them at all. We make mental analyses and syntheses of objects and events. Our unnoticed goal is to categorize and understand. What is this thing, and what is it doing? What has happened and why?

Cognitive curiosity builds on the sensory and manipulation mechanisms, but the intent goes beyond those stages from the beginning. The object may be quite familiar but in the wrong place: Why is that onion hanging by a string from the ceiling? The people and the place may be known but what is happening is not understood: Why is she staring at that bird? The sensory information is commonplace, but the contextual meaning is unusual. That irregularity draws our curiosity. We want to know.

Composition

The complexity of curiosity acts and their place in human life makes it difficult for psychologists to avoid oversimplifying them. The normal-science tendency is to focus on identifiable pieces of action for close study. That leads to descriptions and perhaps theories implying a single primary cause. The piecemeal approach is often necessary in a practical sense, but it is also necessary that the field of view be widened after a time to try to fit different pieces together. Study of curiosity has been a difficult problem in the contexts of the several general psychology theories of past decades, and the result has been about 40 years of unconnected ideas. In this section, we try a framework to patch together the different kinds of curiosity research.

Curiosity is an expression of being human, being enculturated, and being a unique person. These three factors name elements of the relatively permanent basis for curiosity acts. First, being human means being curious. Human biology sets the nature and the limits. Receiving information, learning, and acting intelligently are the ways of human life. We can minimize or exaggerate these natural inclinations, but we cannot be free from them.

At a fundamental level, all people display curiosity.

Second, we develop in ways set by our culture. **Enculturation** is not a single process but a pattern of overlapping social environments. We are individuals in the general culture of the world and recipients of the traditions of Western civilization. Many of us are also citizens of the United States and students receiving higher education. Finer analysis may locate our specific towns, ethnic backgrounds, religions, and styles of family life. Collectively and separately, these different aspects of culture establish relatively permanent tendencies toward being curious or not curious. The cultural learning has formed ideas of places, times, and objects that are appropriate for curiosity acts.

Third, we have each accumulated a unique personal history. The cultural backgrounds have provided the opportunities, and within those possibilities, each of us has learned specific variations. That personal history adds a great measure of complexity to the systemic tendencies to be curious.

Boredom, Optimum, and Overload

Modestly novel stimuli attract curiosity. That is the primary statement of curiosity and also presents the most intriguing challenges for understanding. The new, the changed, and the surprising are the features toward which people direct their attention. Why this should be so and what makes a stimulus attractively novel are the key problems.

Many psychological theories of the past viewed the problem as why people are curious at all. But that is not the puzzle. Rather, it is a matter of fitting curiosity acts into a theoretical picture including other human acts. The question has been how to reconcile curiosity with other assumptions we make about what people do. Several dimensions of novelty have been studied in laboratories, and a great amount of professional knowledge has been acquired in applications such as advertising. We know many principles and details about what attracts our notice. Yet, the psychologist's question remains "Why these things rather than others?"

Studying the facts of curiosity presents some unusual problems. Part of the essence of curiosity is a certain spontaneity and lack of personal goals in the events. Context is an especially important part of the curiosity act. The process of imposing experimental controls is likely to alter that context. We must be wary. As a bit of curiosity is brought into the laboratory, have its causes been altered? Do we look at pictures for the same reasons when they are given in pairs in an empty room as when we walk through a gallery or glance at scenes in life? Has the experimental context changed the rules regulating the act? For example, are our feelings and emotions the same when we sit in a room being observed as when we are in an open, unwatched context? There is reason to be cautious in concluding which factors are important in causing curiosity.

A second problem ties into the first. We bring a personal context to an instance of curiosity. William James called it one's interest. His term summarized the unique complexity that each person holds. Curiosity operates from that personal context. The very nature of curiosity is its personal uniqueness. If a standardized laboratory protocol is used and measures of curiosity are collected from a number of volunteers, the summary may be useful but still pose a problem. The method reveals similar patterns of curiosity acts, but that does not mean that individuals have the same factors regulating their choices. Nevertheless, generalities from averaged experimental studies have value. A first, somewhat crude approximation emerges in experiments that reduce the complexity of social and personal contexts.

At any moment, we have experienced a certain level of past stimulation and have been exposed to specific stimuli. These recent events establish our readiness to seek or receive experiences. We will describe several forms of stimulation history that affect curiosity. Deprived sensory environments establish one extreme, and information overloads are at the other. Within these limits, each of us lives a life of events of varying stimulation. The pattern of curiosity appears to be one of moderating extremes, both in the hills and valleys of life events and in the limited shifts of daily events.

Curiosity toward specific stimuli comes from experiences with narrow ranges of stimulation. I tire of television and pick up a book. Having seen no familiar faces for a time, we seek old friends. Given a choice, we will look at one of a pair of pictures that has changed rather than at one that has not. Recent experiences make some alternatives more attractive than others.

The fundamental facts of curiosity can be assembled in a few statements. First, it is our nature to seek information. The natural response is one of seeking, not of remaining unmoved. Second, we are likely to choose information that is fairly close to, but different from, that which has made up our cumulative life experience to date. Brief experiences of greatly changed levels of information are avoided. Stimulus deprivation provokes strong desire for information, and stimulus overload leads us to seek out more simple environments. Third, with continued exposure to information growth or reduction, our level of stimulus preference follows in that direction.

Preferred Stimulation

Daniel Berlyne at the University of Toronto demonstrated that people prefer to look at novel stimuli. He showed this by presenting a choice of visual material that was new, more complex, surprising, irregular, heterogeneous in elements, or incongruous (Berlyne, 1958). Of course, the ideas were not new. We remember that novelty was mentioned by William James in his instinct theory of curiosity.

Novelty is partly just a renaming of the idea of curiosity from a different direction. Novelty is what attracts curiosity. People are curious about the novel. Yet, *novelty* is a useful and often used term, even though it lacks precision. It summarizes several curiosity dimensions of stimuli. It is a matter of research

to decide what are the limits of novelty, what defines it, and how much exposure reduces its effects. Berlyne's studies of people looking at pictures were a beginning to a very complex research problem.

Berlyne's first stimuli were really rather simple ones. They did not challenge the mind or reflect the limits that there might be. Are people always attracted to stimuli that are more complex and have more material? Is there no end to the incongruity that might be experienced? In further studies in his laboratory, Berlyne (1966) presented people with visual material of increasing complexity. Preference was now not always for the most complex. Each person had a different pattern, but each had a peak in complexity preference. Anything more complex than the personal peak was looked at less if not avoided altogether. This suggested that there may be an optimum of novelty and complexity that is most preferred.

Boredom's Effect

What happens to curiosity if experience is temporarily restricted? An obvious first answer is that there will be an increase in desire to have contact with the world. Anyone who has spent some time in bed recovering from an accident or illness is well aware of that. But with long-term exposure to the reduced context, choice of stimulation should shift toward the simpler. If experience with complexity increases the preferred level, then extended deprivation should reduce it.

One kind of evidence comes from studies of people who submitted to deprivation from changed stimulation in studies at McGill University in the early 1950s (Bexton, Heron, & Scott, 1954). Volunteers were paid well to remain on a bed in a small room. Milky goggles were worn, a constant noise was given, and arm and hand movements were restrained by cardboard cuffs. Brief periods were allowed for food, drink, waste elimination, and testing. Many volunteers did not stay longer than 2 days. After an initial period of sleep, most reported themselves to be very uncomfortable and sometimes frightened. A great number of studies following this pattern were conducted during the 1960s.

The deprivation may be of varying degrees and qualities. At the mildest level, we may be confined to an unchanged environment, as in a hospital room or a jail cell, or be obliged to work at an uneventful job keeping watch. Another degree of deprivation adds social isolation as well; no contacts with others except as absolutely necessary. Social isolation may be a major part of the stress experienced by many people. This stage is experienced by those who have endured a winter alone in a snowbound cabin or tent. Still more isolation results from the arrangements of the McGill experiments described above. These are conditions of elimination of changing or patterns of stimulation. Finally, sensory isolation may be attempted, in which the energy reaching the receptors is reduced as much as possible.

Sensory isolation was attempted in Jack Vernon's (1963) laboratory at Princeton University. His room was dark and quiet, an attempt to reduce the level of stimulation to very low levels as well as reducing its variation. John Lilly (1956) went to an even greater extreme by immersing himself in liquid, in the dark. This removed many of the pressure sensations on the skin that can't be avoided by a person on even the softest bed. He and other volunteers usually escaped this most extreme deprivation before 8 hours were finished. People don't seem to tolerate really low levels of sensation.

A certain amount of apparently pathological activity may have its roots in sensory restriction and boredom. Desmond Morris (1967) noted several outrageous examples among zoo animals. A sloth bear ate and regurgitated its meal, and then repeated that act more than 100 times with the same meal. Birds were seen to continue to groom their feathers until they dropped out, eventually becoming naked with only those feathers on the top of their heads that they couldn't reach. A male lion learned the trick of calling people to his cage with a roar. When a group was close, he lifted his leg and sprayed them with urine. In the same vein, people will also do

their best to keep up an adequate level and variety of stimulation. If necessary, they will do unusual things to get it. A great many socially disruptive acts perhaps have primary causes in boredom.

Change in Stimulus Preference

On a moment-to-moment basis, we adapt to current stimulation. As we gain experience, those elements lose their attractive powers. A different set of stimuli is now attractive. This is a continuous process, illustrated in one way by the pattern of visual inspection of a scene. One point is focused for a time, and then the eye moves on to another (Antes, 1974, 1977). We assume that the informative value of the stimulus is exhausted after examining it for a time. The next most informative stimulus then attracts acts of curiosity.

In a complex setting, we may prefer more and more complex stimuli as we exhaust them. A first look at an instrument and control panel of a new machine will most likely result in searching for and focusing on some familiar elements. From this base, we look at other elements, moving gradually toward the more unfamiliar and novel. The functions and patterns on the panel are learned. Eventually, the whole panel is understood and merits little visual inspection. New panels of a similar kind may now be grasped as a unit and scanned for variations. With time, a model of that kind of instrument panel is formed on our accumulated expertise. The preferred optimal level of that kind of material has shifted markedly toward the complex.

Individual differences in what is optimal are likely to reflect the experience we have had with the stimuli. The greater experience, the more complexity we can handle and will prefer. It is not hard to find life events that corroborate the systematic laboratory studies. The domains of art give many examples. If we are completely ignorant of an art form, it is not likely to please us in any aspect that does not come close to daily experiences. In casual experience with visual arts of photography, painting, and sculpture, we like realism. With continued exposure, we begin to have some interest in variations, symbolism, and abstractions. With great intensity of exposure and training, we may leave our naive friends behind and then marvel at the simplicity of their tastes, the same simpler pleasures we too once had.

There is a similar happening in hearing music. With study and constant exposure, we come to hear it differently and prefer different aspects of it. The kinds of music to which we have not become accustomed are little more than "noise" and are avoided. Each generation speaks poorly of the music of the next, and of the past, partly because they have not heard it in the same ways and to the same extent.

The details of information in any subject fit this pattern. Farmers with continuous needs for market information seek out the daily radio reports from nearby areas and can digest the information readily. To the novice, the sounds are little more than a chant about feeder pigs, pork bellies, December wheat, and so on; something to avoid or wait out until something that makes sense comes on again.

Our optimal level of stimulus preference does not remain constant. It changes with the experiences of the recent past, and some major shifts of the optimal level develop with accumulated experience. We experience a pattern of changes through life. The content of daily work gradually has an effect on our preferences. As we become more sophisticated in a job, trade, or profession, all of that is included in the life picture. We become a part of a new world, and preferences shift accordingly. Problems can arise in relationships with others who are following a different track. We grow more dissimilar in likes and dislikes as we accumulate different experience. As we noted in Chapter 8, love relationships are especially likely to suffer if there is not sufficient communication. Each must be willing to learn parts of the new world of the other and to communicate their world back. Without that sharing, there can be a slow drifting apart of interests that eventually becomes too great a rift to bridge.

The preferred optimum may also shift toward the simpler. Under conditions of little change, we come to prefer a less complex world. In a world of little change, preference moves to that world. The lessened activity adopted by some people in their retirement years may restrict their stimulus world. Their preference follows. The complexity of work is forgotten and the different world of daily survival chores is substituted. Some resort to the dull sameness of daytime television soaps, game shows, and talk shows. They are attracted to materials near to that new level; their lives are reformed to the variety of that presented world. They have not lost their curiosity; they are just curious about different things.

Absorption

When we attend to novelty at our preferred optimum, we feel different. We are absorbed in it, and that makes it different from other common perception. Being absorbed underwrites the range of topics we intend to understand in this chapter on playing. *Being absorbed* is the common theme in enjoying stories from all kinds of media, in liking games and personal challenges, in savoring personal interactions including sexual experiences, and in appreciating music and other forms of art. We lose our sense of self and of conscious control for a time and simply let things happen.

In doing something, the experience can be intense and absorbing. These are feelings that come from the doing, from the carrying through of life segment acts. These feelings are unrelated to the ending or the goal that might come at the end of the activity. The focus is instead on the experiences during the acts themselves. We will look at three perspectives on absorption: diversions, flow, and sensation seeking.

Diversions

Gene Quarrick (1989) presents absorption in terms of levels of diversion. Mildest diversions are games, outdoor activities, and similar forms of playing. He sees these as slightly diluted, everyday reality. We are still conscious of directing our activities but with a reduced personal evaluation of how we are doing. At the next level, he describes absorption. The mark of this second level is our break from reality and being unmindful of our self. Absorption in a good novel has this quality. The third level of diversion is rarer, yielding altered conscious states. Meditation practice and psychoactive drugs are two means to enter the third level.

Quarrick also notes some common misconceptions about what kinds of play yield more intensity of diversion. Physical activity is not necessary and may actually be counterproductive. Playing outdoors is neither necessary nor likely to intensify absorption. The reason may be that both of these present environment conditions that increase demand for our conscious control. Finally, the absorption is not measured by how much fun it is. Fun and pleasure can come from intense purposeful work, and many forms of absorption, such as horror movies and novels, may be frighteningly unpleasant.

Flow of Action

One of the most discussed of the experiences within a life segment is that called flow. Mihalyi Csikszentmihalyi appears to have been the first to elaborate this phenomenon and has followed it with studies and inspiration to many other social scientists.

In one of his earlier studies, Csikszentmihalyi (1975) looked at people as they experience their chosen games and reported that one of their experiences is that of **flow.** Game segments have periods of flow marked by a mental continuity or immersion that maintains a person for a duration. Flow is a

> peculiar dynamic state—the holistic sensation that people feel when they act with total involvement. . . . Action follows upon action according to an internal logic that seems to need no conscious intervention by the actor.

> Games are obvious flow activities and play is the flow experience par excellence. (pp. 36-37)

Csikszentmihalyi focused not just on games, play, and leisure. He also looked for flow experience in other life segments. Similar involvement appears in ritual and in work. The essence is the psychological carrying along of the activity. Once begun, the pieces are put together in a continuous stream. They carry along with a strong resistance to interference.

Victor Turner (1974) added to the concept of flow, it being one of three concepts he used to describe rituals. He saw flow as a feeling of being excitedly engaged and intensely focused on an activity without holding self-awareness.

Sensation Seeking

Marvin Zuckerman (1979) describes a "need for varied, novel, and complex sensations and experiences and the willingness to take physical and social risks for the sake of such experiences" (p. 10). In his view, this sensation seeking is a trait that can be discovered in what people do and in what they report in a paper and pencil test. Its essence is seeking and enjoying awareness of new stimuli.

From several studies of different populations and different countries, four dimensions of sensation seeking emerged. Zuckerman (1983, 1988) lists these:

> Thrill and adventure seeking: seeking sensations through physically risky activities involving elements of speed, danger, novelty, and defiance of gravity

> Experience seeking: seeking novel experience through nonconforming lifestyle, travel, music, art, drugs, and unconventional friends

> Disinhibition: seeking sensation through release in uninhibited social situations

> Boredom susceptibility: becoming restless with and avoiding repeated experience, routine work, and predictable people

Too much emphasis can be put on the risk-taking aspect. Danger and risk are not sought for their sake. Instead, high sensation seekers will not let risk deter them from new experiences. They also tend to be bored readily and will show interest in more things. Over time, the drive to find something new leads them to more risky sports and other activities, simply because those are what they haven't yet done (Rowland, Franken, & Harrison, 1986).

Consequences

A last aspect of the experience of playing and the like is its consequences for the participants. What has changed for the player? Are there nonspecific results of the doing, independent of any product, score, or reward? Some specific feelings appear in overlapping categories. The doing gives pleasure, refreshment, and a sort of resetting.

Our ideas of the consequences of doing and having done a life segment are typically based on our reports. We experience a sort of pleasure in the doing, although it is often not an obvious pleasure we felt at the moment.

The experience comes as a realization after the intense immersion in the doing has lessened. During the activity, we are only occasionally aware that there is an enjoyment. The deeper the degree of the flow experience, the less mental time there is for such higher-order evaluation. In water skiing, we are intent on staying up, zigzagging, and riding the wake. After the ride is over, the feeling of pleasure appears.

Many life segments produce a feeling of refreshment. The change is a kind of regeneration or wiping away of staleness and monotony. Again, these experiences appear after the segment has finished. A battle of puns with a friend leaves us exhilarated and feeling mentally awake. At the end of the golf game, there may be some fatigue but also a lift and light-hearted feeling.

Another variety of consequences of a specific life segment can be called resetting. The activities have brought us back to normal. When we are strung out and angry, a handball game resets us to a normal frame of mind. Mental cobwebs are blown away on an aimless excursion by bicycle. The theme is one of re-establishing oneself.

SECTION SUMMARY:
LOOKING FOR EXPERIENCE

Being curious is natural, part of our basic design. We have sensory curiosity, looking for what a thing appears to be; manipulative curiosity, seeing what it is through how it works; and cognitive curiosity, finding out what it is for. Dimensions of our curiosity are set by human biology and elaborated by cultural and individual experiences.

Curiosity is tricky to examine because of that personal component and because it is embedded in a natural context of experience. Still, we have determined at least two general patterns. First, we prefer and direct our curiosity toward what is moderately changed, taking into account what we have recently encountered and our total life experience. Extreme changes, such as sensory isolation or extreme stimulus complexity, are avoided and produce discomfort. Second, the experiences we have, whether growing or shrinking, lead our preferences in that direction of change. Growth in experience and competence in work or other endeavors lead us to prefer more of those increases. Stimulus complexity reduction in life leads to comparable interest in simpler things.

Some activities take us into them with abandon. Diversions vary in our absorption in them from mild dilution of awareness to total abandon. The common experience of moderately strong immersion in an activity is described as flow. Seeking pleasure by being absorbed in new activities has been characterized as a sensation-seeking trait.

◆

THEORIES OF RITUAL, PLAY, AND LEISURE

"Theories" is not the most exciting heading for a section, implying abstract discussions. But we are not delving into intricate statements of what makes up human adult ritual, play, and leisure, primarily because there are none. What we have to explore are ideas about how we live our lives. Some of those theoretical ideas reach back to make comparisons with what we once did. We sometimes discover the essence by seeing what has changed. We will assume at the outset that the development and fate of ritual, play, and leisure are linked in human history. Ritual and play share some characteristics of social boundedness and special intensity of inward personal experience. Play and leisure have in common an opposition to bounded work. We begin with some descriptions of ritual in our social history.

Ideas of Ritual

To understand play, some scholars have looked into the organization of life events in general. In doing that, they made an interesting comparison between the form of activities in preindustrial and modern Western societies. In overview, people in early societies were bound by social obligations with little choice. They had similar work, social roles, religion, and ceremonies of change. Community activities were undertaken and shared by all members. In modern societies, that sense of common activity and obligation is replaced by specialized work, relative freedom of individual action, and rational awareness of intentionally choosing and doing.

Ritual in Preindustrial Society

In early societies, the daily chores required for survival and comfort were carried out by everyone and not thought of as special. It was the periodic ritual that was the different, separate period of "work." A rite of passage to adulthood, celebration of the coming of spring, religious observances, and the like were matters for all members of the community to share as a matter of obligation. The roles that each played were established, and everyone participated. These rituals were thought of as the "work of the Gods," although we see in them roots of play elements.

Victor Turner (1974) described features in the progress of a preindustrial society ritual that are psychologically interesting and help understand modern ritual, work, and leisure. One of these he called liminality. **Liminality** is a period in many rituals in which one is separated from normal social obligations. This person may be secluded for a time or may perform a special set of acts. Play elements may appear in these liminal periods. The play amounts to variations from what is typical, variations called *liminoid* by Turner. Liminoid experiences provide opportunity for changes, including changes in understanding of social roles and obligations.

Ritual in Modern Society

Our modern ritual is usually a matter of choice by its participants, although frequently constrained by strong social pressures and obligations. It is typically an active performance including vocalizations, movements, and sometimes objects, special costuming, rhythm, and music. In most forms of ritual, participants act seriously, with little make-believe or frivolity, unless that is assigned for the event. Most ritual has a definite start and finish. Prescribed content draws the participants into the activity in an absorbed manner. The clearest example is a service of religious worship. The ritual still serves important psychological functions, but the features of liminality have been liberated into new contexts.

In our modern Western world of individual action in rationally segmented social roles, ritual becomes a bounded event with little tie to or significance for other acts and our place in those other social roles. In experiencing ritual, we share a socially defined structure with patterns of actions and feelings of involvement that exclude other possible world events. Once begun, we resist alteration by other than unusually strong interference. Social rules of ritual insist that the event be protected from casual change until it has reached its defined end. The boundaries, flow of action, and consequences are typically well-defined.

Analysts have identified several ways that rituals serve their participants. As we outline these functions, we can apply them to examples such as marriage ceremonies and birthday parties. First, ritual coordinates the group. The individuals are brought to common values through the ritual acts. Ritual serves a self-correction and maintenance role. Ritual validates the group's structure and the premises on which it is formed (Schwartzman, 1981).

Second, ritual is a means of communication. Although the message may be repetitious in rituals that are regular events, some rituals are unique events. The many communications in the ritual are not questioned, not doubted. In viewing ritual as a vehicle of communication, ritual is seen as integrating the social order, as contrasted with play. Both are instances of social communication in which the difference is indicated by the context. Ritual maintains the same social content, whereas play often appears to change it (Handelman, 1977).

A third function of ritual is marking a change in status. Milestones of social maturation are often marked by rituals as commonplace as birthday parties or as complicated as marriage ceremonies, funerals, and court proceedings.

A fourth aspect of ritual is a learning or reinforcement function. The participants reinstate or strengthen their attention or focus to relevant content.

Finally, ritual can be an effective means of adapting to life stress. Under conditions of anxiety, we may escape life's irritants by disengaging from them and undertaking a time-consuming ritual.

Views of Playing

As we noted, few psychologists have turned their attention to the nature of adult human play. Play has been mentioned by a few of the classic psychology theorists, but they have done little more than assume that there must be some practical purpose for play. They considered it directly or indirectly to be some sort of practice for life's "real" activities. Children playing are thought to be practicing for adult life, and adults are playing at roles to develop their skills. The functional theme of thought has been very powerful.

The dominant idea in defining a theory of play has been its contrast with work. Play is nonwork. Work is made up of activities with goals that are essential to human existence. Therefore, by this line of reasoning, play must not have goals nor be essential. Life segments of play, however, are not that easily categorized.

Traditional Play Theories

There are good sources for examining the different forms of traditional theory about play (Levy, 1978; Witt & Bishop, 1970). We summarize them below only to get an understanding of the types and directions that have been proposed. Table 13.1 provides an outline.

Older theories were attempts to find a practical use for play. Their focus was on some aspect of body energy or activity practice. More recent psychological theories consider play from the window of specific perspectives. Psychoanalysis needs, developmental progress, response to the world, and

TABLE 13.1 Some Classical and Modern Theories Dealing in Some Fashion With Play

Classic theories

Surplus energy	Schiller (1875)	energy not needed for survival
Recreation	Lazarus (1883)	overcome energy deficit
Pre-exercise	Groos (1901)	practice incomplete instincts
Recapitulation	Hall (1906)	replay of evolution development
Relaxation	Patrick (1916)	motor exercise

Psychological theories

Psychoanalytic	Freud (1920/1948)	fill needs to grow and have mastery
Ecology situation	Parten (1933)	evoked by the situation
Compensation	Mitchell & Mason (1934)	compensate for disability or blocked motives
Developmental	Piaget (1952)	changing reality to fit thinking
Ecology stimuli	Berlyne (1966)	optimal flow of stimulation
Attribution	Rotter (1966)	internals seek mastery, externals respond to chance
Conflict/ enculturation	Sutton-Smith (1968)	safe tryouts of life roles

personality needs are their views. The far greater share of effort and emphasis in these theories has been toward the play of children. The cultural biases we discussed at the opening of the chapter effectively shaped this aspect of play theories.

The essence of play as nonwork and the contrast of play with work are given in three classic and modern definitions. Johan Huizinga, Roger Caillois, and Brian Sutton-Smith each provided provocative ideas. Among the ideas that have influenced the study of play, Johan Huizinga's (1950) classic definition, often quoted, is this:

> [Play is] a free activity standing quite consciously outside "ordinary" life as being "not serious," but at the same time absorbing the player intensely and utterly. It is an activity connected with no material interest, and no profit can be gained by it. It proceeds within its own proper boundaries of time and space according to fixed rules and in an orderly manner. It promotes the formation of social groupings which tend to surround themselves with secrecy and to stress their difference from the common world by disguise or other means. (p. 13)

A similar model comes from Roger Caillois (1961). Caillois has incorporated the many dimensions of game forms of play into six adjectives: *free, separate, uncertain, unproductive, governed,* and *make-believe.* Play is free activity, not required or mandated. Play occupies separate time and space of its own. It is uncertain in outcome, and it is unproductive; there are no products. Play is governed by rules. Play is make-believe, not real life. Putting these ideas together, play is free, make-believe, separate activity governed by rules and with uncertain and unproductive outcomes.

In a somewhat historical look, Brian Sutton-Smith and Diana Kelly-Byrne (1984) hold play to be shaped in the social developments of recent Western culture. In their view, play has been idealized because it inherently threatens social order. Because play challenges the rules of social action, it must be disguised to be seen as positive and productive. In this ideal, play is thought to be taken up by free choice, to be pleasant, and to serve purposes for everyone.

Sutton-Smith and Kelly-Byrne (1984) see play as idealized through several forces.

> The work ethic has led to thought of just two states: work and nonwork, the latter being leisure and play.

> The forms of play have been adopted from the wealthy classes, with the view that the function of play shall be to develop the

child to that status. Team sports are the shining example.

Play theories have been developed by experts whose views reflect their privileged status.

Add to this a few other social forces such as the child study movement, toy manufacturers' interests, and the kindergarten tradition of play at school.

More recent ideas of the experience of flow in activities have blurred the difference between play and work. Although there have been different approaches to solving the problem of play's challenge to society, the view that play is a productive part of human experience in its own right has strengthened in Western thought, perhaps through its various mercantile applications. Play has become big business.

Liminoid Origins

Playful elements of preindustrial society were found in the period of liminality leading to work of the gods composing ritual obligations. In modern society, there are no longer universal ritual obligations comparable to those of smaller preindustrial societies. Each of us acts out individual life roles in work and daily affairs that may share few features with others. Daily activities were once essentially the same for everyone and done continuously, but now they are matters of specialization. Work is defined and rationally placed in separate time and space separated from other functions.

Liminoid acts, pieces of playful variation and creation, are still produced, but in modern society, many of them are found in various aspects of rationalized work. We creatively solve problems, analyze and discover in science, and invent novel lifestyles. Institutions such as research laboratories and universities are formalized centers for basically liminoid acts.

Play appears irregularly outside of formal settings. Play is a special segment of life experience, one of many rational activities with a special context and interpretation. The play context is one of thinking differently about what is happening. In playing, we know we have freely chosen to play. We choose what we do and make up the rules and goals.

Play activity is self-constructed and self-defined. The key to it being play, however, is the special awareness we have of it. Play is a matter of knowing it is play and communicating that to others. The exact acts do not matter. Play is not defined by what we do but by what we think about the doing. In Csikszentmihalyi's phrase, "we play when we know we are playing." We move into or out of that play context.

Functioning of Play

In many respects, play in modern society has taken on a character opposing that of ritual. Whereas ritual validates group beliefs, structures, and communications, play casts doubt on and mocks them, providing opportunity to try out change. Play, like ritual, erects a special domain of reality that is at once separate and integral with the normal. Unlike in participants in ritual, players in that special domain are permitted a period of being free from the strictures of normal society while still enjoying its comforts and protection. To play is to feel free of responsibility yet protected.

An important part of the freedom in play is the possibility of communicating disguised messages of frustrations or idealized personal worlds. Righteous aggressive urges cannot be expressed in socially controlled life but can be acted out in play. Unfulfilled needs for dependence or for nurturance become part of the acts of play. Preferred and suppressed worlds may be acted with others in play. Each player is communicating messages that are understood, paradoxically, to be messages of play that are not intended, yet they are also intentional statements about the normal social order. Good examples of this in common use are political cartoons. Drastic caricatures of people and events are acceptable because they are protected by being "just comics," even as we know their intent is an exaggerated criticism.

Such play may enable change in social values. Play gives a safe vantage from which comment on normal society can develop. Playful acts may propose "what can be." Play flows naturally along paths set by its participants, with only partial adherence to social rules. Some of the rules themselves are made up as a part of the play. Because play is by nature creative in a setting without many social rules, models of change for society are demonstrated, even though there are no expressed intentions of change. Play is inherently amoral regarding social values, yet it may lead to change in those values by the examples it provides.

These may be dangerous messages for society, even in play, and hence different ways have been developed to ensure that they are controlled. Some societies have tried to restrict or outlaw play by all but the very youngest children. Most modern Western societies have used the more subtle control of idealizing play. Playful acts are clearly framed so that everyone knows that it is just play. Some patterns of interaction such as aggressive competition are formalized into games with rules and thus broken off as separate from normal social rules. Play is organized and claimed to be educational for various life roles. Each of these is an aspect of preventing the challenging message of the free player from upsetting the social order.

Conceptions of Leisure

Leisure is another term that is used broadly, and many have attempted to extract its essence. The most common and perhaps least reflective meaning suggests that leisure encompasses all activities that are nonwork. Assuming that leisure is just nonwork presupposes a good definition and understanding of work as well as the many small chores of daily life such as eating, sleeping, and toiletry. It also suggests that there are no leisure aspects to ongoing work. The thrust of this common approach is that leisure can be identified by what is being done.

Social History

American leisure followed the fortunes of its people as they developed their society and its production. In the colonial days, people were somewhat equal and united in building a safe and comfortable life. Supporting that were beliefs commonly called the **Protestant ethic.** In these beliefs, work was identified with one's conscience and linked to ideals of progress and development. Work was sacred. The ideal of capitalism was included, leading to the general view that a good life was one of working hard to get ahead and profit, along with brief periods of formal worship. All other aspects of life were immoral unless they aided ideal work or worship. Play in this plan, whether that of children or adults, is seen to be practice for work. Leisure activities, if there was time for any, should hone work skills or provide rest for ensuing periods of productive work. Other leisure is wasting time, and time is a most valuable commodity in the Protestant ethic. Social recreation of sorts was found in getting together to accomplish work that individuals could not do alone, such as raising a barn or rolling logs away to make a farm field. These "bees" and time spent hunting the prolific game were the primary diversions from work, although some socializing also took place in community taverns.

As capitalism was successful, the equality disappeared, and wealthy and working populations emerged, the wealthy having time and interest in leisure. Wealthy landowners of the South, freed from labor by having slaves, took the lead into leisure. With further development of industrial and commercial society, a middle level formed with ideas of shortening the workday. That freed time combined with resources for conspicuous consumption, particularly in new varieties of recreation. Organized recreation was extended to the working population by local, state, and federal government.

In this century, working hours were shortened further giving time to consume as well as produce. Consumption fed further production of ways of leisure and recreation. From playing games, people moved to paying to watch sports. The commercial industries devoted to observing others moved in historical progression from printed materials to radio to television to the World Wide Web. The present variety of possibilities suggests a similar diversity of motivations for choices and intensities of what we choose to do.

Classifications of Leisure

Many analyses of leisure's nature have focused not on what is done but why. These view leisure as a psychologically defined condition centering on personal freedom. Most typical of these ideas, leisure varieties elaborate different concepts of freedom to choose acts or freedom from constraints. The freedom-to and freedom-from are perceptions at the heart of leisure. Understanding the roles of these perceptions of freedoms may be approached by once again looking at theoretical studies of society's evolution.

Those who accept leisure as essentially determined by some aspect of personal freedom have proposed classifications of leisure in those terms. John Kelly (1983) analyzed the freedom, intrinsic, and nonobligatory definitions of leisure that have been proposed. Freedom definitions imply that leisure acts are unconstrained, discretionary activities, that there is choice among acts without coercion. Leisure acts are done for their own sake, according to theories of intrinsic motivation. And leisure is nonobligatory in the sense that it is not in response to the demands of society; leisure acts are those that don't have to be done. Each of these definitions appears to be approaching the free choice element of leisure.

Given the basic element of freedom in choices of leisure acts, the questions now focus on other constraints. Complete freedom is never an option. Anarchy, even in leisure choices, will not survive. Leisure is coordinated with other parts of life in an ongoing plan. John Neulinger (1981) has suggested that in addition to perceived freedom, different leisure states of mind arise from situations varying in degree of intrinsic and extrinsic

motivation. **Pure leisure** comes from acts done entirely for their own sake. This ideal is rarely attained. **Leisure-work** ideas have some mixture of self-determination and anticipation of consequences or products. I choose to build a canoe, but anticipating the final product also motivates me. **Leisure-job acts** give the appearance of choosing but value the end and not the doing. A leisure-job may be running for improved health or playing the lotto to try to get rich. Neulinger's system also includes analogous states without freedom in the work domain called pure work, work job, and pure job. He views leisure to be most valuable when it has high perceived freedom and high intrinsic motivation.

Some leisure is done alone, and some is done with others. Some leisure is a matter of merely filling time meaningfully; other leisure is intense and has periods of flow. John Kelly (1983) put these two dimensions together to identify a pattern of leisure situations. Activity defined by the extreme of each dimension will illustrate his system. Watching routine television programming shows low-intensity, solitary leisure. Low-intensity, social leisure may be found in passing time chatting with others or casually interacting at a party. Solitary, intense leisure marks deep personal involvement in creating or performing, even if others are nearby; perhaps also some reading. Intense, social leisure is illustrated in many team sports and sexual interactions. These two dimensions show some of the variety of forms of leisure. Further dimensions of length of time of the leisure acts and Neulinger's idea of importance of consequences could add to the complexity.

A concept raised by ideas of the influence of the Protestant work ethic is the apparent paradox of serious leisure. Stebbins (1982) has developed some thoughts about serious leisure from the easy observation that we have fairly large periods of time left unfilled by work to earn a living. He suggests that we take up major secondary projects as leisure careers. These projects may be, for example, dedication as amateurs to sports or to intellectual fields, or as volunteers in aid of social projects. You may become an expert in certain coins or steam locomotives, or your serious leisure may turn to environmental activism. Stebbins proposes that these serious leisure acts are motivated by unmet needs to persevere at a task, put effort into it, have feelings of efficacy and accomplishment, and be a part of the changed social world that results. We exercise unused abilities and come to identify with the leisure activity. Stebbins's theme is one of needing to act during the long periods of nonwork time to fill the same needs that motivate wage-earning work. This is compatible with Turner's conten-

tion that such needs are a part of the Protestant ethic of common cultural education.

Further constraint on choice of leisure follows from our perceived social roles and the cultural stereotypes that follow. A truck driver is more likely to bowl than play polo; physicians are more likely to golf than drive stock cars. Seppo Iso-Aholoa and Roger Mannell (1984) wrote of these choices being "rooted either in feelings of (1) *not having or being* something or in feelings of (2) *having or being* something" (p. 114, italics in original). Those feelings involve social and personal competencies, one's cultural roles and obligations, and physical resources.

SECTION SUMMARY: THEORIES OF RITUAL, PLAY, AND LEISURE

Turner presented preindustrial society as normal undifferentiated workaday life broken by frequent periods of ritual in which play elements appeared during periods of liminality. Modern social ritual is a bounded life segment often marked by its functions of coordinating the group, communicating and learning, and marking changes.

Traditionally, play is not handled directly, but as an aspect of a more general theory. Modern definitions mark play as a separated activity with special rules. For example, Caillois described it as free, make-believe, separate activity governed by rules with uncertain and unproductive outcomes. Play exists outside of serious life activities and is primarily self-constructed and self-

defined. Play is protected while happening outside the serious social rules, thereby being able to challenge and mock those rules from its safe vantage.

Recent historical social values, termed the Protestant ethic, picture leisure as preparation for work or rest between work periods. Modern societies' efficiencies allow large time blocks for nonwork activity. Such time can be viewed as freedom-from work or as freedom-to carry on nonwork activities. Others see a continuum from pure leisure to leisure-work to leisure-job, reflecting different goals in the activities. Some leisure is seen as serious leisure in becoming the more important segment of one's life activities.

FORMS OF PLAYING

The forms taken by play are without specific limits or rules. Patterns of creatively divergent acts are performed within the frame of

play, and there are varying degrees of simultaneous conformity to normal rules of social order. Some play takes place in parallel with standard, socially regulated performances. For example, playful language may accompany otherwise serious activity. In some instances, a form of play serves a social role, as in a joking relationship greeting. Pieces of humor are play but are not usually thought of in those terms. Games and their institutionalized forms, labeled sports, have aspects of play experience kept in close check by special forms of social rules. Leisure activities are more indefinite, with some being more physical and others more cognitive in nature. Finally, touring is a special kind of play that has received extensive study. These are the ideas we explore in this section of the text.

Social Interactions

Some play is known by its social contexts. Play is very likely in a scene of partying and celebrating. Holiday events, birthdays, festivals, and the like provide social occasions for playing. It is expected, and it happens (Bowman, 1978).

In other forms, the playful acts are communicated by direct verbal or nonverbal signals. The message is "this is play," and it communicates that what is being done does not mean what it normally means. The cues signify "These acts are done in play and are to be forgiven or ignored." What are the signals that give this play meaning? Adults do not usually begin their play with direct verbalization as do children. Children can easily say "Let's play" to begin a play segment. For adults, play typically involves some other forms of communication. A common nonverbal communication of play is lightheartedness of the participants. The show of smiles and the presence of laughter suggest playful elements to what they are doing.

Some play is shown by the play activity itself. Acts that do not fit in because they are unusual, exaggerated, unexpected, or incongruous may permit viewers to immediately say, "That is playing." A brief segment of the play is enough to form the judgment. Someone intentionally making grotesque faces while another is speaking can be seen to be "trying to break up the speaker," an act of play. A person in business dress skipping along the top of a low wall would be judged

to be playing. Picking up a large scrap of paper, wadding it, and tossing it in a high arc toward a waste receptacle is a common segment of play. In each of these, the observer immediately knows the act is one of play.

Certain segments of play may present the same features of the unexpected or unusual but require a longer viewing time to decide how the acts have progressed. For example, the events leading up to a practical joke are not immediately seen in themselves as play. We must see the developing context and how the play sequence has been ended.

Joking typically takes place between two relatively equal individuals; one teases and "makes fun" of the other, who, in return, does not take offense but may respond with similar acts. Early theory suggested that joking is a form of indirect aggression, but Kathleen Alford (1981) has shown instead that the strongest joking relationships appear between equal and intimate friends. The closer the friendship, the more likely that joking will occur and the more "abusive" it will appear. Joking is not usually hostile; it is a harmonious form of play.

There are different ways that segments of play end. Play often finishes when the participants begin to see their acts in another context. Sometimes it is guilt, aggression, or fear that enters the mind. Self-reflection on the acts changes the mood. Play stops when others are seen to be not approving. The play may develop into intense happiness and laughter breaks it down. Sometimes, the play just suddenly appears no longer fun, as if a feeling of satiation has entered.

Play in Language

Talk does more than communicate bounds and intentions. Some of the more interesting and common kinds of play are those that work with words and their different meanings. The twisted and incongruous meanings of a good pun are playful and enjoyed by almost everyone. Dozens of funny stories end with outrageous puns of famous sayings, although it is conventional to express displeasure by groaning and complaining. That tradition has a history. In the early 1700s, the critic John Dennis expressed the convention with the comment "A man who could make so vile a pun would not scruple to pick a pocket." The elements of play are clear in a pun's brief segments. The boundaries and the inference of play only become apparent after the meaning of the talk has been recognized. Perhaps, it is the element of being tricked that produces the annoyance, leading to the groan.

The "nicknames" and situation labels we use reflect play. We enter conversational play situations and attach labels. Those labels reflect the happenings and salient features of the interaction. Campus newspaper personals columns are filled with such verbal debris. "Pinky, call the three bears." "Will 'the great one' at Danny's Saturday night be there again next week? The Strawberry." These bits and pieces are the leftovers from a period of playful language interaction.

Sometimes, a whole conversation will follow a strange direction in which the play is that strangeness. Appearing bizarre to the nonparticipant observer are the apparently meaningless conversations that people concoct in play. In some, each respondent purposefully says something that makes no sense in following what has been said. It is a sort of diversive creativity. The play is in the unconnectedness of the silly talk.

Apparent boredom sometimes leads to a game of back-and-forth verbal construction. As two people drive along together, one sees a sign and makes the noun into an active verb: "The turns are turning." The other responds with another: "The store is storing." And on it goes for miles with the only rule being no repetition. Variations on this theme are endless and playful.

Segments of culture adopt personal styles of speech. In effect, a new language is built. Such talk among social groups is slang; among professionals, it is jargon. Work groups in the military services form slang of the objects and events with which they work. Groups of young people and local ethnic groups are most known for their creative and constantly changing slang. The play component of slang language seems obvious.

Games

The subject of games has a broad literature, crossing many disciplines of social science and education. Few studies have been made of the psychological role of games and fewer still in which the major thrust is toward adult human beings. The only organizing ideas come from a few older works; there are no recent efforts on a grand scale. We will focus on the 1950s French work of Roger Caillois (1961), published in *Man, Play, and Games*. In that book, he made a rational classification of games and other forms of play and leisure activity.

Caillois intentionally mixed games and other forms of play. In his system, games use rules; other forms of play use imagination or make-believe. Within these two forms, there are four classification headings or quadrants, two aspects of the activities in any quadrant, and normal play versus corrupted forms in each. After making these distinctions, Caillois devotes time to elaborating selected combinations. Only the essentials of the system will be described. The four kinds of activities, or quadrants, are given common names and a special label, as shown in Figure 13.1.

Games of competition are called **agon.** The game is a matter of pitting the skills. Baseball and chess are good examples. We start in an equal fashion, defined by the rules. Teams have the same number of players, often chosen to be of equal skill or suitably handicapped to achieve that initial equality. The playing "pieces" are equal in number or divided to reflect an equal starting condition. The progress of the game follows rules, and the play is under each person's direct responsibility.

Chance games are labeled **alea,** the Latin name for dice. Fair games such as dice or roulette give each player has an equal chance; no skill is involved. The game is structured so that winning is in accordance

		AGON	**ALEA**	**MIMICRY**	**ILINX**
		competition	chance		movement
PAIDIA	(joy)				
↑		wrestle		mask	swing
			dice		
		baseball			dance
			roulette		
↓		chess		acting	
LUDUS	(control)				
INSTITUTIONAL		sports	lotteries	theater	skiing
WORK FORM		business	markets	ceremony	aviation
CORRUPTION		greed	superstition	alienation	intoxication

Figure 13.1. Roger Caillois's (1961) forms of play, examples along the joy/control dimension and some forms found in nonplay living.

with the risk. Players are effectively passive with regard to the outcome. We may produce a variety of stylish acts in the play, but they have no real effect on the outcome.

Mimicry is Caillois's name for simulation activities. We take pleasure in playing or appearing to be like someone or something else. There are no rules in the simplest form of mimicry, other than the demand for invention and novelty. Children imagine they are animals or act the role of attractive adult jobs. Adults wear masks and costumes or take part in theater.

The fourth type is vertigo, which Caillois named **ilinx** after the Greek word for whirlpool. We enjoy rapid dancing, falling, moving rapidly, or twisting about on play machinery. The goal is a period of loss of perceptual stability leading to dizziness and disorder.

Within each of these types of play and game activities, there is a continuum between paidia and ludus. **Paidia** is the spontaneous expression of the energy of a play instinct, marked by a carefree gaiety and joy, uncontrolled fantasy, free improvisation, turbulence, and diversion. Paidia is the bubbling activity of the young child at play or the spurt of unrestrained exuberance of adults. **Ludus** marks the control and enrichment of paidia activity. Ludus is the disciplined form of play. We learn to master skills of play in training,

seek tasks for their gratuitous difficulty, and make games pure and excellent. The paidia-ludus continuum is shown by examples in Figure 13.1.

The game and play activities may become corrupted in their contact with daily life. The pleasures of the games change to perversions, as the game becomes translated into a nongame activity of life. Caillois sees this in stages. The game or play becomes institutionalized at the edge of ordinary life, its forms may become a part of ordinary life activity, and it may become corrupted into an unsociable or immoral form as it loses the controlling context of play, with its rules and standards. Agon becomes obsessive ambition, alea goes to superstitious belief, mimicry to loss of identity, and ilinx to intoxication. The bottom rows of Figure 13.1 give examples.

The paidia and ludus ways of playing also enter ordinary life as styles of preference for disorder or coordination, respectively. Further movement toward those styles may mark a corruption to neurotic mania or obsession for order. These are the highlights of Caillois's analysis.

Sport

The word *sport* has a broad meaning, and it may not be useful to precisely define what it includes and what it does not. Even the international contests have changing standards of what is included. As a general definition, **sport** will be considered to be institutionalized kinetic games. Sports are games in which there is a socially defined structure of process and form and in which a primary defining element is motion.

The motion or kinetic aspect of sport activities separates sports from playing chess or solving puzzles. The latter may be highly charged and organized, but they are not sports in the same sense as those games in which motion is the essence. The moves of the sports players become standardized, refined, and stylized. There are dozens of ways to bring the basketball to the hoop, to catch and throw the baseball, to evade a blocker in football, to pass the puck, and so on. These kinetic acts are named and replayed by the commentators of major spectator sports. Practice and perfection of those moves become at least as important for the nonprofessional playing the sport as is the scoring of points. These kinetic elements become the goals.

The structure of sport shows some of the character of ritual. Both sport and ritual are made up of defined, serious acts by the participants and include prescribed activities of the spectators. Some writers have found that each of the five characteristics of ritual defined earlier is well represented in sports. First, the social coordination aspects of sport are obvious. Second, sports communicate common social messages. Like ritual, sport uses ideas and values that are a part of society. In a sense, the sport becomes another way of expressing or commenting on the social order. Third, sports have aspects of change of status. Making the all-star team, winning the cup, breaking the course record, and so on are changes resulting from sports performance. Fourth, athletes spend time learning to focus their mental and physical skills toward the sport. Finally, sports are the means by which people can handle stress by disengaging from other life for the time of the sport. These benefits come to both the players and the observers.

Sport, as it has become organized and institutionalized, has drifted away from the primary features of play and casual games. Instead of viewing sports as regularized games played primarily for recreation, sports are now most generally seen in prototype in their professionalized form. Football is for the sake of professional games, and baseball is for the sake of major league play. The internal motivation has been altered. As sport becomes a profession, the play becomes work. The individual's choice and spontaneity in style and depth of play shrink. The sport loses the defining element of play, that one knows one is playing. The goals of the sport are outside of the basic game itself, and the outcome becomes important to many people besides the players. At this stage, sport is work for the athlete and has become an example of a leisure diversion for the spectator.

SECTION SUMMARY: FORMS OF PLAYING

Play segments are identified through sophisticated experience with social cues to intentions. A common form of play appears in language and various word games. Games were classed by Caillois into ones of competition, chance, mimicry, and movements, varying along a scale from disciplined control to carefree activity. Sports are marked by formal rules and kinetic (movement) elements.

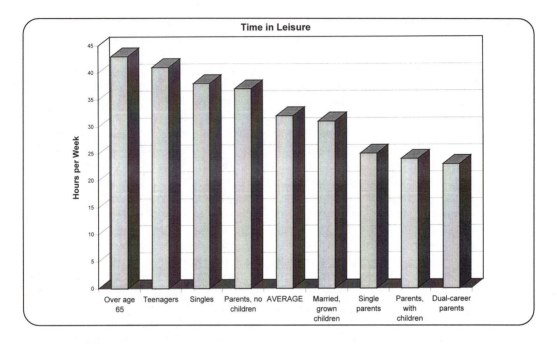

Figure 13.2. Leisure time available to different populations, adapted from United Media Enterprises (1983).

FORMS OF LEISURE

A logical step beyond saying that leisure is just nonwork is the implication that nonwork is activity without goals that are essential to human existence. It is not that simple. Nearly everyone agrees that there are important psychological states that are a part of leisure, although again, there is variety in discussing just what are those states. One focus is on the kind of satisfactions that are commonly thought to be untypical of work. Thus, Sebastian de Grazia (1962) called leisure the "state of being in which activity is performed for its own sake or as its own end" (p. 15).

According to this analysis, leisure includes play and sport but also somewhat more diffuse activities such as social and scheduled amusements, walking, talking, reading, and watching television. All are activities done for their own sake or for their own ends. Others have added to this the idea that we have positive goals in seeking leisure including relaxation, diversion, enjoying a vicarious social life, or exercising creativity.

Time in Leisure

However we account for it, leisure does take a significant chunk of our time. Assuming 8 hr a day in sleeping and related preparations and 9 hours a day in working and ancillary transportation, and so on, about 7 hours a day are left for other life maintenance chores and leisure. A typical analysis suggests we average about 32 hr a week in leisure. Not everyone is the same, though, as Figure 13.2 shows.

Following the idea that leisure is nothing more than what fills unproductive time, Mihalyi Csikszentmihalyi (1975) showed how leisure acts are commonplace. Among his studies of play in work and games, he explored the use of leisure time in general. He asked a group of 20 people to keep a record of the way they spent all of their waking time for 48 hr. He catalogued the different ways time was spent in leisure activities. An abstraction of his results appears in Table 13.2

Note that these are not indications of amount of time spent but the frequency of oc-

TABLE 13.2 Classification of Leisure Episodes From Two-Day Student Records of Activities, Abstracted From Csikszentmihalyi, 1975

Activity	Frequency (not time)
Social	218
Kinesthetic	194
Imagining	144
Attending	124
Oral	57
Creative	25

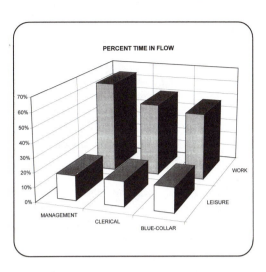

Figure 13.3. Estimates of time in flow experience based on time-sampled reports of workers, based on Csikszentmihalyi and LeFevre, 1989.

currence of each segment of leisure activity. This was just a preliminary attempt to assess the range of leisure acts everyone performs.

Following this measurement, some of the same people were asked a few days later to exclude all of these leisure acts from their activity for another 24-hour period. This was far from an ideal test, but in some ways, it was a very conservative one, because errors of intrusion of leisure acts were likely. Effects were found. Physically, the people were more tired, sleepy, and prone to headache. They tested as less creative, and they reported that they felt, in their words, "unreasonable." This experiment has aspects similar to the sensory isolation and boredom laboratory studies we discussed earlier. Deprivation from leisure activities does have consequences, but serious questions as to actual causes still remain. Particularly, the conditions of continual self-denial would appear to be similar to those defining psychological stress, and the effects are consonant with that.

Csikszentmihalyi and his colleagues have developed more precise means of assessing ongoing life experiences using electronic pagers. In a recent study using volunteers from large companies, they interrogated workers randomly in 2-hour intervals from 7:30 in the morning to 10:30 at night. When paged, volunteers immediately answered a series of questions about their activities at that time, using a prepared booklet (Csik-

szentmihalyi & LeFevre, 1989). Activities were characterized as work, leisure, and other. Work activities were reported 27% of the time, leisure 20%, and other activities in the remaining 53% of the time, including transportation, eating, chores, resting, and shopping. Leisure included television, reading, socializing, active leisure, and daydreaming. From people's reports of experiences at those times, the researchers determined the extent of experiences of flow, and it is here that some surprises appear. Flow experience occurred 54% of the time during work but only 17% of the time during leisure; more than three times less often (see Figure 13.3).

We have then, the paradoxical situation of people having many more positive feelings at work than in leisure, yet saying that they "wish to be doing something else" when they are at work, not when they are in leisure. Apparently, the obligatory nature of work masks the positive experience it engenders. In deciding whether they wish to work or not, people judge their desires by social conventions rather than by the reality of their feelings. (Csikszentmihalyi & LeFevre, 1989, pp. 820-821)

Leisure Variety

In a broad fashion—thinking of leisure as a catchall of nonwork activities—leisure segments have in common that they fill time. Lists of leisure activities reveal a few ideas.

On a primarily cognitive rather than physical act dimension, some leisure time is filled with observing others perform. Some of these performances are artistic, many are athletic, and some just "mental bubblegum"—filling time. Plays, dances, stage shows, television, movies, and graphic arts all provide different mental worlds for a time. They produce temporary change, and tastes for new items develop with experiences. Modest changes overlaid on fundamental consistency are preferred.

Watching television has become a major leisure-time activity for many people, although the study above found only about one quarter of that time was an involving, flow experience. One researcher found that there is a sinister entrapment caused by too much viewing. The more that people watch TV to escape from their lives, the more they feel uncomfortable with their leisure time. They become unable to enjoy other leisure activities. Extended TV watching is most likely to be chosen by people who are not happy with their lives. That TV experience then leads them to be unsatisfied with anything that is not crammed with excitement. They are led "to an increased dependence . . . on prefabricated and preplanned activities" (Kubey, 1986).

A traditional form of cognitive leisure experience is reading. Literature in many forms can take us to another life or a different set of experiences. The scene can be a close approximation of our usual daily life, or it can be a weird world of mayhem or outer space fantasy. Whatever the subject, time can be filled with these experiences.

Other categories of cognitive leisure include mental challenges such as puzzles. Crossword puzzles and jigsaw puzzles are major leisure activities for many. Other people take up leisure learning. Heavy mental investment is placed in learning a skill or a subject just for the sake of knowing it. We learn languages, study astronomy, or memorize woodland plants. Still others invest major time and effort in collecting and becoming experts on stamps, coins, beer cans, or whatever.

A new category of leisure time is just developing, that of using computers. Specialized machines for games have become high fashion, especially for children, and games for conventional personal computers are big business. The era of communicating with others by computer, using information services, "surfing the net," and viewing traditional media prepared for computers is just beginning. Although these leisure activities take great amounts of time now for only a modest percentage of people who have the resources, as with radio and television before them, their future development seems assured.

Forms of leisure emphasizing or requiring physical activity include something for everyone. In addition to common sports and games, the following list of possibilities suggests the scope: bicycling, birding, boating, building, camping, climbing, dancing, drawing, driving, exercising, fishing, flying, gardening, hang gliding, hiking, hobby crafts, hunting, juggling, model-building, motorcycling, painting, parachuting, playing games and sports, horseback riding, running, sailing, sewing, shooting, singing, skating, skiing, sledding, soaring, swimming, walking, and weaving.

Touring

Tourism is a much-studied example of leisure, and it serves to illustrate what future study may uncover in other topics. Touring is a common leisure experience that takes up long periods of time. A distinction between touring and travel has been suggested by some writers. Travel is not necessarily a unique life segment, although it may be an important component of leisure activity. Normal conditions of existence can be maintained while traveling, particularly if the travel is a part of one's work or merely a change of location. Touring, however, is an immersion in a different pattern of life for a time. Its purpose is to experience change. Valene Smith (1977) defined a tourist as a "temporarily leisured person who voluntarily visits a place away from home for the purpose of experiencing a change" (p. 2).

Touring is a definite life segment, apart from normal affairs. It has a purpose that is integral to our personal and social needs. The bounds are especially clear. Going away from home marks the beginning, the duration, and the end. It brings us to confront a different life situation, resulting in significant personal change. The consequences include new or renewed personal meaning and significance. Touring is a revitalization. In touring, we are free to indulge our fantasies, to challenge ourselves, and to develop our potentials. If we have not changed or been renewed by the activity, the touring has not been successful.

Nelson Graburn (1989) describes tourism from the cultural perspective of study of ritual. In the current Western social world,

> A majority of Americans and Europeans see life properly consisting of alternations of these two modes of existence: living at home and working for longish periods followed by taking vacations away from home for shorter periods.
>
> Our two lives, the sacred/nonordinary/touristic and the profane/workaday/stay-at-home, customarily alternate for ordinary people. (pp. 22, 26)

Nelson Graburn (1983) has also separated two forms of tourism. The more typical form is that of regular, scheduled breaks in the work period. Annual vacations or leave, spring breaks, and holidays are common traditions in Western society. These are seen by anthropologists as forms of *rites of intensification*. They give meaning to life and mark the passage of time. The workaday (profane) life is broken by periods of nonordinary (sacred) life. The change from one to the other is celebrated. If the sacred time is a period of touring, those changes are marked by "bon voyage" and "welcome home" parties.

The second form of tourism is similar to the anthropologists' *life crises rites* or rites of passage from one stage to another. Social order marks adulthood, graduation, marriage, and so on with rituals, sometimes challenging, but always socially memorable. The tourist chooses to undertake a similar event, often including testing of personal limits. The self-test is done to prove we are capable.

Amusement parks offer one short-duration example of this form of touring. People pay substantial sums of money to submit to twirling, falling, zigzagging, and other visual and motor frights. Individuals typically begin on tame and calm rides and progress to the more violent and terrifying. They are testing their limits. Eventually, they find the limit or become sated and unwilling to choose more. For many people it ends there, but others return regularly for repeats of the unusual stimulation.

Longer durations of self-test experiences are also common. Primitive camping has become popular, especially as it is linked with a particular way of traveling. Some camp in the wilderness while canoeing. Others follow long hiking trails. A few travel by horseback. People set out alone or in small groups to travel great distances with few resources. For many years, thousands of people have converged on a designated spot in western Iowa to spend a week in July riding their bicycles across the state (called RAGBRAI). All are challenges and allow us to see what we can endure.

Graburn (1989) has also outlined several goals of traditional travel-based touring. He first distinguished culture and nature purposes. Culture touring may be either historical or ethnic. Visiting the castles of England, the churches of Spain, or the battlefields of the American Civil War are historical forms of touring. Ethnic tours take us to observe and perhaps interact with native peoples. The lure may be to live a week in a rural village in China, with a French winemaker, or on a Wyoming family ranch.

Nature touring may be environmental, ecological, or ethnic. Environmental tours take people to a different world. Most typically, people seek the salt air and bright sun of a beach; the cool, clear air and remarkable vistas of mountains; or the tranquillity and varied animal and plant wonders of the deep woods. Some people seek change rather than purity and are willing to be in the city jungle for the wonders to be found there. Environmental touring for some has recreation as its goal. For others there is a need to have experiences and obtain objects: hunting, fishing, rock collecting, shell scavenging, and so on.

Ecological tourists also seek environmental change but try to leave no impact. Theirs is an appreciation of the natural world combined with an ethic of noninterference. They photograph, sketch, and make sound recordings and perhaps collect information of the species and landforms. Several national and international organizations of people with ecological interests (for example, the Sierra Club, National Audubon Society, and National Wildlife Federation) have been developed to further the ecology ethic.

Ethnic nature touring includes the cultural. The difference is a subtle one of primary interest. Nature tourists see native peoples as a part of the natural world, reflecting the beauty of nature. Interacting with such people is another facet of knowing nature.

Graburn believes three factors will predict the nature of tourism: discretionary income, cultural self-confidence, and symbolic inversions or reversals. The effect of the first is obvious. Those with no resources cannot tour, but having extra money does not mean one necessarily will.

Cultural self-confidence is a matter of education and experience. Without some knowledge of our own and other cultural practices, we will choose to stay close to home or to the familiar. With education and experience, we will choose the strange, the exciting, and the unexpected. The best way to develop in this more adventuresome direction is touring itself.

Cautious exploration is begun with some assurance of safety. We will not venture into a setting where we do not know how to act. The "rube" fears the city, and the "slicker" fears the farm. One strategy has been to carry some of our home along. Perhaps the strong

attraction to heavily equipped motor homes and trailers is the feeling of support they give. We can venture out without leaving the safety of our familiar (wheeled) home.

Ritual inversion just means that some of the rules of acting are reversed or modified. Typical changes involve the environment, class or lifestyle, formality, and health. Environment changes are most popular. People flock to the beach from cold climates, whereas others seek the still cold air of the north. Some seek crowds, and others look for the isolation of open spaces or a secluded cabin.

Our social class may be changed from a simple life to a luxury hotel weekend or from affluence to a period of slumming. Thrifty people may throw their money around. A person having a desk-bound lifestyle may seek the thrills of kayaking. Some will go on religious pilgrimages. Others will seek change in sexual experience. The formality of a daily schedule will be thrown out for doing whatever strikes our fancy whenever it happens. Unconventional dress may be worn: The laborer dresses formally, the tycoon becomes a beach bum, and some opt for nudity. Health forces include dieting, exercise, spas, and the like. Others choose the opposites: gluttony, sloth, and saloons.

Ritual inversions are common but are done in moderation. That is, we choose to change only a few things at a time. Those few changes give some of the pleasure or magic to the tourist. Things are done that cannot or won't be done at home.

Taken together, Graburn believes that these three factors of wealth, self-confidence, and inversions make up a matrix of the forces determining tourism. We purposefully choose, depending on the context of our lives. His model provides an understanding of some of the regulation of our touring and goes a long way toward structuring the individual differences in tourism among people, among cultures, and over time.

The effect of touring, the revitalization, is prolonged by memories. Tourists collect memory cues, souvenirs. Pictures, rocks, shells, pressed flowers, and a vast collection of manufactured objects are brought home with the intention of cuing memories of the tour. Photographs, particularly those including the tourists, are especially valued. Rarely, however, do these treasures have value for others with whom the tourist wishes to share them.

The product of touring, like that of rituals, play, games, and other forms of leisure, are those of pleasure, refreshment, and resetting. Essential causes or even complete descriptions are yet to be discovered, but all of these life segments are human ways and necessary parts of human existence.

SECTION SUMMARY: FORMS OF LEISURE

We average about 32 hr per week in leisure, varying according to current life roles, and when experimentally deprived of our leisure activities, we report being tired and uncomfortable. We believe we enjoy leisure activities, but study shows we are more often immersed in flow during work than in leisure.

Leisure touring has had special study and shown to be of two forms: regular breaks and self-testing experiences. Three factors predict the extent and kind of touring one will do: discretionary income, cultural self-confidence or experience with the destination setting, and interest in reversals or inversions of regular daily experience.

CHAPTER CONCLUSIONS

If play is a part of our design heritage, a leftover from information-gathering activity that was necessary for brain function development, then our many curiosity, leisure, play, and related activities will remain a fundamental part of how we function. Their motivational relevance seems clear.

But it is not so simple. As in so many life activities, our cultural ideals put their twist on play. Most work-organized societies view leisure and play as a waste of time, subtracting from the serious needs. At the same time, work is viewed as something we would rather not do in favor of rest and leisure. The slogans put us in a circle that is confused even more by finding that our most absorbing activities exist in work, not in play. This leaves us devaluing leisure and play because it is not in line with high-order serious production, while valuing it as a prime reason why we work.

The puzzles are perhaps more apparent than real. Much of the difficulty lies in defining work and leisure and play in terms of external outcomes rather than in terms of psychological motivations and values. We truly like to do things, engaging in them with our minds and bodies. Whether these activities are called play or work is a social convenience. Perhaps, when we understand these ideas better, separate chapters on work and play will seem unsuitable.

Study and Review Questions

1. What brain development programs and features underwrite play?

2. What are our traditional thoughts and analogies about play?

3. What is the most defensible descriptor of play?

4. How did Aristotle describe curiosity?

5. Compare the sensory, manipulative, and cognitive modalities of curiosity?

6. What do we mean by natural human curiosity?

7. For what reasons is curiosity difficult to study experimentally?

8. What are the three basic principles of curiosity?

9. What stimulus complexity do we prefer?

10. What happens when we experience sensory reduction?

11. How does life experience affect our preference for stimulus complexity?

12. What do we feel when we are absorbed?

13. What is the theory idea called flow?

14. At root, what are sensation seekers looking for?

15. What are the forms of outcomes or consequences of playing?

16. What is Victor Turner's theory idea called liminality?

17. What are the several possible outcomes of modern experiences of ritual?

18. How did Roger Caillois describe play?

19. At its root, how is play best defined?

20. How might play function to alter society?

21. How does the Protestant work ethic view leisure?

22. Compare pure-leisure, leisure-work, and leisure-job perspectives of activities.

23. What is the likely function of "serious leisure"?

24. In what ways do play periods end?

25. In what forms do we play using language?

26. What are Roger Caillois's classification forms of games?

27. Define Roger Caillois's paidia and ludus dimensions of play.

28. What elements define a sport?

29. How much of our time is commonly spent in leisure?

30. What is the result of voluntarily excluding leisure?

31. In what life activity does flow most often occur?

32. What are the two forms of touring?

33. With what factors can we predict touring?

Epilogue: Motivation Ideals

This epilogue brings together some of the facts and thoughts of the text that qualify as noteworthy motivation rules of living. In some ways, the content is my particular view of motivation arising from my many years of looking at these topics. It is reasonable to view it as my motivation instruction booklet.

You can be as motivated or as unmotivated as you and your life circumstances allow you to be.

Motivation is an attitude we have about what we and others are doing. It is neither something we have or don't have, nor a simple condition of our bodies. That attitude is reflected in the ways we choose to do things. Life is always a matter of answering one basic question: What do I do next?

Accept that your physical body always has its influence.

We are wonderfully complex biological machines. Even though we may think our cerebral capacities for thinking and learning are in control, our being is built entirely of a collection of biological adaptations. We cannot understand ourselves or our motivations if we fail to acknowledge that base.

Choose the best time of day for activities.

Evidence of our dependence on biological functions appears in subtle but real variations in sensitivities and performance according to the time of day. It makes a difference when in the day we try to memorize, to do fine motor work, or even to feel sexual interest.

Arise at the same time each morning, no matter what the circumstances.

Adequate and efficient sleep comes from establishing regularity. Once in synchrony with daily life, sleep will strengthen in its optimal pattern of several cycles of deep to light sleep. The most-needed deep sleep will essentially finish in the first half of the sleep period; the later parts of the night show increased time in dreaming.

Enjoy your dreams, but don't obsess over them because they mean little.

Dream material is memories and imagination left without the control of external stimulation and internal mental processes exercising their normal self-correction. Weird or repetitive dreams can and will appear, because that is the stuff of memory and normal mental functioning.

Design your meals with the needs and foods available to your primitive ancestors.

Our food requirements came from a long period of successful adaptations. Recent cultural changes, arising at the beginnings of agricultural civilizations, have distorted our typical diet toward foods easily produced and managed. The consequence is a mismatch with serious health consequences.

Problems caused by eating too much of the wrong things are rarely solved by your eating something else.

Whether our culinary sins are eating too much or the wrong kinds of carbohydrates, consuming too much saturated fat, or just eating too much, there are no magic foods that will compensate. There is no alternative to a sound diet composed of foods meeting our adapted needs.

Dieting is not a way to control your weight.

Weight management follows adopting a lifetime pattern of eating a sound diet appropriate to an adequate pattern of body activity. That is simply stated but notoriously difficult to carry out while in a lifestyle based on tasty foods and too little exertion.

Act the emotion you want to feel and want others to feel as well.

The emotion we show to others influences them in that same feeling. They in turn display it back to you. The mutual reflection builds the feeling in both. Evidence suggests, too, that just expressing an emotion directly builds that feeling and physiology in oneself.

Use anger judiciously to keep order in situations where the rules indicate it.

Cultural rules are formed to establish what rule violations justify being angry and what actions are appropriate to keep the order. Anger along with appropriate aggressive acts are then justified and expected. Failing to be angry under adequate provocation is as serious a "mistake" as to be angry without justification.

Recognize that women and men express anger and use aggression differently.

Traditionally, women's basic social style has been cooperative, and becoming angry and aggressive is a mark of failing to keep self-control. Men use aggression according to rules of fair fighting to manage their reputation and to control situations. With changes toward gender equality in social rules, these differences are weakening.

Develop your children's competency with aggression by models of appropriate experiences.

Children learn how to be aggressive and what it is for by watching others, most important, their adult caregivers. In viewing rewarding and punishing effects, children learn aggression's consequences.

Use your pain to guide your living.

Pain's power to control us reflects its important goal of managing damage. It has to hurt to have that power. Removing all of the hurt takes away the damage-limiting function. Remember, too, that pain is a complicated design of nervous system information flow that is not easily thwarted as long as problems remain.

Understand fear as a necessary guide to danger.

Fear is a natural communication about things that may damage us. Without fear, we literally put ourselves in harm's way.

Regulate stress by achieving control over situations or by managing your mental experience.

Psychological stress comes from what we think about our current life events. By getting control over those situations, we may change their appraised importance, or we may be just exercising our limited mental attention in such a way that we get relief from the circle of worry. Stress therapies work by breaking some chains of thinking about stress events and consequences and thereby change the nature of our personal reality.

Recognize depression early and take appropriate action.

Dwelling in a stresslike depressed state can increase its depth to the point of requiring medical intervention. Therefore, we must take prompt action to cope with the situation and exercise emotion control.

Plan regular monogamous sex to facilitate your health.

Our bodies were designed to have frequent sex. Frequent sex with a regular partner puts a woman's hormone symphony into optimal fertility with consequent good health. For men, too, it raises testosterone production and improves sperm quality. One likely mechanism underwriting this is chemical communication through close body contact.

Grant that men are attracted to sexy women, and women seek men who are interested in them.

Based both on adaptations proposed by evolution theory and on a variety of data about sexual practices, men and women differ somewhat in what attracts them to sexual mates. Sexual opportunity and activity arouse men. Finding a mate who will care for her (and her potential children) arouses women.

Develop a pattern of mutually satisfying sex by communicating to and listening to your partner.

Both evolution theory and social evidence indicate that women have less orgasmic experience than men during sex, but the causes are at least in part based in the ways the sexual act is consummated. Women's stimulation needs change regularly; for their satisfaction, this must be recognized by their men partners and communicated to them by the women.

Welcome sexual fantasies as common experiences.

Both men and women experience sexual fantasies, both during sexual activities and in other settings. Men's fantasies tend to use past experiences, whereas women are inclined to fantasize about exciting possibilities.

Build part of your self-picture with your sexual experiences.

Both what we have done and what we have not done become components in defining who we are. Included are the kinds of partners we choose, the ways we treat others in sexual encounters, and the public reputation we allow to be broadcast.

Learn that youthful romantic love is not the material of successful lifelong love.

Media-reinforced romantic love is built from fantasy, unmet needs, and hopes. It appears rapidly with overtones of obsession and weaknesses but usually fades abruptly when the imagined ideals are not realized.

Grow a love bond with trust, respect, caring, and loyalty.

The real love of adult life is a long-term managed experience of support between people who recognize and celebrate their differences as well as their shared world. It is marked by mutual and successful communication and usually (but not necessarily) sexual activity.

Attract others to a relationship by acting normally and managing its development.

We are attracted to others who are familiar to us, meet our standards of attractiveness, and show interest in us. To ensure that the relationship develops will demand that we be noticed by and interested in others while staying inside of the bounds of what is appropriate in each setting. Progress comes from balanced and careful conversations and activities of sharing.

Get along with others by managing disorderly events according to the rules.

Social living demands order, and we are all motivated to control disruption. The management rules all aim at putting an acceptable public "face" on happenings so that they appear to be within bounds. By the ways we present ourselves in special roles or in verbal communications, the meaning of events is made acceptable.

Change the will of a majority by defending a credible position from inside the group.

Although public decisions may go against the position we present, if we stay within that group and provide a consistent defense, the seeds of change are sown. Others in the group will admire and remember that dissent, and eventually the mental conflict it engenders will be resolved in favor of change. It is important that we stay in the group, even with losses, to keep that mental conflict alive.

Influence others by using social and personality motivation principles.

We all try to follow certain rules of social living and personal expression toward others. We obey and defer to authority. We try to be like those we admire. We do what others are doing. We honor our commitments to others. We balance our actions with those of others. These social mechanisms can be called authority, attraction, conformity, commitment, and reciprocation.

Picture your own thought as the operation of complex fallible machinery.

Our sensory experiences, our sense of willful agency, and our emotional feelings make up experienced awareness or "how-it-seems-to-me." That awareness, being the product of elaborate brain machinery, is not able by itself to observe how its own thinking works. A more accurate picture must be made of collected inferences coming from an outside position.

Learn to control your awareness.

Hypnosis, meditation, and similar demonstrations appear to show unlocked powers of the mind. The only mystery in these phenomena is why we don't learn simple ways to exert control over what we hold in our mind. We can learn control over awareness in a manner not unlike learning any skill: practice, practice, practice. We aren't releasing hidden powers, but developing a latent capability.

Accept the fallibility of your logical thinking but know the likely errors.

Solving problems, deciding, and judging often have correct ways of being done, what we call the normative rules. But we have systematic biases and difficulties brought on by our brain machinery. We are limited in working memory, in breadth of content we can apprehend at a time, and in valuing a variety of personal emotional attachments. The result is a list of likely rules of thumb or mental short-cuts that sometimes lead us to poor thinking.

Be aware that any tough decision will be followed by thinking and activities that protect your choice.

We try to make our perspective consis-tent by altering our perceptions and perfor-mances. Making a tough choice means we have rejected a valued alternative. To build consistency, we come to value more highly what we have chosen and devalue what we did not. This motivational-emotional element accounts for some seemingly illogical think-ing and acting.

Keep yourself happy to improve the quality of your thinking.

When we feel good, we bring out more diverse memories, leading to being more creative and productive. We take less time to choose and decide. Furthermore, we tend to choose thinking and actions that protect that happy state.

Be wary of addiction labels and what they imply.

Addiction is a slippery concept, being largely a legal brand implying what amounts to an unproved medical condition. Wide-spread publicity of extreme failures of control convinces most of us that addiction is like a disease and cannot be shaken without lifelong outside support. Ignored in this public view are the large numbers of us who have changed toward moderation or rejection of previous habits entirely as a matter of our self-control.

Choose your habits with full knowledge of what they do to you.

Forbidden drugs are poor choices, per-haps more for political reasons than medical ones. But we also know that what is legal can be a medically poor choice. With regular moderate use, our celebrated legal drugs—al-cohol, caffeine, and (decreasingly) nico-tine—along with a potpourri of over-the-counter medications, may have more serious consequences than illegal substances. We must be mindful of the influences on us to engage these things, including their physi-ological effects and potential to manage feel-ings, our psychological dependence and incli-nation toward habit, and cultural tradition and social influence.

Decide that you will enjoy your work and be productive.

Our primary life satisfaction comes from what we do as work. We identify ourselves by it. We experience our periods of deepest in-volvement doing challenging work. Yet, we typically believe that other people don't like to work, so we make up reasons why they and we have to do it. By accepting that we will be productive in our work, we rise above the in-consistency and are free to revel in what we truly enjoy.

Ensure that others have opportunity for challenging and satisfying work.

Whether as managers, coworkers, or subordinates, when we give positive opportu-nity to others, the work environment for all improves. Productivity and work quality will follow. We need to accept that successful work is what makes people happy and satis-fied. Gradually, the self-defeating circle of managers who believe they have to coerce workers and workers who believe that they have to be coerced will fade away.

Reject reward schemes attached to work.

Rewards constrain our work perfor-mance into the prearranged scheme. They are implicit threats that make our potential cre-ativity, cooperation, and satisfaction in doing the work counterproductive. Managerial oversight should facilitate our work instead of evaluating it. Necessary compensation schemes should be divorced as far as possible from the specifics of doing the work.

Plan and enjoy periods of play.

Far from being something just children do, play is a normal part of adult functioning. We speculate that play is a normal product of our information-seeking brains. That makes us forever curious, expressed at times in exploring the unreal and the imagined beyond the world experiences we are now living. Play gives us a protected opportunity to try out those divergent activities.

Accept leisure activity as necessary to mental and physical health.

Our leisure acts aren't just rest or random activity. We can be amazed at the variety of what we do when we are not working or meeting other essential life needs. Study shows that we don't tolerate restriction of leisure, mentally or physically. Yet, we also don't find as many periods of deep involvement during leisure as we do during work. We often claim our leisure activity to be the most treasured part of living, although the reality may be that much of it is relatively boring. Still, that boring time seems in some sense necessary. Perhaps we are also not designed to be optimally challenged all of the time.

References

Ackerman, D. (1992). *The moon by whale light.* New York: Vantage.

Adams, J. S. (1963). Toward an understanding of inequity. *Journal of Abnormal and Social Psychology, 67,* 422-436.

Adams, J. S. (1965). Inequality in social exchange. In L. Berkowitz (Ed.), *Advances in experimental social psychology* (Vol. 2, pp. 267-299). New York: Academic Press.

Adler, A. (1930). Individual psychology: Some of the problems fundamental to all psychology. In C. Murchison (Ed.), *Psychologies of 1930* (pp. 395-405). Worcester, MA: Clark University Press.

Agnew, H. W., Webb, W. B., & Williams, R. L. (1967). Comparison of stage four and 1-REM sleep deprivation. *Perceptual and Motor Skills, 24,* 851-858.

Ainsworth, M. D. S., & Bell, S. M. (1977). Infant crying and maternal responsiveness: A rejoinder to Gewirtz and Byrd. *Child Development, 48,* 1208-1216.

Alberti, R. E., & Emmons, M. L. (1990). *Your perfect right: A guide to assertive living.* New York: Impact Publications.

Alderfer, C. P. (1972). *Existence, relatedness, and growth: Human needs in organizational settings.* New York: Free Press.

Alexander, G. M., & Sherwin, B. B. (1993). Sex steroids, sexual behavior, and selective attention for erotic stimuli in women using oral contraceptives. *Psychoneuroendocrinology, 18,* 91-102.

Alford, K. E. (1981). The structure of joking relationships in American society. In A. T. Cheska (Ed.), *Play as context* (pp. 278-289). West Point, NY: Leisure Press.

Allman, W. F. (1994). *The stone age present: How evolution has shaped modern life—from sex, violence, and language to emotions, morals, and communities.* New York: Simon & Schuster.

Alzate, H. (1989). Sexual behavior of unmarried Columbia University students: A follow-up. *Archives of Sexual Behavior, 18,* 239-250.

Alzate, H. (1990). Vaginal erogeneity, the "G-spot," and "female ejaculation." *Journal of Sex Education and Therapy, 16,* 137-140.

Alzate, H., & Hoch, Z. (1986). The "G-spot" and "female ejaculation": A current appraisal. *Journal of Sex and Marital Therapy, 12,* 211-220.

American Psychiatric Association. (1994). *Diagnostic and statistical manual of mental disorders* (4th. ed.). Washington, DC: Author.

Angus, R. G., Heslegrave, R. J., & Myles, W. S. (1985). Effects of prolonged sleep deprivation, with and without chronic physical exercise, on mood and performance. *Psychophysiology, 22,* 276-282.

Antes, J. R. (1974). The time course of picture viewing. *Journal of Experimental Psychology, 103,* 62-70.

Antes, J. R. (1977). Recognizing and localizing features in brief picture presentations. *Memory and Cognition, 5,* 155-161.

Appley, M. H., & Trumbull, R. (1986). Development of the stress concept. In M. H. Appley & R. Trumbull (Eds.), *Dynamics of stress: Physiological, psychological, and social perspectives* (pp. 3-18). New York: Plenum.

Apter, M. J. (1982). *The experience of motivation: Theory of psychological reversals.* New York: Academic Press.

Archer, D., & Gartner, D. (1984). *Violence and crime in cross-national perspective.* New Haven, CT: Yale University Press.

Archer, J. (1991). The influence of testosterone on human aggression. *British Journal of Psychology, 82,* 1-29.

Archer, J., & Lloyd, B. (1985). *Sex and gender.* Cambridge, UK: Cambridge University Press.

Ardrey, R. (1966). *The territorial imperative.* New York: Atheneum.

Ardrey, R. (1976). *The hunting hypothesis.* New York: Atheneum.

Argyle, M., & Henderson, M. (1984). The rules of friendship. *Journal of Social and Personal Relationships, 1,* 211-237.

Argyle, M., & Henderson, M. (1985). *The anatomy of relationships.* London: Methuen.

Aries, P. (1985). Love in married life. In P. Aries & A. Bejin (Eds.), *Western sexuality: Practice and percept in past and present times* (pp. 130-139). Oxford & New York: Basil Blackwell.

Asch, S. E. (1952). *Social psychology.* Englewood Cliffs, NJ: Prentice Hall.

Ashton, H., & Stepney, R. (1982). *Smoking: Psychology and pharmacology.* London & New York: Tavistock.

Asterita, M. F. (1985). *The physiology of stress.* New York: Human Sciences Press.

Atkinson, J. W. (1957). Motivational determinants of risk-taking behavior. *Psychological Review, 64,* 359-372.

Averill, J. R. (1980). A constructivist view of emotion. In R. Plutchik & H. Kellerman (Eds.), *Emotion: Theory, research, and experience* (Vol. 1, pp. 305-339). New York: Academic Press

Averill, J. R. (1982). *Anger and aggression: An essay on emotion.* New York: Springer-Verlag.

Averill, J. R. (1984). The acquisition of emotions during adulthood. In C. Z. Malatesta & C. E. Izard (Eds.), *Emotions in adult development* (pp. 23-43). Beverly Hills, CA: Sage.

Ax, A. (1953). The physiological differentiation between fear and anger in humans. *Psychosomatic Medicine, 15,* 433-442.

Bagatell, C. J., Heiman, J. R., Rivier, J. E., & Bremner, W. J. (1994). Effects of endogenous testosterone and estradiol on sexual behavior in normal young men. *Journal of Clinical Endocrinology and Metabolism, 78,* 711-716.

Baize, H. R., & Schroeder, J. E. (1995). Personality and mate selection in personal ads: Evolutionary preferences in a public mate selection process. *Journal of Social Behavior and Personality, 10,* 517-536.

Baker, R. A. (1990). *They call it hypnosis.* Buffalo, NY: Prometheus.

Baker, R. (1996). *Sperm wars: The science of sex.* New York: Basic Books.

Baker, R. R., & Bellis, M. A. (1993a). Human sperm competition: Ejaculation adjustment by males and the function of masturbation. *Animal Behavior, 46,* 861-885.

Baker, R. R., & Bellis, M. A. (1993b). Human sperm competition: Ejaculation manipulation by females and a function for the female orgasm. *Animal Behavior, 46,* 885-909.

Balasubramaniam, V., Ramanujam, P. B., Kanaka, T. S., & Ramamurth, B. (1972). Stereotaxic surgery for behavior disorders. In E. Hitchcock, L. Laitiner, & K. Taernt (Eds.), *Psychosurgery* (pp. 156-163). Springfield, IL: Charles C Thomas.

Bancroft, J., Tennant, G., Loucas, K., & Cass, J. (1974). The control of deviant sexual behavior by drugs: I. Behavioural changes following oestrogens and anti-androgens. *British Journal of Psychiatry, 125,* 310-315.

Bancroft, J., & Wu, F. C. W. (1983). Changes in erectile responsiveness during androgen replacement therapy. *Archives of Sexual Behavior, 12,* 59-66.

Bandura, A. (1973). *Aggression: A social learning analysis.* Englewood Cliffs, NJ: Prentice Hall.

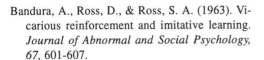

Bandura, A., Ross, D., & Ross, S. A. (1963). Vicarious reinforcement and imitative learning. *Journal of Abnormal and Social Psychology, 67,* 601-607.

Banes, S., Frank, S., & Horwitz, T. (Eds.). (1976). *Our national passion: 200 years of sex in America.* Chicago: Follett.

Barker, R., Dembo, T., & Lewin, K. (1941). Frustration and regression: An experiment with young children. *University of Iowa Studies in Child Welfare, 18*(1, Whole No. 386).

Barkow, J. H. (1992). Beneath new culture is old psychology: Gossip and social stratification. In J. H. Barkow, L. Cosmides, & J. Tooby (Eds.), *The adapted mind: Evolutionary psychology and the generation of culture* (pp. 626-637). New York: Oxford University Press.

Barkow, J. H., Cosmides, L., & Tooby, J. (Eds.). (1992). *The adapted mind: Evolutionary psychology and the generation of culture.* New York and Oxford: Oxford University Press.

Baron, R. A. (1977). *Human aggression.* New York: Plenum.

Barrett, C. (1989). The concept of leisure: Idea and ideal. In T. Winnifrith & C. Barrett (Eds.), *The philosophy of leisure* (pp. 1-19). London: Macmillan.

Bartlett, F. C. (1943). Fatigue following highly skilled work. *Proceedings of the Royal Society,* Series B, *131,* 247-257.

Bartley, S. H., & Chute, E. (1947). *Fatigue and impairment in man.* New York: McGraw-Hill.

Beach, F. A. (1969). Locks and beagles. *American Psychologist, 24,* 971-989.

Beck, A. T. (1976). *Cognitive theory and emotional disorders.* New York: International Universities Press.

Beck, A. T., & Emery, G. (1985). *Anxiety disorders and phobias: A cognitive perspective.* New York: Basic Books.

Beck, R. C. (1990). *Motivation: Theories and principles* (3rd. ed.). Englewood Cliffs, NJ: Prentice Hall.

Becker, H. S. (1963). *Outsiders: Studies in the sociology of deviance.* New York: Free Press.

Beecher, H. K. (1946, April). Pain in men wounded in battle. *The Bulletin of the U. S. Army Medical Department, 5,* 445-454.

Behar, D., Rapoport, J. L., Adams, A. J., Berg, C. J., & Cornblath, M. (1984). Sugar challenge testing with children considered "sugar reactive." *Nutritional Behavior, 1,* 277-288.

Bell, S. M., & Ainsworth, M. D. S. (1972). Infant crying and maternal responsiveness. *Child Development, 43,* 1171-1190.

Bellerose, S. B., & Binik, Y. M. (1993). Body image and sexuality in oophorectomized women. *Archives of Sexual Behavior, 22,* 435-459.

Berg, J. H., & Piner, K. (1990). Social relationships and the lack of social relationships. In S. W. Duck & R. C. Silver (Eds.), *Personal relationships and social support.* London: Sage.

Berger, H. (1929). Uber das Elecktrenkephalogramm des Menschen. *Archiv für Psychiatrie und Neurokrankheiten, 87,* 527-570.

Berkowitz, L. (1965). Some aspects of observed aggression. *Journal of Personality and Social Psychology, 2,* 359-369.

Berkowitz, L. (1970). Aggressive humor as a stimulus to aggressive responses. *Journal of Personality and Social Psychology, 16,* 710-717.

Berkowitz, L. (1989). The frustration-aggression hypothesis: An examination and reformulation. *Psychological Bulletin, 106,* 59-73.

Berkowitz, L. (1990). On the formation and regulation of anger and aggression: A cognitive-neoassociationistic analysis. *American Psychologist, 45,* 494-503.

Berkowitz, L. (1993). *Aggression: Its causes, consequences, and control.* New York: McGraw-Hill.

Berkowitz, L., Cochran, S., & Embree, M. (1981). Physical pain and the goal of aversively stimulated aggression. *Journal of Personality and Social Psychology, 40,* 687-700.

Berkowitz, L., & Geen, R. G. (1966). Film violence and the cue properties of available targets. *Journal of Personality and Social Psychology, 3,* 525-530.

Berkowitz, L., & LePage, A. (1967). Weapons as aggression-eliciting stimuli. *Journal of Personality and Social Psychology, 7,* 202-207.

Berlyne, D. E. (1958). The influence of complexity and novelty in visual figures on orienting responses. *Journal of Experimental Psychology, 55,* 289-296.

Berlyne, D. E. (1966). Curiosity and exploration. *Science, 153,* 25-33.

Bernard, J. (1990). Ground rules for marriage: Perspectives on the pattern of an era. In M. T. Norman & C. C. Nadelson (Eds.), *Women and men: New perspectives on gender differences* (pp. 89-115). Washington and London: American Psychiatric Press.

Berridge, V. (1984). Drugs and social policy: The establishment of drug control in Britain 1900-30. *British Journal of Addiction, 79,* 17-28.

Berridge, V., & Edwards, G. (1981). *Opium and the people.* London: Allen Lane/St. Martin's Press.

Bexton, W. H., Heron, W., & Scott, T. H. (1954). Effect of decreased variation in the sensory environment. *Canadian Journal of Psychology, 8,* 70-76.

Biernacki, P. (1986). *Pathways from heroin addiction: Recovery without treatment.* Philadelphia: Temple University.

Bills, A. G. (1943). *The psychology of efficiency.* New York: Harper.

Birch, L. L. (1981). Generalization of a modified food preference. *Child Development, 52,* 755-758.

Birch, L. L. (1987). The acquisition of food acceptance patterns in children. In R. A. Boakes, D. A. Popplewell, & M. J. Burton (Eds.), *Eating habits: Food, physiology, and learned behaviour* (pp. 107-130). Chichester & New York: John Wiley.

Birch, L. L., Billman, J., & Richards, S. (1984). Time of day influences food acceptability. *Appetite, 5,* 109-112.

Birch, L. L., & Deysher, M. (1985). Conditioned and unconditioned caloric compensation: Evidence for self-regulation of food intake by young children. *Learning and Motivation, 16,* 341-355.

Birch, L. L., & Marlin, D. W. (1982). I don't like it; I never tried it: Effects of exposure on two-year-old children's food preferences. *Appetite, 3,* 353-360.

Birch, L. L., Marlin, D., & Rotter, J. (1984). Eating as the "means" activity in a contingency: Effects on young children's food preference. *Child Development, 55,* 431-439.

Birch, L. L., McPhee, L., Shoba, B. C., Steinberg, L., & Krehbiel, R. (1987). "Clean up your plate": Effects of child feeding practices on the development of intake regulation. *Learning and Motivation, 18,* 301-317.

Birch, L. L., McPhee, L., Sullivan, S., & Johnson, S. (1989). Conditioned meal initiation in young children. *Appetite, 13,* 105-113.

Birch, L. L., Zimmerman, S., & Hind, H. (1980). The influence of social affective context on preschool children's food preferences. *Child Development, 51,* 856-861.

Birken, L. (1988). *Consuming desire: Sexual science and the emergence of a culture of abundance, 1871-1914.* Ithaca, NY: Cornell University Press.

Black, R. M., & Anderson G. H. (1994). Sweeteners, food intake, and selection. In J. D. Fernstrom & G. D. Miller (Eds.), *Appetite and body weight regulation: Sugar, fat, and macronutrient substitutes* (pp. 125-136). Boca Raton, FL: CRC Press.

Blumstein, P., & Schwartz, P. (1983). *American couples.* New York: William Morrow.

Blumstein, P., & Schwartz, P. (1989). Intimate relationships and the creation of sexuality. In B. J. Risman & P. Schwartz (Eds.), *Gender in intimate relationships: A microstructural approach* (pp. 120-129). Belmont, CA: Wadsworth.

Boles, J., & Garbin, A. P. (1974). Stripping for a living: An occupational study of the night club stripper. In C. D. Bryant (Ed.), *Deviant behavior: Occupational and organizational bases* (pp. 312-335). Chicago: Rand McNally.

Bonica, J. J. (1989). Local anaesthesia and regional blocks. In P. D. Wall & R. Melzack (Eds.), *Textbook of pain* (pp. 724-743). New York: Churchill-Livingstone.

Booth, D. (1990). Learned role of tastes in eating motivation. In E. D. Capaldi & T. L. Powley (Eds.), *Taste, experience, and feeding* (pp. 179-194). Washington, DC: American Psychological Association.

Booth, D. (1991). Learned ingestive motivation and the pleasures of the palate. In R. C. Bolles (Ed.), *The hedonics of taste* (pp. 29-58). Hillsdale, NJ: Lawrence Erlbaum.

Booth, D. (1994). Palatability and the intake of food and drinks. In M. S. Westerterp-Plantenga,

E. W. H. M. Frederix, & A. B. Steffens (Eds.), *Food intake and energy expenditure* (47-54). Boca Raton, FL: CRC Press.

Booth, D. A., Conner, M. T., & Marie, S. (1987). Sweetness and food selection: Measurement of sweeteners' effects on acceptance. In J. Dobbing (Ed.), *Sweetness* (pp. 143-160). London: Springer-Verlag.

Booth, D. A., Lee, M., & McAleavey, C. (1976). Acquired sensory control of satiation in man. *British Journal of Psychology, 67,* 137-147.

Booth, D. A., & Weststrate, J. A. (1994). Current issues in intake psychobiology. In M. S. Westerterp-Plantenga, E. W. H. M Frederix, & A. B. Steffens (Eds.), *Food intake and energy expenditure* (pp. 19-29). Boca Raton, FL: CRC Press.

Bowen, B. (1990). Average attractions: Psychologists break down the essence of physical beauty. *Science News, 140,* 232-234.

Bowlby, J. (1969). *Attachment and loss: Vol. 1. Attachment.* New York: Basic Books.

Bowlby, J. (1973). *Attachment and loss: Vol. 2. Separation: Anxiety and anger.* New York: Basic Books.

Bowlby, J. (1980). *Attachment and loss: Vol. 3. Loss.* New York: Basic Books.

Bowman, J. R. (1978). The organization of spontaneous adult play. In M. A. Salter (Ed.), *Play: Anthropological perspectives* (pp. 239-250). West Point, NY: Leisure Press.

Branden, N. (1980). *The psychology of romantic love.* Los Angeles: Tarcher.

Bray, G. A. (1994). Appetite control in adults. In J. D. Fernstrom & G. D. Miller (Eds.), *Appetite and body weight regulation: Sugar, fat, and macronutrient substitutes* (pp. 17-31). Boca Raton, FL: CRC Press.

Brickman, P., Rabinowitz, V. C., Karuza, J., Jr., Coates, D., Cohn, E., & Kidder, L. (1982). Models of helping and coping. *American Psychologist, 37,* 368-384.

Bridges, K. M. B. (1932). Emotional development in early infancy. *Child Development, 3,* 324-341.

Brody, L. R., & Hall, J. A. (1993). Gender and emotion. In M. Lewis & J. M. Haviland (Eds.), *Handbook of emotions* (pp. 447-460). New York: Guilford.

Brown, I. D., Tickner, A. H., & Simmons, D. C. (1970). Effect of prolonged driving on overtaking criteria. *Ergonomics, 13,* 239-242.

Brown, J. S., & Farber, I. E. (1951). Emotions conceptualized as intervening variables—with suggestions toward a theory of frustration. *Psychological Bulletin, 48,* 465-495.

Brown, P., & Levinson, S. (1987). *Politeness: Some universals in language usage.* Cambridge, UK: Cambridge University Press.

Bryan, J. H., & Text, N. (1967). Models and helping: Naturalistic studies in aiding behavior. *Journal of Personality and Social Psychology, 6,* 400-407.

Buena, F., Swerdloff, R. S., Steiner, B. S., Lutchmansingh, P., Peterson, M. A., Pandian, M. R., Galmarini, M., & Bhasin, S. (1993). Sexual function does not change when serum testosterone levels are pharmacologically varied within the normal male range. *Fertility and Sterility, 59,* 1118-1123.

Bullough, V. L. (1976). *Sexual variations in society and history.* New York: John Wiley.

Bullough, V. L. (1994). *Science in the bedroom: A history of sex research.* New York: Basic Books.

Burnham, J. C. (1993). *Bad acts: Drinking, smoking, taking drugs, gambling, sexual misbehavior, and swearing in American history.* New York: New York University Press.

Burris, A. S., Banks, S. M., Carter, C. S., Davidson, J. M., & Sherins, R. J. (1992). A long-term, prospective study of the physiologic and behavioral effects of hormone replacement in untreated hypogonadal men. *Journal of Andrology, 13,* 297-304.

Buss, A. H. (1961). *The psychology of aggression.* New York: Atheneum.

Buss, D. M. (1989). Sex differences in human mate preferences: Evolutionary hypotheses tested in 37 cultures. *Behavioral and Brain Sciences, 12,* 1-49.

Buss, D. M. (1994). *The evolution of desire: Strategies of human mating.* New York: Basic Books.

Buss, D. M., & Schmitt, D. P. (1993). Sexual strategies theory: An evolutionary perspective on human mating. *Psychological Review, 100,* 204-232.

Caillois, R. (1961). *Man, play, and games.* New York: Free Press.

Caldwell, L. S., & Lyddan, J. M. (1971). Serial isometric fatigue functions with variable intertrial intervals. *Journal of Motor Behavior, 3,* 17-30.

Calkins, M. W. (1900). Psychology as a science of selves. *Philosophical Review, 9,* 490-501.

Campbell, A. (1982). Female aggression. In P. Marsh & A. Campbell (Eds.), *Aggression and violence* (pp. 137-150). Oxford, UK: Basil Blackwell.

Campbell, A. (1993). *Men, women, and aggression.* New York: Basic Books.

Campbell, J. P., & Pritchard, R. D. (1976). Motivation theory in industrial and organizational psychology. In M. D. Dunnette (Ed.), *Handbook of industrial and organizational psychology* (pp. 63-130). New York: John Wiley.

Cancian, F. M. (1989). Love and the rise of capitalism. In B. J. Risman & P. Schwartz (Eds.), *Gender in intimate relationships: A microstructural approach* (pp. 12-25). Belmont, CA: Wadsworth.

Cannon, G., & Einzig, H. (1985). *Dieting makes you fat.* New York: Simon & Schuster.

Cannon, W. B. (1915). *Bodily changes in pain, hunger, fear, and rage.* New York: Appleton.

Cannon, W. B. (1927). The James-Lange theory of emotions: A critical examination and an alternative theory. *American Journal of Psychology, 39,* 106-124.

Cannon, W. B. (1929). *Bodily changes in pain, hunger, fear, and rage* (2nd ed.). New York: D. Appleton.

Cannon, W. B. (1932). *Wisdom of the body.* New York: Norton.

Carani, C., Bancroft, J., Del Rio, G., Granata, A. R., Facchinetti, F., & Marrama, P. (1990). The endocrine effects of visual erotic stimuli in normal men. *Psychoneuroendocrinology, 15,* 207-216.

Carmichael, M. S., Humbert, R., Dixen, J., Palmisano, G., Greenleaf, W., & Davidson, J. M. (1987). Plasma oxytocin increases in the human sexual response. *Journal of Clinical Endocrinology and Metabolism, 64,* 27-31.

Carmichael, M. S., Warburton, V. L., Dixen, J., & Davidson, J. M. (1994). Relationships among cardiovascular, muscular, and oxytocin responses during human sexual activity. *Archives of Sexual Behavior, 23,* 59-70.

Carroll, S. J., & Tosi, H. L. (1973). *Management by objectives.* New York: Macmillan.

Cashdan E. (1995). Hormones, sex, and status in women. *Hormones and Behavior, 29,* 354-366.

Chambers, E. A. (1961). Industrial fatigue. *Occupational Psychology, 35,* 44-57.

Chapman, C. R. (1984). New directions in the understanding and management of pain. *Social Science and Medicine, 19,* 1261-1277.

Chiles, W. D. (1955). *Experimental studies of prolonged wakefulness* (Technical Report Number 55-395). Dayton, OH: WADC.

Chisolm, J. S. (1995). Love's contingencies: The developmental socioecology of romantic passion. In W. Jankowiak (Ed.), *Romantic passion: A universal experience?* (pp. 42-56). New York: Columbia University Press.

Churchland, P. M. (1981). Eliminative materialism and the proposition attitudes. *Journal of Philosophy, 78(2),* 67-90.

Churchland, P. S. (1986). *Neurophilosophy: Toward a unified science of the mind-brain.* Cambridge: MIT Press.

Cialdini, R. B. (1984). *Influence: How and why people agree to things.* New York: Morrow.

Clark, R., III, & Hatfield, E. (1989). Gender differences in receptivity to sexual offers. *Journal of Psychology and Human Sex, 2,* 39-55.

Cofer, C. N., & Appley, M. H. (1964). *Motivation theory and research.* New York: John Wiley.

Cole, M. (1980). *Violent sheep: The tyranny of the meek.* New York: Times Books.

Colquhoun, W. P. (1959). The effect of a short rest-pause on inspection efficiency. *Ergonomics, 2,* 367-372.

Colquhoun, W. P. (1971). Circadian variations in mental efficiency. In W. P. Colquhoun (Ed.), *Biological rhythms and human performance* (pp. 39-107). London and New York: Academic Press.

Cosmides, L., & Tooby, J. (1992). Cognitive adaptations for social exchange. In J. H. Barkow, L. Cosmides, & J. Tooby (Eds.), *The adapted mind: Evolutionary psychology and the generation of culture* (pp. 163-228). New York: Oxford University Press.

Costanzo, P. R., & Woody, E. Z. (1985). Domain-specific parenting styles and their impact on the child's development of particular deviance: The example of deviance proneness. *Journal of Social and Clinical Psychology, 3,* 425-430.

Coulter, J. (1979). *The social construction of mind.* London: Macmillan.

Coulter, J. (1989). *Mind in action.* Atlantic Highlands, NJ: Humanities Press International.

Crawford, M., & Marsh, D. (1989). *The driving force: Food evolution and the future.* London: Heinemann.

Csikszentmihalyi, M. (1975). *Beyond boredom and anxiety.* San Francisco: Jossey-Bass.

Csikszentmihalyi, M. (1990). *Flow: The psychology of optimal experience.* New York: Harper-Collins.

Csikszentmihalyi, M., & LeFevre, J. (1989). Optimal experience in work and leisure. *Journal of Personality and Social Psychology, 56,* 815-822.

Cutler, W. B. (1991). *Love cycles: The science of intimacy.* New York: Villard.

Cutler, W. B., Garcia, C. R., & Krieger, A. M. (1979). Sexual behavior frequency and menstrual cycle length in mature premenopausal women. *Psychoneuroendocrinology, 4,* 297-309.

Cutler, W. B., Garcia, C. R., & Krieger, A. M. (1980). Sporadic sexual behavior and menstrual cycle length in women. *Hormones and Behavior, 14,* 163-172.

Cutler, W. B., Preti, G., Huggins, G. R., Erickson, B., Garcia, C. R., & Lawley, H. J. (1985). Sexual behavior frequency and biphasic ovulatory type menstrual cycles. *Physiology and Behavior, 34,* 805-816.

Cutler, W. B., Preti, G., Krieger, A., Huggins, G. R., Garcia, C. V. R., & Lawley, H. J. (1986). Human axillary secretions influence women's menstrual cycles: The role of donor extract from men. *Hormones and Behavior, 20,* 463-473.

Daly, M., & Wilson, M. (1994). Evolutionary psychology of male violence. In J. Archer (Ed.), *The behavioural biology of aggression* (pp. 253-288). Cambridge and New York: Cambridge University Press.

Darley, J. M., & Bateson, C. D. (1973). "From Jerusalem to Jericho": A study of situational and dispositional variables in helping behavior. *Journal of Personality and Social Psychology, 27,* 100-108.

Darley, J. M., & Latané, B. (1968). Bystander intervention in emergencies: Diffusion of responsibility. *Journal of Personality and Social Psychology, 8,* 377-383.

Darwin, C. (1859). *On the origin of species by means of natural selection.* London: Murray.

Davidson, J. M., & Myers, L. S. (1988). Endocrine factors in sexual psychophysiology. In R. C. Rosen & J. G. Beck (Eds.), *Patterns of sexual arousal: Psychophysiological processes and clinical applications* (pp. 158-186). New York & London: Guilford.

Dawkins, R. (1982). *The extended phenotype: The gene as the unit of selection.* Oxford & San Francisco: W. H. Freeman.

Dawkins, R. (1986). *The blind watchmaker: Why the evidence of evolution reveals a universe without design.* New York: Norton.

Dawkins, R. (1989). *The selfish gene* (rev. ed.). Oxford and New York: Oxford University Press.

Dawkins, R. (1995). *River out of Eden: A Darwinian view of life.* New York: Basic Books.

deCharms, R. (1968). *Personal causation: The internal affective determinants of behavior.* New York: Academic Press.

Deci, E. L. (1975). *Intrinsic motivation.* New York: Plenum.

Deci, E. L., & Porac, J. (1978), Cognitive evaluation theory and the study of human motivation. In M. R. Lepper & D. Greene (Eds.), *The hidden costs of rewards* (pp. 149-203). New York: John Wiley.

Deci, E. L., & Ryan, R. M. (1985). *Intrinsic motivation and self-determination in human behavior.* New York: Plenum.

D'Emilio, J., & Freedman, E. (1988). *Intimate matters: A history of sexuality in America.* New York: Harper & Row.

de Grazia, S. (1962). *Of time, work, and leisure.* Garden City, NY: Doubleday.

Dement, W. C. (1960). The effect of dream deprivation. *Science, 131,* 1705-1707.

Dennett, D. C. (1991). *Consciousness explained.* New York: Little, Brown.

Dennett, D. C. (1995). *Darwin's dangerous idea: Evolution and the meanings of life.* New York: Simon & Schuster.

Deslypere, J. P. & Vermeulen, A. (1984). Leydig cell function in normal men: Effect of age, lifestyle, residence, diet, and activity. *Journal of Clinical Endocrinology and Metabolism, 59,* 955-962.

De Waal, F. B. M. (1992). Aggression as a well-integrated part of primate social relationships: A critique of the Seville Statement on Violence. In J. Silverberg & J. P. Gray (Eds.), *Aggression and peacefulness in humans and other primates* (pp. 37-56). New York: Oxford University Press.

Dollard, J., Doob, L. W., Miller, N. E., Mowrer, O. H., & Sears, R. R. (1939). *Frustration and aggression.* New Haven, CT: Yale University Press.

Domhoff, G. W. (1993). The repetition of dreams and dream elements: A possible clue to a function of dreams. In A. Moffitt, M. Kramer, & R. Hoffman (Eds.), *The functions of dreaming* (pp. 293-320). Albany: State University of New York Press.

Donnerstein, E., & Wilson, D. W. (1976). The effects of noise and perceived control upon ongoing and subsequent aggressive behavior. *Journal of Personality and Social Psychology, 34,* 774-781.

Dornan, M. R., & Malsbury, C. W. (1989). Neuropeptides and male sexual behavior. *Neuroscience and Biobehavioral Review, 13,* 1-15.

Drewnowski, A. (1994). Human preferences for sugar and fat. In J. D. Fernstrom & G. D. Miller (Eds.), *Appetite and body weight regulation: Sugar, fat, and macronutrient substitutes* (pp. 137-147). Boca Raton, FL: CRC Press.

Druckman, D., & Bjork, R. A. (Eds.). (1991). *In the mind's eye: Enhancing human performance.* Washington, DC: National Academy Press.

Duck, S. (1991). *Understanding relationships.* New York: Guilford.

Duffy, E. (1941). An explanation of "emotional" phenomena without the use of the concept "emotion." *Journal of General Psychology, 25,* 283-293.

Duffy, E. (1951). The concept of energy mobilization. *Psychological Review, 58,* 30-40.

Duffy, E. (1962). *Activation and behavior.* New York: John Wiley.

Dunwiddie, T. V. (1988). Mechanisms of cocaine abuse and toxicity: An overview. In D. Clouet, K. Asghar, & R. Brown (Eds.), *Mechanisms of cocaine abuse and toxicity* (pp. 337-353). Rockville, MD: National Institute on Drug Abuse.

Duster, T. (1970). *The legislation of morality.* New York: Free Press.

Eaton, S. B., Shostak, M., & Konner, M. (1988). *The paleolithic prescription.* New York: Harper & Row.

Egger, M. D., & Flynn, J. P. (1963). Effect of electrical stimulation of the amygdala on hypothalamically elicited attack behavior in cats. *Journal of Neurophysiology, 26,* 705-720.

Einstein, M. A., & Hornstein, I. (1970). Food preferences of college students and nutritional implications. *Journal of Food Science, 35,* 429-435.

Ekman, P. (1972). Universals and cultural differences in facial expression of emotion. In J. Cole (Ed.), *Nebraska Symposium on Motivation, 1971.* Lincoln: University of Nebraska Press.

Ekman, P. (1973). Cross-cultural studies of facial expression. In P. Ekman (Ed.), *Darwin and facial expression: A century of research in review* (pp. 169-222). New York: Academic Press.

Ekman, P. (1977). Biological and cultural contributions to body and facial movement. In J. Blacking (Ed.), *The anthropology of the body* (pp. 39-84). London: Academic Press.

Ekman, P. (1984). Expression and the nature of emotion. In K. R. Scherer & P. Ekman (Eds.), *Approaches to emotion* (pp. 319-343). Hillsdale, NJ: Lawrence Erlbaum.

Ekman, P. (1992a). Are there basic emotions? *Psychological Review, 99,* 550-553.

Ekman, P. (1992b). Facial expressions of emotions: New findings, new questions. *Psychological Science, 3,* 34-38.

Ellman, S. J., Spielman, A. J., Luck, D., Steiner, S. S., & Halperin, R. (1991). REM deprivation: A review. In S. J. Ellman & J. S. Antrobus (Eds.), *The mind in sleep: Psychology and psy-*

chophysiology (2nd ed., pp. 329-376). New York: John Wiley.

Emde, R. N., Gaensbauer, T. J., & Harmon, R. J. (1976). Emotional expressions in infancy: A biobehavioral study. *Psychological Issues. A Monograph Series, 10*(1). New York: International Universities Press.

Emswiller, R., Deaux, K., & Willits, J. (1971). Similarity, sex, and requests for small favors. *Journal of Applied Social Psychology, 1,* 284-291.

Eron, L. D. (1987). The development of aggressive behavior from the perspective of a developing behaviorism. *American Psychologist, 42,* 435-442.

Ervin, F. R., & Martin, J. (1986). Neurophysiological bases of the primary emotions. In R. Plutchik & H. Kellerman (Eds.), *Emotion: Theory, research, and experience: Vol. 3. Biological foundations of emotion* (pp. 145-170). Orlando, FL: Academic Press.

Escalona, S. K. (1945). Feeding disturbances in very young children. *American Journal of Orthopsychiatry, 15,* 76-80.

Evans, F. J. (1974). The placebo response in pain reduction. In J. J. Bonica (Ed.), *Advances in neurology* (Vol. 4, pp. 289-296). New York: Raven Press.

Farrington, D. P. (1989). Early predictors of adolescent aggression and adult violence. *Violence and Victims, 4,* 79-100.

Fausto-Sterling, A. (1985). *Myths of gender: Biological theories of women and men.* New York: Basic Books.

Feinberg, I., Fein, G., & Floyd, T. C. (1980). EEG patterns during and following extended sleep in young adults. *Electroencephalography and Clinical Neurophysiology, 50,* 467-476.

Feinman, S., & Gill, G. W. (1978). Sex differences in physical attractiveness preferences. *Journal of Social Psychology, 105,* 43-52.

Felson, R. B. (1984). Patterns of aggressive social interaction. In A. Mummendey (Ed.), *Social psychology of aggression: From individual behavior to social interaction* (pp. 107-126). Berlin: Springer-Verlag.

Felson, R. B., & Ribner, S. A. (1981). An attributional approach to accounts and sanctions for criminal violence. *Social Psychology Quarterly, 44,* 137-142.

Ferrence, R. G. (1980). Sex differences in prevalence of problem drinking. In O. J. Kalant (Ed.), *Research advances in alcohol and drug problems: Vol. 5. Alcohol and drug problems in women.* New York: Plenum.

Festinger, L. (1950). Informal social communication. *Psychological Review, 57,* 271-282.

Festinger, L. (1957). *A theory of cognitive dissonance.* Evanston, IL: Row, Peterson.

Festinger, L., Pepitone, A., & Newcomb, T. (1952). Some consequences of deindividuation in a group. *Journal of Abnormal and Social Psychology, 47,* 382-389.

Fieldhouse, P. (1986). *Food and nutrition: Customs and culture.* London: Croom Helm.

Fillmore, K. M. (1988). *Alcohol use across the life course: A critical review of 70 years of international longitudinal research.* Toronto: Addiction Research Foundation.

Fisher, H. E. (1992). *Anatomy of love: The natural history of monogamy, adultery, and divorce.* New York: Norton.

Fisher, H. (1995). The nature and evolution of romantic love. In W. Jankowiak (Ed.), *Romantic passion: A universal experience?* (pp. 24-41). New York: Columbia University Press.

Fisher, M. (1990). *Personal love.* London: Duckworth.

Fisher, S. (1973). *The female orgasm: Psychology, physiology, and fantasy.* New York: Basic Books.

Fodor, J. A. (1983). *Modularity of mind.* Cambridge: MIT Press.

Folkard, S. (1982). Circadian rhythms and human memory. In F. M. Brown & R. C. Graeber (Eds.), *Rhythmic aspects of behavior* (pp. 241-272). Hillsdale, NJ: Lawrence Erlbaum.

Folkard, S. (1983). Diurnal variation. In G. R. J. Hockey (Ed.), *Stress and fatigue in human performance* (pp. 245-272). New York: John Wiley.

Folkard, S., & Monk, T. H. (1980). Circadian rhythms in human memory. *British Journal of Psychology, 71,* 295-307.

Folkman, S., & Lazarus, R. (1980). An analysis of coping in a middle-aged community sample. *Journal of Health and Social Behavior, 21,* 219-239.

Fordyce, W. E. (1976). *Behavioral methods for chronic pain and illness.* St. Louis, MO: C. V. Mosby.

Forgas, J. P. (1986). Cognitive representations of aggressive situations. In A. Campbell & J. J. Gibbs (Eds.), *Violent transactions: The limits of personality* (pp. 41-58). Oxford, UK: Basil Blackwell.

Foulkes, W. D. (1985). *Dreaming: A cognitive-psychological analysis.* Hillsdale, NJ: Lawrence Erlbaum.

Foulkes, W. D., & Schmidt, M. (1983). Temporal sequence and unit composition in dream reports from different stages of sleep. *Sleep, 6,* 265-280.

Fox, R. (1982). The violent imagination. In P. Marsh & A. Campbell (Eds.), *Aggression and violence* (pp. 6-26). Oxford, UK: Basil Blackwell.

Frank, G., Halberg, F., Harner, R., Mathews, J., Johnson, E., Gravem, H., & Andrus, V. (1966). Circadian periodicity, adrenal corticosteroids, and the EEG of normal man. *Journal of Psychiatric Research, 4,* 73-86.

Franken, R. E. (1993). *Human motivation* (3rd ed.). Pacific Grove, CA: Brooks/Cole.

Frankenhaeuser, M. (1986). A psychobiological framework for research on human stress and coping. In M. H. Appley & R. Trumbull (Eds.), *Dynamics of stress: Physiological, psychological, and social perspectives* (pp. 101-116). New York: Plenum.

Freedman, J. L. (1975). *Crowding and behavior.* San Francisco: W. H. Freeman.

Freeman, G. L. (1948). *The energetics of human behavior.* Ithaca, NY: Cornell University Press.

Freeman, J. L., Sears, D. O., & Carlsmith, J. M. (1978). *Social psychology* (3rd ed.). Englewood Cliffs, NJ: Prentice Hall.

Freud, S. (1948). *Beyond the pleasure principle.* London: Hogarth. (Original work published 1920)

Freud, S. (1950). *Interpretation of dreams* (A. A. Brill, Trans.). New York: Modern Library. (Original work published 1900)

Freud, S. (1959). Inhibitions, symptoms, and anxiety. In J. Strachey (Trans.), *Standard edition of the complete psychological works of Sigmund Freud* (Vol. 20, pp. 77-175). London: Hogarth. (Original work published 1926)

Freud, S. (1962). *Three essays on the theory of sexuality* (J. Stachey, Ed. and Trans.). New York: Basic Books.

Freud, S. (1963). Introductory lectures on psychoanalysis. In J. Strachey (Trans.), *Standard edition of the complete psychological works of Sigmund Freud* (Vol. 16, pp. 243-496). London: Hogarth. (Original work published 1917)

Frey, D. (1986). Recent research on selective exposure to information. In L. Berkowitz (Ed.), *Advances in experimental social psychology* (Vol. 19, pp. 41-80). New York: Academic Press.

Friedman, M., & Rosenman, R. H. (1974). *Type A behavior and your heart.* New York: Knopf.

Friedmann, J., Globus, G., Huntley, A., Mullaney, D., Naitoh, P., & Johnson, L. (1977). Performance and mood during and after gradual sleep reduction. *Psychophysiology, 14,* 245-250.

Frodi, A. (1975). The effect of exposure to weapons on aggressive behavior from a cross-cultural perspective. *International Journal of Psychology, 10,* 283-292.

Funkenstein, D. H. (1956). Nor-epinephrine-like and epinephrine-like substances in relation to human behavior. *Journal of Mental Disease, 124,* 56-68.

Gal, R., & Lazarus, R. S. (1975). The role of activity in anticipating and confronting stressful situations. *Journal of Human Stress, 1,* 4-20.

Garn, S. M. (1985). Continuities and changes in fatness from infancy through adulthood. *Current Problems in Pediatrics, 15*(2).

Gaskell, G. (1990). Collective behavior in a societal context. In H. T. Himmelweit & G. Gaskell (Eds.), *Societal psychology* (pp. 252-272). Newbury Park, CA: Sage.

Gauld, A. (1992). *A history of hypnosis.* Cambridge, UK: Cambridge University Press.

Geen, R. G. (1978). Effects of attack and uncontrollable noise on aggression. *Journal of Research in Personality, 12,* 15-29.

Geer, J. H., & Maisel, E. (1972). Evaluating the effects of the prediction-control confound. *Journal of Personality and Social Psychology, 23,* 314-319.

Gibbs, J. J. (1986). Alcohol consumption, cognition, and context: Examining tavern violence. In A. Campbell & J. J. Gibbs (Eds.), *Violent transactions: The limits of personality* (pp. 133-151): Oxford, UK: Basil Blackwell.

Giddens, A. (1992). *The transformation of intimacy: Sexuality, love, and eroticism in modern societies.* Stanford, CA: Stanford University Press.

Gillis, J. R. (1988). From ritual to romance: Toward an alternative history of love. In C. Z. Stearns & P. N. Stearns (Eds.), *Emotion and social change: Toward a new psychohistory* (pp. 87-121). New York & London: Holmes & Meier.

Givens, D. B. (1983). *Love signals: How to attract a mate.* New York: Crown.

Goffman, E. (1955). On face-work: An analysis of ritual elements in social interaction. *Psychiatry: Journal for the Study of Interpersonal Processes, 18,* 213-231.

Goffman, E. (1959). *The presentation of self in everyday life.* New York: Doubleday.

Goldblatt, P. B., Moore, M. E., & Stunkard, A. J. (1965). Social factors in obesity. *Journal of the American Medical Association, 192,* 1039-1044.

Goldstein, J. H. (1986). Sport and aggression. In A. Campbell & J. J. Gibbs (Eds.), *Violent transactions: The limits of personality* (pp. 249-257). Oxford, UK: Basil Blackwell.

Goldstein, J. H. (1989). Beliefs about human aggression. In J. Groebel & R. A. Hinde (Eds.), *Aggression and war: Their biological and social bases* (pp. 10-19). Cambridge, UK: Cambridge University Press.

Goodman, J. (1993). *Tobacco in history: The cultures of dependence.* London and New York: Routledge.

Goodman, P. S. (1974). An examination of referents used in the evaluation of pay. *Organizational Behavior and Human Performance, 12,* 170-195.

Graburn, N. H. (1983). The anthropology of tourism. *Annals of Tourism Research, 10,* 9-33.

Graburn, N. H. (1989). Tourism: The sacred journey. In V. Smith (Ed.), *Hosts and guests: The anthropology of tourism* (pp. 21-36). Philadelphia: University of Pennsylvania.

Graham, C. A., & McGrew, W. C. (1980). Menstrual synchrony in female undergraduates living on a coeducational campus. *Psychoneuroendocrinology, 5,* 245-252.

Gray, J. A. (1987). *The psychology of fear and stress* (2nd ed.). Cambridge, UK: Cambridge University Press.

Griffitt, W. (1970). Environmental effects on interpersonal affective behavior: Ambient effective temperature and attraction. *Journal of Personality and Social Psychology, 15,* 240-244.

Griggs, R. A., & Cox, J. R. (1982). The elusive thematic-materials effect in Wason's selection task. *British Journal of Psychology, 73,* 407-420.

Groos, K. (1901). *The play of man.* New York: D. Appleton.

Gruen, R. J. (1993). Stress and depression: Toward the development of integrative models. In L. Goldberger & S. Breznitz (Eds.), *Handbook of stress: Theoretical and clinical aspects* (2nd ed., pp. 550-569). New York: Free Press.

Gruenberg, B. (1980). The happy worker: An analysis of educational and occupational differences in determinants of job satisfaction. *American Journal of Sociology, 86,* 247-271.

Gulevich, G., Dement, W., & Johnson, L. (1966). Psychiatric and EEG observations on a case of prolonged (264 hours) wakefulness. *Archives of General Psychiatry, 15,* 29-35.

Guyton, A. C. (1991). *Textbook of medical physiology* (8th ed.). Philadelphia: Saunders.

Hackman, J. R. (1991). Work design. In R. M. Steers & L. W. Porter (Eds.), *Motivation and work behavior* (5th ed., pp. 418-444). New York: McGraw-Hill.

Hackman, J. R., & Oldham, G. R. (1975). Development of the job diagnostic survey. *Journal of Applied Psychology, 60,* 159-170.

Hackman, J. R., & Oldham, G. R. (1976). Motivation through the design of work: Test of a theory. *Organizational Behavior and Human Performance, 16,* 250-279.

Hagen, R. (1979). *The bio-sexual factor.* Garden City, NY: Doubleday.

Halberg, F. (1959). Physiologic 24-hour periodicity: General and procedural considerations with reference to the adrenal cycle. *Z. Vitamin-Hormon-Fermentforsch, 10,* 225-296.

Haldeman, S. (1989). Manipulation and massage for the relief of pain. In P. D. Wall & R. Melzack (Eds.), *Textbook of pain* (pp. 942-951). New York: Churchill-Livingstone.

Halgren, E. (1981). The amygdala contribution to emotion and memory: Current studies in humans. In Y. Ben-Ari (Ed.), *The amygdaloid complex* (pp. 395-408). Amsterdam: Elsevier.

Hall, G. S. (1906). *Youth.* New York: Appleton.

Hammerton, M. (1971). Violent exercise and a cognitive task. *Ergonomics, 14,* 265-267.

Hammerton, M., & Tickner, A. H. (1968). Physical fitness and skilled work after exercise. *Ergonomics, 11,* 41-45.

Handelman, D. (1977). Play and ritual: Complementary forms of metacommunication. In A. J. Chapman & H. Foot (Eds.), *It's a funny thing, humour* (pp. 185-192). London: Pergamon.

Hannay, A. (1990). *Human consciousness.* London and New York: Routledge.

Hariton, E. B., & Singer, J. L. (1974). Women's fantasies during sexual intercourse: Normative and theoretical implications. *Journal of Consulting and Clinical Psychology, 42,* 312-322.

Harré, R. (Ed.). (1986). *The social construction of emotions.* Oxford: Basil Blackwell.

Harré, R. (1988). Wittgenstein and artificial intelligence. *Philosophical Psychology, 1,* 105-115.

Harris, M., & Ross, E. B. (Eds.). (1987). *Food and evolution: Toward a theory of human food habits.* Philadelphia: Temple University Press.

Hartman, E. L. (1973). *The functions of sleep.* New Haven, CT: Yale University Press.

Hatfield, E. (1988). Passionate and companionate love. In R. Sternberg & M. L. Barnes (Eds.), *The psychology of love* (pp. 191-217). New Haven, CT: Yale University Press.

Hatfield, E., & Walster, G. W. (1978). *A new look at love.* Lanthan, MA: University Press of America.

Hays, R. B. (1989). The day-to-day functioning of close versus casual friendship. *Journal of Social and Personal Relationships, 7,* 21-37.

Hazan, C., & Shaver, P. (1987). Romantic love conceptualized as an attachment process. *Journal of Personality and Social Psychology, 52,* 511-524.

Hazen, H. (1983). *Endless rapture: Rape, romance, and the female imagination.* New York: Scribner's.

Hebb, D. O. (1946). On the nature of fear. *Psychological Review, 53,* 259-286.

Hebb, D. O. (1949). *The organization of behavior.* New York: Wiley-Interscience.

Heidbreder, E. (1933). *Seven psychologies.* New York: Appleton-Century-Crofts.

Heider, F. (1944). Social perception and phenomenal causality. *Psychological Review, 51,* 358-374.

Heider, F. (1946). Attitudes and cognitive organization. *Journal of Psychology, 21,* 107-112.

Heider, F. (1958). *The psychology of interpersonal relations.* New York: John Wiley.

Helgeson, V. S., Shaver, P. R., & Dyer, M. (1987). Prototypes of intimacy and distance in same-sex and opposite-sex relationships. *Journal of Social and Personal Relationships, 4,* 195-233.

Helzer, J. E., Canino, G. J., Hwu, H.-W., Bland, R. C., Newman, S., & Yeh, S.-K. (1988). Alcoholism: A cross-national comparison of population surveys with the Diagnostic Interview Schedule. In R. M. Rose & J. E. Barrett (Eds.), *Alcoholism: Origins and outcome.* New York: Raven.

Hendrick, S. S., & Hendrick, C. (1992). *Romantic love.* Newbury Park, CA: Sage.

Henne, D., & Latham, G. P. (1985). Job dissatisfaction: What are the consequences? *International Journal of Psychology, 20,* 221-240.

Henry, J. P. (1986). Neuroendocrine patterns of emotional response. In R. Plutchik & H. Kellerman (Eds.), *Emotion: Theory, research, and experience: Vol. 3. Biological foundations of emotions* (pp. 37-60). San Diego, CA: Academic Press.

Herman, C. P., & Polivy, J. (1993). Mental control of eating: Excitatory and inhibitory food thoughts. In D. M. Wegner & J. W. Pennebaker (Eds.), *Handbook of mental control* (pp. 491-505). Englewood Cliffs, NJ: Prentice Hall.

Herzberg, F. (1966). *Work and the nature of man.* Cleveland: World Publishing.

Herzberg, F., Mausner, B., & Snyderman, B. B. (1959). *The motivation to work.* New York: John Wiley.

Hesselund, H. (1976). Masturbation and sexual fantasies in married couples. *Archives of Sexual Behavior, 5,* 133-147.

Hewitt, J. P., & Stokes, R. (1975). Disclaimers. *American Sociological Review, 40,* 1-11.

Hilgard, E. (1965). *Hypnotic suggestibility.* New York: Harcourt, Brace & World.

Hinde, R. A. (1982). *Ethology: Its nature and relations with other sciences.* New York & Oxford: Oxford University Press.

Hite, S. (1974). *Sexual honesty: By women for women.* London: Arrow.

Hite, S. (1976). *The Hite report.* New York: Macmillan.

Hite, S. (1981). *The Hite report on male sexuality.* New York: Macmillan.

Hite, S. (1987). *Women and love: A cultural revolution in progress.* New York: Knopf.

Hochschild, A. R. (1983). *The managed heart: Commercialization of human feeling.* Berkeley: University of California Press.

Holding, D. H. (1983). Fatigue. In G. R. J. Hockey (Ed.), *Stress and fatigue in human performance* (pp. 145-167). New York: John Wiley.

Holmes, T. H., & Rahe, R. H. (1967). The social adjustment rating scale. *Journal of Psychosomatic Research, 11,* 213-218.

Horne, J. A. (1976). Recovery sleep following different visual conditions during total sleep deprivation in man. *Biological Psychology, 4,* 107-118.

Horne, J. A. (1988). *Why we sleep.* Oxford and New York: Oxford University Press.

Horney, K. (1937). *The neurotic personality of our time.* New York: Norton.

Hovland, C. I., & Sears, R. R. (1940). Minor studies of aggression: VI Correlation of lynchings with economic indices. *Journal of Psychology, 9,* 301-310.

Hoyenga, K. B., & Hoyenga, K. T. (1993). *Gender-related differences: Origins and outcomes.* Boston: Allyn & Bacon.

Huizinga, J. (1950). *Homo ludens: A study of the play element in culture.* New York: Roy.

Hull, C. L. (1933). *Hypnosis and suggestibility: An experimental approach.* New York: Appleton-Century.

Hull, C. L. (1943). *Principles of behavior.* New York: Appleton-Century-Crofts.

Hunt, H. T. (1989). *The multiplicity of dreams: Memory, imagination, and consciousness.* New Haven, CT: Yale University Press.

Hunt, M. (1960). *The natural history of love.* London: Hutchinson.

Husserl, E. (1973). *Experience and judgment: Investigations in a genealogy of logic* (J. S. Churchill & K. Ameriks, Trans.). Evanston, IL: Northwestern University Press.

Inglis, B. (1989). *Trance: A natural history of altered states of mind.* London: Grafton.

Isen, A. M. (1993). Positive affect and decision making. In M. Lewis & J. M. Haviland (Eds.), *Handbook of emotions* (pp. 261-277). New York: Guilford.

Isen, A. M., & Leven, P. F. (1972). Effect of feeling good on helping: Cookies and kindness. *Journal of Personality and Social Psychology, 21,* 384-388.

Isen, A. M., & Means, B. (1983). The influence of positive affect on decision-making strategy. *Social Cognition, 2,* 18-31.

Isen, A. M., Rosenzweig, A. S., & Young, M. (1991). The influence of positive affect on clinical problem solving. *Medical Decision Making, 11,* 221-227.

Iso-Ahola, S. E., & Mannell, R. (1984). Social and psychological constraints on leisure. In M. G. Wade (Ed.), *Constraints on leisure* (pp. 111-151). Springfield, IL: Charles C Thomas.

Izard, C. (1971). *The face of emotion.* New York: Appleton-Century-Crofts.

Izard, C. (1977). *Human emotions.* New York: Plenum.

Izard, C. E. (1984). Emotion-cognition relationships and human development. In C. E. Izard, J. Kagan, & R. B. Zajonc (Eds.), *Emotions, cognition, and behavior* (pp. 17-37). New York: Cambridge University Press.

Izard, C. E. (1991). *The psychology of emotions.* New York & London: Plenum.

Izard, C. E. (1992). Basic emotions, relations among emotions, and emotion-cognition relations. *Psychological Review, 99,* 561-565.

Izard, C. E. (1993). Four systems for emotion activation: Cognitive and noncognitive processes. *Psychological Review, 100,* 68-90.

Izard, C. E., & Malatesta, C. Z. (1987). Perspectives on emotional development: I. Differential emotions theory of early emotional development. In J. D. Osofsky (Ed.), *Handbook of infant development* (2nd ed., pp. 494-554). New York: Wiley-Interscience.

Jacobson, E. (1938). *Progressive relaxation.* Chicago: University of Chicago Press.

James, W. (1884). What is an emotion? *Mind, 9,* 188-205.

James, W. (1890). *Principles of psychology.* New York: Holt.

James, W. (1894). The physical basis of emotions. *Psychological Review, 1,* 516-529.

Janis, I. L., & Mann, L. (1977). *Decision making: A psychological analysis of conflict, choice, and commitment.* New York: Free Press.

Jankowiak, W. R., & Fischer, E. F. (1992). A cross-cultural perspective on romantic love. *Ethnology, 31,* 149-155.

Jasper, H. H., & Rasmussen, T. (1958). Studies of clinical and electrical responses to deep temporal stimulation in man with some consideration of functional autonomy. *Association for Research in Nervous and Mental Diseases Proceedings, 36,* 316-334.

Jessup, B. A. (1989). Relaxation and biofeedback. In P. D. Wall & R. Melzack (Eds.), *Textbook of pain* (pp. 989-1000). New York: Churchill-Livingstone.

Johnson, R. N. (1970). *Aggression in man and animals.* Philadelphia: Saunders.

Jones, J., & Barlow, D. (1990). Self-reported frequency of sexual urges, fantasies, and masturbatory fantasies in heterosexual males and females. *Archives of Sexual Behavior, 19,* 269-279.

Jung, C. G. (1936). *Analytic psychology: Its theory and practice.* New York: Random House.

Jurgensen, C. E. (1978). What makes a job good or bad? *Journal of Applied Psychology, 63,* 267-276.

Kagan, J. (1984). The idea of emotion in human development. In C. E. Izard, J. Kagan, & R. B. Zajonc (Eds.), *Emotions, cognition, and behavior* (pp. 38-72). New York: Cambridge University Press.

Kahn, E., & Fisher, C. (1969). The sleep characteristics of the normal aged male. *Journal of Nervous and Mental Disorders, 148,* 477-494.

Kaplan, H. S. (1974). *The new sex therapy: Active treatment of sexual dysfunctions.* New York: Brunner/Mazel.

Kaplan, H. S. (1979). *Disorders of sexual desire and other new concepts and techniques in sex therapy.* New York: Simon & Schuster.

Karan, L. D., Haller, D. L., & Schnoll, S. H. (1991). Cocaine. In R. J. Frances & S. I. Miller (Eds.), *Clinical textbook of addictive disorders* (pp. 121-145). New York and London: Guilford.

Karli, P. (1991). *Animal and human aggression.* New York & Oxford: Oxford University Press.

Kelley, H. H. (1983). Love and commitment. In H. H. Kelley [and 8 others] (Eds.), *Close relationships* (pp. 265-314). New York: Freeman.

Kelly, J. R. (1983). *Leisure identities and interactions.* London & Boston: Allen & Unwin.

Kierkegaard, S. A. (1957). *The concept of dread* (2nd ed.). Princeton, NJ: Princeton University Press. (Original work published 1844)

King, H. E. (1961). Psychological effects of excitation in the limbic system. In D. E. Sheer (Ed.), *Electrical stimulation of the brain* (pp. 447-486). Austin: University of Texas Press.

King, N. (1970). A clarification and evaluation of the two-factor theory of job satisfaction. *Psychological Bulletin, 74,* 18-31.

Kinsey, A. C., Pomeroy, W. B., & Martin, C. E. (1948). *Sexual behavior in the human male.* Philadelphia: W. B. Saunders.

Kinsey, A. C., Pomeroy, W. B., Martin, C. E., & Gebhard, P. H. (1953). *Sexual behavior in the human female.* Philadelphia: W. B. Saunders.

Klama, J. (1988). *Aggression: The myth of the beast within.* New York: John Wiley.

Kleitman, N. (1963). *Sleep and wakefulness* (rev. ed.). Chicago: University of Chicago Press.

Klinnert, M. D., Campos, J. J., Sorce, J. F., Emde, R. N., & Svejda, M. (1983). Emotions as behavior regulators: Social referencing in infancy. In R. Plutchik & H. Kellerman (Eds.), *Emotion: Theory, research, and experience: Vol. 2. Emotions in early development* (pp. 57-86). New York: Academic Press.

Knussmann, R., Christiansen, K., & Couwenbergs, C. (1986). Relations between sex hormone levels and sexual behavior in men. *Archives of Sexual Behavior, 15,* 429-445.

Koestner, R., & Wheeler, R. (1988). Self-presentation in personal advertisements: The influence of implicit notions of attraction and role expectations. *Journal of Social and Personal Relationships, 5,* 149-160.

Kohn, A. (1993). *Punished by rewards: The trouble with gold stars, incentive plans, A's, praise, and other bribes.* Boston: Houghton Mifflin.

Kolb, L. (1925). Pleasure and deterioration from narcotic addiction. *Mental Hygiene, 9,* 699-724.

Kovach, K. A. (1987, September-October). What motivates employees? Workers and supervisors give different answers. *Business Horizons,* pp. 58-65.

Kreskin. (1973). *The amazing world of Kreskin.* New York: Random House.

Kreuz, L. E., & Rose, R. M. (1972). Assessment of aggressive behavior and plasma testosterone in a young criminal population. *Psychosomatic Medicine, 34,* 321-322.

Kubey, R. (1986). Television use in everyday life: Coping with unstructured time. *Journal of Communication, 36*(3), 108-123.

Kurucz, C. N., & Khalil, T. M. (1977). Probability models for analyzing the effects of biorhythms on accident occurrence. *Journal of Safety Research, 9,* 150-158.

Lacey, J. I. (1967). Somatic response patterning and stress: Some revisions of activation theory. In M. H. Appley & R. Trumbull (Eds.), *Psychological stress* (pp. 14-37). New York: Appleton-Century-Crofts.

Landis, C., & Hunt, W. A. (1939). *The startle pattern.* New York: Holt, Rinehart.

Langer, E., Blank, A., & Chanowitz, B. (1978). The mindlessness of ostensibly thoughtful action: The role of "placebic" information in interpersonal interaction. *Journal of Personality and Social Psychology, 36,* 635-642.

Lasagna, L., Mostellar, F., von Felsinger, J. M., & Beecher, H. K. (1954). A study of the placebo response. *American Journal of Medicine, 16,* 770-779.

Latané, B., & Darley, J. M. (1970). *The unresponsive bystander: Why doesn't he help?* New York: Appleton-Century-Crofts.

Latané, B., & Rodin, J. A. (1969). A lady in distress: Inhibiting effects of friends and bystanders on bystander intervention. *Journal of Experimental Social Psychology, 5,* 189-202.

Latham, G. P., & Locke, E. A. (1979, Autumn). Goal setting: A motivational technique that works. *Organizational Dynamics,* pp. 68-80.

Latham, G. P., & Yukl, G. A. (1975). Assigned versus participative goal setting with educated and uneducated woods workers. *Journal of Applied Psychology, 60,* 299-302.

Laumann, E. O., Gagnon, J. H., Michael, R. T., & Michaels, S. (1994). *The social organization of sexuality: Sexual practices in the United States.* Chicago: University of Chicago Press.

Lavie, P. (1985). Ultradian rhythms: Gates of sleep and wakefulness. In H. Schulz & P. Lavie (Eds.), *Ultradian rhythms in physiology and behavior* (pp. 148-164). Berlin: Springer-Verlag.

Lawler, E. E., III. (1973). *Motivation in work organizations.* Monterey, CA: Brooks/Cole.

Lawler, E. E., III, & Mohrman, S. A. (1987, Spring). Quality Circles: After the honeymoon. *Organizational Dynamics,* pp. 42-54.

Lazarus, M. (1883). *About the attractions of play.* Berlin: F. Dummler.

Lazarus, R. S., & Alfert, E. (1964). Short-circuiting of threat by experimentally altering cognitive appraisal. *Journal of Abnormal and Social Psychology, 69,* 195-205.

Lazarus, R. S., Coyne, J. C., & Folkman, S. (1984). Cognition, emotion, and motivation: The doctoring of Humpty-Dumpty. In K. R. Scherer & P. Ekman (Eds.), *Approaches to emotion* (pp. 221-237). Hillsdale, NJ: Lawrence Erlbaum.

Lazarus, R. S., & Folkman, S. (1984). *Stress, appraisal, and coping.* New York: Springer.

Lazarus, R. S., Speisman, J. C., Mordkoff, A. M., & Davison, L. A. (1962). A laboratory study of psychological stress produced by motion picture film. *Psychological Monographs, 76*(34, Whole No. 553), 1-35.

Leahey, T. H. (1992). *A history of psychology: Main currents in psychological thought* (3rd ed.). Englewood Cliffs, NJ: Prentice Hall.

Leakey, R. E. (1981). *The making of mankind.* London: Michael Joseph.

Leakey, R. (1994). *The origin of humankind.* New York: Basic Books.

Leakey, R. E., & Lewin, R. (1977). *Origins.* London: MacDonald and Jane's.

LeBon, G. (1960). *The crowd: A study of the popular mind.* New York: Viking. (Original work published 1895)

LeDoux, J. E. (1987). Emotion. In F. Plum (Ed.), *Handbook of physiology: Sec. 1. The nervous system: Vol. 5. Higher functions of the brain* (pp. 419-459). Bethesda, MD: American Physiological Association.

LeDoux, J. E. (1993). Emotional networks in the brain. In M. Lewis & J. M. Haviland (Eds.), *Handbook of emotions* (pp. 109-118). New York: Guilford.

Lee, J. A. (1988). Love-styles. In R. J. Sternberg & M. L. Barnes (Eds.), *The psychology of love* (pp. 38-67). New Haven, CT: Yale University Press.

Lee, R. (1979). *The !Kung San: Men, women, and work in a foraging society.* New York: Cambridge University Press.

Lehmann, B. J., & de Lateur, B. J. (1989). Ultrasound, shortwave, microwave, superficial heat, and cold in the treatment of pain. In P. D. Wall & R. Melzack (Eds.), *Textbook of pain* (pp. 932-941). New York: Churchill-Livingstone.

Leitenberg, H., & Henning, K. (1995). Sexual fantasy. *Psychological Bulletin, 117,* 469-496.

Leites, E. (1986). *The Puritan conscience and modern sexuality.* New Haven, CT: Yale University Press.

Lender, M. E., & Martin, J. K. (1982). *Drinking in America: A history.* New York: Free Press.

Lepper, M. R., & Greene, D. (Eds.). (1978). *The hidden costs of reward: New perspectives on the psychology of human motivation.* Hillsdale, NJ: Lawrence Erlbaum.

Lerner, M. J. (1977). The justice motive: Some hypotheses as to its origin and forms. *Journal of Personality, 45,* 1-52.

Levenson, R. W., Carstensen, L. L., Friesen, W. V., & Ekman, P. (1991). Emotion, physiology, and expression in old age. *Psychology and Aging, 6,* 28-35.

Levenson, R. W., Ekman, P., & Friesen, W. V. (1990). Voluntary facial expression generates emotion-specific nervous system activity. *Psychophysiology, 27,* 363-384.

Levenstein, H. A. (1988). *Revolution at the table: The transformation of the American diet.* New York: Oxford University Press.

Leventhal, H., Brown, D., Shacham, S., & Enquist, G. (1979). Effects of preparatory information about sensations, threat of pain, and attention on cold pressor distress. *Journal of Personality and Social Psychology, 37,* 688-714.

Levi, L. (1965). The urinary output of adrenaline and noradrenaline during pleasant and unpleasant emotional states. *Psychosomatic Medicine, 27,* 80-85.

Levitsky, D. A., & Strupp, B. J. (1994). Imprecise control of food intake on low-fat diets. In J. D. Fernstrom & G. D. Miller (Eds.), *Appetite and body weight regulation: Sugar, fat, and macronutrient substitutes* (pp. 179-190). Boca Raton. FL: CRC Press.

Levy, J. (1978). *Play behavior.* New York: John Wiley.

Leyens, J. P., Camino, L., Parke, R. D., & Berkowitz, L. (1975). Effects of movie violence on aggression in a field setting as a function of group dominance and cohesion. *Journal of Personality and Social Psychology, 32,* 346-360.

Liebowitz, M. R. (1983). *The chemistry of love.* Boston: Little, Brown.

Lilly, J. C. (1956). Mental effects of reduction of ordinary levels of physical stimuli on intact, healthy persons. *Psychiatric Research Reports, No. 5.*

Locke, E. A., & Latham, G. P. (1990a). Work motivation: The high performance cycle. In U. Kleinbeck, H.-H. Quast, H. Thierry, & H. Häcker (Eds.), *Work motivation* (pp. 3-25). Hillsdale, NJ: Lawrence Erlbaum.

Locke, E. A., & Latham, G. P. (1990b). Work motivation and satisfaction: Light at the end of the tunnel. *Psychological Science, 1,* 240-246.

Locke, E. A., & Latham, G. P. (1994). Goal setting theory. In H. F. O'Neil, Jr., & M. Drillings (Eds.), *Motivation: Theory and research* (pp. 13-30). Hillsdale, NJ: Lawrence Erlbaum.

Locke, E. A., & Schweiger, D. M. (1979). Participation in decision making: One more look. *Research in Organizational Behavior, 1,* 265-339.

Logue, A. W. (1991). *The psychology of eating and drinking* (2nd ed.). New York: W. H. Freeman.

Lore, R. K., & Schultz, L. A. (1993). Control of aggression: A comparative perspective. *American Psychologist, 48,* 16-25.

Lorenz, K. (1966). *On aggression.* London: Methuen.

Luce, G. G. (1971). *Biological rhythms in human and animal physiology.* New York: Dover.

Lutz, C. A. (1990). Engendered emotion: Gender, power, and the rhetoric of emotional control in American discourse. In C. A. Lutz & L. Abu-Lughod (Eds.), *Language and the politics of emotion* (pp. 69-91). Cambridge and New York: Cambridge University Press.

Lyman, B. (1989). *A psychology of food: More than a matter of taste.* New York: AVI, Van Nostrand Reinhold.

MacDonald, A. J. R. (1989). Acupuncture analgesia and therapy. In P. D. Wall & R. Melzack (Eds.), *Textbook of pain* (pp. 906-919). New York: Churchill-Livingstone.

Mackworth, J. F. (1970). *Vigilance and attention: A signal detection approach.* Harmondsworth, UK: Penguin.

MacLean, P. D. (1949). Psychosomatic disease and the "visceral brain": Recent developments bearing on the Papez theory of emotions. *Psychosomatic Medicine, 11,* 338-353.

MacLean, P. D. (1970). The limbic brain in relation to the psychoses. In P. D. Black (Ed.), *Physiological correlates of emotion* (pp. 129-146). New York: Academic Press.

MacLean, P. D. (1980). Sensory and perceptive factors in emotional functions of the triune brain. In A. O. Rorty (Ed.), *Explaining emotions* (pp. 9-36). Berkeley: University of California Press.

MacLean, P. D. (1993). Cerebral evolution of emotion. In M. Lewis & J. M. Haviland (Eds.), *Handbook of emotions* (pp. 67-83). New York: Guilford.

Maidini, E. A. (1991). Comparative study of Herzberg's two-factor theory of job satisfaction among public and private sectors. *Public Personnel Management, 20,* 441-448.

Maier, N. R. F. (1949). *Frustration: The study of behavior without a goal.* New York: McGraw-Hill.

Mandler, G. (1985). *Cognitive psychology: An essay in cognitive science.* Hillsdale, NJ: Lawrence Erlbaum.

Mandler, G. (1975). *Mind and emotion.* New York: John Wiley.

Mangan, G. L., & Golding, J. F. (1984). *The psychopharmacology of smoking.* Cambridge, UK: Cambridge University Press.

Marks, V. H., Ervin, F. R., & Sweet, W. H. (1972). Deep temporal lobe stimulation in man. In B. E. Eleftheriou (Ed.), *The neurobiology of the amygdala* (pp. 485-507). New York: Plenum.

Marsh, P. (1982). Rhetorics of violence. In P. Marsh & A. Campbell (Eds.), *Aggression and violence* (pp. 102-117). Oxford: Basil Blackwell.

Marsh, P., Rosser, E., & Harré, R. (1978). *The rules of disorder.* London: Routledge & Kegan Paul.

Maslow, A. H. (1970). *Motivation and personality* (2nd ed.). New York: Harper & Row.

Masters, W. H., & Johnson, V. E. (1966). *Human sexual response.* Boston: Little, Brown.

Mattes, R. D. (1987). Sensory influences on food intake and utilization in humans. *Human Nutrition: Applied Nutrition, 41A,* 77-95.

Mattsson, A., Schalling, D., Olweus, D., Low, H., & Svensson, J. (1980). Plasma testosterone: Aggressive behavior and personality dimensions in young male delinquents. *Journal of the American Academy of Child Psychiatry, 19,* 476-490.

Mayer, J. (1955). Regulation of energy intake and body weight, the glucostatic theory, and the lipostatic hypothesis. *Annals of the New York Academy of Sciences, 63,* 15-43.

Maynard Smith, J. (1982). *Evolution and the theory of games.* Cambridge, UK: Cambridge University Press.

Mazur, A. (1983). Hormones, aggression, and dominance in humans. In B. B. Svare (Ed.), *Hormones and aggressive behavior.* New York: Plenum.

McCaghy, C. H., & Skipper, J. K., Jr. (1972). Stripping: Anatomy of a deviant life style. In S. D. Feldman & G. W. Thiebar (Eds.), *Life styles: Diversity in American society.* Boston: Little, Brown.

McCauley, C., & Swann, C. P. (1978). Male-female differences in sexual fantasy. *Journal of Research in Personality, 12,* 76-86.

McClelland, D. C. (1961). *The achieving society.* Princeton, NJ: Van Nostrand.

McClelland, D. C. (1965). Toward a theory of motive acquisition. *American Psychologist, 20,* 321-333.

McClintock, M. K. (1971). Menstrual symphony and suppression. *Nature, 229,* 244-245.

McFarland, R. A. (1953). *Human factors in air transportation.* New York: McGraw-Hill.

McGinn, C. (1991). *The problem of consciousness.* Oxford and Cambridge, MA: Basil Blackwell.

McGinty, D. J., Harper, T. M., & Fairbanks, M. K. (1974). Neuronal unit activity and the control of sleep states. In E. Weitzman (Ed.), *Advances in sleep research* (Vol. 1). New York: Spectrum.

McGregor, D. M. (1960). *The human side of enterprise.* New York: McGraw-Hill.

McPhail, C. (1991). *The myth of the madding crowd.* New York: Aldine de Gruyter.

McPhail, C., & Wohlstein, R. (1983). Individual and collective behavior within gatherings, demonstrations, and riots. *Annual Review of Sociology, 9,* 579-600.

Mead, G. H. (1934). *Mind, self, and society.* Chicago: University of Chicago Press.

Mead, M. (1975). Review of Darwin and facial expression. *Journal of Communication, 25,* 209-213.

Meddis, R. (1977). *The sleep instinct.* London and Boston: Routledge & Kegan Paul.

Mednick, R. A. (1977). Gender-specific variables in sexual fantasy. *Journal of Personality Assessment, 41,* 248-254.

Mednick, S. A., Pollock, V., Volavka, J., & Gabrielli, W. F., Jr. (1982). Biology and violence. In M. E. Wolfgang & N. A. Weiner (Eds.), *Criminal violence.* Beverly Hills, CA: Sage.

Mehrabian, A. (1967). Substitute for apology: Manipulation of cognitions to reduce negative attitude toward self. *Psychological Reports, 20,* 687-692.

Meichenbaum, D., & Fitzpatrick, D. (1993). A constructivist narrative perspective on stress and coping: Stress inoculation applications. In L. Goldberger & S. Breznitz (Eds.), *Handbook of stress: Theoretical and clinical aspects* (2nd ed., pp. 706-723). New York: Free Press.

Meller, R. (1982). Aggression in primate social groups: Hormonal correlates. In P. Marsh & A. Campbell (Eds.), *Aggression and violence* (pp. 118-136). Oxford: Basil Blackwell.

Melzack, R. (1975). The McGill Pain Questionnaire: Major properties and scoring methods. *Pain, 1,* 277-299.

Melzack, R. (1986). Neurophysiological foundations of pain. In R. A. Sternbach (Ed.), *The psychology of pain* (2nd ed., pp. 1-24). New York: Raven.

Melzack, R. (1989). Folk medicine and the sensory modulation of pain. In P. D. Wall & R. Melzack (Eds.), *Textbook of pain* (pp. 897-905). New York: Churchill-Livingstone.

Melzack, R., & Casey, K. L. (1968). Sensory, motivational, and central control determinants of pain: A new conceptual model. In D. Kenshalo (Ed.), *The skin senses* (pp. 423-443). Springfield: Charles C Thomas.

Melzack, R., & Wall, P. D. (1965). Pain mechanisms: A new theory. *Science, 150,* 971-979.

Melzack, R., & Wall, P. D. (1982). *The challenge of pain.* New York: Basic Books.

Melzack, R., & Wall, P. D. (1988). *The challenge of pain* (2nd ed.). New York: Penguin.

Merskey, H., & 13 others. (1979). Pain terms: A list with definitions and notes on usage. Recommended by the IASP Subcommittee on Taxonomy. *Pain, 6,* 249-252.

Meyer, M. (1921). *The psychology of the other one.* Columbia: Missouri Book Store.

Michael, R. T., Gagnon, J. H., Laumann, E. O., & Kolata, G. (1994). *Sex in America: A definitive survey.* Boston: Little, Brown.

Milgram, S. (1974). *Obedience to authority.* New York: Harper & Row.

Miller, N. E. (1948). Studies of fear as an acquirable drive: I. Fear as motivation and fear-reduction as reinforcement in the learning of new responses. *Journal of Experimental Psychology, 38,* 89-101.

Mills, J. N. (1964). Circadian rhythms during and after three months in solitude underground. *Journal of Physiology, 174,* 217-231.

Minors, D. S., & Waterhouse, J. M. (1981). *Circadian rhythms and the human*. Bristol, UK: John Wright.

Mitchell, E. D., & Mason, B. S. (1934). *The theory of play*. New York: Barnes.

Money, J., & Erhardt, A. A. (1972). *Man & woman, boy & girl*. Baltimore, MD: Johns Hopkins University Press.

Money, J., & Schwartz, M. (1976). Fetal androgens in the early treated androgenital syndrome of 46XX homaphroditism: Influences on assertive and aggressive types of behavior. *Aggressive Behavior, 2*, 19-30.

Monk, T. H., & Folkard, S. (1983). Circadian rhythms and shiftwork. In G. R. J. Hockey (Ed.), *Stress and fatigue in human performance* (pp. 97-121). New York: John Wiley.

Morgan, E. (1982). *The aquatic ape*. New York: Stein & Day.

Morgan, E. (1990). *The scars of evolution*. London: Souvenir Press.

Morris, D. (1967). *The naked ape*. New York: McGraw-Hill.

Morris, D. (1969). *The human zoo*. New York: McGraw-Hill.

Morris, D. B. (1991). *The culture of pain*. Berkeley: University of California Press.

Moruzzi, G., & Magoun, H. W. (1949). Brain stem reticular formation and activation of the EEG. *EEG and Clinical Neurophysiology, 1*, 455-473.

Moscovici, S. (1976). *Social influence and social change*. London: Academic Press.

Moscovici, S. (1985). *The age of the crowd: A historical treatise on mass psychology*. Cambridge and New York: Cambridge University Press.

Mosher, D. L., & Abramson, P. R. (1977). Subjective sexual arousal to films of masturbation. *Journal of Consulting and Clinical Psychology, 45*, 796-807.

Moss, C. S. (1965). *Hypnosis in perspective*. New York: Macmillan.

Mowrer, O. H. (1939). Stimulus-response analysis of anxiety and its role as a reinforcing agent. *Psychological Review, 46*, 553-565.

Moyer, K. E. (1985). *Violence and aggression: A physiological perspective*. New York: Paragon House.

Much, N. C., & Shweder, R. A. (1978). Speaking of rules: The analysis of culture in breach. In W. Damon (Ed.), *Moral development* (New Directions for Child Development, No. 2). San Francisco: Jossey-Bass.

Mullaney, D. J., Johnson, L. C., Naitoh, P., Friedmann, J. K., & Globus, G. G. (1977). Sleep during and after gradual sleep reduction. *Psychophysiology, 14*, 237-244.

Murphy, C. (1986). The chemical senses and nutrition in the elderly. In M. R. Kare & D. E. Ingle (Eds.), *Interaction of the chemical senses with nutrition* (pp. 87-105). Orlando, FL: Academic Press.

Murphy, M. R., Checkley, S. A., Seckl, J. R., & Lightman, S. L. (1990). Nalone inhibits oxytocin release at orgasm in man. *Journal of Clinical Endocrinology & Metabolism, 71*, 1056-1058.

Murray, H. A. (1938). *Explorations in personality*. New York: Oxford University Press.

Murstein, B. I. (1974). *Love, sex, and marriage through the ages*. New York: Springer.

Musto, D. (1973). *The American disease: Origins of narcotic policy*. New Haven, CT: Yale University Press.

Naatanen, R. (1973). The inverted-U relationship between activation and performance: A critical review. In S. Kornblum (Ed.), *Attention and performance* (Vol. 4, pp. 155-174). New York: Academic Press.

Nankin, H. R., & Calkins, J. H. (1986). Decreased bioavailable testosterone in aging normal and impotent men. *Journal of Clinical Endocrinology and Metabolism, 63*, 1418-1420.

Neiss, R. (1988). Reconceptualizing arousal: Psychobiological states in motor performance. *Psychological Bulletin, 103*, 345-366.

Neulinger, J. (1981). *The psychology of leisure* (2nd ed.). Springfield, IL: Charles C Thomas.

Newman, R. I., & Seres, J. (1986). The interdisciplinary pain center: An approach to the management of chronic pain. In A. D. Holzman & D. C. Turk (Eds.), *Pain management: A handbook of psychological treatment approaches*. New York: Pergamon.

Nicolaidis, S. (1977). Sensory-neuroendocrine reflexes and their anticipatory and optimizing role on metabolism. In R. Kare & O. Maller

(Eds.), *The chemical senses and nutrition* (pp. 123-143). New York: Academic Press.

Nisbett, R. E. (1972). Hunger, obesity, and the ventromedial hypothalamus. *Psychological Review, 79,* 433-453.

Olweus, D. (1979). Stability of aggressive reaction patterns in males: A review. *Psychological Bulletin, 86,* 852-875.

Orne, M. T., & Dinges, D. F. (1989). Hypnosis. In P. D. Wall & R. Melzack (Eds.), *Textbook of pain* (pp. 1021-1031). New York: Churchill-Livingstone.

Ornstein, R. E. (1977). *The psychology of consciousness* (2nd ed.). New York: Harcourt, Brace & Jovanovich.

Ortony, A., & Turner, T. J. (1990). What's basic about basic emotions? *Psychological Review, 97,* 315-331.

Oswald, I. (1974). *Sleep.* Harmondsworth, UK: Penguin.

Paicheler, G. (1988). *The psychology of social influence.* Cambridge and New York: Cambridge University Press.

Pananicolaou, A. C. (1989). *Emotion: A reconsideration of the somatic theory.* New York: Gordon and Breach Science Publishers.

Pangborn, R. M., Witherly, S. A., & Jones, F. (1979). Parotid and whole-mouth secretion in response to viewing, handling and sniffing food. *Perception, 8,* 339-346.

Panksepp, J. (1982). Toward a general psychobiological theory of emotions. *The Behavioral and Brain Sciences, 5,* 407-467.

Panksepp, J. (1985). Mood changes. In P. J. Vinken, G. W. Bruynm, & H. L. Klawans (Eds.), *Handbook of clinical neurology: Vol. 1(45). Clinical neuropsychology* (pp. 271-285). Amsterdam: Elsevier Science.

Panksepp, J. (1986). The anatomy of emotions. In R. Plutchik & H. Kellerman (Eds.), *Emotion: Theory, research, and experience. Vol. 3: Biological foundations of emotions* (pp. 91-124). San Diego, CA: Academic Press.

Panksepp, J. (1992). A critical role for "affective neuroscience" in resolving what is basic about basic emotions. *Psychological Review, 99,* 554-560.

Panksepp, J., Sacks, D. S., Crepeau, L. J., & Abbott, B. B. (1991). The psycho- and neurobiology of

fear systems in the brain. In M. R. Denney (Ed.), *Fear, avoidance, and phobias: A fundamental analysis* (pp. 7-59). Hillsdale, NJ: Lawrence Erlbaum.

Papez, J. W. (1937). A proposed mechanism of emotion. *Archives of Neurology and Psychiatry, 38,* 725-743.

Parke, R. D., Berkowitz, L., Leyens, J. P., West, S. G., & Sebastian, R. J. (1977). Some effects of violent and nonviolent movies on the behavior of juvenile delinquents. In L. Berkowitz (Ed.), *Advances in experimental social psychology* (Vol. 10, pp. 135-172). New York: Academic Press.

Parten, M. B. (1933). Social play among preschool children. *Journal of Abnormal and Social Psychology, 28,* 136-147.

Pátkai, P. (1971). Catecholamine excretion in pleasant and unpleasant situations. *Acta Psychologica, 35,* 352-363.

Patrick, G. T. W. (1916). *The psychology of relaxation.* Boston: Houghton Mifflin.

Patterson, G. R. (1986). Performance models for antisocial boys. *American Psychologist, 41,* 432-444.

Pavlov, I. P. (1927). *Conditioned reflexes.* Oxford, UK: Oxford University Press.

Peele, S. (1986). The implications and limitations of genetic models of alcoholism and other addictions. *Journal of Studies on Alcohol, 47,* 63-73.

Peele, S. (1988). A moral vision of addiction: How people's values determine whether they become and remain addicts. In S. Peele (Ed.), *Visions of addiction: Major contemporary perspectives on addiction and alcoholism* (pp. 201-233). Lexington, MA: Lexington Books.

Pelchat, M. L., & Rozin, P. (1982). The special role of nausea in the acquisition of food dislikes by humans. *Appetite, 3,* 341-351.

Pennebaker, J. W., Burnham, M. A., Schaeffer, M. A., & Harper, D. C. (1977). Lack of control as a determinant of perceived physical symptoms. *Journal of Personality and Social Psychology, 35,* 167-184.

Perper, T. (1985). *Sex signals: The biology of love.* Philadelphia: ISI Press.

Perry, J. D., & Whipple, B. (1981). Pelvic muscle strength of female ejaculators: Evidence in support of a new theory of orgasm. *Journal of Sex Research, 17,* 22-39.

Persinger, M. A., Cooke, W. J., & Janes, J. T. (1978). No evidence found for relationship between biorhythms and industrial accidents. *Perceptual and Motor Skills, 46,* 423-426.

Persky, H., Charney, N., Lief, H. I., O'Brien, C. P., Miller, W. R., & Strauss, D. (1978). The relationship of plasma estradiol level to sexual behavior in young women. *Psychosomatic Medicine, 40,* 523-535.

Persky, H., Lief, H. I., O'Brien, C. P. & Strauss, D. (1977). Reproductive hormone levels and sexual behaviors of young couples during the menstrual cycle. In R. Gemme & C. C. Wheeler (Eds.), *Progress in sexology* (pp. 293-310). New York: Plenum.

Petersen, D. M., & Dressel, P. L. (1982). Equal time for women: Social notes on the male strip show. *Urban Life, 11,* 185-208.

Piaget, J. (1952). *The origins of intelligence in children.* New York: International Universities Press.

Plomin, R., Foch, T. T., & Rowe, D. C. (1981). Bobo clown aggression in childhood: Environment not genes. *Journal of Research in Personality, 15,* 331-342.

Plutchik, R. (1980). *Emotion: A psychoevolutionary synthesis.* New York: Harper & Row.

Plutchik, R. (1984). Emotions: A general psychoevolutionary theory. In K. R. Scherer & P. Ekman (Eds.), *Approaches to emotion* (pp. 197-219). Hillsdale, NJ: Lawrence Erlbaum.

Plutchik, R., & Kellerman, H. (Eds.). (1983). *Emotion: Theory, research, and experience: Vol. 2. Emotions in early development.* New York: Academic Press.

Powers, R. J., & Kutash, I. L. (1978). Substance-induced aggression. In I. L. Kutash, S. B. Kutash, L. B. Schlesinger, & associates (Eds.), *Violence: Perspectives on murder and aggression* (pp. 317-342). San Francisco: Jossey-Bass.

Pribram, K., & McGuinness, D. (1975). Arousal, activation, and effort in the control of attention. *Psychological Review, 82,* 116-149.

Quadagno, D. M., Shubeita, H. E., Deck, J., & Francoer, D. (1981). Influence of male social contacts, exercise, and all-female living conditions on the menstrual cycle. *Psychoneuroendocrinology, 6,* 239-244.

Quarrick, G. (1989). *Our sweetest hours: Recreation and the mental state of absorption.* Jefferson, NC: McFarland.

Rahe, R. H. (1975). Life changes and near-future illness reports. In L. Levi (Ed.), *Emotion: Their parameters and measurements* (pp. 511-529). New York: Raven.

Rahe, R. H., & Arthur, R. J. (1978). Life change and illness studies: Past history and future directions. *Journal of Human Stress, 4,* 3-15.

Raskin, M., Bali, L. R., & Peeke, H. V. (1980). Muscle biofeedback and transcendental meditation: A controlled evaluation of efficiency in treatment of chronic anxiety. *Archives of General Psychiatry, 37,* 93-97.

Read, S. J. (1992). Constructing accounts: The role of explanatory coherence. In M. L. McLaughlin, M. J. Cody, & S. J. Read (Eds.), *Explaining one's self to others: Reason giving in a social context* (pp. 3-19). Hillsdale, NJ: Lawrence Erlbaum.

Reason, J., & Mycielska, K. (1982). *Absentminded? The psychology of mental lapses and everyday errors.* Englewood Cliffs, NJ: Prentice Hall.

Rechtschaffen, A., & Kales, A. (Eds.). (1968). *A manual of standardized terminology: Techniques and scoring system for sleep stages of human subjects* (National Institute of Health, Publication No. 204). Washington, DC: Government Printing Office.

Reinberg, A., & Lagoguey, M. (1978). Circadian and circaannual rhythms in sexual activity and plasma hormones (FSH, LH, testosterone) of five human males. *Archives of Sexual Behavior, 7,* 13-30.

Reinberg, A., Smolensky, M. H., & Hallek, M. (1988). Annual variation in semen characteristics and plasma hormone levels in men undergoing vasectomy. *Fertility and Sterility, 49,* 309-315.

Reis, H. T. (1986). Gender effects in social participation: Intimacy, loneliness, and the conduct of social interaction. In R. Gilmour & S. W. Duck (Eds.), *The merging field of personal relationships.* Hillsdale, NJ: Lawrence Erlbaum.

Reiss, S. (1991). Expectancy model of fear, anxiety, and panic. *Clinical Psychology Review, 11,* 141-153.

Rice, K. M., & Blanchard, E. B. (1982). Biofeedback in the treatment of anxiety disorders. *Clinical Psychology Review, 2,* 557-577.

Robins, L. N., Helzer, J. E., & Davis, D. H. (1975). Narcotic use in Southeast Asia and afterward. *Archives of General Psychiatry, 32,* 955-961.

Robins, L. N., Helzer, J. E., Hesselbroack, M., & Wish, E. (1980). Vietnam veterans three years after Vietnam: How our study changed our view of heroin. In L. Brill & C. Winick (Eds.), *The yearbook of substance use and abuse* (Vol. 2). New York: Human Sciences Press.

Robins, L. N., Helzer, J. E., Przybeck, T. R., & Regier, D. A. (1988). Alcohol disorders in the community: A report from the Epidemiological Catchment Area. In R. M. Rose & J. E. Barrett (Eds.), *Alcoholism: Origins and outcome.* New York: Raven.

Roffwarg, H. P., Muzio, J. N., & Dement, W. C. (1966). Ontogenetic development of the human sleep-dream cycle. *Science, 152,* 604-619.

Rogers, C. R. (1963). Toward the science of the person. *Journal of Humanistic Psychology, 3,* 79-92.

Rolls, B. J., & Shide, D. J (1994). Dietary fat and control of food intake. In J. D. Fernstrom & G. D. Miller (Eds.), *Appetite and body weight regulation: Sugar, fat, and macronutrient substitutes* (pp. 167-177). Boca Raton, FL: CRC Press.

Rolls, B. J., Shide, D. J., Hoeymans, N., Jas, P., & Nichols, A. (1992). Information about fat content of preloads influencing energy intake in women. *Appetite, 19,* 123.

Romanes, G. (1886). The springs of conduct. *Nature, 33,* 436-437.

Rotter, J. B. (1966). Generalized expectancies for internal versus external control of reinforcement. *Psychological Monographs, 80*(609).

Routtenberg, A. (1968). The two-arousal hypothesis: Reticular formation and limbic system. *Psychological Review, 75,* 51-80.

Rowland, G. L., Franken, R. E., & Harrison, K. (1986). Sensation seeking and participation in sporting activities. *Journal of Sports Psychology, 8,* 212-220.

Rozin, J., & Schiller, D. (1980). The nature and acquisition of a preference for chili peppers by humans. *Motivation and Emotion, 4,* 77-101.

Rozin, P., & Kalat, J. W. (1971). Specific hungers and poison avoidance as adaptive specializations of learning. *Psychological Review, 78,* 459-486.

Rubin, R., Govin, P., Lubin, A., Poland, R., & Pirke, K. (1975). Nocturnal increase of plasma testosterone in men: Relation to gonadotrophins and prolactin. *Journal of Clinical Endocrinology and Metabolism, 40,* 1027-1033.

Rubin, Z. (1970). Measurement of romantic love. *Journal of Personality and Social Psychology, 16,* 265-273.

Rule, B. G., Taylor, B., & Dobb, A. R. (1987). Priming effects of heat on aggressive thoughts. *Social Cognition, 5,* 131-144.

Russell, M. J., Switz, G. M., & Thompson, K. (1980). Olfactory influences on the human menstrual cycle. *Pharmacology, Biochemistry, and Behavior, 13,* 737-738.

Russett, C. E. (1989). *Sexual science: The Victorian construction of womanhood.* Cambridge, MA: Harvard University Press.

Rutledge, L. L., & Hupka, R. B. (1985). The facial feedback hypothesis: Methodological concerns and new supporting evidence. *Motivation and Emotion, 9,* 219-240.

Sanders, A. F. (1986). Energetical states underlying task performance. In G. R. J. Hockey, A. W. K. Gaillard, & M. G. H. Coles (Eds.), *Energetics and human information processing* (pp. 139-154). Dordrecht and Boston: Martinus Nijhoff.

Sapolsky, R. M. (1994). *Why zebras don't get ulcers.* New York: Freeman.

Schacter, F. (1951). Deviation, rejection, and communication. *Journal of Abnormal and Social Psychology, 46,* 190-207.

Schachter, S. (1982). Recidivism and self-cure of smoking and obesity. *American Psychologist, 37,* 436-444.

Schachter, S., & Singer, J. E. (1962). Cognitive, social, and physiological determinants of emotional state. *Psychological Review, 69,* 379-399.

Scherer, K. R., & Ekman, P. (Eds.). (1984). *Approaches to emotion*. Hillsdale, NJ: Lawrence Erlbaum.

Schiller, F. V. (1875). *Essays aesthetical and philosophical*. London: George Bell.

Schlenker, B. R., & Darby, B. W. (1981). The use of apologies in social predicaments. *Social Psychology Quarterly, 44,* 271-278.

Schnarch, D. M. (1991). *Constructing the sexual crucible: An integration of sexual and marital therapy*. New York: Norton.

Schultz, D. P., & Schultz, S. E. (1996). *A history of modern psychology* (6th ed.). Fort Worth, TX: Harcourt, Brace & Jovanovich.

Schulz, H., & Lavie, P. (Eds.). (1985). *Ultradian rhythms in physiology and behavior*. Berlin: Springer-Verlag.

Schwab, R. S. (1953). Motivation in measurements of fatigue. In W. F. Floyd & A. T. Welford (Eds.), *Symposium on fatigue* (pp. 143-148). London: H. K. Lewis.

Schwartz, S. H., & Clausen, G. T. (1970). Responsibility, norms, and helping in an emergency. *Journal of Personality and Social Psychology, 16,* 299-310.

Schwartzman, J. (1981). Play: Epistemology and change. In A. T. Cheska (Ed.), *Play as context* (pp. 52-59). West Point, NY: Leisure Press.

Scott, M. B., & Lyman, S. (1968). Accounts. *American Sociological Review, 33,* 46-62.

Searle, J. (1980). Minds, brains, and programs. *Behavioral and Brain Sciences, 3,* 417-458.

Searle, J. (1988). The realistic stance. *Behavioral and Brain Sciences, 11,* 527-529.

Sears, B. (1995). *The zone: A dietary road map*. New York: Regan Books.

Sears, R. R., Maccoby, E. E., & Lewin, H. (1957). *Patterns of child rearing*. New York: Harper.

Seidman, S. (1991). *Romantic longings: Love in America, 1830-1980*. New York & London: Routledge.

Seligman, M. E. P. (1975). *Helplessness: On depression, development, and death*. San Francisco, CA: Freeman.

Selye, H. (1936). A syndrome produced by diverse nocuous agents. *Nature, 138,* 32.

Selye, H. (1976). *The stress of life* (rev. ed.). New York: McGraw-Hill.

Semin, G. R., & Manstead, A. S. R. (1983). *The accountability of conduct: A social psychological analysis*. London & New York: Academic Press.

Sherwin, B., & Gelfand, M. (1987). The role of androgen in the maintenance of sexual functioning on oophorectomized women. *Psychosomatic Medicine, 49,* 397-409.

Sherwin, B. B., Gelfand, M. M., & Brender, W. (1985). Androgen enhances sexual motivation of females: A prospective cross-over study of sex steroid administration in the surgical menopause. *Psychosomatic Medicine, 47,* 339-351.

Shields, S. (1987). Women, men, and the dilemma of emotion. In P. Shaver & C. Hendrick (Eds.), *Sex and gender* (pp. 229-250). Newbury Park, CA: Sage.

Shirley, G. (1901). *Twentieth-century lovers' guide of love, courtship and marriage*. Philadelphia: David McKay.

Siann, G. (1985). *Accounting for aggression: Perspectives on aggression and violence*. Boston: Allen & Unwin.

Siever, L. J. (1987). Role of noradrenergic mechanisms in the etiology of the affective disorders. In H. Y. Meltzer (Ed.), *Psychopharmacology: The third generation of progress*. New York: Raven.

Siffre, M. (1975). Six months alone in a cave. *National Geographic, 147,* 426-435.

Silver, B. V., & Blanchard, E. G. (1978). Biofeedback and relaxation training in the treatment of psychophysiological disorders: Or, are the machines really necessary? *Journal of Behavioral Medicine, 1,* 217-239.

Simmel, G. (1955). *Conflict: The web of group affiliation*. New York: Free Press.

Simon, W., & Gagnon, J. H. (1987). A sexual scripts approach. In J. H. Geer & W. T. O'Donohue (Eds.), *Theories of human sexuality* (pp. 363-383). New York: Plenum.

Simoons, F. J. (1961). *Eat not this flesh*. Madison: University of Wisconsin Press.

Simoons, F. J. (1982). Geography and genetics as factors in the psychobiology of human food selection. In L. M. Barker (Ed.), *The psychobiology of human food selection* (pp. 205-224). Westport, CT: AVI Publishing.

Singh, D. (1993). Body shape and female attractiveness: The critical role of waist-to-hip ratio. *Human Nature, 4*, 297-321.

Sjostrom, L. (1980). Fat cells and body weight. In A. J. Stunkard (Ed.), *Obesity* (pp. 72-100). Philadelphia: W. B. Saunders.

Smith, D. (1974). Theorizing as ideology. In R. Turner (Ed.), *Ethnomethodology*. Harmondsworth, UK: Penguin.

Smith, V. (Ed.). (1977). *Hosts and guests: The anthropology of tourism*. Philadelphia: University of Pennsylvania.

Smith, V. (Ed.) (1989). *Hosts and guests: The anthropology of tourism* (2nd ed.). Philadelphia: University of Pennsylvania.

Solomon, R. C. (1976). *The passions*. Garden City, NY: Doubleday.

Solomon, R. C. (1987). Heterosex. In E. E. Shelp (Ed.), *Sexuality and medicine: Vol. 1. Conceptual roots* (pp. 205-224). Dordrecht and Boston: D. Reidel.

Solomon, R. C. (1989). Emotions, philosophy, and the self. In L. Cirillo, B. Kaplan, & S. Wapner (Eds.), *Emotions in ideal human development* (pp. 135-149). Hillsdale, NJ: Lawrence Erlbaum.

Solomon, R. L., & Corbit, J. D. (1974). An opponent process theory of motivation: I. Temporal dynamics of affect. *Psychological Review, 81*, 119-145.

Speisman, J. C., Lazarus, R. S., & Mordkoff, A. (1964). Experimental reduction of stress based on ego-defense theory. *Journal of Abnormal and Social Psychology, 68*, 367-380.

Spence, K. W. (1956). *Behavior theory and conditioning*. New Haven, CT: Yale University Press.

Spence, K. W. (1958). A simple theory of emotionally based drive (D) and its relation to performance in simple learning situations. *American Psychologist, 13*, 131-141.

Sprecher, S. (1987). The effects of self-disclosure given and received on affection for an intimate partner and stability of the relationship. *Journal of Social and Personal Relationships, 4*, 115-127.

Sprecher, S., & McKinney, K. (1993). *Sexuality*. Newbury Park, CA: Sage.

Spring, B. (1986). Effects of foods and nutrients on the behavior of normal individuals. In R. J. Wurtman & J. J. Wurtman (Eds.), *Nutrition and the brain: Vol. 7. Food constituents affecting normal and abnormal behaviors* (pp. 1-47). New York: Raven.

Stacey, M. (1994). *Consumed: Why Americans love, hate, and fear food*. New York: Simon & Schuster.

Stahl, M. J. (1986). *Management and technical motivation: Assessment needs for achievement, power, and affiliation*. New York: Praeger.

Staw, B. (1979). The self-perception of motivation. In R. M. Steers & L. W. Porter (1979), *Motivation and work behavior* (pp. 253-269). New York: McGraw-Hill.

Stearns, C. Z., & Stearns, P. N. (1986). *Anger: The struggle for emotional control in America's history*. Chicago: University of Chicago Press.

Stearns, P. N. (1988). Anger and American work: A twentieth-century turning point. In C. Z. Stearns & P. N. Stearns (Eds.), *Emotion and social change: Toward a new psychohistory* (pp. 123-148). New York and London: Holmes and Meier.

Stebbins, R. A. (1982). Serious leisure: A conceptual statement. *Pacific Sociological Review, 25*, 251-272.

Steers, R. M., & Porter, L. W. (1975, 1979, 1983, 1987, 1991). *Motivation and work behavior*. New York: McGraw-Hill.

Steinman, D. L., Wincze, J. P., Sakheim, Barlow, D. H., & Mavissakalian, M. (1981). A comparison of male and female patterns of sexual arousal. *Archives of Sexual Behavior, 10*, 529-547.

Sternbach, R. A., & Tursky, B. (1965). Ethnic differences among housewives in psychophysical and skin potential responses to electric shock. *Psychophysiology, 1*, 241-246.

Sternberg, R. J. (1986). A triangular theory of love. *Psychological Review, 93*, 119-135.

Sternberg, R. J. (1988). *The triangle of love*. New York: Basic Books.

Stich, S. P. (1983). *From folk psychology to cognitive science*. Cambridge: MIT Press.

Stroebe, W. (1977). Self-esteem and interpersonal attraction. In S. W. Duck (Ed.), *Theory and practice in interpersonal attraction* (pp. 79-104). London: Academic Press.

Strominger, J. L., & Brobeck, J. R. (1953). A mechanism of regulation of food intake. *Yale Journal of Biology and Medicine, 25,* 383-390.

Stuart, R. B., & Davis, B. (1972). *Slim chance in a fat world: Behavioral control of obesity.* Champaign, IL: Research Press.

Sue, D. (1979). Erotic fantasies of college students during coitus. *Journal of Sex Research, 15,* 299-305.

Sullivan, S., & Birch, L. L. (1990). Pass the sugar; pass the salt: Experience dictates preference. *Developmental Psychology, 26,* 546-551.

Sunshine, A., & Olson, N. Z. (1989). Non-narcotic analgesics. In P. D. Wall & R. Melzack (Eds.), *Textbook of pain* (pp. 670-685). New York: Churchill-Livingstone.

Sutton-Smith, B. (1968). Novel responses to toys. *Merrill-Palmer Quarterly, 14,* 151-158.

Sutton-Smith, B., & Kelly-Byrne, D. (1984). The idealization of play. In P. K. Smith (Ed.), *Play in animals and humans* (pp. 305-321). Oxford, UK: Basil Blackwell.

Swensen, C. H., Jr. (1972). The behavior of love. In H. A. Otto (Ed.), *Love today: A new exploration* (pp. 86-101). New York: Association Press.

Symons, D. (1979). *The evolution of human sexuality.* New York: Oxford University Press.

Symons, D. (1987). An evolutionary approach: Can Darwin's view of life shed light on human sexuality? In J. H. Geer & W. T. O'Donohue (Eds.), *Theories of human sexuality* (pp. 91-125). New York: Plenum.

Taylor, F. W. (1911). *Principles of scientific management.* New York: Norton.

Taylor, J. A. (1953). A personality scale of manifest anxiety. *Journal of Abnormal and Social Psychology, 48,* 285-290.

Taylor, S. P., & Leonard, K. E. (1983). Alcohol and human physical aggression. In R. G. Geen & E. I. Donnerstein (Eds.), *Aggression: Theoretical and empirical reviews: Vol. 2. Issues in research.* New York: Academic Press.

Tedeschi, J. T., Gaes, J., & Rivera, A. N. (1977). Aggression and the use of coercive power. *Journal of Social Issues, 33,* 101-125.

Terry, C. E., & Pellens, M. (1928). *The opium problem.* New York: Bureau of Social Hygiene.

Thayer, R. E. (1989). *The biopsychology of mood and arousal.* New York & Oxford: Oxford University Press.

Thierry, H. (1990). Intrinsic motivation reconsidered. In U. Kleinbeck, H.-H. Quast, H. Thierry, & H. Häcker (Eds.), *Work motivation* (pp. 67-82). Hillsdale, NJ: Lawrence Erlbaum.

Thommen, A. A. (1973). *Is this your day?* New York: Crown.

Tinbergen, N. (1951). *The study of instinct.* Oxford, UK: Oxford University Press.

Tinbergen, N. (1968). On war and peace in animals and man. *Science, 160,* 1411-1418.

Tooby, J., & Cosmides, L. (1992). Chapter 1 (part): The psychological foundations of culture. In J. H. Barkow, L. Cosmides, & J. Tooby (Eds.), *The adapted mind: Evolutionary psychology and the generation of culture* (pp. 17-136). New York and Oxford: Oxford University Press.

Townsend, J. M., & Levy, G. D. (1990). Effect of potential partner's physical attractiveness and socioeconomic status on sexuality and partner selection. *Archives of Sexual Behavior, 371,* 149-164.

Trevarthen, C. (1984). Emotions in infancy: Regulators of contact and relationships with persons. In K. R. Scherer & P. Ekman (Eds.), *Approaches to emotion* (pp. 129-157). Hillsdale, NJ: Lawrence Erlbaum.

Tucker, D. M., & Williamson, P. A. (1984). Asymmetric neural control systems in human self-regulation. *Psychological Review, 91,* 185-215.

Tune, G. S. (1969). Sleep and wakefulness in 509 normal adults. *British Journal of Medical Psychology, 49,* 75-80.

Turk, D. C., Meichenbaum, D. H., & Berman, W. H. (1979). Application of biofeedback for the regulation of pain: A critical review. *Psychological Bulletin, 86,* 1322-1338.

Turk, D. C., Meichenbaum, D. H., & Genest, M. (1983). *Pain and behavioral medicine.* New York: Guilford.

Turner, C. W., & Simons, L. S. (1974). Effects of subject sophistication and evaluation apprehension on aggressive responses to weapons.

Journal of Personality and Social Psychology, 30, 341-348.

Turner, C. W., Simons, L. S., Berkowitz, L., & Frodi, A. (1977). The stimulating and inhibiting effects of weapons on aggressive behavior. *Aggressive Behavior, 3,* 355-378.

Turner, V. (1974). Liminal to liminoid in play, flow, and rituals: An essay in comparative symbology. In E. Norbeck (Ed.), *The anthropological study of play* (pp. 53-92). Houston, TX: William Marsh Rice University.

Twycross, R. G., & McQuay, H. J. (1989). Opioids. In P. D. Wall & R. Melzack (Eds.), *Textbook of pain* (pp. 686-701). New York: Churchill-Livingstone.

United Media Enterprises. (1983). *Where does the time go?* New York: Newspaper Enterprise Association.

Vaillant, G. E. (1983). *The natural history of alcoholism.* Cambridge, MA: Harvard University Press.

Vazques, M., Pearson, P. B., & Beauchamp, G. K. (1982). Flavor preferences in malnourished Mexican infants. *Physiology and Behavior, 28,* 513-519.

Vernon, J. (1963). *Inside the black room.* New York: Potter.

von Krafft-Ebing, R. (1887). *Psychopathia sexualis* (Sexual psycho-pathology). Stuttgart: Enke.

Vroom, V. H. (1964). *Work and motivation.* New York: Wiley.

Walker, W. O. III. (1991). *Opium and foreign policy: The Anglo-American search for order in Asia, 1912-1954.* Chapel Hill and London: University of North Carolina Press.

Wall, P. D. (1979). On the relation of pain to injury. *Pain, 6,* 253-264.

Wall, P. D. (1989). Introduction. In P. D. Wall & R. Melzack (Eds.), *Textbook of pain* (pp. 1-18). New York: Churchill-Livingstone.

Wall, P. D., & Melzack, R. (Eds.). (1989). *Textbook of pain.* New York: Churchill-Livingstone.

Wallace, B., & Fisher, L. E. (1987). *Consciousness and behavior* (2nd ed.). Boston: Allyn & Bacon.

Waller, N., & Shaver, P. (1994). The importance of nongenetic influences on romantic love styles: A twin-family study. *Psychological Science, 5,* 268-274.

Wason, P. (1966). Reasoning. In B. M. Foss (Ed.), *New horizons in psychology.* Harmondsworth, UK: Penguin.

Watson, J. B. (1929). *Psychology from the standpoint of a behaviorist* (3rd ed.). Philadelphia: J. B. Lippincott.

Watson, J. B., & Raynor, R. (1920). Conditioned emotional reactions. *Journal of Experimental Psychology, 3,* 1-14.

Watson, R. (1985). *The philosopher's diet: How to lose weight and change the world.* Boston: The Atlantic Monthly Press.

Webb, W. B. (1975). *Sleep: The gentle tyrant.* Englewood Cliffs, NJ: Prentice Hall.

Webb, W. B. (1979). Theories of sleep functions and some clinical implications. In R. Drucker-Colin, M. Shkurovich, & M. B. Sterman, (Eds.), *The functions of sleep* (pp. 19-35). New York: Academic Press.

Webb, W. B. (1982). Sleep in older persons: Sleep structures of 50- to 60-year old men and women. *Journal of Gerontology, 37,* 581-586.

Webb, W. B., & Agnew, H. W. (1970). Sleep stage characteristics of long and short sleepers. *Science, 168,* 146-147.

Webb, W. B., & Agnew, H. W. (1974). The effects of a chronic limitation of sleep length. *Psychophysiology, 11,* 265-274.

Weeks, J. (1981). *Sex, politics, and society: The regulation of sexuality since 1800.* London & New York: Longman.

Weeks, J. (1985). *Sexuality and its discontents: Meanings, myths, and modern sexualities.* London: Routledge & Kegan Paul.

Wever, R. A. (1975). The circadian multi-oscillator system of man. *International Journal of Chronobiology, 3,* 19-55.

Wever, R. A. (1979). *The circadian systems of man: Results of experiments under temporal isolation.* New York: Springer-Verlag.

White, R. W. (1959). Motivation reconsidered: The concept of competence. *Psychological Review, 66,* 297-333.

Williams, D. L., MacLean, A. W., & Cairns, J. (1983). Dose-response effects of ethanol on the sleep of young women. *Journal of Studies on Alcohol, 44,* 515-523.

Williams, H. L., Lubin, A., & Goodnow, J. J. (1959). Impaired performance with acute sleep loss. *Psychological Monographs, 73*(14, Whole No. 484).

Wilson, T. B. (1994). *Innovative reward systems for the changing workplace.* New York: McGraw-Hill.

Winger, G., Hofmann, F. G., & Woods, J. H. (1992). *A handbook on drug and alcohol abuse.* New York, Oxford: Oxford University Press.

Witt, P. A., & Bishop, D. W. (1970). Situational antecedents to leisure behavior. *Journal of Leisure Research, 2,* 64-77.

Wittgenstein, L. (1953). *Philosophical investigations* (G. E. M. Anscombe, Trans.). Oxford, UK: Basil Blackwell.

Wolcott, J. H., McMeekin, R. R., Burgin, R. E., & Yanowitch, R. E. (1977). Correlation of general aviation accidents with the biorhythm theory. *Human Factors, 19,* 283-293.

Wolpe, J. (1958). *Psychotherapy by reciprocal inhibition.* Stanford, CA: Stanford University Press.

Wood, W., Wong, F. Y., & Chachere, J. G. (1991). Effects of media violence on viewers' aggression in unconstrained social interaction. *Psychological Bulletin, 109,* 371-383.

Woodworth, R. S. (1918). *Dynamic psychology.* New York: Columbia University Press.

Woolf, C. J. (1989). Segmental afferent fibre-induced analgesia: Transcutaneous electrical nerve stimulation (TENS) and vibration. In P. D. Wall & R. Melzack (Eds.), *Textbook of pain* (pp. 884-896). New York: Churchill-Livingstone.

Wright, R. (1994). *The moral animal: Evolutionary psychology and everyday life.* New York: Pantheon Books.

Wright, S. (1978). *Crowds and riots: A study in social organization.* Beverly Hills, CA: Sage.

Wurtman, J. J. (1984). The involvement of brain serotonin in excessive carbohydrate snacking by obese carbohydrate cravers. *Journal of the American Dietetic Association, 84,* 1004.

Wurtman, R. (1988). Neurotransmitters, control of appetite, and obesity. In M. Winick (Ed.), *Control of appetite* (pp. 27-34). New York: John Wiley.

Wurtman, R. J., & Wurtman, J. J. (1984). Nutrients, neurotransmitter synthesis, and control of food intake. In A. J. Stunkard & E. Stellar

(Eds.), *Eating and its disorders* (pp. 77-86). New York: Raven.

Yerkes, R. M., & Dodson, J. D. (1908). The relation of strength of stimulus to rapidity of habit-formation. *Journal of Comparative Neurology of Psychology, 18,* 459-482.

Yukl, G. A. (1981). *Leadership in organizations.* Englewood Cliffs, NJ: Prentice Hall.

Zavos, P. M., & Goodpasture, J. C. (1989). Clinical improvements of specific seminal deficiencies via intercourse with a seminal collection device versus masturbation. *Fertility and Sterility, 51,* 190-191.

Zborowski, M. (1952). Cultural components in response to pain. *Journal of Social Issues, 8*(4), 16-30.

Zborowski, M. (1969). *People in pain.* San Francisco: Jossey-Bass.

Zepelin, H. (1973). A survey of age differences in sleep patterns and dream recall among well-educated men and women. *Sleep Research, 2,* 81.

Zepelin, H., & Rechtschaffen, A. (1974). Mammalian sleep, longevity, and energy metabolism. *Brain, Behavior, and Evolution, 10,* 425.

Zillman, D., & Cantor, J. (1976). Effect of timing of information about mitigation circumstances on emotional responses to provocation and retaliatory behavior. *Journal of Experimental Social Psychology, 12,* 38-55.

Zimbardo, P. (1969). Individuation, reason, and order vs. deindividuation, impulse, and chaos. In W. J. Arnold & D. Levine (Eds.), *Nebraska Symposium on Motivation* (Vol. 17, pp. 237-309). Lincoln: University of Nebraska Press.

Zinberg, N. E., & Jacobson, R. C. (1976). The natural history of chipping. *American Journal of Psychiatry, 133,* 37-40.

Zuckerman, M. (1979). *Sensation seeking: Beyond the optimal level of arousal.* Hillsdale, NJ: Lawrence Erlbaum.

Zuckerman, M. (1983). A biological theory of sensation seeking. In M. Zuckerman (Ed.), *Biological bases of sensation seeking, impulsivity, and anxiety* (pp. 37-76). Hillsdale, NJ: Lawrence Erlbaum.

Zuckerman, M. (1988). Behavior and biology: Research on sensation seeking and reactions to the media. In L. Donohew, H. E. Sypher, & E. T.

Higgins (Eds.), *Communication, social cognition, and affect* (pp. 173-194). Hillsdale, NJ: Lawrence Erlbaum.

Zuti, W. B., & Golding, L. A. (1976). Comparing diet and exercise as weight reduction tools. *Physician and Sportsmedicine, 4,* 49-53.

Index

Absentmindedness, 321
Absorption:
  food, 65
  mental condition, 404
Abstinence from drug use,
  337-339
Accounts, 19-20
Ackerman, Diane, 302
Acts, 20
Acupuncture, 172
Adams, J. Stacey, 374
Addiction, 329-357
  abstinence, 337-339
  components of, 330-335
  craving, 332
  cultural origins, 333
  economical affect
    maintenance, 334-335
  fatalism, 335-336
  feelings maintenance,
    334-335
  habits, 332-333
  history of drug use,
    341-347
  medical (disease) model of,
    330, 336-338, 346-347,
    353
  models of, 336-339
  personal efficacy, 335
  physical dependence,
    330-331
  politics of drug illegality,
    344-347

self-represntation, 335
social response, 334
to drug use, 331-332, 334,
  337-347
to opiates, 340-347
tolerance, 331
wars on drugs, 346
withdrawal, 331-332
Adenosine triphospate (ATP),
  377-378
Adipose tissue. See Fat, tissue
Adler, Alfred, 6
Adrenal glands, 184-187
  See also Epinephrine
Advertising, 84-85
Affect, 17
Affect programs, 104
Agency, 294-301
Aggression, 129-157, 272
  accounts, 149-150
  developmental, 151-152,
    155-156
  dominance ranking,
    137-138
  feeling bad, 143-145
  gender roles, 151-152
  imitation, 143-144
  impulsive, 143-145
  instrumental, 148-152
  intentions, 131-132
  passive, 132
  priming thoughts, 144-145
  rules of disorder, 149-150

territoriality, 137
Alcohol use, 136, 272,
  330-334, 337-339
  consumption records,
    348-349, 353
  prohibition laws, 351-352
  social history, 348-353
Alderfer, Clayton, 365-366,
  369
Alford, Kathleen, 414
Alpha waves. See
    Electroencephalograph
    (EEG)
Altruism, 280-282
Amygdala, 32, 110-111,
  134-135, 146
Anger, 130, 13, 140-141,
  144-148, 151-156
  historical emotionology,
    155-156
  rules, 146-148
Animal psychology, 13-14
Anorexia nervosa, 356-357
Anxiety, 178-180
  disorders, 189-190
  Manifest Anxiety Scale,
    179-180
  theories, 178-180
Appetite, 72-76
Appraisal, 146-147, 182
  of emotion, 104, 120-121
Apologies, 277

Arousal, 9-11, 15-16, 33, 121, 142-143
Ascending reticular activating system (ARAS), 31
Asch, Solomon, 284
Aspirin, 171
Assertiveness training, 195
Atkinson, John, 366-367
Attention, 297-298
Attraction:
    in social influence, 289-290
    to others, 253-255
Attribution of responsibility, 275, 278-279
Atwater, Wilbur, 84
Authority in social influence, 288-289
Averill, James, 123-124, 146-148, 154
Awareness. *See* Consciousness

Baker, Robert, 311, 313
Balance theory, 322-323
Bandura, Albert, 153
Barker, Jerome, 298
Basic rest and activation cycle (BRAC), 48
Beck, Aaron, 190, 192
Beecher, Henry, 164
Behavior modification, 174, 388
Behaviorism, 6-7, 107
Berkowitz, Leonard, 142-145, 154
Berlyne, Daniel, 402
Beta waves. *See* Electroencephalograph (EEG)
Biernacki, Patrick, 338-339
Biofeedback, 173-174, 195-196
Biological rhythms, 35-44
Biorhythms, 43-44
Booth, David, 75-76
Boredom, 401-403
Branden, Nathaniel, 248, 261-262
Bridges, Kathryn, 113-114
Bulimia, 357
Buss, Arnold, 143
Bystander apathy, 280-282

Caillois, Roger, 409, 415-416
Campbell, Anne, 149, 151-152
Cannon, Walter, 10, 23, 101, 108-109, 183-184
Carbohydrates, 62-63, 66, 69-70, 73-75, 90-92, 377
Catharsis, 138
Causal fantasy, 315
Cephalic phase response, 71
Cerebral cortex, 32-34, 135
Chisolm, James, 248-251
Cialdini, Robert, 288
Circadian rhythms, 37-43, 221
Cocaine, 171
Cognition, 295-327, 330-331, 340-341, 394
    mind theories of, 302-309
Cognitive appraisal. *See* Appraisal
Cognitive dissonance, 323-325, 373
Cognitive science, 21-22
Cole, Michele, 132
Commitment:
    as social influence, 291
    in love relationships, 251-252
    in stress, 182
Competence, 372
Compliance, 284, 289
Conflict, 286
Conformity, 284, 290
Consciousness, 17-18, 296-313
Consistency, 321-325
Coping. *See* Stress, coping
Cortisol, 38, 146, 186-187
Craving, 333, 338
Crawford, Michael, 67-68
Crowds, 282-283
Csikszentmihalyi, Mihalyi, 405, 418-419
Curiosity, 399-404
Cutler, Winifred, 219-220, 225

Darwin, Charles, 11, 104, 115, 207, 226, 273
Dawkins, Richard, 139-140, 307
Deci, Edward, 373
deCharms, Robert, 373
Decisions, 316-321, 324
Defensive practices, 274

Deindividuation, 282
Delta waves. *See* Electroencephalograph (EEG)
Dennett, Daniel, 19
Depression, 191-192
    biological, 191
    negative thinking, 191-192
Descartes, René, 303
Desynchronization, 40-43
Deviance of social acts, 286-287
Dieting, 93, 356-357
Diffusion of responsibility, 281
Digestion, 64-65
Diurnal variation, 37, 39-40
Domhoff, William, 55-56
Dreams, 54-57
Drewnowski, Adam, 75
Drives, 5-7, 23, 142
Drucker, Peter, 386
Drug use. *See* Addiction, to drug use
Dualism, 303
Duck, Steve, 256-257
Duffy, Elizabeth, 10

Eating, 61-93
    cultural influences, 81-86
    overeating, 89-93, 356
    social factors, 78-81, 93
Electroencephalograph (EEG)
    alpha waves, 33, 38, 46-47
    beta waves, 33, 46-47
    delta waves, 33, 46-47, 49
    theta waves, 33, 46-47
Effectance, 372
Ekman, Paul, 104-105, 117-118
Emde, Robert, 114-115
Emotion, 97-126
    cultural influences in, 119-125
    development, 113-115
    experience, 98-102
    face expression in, 105, 115-119
    facial feedback hypothesis, 105, 117-118
    gender roles in, 124-125
    managing expression of, 118-119

primary, 102-103
social construction of, 122-124
social influences in, 119-125
social rules, 123-124
Endocrine glands, 34-35, 38-39, 185-187, 218-219
Endorphins, 111, 146, 166, 250
Energetics, 10
Energy, 9, 15, 17
Epinephrine, 109, 185-187
Equity theory, 374-375
ERG work theory, 365-366
Erogenous zones, 223-224
Eron, Leonard, 151
Ethology, 137-139
Evolution theory, 11-14, 209, 273
  diet, 67-70, 73-75
  sleep, 46
Evolutionary psychology, 12-13
  of aggression, 139-141
  of emotion, 104-106
  of gossip, 298-299
  of love relationships, 248-250, 265
  of play, 396-397
  of sexuality, 226-229
  of thinking, 318-319
Evolutionary stable strategy (ESS), 139-140
Exercise, 92-93

Facework, 274-276
Fashions, 272-274
Fatalism, 335-336
Fatigue, 375-382
  management of, 381-382
  muscle physiology, 377-378
  objective, 376-377
  psychological, 378-380
  transfer of, 381
Fat:
  in body tissue, 65-66, 70-71, 89-92, 220
  in the diet, 63-64, 66-67, 69-70, 74-75, 90-92
Fear, 144, 175-178
  elicitors, 176-177
  responses, 177-178

Feelings, 16-17
  and food, 78
  of happiness, 325
Felson, Richard, 150
Festinger, Leon, 23, 323-325
Fisher, Helen, 257-258
Fletcher, Horace, 84
Flow, 372-373, 405
Folkman, Susan, 182-183, 193-194
Food:
  magic, 86
  motivation, 87-88
  sensation, 76-77
Forebrain, 32-34
Forgas, Joseph, 150
Foulkes, David, 55-56
Fox, Robin, 150-151
Frankenhaeuser, Marianne, 186-187
Freud, Sigmund, 6, 54, 56, 142, 179, 208, 211, 313
Frustration, 142-143
Functionalism, 5-6
Funt, Alan, 284-285

Gagnon, John, 239
Gambler's fallacy, 317
Games. See Play, as games
Gender roles
  in aggression, 140-141
  in emotion, 124-125
  in sexual fantasy, 240-241
  in sexuality, 208-210, 223-232
  in social manners, 271
  in thinking, 319
General adaptation syndrome, 181-193
Glucagon, 65, 70-71, 186
Glucose, 62, 65, 70-71, 91, 377
Glucostat theory, 70-71
Glycogen, 63, 186, 377
Goffman, Erving, 2740275
Goldstein, Jeffrey, 133, 153-154
Gossip, 298-299
Graburn, Nelson, 421-422
Graham, Sylvester, 83

Hagen, Richard, 226, 229-230

Hall, G. Stanley, 211
Happiness, 325
Harré, Rom, 123, 148
Harrison Narcotic Act, 344-345
Hatfield, Elaine, 247-248
Hazen, Helen, 243
Heider, Fritz, 23, 278-279, 322-323
Helping others, 280-282
Helplessness. See Learned helplessness
Henry, James, 111-112
Heroin, 340
Herzberg, Frederick, 369-370
Hindbrain, 31-32
Hilgard, Ernest, 312
Hite, Shere, 230, 242-243
Hochschild, Arlie, 118-119
Homeostasis, 23, 184
Hormones, 34-35, 135-136, 146, 185-187
  in sex. See Sex, hormones in
Horne, James, 45, 48, 51
Horney, Karen, 6
Huizinga, Johan, 409
Hull, Clark, 313
Hunt, Harry, 55, 57
Husserl, Edmund, 316-317
Hypnosis, 174, 311-313
Hypothalamus, 32, 111, 185-186

Instinct, 99-100
Insulin, 65, 70-71
Intrinsic motivation, 372-374
Inverted-U theory, 15-16
Isen, Alice, 325
Izard, Carroll, 105-106, 116-117

James, William, 3, 98-101, 108, 121-122, 148, 296-298, 310, 313-314, 316
Jet-lag, 40-41
Job:
  enhancement, 370-372
  enlargement, 370
  enrichment, 370-372
Jung, Carl, 6

Kagan, Jerome, 115
Kaplan, Helen, 217-218
Karli, Peter, 135-138
Kelley, Harold, 221
Kellogg, John, 83-84, 86
Kelly, John, 412
Kelly-Byrne, Diana, 409-410
Kierkegaard, Soren, 178-179
Kinsey, Alfred, 212, 229, 241
Klinnert, Mary, 114-115
Kohn, Alfie, 390
Latham, Gary, 386-388

Lazarus, Richard, 120-121,
    182-183, 193-194
Learned helplessness, 191-192
LeBon, Gustave, 282
LeDoux, Joseph, 110-111
Lee, John, 250-251
Leisure, 411-413, 418-423
    theories and ideas, 411-413
    time in, 418
Libertarian, 213
Libido, 223-224
Limbic system, 32, 109-111,
    134-135, 146
Liminality in play and ritual,
    407, 410
Lipostat theory, 71
Locke, Edwin, 386-388
Lorenz, Konrad, 137-138, 396
Love, 201-210, 247-265
    committed, 248-250
    cultural history, 201-206
    differentiation in, 262-263
    experiences in
        relationships, 260-261
    pragmatic, 247-248
    romantic, 206, 247-250,
        252
    mutual visibility, 261-262
    relationship break-ups,
        263-265
Lutz, Catherine, 125

MacLean, Paul, 109-110
Malatesta, Carol, 116-117
Management by objectives,
    386
Mandler, George, 180,
    305-306
Manners, 270-272

Marijuana, 341, 345-346
Marsh, David, 67-68
Marsh, Peter, 148-149
Maslow, Abraham, 23,
    364-370, 372
Masters and Johnson, 212,
    217-218
Maturity in relationships,
    255-256
McClelland, David, 367-368
McClintock, Martha, 225
McFarland, Ross, 377-378
McGinn, Colin, 305
McGregor, Douglas, 362
McKinley, Kathleen, 244
Medical model. *See*
    Addictions, medical
    (disease) model of
Meditation, 196, 310-311
Melzack, Ronald, 161-162,
    167-169
Memes, 307
Memory, 39-40
Mental experience. *See*
    Consciousness
Mesmer, Anton, 312
Metabolism, 71, 89-90
Midbrain, 32
Milgram, Stanley, 284
Mobs, 282-283
Modeling, 143-144
Morphine, 340
Morris, Desmond, 403
Motive talk, 274-278
Moyer, Kenneth, 1345-135
Murray, Henry, 6, 23, 364,
    366-367

Narcotics, 340
National Health and Social
    Life Survey, 213-215,
    228-231, 243, 253
Needs, 23, 364-368
    achievement, 366-368
    affiliation, 367-368
    power, 367-368
Nervous systems, 29-34, 105
    in aggression, 133-135
    in pain, 166-169
    in sex, 218
    in stress, 183-187
Neulinger, John, 412
Neurotransmitters, 34-36, 88

in aggression, 135-136
    in love, 250
    in pain, 166
    in sex, 222
Nicotine, 354
Nociception, 166
NREM sleep and dreaming,
    55
Nutrition, 62-72

Obedience, 284
Obesity, 89-93
Olweus, Dan, 151
Omega-3 fatty acid, 64, 68
Opiates, 171
Opponent process theory, 23
Orgasm. *See* Sex, orgasm in
Overjustification, 373
Oxytocin, 222

Paicheler, Geneviève, 286
Pain, 159-174
    causalgia, 162
    chronic, 161, 169
    clinics, 174
    cultural influences, 162-164
    drug treatment of, 170-171
    experiences of, 160-165,
        195
    Gate Control theory,
        167-168
    meaning, 164-165
    neuralgia, 162-163
    phantom limb, 162
    physiology, 165-169
    psychological control,
        173-174
    referred, 161-162
    stimulation treatment,
        172-173
    surgery treatment, 172
Panksepp, Jaak, 111, 184
Paradoxical sleep, 47
Passive aggression, 132
Personal efficacy in addiction
    control, 335
Pheromones, 222, 224-225
Pituitary, 185
Placebo, 164-165, 316
Play, 395-399, 407-411,
    413-417
    and society rules, 410-411

as games, 415-416
as social interactions, 414
definitions and ideas,
    397-398
in language, 414-415
theories, 408-411
Pleasure:
in sex, 244
Plutchik, Robert, 106-107
Pornography, 241-243
Positive regard, 254-255
Premenstrual syndrome, 219
Problem solving, 319-321
Prostaglandins, 169
Protective practices, 274
Protein, 63-64, 66, 69-70,
    73-75, 90-92
Protestant ethic, 411
Psychoanalysis, 6, 142
Punishment, 151, 154
Pure Food and Drug Act,
    343-344

Quality Circles, 384-385
Quarrick, Gene, 404-405

Rapid eye movement (REM),
    46-55
Read, Stephen, 277
Reasoning, 315-316
Reciprocation, 291
Relaxation training, 173, 196
Reticular activating system.
    See Ascending reticular
    activating system
Rewards for work, 388-390
Ritual, 407-408
Romantic love. See Love,
    romantic
Rosser, Elisabeth, 148-149
Rubin, Zick, 261

Schachter, Stanley, 121-122,
    338
Schemas, 305-306
Schnarch, David, 262-263
Scientific Management,
    381-383
Scientism, 273-274
Sears, Barry, 70
Sears, Robert, 151

Self-defense, 148
Self-esteem, 148-149, 152,
    256
Self-picture, 148-149,
    332-333, 335
Seligman, Martin, 192
Selye, Hans, 181
Sensation Seeking, 405-406
Sensory isolation and
    deprivation, 402-403
Set-point theory, 71
Sex, 201-232, 237-246
erotic, 223, 237-244
estrogen in, 219-222
hormones in, 217-222
in love relationships, 263
orgasm in, 211, 217-218,
    221, 226, 232-230
short-term mating, 228
social roles in, 245-246
stages in, 217-218
testosterone in, 219,
    221-222, 224, 241
Sexology, 208, 210-213
Sexual:
attitudes, 213-215
attraction, 227-229
desire, 221-222
dysfunction, 212, 215, 230
ethics, 245
fantasy, 222, 240-241
identity, 245
ideology, 213-215
interest, 229-232
marketing, 215
orientation, 245
politics, 213-215
scripts, 238-239
sensual arousal in, 223-225
Shift work, 42-43
Shirley, Grace, 210, 256, 258
Simon, William, 239
Singer, Jerome, 121-122
Skinner B. F., 388
Sleep:
core, 45, 48, 51-52
length, 50-52
loss, 52-54
reduction, 51-52
slow-wave (SWS), 47-48,
    51-54
spindles, 46-47
theory, 45-46
Smith, Valene, 420-421

Smoking, 221, 272, 330-338,
    354-356
social history, 354-356
Social:
change, 285-287
comparison, 284-285
conformity, 284
constructionism, 122-124
deviance, 286-287
disruption, 280-283
influences, 281, 284-291
manners, 270-272
order, 270-274
referencing, 114-115
Solomon, Robert, 101-102
Spinal cord, 30-31
in pain, 167-168
Sport, 416-417
Sprecher, Susan, 244
Stacey, Michelle, 86
Startle reflex, 177
Staw, Barry, 373
Stearns, Carol and Peter,
    155-156
Sternberg, Robert, 251-252
Stress, 109, 181-196
coping, 193-196
crowding, 188
life changes, 187-188
type A coronary-prone,
    188-189
Structuralism, 3-4
Sutton-Smith, Brian, 409-410
Symons, Donald, 226-227,
    229
Sympathetic nervous system,
    29-30, 108-108, 121,
    184-186, 217

Taste of foods, 75-78
Taylor, Frederick, 383
Tedeschi, James, 150
Temperance in alcohol
    politics, 349-352
Testosterone, 39, 111, 136,
    146, 186
in sex, 219, 221-222, 224,
    241
Thalamus, 32
Theory X of work, 362
Theta waves. See
    Electroencephalograph
    (EEG)

Thinking. *See* Cognition
Titchener, Edward, 3
Tobacco. *See* Smoking
Tolerance, 331
Touring, 420-423
Transcutaneous electrical
    nerve stimulation
    (TENS), 172
Turner, Victor, 405, 407
Type A. *See* Stress, type A
    coronary-prone

Vegetarianism, 83
Vernon, Jack, 403
Victorian culture, 205, 207,
    214
VIE theory of work, 385-386
Vigilance, 388
Violence, 150-151

Vitamins, 64, 90
von Krafft-Ebing, Richard,
    211
Vroom, Victor, 385

Wall, Patrick, 160, 164, 167,
    170
Wason, Peter, 318-319
Watson, John, 6-7, 107-108,
    211
Webb, Wilse, 45, 49-50, 54
Weight control, 91-93
White, Robert, 372
Wilson, Thomas, 390
Withdrawal, 331-332, 338
Wood, Wendy, 159
Woodworth, Robert, 5
Work motivation, 361-391
    and satisfaction, 387-388

    definitions and ideas,
      361-364
    goal-setting theory,
      386-387
    hygiene factors, 369
    motivator factors, 369
    needs theories, 364-368
    participation in
      management, 383-385
    two-factor theory, 369-
      370
    Vie theory, 385-386
Wright, Hamilton, 344-345
Wundt, Wilhelm, 2-3

Zborowski, Mark, 163
Zeitgebers, 41
Zuckerman, Marvin, 405-406

About the Author

David C. Edwards is Professor of Psychology at Iowa State University. He was chair of psychology at Iowa State from 1975 to 1984. His early experimental work focused on topics in animal learning, memory, and perception. Current scholarly interests include the many topics of motivation plus turn-of-the-century American psychology, modern evolutionary psychology, and human factors principles applied to general aviation. He is the author of *General Psychology* (1968, 1972) and *Pilot: Mental and Physical Performance* (1990). His degrees are from the University of Wisconsin-Milwaukee (1959, B.S. degree in psychology) and the University of Iowa (1961, M.A. in psychology; 1962, Ph.D. in psychology).